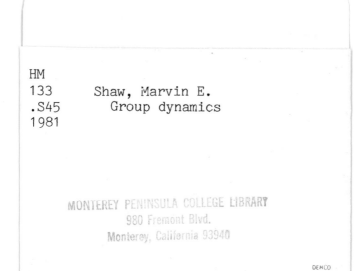

# Group Dynamics

## The Psychology of
## Small Group Behavior

# McGraw-Hill Series in Psychology

## CONSULTING EDITOR

Norman Garmezy

**Adams** Human Memory
**Berlyne** Conflict, Arousal, and Curiosity
**Bernstein and Nietzel** Introduction to Clinical Psychology
**Blum** Psychoanalytic Theories of Personality
**Block** Multivariate Statistical Methods in Behavioral Research
**Brown** The Motivation of Behavior
**Campbell, Dunnette, Lawler, and Weick** Managerial Behavior, Performance, and
  Effectiveness
**Crites** Vocational Psychology
**D'Amato** Experimental Psychology: Methodology, Psychophysics, and Learning
**Dollard and Miller** Personality and Psychotherapy
**Ferguson** Statistical Analysis in Psychology and Education
**Fodor, Bever, and Garrett** The Psychology of Language: An Introduction to
  Psycholinguistics and Generative Grammar
**Forgus and Melamed** Perception: A Cognitive-Stage Approach
**Franks** Behavior Therapy: Appraisal and Status
**Gilmer and Deci** Industrial and Organizational Psychology
**Guilford** Psychometric Methods
**Guilford** The Nature of Human Intelligence
**Guilford and Fruchter** Fundamental Statistics in Psychology and Education
**Guion** Personnel Testing
**Hetherington and Parke** Child Psychology: A Contemporary Viewpoint
**Hirsh** The Measurement of Hearing
**Hjelle and Ziegler** Personality Theories: Basic Assumptions, Research, and
  Applications
**Horowitz** Elements of Statistics for Psychology and Education
**Hulse, Egeth, and Deese** The Psychology of Learning
**Hurlock** Adolescent Development
**Hurlock** Child Development
**Hurlock** Developmental Psychology

# Group Dynamics

## The Psychology of Small Group Behavior

### Third Edition

Marvin E. Shaw
*Professor of Psychology*
*University of Florida*

## McGraw-Hill Book Company

New York   St. Louis   San Francisco   Auckland   Bogotá   Hamburg
London   Madrid   Mexico   Montreal   New Delhi
Panama   Paris   São Paulo   Singapore   Sydney   Tokyo   Toronto

This book was set in Times Roman by Black Dot, Inc. (ECU)
The editors were Rhona Robbin and James R. Belser;
the production supervisor was Richard A. Ausburn.
The drawings were done by VIS.
The cover was designed by Antonia Goldmark.

**GROUP DYNAMICS**
The Psychology of Small Group Behavior

Copyright © 1981, 1976, 1971 by McGraw-Hill, Inc. All rights reserved. Printed in the United States of America. No part of this publication may be reproduced, stored in a retrieval system, or transmitted, in any form or by any means, electronic, mechanical, photocopying, recording, or otherwise, without the prior written permission of the publisher.

9 0 EDWEDW 8 9 8 7

Library of Congress Cataloging in Publication Data

Shaw, Marvin E
    Group dynamics.

    (McGraw-Hill series in psychology)
    Bibliography:  p.
    Includes indexes.
    1.  Small groups.   2.  Sociometry.   I.  Title.
HM133.S45   1981      302.3′4       80-14375
ISBN 0-07-056504-X

To L. M. S.

# Contents

# Preface

Participation in groups is a way of life in our culture. People form groups for almost every conceivable purpose: to make decisions, to solve problems, to rear families, to satisfy social needs, and many more. It is not surprising, then, that interest in group dynamics continues to be evident. Each year, new contributions are made to our understanding of group behavior, including both theory and research. Thus a major purpose of any revision must be to incorporate new information and new theoretical formulations that enhance our knowledge of groups. Additional purposes of this revision are to expand the coverage to include materials that are inadequately covered or omitted from previous editions, to eliminate outdated or less useful materials, and to reorganize the presentation to facilitate communication. Therefore, new information has been added throughout the text, especially with respect to group polarization, group development, coalition formation, social density and crowding, leadership, and group tasks and goals. Two chapters (Chapter 10 on experiential groups and Chapter 11 on children's groups) have been eliminated and relevant materials incorporated  in other chapters. The treatment of leadership has been expanded to compose an entire chapter. Finally, a chapter dealing with groups in action has been added which includes examples from problem-solving groups, educational groups, and experiential groups.

With respect to objectives, the third edition is similar to earlier editions. The text is written for the student who has been introduced to social psychology and its terminology but who has not delved deeply into the study of small groups. The audience for which it is intended include college seniors and first-year graduate students. It assumes that the reader is familiar with basic social-psychological concepts and terminology and has some knowledge of social processes. Thus the book does not purport to meet the needs of everyone who is interested in groups. However, the reader who does not have the backgound to fully appreciate some of the finer distinctions and nuances should, nevertheless, be able to understand, and benefit from, the major ideas that are presented.

It has been my purpose to examine many aspects of small group behavior, not as isolated phenomena, but as interrelated processes of social interaction. Unfortunately, it is easier to state this goal than to achieve it. Group processes are so complex, and so many variables influence behavior in groups, that it is impossible to discuss them all at the same time. Consequently, it has been necessary to discuss various aspects of group dynamics in different chapters. Whenever possible, I have tried to indicate interrelated processes by cross references and, I fear, some redundancy.

Emphasis has been placed on data obtained from empirical studies rather than on theoretical or logical analyses of groups. All kinds of empirical approaches were acceptable, provided only that observations were made under controlled conditions. (This does not mean that the investigator must have controlled *all* relevant variables, but only that he or she knows enough about the situation to make valid inferences about casual relationships.) However, in the review of relevant research, the intent was to be representative rather than exhaustive. Several representative studies are cited to support each of the conclusions drawn about a given process whenever such studies are available, but many relevant studies are not mentioned if essentially the same conclusions can be drawn from those cited. Emphasis has also been placed on task-oriented, rather than experiential, groups.

Finally, each substantive chapter ends with a list of plausible hypotheses about the phenomena discussed in the chapter. It is hoped that these lists will serve as summaries of the materials presented in the main part of the chapters and as a guide for future explorations.

I am deeply indebted to the many persons who contributed, directly or indirectly, to this revision. Bruce Caine, Louis Kamfer, Soro Kano, Robert Montgomery, Barry Schlenker, and David Senn offered many suggestions that significantly improved the current work. Harvey Bertcher and Homer E. Stavely, Jr., analyzed the second edition of the text and offered many good suggestions for improvement, and Daniel J. Isenberg, Charles R. Petrie, Denzel E. Benson, as well as Homer E. Stavely, Jr., read the entire manuscript for the present edition and their comments and suggestions were especially helpful. I am most grateful to all those persons listed above and to those contributors whose names I neglected to record. Obviously, these persons should not be held responsible for any deficiencies of the final product, but their contributions are greatly appreciated. Barbara Mitchell typed the final manuscript and I am grateful for her professional assistance. Finally, materials from the works of many authors made this work possible; I thank them one and all. The materials from works published by the following organizations were used and are much appreciated: Academic Press, Inc.; Acta Psychologica; Addison-Wesley Publishing Co., Inc.; American Psychological Association, Inc.; American Sociological Association, Inc.; Cornell Journal of Social Relations; Duke University Press; The Free Press; General Learning Press; Harcourt, Brace & World, Inc.; Harper & Row, Publishers, Inc.; Institute of Management Sciences; John Wiley & Sons, Inc.; McGraw-Hill Book Company; Oxford University Press; Penguin Books, Inc.; Plenum Publishing Corporation; Prentice-Hall, Inc.; Psychonomic Journals, Inc.; Sage Publications, Inc.; Tavistock Publications, Ltd.; The Journal Press; The Ronald Press Company; The Society for Research in Child Development, Inc.; and the University of Chicago Press.

*Marvin E. Shaw*

# Group Dynamics

## The Psychology of
## Small Group Behavior

# Chapter 1

# An Introduction
# to Small Groups

Throughout history people have joined together in groups to accomplish a wide range of purposes. Men and women form personal relationships to procreate, to raise families, and/or to make the business of day-to-day living more interesting and meaningful. These family groups are probably among the oldest and most basic types of groups, but many other types come readily to mind: decision-making groups, discussion groups, social groups, professional groups, political groups, athletic teams, committees, fraternities. . . . The list could be extended ad nauseam. It is apparent that a large proportion of human behavior occurs in groups. Governments conduct much of their business in groups, whether they be the Central Committee of a socialistic society, the President's Cabinet in a republic, or a group of select advisers to the head of a dictatorship. Industrial organizations employ committees to improve quality of decisions or to reduce the probability of defective decisions or products; educators employ group discussion to facilitate learning; college students form groups to facilitate social interaction, to promote common causes, or to protest injustices. It has been estimated that there are four or five million groups in existence at any given time (James, 1951).

Some groups achieve the goals for which they are established, but many do not. Consider two hypothetical student groups that experience contrasting processes and outcomes. Committee A is composed of five men selected to represent the various fraternities on campus. The members are all of about average intelligence; they have similar needs, but their interests vary widely. The members arrived at the meeting dressed in casual clothing (one member came directly from the tennis court still wearing his sweaty uniform, another had been sleeping and did not take time to change his clothes or comb his hair, and others were equally careless about their appearance). The meeting was held in the basement of the Student Union for the purpose of deciding what projects to recommend to campus fraternities for the current academic year. The room in which the meeting was held had been given little janitorial attention. The chairs around the rectangular table were in disarray, papers were scattered on the floor, and ashtrays had not been emptied. When members came into the room, one member chose to sit at the head of the table, thus forcing the chairman to sit on one side.

The meeting got off to a bad start. One member who held no official position in the group began discussing the projects but was sharply reminded by the chairman that he was not running the meeting. The chairman then gave a short lecture on the rights and privileges of chairpersons, during which group members displayed evidences of discomfort. A wide-ranging discussion followed, but few comments were relevant to the committee's task. Person-directed observations were not infrequent. The meeting adjourned at the end of the hour with no visible progress having been made toward goal achievement.

The second hypothetical group, Committee B, is composed of three men and three women who are elected by social and academic associations on a college campus. Their task is to decide how to award a $500 prize for the greatest contribution to the community by a senior during the current academic year. The members of Committee B represent a wide range of needs and abilities, although their values and interests are similar. The members arrived at the meeting neatly dressed and well-groomed (the men wore slacks and sport jackets with matching ties; the women were dressed in blouses and skirts or pantsuits). The meeting was held in the conference room of the Student Union, a room reserved for the use of student government and committees. The room was clean and orderly, with chairs carefully placed around the circular table on which clean ashtrays and note pads had been placed.

The meeting began promptly and proceeded smoothly throughout the forty-eight-minute session. The chairperson opened the meeting with a brief summary of the task assigned the Committee and reviewed the work that had already been done. She then stated that all opinions and ideas were welcome and would be given careful consideration. During the course of the discussion she was careful to elicit minority opinions and skillfully guided the discussion to evaluate each suggestion before either accepting or rejecting it. A unanimous decision was reached amicably, and the meeting adjourned amid expressions of praise for various members of the Committee. After adjournment, several members remained to chat about various matters unrelated to the Committee functions.

It is evident from the preceding accounts that the meetings of Committee A and Committee B were very different experiences for their members. The meeting of Committee A was characterized by disorganization, inefficiency, and interpersonal conflict; the meeting of Committee B was congenial, organized, and effective. How can we account for these differences? What factors contribute to group compatibility and effectiveness? It is obvious that the two groups differ in many ways. They differ in composition (same-sex versus mixed-sex, "grubby" versus well-dressed, homogeneity versus heterogeneity of abilities, etc.), with respect to meeting room (disarrayed, rectangular table versus orderly, circular table), in kind of task (unstructured versus structured task), and probably in many other ways. Which of these many differences account for the great differences in group functioning? In this book we shall explore the methods and procedures used in attempting to answer these questions, review the research evidence concerning group process, and consider some of the ways our knowledge of group behavior can be used to improve group relations and outcomes.

The title of this book and this chapter indicate that our concern is with *small* groups. It is legitimate, therefore, to ask just how small is a "small group" and how many of the groups in existence fall into this category. Actually, there is no clear-cut dividing line between small and large groups. A group having ten or fewer members is certainly a small group; one with thirty or more members is definitely a large group. But there is a gray area between ten and thirty where the appropriate designation is unclear and often is made on bases other than the number of group members. For example, a group of thirty persons might function as a small group if all its members were closely related to one another and highly motivated to cooperate toward the achievement of a common goal. Fortunately, the maximum size of a small group usually does not become a problem, since the great majority of research studies deal with groups of five or fewer members. However, this fact does create a problem in generalizing laboratory findings to natural situations.

The question concerning the proportion of extant groups that can be considered small is much easier to answer. A survey study of group memberships by James (1951) revealed that 92 percent of all group memberships observed were in groups of two or three persons, and only 2 percent of the remaining groupings included five or more persons. It is important to note that James observed spontaneous groupings in everyday activities. This procedure probably resulted in a bias toward smaller groups. However, his findings strongly suggest that the study of small groups encompasses the majority of group memberships. Similar findings were reported by Wheeler and Nezlek (1977). They found that, on the average, 48 percent of a person's interactions were with one other person, 19 percent with two other persons, 11 percent with three other persons, and 22 percent with four or more other persons. One cannot infer from these data, however, that small groups are the most important social aggregations, although it seems likely that they are most significant from the standpoint of the individual group member. As shall be seen from studies cited in the following chapters, the small group exerts strong influence on almost every phase of the member's life. The norms (standards of conduct) of the group provide a basis for the determination of "appropriate" behavior in otherwise ambiguous situations; the presence of others often leads to the satisfaction of individual needs for affiliation and may arouse the individual to unusual performance levels; goals can be achieved in groups that cannot be achieved alone; and much more.

Perhaps enough has been said to arouse the curiosity of the reader to the extent that he or she is willing to examine the data from small group research or at least to ask the question: What is a *group?* This is a fair question. When we presume to discourse upon a significant subject, we should be prepared to define our terms as clearly as possible. It would be easy to state our own definition of group and proceed to more exciting topics. However, there is no single definition that is generally accepted by all (or even most) students of small group behavior. It will be more instructive therefore to consider the diverse meanings of this concept.

## DEFINITIONS OF GROUP

It is not our purpose to present a comprehensive listing of definitions of group; rather, we shall sample definitions representing the various approaches to conceptualization. These approaches are not necessarily unique. On the contrary, there is much overlap, and it is evident that different authors are simply looking at different aspects of the same phenomenon. Indeed, some authors are able to discuss group phenomena at great length without presenting a specific definition of the term (for example, Collins & Guetzkow, 1964; McGrath & Altman, 1966; Roby, 1968; Schutz, 1958). These authors have judged that it is more appropriate to specify the characteristics of small groups than to offer a single definition. Others have proposed definitions that emphasize one (or a few) of the many characteristics of groups. It may be instructive to review some of these attempts to define *group.*

A definition of group that has been widely adopted and cited is one proposed by Bales:

> A small group is defined as any number of persons engaged in interaction with one another in a single face-to-face meeting or series of such meetings, in which each member receives some impression or perception of each other member distinct enough so that he can, either at the time or in later questioning, give some reaction to each of the others as an individual person, even though it be only to recall that the other was present (Bales, 1950, p. 33).

The major characteristic emphasized by this definition is *perception*. Although Bales rigorously delimits the situation in which the perceptions occur and specifies precisely the circumstances in which member perceptions may be revealed, the sine qua non is that group members perceive the existence of the group.

Another aspect of groups that has impressed students of groups is the motivation that leads individuals to join groups. It is a common observation that individuals join a group because they believe that it will satisfy some need. Thus, people in business may join civic clubs in order to improve their business opportunities, college students affiliate with a fraternity to satisfy social needs, and proponents of civil rights may join action-oriented groups because they believe that such groups can satisfy their motivations to improve society. Groups that fail to satisfy the need or needs of individual group members usually disintegrate. The following definition is representative of those that emphasize *motivation* as the essential characteristic of *group:*

> We define "group" as a collection of individuals whose existence as a collection is rewarding to the individuals (Bass, 1960, p. 39).

This definition clearly implies that need satisfaction is the necessary element for identifying an aggregate as a group. In fact, Bass asserted that other characteristics included in other definitions are superfluous. In his view, shared perceptions of unity, commonality of goals, and interaction are irrelevant for purposes of definition unless these ascribed characteristics are related to the potentially rewarding aspects of the collectivity. A practical difficulty in the definition of "group" in terms of need satisfaction is obvious: How does one determine what needs are operating and whether needs are in fact being satisfied by the collection of persons?

Some authors define group in terms of *group goals,* an emphasis shown in the following definition:

> Just what *are* these small groups we are referring to? To put it simply, they are units composed of two or more persons who come into contact for a purpose and who consider the contact meaningful (Mills, 1967, p. 2).

Presumably, goal achievement is rewarding, and to the extent that this is so, definitions in terms of goals are quite similar to definitions in terms of motivation.

A different kind of concern is revealed in definitions of group that are based upon *organizational* characteristics. Those who emphasize organization reveal a greater interest in the group as a unit in contrast to the preceding definitions which reflected greater interests in the individual as the unit of analysis. Persons with this orientation are impressed by the structural elements of groups (roles, statuses, norms) and the relationships among them. According to McDavid and Harari, the essential properties of organization which define a group are unitary functioning, interrelated elements, and regulatory mechanisms. They define group as follows:

> A social-psychological group is an organized system of two or more individuals who are interrelated so that the system performs some function, has a standard set of role relationships among its members, and has a set of norms that regulate the function of the group and each of its members (McDavid & Harari, 1968, p. 237).

Definitions in terms of organization seem to limit consideration of structural properties to statuses, roles, and norms, although it is evident that many other structural elements are involved in group structure (for example, power relations, affective relations, etc.). However, the main objection to definitions of this type is that they are merely partial descriptions of one aspect of groups, namely group structure.

Many years ago, Lewin argued cogently that the essential aspect of a collection of individuals which makes it a group is the interdependency of individuals on one another. He was particularly concerned that some writers seemed to view similarity of members as the critical characteristic of groups. In Lewin's view, even definitions of group in terms of group goals are based on similarity. In his words:

> Conceiving of a group as a dynamic whole should include a definition of group which is based on interdependence of the members (or better, of the subparts of the group). It seems to be rather important to stress this point because many definitions of a group use the similarity of group members rather than their dynamic interdependence as the constituent factor. . . . One should realize that even a definition of group membership by equality of goal or equality of an enemy is still a definition by similarity (Lewin, 1951, pp. 146–147).

More recently, Fiedler proposed a similar definition:

> By this term [group] we generally mean a set of individuals who share a common fate, that is, who are *interdependent* in the sense that an event which affects one member is likely to affect all (Fiedler, 1967, p. 6).

The term *interdependence* can have a variety of meanings, since group members may be interdependent with respect to one or more dimensions. In many cases, interdependence is essentially the same as *interaction*, since interaction is one form of interdependence. Many authors believe that this form of interdependence is the essence of "groupness" and hence have based definitions of groups on this aspect. For example:

> A group may be regarded as an open interaction system in which actions determine the structure of the system and successive interactions exert coequal effects upon the identity of the system (Stogdill, 1959, p. 18).

In addition to these definitions that are largely limited to single characteristics of groups, some authors suggest definitions that include multiple characteristics, as evidenced by the following:

> A comprehensive definition of "group" can be formulated in terms of the following properties: interaction between individuals, perceptions of other members and the development of shared perceptions, the development of affective ties, and the development of interdependence or roles (DeLamater, 1974, p. 39).

> A social group is "A collectivity that has psychological implications for the individual, based upon the person's awareness of other group members, his or her membership (or desired membership) in the group, and the emotional significance of the group" (Shaver, 1977, p. 557).

## A Minimal Definition of Group

These definitions are all correct in that each points to some important aspect(s) of the concept "group" and/or delimits it in some way. It appears that different theorists look at different facets of the group, and each assumes that his or her view reveals its essential characteristics. Differences among definitions in some cases appear to be due to variations in levels of analysis, e.g., differences between definitions in terms of perceptions and in terms of organization. In other cases, such differences seem to be due largely to semantic variations, e.g., differences between definitions in terms of interdependency and in terms of interaction. Even when definitions are based upon the same characteristic, there often are differences in minor details, such as the requirement that there be face-to-face communication or that some of the consequences of group processes be uniform for all group members. Nevertheless, there is sufficient commonality among definitions to indicate that they are all referring to the same basic concept.

In our view, definitions in terms of interdependency or interaction more directly delineate the basic elements of the concept "group." If a group exists, then it may be assumed that its members (1) are motivated to join the group (and hence that it will satisfy some of their needs), and (2) are aware of its existence, i.e., their perceptions are veridical. Furthermore, it is a common observation that when individuals interact, even for brief periods, differentiations begin to develop. Some persons contribute more to group processes than others, some are valued more than others, and certain approved patterns of behavior appear. In short, group organization begins to take place. Finally, it is not obvious that a common goal is an essential characteristic of a group. It is at least theoretically possible for a group to meet only individual goals. To summarize: Motivations of members may account for the *formation* of a group; the group members may *veridically perceive* that the group exists or that they are members of a group; and organization (the formation and interrelation of roles, statuses, and norms) may be an inevitable *consequence* of group process. But none of these aspects is either necessary or sufficient to define "group." Therefore, for purposes of this book, *a group is defined as two or more persons who are interacting with one another in such a manner that each person influences and is influenced by each other person.* A *small group* is a group having twenty or fewer members, although in most instances we will be concerned with groups having five or fewer members.

Some examples of aggregates that are groups and of some that are not may help to clarify this conception of group. If one person, A, sees another person, B, with whom she wishes to speak and so approaches him, A is influenced by B but not vice versa; hence *interaction* does not occur, and A and B do not constitute a group. However, if B notices that A is attempting to get his attention, B may be influenced to also approach A. In this case, A and B are interacting and so compose a group. Or consider the case of a person, A, who is looking up at the sky and is approached, independently, by two other persons, B and C, who also begin looking in the same direction. Again, no group exists, despite the fact that B and C have been influenced by A, because A has not been influenced by B or C. These three persons become a group if they enter into a discussion (interaction) concerning the object of their attention. It should be clear that interaction requires *mutual* influence, and an aggregate of individuals is a group only if interaction occurs.

Although interaction is the essential feature that distinguishes a group from an aggregate, other aspects of a group are important. In general, the group dynamicist is interested in groups that (1) endure for a reasonable period (longer than a few minutes, at least), (2) have a common goal or goals, and (3) have developed at least a rudimentary group structure.

## REALITY OF GROUPS

Are groups real? This may appear to be a strange question to raise after devoting several pages to the definition of group. Nevertheless, it is a question that must be considered, since the "realness" of groups has been debated for many years. Some social scientists have maintained that the concept of group is a mere analogy, an abstraction that we use to account for collective individual behavior. F. H. Allport (1924) argued cogently that only individuals are real; groups are no more than sets of values, ideas, thoughts, habits, etc., that exist simultaneously in the minds of the individuals in collectivities. In short, groups exist only in the minds of human beings. Others (Durkheim, 1898; Warriner, 1956) have argued just as strongly that groups are entities and should be treated like other unitary objects in our environment. Those who take this position assert that group phenomena cannot be explained in psychological terms; hence any valid explanation of group processes must be at the level of the group. Somewhere between these two extreme positions are those theorists who maintain that entities, including groups, vary in the degree to which they are "real" and that the problem is one of determining the degree of being an entity (Campbell, 1958; K. W. Deutsch, 1954; Rice, 1928; Spencer, 1876).

As in many controversies the more moderate position turns out to be the more reasonable one. The most articulate representative of this view is probably Donald T. Campbell (1958). He noted that certain objects in our environment, such as stones and teacups, appear to be more solid and unitary than other objects, such as social groups, and therefore more "real." Somehow, this makes objectionable the use of the same term to refer to both categories of objects. He argued, however, that the differences in objects of this sort are really differences in our perceptions of them. That is, physical objects such as tables and chairs are more solid, have sharper boundaries, and are more multiply confirmed than are social groups. For example, we not only can see a chair, but we can also touch it, feel its temperature, hear the sound that results from tapping it, etc. Information about it can be obtained from multiple sense modalities. Information about a group, however, comes from fewer sources and often seems to be less immediate and compelling than that obtained about physical objects. Therefore, although the process is essentially the same, social groups are seen as less real than physical objects. Campbell suggested that the term "entity" has an all-or-none connotation and hence is inadequate to express the notion of degree of "realness." He therefore coined the term "entitativity" to refer to the degree of having real existence.

Once it is admitted that objects may vary in degree of realness, or at least in the degree to which they are perceived as real, then a question arises concerning the factors determining the perception of entitativity. Campbell has proposed that the gestalt principles of perceptual organization are adequate to account for the perception of entitativity. These well-known principles are proximity, similarity, common fate, and pregnance. Let us examine in greater detail how these principles apply to the perception of the reality of groups.

## Perception of Entitativity

The identification of an aggregate of several units as an entity is basically a process of establishing boundaries which separate the units belonging to the entity from other units that are not a part of the entity. Thus, through the use of principles of organization Campbell sought to determine the circumstances under which such boundaries are established. He believed that an analysis of this type would be equally applicable to physical objects, e.g., stones and chairs, and to social phenomena, e.g., social groups. According to Campbell, common fate seems to be most important in establishing boundaries, followed by similarity and proximity. Pregnance, which refers to the fact that elements forming a pattern tend to be perceived as the best figure possible, plays a very secondary role in the perception of entitativity. Campbell used this principle only to examine the degree of closure or completeness obtained by application of the other three principles.

In attempting to show how common fate may be used to establish entitativity, Campbell suggested that it might be possible to compute a "coefficient of common fate" which would reflect the degree to which two or more units have been in the same general place at the same time. For example, if a stone is multicolored, it may not be immediately obvious that the differently colored parts constitute a single entity. However, if the stone is moved about, it can be seen that the various parts generally move together; that is, the parts maintain their same relative position regardless of the location of the stone in space. The various parts thus experience a common fate, and this is a clue to entitativity. In the same way, we may observe the extent to which a collection of individuals experience a common fate. For example, if we note that a man and a woman are walking down the street side by side, we may be uncertain about their relationship. If they both turn the corner in the same direction, get into the same automobile, etc., then we perceive that they are together, that is, that they constitute a unit or a group. The essence of common fate, then, is that all components of a unit experience similar outcomes. The degree to which the outcomes of several individuals covary serves as an index or cue for the perception of them as a group; the greater the covariation the greater the degree of entitativity attributed to them.

Although similarity does not appear to be as primary as common fate, it does serve an important role in the perception of entitativity. Units that are similar in some noticeable respect tend to be perceived as an entity. Soldiers in military uniform are seen as a group; horses are seen as one group, cats another, etc. Of course, similarity may often lead us to make perceptual errors. Tall persons may be seen as a group (for example, as members of a basketball team) when in fact they just happened to be in the same vicinity at the same time and really do not know each other. Similarity often serves as a preliminary cue for the perception of entitativity, which can later be checked by application of the common fate principle.

The reader may have noted that in the example of tall persons being perceived as a basketball team there was at least the implicit assumption that these similar persons were in close proximity. This is not necessary, however; several tall men might be perceived as belonging to a basketball team even if they were seen in different parts of the city and at different times, assuming that the perceiver had reason to believe a basketball team was in town. But this example does illustrate the role of proximity. The tall men might have been perceived as belonging together even if they were not in proximity to one another, but the probability that they will be so perceived is enhanced by proximity. A collection of individuals occupying a common space is more likely to be perceived as a group than are dispersed individuals, even if there is no other basis for the perception of entitativity. As in the case of similarity, proximity often serves as a basis for preliminary groupings which can be checked by common fate indices.

A collection of individuals who experience a common fate on several different occasions, who are similar in one or more respects, and who are in close proximity will undoubtedly be perceived as an entity. The degree of "realness" attributed to the entity will vary with the strength of these principles of perceptual organization. Since the only basis we have for attributing reality to any object derives from our perception of it, we must conclude (with Campbell) that a group is real to the extent that it is perceived as an entity.

## ISSUES IN GROUP DYNAMICS

Although there is disagreement among both psychologists and sociologists concerning the reality of groups, this is not an issue for students of group dynamics. The person who is interested in the scientific study of groups does not doubt that they exist. However, there are a number of issues upon which there is disagreement among group dynamicists. This is not surprising, since group dynamics is a relatively new area of research. It is the nature of the scientific endeavor to continually question and probe for "truth," and the path to truth is never clear. It is inevitable that differences arise regarding the proper questions to be asked and the proper theoretical and empirical procedures to be used in answering them.

There are numerous "mini-issues" in group dynamics, such as definition of group and the ideal group size, but the most important issues center around two major questions: What is the best approach to the study and analysis of groups? Do we need groups? The first question is complex and is answered in many ways, whereas the latter question is somewhat simpler and is usually answered either yes or no (albeit with elaborations).

## Methods of Analysis

Disagreements about the proper approach to the analysis of groups begin with the problem of definition, which was explored in an earlier section. But having accepted a working definition of group, we find that there are still wide differences concerning the most fruitful method of studying groups. At the most general level, there is a division of opinion regarding whether the approach should be theoretical or empirical. Some maintain that the only way we can ever hope to "really" understand group process is by way of theoretical analysis. Others argue that theory is premature at best and, at worst, a waste of time. The extreme empiricist position holds that any phenomenon can be understood only through the careful analysis of empirical observations. (Parenthetically, it might be noted that both the extreme theoretician and the extreme empiricist are wrong; both theory and empirical studies are needed. On the one hand, it is probably impossible to build a theory without some "facts" to use as elements or units of the theoretical structure; and incorrect "facts" lead to incorrect theories. Empirical studies can increase the probability that the elements of the theory are valid. On the other hand, a mass of unorganized and unrelated facts, no matter how correct they may be, is not likely to prove very useful in the understanding of any complex phenomenon. Theory provides the organization of data that is necessary for understanding their implications beyond the specific situations in which the data were obtained.)

In any case, group dynamicists must decide what theory and/or what empirical methods they will use in their approach to the study of small group behavior. At the level of theory, they may choose among a wide variety of approaches. Cartwright and Zander (1968) listed eight theoretical orientations that have been adopted for the analysis of groups:

1   *Field theory* holds that behavior is the result of a field of interdependent forces. In group dynamics, the major proponent of the field theory orientation was Kurt Lewin, who analyzed both individual and group behavior as parts of a system of interrelated events. The method of analysis is similar to that of physics and assumes that the properties of any given behavioral event are determined by its relations to other events in the same system. Field theory provides an excellent basis for the description of group behavior, but, unfortunately, it has not led to a systematic theoretical formulation of group processes.

2   *Interaction theory* views the group as a system of interacting

individuals. In its most common form, three basic elements are identified: activity, interaction, and sentiment. The theory holds that all aspects of group behavior can be understood by spelling out the relations among these three basic elements. This approach has been adopted primarily by sociologically oriented social psychologists and has proved to be most useful in the description of natural groups.

3  *Systems theory* adopts a position very similar to that proposed by interaction theory, and, indeed, there is some question that these are two different orientations. In both, there is an attempt to understand complicated processes from an analysis of basic elements. The chief difference between interaction theory and systems theory is the kinds of elements that are identified and used for analysis. Whereas interaction theory appeals to activity, interaction, and sentiment, systems theory describes the group as a system of interlocking elements such as positions and roles, with much emphasis upon group inputs and outputs.

4  The *sociometric orientation* emphasizes interpersonal choices among group members. The morale and performance of the group are seen as depending upon the interpersonal relations among group members that are reflected in sociometric choices. This orientation has stimulated much research and, as we shall see later, has contributed to our understanding of certain aspects of group behavior. On the other hand, its effect upon systematic theory has been minimal.

5  The *psychoanalytic orientation,* of course, derives from Freudian psychology. It is concerned with motivational and defensive processes of the individual as related to group life. The psychoanalytic orientation has led to at least one theory of group process and has contributed to many more. It has not, however, stimulated much empirical research; hence, the empirical bases of psychoanalytically oriented theoretical formulations are not as strong as would be desirable.

6  The *general psychology orientation* attempts to extend theoretical analyses of individual behavior to group behavior. Thus, the various theoretical formulations with regard to such individual processes as learning, motivation, and perception are applied directly to group processes. There is some question whether this approach should be called an orientation or merely a denial that there is anything unique about group behavior. We shall see that this denial is incorrect.

7  The *empirical-statistical orientation* holds that the basic concepts of group theory can be discovered through the application of statistical procedures. The work of Cattell (1948) exemplifies this approach. He attempted to discover the basic aspects of group behavior from a statistical analysis of data about individuals, primarily by means of factor analysis.

8  The *formal models orientation* was most popular during the 1950s. Theorists adopting this approach attempt to construct formal models of group behavior, using rigorous mathematical procedures. Model builders are often more concerned with the internal consistency of their models than with the degree of correspondence between model and natural situations. For this reason, perhaps, this orientation has produced only

restricted theoretical models which have had limited influence upon group dynamics.

In addition to the eight orientations mentioned by Cartwright and Zander, two other orientations have been proposed for analyzing group behavior:

**9** *Reinforcement theory* attempts to explain interpersonal behavior in terms of the outcomes for group members, i.e., the rewards and costs that accrue to each group member as a consequence of participating in the group. An example of this approach is Thibaut and Kelley's exchange theory which is outlined in Chapter 2, page 22ff.

**10** The *transactional approach* explains group behavior as an interchange of inputs and outputs. Each group member is seen as making contributions that are valued by other group members. For example, the leader who is able to help the group achieve its goals and who otherwise meets the expectations of others in the group may exchange these valuable resources for influence, status, and esteem (Hollander, 1978).

It will be obvious that there are many similarities among these several approaches to groups. What is not so obvious is that relatively few of these approaches have contributed greatly to the theoretical analysis of group behavior. However, some examples of derived theories that have made important contributions are presented in Chapter 2.

At the empirical level of analysis, the investigator again may select from a large number of possible techniques. The methods available range from loosely controlled descriptive-exploratory studies, on the one hand, to rigorously controlled laboratory or simulation studies, on the other. Proponents of the former approach assert that the more rigorously controlled studies deal with artificial situations and phenomena; hence their findings are irrelevant to "real life." Supporters of the more highly controlled designs take the position that descriptive-exploratory studies can yield only suggestive data; only rigorously controlled studies can provide a degree of certainty that one has established valid principles of group behavior. For them, the question of relevance to "real life"* is an empirical question that can be answered only by testing laboratory-established principles in natural situations.

Methods for studying group behavior may be classified into three major classes or categories, ranging from the most natural and least rigorously controlled to the most "artificial" and most highly controlled: (1) field studies, (2) laboratory experiments, and (3) role playing.

---

*The common expression "real life" is actually inappropriate. Behavior in a laboratory is just as real as behavior in a factory or in the street. The term is usually intended to mean that which occurs in everyday situations, without interference by the investigator. Hence, more acceptable terms would be "natural situations" and "natural groups." In the remainder of this book we will use the more appropriate terms, except when citing the views or statements of others who have used the less accurate phrasing.

Field studies and laboratory experiments are distinguished by the settings in which they occur and by the kinds of subjects typically investigated. Field studies are conducted in naturally occurring situations, i.e., in the field. The units of study are usually experienced groups, i.e. natural groups that have a history, such as family groups or basketball teams. Field studies may vary considerably, however, in purpose and method: They may take the form of descriptive-exploratory studies, natural experiments, or field experiments. The descriptive-exploratory study examines a natural situation for the purpose of describing it and exploring possible relationships among naturally occurring variables. The phenomena under investigation are not interfered with in any way—at least not deliberately. The natural experiment also investigates the phenomena, in this case group behaviors, without interfering with them. It differs from the descriptive-exploratory study in that the investigator tries to take advantage of naturally occurring events in order to study their effects upon group behavior. For example, the researcher might take advantage of forced integration of schools to study racially mixed groups. In the field experiment, the investigator deliberately produces variations in the natural situation in order to study their effects upon the group.

The essential features of a laboratory study are that (1) it is conducted in a laboratory setting and (2) the situation is arranged deliberately for the investigation of specified phenomena. The groups that are brought into the laboratory may be experienced, as in the field study, or they may be näive in that the members of the group have never interacted with each other before the beginning of the experiment. Such näive groups may, of course, be formed by random assignment of members or by selecting the members according to specified criteria, such as mental ability, personality charac- teristics, age, sex, and so on.

Role playing is a "make-believe" approach to the study of groups. Participants are asked to assume particular roles for the duration of the investigation and to behave in accordance with role prescriptions. Role playing is most often used when one is interested in effects of particular kinds of behavior upon group process. This approach will be discussed in greater detail in Chapter 2.

### The Value of Groups

A recent controversy about groups was precipitated by a proposal that humans would do better without groups (Buys, 1978). This proposal was based upon research in social psychology which shows that in some instances groups have socially undesirable consequences. Buys cited the following "unpleasant and unhealthful" consequences:

1  Deindividuation, a presumed state of affairs in which group

members lose their identity and are not attended to as individuals, produces negative effects (Zimbardo, 1970).

**2** The anonymity resulting from deindividuation leads to increased rowdyish behavior (Diener, Westford, Dineen, & Fraser, 1973), shocking behavior (Milgram, 1974), and stealing (Fraser, Kelem, Diener, & Beaman, 1975).

**3** Another consequence of deindividuation, diffusion of responsibility, has been related to the failure of many persons to help those in need (Darley & Latane, 1968; Latane & Darley, 1968; Latane & Rodin, 1969). Buys noted that small tips have also been attributed to diffusion of responsibility (Freeman, Walker, Borden, & Latane, 1975), although whether this effect is positive or negative may be debatable.

**4** Modeling the uninhibited behavior of others in groups where members feel anonymous encourages impulsive and antisocial behavior (Diener, Dineen, Endresen, Beaman, & Fraser, 1975).

**5** People often make riskier decisions in groups than when alone (Stoner, 1961; Wallach, Kogan, & Bem, 1964). (Buys did not, however, mention that conservative decisions may also occur in groups.)

**6** Highly cohesive groups may become victims of "groupthink," a process in which critical thinking is suspended and decisions are made without adequate information or consideration of alternatives (Janis, 1972).

**7** Group contagion may result in collective panic (Brown, 1965).

**8** Social movements may engulf millions of people who become victims of the distorted visions of political leaders (Toch, 1965).

**9** Pressures toward uniformity lead to conformity in groups and may have undesirable consequences (Asch, 1951, 1956; Milgram, 1974).

**10** Group leadership often results from appointment, communication networks, type and amount of communication, and the leader's similarity to other group members (Freedman, Carlsmith, & Sears, 1974). Buys implies that leadership should be based upon positive personal characteristics of leaders but fails to explain why leadership based upon the determinants listed by Freedman et al. is necessarily bad.

The proposal by Buys described above stimulated numerous counterarguments. The most detailed rebuttal (Anderson, 1978) noted several weaknesses of the Buys' analysis.

**1** The article by Buys fails to review the literature on the behavior of humans who are alone. It is likely that the same negative kinds of behavior occur when people are *not* in groups, or perhaps different but equally negative behavior may be engaged in by individuals. This particular view is presented forcefully by Kravitz, Cohen, Martin, Sweeney, McCarty, Elliott, and Goldstein (1978) who suggest that the trouble is not in groups as such but in other individuals in situations. All we need do, they maintain, is just eliminate the individuals and groups will not be a problem!

Buys omitted from his review the literature which shows enhancement effects due to group membership. This omission was also noted by Green and Mack (1978).

**2** Buys failed to consider the new developments in role theory (Sarbin & Allen, 1968), systems theory (Berrien, 1976), and task analysis (Hackman, 1968) which make it possible to design a near-perfect group by relating role prescriptions, task dimensions, and desired outcomes.

**3** Many of the consequences of group behavior cited by Buys as evidence of the negative effects of groups may often be desirable. Both Anderson (1978) and Green and Mack (1978) noted that risky decisions are better than conservative decisions in many situations. Green and Mack also pointed out that modeling of desirable behaviors, such as cooperative behavior in juvenile groups, leads to desirable prosocial behavior.

In addition to those problems identified by Anderson, Green and Mack (1978) noted that Buys reported selectively, choosing only those findings that are in accord with his hypothesis. Shaffer (1978) argued that Buys confused collective behavior with group behavior and pointed out that most of his examples are drawn from research on collectivities that are relatively spontaneous, transient, and unstable.

It is clear that there are arguments to support both sides of this controversy and it will be resolved only by careful delimitation of the kinds of groups and collectivities that are being discussed and by careful review and interpretation of *all* relevant literature. In the remainder of this book we will be presenting and discussing a wide range of theory and research that should provide much of the material needed to properly evaluate the claims and counterclaims of participants in this controversy. The student is invited to continuously appraise the value (or lack of value) of groups as he or she learns about group behavior.

## SUGGESTED READINGS

Campbell, D. T. Common fate, similarity, and other indices of the status of aggregates of persons as social entities. *Behavioral Science,* 1958, **3,** 14–25.

DeLamater, J. A definition of "group." *Small Group Behavior,* 1974, **5,** 30–44.

Shaffer, L. S. On the current confusion of group-related behavior and collective behavior: A reaction to Buys. *Personality and Social Psychology Bulletin,* 1978, **4,** 564–567.

# Chapter 2

# Approaches to
# the Study of Groups

The analysis of group behavior has been approached from many points of view, and there is disagreement concerning the most appropriate form of analysis. Some persons believe a theoretical approach is likely to be most productive, whereas others maintain that empirical analysis is the best method for analyzing group process. Those who prefer the theoretical approach believe that emphasis should be placed upon the systematic organization of data and ideas about group process; those who prefer empirical analysis believe that emphasis should be placed upon the accumulation of reliable data about group process. This controversy often turns out to be no more than a difference in the emphasis placed on theory or research or perhaps only a difference in personal preference for one or the other approach.

Probably no one would deny that theorizing and empirical research are interrelated processes and that both are needed for the complete analysis of group behavior. Empiricism provides the evidence necessary for the construction of a meaningful theory. Theory, in turn, organizes and extends known data and thus serves as a framework for further empirical work. Theory often suggests new directions for future research that otherwise might be overlooked. New empirical evidence either strengthens the theory, if consistent with it, or forces rejection or modification if not. Thus, scientific knowledge escalates through successive increments from both theory and research. The important choice, then, is not between theoretical and empirical approaches, but between kinds of theories and between kinds of empirical methods.

## THEORETICAL APPROACHES

A theory may be defined as "... *a set of interrelated hypotheses or propositions concerning a phenomenon or set of phenomena*" (Shaw & Costanzo, 1970, p. 4). Thus, theoretical approaches may vary from very general systems or orientations, such as field theory and stimulus-response reinforcement theory, to more limited theories dealing with a specific phenomenon such as leadership or conformity behavior. Shaw and Costanzo (1970) used the term *theoretical orientation* to refer to the more general approach and reserved the term *theory* for the more limited approach. The theoretical approaches examined here deal with "middle range" phenomena, namely, small group behavior.

Many theoretical approaches have been proposed, and each has made a contribution to the understanding of group behavior. It is not the purpose here, however, to exhaustively review theories of group process. Instead, four selected theories will be described briefly to give the student some familiarity with differing viewpoints and to provide a basis for organizing the empirical data presented in later portions of this text. The four theories selected are group syntality theory, exchange theory, FIRO, and group congruency theory. More detailed accounts of the first three of these theories may be found in *Theories of Social Psychology* (Shaw & Costanzo, 1970), but the best source is the original treatise by the author of each theory.

### Group Syntality Theory

Group syntality theory was formulated by Cattell (1948). This approach was called "empirical-statistical" by Cartwright and Zander (1968) and "transorientational" by Shaw and Costanzo (1970). Cartwright and Zander were impressed by the method that Cattell used in obtaining the data that went into his theory. Cattell relied heavily on factor analysis as an analytic tool, it is true, but this only provided the raw materials for the theory and probably should not be considered a theoretical approach per se. Shaw and Costanzo, on the other hand, were impressed by the degree to which syntality theory incorporated aspects of different theoretical orientations. For example, Cattell's use of vectors in regard to synergy (group energy) draws upon Lewin's field orientation, whereas his appeal to the law of effect in explaining the acquisition of patterns of group behavior makes use of the reinforcement orientation. Regardless of its classification, syntality theory represents an interesting approach to the analysis of groups, and one that is strikingly different from the other three summarized in this chapter.

Cattell's theory consists of two interrelated parts, one part dealing with the dimensions of groups and the other with the dynamics of syntality. The dimensions of groups consist of three categories or "panels." These panels were labeled *population traits, syntality traits,* and *characteristics of internal structure.* Thus, each panel is really a set of variables or characteristics that describe some aspect of the group.

Population traits are merely the characteristics of the individual members who compose the group. Such personal characteristics exist independently of the group and are brought to it when the individual becomes a member. In describing the dimensions of the group in terms of population traits, Cattell (1948) used the averages of these characteristics. The population panel of a given group, therefore, consists of average intelligence, attitude, personality, and the like of the members of the group.

Syntality is defined as the personality of the group, or, more precisely, as any effect that the group has as a totality. It is that which makes the group a unique entity. Syntality traits, then, are those effects which the group has, acting as a group. Such effects may be in relation to another group or to the environment in which the group exists. Syntality traits are inferred from the external behavior of the group and may include such behaviors as decision making, aggressive acts, and the like.

Internal structure refers to the relationships among group members, and structural characteristics describe the organizational patterns within the group. Roles, cliques, status positions, communication networks, and the like are examples of characteristics of internal structure.

The three panels are characterized by interdependency. If all the laws of group behavior were known, then it should be possible to predict any one panel from a knowledge of the other two. For example, if laws of group behavior were completely understood and if the population traits and internal structure of a given group were known, it would be possible to predict precisely the group's syntality traits, i.e., the group's behavior.

Cultural influences are found in all three panels. For example, the characteristics of an individual group member (population traits) are determined in large part by the cultural experiences that the individual has undergone earlier in life. The kinds of interrelationships that develop within a group are also influenced by cultural tradition. Since group syntality is influenced by population traits and structure, it is also indirectly influenced by cultural variables.

Cattell's major concept for analyzing the dynamics of syntality is *synergy*. Each individual joins the group for the purpose of satisfying some psychological need or needs and thus brings to the group a degree of energy that he or she has committed to the group's activities. Synergy is the total of this individual energy that is available to the group. Typically, the activities of the group are of two kinds: activities directed toward the maintenance of the group and those directed toward achievement of the group's goal(s). That is, some major portion of the group's synergy must be used to deal with interpersonal relations in the group. In any group there is a certain amount of friction among group members resulting from status striving, power seeking, member incompatibility, etc. The portion of synergy that must be diverted to establishing cohesion and harmony in the group is called *maintenance synergy*. This requirement for synergy is met first, since the group would otherwise disintegrate. After these activities have been supplied with synergy, that which is left over (called *effective synergy*) can be used to achieve the goals of the group. It is clear from this analysis that groups characterized by much interpersonal conflict are likely to be ineffective in achieving the goals of the group.

Seven "theorems" were proposed by Cattell (1948) in his analysis of the dynamics of syntality, which are largely specifications of the characteristics of synergy. Briefly stated, these theorems are:

**1** Groups are formed to satisfy individual needs and cease to exist when they no longer serve this purpose.

**2** The total synergy of a group is the vectorial resultant of the attitudes of all members toward the group. (Synergy thus depends upon the number of persons in the group, the strength and direction of the satisfactions each person obtains from the group, and the relation of such satisfactions to other groups.)

**3** Effective synergy may be directed toward goals outside the group; hence groups may establish patterns of reacting which are subsidiary to some ultimate goal of the group. (For example, a nation may establish an army as a means of attaining its goal of security.)

**4** Individual group members may also use groups to achieve personal goals; that is, group activities may be subsidiary to some ultimate personal goal. [For example, a man may join a trade union (group) in order to join a ship's company (group) in order to travel to see his friend (personal goal).]

**5** Patterns of behavior in groups, such as loyalty, subsidiation,* and subordination, are learned in accordance with the law of effect.

**6** Group memberships may overlap, but the total synergy in such overlapping groups remains constant so long as individual energy directed toward nongroup goals remains constant and group activities relative to goal distance do not vary. (Note that this does *not* mean that individuals

*Cattell coined the term "subsidiation" to refer to the formation or partial support of other groups.

cannot join a new group without taking energy from groups to which they already belong. On the contrary, they may do so if the goals of the new group are consistent with their interests. For example, a person who is interested in golf may join a committee to improve the golf course without developing new energy or using energy devoted to other groups. On the other hand, if a person is a member of a group committed to aiding the physically handicapped and joins a group devoted to helping the culturally disadvantaged, some synergy would probably be drained off from the first group, since the source of synergy is the member's concern for hapless persons in both groups.)

7   There exists a close parallelism between the personality traits of the group members and the syntality traits of the group. (For example, individual disposition rigidity parallels syntal conservatism, personal intelligence level parallels syntal integration.)

Many of the terms used by Cattell appear to be unnecessarily recondite. Nevertheless, syntality theory contains some interesting implications for group process. For example, the energies available to groups having common members are interrelated, so that energy which a member commits to one group may, in certain instances, detract from that available for use by other groups (theorem 6). This might account for some cases of intergroup conflict. Theorem 7 suggests that the researcher can probably learn as much from the study of the individual group members as from studying the group as a whole, and vice versa. This implication is, of course, related to the implications from theorem 5: The law of effect works on individuals, and the patterns of behavior in the group can be established through the reinforcement of selected patterns of individual behavior. For greater detail, the interested reader may wish to refer to Cattell (1951a, 1951b), Cattell and Wispe (1948), and Cattell, Saunders, and Stice (1953). These reports show how some of the panels of group behavior can be measured and how the ideas discussed above are related to the empirical-statistical orientation discussed in Chapter 1.

## Exchange Theory

Thibaut and Kelley (1959) proposed a much more ambitious theory (or "framework" as they preferred to call it) than that of Cattell. Their intention was to explain interpersonal behavior and group processes. They viewed their approach as primarily functionalistic, since their focus was upon what is useful or effective from the viewpoint of the group. The theory assumes that the existence of the group is based solely upon the participation and satisfaction of individuals in the group. Therefore, the analysis of group processes must be in terms of the adjustments that *individuals* make in attempting to solve the problems of interdependency. It is not too difficult to see that this viewpoint leads almost inevitably to the adoption of a reinforcement orientation. Although their analysis was limited largely to the dyad, Thibaut and Kelley believe that their theory applies to larger groups as well.

The theory can best be described by examining the authors' analysis of interaction, which involves (1) definitions of the key concepts used in the theory, (2) a consideration of the consequences of interaction, and (3) an analysis of members' evaluation of interpersonal relationships.

The key concepts in the theory are *interaction, interpersonal relationship, behavior sequence,* and *behavior repertoire. Interaction* and *interpersonal relationship* are interdependent and hence are defined together. The central feature of interaction is the interpersonal relationship, and two persons are said to have formed a relationship if they interact on several different occasions. This statement is meaningful, of course, only when "interaction" has been defined. It is perhaps best to quote Thibaut and Kelley's definition: "By interaction is meant that they emit behavior in each other's presence, they create products for each other, or they communicate with each other. In every case that we would identify as an instance of interaction there is at least the possibility that the actions of each person affect the other" (Thibaut & Kelley, 1959, p. 10).

For example, if person A meets person B on the street, stops and chats about the weather, listens to the troubles of the day, and then each proceeds on his or her way, they are said to have interacted; that is, their conversation was an instance of interaction.

The *behavior sequence* was chosen as the unit for the analysis of behavior. Each behavior sequence is said to consist of a number of specific motor and verbal acts that are sequentially organized and directed toward some immediate goal. In the example given above, A's motor and verbal acts during the chat about the weather might be considered a sequence of acts directed toward the goal of being friendly, and hence would be treated as a behavior sequence. Each individual, of course, is capable of enacting a tremendous number and variety of behavior sequences. Thibaut and Kelley used the term *behavior repertoire* to refer to all the possible behavior sequences that a given person might enact during interaction with another person, including combinations of possible behavior sequences. Interaction is selective both with respect to who interacts with whom and with respect to what behavior sequences are enacted. Probably no person interacts with every other person that it would be possible to interact with, nor does a person enact all possible behavior sequences. For example, it is possible for most persons to enact a behavior sequence leading to murder, but few persons do so.

The consequences (outcomes) of interaction are described in terms of *rewards* and *costs.* When two persons interact, each one typically enjoys some part of the interaction, but finds other parts less enjoyable or even unpleasant. The concept of *reward* refers to those aspects which the individual finds pleasurable, enjoyable, gratifying, or otherwise satisfying. "The provision of a means whereby a drive is reduced or a need fulfilled constitutes a reward" (Thibaut & Kelley, 1959, p. 12). *Costs* refer to anything that inhibits the performance of a behavior sequence. That is, the greater the inhibition that the person must overcome in order to perform a given behavior sequence, the more costly the enactment of that behavior. Outcomes are the resultant of rewards minus costs.

Rewards and costs may be determined by either exogenous or endogenous factors. Exogenous factors are those that are external to the interpersonal relationship. For example, rewards and costs that are due to individual characteristics such as values, skills, needs, tools, and the like are regarded as exogenous. An individual who is highly skilled in the performance of a given act may find it enjoyable to enact that behavior sequence in the presence of others; for one who is unskilled, the enactment of that same behavior sequence may incur a cost. Endogenous factors are those that are inherent in the relationship itself; that is, the reward or cost depends not only upon the actions of the individual but also upon the behaviors of the other person. Two musicians may enjoy a musical interaction only if they harmonize; each one trying to play a different tune would probably be costly to both, owing to response interference. Other kinds of endogenous costs are due to satiation, fatigue, or incompatible responses.

In applying these concepts to the analysis of group behavior, Thibaut and Kelley (1959) made use of a behavior matrix, modeled after game theory formulations. An example of this matrix is shown in Figure 2-1, which represents the possible outcomes of interactions of persons A and B. The columns of the matrix represent the behavior repertoire of person A and the rows represent that of person B. The numbers in the upper portion of each cell indicate the outcome of the interaction for person A whenever the interaction falls within that cell, and the number in the lower portion indicates B's outcomes for that same interaction. For example, if A enacts behavior sequence $a_1$ and B enacts behavior sequence $b_1$, the interaction falls in the upper left-hand corner of the matrix; hence A's outcome is 6 units and B's outcome is 2 units. In this example, these are, of course, arbitrary units which represent the resultant of costs incurred and rewards received during the course of that particular interaction. Parenthetically, it might be noted that the determination of exact values for rewards and costs in a natural situation is one of the unsolved problems for exchange theory—indeed, for all psychology.

According to Thibaut and Kelley, interaction outcomes are evaluated by comparison with certain internal standards, which they called the *comparison level* (CL) and the *comparison level for alternatives* (CL$_{alt}$).

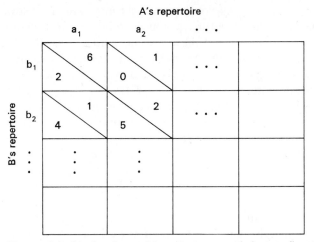

**Figure 2-1** Matrix of possible outcomes, scaled according to overall goodness of outcomes. (Reprinted with permission from J. W. Thibaut & H. H. Kelley. *The social psychology of groups.* New York: Wiley, 1959, Table 2-2, p. 15.)

The CL is the standard against which an individual evaluates the attractiveness of an interpersonal relationship, or how satisfactory it is. The CL is a subjective standard that is developed as a consequence of the interpersonal relationships the individual has experienced during his or her lifetime. In general, the CL will be somewhere near the middle of the range of relationships that the person has experienced, ordered according to the goodness of the outcomes, that is, how satisfactory the outcome is for the individual. Once the CL has been established, the individual will evaluate positively any relationship that falls above the CL in terms of outcomes, and negatively any relationship that falls below the CL. Presumably, each new experience leads to some modification of the CL, although the increment (or decrement) from any one interaction may be negligible. This conception of the CL is similar to other formulations regarding subjective standards; for example, reference scales (Tresselt, 1947), adaptation level (Helson, 1948), and judgment scales (Sherif & Hovland, 1961).

The CL$_{alt}$ is the standard which an individual uses to decide whether to remain in a relationship or to leave it. The CL$_{alt}$ is the lowest outcome that a person will accept in view of alternative relationships. Theoretically, an individual might choose to enter into or to maintain a relationship that is unattractive (below his CL) if it is the most attractive one available at the time, that is, if it is above his or her CL$_{alt}$. For example, if a young man wishes to attend the high school prom, he may elect to escort a young lady who is not particularly attractive to him if she is the best alternative that he has available for that affair. His relationship with her may well fall below his CL but, nevertheless, be above his $CL_{alt}$. On the other hand, a person may leave an attractive relationship if there are more attractive alternatives. It should be noted that these considerations assume that the relationship is voluntary; the individual may be forced to remain in a relationship that is below both his or her CL and $CL_{alt}$. Some support for the CL concept is available. In one study (Friedland, Arnold, & Thibaut, 1974), CLs were established by varying the rate of payoff in a series of interactions and the effects of differing levels of reward on cooperative behavior examined. Two levels of reward and two different CLs were tested. Absolute level of reward did not influence cooperative behavior, but outcomes that were above the CL yielded more frequent cooperative behavior than outcomes below the CL.

This analysis of dyadic interaction, as a prototype of group interaction, can be used to predict the course of interaction if one can identify the rewards and costs in the situation. Thibaut and Kelley proposed that an individual generally repeats a rewarded response but does not repeat a costly response. Consider, for example, the interaction matrix depicted in Figure 2-2. This represents a situation which Thibaut and Kelley called an instance of *mutual fate control*. In this situation, persons A and B can each determine the other's outcomes regardless of the other's behavior. Thibaut and Kelley predict that A will eventually enact $a_1$ and B will enact $b_1$ after a series of exchanges. For example, if A enacts $a_1$ and B enacts $b_2$, then A is punished (the interaction is costly) and B is rewarded; hence A will tend to change his or her response and B will tend to repeat the same response. This means that on the next exchange, the interaction will be in the lower right-hand cell, and the interaction will be costly for both persons. On the next exchange, both should shift responses, putting the interaction into the $a_1/b_1$ cell. Both are rewarded and the interaction should continue in this manner. No matter where the interaction starts, it should always lead to the same final pattern of interaction in which both A and B are rewarded. Although this example deals with mutual fate control, the same principles

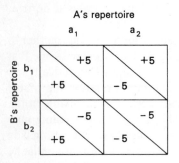

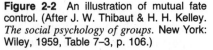

**Figure 2-2** An illustration of mutual fate control. (After J. W. Thibaut & H. H. Kelley. *The social psychology of groups.* New York: Wiley, 1959, Table 7–3, p. 106.)

should apply to other outcome matrices. Several empirical studies (Bixenstine, Potash, & Wilson, 1963; M. E. Shaw, 1962; Willis & Joseph, 1959) have yielded results opposite to those predicted by the theory; for example, interacting dyads tend to develop an interaction pattern in which the outcomes are *low* for both persons. However, it is unclear whether these findings are due to failure to manipulate rewards and costs or to inaccuracy of the theory. That is, rewards and costs for the individual may be determined by the value of his or her outcomes *relative* to the value of the other person's outcomes, rather than by the absolute value of his or her own outcomes.

Exchange theory has many other important implications which cannot be covered here. Its greatest contribution at this stage is probably to the organization of empirical data rather than to the prediction of interpersonal behavior. This is due in part to the difficulty of determining rewards and costs for particular persons and in part to the fact that as yet the theory has not been widely tested (see McNeel, 1973; McNeel, Sweeney, & Bohlin, 1974).

### FIRO: A Theory of Interpersonal Relations

FIRO is a theory of interpersonal behavior that derives from the psychoanalytic orientation. It was formulated by Schutz in 1955 and was later expanded and modified (Schutz, 1958, 1967). FIRO stands for Fundamental Interpersonal Relations Orientation. As the name indicates, the theory attempts to explain interpersonal behavior in terms of orientations to others. The theory holds that people orient themselves toward others in certain characteristic patterns, which are major determinants of interpersonal behavior. The particular characteristic that an individual exemplifies can be explained in terms of three interpersonal needs: *inclusion, control, and affection.* These needs are present during childhood, and the characteristic interaction pattern that an individual develops with respect to each need area is a consequence of the way the child was treated by his or her parents or other adults and of the manner in which he or she responded to these treatments.

*Inclusion* refers to the need for togetherness, the need to associate with others. The need manifests itself through behaviors designed to attract the attention and interest of others (Schutz, 1967). The person who has a strong need for inclusion will reveal it through strivings for prominence, recognition, prestige, etc. For example, the person who has a strong need for inclusion may be overly friendly, amiable, deferent; the person may also be possessive and try to punish friends when they attempt to establish friendships with others.

*Control* refers to the decision-making process between people. The need for control varies from the need to dominate others (to have power and authority over them) to the need to be controlled. At one extreme, the person wants to control others completely; at the other extreme, the person wants others to control him or her completely. Again, this need is manifested through the person's behavior vis-à-vis others. The person with a high need to control displays rebellion and refusal to be controlled; the person with a high need to be controlled is compliant and submissive to others.

*Affection* refers to close personal and emotional feelings between two individuals, and its extremes are represented by love and hate. The person with a strong need for affection will be friendly, make overtures to others, and generally try to establish close emotional ties with others. At the other extreme, the low-need person will avoid close interpersonal relations.

When two or more persons interact, each one typically enacts in each need area the characteristic behavior pattern that he or she developed in childhood. The interaction patterns of any two given individuals may be either compatible or incompatible. If they are compatible, then the interaction is likely to be easy and productive; if incompatible, difficult and unproductive. Schutz (1958) identified three types of compatibility-incompatibility that could occur in each of the three need areas: interchange compatibility, originator compatibility, and reciprocal compatibility. *Interchange compatibility* is based upon the mutual expression of inclusion, control, or affection. Some persons prefer a great deal of exchange of behavior relevant to the need area under consideration, whereas others prefer neither to receive nor to send inclusion, control, or affection. Interchange compatibility exists when the two persons interacting are similar with respect to the amount of exchange desired; incompatibility results from dissimilarity in this respect. For example, if two persons are interacting and both prefer either a high rate of exchange or a low rate of exchange in the area of affection, they will be compatible; if one person prefers a high rate of exchange and the other prefers a low rate of exchange, they will be incompatible. Thus exchange compatibility depends upon the degree to which both members of a dyad agree concerning the amount of mutual interaction that is desirable.

*Originator compatibility* derives from the originator-receiver dimension of interaction. In general, two persons are compatible to the degree that the expression of inclusion, control, or affection corresponds to that which the other person wishes to receive in each area. For example, if one person needs to control and tries to dominate another, and that other needs to be submissive, they will be compatible. On the other hand, if both persons need to control and try to dominate each other, they will be incompatible. Similarly, if one person actively initiates (originates) group activities for another person who wants to be included in group activities, the dyad will be compatible, whereas the same initiation of group activities for a person who does not want to be included will lead to incompatibility. The important thing here is the degree to which the activities originated by one person are in accord with the needs of the other member of the dyad.

*Reciprocal compatibility* reflects the degree to which two persons "reciprocally satisfy each other's behavior preferences" (Schutz, 1958, p. 108). Thus if one person wants the other to express much affection and the other does so, the dyad is compatible in the area of affection. But if one member is frustrated because the other does not express enough affection or if one member cannot express his preferred behavior toward the other (e.g., affection or control), the dyad will be incompatible. In general, reciprocal compatibility depends upon the degree to which each person's behavior is in accord with the other person's needs.

The general assumption of Schutz's theory is that compatible groups will be more efficient than incompatible groups. This effect is reflected in the initial formation of groups, in the degree to which the groups are likely to continue to function, and in the productivity of groups. Research reported by Schutz (1955, 1958, 1967) generally supports the theory. Research by other investigators has also revealed some evidence supporting the theory (e.g., Lundgren, 1975; Reddy & Byrnes, 1972), but some researchers have failed to find the expected relationships between interpersonal needs and behavior in groups (e.g., Armstrong & Roback, 1977; Lundgren & Knight, 1977; Moos & Speisman, 1962). However, in some cases the investigators may have failed to create the kinds of situations in which one might expect interpersonal needs to be related to group behavior. Research relevant to Schutz's theory will be discussed more fully in Chapter 7.

### Group Congruency Theory

The origins of group congruency theory are blurred in history, but the basic ideas inherent in the theory may be traced at least to Benoit-Smullyan (1944). He observed that a person in a given society can be ranked on a variety of dimensions such as age, education, income, occupational prestige, and power and suggested that such rankings tend toward equilibration; i.e., a person strives to achieve a balance such that status or rankings on various dimensions are approximately equal. So long as status incongruency exists, the person is likely to desire social change (Lenski, 1954), to display more psychosomatic symptoms (Jackson, 1962), and to withdraw from social situations (Lenski, 1956).

Status congruency has also been shown to be a variable in small group performance. For instance, Adams (1953) proposed that status congruency contributes to the development of stable expectations for behavior and thus enhances smooth interpersonal interaction. He computed a status congruency index for groups of Air Force flight crews and related this index to intergroup trust, friendship, and satisfaction. Groups that were lowest in status congruency were generally lower in friendship, trust, and satisfaction. Similar effects were observed in laboratory groups constructed to vary in degree of status congruency (Brandon, 1965; Sampson, 1969).

From the studies cited above, it was just a small step to a more generalized conceptualization of congruency in groups and its consequences for group process and outcome. Thus, Hrycenko and Minton (1974) hypothesized that satisfaction with one's power position in a group will be determined by the interaction of preference for locus of control (internal or external) and the actual degree of power possessed. That is, a person who believes that he or she has internal control will find a high-power position more congruent with this belief than a low-power position, whereas a person who believes that his or her behavior is externally controlled will perceive the low-power position to be more appropriate. Thus, one's beliefs about control may be either congruent or incongruent with one's position in the group, and satisfaction with the group position should vary with congruency. The experimental data supported the hypothesis for men but not for women. In a similar vein, Shaw and Harkey (1976) proposed that behavioral tendencies of group members which are congruent with their positions in the group should facilitate group performance, whereas those which are not congruent should impede group performance. Experimental evidence supported the hypothesis for both male and female groups.

Group congruency theory, in its present form, is an "emergent" from the theory and research described above. Group performance is assumed to be the consequence of a complex set of variables or group elements and the interactions among those elements. The term *group elements* refers to all those aspects of the group and the group situation that influence or may be expected to influence group process. Group elements that affect group performance may be either intrinsic or extrinsic with respect to the group. Extrinsic elements include such things as member characteristics (for example, abilities, personality characteristics, attitudes) and group tasks. Intrinsic elements include those aspects of the group that result from group interaction (for example, group structure, group cohesiveness, group compatibility). (Of course, group structure may be extrinsic in the sense that it can be imposed by forces outside the group, but even in those instances an informal structure usually emerges in the group and functions as an intrinsic variable.) In general, the effects produced by the interaction of group elements are intrinsic to the group.

Some group elements affect group behavior more or less directly. For example, task difficulty influences group performance independently of variations in group interaction effects. However, the effects of group elements on group performance and member behavior are often mediated by group process, and this is especially true of effects produced by the interaction of group elements. In general, when the group is harmonious and nonconflictual, the energy available to the group can be used in the interest of goal attainment. But if the group process is characterized by tension, interpersonal conflict, and member discontent, much of the group's available energy must be devoted to resolving these internal problems, and less energy will be available for goal-directed activities (cf. syntality theory). *Group congruency* refers to nonconflicting, harmonious relationships among group elements; hence, congruent groups should be characterized by harmonious group process and greater productivity.

**Propositions** The above considerations may be formalized in the following theoretical propositions:

**Proposition 1** Groups vary in the degree to which elements of the group fit together harmoniously, that is, in degree of group congruency.

**Proposition 2** The less congruent the group elements, the greater the disruption of the internal functioning of the group.

**Proposition 3** The more the internal functioning of the group is disrupted, the poorer the performance of the group.

**Proposition 4** The more the internal functioning of the group is disrupted, the lower the morale (general satisfaction) of the group members.

It follows from these propositions that both the performance of the group and the morale of group members should vary with group congruency. Although the evidence relative to these hypotheses is limited, it is generally supportive (see Hrycenko & Minton, 1974; Shaw, 1959b; Shaw & Harkey, 1976). The theory provides a convenient framework for evaluating those aspects of group behavior that derive from the interrelationships among group elements. It does not apply to those variables that influence group process more or less independently of other variables (e.g., task-related abilities of group members). In addition to its limited scope, the theory provides no objective basis for determining whether two group elements are congruent or incongruent. Such identification derives from logical analysis and depends upon consensus for a priori validation. In practice, it is relatively easy to determine whether elements are or are not congruent, and the lack of rigorous objectivity may be less of a problem than it appears to be.

## A Brief Comparison of Theories

Each of these theories attempts to explain group behavior, although they differ in the range of group processes encompassed. The most comprehensive theory probably is exchange theory, which can be applied to any aspect of group behavior. Group syntality theory, FIRO, and congruency theory aspire to generality but are not as easily extended to all forms of group behavior as is exchange theory.

The theories also differ in precision, although it is difficult to compare them in terms of overall precision. Syntality theory lacks precision in the definition of some terms and in the measurement of variables. Congruency theory lacks precision in that there is no specification of rules for determining objectively just which group elements are or are not congruent. Exchange theory and FIRO permit relatively precise predictions about group behavior, but both suffer from measurement problems. Exchange theory requires the identification and measurement of reinforcers, and this has proved a difficult undertaking. FIRO requires the measurement of needs and the combining of these measures to predict compatibility. Schutz's need scales are moderately satisfactory, but some of the formulas for computing compatibility are of questionable validity.

In spite of these problems, each theory aids in the understanding of group process, and each will be referred to again in later discussions of small group phenomena.

## EMPIRICAL APPROACHES

The variety of empirical approaches to the study of group behavior is limited only the ingenuity of investigators. However, as noted in Chapter 1, the empirical studies of small groups fall into three general classes: field studies, laboratory experiments, and role playing. Role-playing studies may be conducted either in the laboratory or in the field and, therefore, do not represent a distinctly different class of studies. For convenience, they will be discussed in a separate section.

### Field Studies

The basic characteristic of a field study is that the phenomenon under investigation is studied as it exists "naturally." That is, the investigator does not create the situation or situations being studied; instead, he or she examines the phenomenon as it occurs in natural ongoing social events. The study is conducted "in the field" rather than in a laboratory. The form of field studies may differ, depending upon the purposes and biases of the investigator. If the purpose of the investigator is to explore and describe, the field study is likely to begin with few or no hypotheses, and the researcher will make no attempt to manipulate any aspect of the situation. This is also likely to be the case if the investigator believes strongly that valid data can be obtained only by avoiding any obtrusion into the phenomenon being studied. On the other hand, the investigator may be primarily interested in testing hypotheses and may believe that interference with the phenomenon is the only way one can be certain that the observed relationships among variables are true cause-effect relationships.* In this case, the form of the field study will probably be a "field experiment." That is, the investigator manipulates the variable(s) of interest to him or her but does so in natural situations rather than in the laboratory. A compromise between these two extreme types of field studies is the "natural experiment." In this approach, the investigator takes advantage of naturally occurring events in order to examine their consequences for group behavior. Each of these variations merits further consideration.

**Descriptive-Exploratory Studies** The purpose of a descriptive-exploratory field study is to describe the groups under investigation, often with the intention of identifying relationships among variables. The exact purpose served by this approach varies from a mere description of the characteristics of groups to the formulation of precise hypotheses about functional relationships. If the purpose is to formulate hypotheses and/or to establish functional relationships, researchers may take one of two possible approaches. They may select groups randomly, measure several variables or characteristics of the groups, and look for relationships among them; or they may select groups according to specified criteria, so that the groups represent different degrees or levels of the variable of interest, and compare sets of groups with respect to other characteristics. An example of the first approach is a study by Polansky, Lippitt, and Redl (1950) of behavioral contagion in groups. These investigators studied eight boys' groups and eight girls' groups in two summer camps. Data consisted of counselor ratings, observations by the experimenters, and questionnaire responses by the boys and girls. The investigators then examined the relationship of the group member's prestige rating to his or her influence in the group. High-prestige members attempted influence more often and initiated "contagion" more often than low-prestige members. This observation led to the formulation of hypotheses about the effects of prestige position upon social influence in groups.

The second approach may be illustrated by a study of social welfare agencies conducted by Blau (1959-1960). Among other things, Blau was interested in the effects of the size of the agency upon the behavior of welfare workers. He therefore selected several small agencies and several large ones and compared the role characteristics found in agencies of each size. At the time the study was planned, Blau believed that the differences between large and small agencies could be attributed to the size variable. However, during the study he became aware that the small agencies were

---

*The intent is to avoid philosophical arguments concerning the nature of causality. "Cause-effect relationship" means only that there is a high probability that if X is manipulated (varied), corresponding and systematic changes will occur in Y.

located in small towns and the large agencies in large towns. This led him to examine other aspects of the two situations which strongly indicated that differences were due to the environmental setting rather than to the size of the agency.

Descriptive-exploratory studies are attractive to investigators concerned with the relevance of empirical studies to natural situations. Since the situations studied are natural ones, there is no question of relevance to other similar situations. However, since there are many natural settings that might be chosen for investigation and since only a few can be selected, one might still question the generality of the findings. This is a question that can be raised with respect to any empirical study and probably is less serious in this approach than in more restricted approaches. The most serious problem with the descriptive-exploratory approach is the relative uncertainty of the validity of conclusions. The investigator measures only a few of the many uncontrolled variables operating in the field, and he or she has no good basis for determining cause-effect relations or, indeed, the validity of observed relationships. The study of welfare agencies cited above provides a good example of this problem. Had Blau been less observant, he might very well have concluded that size of welfare agency is a determinant of role characteristics, although it appears more likely that the environmental setting is the major variable. But even this conclusion may not be valid; some other unnoticed variable may be the real determinant of the role characteristics.

**Natural Experiments** The natural experiment differs from the descriptive-exploratory study in that investigators take advantage of naturally occurring changes to study their effects upon group process. This sometimes can be planned in advance if researchers know that the change is about to occur or will occur at a definite time. For example, if they know that certain classrooms will be desegregated on a given date, they can design a before-after study, or they can select other similar classrooms that will not be desegregated and compare those which are with those which are not. In this way the effects of desegregation can be evaluated.

An example of this approach is the study by Cook, Havel, and Christ (1957). They learned that certain foreign students would be selected to attend a summer orientation program in the United States (although they had no voice in the selection) and planned an experiment to study the effects of the orientation on the students. A control group was selected which was roughly matched to the experimental group (those attending the orientation) on such characteristics as nationality, field of study, and age. The two groups could then be compared on the dependent measures of interest to the investigators.

The natural experiment has an added advantage over the descriptive-exploratory study in that cause-effect relationships are somewhat more impelling. However, since the investigator does not have control over the manipulation, uncontrolled and unknown variables may be contaminating the results.

**Field Experiments** The field experiment carries the degree of experimental control one step further: The investigator controls the manipulation of certain variables but does so in a field setting. A classic example of this approach is the study of resistance to change conducted by Coch and French (1948). The subjects for this study were four groups of factory workers. Groups contained from seven to fourteen members. At the beginning of the study, the four groups were roughly equivalent on cohesiveness, efficiency, and the amount of change that would be necessary to carry out the study. All groups were subjected to a change in work procedure, but preparation for the change was different for different groups. In one group representatives of the workers participated in planning the change, in two groups all workers participated in planning the change, and in the fourth group the members were merely informed of the change. Effects of the various treatments were measured by determining the time required for the groups to attain a set standard of efficiency. Total participation produced the fastest learning of the new procedure, representative participation produced the next best rate, and no participation (the control group) produced the slowest rate of all. This group failed to attain the standard.

A similar kind of field study was conducted by Morse and Reimer (1956). These researchers studied the effect of increasing the decision-making role of the rank-and-file employees in an industrial organization. Four clerical groups were selected to be as similar as possible on a number of characteristics related to group satisfaction and productivity. Two of the groups were randomly assigned to an "autonomy" condition and the other two to a "hierarchically controlled" condition. Members of the autonomy groups were given increased control over their activities, whereas members of the hierarchically controlled groups experienced a decrease in such control. Pre-post measures of satisfaction and productivity indicated that satisfaction increased in the autonomy groups but decreased in the hierarchically controlled groups. All groups increased in productivity, but the increase was greater in the hierarchically controlled groups.*

The advantage of the field experiment over the natural experiment is evident. Since experimenters control the introduction of changes in the former, they can be more confident that they have controlled for the effects of unwanted variables. In the latter, the change is introduced by natural events or by others. Field experiments represent the best compromise

*This difference in productivity may have been due to an artifact inherent in the method of measuring productivity. This experiment will be discussed in greater detail in Chapter 9.

between the need to control significant variables and the desire to extend findings to everyday events and situations, although there is still some question about the degree of control over other variables that might influence the phenomena under investigation.

## Laboratory Experiments

The major difference between the laboratory experiment and the field study is the locus of the investigation, that is, a self-contained laboratory rather than a natural setting. This difference, however, is highly significant because it carries with it many implications for the control of variables and the generality of findings. The greatest advantage of the laboratory experiment is the degree of control that the experimenter can exercise over variables. If experimenters are ingenious enough, they can control all or most of the variables that might influence the phenomenon under consideration, except the one(s) that they are interested in studying. Cause and effect can be established with considerably greater confidence than when such controls are lacking. On the other hand, this degree of control makes the laboratory situation unlike any situation that one is likely to encounter in the "real world." Critics of the laboratory approach have used this fact to deny that such studies have any validity for group behavior outside the laboratory. However, Festinger (1953b) has argued cogently that the situation in which group members find them is real to them, whether it is in the laboratory or in a natural setting. There are actually two issues here: (1) the validity of the behavior, given the conditions under which it occurs, and (2) whether effects that occur in the laboratory also occur outside the laboratory, i.e., in natural situations. The question of the extent to which data from the laboratory apply in natural situations has been called *generalizability, external validity,* and (the currently popular term) *ecological validity.* Observations made in either laboratories or natural settings may be valid or invalid, depending upon the conditions under which the observations are made. But the mere fact that data are obtained in the laboratory does not invalidate them. Nevertheless, it is true that the strength of variables operating in the laboratory is usually much less than the strength of similar variables found in natural situations. It is often implicitly assumed that if weak variables produce small effects in the laboratory, strong variables of the same type will produce large effects in natural settings. This is a hazardous assumption which few, if any, investigators would accept when it is stated explicitly, and the careful student of group behavior will be on guard against making such an assumption implicitly.

Whether effects that occur in the laboratory can be generalized to natural situations is a more complex problem. It may be that the variables studied in the laboratory are basically different from those operating in natural settings; if so, laboratory results obviously cannot be generalized to situations outside the laboratory. It is also true that conclusions formulated from laboratory results may not hold in natural settings where many other variables are operating. In natural groups another variable may be so powerful that the effects of the "laboratory variable" are negated.

Like other approaches, laboratory experimentation has many variations. The laboratory experiment most similar to the field experiment is that in which experienced or natural groups are brought into the laboratory and subjected to experimental treatments. The more common method, however, involves the formation of "artificial" or naïve groups for the sole purpose of experimentation. Naïve groups may be formed by random assignment of members or by systematic selection of members to represent specific populations.

**Experienced Groups**   When natural groups are brought into the laboratory, they are already experienced groups; that is, the members of the groups have already established relationships among themselves, and many of the processes of group formation have already been completed. This means that the initial phases of group formation cannot be studied with such groups. Often, however, the experimenter is interested in studying processes that are interfered with by group formation processes. Experienced groups are preferable for such studies, as well as for those designed for generalization to natural ongoing groups.

This approach is illustrated by a study conducted by Bowen (1966) in which family groups were brought into the laboratory for the purpose of studying coalition patterns. By bringing three families (father, mother, and teen-age son) into the laboratory at the same time, and systematically rotating group memberships, Bowen not only was able to examine patterns of coalition formation in family groups, but also was able to compare such patterns in family, simulated family (father, mother, and son, each from a different family), and ad hoc groups (three fathers, three mothers, or three sons).

The advantages of using experienced groups are obvious, but it should also be evident that intragroup relationships that are brought with the group into the laboratory may influence the experimental results. That is, there is a greater probability of unknown variables contaminating the results of experiments using experienced groups than of those using naïve groups. Nevertheless, if the intent is to generalize to experienced groups, then the results of studies using such groups are clearly more relevant.

**Selected Naive Groups**   Often an investigator is interested in studying variables that can be manipulated only through selection. For example, the investigation of group composition effects almost necessarily requires selection of group members. This can be illustrated by an experimental test of FIRO in which Schutz (1955) selected group members according to their scores on need scales. On the basis of these scores, groups were formed to be either compatible or incompatible, and Schutz was able to show that compatible groups were more effective than incompatible groups when faced with tasks requiring intragroup cooperation. This technique has the advantage of permitting relatively precise specification of group characteristics, but care must be taken to ensure that such selection does not result in the unwitting variation of other significant variables.

**Random Naive Groups**  In laboratory experimentation, the common approach is to use random näive groups. Subjects are randomly assigned to groups; the groups thus composed are then randomly assigned to sets of groups which are exposed to differential treatments. The purpose of this procedure is to ensure that members of groups exposed to differential experimental treatments are not initially different. Since randomization ensures that each subject has the same chance of being assigned to any given group as any other subject, it is unlikely that any sizable sets of groups assigned to different experimental treatments will be different at the beginning of the experiment. Any differences that are observed following experimental manipulations are attributed to the treatment differences. It should be kept in mind, however, that randomization does not guarantee initial comparability of groups. Even strictly random assignment occasionally can result in differences in group composition, which in turn can influence experimental results.

Both random and selected näive groups are subject to the criticism that they are "artificial" and hence have no meaning for the real world. Actually, this is both a strength and a weakness. Just because a group *is* artificial, investigators can contrive situations that do not occur naturally. For example, it is probable that certain combinations of group memberships never occur in a natural group. It would be surprising to find a group composed solely of highly dominant individuals or of submissive individuals. By means of the selected näive group procedure, however, it is easy to construct such groups in the laboratory. Also, as Cartwright and Zander (1968) pointed out, research on artificial groups in the laboratory can help resolve questions about the direction of causality or about which of several variables may be producing an observed effect found in studies of natural groups. There is nevertheless, a problem of generalizing to nonlaboratory situations. The best approach is to examine hypotheses in both field and laboratory settings.

### Role-Playing Experiments

The term *role playing* has been used in a variety of ways. Sociologists often use the term to denote overt enactment of one's own role (the set of behaviors that one judges to be appropriate in a given situation) (Coutu, 1951), whereas psychologists more often employ role playing as a label for the enactment of an assumed role (the set of behaviors that one believes appropriate for a position other than one's own, such as leader, teacher, or observer). The latter kind of role playing has long been used to try to understand and/or change behavior (e.g., Moreno, 1946) and is the type of role playing that is ordinarily used in experimentation. In practice, two rather different role-playing methods have been employed to study interpersonal behavior, which we have labeled *role visualization* and *role enactment.*

**Role Visualization Experiments**   This approach requires the subject to passively visualize another person's role and to predict the other person's behavior (Bem, 1967). Typically, a situation is described in detail to a subject so that he or she has approximately the same information as the person actually in the situation. The subject is then asked to predict how the other person will or did behave in the situation. This role visualization procedure is often used to test some theory about psychological processes occurring in typical social psychological experiments. For example, Bem (1967) argued that participants' responses in dissonance studies are the result of self-observation of behavior and not the consequences of internal states of arousal. Since subjects employing role visualization yielded results similar to those by actual subjects in such experiments, he concluded that his theory was correct. Similarly, Mixon (1972) employed the technique to test his theories about the well-known studies of obedience to authority (Milgram, 1963). You will probably recall that Milgram told participants that they were teachers who could use electric shock to help their "students" learn the assigned material. "Teachers" had control of a shock generator having voltage levers ranging from 15 to 450 volts. Verbal labels were also supplied, ranging from "slight shock" to "danger: severe shock." The "students" were actually confederates who received no shock regardless of the subject's manipulation of the shock levers, but the subjects did not know this. Surprisingly, twenty-six of the forty subjects tested administered the highest shock level available. Mixon (1972) described this situation in detail to his subjects, including descriptions of the confederate's and the experimenter's behavior during the course of the experiment. His subjects also knew that the shock generator did not actually deliver shocks. Nevertheless, they behaved much like the subjects in Milgram's study. Mixon concluded that in both Milgram's and his own experiments, subjects were responding to stipulated false beliefs; that is, they knew they were being judged in the context of the experimental situation and behaved accordingly.

**Role Enactment Experiments**   The role enactment procedure is usually employed for purposes quite different from those of the role visualization type. The investigator is ordinarily interested in the behavior of other persons in response to the behavior of the role player(s) and/or in the consequences of specific role enactments for group process and outcome. This method of studying group behavior has a long history and has been used to study many different aspects of small group behavior. The method can best be presented by describing some examples of its application. An early example of role-playing experimentation is the classic study of "social climates" by Lewin, Lippitt, and White (1939). They were interested in the effects of different styles of leadership on group productivity and morale. Adult leaders played the role of either a democratic, autocratic, or laissez-faire leader in groups of 10-year-old boys. The democratic leader allowed the boys to participate in choosing the product they wanted to work on, to decide how they wanted to proceed, etc.; the autocratic leader determined all policy and generally dictated procedures; and the laissez-faire leader was essentially a non-leader who provided help when asked but otherwise allowed the boys to do what they wanted. The task was to produce objects like paper masks. The results showed that boys in the democratic-led groups were better satisfied, showed less hostility and aggression, and produced slightly fewer products than boys led by autocratic leaders. Laissez-faire groups were intermediate, but more similar to the democratic than to the autocratic groups. (This study will be discussed in greater detail in Chapter 9.)

Role enactment studies are not necessarily limited to a single role within the group. For instance, Hoffman (1959) asked one member of a four-person group to assume the role of supervisor and the other three to assume the roles of workers. Each person was asked to assume specified attitudes and beliefs about the situation in which they were placed. The task of the supervisor was to convince the workers to accept a change in work procedure suggested by an efficiency expert. This research paradigm was used to study the effects of various group compositions upon group behavior. (See Chapter 7 for a more complete report of this investigation.) For a somewhat different purpose, Shaw and Breed (1970) employed the same task and role-playing procedure but varied the beliefs held by workers about the past behavior of the supervisor. In this study, the beliefs of the workers embedded in their assigned roles constituted the independent variable of interest to the researchers. (See Chapter 10 for a more complete report of this study.) The Hoffman experiment thus employed multiple role playing only as a vehicle for examining the effects of variables manipulated independently of the role playing itself, whereas the Shaw and Breed study employed role playing as a means of manipulating experimental variables.

Role playing as an experimental method has been more controversial than other procedures used to study group behavior. In part, disagreements are the result of confusion about the nature of role playing as a methodology. For instance, Alexander and Scriven (1977) noted that concern about the widespread use of deception in experimentation encouraged the use of role playing as an alternative procedure. One consequence of this has been a confusion of questions about role-playing validity with the controversy about deception versus role playing. But there are also disagreements about the validity and/or effectiveness of the role-playing technique that derive from strongly held beliefs. One of the most persistent criticisms of the method is that it lacks "experimental realism," involvement, and/or spontaneity (Aronson & Carlsmith, 1968; Cooper, 1976; Freedman, 1969). Another criticism is that role playing introduces an additional variable—the observer who is also the subject (Miller, 1972). The consequences of this variable are unknown and may be unknowable. These various criticisms have been strongly refuted by several researchers (e.g., Alexander & Scriven, 1977; Krupat, 1977; Mixon, 1977).

Despite the controversies surrounding role playing as an experimental method, the research evidence is reasonably clear: role playing is useful for some purposes but not for others. Role visualization is an acceptable procedure for determining whether data from other kinds of research are consistent with "conventional wisdom," that is, whether subjects behave in ways that persons from the target population expect them to behave in particular situations (e.g., see Bem, 1967; Mixon, 1972). Role enactment is useful as a vehicle for testing the effects of other variables manipulated by some other procedure (e.g., Hoffman, 1959) or as a means of manipulating variables (e.g., Lewin, Lippitt, & White, 1939; Shaw & Breed, 1970). On the other hand, neither role visualization nor role enactment appears to be effective as a means of inducing or arousing emotional states, such as fear and anxiety (e.g., Greenberg, 1967). As in the use of any other research technique, role playing must be theoretically justified in relation to the particular research problem being investigated (Movahedi, 1977).

## THEORY AND RESEARCH

Theory and research are complementary processes. A theory organizes information so that its implications can be recognized and subjected to further empirical test. This is really what science is all about. It is an attempt to understand our world through successive approximations to truth. Each theoretical proposition or hypothesis represents one level of understanding, but it must be consistent with known data as well as with data that may accumulate in the future. In one sense, a theory (or better, its propositions) is merely a guess about the nature of the phenomena it purports to explain. To be sure, it is the best guess that the theorist can make at the time with the facts available. But the scientist continually questions propositions and attempts to test their validity by comparing them against some external criteria. The empirical methods discussed in the previous section serve this function. Campbell and Stanley (1963) noted that the task of data collection, when its purpose is to test a theory, is primarily one of rejecting inadequate hypotheses. In designing data-collection procedures, one must, therefore, arrange conditions so that certain results will call for a rejection of the hypothesis being tested. Understanding the nature of this process requires a knowledge of the nature of "proof" as well as an awareness of empirical approaches used in the study of small groups.

## The Nature of Proof

Upon reading a report of an empirical study of small group behavior, the beginning student frequently asks, "What does that prove?" The simple answer to that question is, "Nothing." No single investigation is sufficient to establish the truth of any but the most limited hypothesis. In order to be absolutely sure that a proposition is true, one must examine every possible instance to which the proposition applies. For example, it cannot be "proved" that the sun always rises in the east, since we obviously have not examined every possible sunrise. It is at least theoretically possible that one fine morning the sun will rise in the west. All would agree that this is an extremely unlikely possibility, but it does illustrate two points about the nature of proof: (1) the impossibility of absolute proof without complete data, and (2) the fact that most of the propositions we accept as "proved" refer to events that have so much supporting evidence that few or no persons reject them.

If we cannot prove a theory or a proposition, then what can we do to establish its validity? Any given phenomenon occurring under a specific set of conditions can be "explained" plausibly by a number of hypotheses. Campbell and Stanley (1963) referred to these several hypotheses as *plausible rival hypotheses,* and they proposed that the purpose of experimentation is to reduce their number. The smaller the number of rival hypotheses, the greater the probability that each of the remaining plausible hypotheses is the correct one. An empirical study designed to test a theory, therefore, should yield evidence that allows the rejection of one or more plausible rival hypotheses.

Reducing the number of plausible rival hypotheses involves a process which Garner, Hake, and Eriksen (1956) called *converging operations.* If an investigator observes a specific phenomenon, X, it can usually be explained by a number of hypotheses of the form "X is the result of A," "X is the result of B," . . . "X is the result of E." In attempting to decide which hypothesis is the correct one, the investigator might try to test each hypothesis in turn; if it can be shown that X occurs in the presence of one factor, say A, but not in the presence of others, there would be some basis for concluding that X is due to A. Or perhaps there is reason to believe that A is responsible and one can test for X with A present and all other factors controlled, or with all other present except A. In the first instance, such one-by-one testing of hypotheses is likely to be costly in time and energy, or separating variables in this way may not be feasible. The second approach is possible, but the investigator is not likely to be lucky enough (or smart enough) to pick the correct hypothesis so easily. In the more typical case, perhaps, it can be shown that the effect occurs when A, B, and C are operating, with D and E controlled; when A, B, and E are operating, with C and D controlled; and that X does not occur when B, C, and D are operating, with A and E controlled. On the basis of these converging operations the investigator would have reason to conclude that the correct hypothesis is: X is the result of A. This conclusion, of course, rests upon the assumption that all significant variables have been considered. To the extent that this assumption is not met, errors are likely to occur.

Perhaps this process can be explicated more clearly by an example from the research literature. Lewin and his associates (see Lewin, 1953) conducted a series of studies on the effects of group decision* on behavior change.

In the first study Lewin (1943) attempted to change the food habits of housewives. Specifically, he was interested in encouraging them to use more undesirable meat products such as kidneys and sweetbreads. The subjects were six groups of Red Cross volunteers; groups ranged from thirteen to seventeen members. Half of the groups were given an interesting lecture arguing for greater use of these meat products, and the other half were led through group discussion to develop the same arguments as those presented in the lecture. At the end of the group discussion, the group leader asked for a show of hands by those willing to try one of the undesirable meat products. A follow-up survey revealed that only 3 percent of those in the lecture groups had served one of these meats, whereas 32 percent of those in the group decision groups had served them. Lewin suggested six factors that might logically account for the observed differences:

**1** *The kind of group.* The Red Cross groups had been working together and were well organized. Perhaps organized groups are more responsive to group discussions.

**2** *The degree of involvement.* In the lecture situation the audience is essentially passive. Thus the group decision situation might have created greater involvement which could account for the observed difference.

---

*"Group decision" was used in these studies to refer to an individual decision made in a group setting.

**3** *Expectation.* Only the groups in the group decision situation were informed that a follow-up would be made. This expectation of surveillance might have produced the difference.

**4** *The act of making a decision.* Presumably, the act of decision is a transition from a state of indecisiveness to one in which the individual is ready to act. This means that one alternative (in this instance, to serve a new meat product) is given greater potency than the other. Since the act of decision occurred only in the group decision situation, this might have accounted for the observed difference.

**5** *Leader personality.* The lecturers and the leader of the group discussion were different persons; hence the effect could have been due to differences in leaders' personalities.

**6** *Conformity to group standards.* Although the individual is in a group during the lecture situation, he or she may feel psychologically alone. Thus, the difference might have been due to a greater effect of group standards in the group decision situation.

A second study (Radke & Klisurich, 1947) was conducted with six groups of housewives, with groups ranging from six to nine members. The attempt here was to increase the consumption of milk. The groups were not organized, and the same person served as both lecturer and group decision leader. A follow-up was made after two weeks and again after four weeks. In both instances, the increase was greater in the group decision situation. As in the first experiment, the group decision subjects had been told that a check would be made, but the lecture subjects had not; however, neither group was told that a second checkup would be made. Lewin and his associates concluded from these results that the greater effectiveness of the group decision procedure could not be explained by differences in kind of group, expectation, or leader personality.

A third study was then conducted (Radke & Klisurich, 1947) in which an attempt was made to increase the consumption of orange juice and cod-liver oil by babies. The subjects were farm mothers with their first baby. In this study, an individual instruction condition was substituted for the lecture. The investigators reasoned that if the group decision effect was due to greater involvement, then individual instruction should create even greater involvement and thus should be more effective than group decision. Again, the group decision procedure was more effective. It was concluded that the group decision effect was not due to involvement.

Through this series of experiments (converging operations), Lewin et al. were able to reduce the number of plausible rival hypotheses to two: the act of decision and conformity to group standards. The point we wish to make here is not that these two factors are sufficient to account for the group decision effect, but rather that the series of experiments demonstrate the way in which converging operations can reduce the number of plausible rival hypotheses.

## SUGGESTED READINGS

Cook, T. D., & Campbell, D. T. *Quasi-experimentation: Design and analysis for field settings.* Chicago: Rand McNally, 1979.

Movahedi, S. Role Playing: An alternative to what? *Personality and Social Psychology Bulletin,* 1977, **3,** 489–497.

Schlenker, B. R. Social psychology and science. *Journal of Personality and Social Psychology,* 1974, **29,** 1–15.

Schutz, W. C. *FIRO: A three-dimensional theory of interpersonal behavior.* New York: Rinehart, 1958. Pp. 1–80.

Shaw, M. E., & Costanzo, P. R. *Theories of social psychology.* New York: McGraw-Hill, 1970. Chap. 1.

Thibaut, J. W., & Kelley, H. H. *The social psychology of groups.* New York: Wiley, 1959. Pp. 1–99.

Chapter 3

# Individuals and Groups

We noted in Chapter 1 that not all persons are enthralled with groups and that some even question the reality of groups. Those persons point out that only individuals are capable of behaving and, therefore, that group behavior is real only in the mind of the beholder. Of course, everyone knows that groups are composed of individuals and that group products are the consequences of individual contributions. This does not mean that group behavior is merely the sum of individual contributions. It is not always clear to what extent an individual's behavior is influenced by others, but it is at least theoretically possible that each group member's actions are determined in part by other group members. As we shall see, evidence from research indicates that people do, in fact, behave differently in groups than when alone.

The way in which behavior is influenced by others represents the domain of social psychology. A major question for group dynamics, which is a subdivision of social psychology, is "How is behavior influenced by others *in a group?*" The demarcation line between "influence by others in a group" and other aspects of social psychology is indistinct; individual social behavior sometimes merges into group behavior almost imperceptibly. This fact is reflected in the research relative to group processes. The early studies of the influence of others merely required the presence of other persons during the time the actor was performing; only later were interacting groups examined. Initially, these groups were studied only in comparison with individuals, a research area that continues to stimulate interest even today.

Although these types of investigations are not, strictly speaking, studies of group processes, they nevertheless contribute to our understanding of group behavior and provide a transition point between individual social psychology and group dynamics. In this chapter three areas of investigation are considered: (1) social facilitation (2) individual versus group performance, and (3) group polarization effects. Social facilitation studies are concerned with the influence of the mere presence of others on individual behavior, whereas the other two deal with comparisons of behavior when the subject is alone and behavior in psychological groups.

## SOCIAL FACILITATION

The study of social facilitation is one of the earliest areas of investigation to be brought into the laboratory. In 1897 Triplett conducted a field study and also a laboratory experiment on social facilitation, although he did not use that term. He was interested primarily in the effects of competition on individual behavior. His studies are most interesting from a historical point of view, but also are enlightening with respect to present-day theory and methodology. Triplett (1897) began by collecting data from the official records of bicycle races as maintained by the Racing Board of the League of American Wheelmen. The League conducted three types of competitions: *unpaced,* in which a single rider attempted to beat an established time on a given course; *paced,* in which a lone rider also attempted to beat an established time, but with a swift multicycle setting the pace; and *competition,* in which several riders competed in an ordinary race. The results of this comparison revealed that the times were fastest for competition, next fastest for paced, and slowest for unpaced events.

Subsequent studies of social facilitation differ with respect to the nature of the audience. In some instances, other people are merely present while an individual attempts an assigned task; in other studies, several persons may work on the same task at the same time, but each person works individually. Whether the audience is passive or coacting, the relationships, real or imagined, may vary from study to study. Since social facilitation effects are similar in both the passive and coacting situations, these investigations may be considered together.

It may be instructive to review some of the early research on the effects of the mere presence of others upon individual behavior. The effects of a passive audience upon eye-hand coordination were studied by Travis (1925). Twenty-two college students were tested on a pursuit-rotor task. Each subject practiced twenty trials per day until Travis judged that the subject had reached maximum efficiency. A passive audience was then admitted, after which the subject was given ten additional trials. The average performance on the ten highest alone trials was compared with the average performance on the ten trials with audience present. Eighteen of the twenty-two subjects had higher average scores with an audience, and sixteen earned their highest single score when an audience was present. The average alone score was 172.76 versus 177.42 for the audience present mean score, although this difference was not statistically significant. The presence of an audience was said to have facilitated the performance of the eye-hand coordination task, although the effect was not great.

Pessin and Husband (1933) investigated the effects of an audience upon the learning of a finger relief maze.* Groups of thirty college subjects were tested either alone with the experimenter or with one or two spectators present. In the spectator situation, subjects were tested either blindfolded or with vision but the maze was shielded from view. No significant difference was found. A study by Begum and Lehr (1963) was somewhat more successful. One group of twenty subjects was tested on a light-monitoring task alone, whereas another group of twenty subjects worked alone but with the knowledge that commissioned or noncommissioned officers would visit them at random. The average detection rate was 45 percent in the alone condition and 79 percent in the observation condition, a highly reliable difference. In this study, however, the subjects were Army National Guard trainees and the audience consisted of their superior officers. Thus an additional variable was operating.

These early studies do not provide compelling evidence that the mere presence of others exerts a consistent influence on individual behavior. From the research cited above one might conclude that whether a passive audience facilitates performance depends upon other variables in the situation. More recent research is in accord with such a conclusion. For instance, Markus (1978) found that the mere presence of others enhanced a well-learned task (dressing and undressing with one's own clothing) but hindered performance on a not so well-learned task (dressing or undressing with unfamiliar clothing). Similarly, Baron, Moore, and Sanders (1978) reported that individuals performed a simple task (learning a noncompetitional word list) more efficiently when in the presence of others than when alone, but performed less efficiently on a complex task (learning a

---

*A finger relief maze has elevated pathways so that it can be solved by touch, without the aid of sight.

competitional word list) when others were present. These investigations will be discussed more fully after we have reviewed research involving coacting audiences.

The early studies by F. H. Allport (1920) appear to be the first in which the term *social facilitation* was used to label the effects of others on individual performance. Allport conducted a series of experiments which he believed demonstrated the facilitating effects of the presence of others. In the first experiment, subjects were given a sheet of paper with a single word at the top. Starting with this stimulus word, they wrote as many disconnected words as they could in a given period. Subjects alternated between working alone and working together in the same room. Competition and rivalry were minimized through instructions. Fourteen of the fifteen subjects tested showed a "social increment" (they worked faster) in the together situation, and twelve of the fifteen wrote more personal associations when alone.

In the second experiment the procedure was the same except that subjects were required to write only every fourth word that came to mind. Relative to the alone situation, eight subjects gained, four lost, and two were not affected by the together situation. In the third study, subjects wrote every third word; six gained and two lost in the together situation as compared with the alone situation.

In a fourth experiment half of the subjects wrote words about winter and half words about summer. No differences in facilitating effects were found between the situation in which all subjects wrote on the same topic and that in which the two halves wrote on different topics. Subjects in a fifth experiment were asked to write down arguments to disprove certain passages from Marcus Aurelius. Twenty tests were done alone and twenty in a group setting in which subjects were informed that all were working on the same task. Eight of the nine subjects tested wrote more arguments in the group situation, but six of the nine had a higher percentage of ideas rated superior by the experimenter in the alone condition. Two additional experiments involving a cancellation test and a multiplication test gave similar results; subjects produced more in the together situation, but the quality was poorer.

Subsequent studies yielded results that were not altogether consistent with Allport's findings. Weston and English (1926) reported that individuals given intelligence tests consisting of reasoning items generally did much better (eight of ten subjects tested) in the together situation than in the alone condition. This seems to be inconsistent with Allport's results concerning quality of performance; however, Farnsworth (1928) found no consistent differences between the two situations when intelligence testing was the task. He argued that Weston and English had not equated either their groups of subjects or the test forms. When these factors were controlled, no reliable difference was found between alone and together intelligence test scores. Further negative evidence was reported by Travis (1928) who found that stutterers were adversely influenced by the presence of others on a word-association task similar to that used by Allport. His subjects wrote an average of 68.1 words alone versus an average of 65.3 words when they were together.

The evidence from early studies of social facilitation appears to be inconsistent. Whether the presence of others is facilitating, inhibiting, or irrelevant seems to be unpredictable without knowledge of other factors. Just what these other factors are and how they influence so-called social facilitation effects are controversial. Several theoretical explanations have been proposed, and more recent research has been directed toward testing one or more of these theories. A consideration of these explanations will be instructive, including the several possible explanations advanced by Triplett in 1897.

## Triplett's Hypotheses

Triplett reviewed several theories that had been advanced to account for these differences and proposed one of his own. Consider these interesting proposals:

*The Suction Theory* held that a vacuum is left by the pacing machine which pulls the rider along without as much effort on his or her part. In regular races, part of the strategy was to hold back during the early parts of the race and let others set the pace. This conserved energy for the final dash at the end and also allowed the rider to take advantage of the "vacuum" created by the leaders. This is not unlike the strategy employed by present-day automobile race drivers.

*The Shelter Theory* is similar to the suction theory. It assumed that the front riders provided a shield against wind pressure, and thus less effort was required of those following.

*The Encouragement Theory* suggested that the presence of a friend keeps up the spirits of the rider and thus encourages a stronger effort on the rider's part.

*The Brain Worry Theory* explained that it requires greater worry to keep the pace than to follow; the pacer exhausts his or her energy by worrying about the task.

*The Theory of Hypnotic Suggestion* proposed that the follower concentrated his or her attention on the revolving wheel of the pacer, thus becoming hypnotized. The hypnosis created muscular exaltation, which increased the rider's energy output.

*The Automatic Theory* held that the leader must use his or her brain to direct the muscles to stay on course, whereas the follower need not attend to such factors but can ride automatically and thus devote all energy to pedaling the bicycle.

Triplett admitted that each of these factors might play a part in producing the observed differences between individual performances alone and in the presence of others, but he believed that "dynamogenic factors" probably played a bigger role. He suggested that the presence of others releases latent energy that is not usually available to the individual. In order to test this hypothesis, he constructed a gadget from fishing reels which could be operated by either one or two persons. It consisted of two reels (one for each operator) which were connected to silk bands. By turning a reel, one could move the band around a 4-meter course. After initial practice with the apparatus, forty children were asked to turn the reel at the highest possible rate for four circuits of the 4-meter course. Half of the children worked first alone, then in pairs, then alone, etc., through six efforts. The other half worked in the reverse order. Triplett found that the together (competition) situation produced much faster rates and thus concluded that this dynamogenic theory was verified.

## Zajonc's Drive Theory

Zajonc (1965a) reviewed the findings of social facilitation studies and noted that the presence of others sometimes enhanced and sometimes interfered with individual performance when compared with performance in isolation. He suggested that the mere presence of others has arousal consequences; that is, an audience is drive-producing. This drive has the effect of facilitating dominant responses (simple, well-learned responses) but inhibits nondominant responses (complex, poorly learned responses). The term *mere presence of others* refers to what is left when the person or persons present cannot control reinforcers for the actor, cannot be imitated, are unable to evaluate the actor's performance, etc. (Markus, 1978). According to Zajonc's theory, then, the mere presence of another is sufficient to produce drive and hence to influence performance.

The drive arousal explanation is, of course, essentially a revival of Triplett's dynamogenic theory (1897) which held that the presence of others releases latent energy that the individual is unable to release when alone. Zajonc's analysis, however, does have the advantage of being related to a considerable amount of theory and research concerning motivation and learning. Zajonc reasoned that if his hypothesis were correct, then the presence of others should have the same effects as those obtained by increasing the generalized drive state. One such effect is the enhancement of dominant responses. A test of this effect was conducted by Zajonc and Sales (1966), with generally positive results. Subjects were shown a number of "foreign" words and asked to pronounce them. Some words were shown only a few times, whereas others were shown and practiced several times. The subjects were then asked which of the words had been projected on a screen, where the projected pattern was actually a meaningless set of lines. Subjects generally responded more frequently with the more highly practiced words, and this effect was greater when others were present than when subjects were alone. These results were interpreted as demonstrating that the mere presence of others facilitates dominant responses (those more frequently practiced) but inhibits non-dominant responses (less frequently practiced ones).

Evidence from related areas of investigation is generally consistent with Zajonc's theory. It is known, for example, that stutterers tend to stutter more when they are highly motivated than when they are more relaxed; similar effects might be expected in other kinds of behavior, which could account for the findings of Travis (1928). Kelley and Thibaut (1969) cited additional evidence to support the notion that motivation level is increased under social conditions. First, subjects report that activity by others produces an urge to greater speed and greater emotional excitement than that experienced when alone. Second, subjects can be aroused to activity even after having been satiated in social isolation, as indicated by studies of children's activities (Burton, 1941). Third, subjects who appear to be least interested in the task itself show the greatest performance gains in the audience situation. And fourth, individual variations from time to time are greater under social conditions. Thus it appears that one strong effect of an audience is to increase motivation for high task performance; the consequences of this high motivation may result either in increased effectiveness or decreased effectiveness, depending upon the nature of the task, the measure of effectiveness, the initial level of motivation, and other factors. For example, competition seems to arouse higher motivation than either individual or cooperative situations, but this motivation is detrimental to a tracking task, which requires both mental concentration and eye-hand coordination (M. E. Shaw, 1958a). Dashiell (1930) argued that the effects of the audience could be accounted for solely by the fact that the audience instigates competitiveness and rivalry, which, of course, are forms of motivation, although such motivations are not always task-related. These factors must also be considered when attempting to understand the effects of others upon individual behavior.

More recent research relevant to Zajonc's drive theory has yielded mixed results. For example, Markus (1978) employed a task that had been practiced many times (dressing and undressing in one's own clothing) and one that had not been practiced (dressing and undressing in clothing other than one's own). Presumably, the responses associated with the former task should be dominant whereas the latter should not. The two tasks were performed alone, in the presence of an attentive observer, and in the presence of a passive, inattentive observer. Both the presence of an attentive and the presence of an inattentive observer enhanced performance on the well-learned task but hindered performance on the unfamiliar task, as predicted by drive theory. On the other hand, investigations by Blank, Staff, and Shaver (1976) and Grush (1978) found evidence that could not easily be explained by the drive hypothesis. Blank and his associates asked subjects to give word-association responses to a list of words while in the presence of an observer or while alone. In both the observer and the alone conditions, half of the subjects were given an explanation for the observer's presence (a student interested in word-associations) and half were not. According to the drive hypothesis, persons will give more common responses in the observer condition, and the latency of the responses should be shorter than in the alone condition (Matlin & Zajonc, 1968). Although subjects gave more common responses when observed, latency of responses did not differ. Furthermore, detailed analysis of responses revealed that the presence of observers primarily affected words for which there was little consensus regarding the word response and did this by reducing the number of idiosyncratic responses. This latter finding, of course, is not consistent with the drive arousal hypothesis.

Grush (1978) approached the problem from a different viewpoint. If the mere presence of an audience is drive-producing, then the nature of the audience should be unimportant. He selected persons who had revealed a dominant response of competition when playing a prisoner's dilemma game alone and asked them to play the game either with no audience, with an audience identified as previous winners, or with an audience identified as a human relations group. As compared with the no-audience conditions, the presence of previous winners facilitated the competitive response, as predicted by the drive hypothesis, but the presence of the human relations group *inhibited* competition.

These, and other similarly inconsistent findings, cast doubt on the drive-arousal hypotheses—at least with respect to the drive-producing consequences of the mere presence of others. Results inconsistent with the mere presence interpretation have also been reported by Cottrell, Wack, Sekerak, and Rittle (1968), Henchy and Glass (1968), Klinger (1969), Martens and Landers (1972), and Paulus and Murdoch (1971). Consequently, other theories have been proposed to either modify or replace the drive-arousal explanation of social facilitation effects.

### Cottrell's Theory of Learned Social Drive

In some respects, Cottrell's (1972) theory may be viewed as a modification of Zajonc's drive theory. Based upon a review of the research on social facilitation, he suggested that the presence of other people does not increase drive unless it arouses anticipations of positive or negative outcomes. He proposed that individuals learn that others may be sources of evaluation and that their evaluations may be either positive or negative. He concluded that it is the expectation of positive or negative outcomes that generates social facilitation effects.

Research data are generally in accord with Cottrell's theory. In one study (Good, 1973), thirty-two females were led to believe that they would perform well on a word association test and thirty-two were led to believe that they would perform poorly. Half of the individuals in each group were led to believe that the experimenter would evaluate their performance and half that he would not. Cottrell's theory predicts facilitation effects (i.e., faster and more common responses to the stimulus words in the association test) when the person being tested believed that the experimenter would evaluate her, regardless of whether she expected to do well or poorly. Good found the expected effects only for those persons who expected to do well.

Martens and Landers (1972) observed persons as they performed a task requiring motor skill (a commercial game called "roll-up"), working alone or in dyads, triads, or tetrads. Three evaluation conditions were established: (1) a normal coaction situation (direct evaluation), (2) removal of visual cues but knowledge of others' outcomes available (indirect evaluation), and (3) removal of both visual cues and knowledge of others' outcomes (no potential for evaluation). Cottrell's theory predicts that social facilitation effects should be greater (i.e., motor performance should be poorer) for direct evaluation than for indirect evaluation, which in turn should be greater than for the no-evaluation condition. The results reported by Martens and Landers were in agreement with this prediction; mean scores were 2.42 for direct evaluation, 2.93 for indirect evaluation, and 3.00 for the no-evaluation condition. These findings call into question the hypothesis that the mere presence of others is drive-arousing, but the findings are not inconsistent with the view that an audience is drive-producing under some conditions.

In another study (Sasfy & Okun, 1974), a more stringent test was made of Martens and Landers' conclusion that direct evaluation of performance and outcomes impairs performance more than indirect evaluation of outcomes only. Expert and nonexpert audiences observed subjects performing the "roll-up" task either with visual information and knowledge of outcomes (direct evaluation), with no visual information but with knowledge of outcomes (indirect evaluation), or with neither visual information nor knowledge of outcomes (no evaluation). Both direct and indirect evaluation conditions impaired performance relative to the no-evaluation condition. They concluded that these findings directly support Cottrell's hypothesis that the potential for evaluation is the chief source of social facilitation effects. Support for the theory of learned social drive has also been provided by VanTuinen and McNeel (1975) and by Rittle and Bernard (1977).

However, not all research data unambiguously support the theory. For example, Atkinson (1974) conducted an experiment using ambiguous pictures (thematic apperception) to elicit descriptive responses from subjects performing alone or in the presence of others. Since the outcomes on this task are difficult to evaluate, he concluded that social facilitation effects are due to a generalized desire (tendency) for social approval. It is not clear, however, that the desire for social approval is basically different from concern about the potential for evaluation. Sanders and Baron (1975) also found results that they believed led to a different interpretation, which we will outline in the next section.

## Distraction-Conflict Theory

Distraction-conflict theory holds that socially mediated drive-arousal will occur whenever there is some reason to shift attention from the task to social stimuli. In humans, the presence of others when a person is performing a task may be distracting, thus creating a conflict between attending to the task and attending to the distractor. (*Distraction* was defined as any stimulus or response requirement that is irrelevant to the task, and *conflict* was defined as the desire or duty to make two mutually exclusive responses either simultaneously or when there is not enough time to make both.) In support of their hypothesis, Sanders and Baron (1975) found that persons who were induced to shift their attention while working on copying tasks performed better on simple tasks but more poorly on complex tasks than persons not so distracted (see Figure 3-1).

Subsequent studies designed to test this theory yielded results that were interpreted as supporting it. In one study, Sanders, Baron, and Moore (1978) demonstrated that social facilitation effects occurred only when subjects were motivated to obtain comparison information and when comparison information was available. The need to monitor the coactor's work in order to compare it with one's own work was presumably distracting and thus produced the social facilitation effects. In a related study (Baron, Moore, & Sanders, 1978), evidence was provided showing that individuals were, in fact, more distracted in the presence of an audience than when alone.

Now that we have reviewed the research and theory, what can be said about social facilitation? First, it is clear that the presence of others is not always facilitating, as originally believed (see F. H. Allport, 1920). Social facilitation effects may be either enhancing or inhibiting, depending upon the nature of the task. In general, simple, well-learned tasks are performed better when others are present, whereas complex, poorly learned tasks are performed less adequately in the presence of others than when alone. But which of the explanations that have been proposed is the correct one? The answer to that question is not clear at all. It does appear, however, that Zajonc's drive theory, in its most extreme form, is not supported by research. Only under certain conditions does the presence of others produce facilitation effects; *mere* presence, isolated from its typically

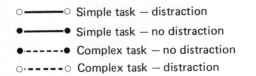

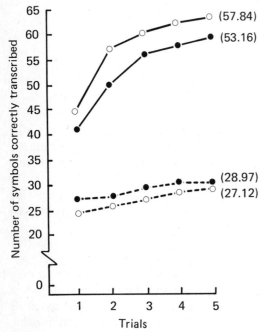

**Figure 3-1** Mean performance scores as a function of type of task and degree of distraction (with composite means, collapsed across trials, in parentheses to right of their respective curves). (Reprinted with permission from G. S. Sanders and R. S. Baron. The motivating effects of distraction on task performance. *Journal of Personality and Social Psychology,* 1975, **32,** 956–963. Copyright 1975 by the American Psychological Association. Reprinted by permission.)

concomitant variables, does not. Whether the culprit is potential for evaluation, desire for social approval, distraction, or some other variable has not yet been established. The reader should keep in mind that demonstration that an effect can be produced by manipulating one variable does not necessarily mean that it cannot also be produced by manipulating some other (and different) variable. For instance, following an unsuccessful attempt to conduct a crucial test between Zajonc's drive theory and Atkinson's social approval hypothesis, Kawamura-Reynolds (1977) made the reasonable suggestion that the presence of others may produce both kinds of motivational effects.

## INDIVIDUAL VERSUS GROUP PERFORMANCE

The comparison of individual and group performance introduces a new variable into the study of interpersonal effects, namely, interaction. This new element is important because, unlike the audience and coaction situations, individual performance is compared with the performance of true psychological groups. Therefore, research in this area relates individual and group behavior more directly than the investigations that have been considered up to this point. Research has centered around three types of behavior—judgment, problem solving, and learning. The risky shift phenomenon may also represent a type of individual versus group performance, but it has somewhat different implications for group behavior and is discussed separately.

### Individual Versus Group Judgment

The major question asked by investigators of individual versus group judgment is: To what extent does the quality of group performance exceed or fall short of the performance of individuals? There are two subsidiary questions: (1) Does the quality of group judgment exceed that of the average individual performance of group members? (2) Does the quality of group performance exceed that of the most proficient member of the group? Two general approaches have been adopted in attempting to answer these questions, although the methods are not related to specific questions. The first method has been referred to as the "statisticized" group technique (Lorge, Fox, Davitz, & Brenner, 1958). The technique compares individual judgments with the result obtained by averaging the products of independent, noninteracting individuals. Actually, this is not a group at all, but rather an aggregate of individual judgments. This method appears to have been used for the first time by Knight (1921) in her investigation of judgments of temperature in a college classroom. She had students estimate the temperature of the classroom and then computed the average judgment for the group. The "group" judgment was better than 80 percent of the individual judgments. A second study was conducted using the same method, but requiring judgments of intelligence from photographs. The "group" rank order did not correlate with the true rank order any better than the individual ranks.

The statisticized group method was employed by Gordon (1923) in a study of aesthetic judgments and again in a study of judgment of weights (Gordon, 1924). Individual judgments of lifted weights correlated .41 with true weights; "group" judgments yielded much higher correlations, reaching .94 with an aggregate of fifty individual judgments. Gordon concluded that "group" judgments are distinctly superior to the judgments of the average individual and equal to that of the best individual. An obvious flaw in this technique is that the number of judgments varies with the size of the group, and it is well known that the average of several judgments (measurements, estimates, etc.) will approximate the true value more closely than most single judgments, so long as the error of measurement is random, that is, so long as any single judgment is just as likely to be too low as it is to be too high. Thus, Stroop (1932) argued that Gordon's findings could be accounted for by the number of judgments alone, without regard to the source of the judgments. In other words, one would expect the same results from several judgments made by one individual and averaged as one would expect from the same number of judgments made by several individuals, each contributing one judgment, as in the Gordon studies. Stroop confirmed Gordon's results and then conducted a second study in which the same individual made varying numbers of judgments. His findings are compared with those reported by Gordon in Table 3-1. The correspondence between the two sets of results is obvious. Stroop's hypothesis of a statistical artifact, therefore, seems to be supported.

Investigations using statisticized groups may also be criticized on other grounds. Preston (1938) noted that such studies give no evidence concerning psychological processes in group interaction. Fortunately, the second method of investigation mentioned above is not so sterile with respect to group behavior. In these studies, the judgments of individuals are compared with the judgments of interacting groups or with individual judgments made after group discussion. As early as 1920, Burtt conducted a series of studies of jury decisions in which individual judgments were compared with judgments by the same individuals after group discussion. In the study most relevant to the present issue, confederates "testified" before subjects about an imaginary crime. Some of the confederates lied and others told the truth. Subjects judged the veracity of the "witness" individually. They then discussed the testimony for five minutes, after

**Table 3-1 A Comparison of Correlations between Actual Weight and Judged Weight as a Function of Size of "Group" and of Number of Judgments**

| Gordon's findings | | | | | |
|---|---|---|---|---|---|
| Size of group | 1 | 5 | 10 | 20 | 50 |
| Correlation | .41 | .68 | .79 | .86 | .94 |
| **Stroop's findings** | | | | | |
| Number of judgments | 1 | 5 | 10 | 20 | 50 |
| Correlation | .43 | .72 | .82 | .87 | .97 |

which they again judged the veracity of the witness. Subjects frequently changed their judgment after group discussion, but they changed in the wrong direction about as often as in the right direction. A similar study by Marston (1924) produced similar results. Students witnessed a staged classroom incident and were then asked to describe what happened, either individually or in groups acting as a jury. Findings of fact were slightly (but not significantly) less accurate by the jury than by the average individual witness. Marston also found that a trained "judge" was more accurate than a jury. The results of these studies suggest that although group judgments are different from individual judgments, they are not necessarily better, and the judgment of a trained individual may be more accurate than that of untrained groups.

The effect of group discussion on the accuracy of individual judgment was also studied by Jenness (1932). Individuals estimated the number of beans in a bottle, discussed their estimates in groups of three and made a group estimate, and then made a final individual estimate. The discussion groups were selected either to disagree maximally or to agree maximally. Finally, there was a control group in which individuals made two estimates with no intervening group discussion or estimate. With maximum disagreement initially, group estimates were less accurate than individual estimates; however, final individual estimates were better than initial estimates in twenty of twenty-six cases. This represented an average reduction in error of 60 percent as compared with a 4 percent reduction in the control group. When initial agreement was maximum, group estimates were more accurate than initial estimates, but final individual estimates were not significantly different from those of the control group. Again groups are not necessarily better than individuals, and group discussion does not always improve individual judgments. Jenness correctly noted the role of individual differences in knowledge in improving group judgments, a fact that will be considered in greater detail in Chapter 6.

A combination of the statisticized group technique and the use of interacting groups was employed by Gurnee (1937). Individuals were required to make their judgments on a written true-false test, after which a vote was taken by a show of hands in groups of 18, 53, 57, and 66. In every group the group judgment was better than the average individual judgment and about equal to the judgment of the best individual. Statisticized group judgments were also computed, but face-to-face groups were generally superior.

In general, it appears that group judgments are seldom less accurate than the average individual judgment and are often superior. This can be accounted for by the number of judgments contributing to the estimate (Stroop, 1932), by the range of knowledge represented by the individual group members (Jenness, 1932), and by the effects of others on the less confident group members (Gurnee, 1937). It is also apparent that the kind of task may determine whether group judgment will be superior to individual judgments. Finally, it is evident that a single capable individual may perform as well as or better than a group (Burtt, 1920; Marston, 1924). The answer to the first question (see page 57), "Does the quality of group judgment exceed that of the average individual performance of group members?" is therefore a qualified "Yes." The second question, "Does the quality of group performance exceed that of the most proficient member of the group?" must be answered negatively, although under some circumstances the group performance might be better than that of any individual in the group.

The research we have reviewed to this point concerned the *accuracy* of individual versus group judgments. But at least one series of studies examined judgments of the proportion of successes and failures; i.e., the *perception* of accuracy in making judgments (Janssens & Nuttin, 1976). Subjects were assigned to serial tasks (estimation of the number of objects presented on slides) in which the outcome (right or wrong) was known immediately after each judgment. Subjects were told that they were right 50 percent of the time and wrong 50 percent of the time. Perceptions of the number of rights and wrongs were obtained at the end of each series of trials. In one experiment, individuals were compared with four-person groups in both competing and noncompeting conditions, and in a second experiment individuals were compared with groups with and without communication among group members. Group members overestimated the number of successes as compared with individuals in all conditions (although group members overestimated more in the competitive than in the noncompetitive condition, and those with communication more than those without communication). Apparently, people in groups see themselves as more accurate than do people who work alone.

## Individual versus Group Problem Solving

Investigators of individual versus group problem solving have used a variety of experimental designs as well as a variety of problems which subjects are asked to solve. The two most common designs are: (1) Individuals are required to solve problems alone and the same individuals attempt to solve similar problems in groups, usually with order and problems counterbalanced, and (2) one sample of individuals attempts a set of problems and another sample of groups attempts to solve the same set of problems. The kinds of problems vary from complex syllogistic reasoning tasks to simple puzzles. There are also variations in the measures of performance, including (1) number of problems solved, (2) time required to solve, either taking into account the number of individuals or not, (3) number of trials, (4) amount of interaction, and (5) quality of solution. Despite all these variations in design and procedure, the results are remarkably consistent when the same measures of performance are compared. A review of several studies may be instructive.

An early study by G. B. Watson (1928) compared individuals and groups on a word-construction task. Beginning with a given word, the subject was to construct as many new words as possible from the letters in the stimulus word. Subjects were 108 graduate students in education. The subjects first worked individually for ten minutes, then in groups (ranging from three to ten persons) for another ten minutes with a secretary recording words for them, followed by a third period in groups, and finally a fourth period as individuals. The best individual in the group averaged 49 words per ten minutes in the individual situation, whereas the groups averaged 75 words per ten-minute period. When the words produced by all individuals in the group working alone were summed to obtain a "group" product, the average was 86.8 words per test period. Note, however, that this procedure did not take into account overlap, that is, the same word produced by several individuals who were grouped together. There was also greater variability among groups than among individuals. Watson concluded that groups are superior to individuals, but that with simple tasks, division of labor, and summation of individual contributions individuals are better. (As noted above, the latter conclusion may be based upon improper procedures.) Watson also concluded that variability among groups depends more upon the ability of the best member than upon others in the group. This conclusion was based upon the observation that the performance of the group corresponded more closely to that of the best group member than to the performance of others in the group, a consequence that is inevitable in this kind of situation.

A somewhat more elegant experimental design was employed by Marjorie E. Shaw (1932) in a now-classic comparison of individual and group problem solving. The subjects were members of a class in social psychology at Columbia University. In the first half of the experiment, half of the students worked in five groups of four persons each and the other half worked as individuals. In the second half, the roles of subjects were reversed, with some substitutions of subjects. The problems in the first part of the study were puzzles, such as the cannibal problem of parlor-game fame. In this particular task, three cannibals and three missionaries must cross a river in a boat that will carry only two persons. One of the cannibals and all of the missionaries know how to row the boat. However, the crossing must be arranged so that the number of cannibals never outnumbers the missionaries—for obvious reasons! The problem is to determine how the crossing can be made in the fewest trips. Another task was similar to this except that the persons involved were husbands and wives. The third task was a disk transfer problem which required that a stack of disks of different sizes be moved from one spot to another, one at a time, using only three positions and never placing a larger disk on a smaller one. The problems in the second half were somewhat more "mentalistic." One required that subjects identify the best location for a school and the best routes for two school buses, given the possible routes, the location and number of children to be picked up, and the capacity of the buses. The second and third problems called for the rearrangement of letters to form the last sentence of a passage of prose and the last few lines of a sonnet, respectively.

In the first half of the experiment, individuals produced 5 correct solutions of 63 possible (7.9 percent) as compared with 8 of 15 possible (53 percent) for the groups. The time required, however, was greater for groups than for individuals. The average number of minutes for groups was 6.5, 16.9, and 18.3, for problems 1, 2, and 3, respectively, as compared with 4.5, 9.9, and 15.5 for individuals. In the second half, the number of correct solutions was again in favor of groups (27 percent correct as compared with 5.7 percent correct by individuals). The average times, however, were shorter for groups on two of the three problems. Shaw's results indicated, therefore, that groups produced more correct solutions, but often at a cost in time. As we shall see later, this cost is much greater if time per individual is taken into account. In addition, Shaw noted that (1) there was an unequal amount of participation by group members, and (2) in erroneous solutions, groups did not err as early in the process as did the average individual.

The relative superiority of groups with respect to accuracy was interpreted by Shaw as due to the rejection of incorrect suggestions and the checking of errors in the group. She also found that more incorrect suggestions were recognized and rejected by someone in the group other than the one who had made the error. This process is, of course, not available to individuals working alone.

A similar study was undertaken by Husband (1940) in a study contrasting individuals and groups in terms of the man-hours required to arrive at a solution and the quality of the solution. The problems included arithmetic problems, a jigsaw puzzle, and code deciphering. Subjects were 120 college students, 40 of whom worked alone and 80 in pairs. He found that pairs were significantly better on the deciphering task and the jigsaw puzzle, but there was no significant difference between pairs and individuals on the arithmetic problems. On the latter, it appeared that one member of the pair took the lead and did all the work; hence, the comparison was really between two individuals. These findings are consistent with those reported by G. B. Watson (1928) and Marjorie E. Shaw (1932). However, Husband noted that the time saved by pairs was never more than one-third, rather than the one-half needed to equate individuals and groups in terms of man-hours required for solution. He concluded that pairs are relatively less efficient than individuals. This conclusion, of course, fails to take into account the improved quality of the solution by pairs.

Many other investigators have reported results that are consistent with those cited above. Taylor and Faust (1952) compared individuals with groups of two and four persons on a modified version of "twenty questions," and found that individuals required more time and questions to identify objects than did groups. Again, groups were relatively more costly in terms of man-minutes (an average of 7.40 minutes for two-person groups, 12.60 minutes for four-person groups, and 5.06 for individuals). Marquart (1955) used problems similar to those used by Marjorie E. Shaw (1932) and reported similar results. However, Marquart computed a "concocted" group score by crediting the hypothetical group with a correct solution if any subjects solved the problem individually, and found that this score indicated that individuals were superior to groups. Lorge, Aikman, Moss, Spiegel, and Tuckman (1955) tested groups and individuals on four tasks varying in degree of "remoteness from reality," and found that the solutions of groups were superior on all problems. Using a complex intellectual problem, Barnlund (1959) compared the performances of individuals working alone, under majority rule, and as members of discussion groups. Decisions made by discussion groups were better than those made either by individuals or by majority rule. A study by Tuckman and Lorge (1962) also demonstrated that groups of five persons had a greater probability of producing good solutions than did individuals.

Finally, Kanekar and Rosenbaum (1972) compared the performance of individuals, four-member groups, and four-person nominal groups (i.e., groups composed by pooling the outputs of four individuals who had worked alone) on anagram tasks. Nominal groups performed better than real groups, but both real and nominal groups performed better than individuals. Davis and Restle (1963), using three puzzle problems, compared four-person groups with individuals. The proportion of solutions was greater for groups than for individuals on all three problems. There was no difference in overall time, although individuals required fewer man-hours for solution.

The evidence thus strongly supports the conclusion that groups produce more and better solutions to problems than do individuals, although the differences in overall time required for solution are not consistently better for either individuals or groups. When the amount of effort invested, as measured by man-hours required for solution, is considered, individuals are found to be superior. There is at least one investigation, however, that yielded results not in complete accord with the studies cited thus far. Moore and Anderson (1954) compared six individuals with six groups of three persons each on the solution of problems from the calculus of symbolic logic. In general, there were few significant differences between individuals and groups in accuracy or time for solution, although individuals required fewer man-hours. It should be noted that Moore and Anderson's subjects were Navy enlisted men who may not have been experts in the calculus of symbolic logic; if few individuals can solve a problem, it may not help to work together in groups.

A number of hypotheses have been advanced to explain the relative superiority of group problem solving. These include (1) summation of individual contributions (Marquart, 1955; G. B. Watson, 1928); (2) rejection of incorrect suggestions and the checking of errors (Barnlund, 1959; Marjorie E. Shaw, 1932); (3) the greater influence of the ablest group member (G. B. Watson, 1928); (4) the social influence of the most confident member (Thorndike, 1938); (5) the greater interest in the task aroused by group membership (Barnlund, 1959); and (6) the greater amount of information available to the group. Some evidence relevant to these proposed explanations is provided by a study by Zaleska (1978). Members of groups were given different solutions to a problem so that some members had the correct answer and some had an incorrect answer. Group members who had the correct answer were more certain that they were correct, talked more, and were perceived as more confident than members who had incorrect answers.

It is probable that all the factors mentioned above contribute to the relatively greater effectiveness of group problem solving. The degree to which each one operates probably depends upon such additional factors as task characteristics. More will be said about these additional variables later in this chapter (see page 67).

### Individual versus Group Learning

Implicit in the studies on group judgment and group problem solving is the hypothesis that interaction contributes something to the group product that is more than the mere combination of individual products. This hypothesis suggests that group members somehow exert an influence on their fellow members which leads to behavior that would not occur when members are alone. It is possible that such group effects lead to gains in group productivity (see pp. 372–374), an assumption adopted by most researchers on individual versus group performance. If this is true, then the effect should not be limited to judgment and problem solving but should also appear in learning phenomena.

As early as 1926, Barton conducted a study using high school pupils in an algebra class. He selected two sections which were alike in IQ, preliminary training in algebra, and prior test performance. One section worked on assignments on an individual basis and the other section worked on the same assignments in small groups. The groups gained significantly more on subsequent test performance. A decade later, Gurnee (1937, 1939) reported two experiments on maze learning by individuals and by groups. In the first study, groups made fewer errors and achieved a perfect trial sooner than did individuals on the first six trials, but on the seventh trial there was no difference between group and individual performance. The second study was similar in design, but the results were slightly different: On the seventh trial those who had worked in groups did significantly better than those who had worked alone on the first six trials.

Later studies used somewhat more sophisticated experimental designs, with correspondingly more interesting results. Perlmutter and de Montmollin (1952) compared individuals and groups on a nonsense-syllable learning task. The study was conducted at the Sorbonne and the subjects were mostly French students, although some other Europeans were included. Half of the subjects (G-I groups) worked in three-person groups, rested fifteen minutes, and then worked individually but in the presence of others (G-I individuals). For the other half, this order was reversed (I-G individuals and I-G groups, respectively). Order of nonsense lists was also systematically varied. In the group situation, group consensus was required. The results are shown in Figure 3-2. There was no significant difference between the G-I and I-G groups; hence they are combined in Figure 3-2. Note that groups learned more and learned faster than either

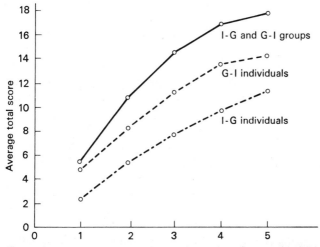

**Figure 3-2** Average curves of group-learned products and individual learning. (Reprinted with permission from H. V. Perlmutter & G. de Montmollin. Group learning of nonsense syllables. *Journal of Abnormal and Social Psychology,* 1952, **47,** 762–769. Copyright 1952 by the American Psychological Association. Reprinted by permission.)

G-I or I-G individuals. It is also important to note that individuals who had had previous experience in groups (G-I individuals) learned faster than did persons who had not had group experience (I-G individuals). These findings demonstrated the superiority of groups over individuals in learning nonsense syllables, as well as the effects of group experience on subsequent learning by individuals.

Similar results were reported by Beaty and Shaw (1965) in a very different kind of learning situation: the probability learning or probability matching situation. In this situation, the subject must choose between two possible outcomes on each trial, such as which of two lights will come on. Individuals learn to "match" their choices to the probabilities associated with each alternative (Gardner, 1957; Gardner, 1958; Goodnow, 1955). Beaty and Shaw reasoned that groups should achieve matching faster than individuals because of benefits derived from group process. They compared individual decisions, individual choices made in groups after a two-minute discussion, and group decisions. In the last two conditions, subjects were run in groups of five. The task was to choose which of two lights would come on where the objective probabilities were 70:30. The results are shown in Figure 3-3. Both groups and individuals in groups learned to match with fewer trials than did individuals alone.

Yuker (1955) demonstrated the same effects in a learning task involving prose materials. He studied 160 subjects divided into forty groups of four persons each. The "War of the Ghosts," a rather bizarre story of ghosts and Indians, was read to individuals in groups, after which they were asked to recall it individually, then as a group, and finally as individuals. Prior to scoring recall data, the investigators segmented story content according to unique ideas. The recall data were scored by assigning a score from 0 (no recall) to 4 (complete recall) to each segment of the story. The recall score was the average of scores on all segments and could, therefore, range from 0 to 4. Mean scores were 1.26 for initial individual recall, 1.88 for group recall, and 1.65 for final individual recall. The best initial individual recall in each group averaged 1.64. The group performance was better than the initial individual recall in 38 of the 40 groups and better than the best initial recall in 29 of the 40 groups. Yuker suggested that groups will learn more than individuals on tasks (1) on which several persons can work without getting in one another's way, (2) which can be solved through the addition of individual contributions, and (3) in which the parts of the solution are at least partially independent.

The results of studies of individual versus group learning are remarkably consistent in showing that groups learn faster than individuals, both in natural situations (Barton, 1926) and in contrived laboratory situations (Beaty & Shaw, 1965; Perlmutter & de Montmollin, 1952; Yuker, 1955). Studies comparing the lecture method with group discussion in the

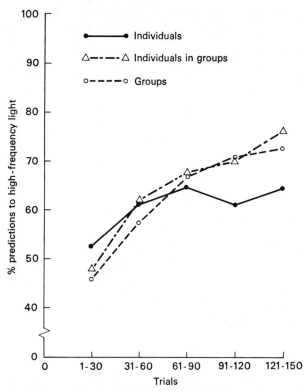

**Figure 3-3** Percent frequency of high-probability responses plotted against blocks of 30 trials. (Reprinted with permission from W. E. Beaty & M. E. Shaw. Some effects of social interaction on probability learning. *Journal of Psychology,* 1965, **59,** 299–306.)

classroom are sometimes cited as evidence that individual learning is sometimes better than group learning (cf. Spence, 1928; Thie, 1925; Zeleny, 1940). However, these studies do not really involve individuals and groups so much as different teaching techniques; differences in learning seem to depend more on the personality of the teacher than on interpersonal factors.

In summary, data concerning individual versus group performance indicates that whether individuals or groups are more effective depends upon the past experience of the persons involved, the kind of task they are attempting to complete, the process that is being investigated, and the measure of effectiveness. For example, expert and/or experienced individuals may perform better than groups of less expert persons. Groups are more effective than individuals on tasks which require a variety of information, which can be solved by adding individual contributions, and which require a number of steps that must be correctly completed in a definite order; individuals are better on tasks that call for centralized organization of parts. Groups perform better than individuals when the process is learning or problem solving, but not necessarily when the process investigated is judgment. These conclusions are based upon measures of outcome; when the measure of effectiveness is the amount of investment per man, individuals are generally shown to be more efficient.

## GROUP POLARIZATION EFFECTS

When people discuss an issue, decision, opinion, or similar topic, the result is often a group-produced enhancement of the prevailing individual tendency; i.e., the average postgroup response will tend to be more extreme *in the same direction* as the average of the pregroup responses. This increase in the extremity of the average response following group discussion has been called *group polarization* (Moscovici & Zavalloni, 1969). The research and theory relevant to group polarization grew out of research on the so-called risky shift. Therefore, it may be instructive to review the history of work on this phenomenon before considering some of the explanations of group polarization effects.

Historically, it was commonly believed that group products tend to be conservative, that is, that groups make more conservative decisions than individuals (e.g., W. H. Whyte, 1957). Although one early study (Ziller, 1957a) suggested that groups may not be as conservative as individuals, the first direct attempt to compare the "riskiness" of individual and group decision making was conducted by Stoner (1961). He found that decisions by groups were riskier than decisions made by individual group members prior to group discussion. This research served as the starting point for a series of studies designed to determine the generality of this finding and to explain the process that produces the effect when it does occur. As we shall see, group decisions may be either more or less risky than individual decisions, depending upon the circumstances surrounding the decision. However, a brief history of the early research may be enlightening.

Wallach, Kogan, and Bem (1962) were taken by surprise by the Stoner findings and apparently experienced some doubt that the risky shift phenomenon could be reliably demonstrated. They noted that Stoner's subjects were male graduate students in industrial management and that the presence of peers in the group situation might have reminded them of the positively sanctioned role that the business manager is expected to play. That is, business managers are expected to be willing to take risks in their decision making; hence, graduate students in business might simply have been conforming to role expectations in the group decision situation. Wallach et al. also suggested that males, regardless of their professional roles, might make more risky decisions in groups because they perceive risk taking to be an attribute of manliness. They therefore designed a study using as subjects both male and female undergraduates enrolled in a liberal arts college program. They argued that if the risky shift could be demonstrated in both male and female subjects drawn from this population, there would be reason to believe that the phenomenon was not due to the role expectations of the particular subjects used by Stoner. In effect, they were trying not only to test the generality of the phenomenon, but also to reduce the number of plausible hypotheses.

The task used in this study (and in many subsequent investigations) consisted of descriptions of twelve hypothetical situations in which the central person must choose between two courses of action which vary in riskiness and in degree of reward achieved if the chosen course is successful. For each description, the subject must indicate the lowest probability of success that he would demand before recommending the potentially more rewarding alternative. Probabilities were listed as 1, 3, 5, 7, and 9 chances of success in 10, with a refusal category (scored 10) to be used if the subject would never recommend the risky alternative. The following is an example of the kind of description used: "An electrical engineer may stick with his present job at a modest but adequate salary, or may take a new job offering considerably more money but no long-term security" (Wallach et al., 1962, p. 77). This instrument is usually referred to as the Wallach-Kogan-Bem choice-dilemma (CD) questionnaire.

Subjects responded to the CD questionnaire individually, then as a group (group consensus after discussion), and again individually after the group decision process. Some of the subjects made individual decisions in subsequent sessions held two to six weeks later. The group decision showed a risky shift from the mean of initial individual decisions on ten of the twelve items, and an overall shift of $-9.4$ for both male and female subjects. A similar shift was found between initial and postdiscussion individual decisions. The effect persisted over the two- to six-week period between the postdiscussion individual decision and the final individual test. The shift in a risky direction did not occur in a control group that responded to the questionnaire twice without intervening group discussion. Wallach et al. concluded that group interaction and achievement of consensus on matters of risk produce a willingness to make more risky decisions than would be made by individuals working alone. They found a significant relationship between the riskiness of initial individual decisions and the influence the individual had on the group decision; this suggests that the risky shift effect may be due to the influence of risk-taking individuals. Two alternative interpretations of this effect were suggested: (1) Since the individual knows that the responsibility for the decision is spread among several others, he or she may experience feeling of decreased personal responsibility. This feeling of less personal responsibility might account for the greater willingness to make a risky decision in the group situation and also for the observed relationship between individual risk taking and influence in the group. (2) The influence of the high risk takers could be the cause of the group's shift toward more risky decisions. They favored the first alternative.

The results of these initial studies were generally accepted as demonstrating that the risky shift phenomenon is real, that is, that it can be reliably demonstrated under controlled conditions. Subsequent investigations were directed largely toward either the identification of variables influencing the phenomenon (i.e., its generality) or toward a determination of the process by which the effect is produced. When the choice-dilemma (CD) questionnaire is the instrument used for investigating the risky shift, it appears to be demonstrable under a variety of circumstances. Wallach, Kogan, and Bem (1964) found that the risky shift occurred when actual risks in the form of monetary payoffs were involved, but only under conditions of group discussion and consensus. An extension of this finding was reported by Bem, Wallach, and Kogan (1965) in a study using aversive stimuli such as olfactory stimulation that might produce unpleasant side effects, chromatic stimulation that might produce severe headache, and the like. Monetary payoffs were varied directly with the probability that the side effects would occur. The risky shift after group discussion was again demonstrated. Similarly, Runyan (1974) found that the risky shift occurred even when decisions had consequences for real persons (friends), and Spector, Cohen, and Penner (1976) found that the risky shift occurred in both real and hypothetical situations involving choice of a date. These experiments seem to demonstrate conclusively that the shift toward risky decisions in group situations is not limited to the particular population, to the particular content of the CD questionnaire items, or to situations in which the risks are hypothetical.

However, as we noted earlier, group-induced shifts toward caution (a cautious or conservative shift) also occur. For instance, Myers and Lamm (1975) found that the mean risky shift was linearly related to the mean individual (initial) risk selected on a scale of 1 to 10 (r = .89). That is, the more risky the initial individual opinions of group members, the greater the shift in the risky direction induced by group discussion. Cautious shifts occurred on items that usually elicit conservative decisions by individuals (called "cautious items"). Group-induced shifts in the conservative direction were also observed on "cautious items" by Morgan and Aram (1975). In betting situations (e.g., in blackjack) both risky and cautious shifts have been observed (Blascovich & Ginsburg, 1974; Blascovich,

Ginsburg, & Howe, 1976). Gambling at the racetrack also appears to induce cautious shifts, especially if the stakes are moderately high (Knox & Safford, 1976; Sanders, 1978).

These several investigations make it clear that group polarization effects occur in groups making decisions and that these effects may be either risky or cautious. As we shall see, several variables influence group polarization.

Early explanations of group polarization outcomes were based on the assumption that group decisions are generally riskier than individual decisions. For instance, it was observed that Stoner's (1961) initial study used only male graduate students enrolled in an industrial management program; therefore, it was suggested that risk is a value for certain roles, such as business leader (Wallach, Kogan, & Bem, 1962). This hypothesis was quickly shown to be incorrect. Wallach et al. (1962) found that students in a liberal arts program and females also showed the risky shift in groups, and other studies found results that argue against this proposal (Bem, Wallach, & Kogan, 1965; Wallach, Kogan, & Bem, 1964). Familiarization with the task was also proposed as an explanation, and initial findings appeared to support this theory (Bateson, 1966; Flanders & Thistlethwaite, 1967). Later attempts to support the familiarization hypothesis, however, were unsuccessful (Teger, Pruitt, St. Jean, & Haaland, 1970).

In addition to those explanations already mentioned, at least two others were proposed by early investigators, namely, that risk taking is a cultural value and that the most risky person in the group is more influential in group discussions. There is little research evidence to support the latter hypothesis, but the cultural value hypothesis has some merit and has been extended to include other normative influences on behavior in decision-making groups. We will discuss this interpretation under the title *social comparison theory* and follow it by considerations of the diffusion of responsibility hypothesis and the persuasive arguments explanation.

## Social Comparison Theory

Social comparison theory was introduced many years ago to help explain how people validate their attitudes, opinions, and beliefs (Festinger, 1954). Here we are concerned with a number of related explanations of group polarization effects that are based upon the original formulation of this theory. The general proposition underlying all these is that the values and norms in a group are used for comparison purposes by individuals. When they learn that their opinions or decisions are not the right distance from the norm in the valued direction, they change in order to be more in accord with the values and/or norms of the group, to make a more favorable impression on others, etc. The particular aspect that is emphasized varies, depending on the orientation of the investigator.

The application of social comparison theory to group polarization phenomena probably originated in the "risk is a value" theory proposed by Brown (1965). The general idea is that people in our society value risk, and in the group situation most individuals want to appear to be willing to take greater risks than the average person in order to enhance their status in the group. Information exchange is, therefore, essential, since group discussion permits the individual to learn about his or her relative standing as a risk taker. When people find that they are not as risky as others, or as they had previously believed, they change in the more risky direction. This theory was later placed in a more general framework (Brown, 1974). The newer version suggested that there are many situations in which people will be motivated to conform (e.g., when being like others is valued), but there is another class of situations in which people will be motivated to fall on one or the other side of the majority position because they seek not to be just average, but better than average. In many situations, to be better than average is virtuous. For instance, people ordinarily want to be better than average on such dimensions as honesty, intelligence, patriotism, and similar characteristics. But people often do not know what the average position is and, consequently, do not know what to do to demonstrate that they are different from the average in the more positive direction. Group discussion is one way of learning about the average position (or norm) and one's own position relative to it. Hence, group discussion will lead to changes in the more desirable direction for those persons who discover that they are not in as favorable a relative position as they had believed.

Several investigations were conducted to examine this general proposition. Levinger and Schneider (1969) suggested that most people regard themselves as above average risk takers; if they learn through group discussion that they are only average or below, they shift to be in accord with their self-image, which is determined by the risk-value norm. These investigators attempted to test the value hypothesis by asking 250 subjects to give their own choice on the CD questionnaire, the choice they believed their fellow students would make, and the choice they would most admire. Their results showed that the average student believed his or her fellow students to be more conservative than himself or herself and most admired a choice more risky than his or her own. The latter finding is especially relevant to the value hypothesis and provides evidence that the underlying assumption of that hypothesis is correct.

Evidence supporting this hypothesis has also been reported by Stoner (1968) and by Wallach and Wing (1968). Stoner reported the risky shift in connection with items on the CD questionnaire for which "widely held values" favored the risky decision, but for items for which widely held values favored a conservative decision there was a conservative shift. Wallach and Wing (1968) found that on a set of six items from the CD questionnaire, male and female undergraduates at Duke University saw themselves as more risky than other students at that university.

Several recent studies have also obtained results that support social comparison theory, although the interpretations no longer assume that the culturally approved value or norm necessarily favors risk. Instead, it is assumed that norms which emerge in groups may favor either risk or caution and that the resulting shift will be in accord with the norm. For instance, in a study cited earlier (Blascovich & Ginsburg, 1974) it was demonstrated that either risky or conservative shifts can be produced in groups by appropriate manipulation of emergent norms. Subjects played blackjack alone and then with two confederates. In some groups, confederates placed high bets (50 cents), in some, medium bets (30 cents), and in still others, low bets (10 cents). Presumably, the bets of the confederates established either high, medium, or low norms, and the näive subjects shifted their own bets in accordance with these norms. Similar variations in risk taking as a function of group norms were observed in a large Nevada casino (Blascovich, Ginsburg, & Howe, 1976).

Cultural differences in risk taking have also been observed and interpreted as supporting the normative explanation (Hong, 1978). It was found that Chinese make more cautious decisions than Americans when alone and that cautious shifts occurred in Chinese groups whereas risky shifts occurred in American groups.

Other investigators have attempted to manipulate the value of responses directly, with mixed results. For instance, when subjects were told that people who see a light move larger distances are more intelligent than those who see it move lesser distances, hearing others in a group express their judgments led to greater estimates of the distance a stimulus light moved; however, those who were told that persons who perceive lesser movement are more intelligent did *not* alter their estimates in the direction of perceiving less movement of the light (Baron & Roper, 1976). Several other investigators have reported evidence that generally supports social comparison theory (e.g., Kerr, Davis, Meek, & Rissman, 1975; Muehleman, Bruker, & Ingram, 1976).

Although most findings are consistent with social comparison theory, the evidence is not overwhelming, and other studies have found results that are not altogether in accord with the theory. For example, when people have knowledge about the responses of others, they can estimate the average or modal position of the group and their position relative to it. Therefore, social comparison theory would predict that mere exposure to the responses of others should be sufficient to produce group polarization effects. However, Wallach and Kogan (1965) found that information exchange alone was not sufficient to reliably produce the risky shift. Similarly, a study by Clark, Crockett, and Archer (1971) found that both unlimited group discussion and group discussion that was limited to arguments only resulted in a statistically significant shift in the risky direction, whereas information exchange resulted in a small, nonsignificant shift. In this same study, Clark et al. tested the prediction, derived from the value hypothesis, that persons who see themselves as more cautious than their peers should not change toward risk, whereas those who see themselves as more risky than their peers should show relatively greater risky shifts after group discussion. The results of the study supported the prediction. Nevertheless, it is curious that cautious persons who learn that they are not as cautious as they thought relative to peers did not change in a cautious direction, an outcome that would be expected from social comparison explanations. Similarly, Burnstein, Vinokur, and Pichevin (1974) found that a person's own choices are *more* extreme than he or she predicts others would make because of greater confidence about his or her own than about others' decisions. They argued that people admire extreme choices because they appear to be based on well-founded arguments and not because they adhere to a social norm. Although these findings do not necessarily refute the social comparison theory, they raise some doubts about the validity of the hypothesis that individuals shift their decisions in order to make them agree with their self-images. This conclusion does not rule out the possibility that the individual shifts after group discussion in order to conform to the perceived expectations of group members.

## The Persuasive Arguments Hypothesis

A rather different explanation of group polarization effects is represented by the persuasive arguments hypothesis (St. Jean,1970; Vinokur & Burnstein, 1974). This explanation asserts that knowledge of others' choices has no direct effect on choice shifts; instead, shifts occur in group discussions because group members are exposed to persuasive arguments and information not available to them at the time they made their initial choices. Several studies provide data supporting this explanation (e.g., Burnstein, Vinokur, & Trope, 1973; Burnstein, Vinokur, & Pichevin, 1974; Ebbesen & Bowers, 1974; Madsen, 1978; Vinokur & Burnstein, 1974). For example, Burnstein, Vinokur, and Trope (1973) found that increasing argumentation produced choice shifts but increasing information about others' choices did not. Similarly, Burnstein and Vinokur (1975) found that writing arguments in support of alternatives given by others led to choice shifts, whereas information about others' choices produced choice shifts only if the person had an opportunity to think about others' choices. It has also been shown that strong depolarization effects (shifts toward less extreme positions) occur when, following discussion, the group is initially split into similar-size subgroups, each favoring a different side of the issue (Vinokur & Burnstein, 1978). This effect is predicted by the persuasive arguments hypothesis but not by the social comparison theory.

Not all research designed to test persuasive arguments theory yielded such unequivocal results, however. At least two studies find evidence suggesting that group polarization effects cannot be completely explained by either the social comparison theory or the persuasive arguments theory alone (Morgan & Aram, 1975; Sanders & Baron, 1977). In one study, for instance, it was found that the degree of risky shift was significantly related to the percent of risky expressions in the group discussion, whether items were risky or cautious types (Morgan & Aram, 1975). It appears likely, then, that persuasive arguments are only one factor instigating group polarization. Social comparison processes and perhaps diffusion of responsibility also contribute to choice shifts in groups.

## Diffusion of Responsibility

As noted earlier in this discussion, Wallach et al. (1962) favored the diffusion of responsibility hypothesis, and they have reported the results of several studies which support their view. Wallach, Kogan, and Bem (1964) examined the risky shift effect under four conditions: personal responsibility—group decision, group responsibility—individual decision, group responsibility—group decision—chance designation of responsible group member, and group responsibility—group decision—group designation of responsible group member. The mean shift indices for the several conditions were 5.6, —1.6, 9.4, and 12.5, respectively, as compared with a mean shift of 2.4 for a control condition. Thus, responsibility for others per se produced a conservative shift, whereas group decision per se produced the usual risky shift. However, when both variables were operating together, a very strong risky shift was found. Wallach et al. (1964) interpreted this as showing that responsibility changes its meaning when linked with group decision. They concluded that group decision brings about a diffusion of responsibility with respect to the decision itself and also reduces the felt responsibility of any group member designated to act as the group's representative. In both instances, the result is to push decisions in a more risky direction.

Most of the evidence reported by Wallach and his associates has been directed toward the systematic rejection of plausible alternative hypotheses. Wallach et al. (1964) and Bem et al. (1965) presented evidence against the role-value hypothesis; Wallach and Kogan (1965) and Kogan and

Wallach (1967a) found that exchange of information alone did not produce the risky shift, thus calling into question the cultural value hypothesis; and Wallach et al. (1962) found only low positive correlations between inital risk level and perceived influence (r = .32 for males and r = .22 for females). Thus, by successively eliminating alternative hypotheses, these investigators have built up a good case for their diffusion of responsibility hypothesis. However, Pruitt and Teger (1969) failed to find a risky shift in groups that were permitted to discuss other issues but not the current issue, a result they interpreted as casting doubt on the diffusion of responsibility theory. Willems and Clark (1971) found that creating emotional bonds between group members does not produce the risky shift, a finding they also interpreted as being inconsistent with the diffusion of responsibility hypothesis. The extent to which these findings discredit the diffusion of responsibility hypothesis is debatable, since group discussions were irrelevant to the decision.

It is clear from the data presented in the preceding pages that group participation often induces group polarization. The direction of this effect may be either toward a riskier decision than the mean individual decisions of group members or toward more conservative or cautious decisions. Furthermore, there is good evidence that group polarization is not limited to the question of risky versus cautious shifts but is a more pervasive phenomenon that occurs in a variety of situations. For example, reviews of the literature reveal that group polarization effects have been observed in such diverse areas as attitude change, ratings of the importance of values, evaluation of given courses of action, gambling, impressions of others, prosocial behavior, antisocial behavior, conflict situations, mock jury decisions, and religious beliefs (Myers & Lamm, 1976; Lamm & Myers, 1978). At least three processes have been shown to be involved in group polarization effects: social comparison processes, persuasive arguments, and diffusion of responsibility. Although proponents of one or another of these explanations often appear to believe that these effects can be produced by only one process, it is plausible that each process may induce group polarization, either alone or in combination.

## PLAUSIBLE HYPOTHESES ABOUT INDIVIDUALS AND GROUPS

The various researches reported in the preceding pages have had the effect of reducing the number of plausible or reasonable hypotheses concerning differences between individual and group processes. The hypotheses that were rejected as a result of research findings are of interest only in a negative way; that is, it is now known that these hypotheses are not valid and need not be considered further. The remaining plausible hypotheses are considerably more significant because they represent the best generalizations that we can make at this time, given the present state of knowledge about individual and group behavior. At this point, it is worthwhile to identify these surviving plausible hypotheses and to state them explicitly so that their implications can be examined and tested more fully. It is well to keep in mind that these hypotheses are generalizations which appear to be valid under most conditions; one should not expect them to hold true under every conceivable set of circumstances. Furthermore, the amount and consistency of the evidence supporting hypotheses may vary greatly. Finally, since they are *hypotheses,* future research may demonstrate that all or some of them are invalid.

*Hypothesis 1   The mere presence of others increases the motivation level of a performing individual when the individual expects to be evaluated.*

The basis for this hypothesis lies in the studies of social facilitation. The various studies involving motor tasks generally revealed that individuals perform better in the presence of others than they do alone, whether the others represent a passive audience (Travis, 1925) or coacting individuals (Triplett, 1897). Similar findings were reported with verbal tasks, such as word association, that require no complex mental operations (F. H. Allport, 1920). However, on tasks which do require higher mental processes, the presence of others may have either no effect (Farnsworth, 1928; Pessin & Husband, 1933) or an adverse effect on performance (Travis, 1928). The dynamogenic theory proposed by Triplett (1897) and the arousal hypothesis formulated by Zajonc (1965a) suggest that these findings can be explained on the assumption that the presence of others increases motivation to perform well. An implication of this proposition is that the presence of others should produce effects similar to those produced by increased motivation. Research by Zajonc and Sales (1966) yielded results compatible with this expectation. Research by Good (1973), Martens and Landers (1972), Blank, Staff, and Shaver (1976), and Grush (1978) provide evidence suggesting that the social facilitation effect does not occur when there is no expectation that the performer will be evaluated by others who are present.

*Hypothesis 2   Group judgments are superior to individual judgments on tasks that involve random error.*

This hypothesis derives from the studies of group judgment that generally show groups more accurate than individuals when the group judgment can be built up from a number of individual judgments, each of which is subject to random error (e.g., Gordon, 1923; Jenness, 1932; Knight, 1921). This effect can be accounted for by the increased number of judgments in the group (Stroop, 1932), the wider range of knowledge in the group (Jenness, 1932), and the influence of the more confident (and more accurate) individuals in the group (Gurnee, 1937). The implication of this hypothesis is that the average of several judgments by one individual is likely to be as accurate as a group judgment when the errors of judgment are expected to be randomly distributed around the true value of the stimulus being judged.

*Hypothesis 3  Groups usually produce more and better solutions to problems than do individuals working alone.*
Data supporting this generalization come from studies by Marjorie E. Shaw (1932), G. B. Watson (1928), Husband (1940), Taylor and Faust (1952), and others. The kinds of problems employed in these investigations varied greatly, but there were sufficient similarities to suggest that the superiority of groups in problem solving is probably limited to tasks having the following characteristics: The contributions of several individuals can be combined; i.e., there can be a division of labor (Marquart, 1955; G. B. Watson, 1928); the creation of ideas or the remembering of information is required (Taylor & Faust, 1952; Yuker, 1955); and it is possible for others to recognize and correct individual errors (Marjorie E. Shaw, 1932). The degree to which the group superiority effect occurs has also been related to the ability of the best group member (G. B. Watson, 1928), to the greater interest in the task aroused by group membership (Barnlund, 1959), and to the influence of the most confident member (Thorndike, 1938). An implication of this hypothesis is that groups should be utilized when the accuracy or quality of the solution is the primary concern.

*Hypothesis 4  Groups usually require more time to complete a task than do individuals working alone, especially when time is measured in man-minutes.*
An important assumption of the above hypothesis is that the task can be done by a single individual. The general findings indicate that groups often (but not always) require more total time to complete a given task than do individuals, even when the measure is overall time required for completion. The important aspect pointed to by Hypothesis 4 is that the time of several persons is invested in a group action as compared with one person in the individual problem-solving situation. Several persons have noted that individuals are far more efficient than groups in terms of man-minutes invested in the solution (e.g., Davis & Restle, 1963; Husband, 1940; Taylor & Faust, 1952). The implication of this hypothesis is obvious: If one is concerned primarily in cost of efficiency, individuals are better than groups in the solution of problems.

*Hypothesis 5   Groups learn faster than individuals.*
Data supporting this hypothesis appear to be universally positive (e.g., Beaty & Shaw, 1965; Perlmutter & de Montmollin, 1952; Yuker, 1955). This hypothesis clearly bears important implications for teaching and classroom activities. Greater use of group activities in the classroom should facilitate learning, which, after all, is the primary purpose of teaching. This is already being done in many classrooms (see, e.g., Johnson & Hunt, 1968), although it is not clear to what extent the process is based upon research findings. It should not, however, be confused with the so-called discussion method of teaching.

*Hypothesis 6   Group discussion often produces group polarization effects, leading to either more risky or more cautious group decisions than decisions made by the average group member prior to group discussion.*

Although the evidence for this proposition is derived largely from research using the choice-dilemma (CD) questionnaire, there is some evidence that the effect is not limited to responses to this instrument. The effect of use of the CD questionnaire has been observed in a variety of situations, among diverse subject populations, and with various payoff functions (e.g., see Bem et al., 1965; Levinger & Schneider, 1969; Wallach et al., 1962; Wallach et al., 1964). Polarization effects have also been observed in both real and hypothetical choices of dates (Spector, Cohen, & Penner, 1976), in blackjack games (Blascovich & Ginsburg, 1974; Blascovich, Ginsburg, & Howe, 1976), and in gambling at the racetrack (Knox & Safford, 1976). The explanation of these effects is still in dispute, but social comparison processes, persuasive arguments, and diffusion of responsibility appear to be involved. The fact that groups often make riskier decisions than individuals, contrary to a once-common belief, is important with respect to many functions of society, such as the jury system, congressional committees, and other decision-making groups.

The consideration of individual and group processes has thus suggested a number of interesting and plausible hypotheses concerning similarities and differences of individual and group performances. The relationship of these to the internal processes of group interaction should become evident in the following chapters as we examine other aspects of the group and the behavior of group members.

## SUGGESTED READINGS

Lamm, H., & Myers, D. G. Group-induced polarization of attitudes and behavior. In L. Berkowitz (Ed.), *Advances in experimental social psychology*. Vol. 11. New York: Academic Press, 1978, Pp. 145–195.

Grush, J. E. Audiences can inhibit or facilitate competitive behavior. *Personality and Social Psychology Bulletin,* 1978, **4,** 119–122.

Markus, H. The effect of mere presence on social facilitation: An unobtrusive test. *Journal of Experimental Social Psychology,* 1978, **14,** 389–397.

Shaw, Marjorie E. A comparison of individuals and small groups in the rational solution of complex problems. *American Journal of Psychology,* 1932, **44,** 491–504.

Yuker, H. E. Group atmosphere and memory. *Journal of Abnormal and Social Psychology,* 1955, **51,** 17–23.

Zaleska, M. Individual and group choices among solutions of a problem when solution verifiability is moderately low. *European Journal of Social Psychology, 1978,* **8,** 37–53.

# Chapter 4

# Group Formation and Development

The initial event in group interaction, the establishment of a relationship between two or more persons, is often referred to as *group formation*. It is evident, however, that the formation of a group is a continuous process. That is, the formation of the initial relationship is a necessary condition for group existence, but the group during its existence is in a never-ending process of change. The relationships among group members may often appear to be stable, with little change from time to time, and indeed such stability may be possible in certain static groups. In the more general case, however, relationships are modified from day to day. The modifications are relatively large early in the life of the group; after the group has established quasi-stable relationships, the changes may be so slow and of such lesser magnitude as to be almost imperceptible. In this chapter, then, consideration will be given not only to the initial attraction of group members, but also to some of the formative processes that occur in the course of group development.

## WHY PEOPLE JOIN GROUPS

If we assume that people join groups voluntarily, the first question that must be asked is, Why do people join groups? The question can, of course, be answered at many levels. At the most general level, we may say that people join groups because the group meets some individual need. There are some tasks that can be accomplished only by groups, there may exist a personal need for affiliation, etc. In fact, a number of theorists have proposed theories of interpersonal attraction based upon the notion of reinforcement. Chapter 2 outlined briefly the exchange theory proposed by Thibaut and Kelley (1959) in which they formulated the concepts of *comparison level* (CL) and *comparison levels for alternatives* ($CL_{alt}$). According to this theory, the comparison level is the standard which an individual uses to evaluate an interpersonal relationship. If the outcomes that accrue from the relationship are above the CL, the relationship is evaluated favorably; if they are below the CL, the relationship is evaluated unfavorably. The $CL_{alt}$ is the standard the individual uses to determine whether to enter into a new relationship or to remain in an already existing one. If the net reward-cost outcome is above that expected from other available relationships, the individual will enter into or continue the relationship; if below available alternatives, he or she will not enter (or continue) the relationship. Clearly, this theory assumes that the individual establishes and maintains an interpersonal relationship because of the rewards that accrue from it. This assumption is supported by the Friedland, Arnold, and Thibaut (1974) study cited in Chapter 2. It will be recalled that after CLs had been established, individuals cooperated more when rewards were above the CL than when they were below it, but cooperation was unrelated to the absolute level of reward.

A similar theory was proposed by Newcomb (1956), who equated attraction and repulsion to another person with positive or negative attitudes toward that person. These attitudes are established according to reinforcement principles, and hence the individual is attracted or repulsed, depending upon the rewards or punishments that derive from the relationship with another. More will be said about these theories after some of the relevant research findings have been discussed.

General explanations have a certain appeal because they seem intuitively correct. But it is not enough to offer general explanations. One may well ask, What are the needs that are satisfied by group membership? What constitute rewards and punishments? The next level of explanation is represented by Cartwright and Zander's (1960) statement that the group itself may be the object of need or the group may simply be the means for satisfying some need that lies outside the group. When these two general classes are examined more closely, it becomes evident that each of them can be analyzed into several smaller classes, which in turn can be subdivided even further. Sources of need satisfaction residing in the group include at least (1) attraction to the members of the group (interpersonal attraction), (2) attraction to the activities of the group, (3) attraction to the goals of the group (i.e., the goals of the group are valued by the individual), and (4) group membership per se. Needs outside the group that may be satisfied through group membership include at least (1) attraction to others outside the group and (2) attraction to goals outside the group. Let us examine these factors in greater detail.

### Interpersonal Attraction

The variables influencing the attraction of one person to another have probably been studied more extensively than any other determinant of group formation. The early studies tended to consider secondary determinants, such as propinquity (Festinger, 1953a) and interaction (Bovard, 1956; Palmore, 1955). However, these variables merely provide the opportunity for the operation of primary variables, such as attitude similarity, value congruence, personality characteristics, and the like. Nevertheless, it is instructive to consider some of the environmental factors that make it possible for other variables to exert their effects on interpersonal attraction.

**Proximity, Contact, and Interaction**    Investigations of environmental and group process variables as determinants of group formation and interpersonal attraction are usually discussed under one of three headings: proximity, contact, or interaction. These factors are closely related and represent varying degrees of association rather than unique variables. In general, *proximity* (or propinquity) has been used to refer to the physical distance between individuals, *contact* to situations in which individuals are likely to be in each other's presence frequently, and *interaction* to situations in which the behavior of each person influences the other.

In a number of field studies the physical distance between individuals has been found to be related to affiliation. The classic study of the formation of friendships in a student housing complex (Festinger, Schachter, & Back, 1950) clearly revealed the role of proximity in the establishment of interpersonal relationships. Married couples were assigned to housing by the university housing office in order of application, without regard to college major, classification, or other variables that might influence the formation of friendships. Festinger et al. found that in this setting interpersonal relationships were determined largely by proximity. Persons living next door to each other often became friends. Couples who occupied corner units or end units which faced the street frequently became social isolates. The results of other investigations agree in showing a positive relationship between attraction and proximity; e.g., Maissonneuve, Palmade, and Fourment (1952) observed that propinquity and liking choices were related in boarding school classes; Byrne and Buehler (1955) found that seat neighbors in college classes were more likely to become acquainted; and Sommer (1959) noted that persons who sat near each other in the cafeteria of a large mental hospital interacted more than persons in more distant positions. Similarly, naval recruits who bunked adjacent to one another interacted more frequently than nonadjacent recruits (Sykes, Larntz, & Fox, 1976), a finding that was interpreted as reflecting interpersonal attraction. Clearly, persons who are physically closer to each other are more likely to form affiliative relationships than those who are more distant from each other.

There has been considerable interest in the degree to which contact between minority groups affects the relationships between such groups. Many investigations reveal that contact results in more favorable attitudes toward members of minority groups and an increased willingness to affiliate with them. During World War II, Stouffer, Suchman, DeVinney, Star, and Williams (1949) observed that the degree to which white soldiers thought it was a good idea to have Negroes in the company varied directly with the amount of contact they had had with Negroes. Results consistent with this finding have been obtained in a variety of settings. Deutsch and Collins (1951) compared black-white relations in a housing project in which black and white families were assigned to buildings in segregated areas with those in an integrated apartment house. They found there were more frequent and more intimate interpersonal relations among blacks and whites in the integrated project than in the segregated one. Furthermore, they were able to demonstrate that this difference did not exist prior to residence in the housing projects. Similarly, Jahoda (1961) found a considerable reduction in preferences for residential segregation following black-white contact as neighbors or on the job, and Harding and Hogrefe (1952) found that white persons who had worked with Negroes on an equal basis were more willing to do so again than those who had not.

Anticipated interaction may lead to increased liking, even if the other person is initially dislikable (Tyler & Sears, 1977). In one experiment, information was given about another person with whom the subject was to interact later, and in another experiment the subject actually interacted with the stimulus person. In each instance, the stimulus person was either likable, dislikable, or "ambiguous." Anticipated interaction increased liking for both the initially ambiguous and the initially dislikable stimulus person, but not for the initially likable person.

It has already been suggested that proximity, contact, and interaction probably are not primary determinants of attraction; i.e., proximity makes it possible for individuals to come into contact and interact with each other, and such interaction makes it possible for them to learn about characteristics of others that make them attractive (e.g., their physical attractiveness, their attitudes, etc.). This interpretation is supported by evidence that proximity and interaction do not always lead to increased attraction. Festinger (1953a) described a housing project in which few group memberships existed among residents. In this project, the residents felt they were forced to live in the project because of a housing shortage, and their attitudes toward fellow residents were quite negative. Gundlach (1956) reported similar negative attitudes on the part of white women workers who had been assigned to work with Negroes with similar educations and backgrounds. At least two other studies have found no relationship between amount of interaction and liking (Stotland & Cottrell, 1962; Stotland, Cottrell, & Laing, 1960). Further evidence that proximity exerts an indirect influence on interpersonal attraction is provided by a study of friendships among 270 residents of a city housing project (Nahemow & Lawton, 1975). Friendships among people of different races and ages were almost exclusively among those who lived close together, but there was an inverse relationship between similarity of friends and proximity of residence.

It is perhaps worth noting that proximity does not always result in interaction. A study of biracial interactions in an elementary school (M. E. Shaw, 1973b) reveals some of the factors influencing black-white interactions, given that they are in proximity and thus have opportunity to interact. Pupils in grades one through six were observed for ten minutes on five separate occasions during which the number of same race (black-black and white-white) and cross-race (black-white) interactions were recorded by two observers. It was found that the frequency of biracial interactions was a function of the proportion of black students in the class: the larger the number of blacks relative to the number of whites, the less frequent biracial interactions. This relationship may be due to the increased opportunity for same-race interaction when the black membership is large, since, as we shall see, similarity induces interpersonal attraction.

If the belief that proximity and interaction merely provide the opportunity for individuals to learn about the characteristics of others that make them attractive is correct, it is important to know what these other characteristics are and to explore just how they function to determine attractiveness.

**Physical Attractiveness**   Probably the most obvious source of attraction between two persons is sheer physical attractiveness. When a person exemplifies the physical characteristics which contribute to the perception of beauty or handsomeness (in a given culture), others are prone to be attracted to, and to want to associate with, him or her. The importance of physical attractiveness in dating behavior, for example, has been demonstrated by Walster, Aronson, Abrahams, and Rottman (1966). They conducted a field study in which subjects were randomly paired at a "computer dance." They found that, regardless of a male subject's attractiveness, how much he liked his partner, how much he wanted to date her again, and how often he actually asked her out again were a function of her physical attractiveness. Scores on the Minnesota Multiphasic Personality Inventory, the Minnesota Counseling Inventory, Berger's (1952) Scale of Self-Acceptance, the Minnesota Scholastic Aptitude Test, and high school percentile rank—all were found to be unrelated to how much the partner wanted to continue the interaction.

A laboratory study using college men also revealed the role of physical appearance in interpersonal attraction (Kleck & Rubenstein, 1975). Female confederates were made up to be either physically attractive or unattractive and participated in either an interview-type discussion or a short-term memory task. Males' liking for the females varied with attractiveness. Furthermore, self-report measures obtained two to four weeks later revealed that the men had thought more about their partner in the interim, continued to like her more, and remembered more details of her appearance if she had been attractive rather than unattractive. There is some evidence, however, that physical attractiveness may be more important for males' liking of females than vice versa. In one experiment (Krebs & Adinolfi, 1975), sixty males and sixty females were rated on physical attractiveness by independent judges, and self-reports of frequency of dating were obtained. There was a positive relationship between physical attractiveness and dating for females, but not for males.

**Similarity**  It has been proposed by a number of authors that individuals are attracted to those who are similar to themselves. For example, Newcomb (1956) suggested that it is more likely that an interaction will be rewarding when the two interactors are similar, since one of the rewards deriving from interaction is social support for one's attitudes, beliefs, and opinions. Heider (1958) also theorized that similarity should produce interpersonal attraction. It is important to remember, however, that similarity is not a general quality. It is appropriate to consider similarity only with respect to specified characteristics (see Cronbach & Gleser, 1953). Hence, it is reasonable to expect that interpersonal attraction is related to similarity with respect to those characteristics that are judged important by the persons involved in the interaction. The variable most widely investigated within this general category of significant characteristics is probably *attitude similarity*. For instance, Newcomb (1961) invited students to live in a house rent-free in exchange for serving as research subjects. Seventeen men were selected for each of two years. At the time they moved into the house, no one knew any other member of the group. The men completed a series of attitude and value inventories and also estimated the attitudes of others in the group. Initially, proximity of room assignments was the primary determinant of attraction. Later, attraction was found to be a function of perceived similarity of attitudes.

The effects of attitude similarity on interpersonal attraction have been studied extensively by Byrne and his associates. In an initial study, Byrne (1961) followed Newcomb in assuming that reciprocal rewards and punishments are important determinants of attraction and that perceived similarity-dissimilarity is rewarding-punishing. Byrne devised the following technique for examining the similarity-attraction hypothesis, using twenty-six issues ranging from such relatively important things as integration, God, and premarital sexual relations to such relatively unimportant things as western movies and television programs. Subjects were asked to express their attitudes on these issues on a 7-point rating scale and to indicate how important each item was to them. Two weeks later subjects were falsely informed that the scale had been given as part of a study of interpersonal prediction, that students in another class had taken the same test, and that they were now to be given each other's test with the name removed in the hope that they could learn about one another from this information. Actually, fake scales were made up to represent four conditions: the other's attitudes were (1) the same as those expressed by the subject, (2) exactly opposite to those expressed by the subject, (3) the same on important issues but opposite on unimportant issues, and (4) the same on unimportant but opposite on important issues. The subjects then indicated how well they liked the other person and how much they would enjoy working with him. Attraction was significantly higher when the other person's attitudes were similar than when they were dissimilar according to both measures. Importance of issues had a significant effect only for the liking ratings. Using essentially the same technique, Byrne and Nelson (1964, 1965b) systematically varied both attitude similarity and topic importance, and found only similarity to be related to attraction. However, in a subsequent study, Byrne, London, and Griffitt (1968) demonstrated that importance signficantly influenced attraction only when importance is defined by individual rather than group judgment.

Several subsequent studies by Byrne and his coworkers have consistently found attitude similarity to be a determinant of attraction (Byrne & Griffitt, 1966; Byrne & Nelson, 1965a; Byrne, Nelson, & Reeves, 1966; Byrne & Rhamey, 1965). The study by Byrne and Rhamey probably illustrates the relationship between attraction and attitude similarity most clearly. They required 180 subjects to read questionnaires purportedly filled out by an anonymous stranger and to evaluate him on a number of variables, including attraction. The stranger's responses agreed with those of the subject on 100 percent, 67 percent, 33 percent, or none of the items. Subjects were also given information about the stranger's evaluation of them, which was positive, neutral, or negative. The attraction scores, which could vary from 2 to 14, are shown graphically in Figure 4-1. It is quite evident that attraction is a positive, increasing function of the proportion of attitudes that are similar to those expressed by the subject. The effects are most strongly operative in the neutral evaluation condition, which suggests that evaluation by the other person also influences one's attraction to that person.

One may wonder whether the clear-cut relationship between laboratory-manipulated attitude similarity and attraction also occurs in natural situations. Indeed, Kleck and Rubenstein (1975) suggested that the relationship may not hold in situations involving actual face-to-face interaction. In their study which we cited earlier, they found no relationship between attitude similarity and attraction when subjects interacted

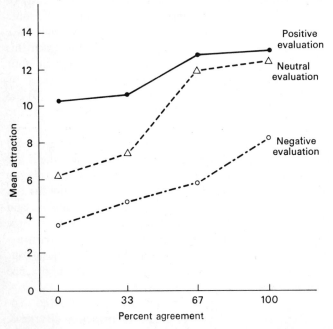

**Figure 4-1**  Mean attraction to a stranger as a function of degree of attitude similarity and quality of the stranger's evaluation of the person. (Plotted with permission from data reported by D. Bryne & R. Rhamey. Magnitude of positive and negative reinforcements as a determinant of attraction. *Journal of Personality and Social Psychology,* 1965, **2,** 884–889. Copyright 1965 by the American Psychological Association. Reprinted by permission.)

with each other. On the other hand, the study by Newcomb (1961) of students living together for long periods observed such a relationship. Similarly, Griffitt and Veitch (1974) observed thirteen previously unacquainted males who lived together for ten days under simulated fallout shelter conditions. Attitudes about 44 issues were assessed just prior to confinement, and sociometric choices were obtained at the end of the first, fifth, and ninth days of confinement. Attitude similarity and attraction were significantly and positively related on each of the three assessments of attraction. These findings make· it clear that, although other factors may sometimes be stronger determinants of attraction than attitude similarity, the attitude similarity–interpersonal attraction relationship occurs when similarity-dissimilarity are not explicitly communicated to the persons being studied and when they have an opportunity to interact face-to-face over a relatively long period of time. Similarity of attitudes also affects attraction to social organizations such as college fraternities and sororities (Good & Good, 1974).

Similarity with respect to other characteristics has also been shown to be a determinant of attraction. *Similarity of personality* as a determinant of attraction was studied by Griffitt (1966), using the Byrne technique of evaluation of a stranger on the basis of his or her responses to a self-concept inventory. When the self-descriptions of the subject and those of the stranger agreed on 33 percent of the items, the mean attraction score was 8.76 as compared with a mean score of 11.61 when there was 100 percent agreement. Byrne, Griffitt, and Stefaniak (1967) had 151 subjects examine the responses of strangers to a repression-sensitization scale. The stranger had responded as the subject did on 25 percent, 50 percent, or 80 percent of the items. The subjects then rated the stranger's attractiveness; mean attraction scores were 6.17, 8.29, and 9.70 for the three degrees of response agreement, respectively. The evidence, therefore, indicates that similarity of personality characteristics is also positively related to interpersonal attraction. This conclusion is supported by Izard (1960a, 1960b), who found that friends were more alike on personality profiles than were random pairs.

These studies demonstrate that similarity of certain personality characteristics is related to interpersonal attraction, at least under some conditions. However, it should be evident that the similarity of personality traits must be perceived by the individual in order for it to influence his or her attraction to the other person. The relation between perceived or assumed similarity and interpersonal attraction was investigated many years ago by Fiedler, Warrington, and Blaisdell (1952). Members and pledges of a college fraternity sorted seventy-six statements descriptive of personality traits four times: (1) describing self, (2) describing how one would ideally like to be, (3) predicting how one's best-liked fellow group member would describe himself, and (4) predicting how one's least-liked fellow group member would describe himself. There was no correlation between real similarity (descriptions of self) and choices of best-liked or least-liked group member. However, subjects perceived persons whom they liked best as more similar to their ideal self and as more similar to themselves than others whom they liked least. A later study by Fiedler, Hutchins, and Dodge (1959) yielded similar findings.

*Economic similarity* has been shown to be a determinant of attractiveness by Byrne, Clore, and Worchel (1966). High and low economic status subjects evaluated strangers on the basis of responses to economic items dealing with spending money. Ratings of attractiveness were higher when the stranger's responses indicated an economic status similar to that of the subject.

*Similarity of race and similarity of sex* as determinants of attraction were investigated by Smith, Williams, and Willis (1967). White and black subjects rated a stimulus person on acceptability as a friend. The stimulus person was described as to race, sex, and belief congruence relative to the subject. Race and sex were found to be related to attractiveness, but neither was as strong as belief congruence. Since the investigators' manipulation of belief congruence was essentially the same as the variations used in the studies of attitude similarity-dissimilarity, their findings support earlier studies concerning the importance of attitude similarity as a determinant of attraction. It has also been shown that both blacks and whites in integrated classrooms state that they prefer to be with members of their own race more than with members of the other race (M. E. Shaw, 1973b). The study of naval recruits cited earlier (Sykes, Larntz, & Fox, 1976) also showed that persons of similar "color" interacted more frequently than persons who were dissimilar in color.

Similarity with respect to several sociodemographic variables was found to be related to attractiveness among high school boys and girls (Kandel, 1978). Data were collected by questionnaires administered in the classroom. Although attraction was related to similarity on a large number of characteristics (e.g., leisure time activities, use of drugs, political affiliation), the highest correlations were for similarity with respect to grade in school (.83), sex (.81), ethnicity (.65), and age (.63).

There is evidence to suggest, however, that similarity may not always be a determinant of attractiveness. A case in which attitude similarity is not positively related to attraction has been reported by Novak and Lerner (1968). Forty-eight males and forty-eight females evaluated a "partner" who held either similar or dissimilar attitudes and who was described as either normal or emotionally disturbed. Subjects were less willing to interact with an emotionally disturbed person who held similar attitudes than with one who held dissimilar attitudes. Rychlak (1965) examined the effects of similarity and compatibility of needs upon preferences for interpersonal role relationships. Similarity was based upon two persons having the same need (e.g., both have a need for dominance), compatibility upon two persons having complementary needs (e.g., one has a need for nurturance and the other a need for succorance), and incompatibility upon one person's having a need that is inconsistent with that of the other (e.g., one has a need for order and the other a need for change). After participation in two small group problems, subjects selected most and least preferred coworkers for the roles of boss, employee, and neighbor. Rychlak's findings supported the hypothesis that need compatibility is a determinant of attraction, whereas need similarity and need incompatibility are not related to attraction. A study by Jellison and Zeisset (1969) indicated that the degree to which trait similarity is related to attractiveness depends upon the desirability of the trait and also upon the degree to which the trait is common in the general population. When a desirable trait is shared by another, the other is more attractive when the shared trait is uncommon in the general population than when it is common; however, when the shared trait is undesirable, the other person is more attractive when the trait is common than when it is uncommon. A. R. Cohen (1956) found similarity of ego defenses to be related to attraction, whereas similarity based on projection preferences had the opposite effect.

**Perceived Ability of Others** The perceived ability of others also appears to be a determinant of the degree to which an individual desires to affiliate with another. Gilchrist (1952) demonstrated that subjects in a problem-solving situation prefer to work with individuals who have been successful previously in solving problems. Apparently, similar results were reported by Senn (1971). Thirty male dyads performed a reaction time task, after which interpersonal attraction was assessed. Attraction toward the other person in the dyad was reliably greater when both persons were successful than when both were unsuccessful or one was successful and the other unsuccessful. Unfortunately, data were reported only for dyads, rather than for individuals; hence, it is not possible to say whether the successful person was seen as more attractive than the unsuccessful one in the successful-unsuccessful dyad. In a study by Shaw and Gilchrist (1955) it was found that although successful persons were initially chosen by both previously successful and previously unsuccessful persons, there was an increasing tendency (over time) for unsuccessful persons to shift to choices of other unsuccessful persons for affiliation. There is some suggestion, then, that similarity of perceived ability may also be a determinant of attraction. Zander and Havelin (1960) reported results consistent with this interpretation; subjects preferred to associate with others having similar ability.

The relationship between perceived ability and attraction has also been demonstrated in an experiment that involved cooperating interracial groups (Blanchard, Adelman, & Cook, 1975). Subjects exhibited greater attraction for groupmates after success than after failure. Race and level of cooperation had no effect on interpersonal attraction. However, in a somewhat similar study (Blanchard, Weigel, & Cook, 1975), the success/failure-attraction relationship was observed with respect to black group members, but not for white group members. To complicate things further, one study found that although success increased attraction and failure decreased attraction for competitive groups, both success and failure increased the attractiveness of group members who were cooperating (Worchel, Andreoli, & Folger, 1977). It seems evident, then, that the relationship between perceived ability of others, as reflected by group success or failure, and attraction is not a simple one. Other circumstances may alter or eliminate the relationship.

Some experimenters have attempted more direct tests of the effects of perceived ability on interpersonal preferences for group membership. In one study (Wilke, Kuyper, Rouwendal, & Visser, 1978), male and female students in a secondary school (aged 15 to 18 years) were administered three tests that supposedly measured ability. The tests were administered in groups ranging in size from 14 to 24 members. After the tests had been scored, scores of others were made known and students stated their first and second choices of persons as work partners. Most of the students preferred to affiliate with a person of higher ability than their own.

Two somewhat similar studies were performed by Suls and Miller (1978). In both experiments subjects were given data regarding the others' performance level, i.e., either very good, good, average, or poor. They were then asked to choose those persons whom they preferred as associates. Overall, subjects chose those identified as good or very good.

Obviously, there are other factors that determine preferences for affiliation, but these various studies provide strong evidence that the perceived ability of the other person is one important determinant, especially in task-oriented group situations. When one anticipates working with others in situations that require ability for effective performance, it is reasonable that persons with ability should be preferred, with the usual caveat, "other things being equal."

In summary, the degree to which one person is attracted to another has been shown to be due to physical attractiveness of the other person, the degree to which the two persons are similar with respect to a variety of characteristics, and the perceived ability of the other person. Similarity has been studied far more extensively than other determinants of attractiveness and the evidence is highly consistent: Attraction is a function of attitude similarity, belief congruence, personality similarity, race similarity, sex similarity, and economic similarity. It is also evident that under some circumstances similarity of characteristics may lead to reduced attraction, e.g., when the other person is seen as emotionally disturbed or when needs are the characteristic under consideration. In the latter case, need compatibility appears to be the important factor. The implicit assumption in the foregoing discussion is, of course, that attraction between two persons will influence the formation of groups with these persons as members. Undoubtedly, there are many other determinants of interpersonal attraction that have not been considered here.

## Group Activities

An individual may be attracted to a group because he or she enjoys the things the group members do. A woman may join a bridge club, not because she enjoys playing bridge (although she might enjoy it), but because she finds the social activities pleasant. A man may join the Kiwanis Club merely because he enjoys meetings and civic activities, although, of course, he may be in agreement with the goals of the club. One could cite many examples of this kind of attraction to the activities of a group, but data from controlled studies are scarce.

Perhaps the most convincing evidence was provided by Sherif and Sherif (1953), who studied group formation in summer camps for boys. They were able to demonstrate, among other things, that boys who were interested in the same activities tended to form groups. Related evidence has also been provided by Thibaut (1950). He found that the attractiveness of the activities in a group affected the attractiveness of group membership. Thus, although the empirical evidence is not extensive, it generally supports the proposition that group activities constitute one source of attraction to the group.

## Group Goals

In many ways it is difficult to separate the activities of a group from its goals, and individuals may be attracted to a group because they enjoy its activities and also value its goals or purposes. For example, a person may join a group formed for the purpose of raising funds to support the local church because he enjoys fund-raising activities and because he believes it is good to support the church. On the other hand, a person who very much disliked soliciting funds might join this group if she valued highly the goal of church support. It is improbable, however, that individuals who enjoyed the activities in a particular group would join it if they negatively valued the group's goals and purposes.

The role of group goals in group formation has been demonstrated most clearly in the investigations of group relations by Sherif and Sherif (1953). After initially establishing intergroup hostility and tension through a series of ingenious manipulations, they attempted to reestablish harmony and integration. In the initial stages of the study, members of a boys' summer camp were formed into two groups on the basis of selected activities. For approximately five days, situations were arranged in which it seemed that one group interfered with or frustrated the other group. For example, following an athletic victory by one group (the Bull Dogs) over the other (the Red Devils), both were invited to attend a party in the mess hall with the stated purpose of reducing intergroup conflict. However, it was arranged so that the Red Devils got to the mess hall first and found ice cream and cake on a table. Half of the refreshments were battered and broken whereas the other half were in good condition. The Red Devils were told to serve themselves and leave the Bull Dogs their share. Without comment, they chose the good half and carried it to their table. The reaction of the Bull Dogs to this treatment was predictable: They called the Red Devils "pigs," "bums," etc., and generally derogated them. When the intergroup conflict created by procedures of this sort had been firmly established, Sherif and Sherif attempted to reduce the conflict and to rearrange group boundaries by introducing common "supraordinate" goals. The most effective of these was a campwide softball game in which a team of best players from both groups were elected by the boys from the entire camp to compete with a team coming from a neighboring camp. Although the supraordinate goal approach did not completely eliminate the hostilities produced by the earlier manipulations, there was a significant reduction in the amount of hostility and tension and some realignment of group boundaries.

The results of this extensive series of studies demonstrate two ways in which attraction to group goals can contribute to group formation. In the early stages of group development, the conflict between groups led to increased group cohesiveness. One element of this cohesiveness was the "common enemy." Or to say it another way, one of the goals of the Bull Dogs was to get even with the Red Devils. More significant, perhaps, is the demonstration that a common group goal can produce new group memberships.

The effects that being in a common predicament has on group attraction are also demonstrated by a study of the consequences of shared stress on interpersonal liking (Latane, Eckman, & Joy, 1966). The investigators proposed that people who are undergoing stress together do something for one another that serves to reduce the stress, thus positively reinforcing each other. Female subjects were assigned to either an experimental condition in which they shared an electric shock or a condition in which each received the same shock but not together. It was found that the ratings of liking for the other person were significantly greater in the shared condition, but only when subjects were firstborns.

The treatment in such a study is certainly rather weak, and perhaps it is surprising that it had any effect at all. To the extent that it did, however, the results support the hypothesis that attraction to goals constitutes one basis for group attraction.

A more convincing demonstration of the effects of group goals upon group composition preferences has been provided by Reckman and Goethals (1973). Thirty-three male and female students who had just graduated from high school were told that they would participate in a group to view a videotape of college students discussing several topics. Then they filled out a fictitious interpersonal judgment scale; their alleged scores were reported to them, along with a "cumulative difference score" which indicated that each student was either similar or dissimilar to others. Next, the purposes of the group session were described as either (1) to make accurate judgments about the central character in the tape or (2) to discuss questions such as whether the student was likable or would make a good leader. When the goal of the group was to make accurate judgments, students indicated that they preferred to work with persons different from themselves (mean difference on an 8-point similarity scale = 4.40); when the goal was congenial discussion, they chose persons more similar to themselves (mean = 2.75). Thus, preferences concerning group composition were clearly influenced by the established goals of the group.

### Group Membership

It has also been proposed that membership in a group per se may be rewarding to an individual, quite apart from the particular individuals who are members of the group, the group activities, or the purposes of the group. It was suggested many years ago that there exists an "affiliation want" (Trotter, 1920), which is one of four instincts that govern human life. Later theorists have denied the instinctual nature of the need for affiliation but nevertheless posit such a need as playing an important role in social groupings (McClelland, Atkinson, Clark, & Lowell, 1953; Schachter, 1959). Schachter proposed that one of the functions of affiliation is to reduce anxiety, and his research generally supported this view. Research by others also agrees with this hypothesis. Pepitone and Kleiner (1957) varied the amount of threat experienced by group members and found that high threat yielded greater increases in attraction to the group than low threat. In a second study (Kleiner, 1960) it was found that reduction of threat increased the attractiveness of a confederate who played the role of group member.

Another reason for need affiliation was suggested by Singer and Shockley (1965), namely, that people affiliate in order to compare abilities (cf. Festinger, 1954). Thirty-nine female students were randomly assigned to either a condition in which they had knowledge concerning their performance on an experimental task or one in which they did not have this information. All subjects were then given a choice of waiting for the next part of the study alone or with others. Those who had no knowledge of their performance chose to affiliate significantly more than did those who had such information (6 of 8 versus 2 of 22). The research by Wilke et al. (1978) and by Suls and Miller (1978) cited earlier provide data that are in accord with this interpretation (see page 92).

The strongest support for the existence of a need for affiliation is provided by a series of investigations which attempted to show that the need for affiliation can be manipulated through deprivation in the same manner as a physiological need such as hunger.

Gewirtz and Baer (1958b) invited children, aged from 3 years 10 months to 5 years 3 months, to play a game using toys. In a deprivation condition, the subject was deprived of social contact for twenty minutes before playing the game. When the child arrived at the laboratory, a familiar adult appeared and announced that the toy was broken but was being repaired. The child was given plausible assurance that the toy would be repaired in a few minutes, and, since the experimenter did not want the child to miss a turn, he or she was to wait. The adult then left the child alone in a relatively barren room for the twenty-minute period. In the control (nondeprivation) condition, the child began the game immediately upon arrival at the laboratory. Each child played a game which required him or her to drop marbles into holes in the toy. After a four-minute period to establish a base-line rate, the experimenter dispensed social reinforcements according to a predetermined schedule immediately after the subject had dropped a marble into the least preferred hole (as determined during the base-line period). Reinforcements were verbal expression of approval such as "good," "fine," "good one," etc. The reinforcements increased the rate of dropping marbles in the nonpreferred hole significantly more in the deprivation condition than in the nondeprivation condition, but only when the experimenter was a member of the opposite sex. In a follow-up study (Gewirtz & Baer, 1958a), a satiation condition was added in which the experimenter maintained a steady stream of conversation with the subject for twenty minutes before the game was started. The effects of reinforcement were significantly greater in the deprivation than in the nondeprivation condition, and greater in the nondeprivation than in the satiation condition. Both boys and girls served as subjects, but only a female experimenter was used. The opposite-sex effect observed in the first study was not found.

Gewirtz and Baer concluded that social deprivation enhances the effectiveness of a social reinforcer, thus supporting the hypothesis that there exists a need for affiliation. However, Walters and Karal (1960) were unable to replicate these findings with college students. Obviously, there is some question whether a twenty-minute period of deprivation is sufficient to arouse the need for affiliation in adults. In a second study (Walters & Ray, 1960), it was found that anxious isolated subjects differed in their response to deprivation whereas nonanxious subjects did not. These investigators concluded that the results reported by Gewirtz and Baer were due to anxiety aroused in the isolated subjects. On the other hand, Stevenson and Cruse (1961) found that social reinforcements were effective in changing behavior, and Stevenson and Odom (1962) demonstrated that the enhanced effects of social reinforcements after social deprivation could not be accounted for in terms of general deprivation. Thus, although there are some conflicting findings, the bulk of the evidence supports the hypothesis that need for affiliation can be manipulated in a manner similar to the manipulation of physiological needs, and that such manipulation has similar effects on responses to reinforcers.

## Instrumental Effects of Group Membership

It is perhaps unnecessary to note that an individual may join a group in order to achieve some goal outside the group. A young man may join a college fraternity as a means of meeting young ladies who are members of college sororities. In this case, the source of attraction to the group resides in the person(s) of others who are not members of the group; that is, the joiner is attracted to persons outside the group whom he believes he can affiliate with more readily if he becomes a member of the group in question. As another example, a business person may join a civic club because of a belief that such membership will "be good for business." It is not always easy to separate attraction to others outside the group and attraction to more impersonal goals outside the group. Therefore, we will examine the general proposition that the sources of reinforcement attainable from group membership may reside outside the group itself.

A number of studies have shown that a group may be perceived as a means to an end outside the group. In a study of labor unions Rose (1952) found that members of local unions report that the major benefits from membership are higher wages and greater job security. However, since attainment of such benefits is a major goal of labor unions, this finding could just as easily be interpreted in terms of attraction to group goals. A more direct bit of evidence was provided by Willerman and Swanson (1953) in their study of college sororities. They found that one important reason for joining a sorority was the increased prestige in the college community that can be achieved through sorority membership. A similar study of reasons for belonging to a business organization demonstrated that goals outside the group, such as need for recognition and autonomy, were important factors in the desire to remain in the organization (Ross & Zander, 1957). Although not extensive, the empirical data thus support the hypothesis that individuals sometimes join groups to achieve goals that lie outside the group. Group membership is seen as instrumental in achieving these outside goals.

So, why do people join groups? After reviewing the multitude of factors related to group formation and membership, the answer still seems to be: because the group is perceived as a means of satisfying some individual need or needs. But some of the things about group membership that are perceived as sources of need satisfaction have been identified and examined. For example, Newcomb (1956) has shown how similarity may affect attraction via generalization. It is more likely that an individual will receive reward from another person if that other person is similar to persons who have been rewarding in the past. The effects of need complementarity also may be interpreted in terms of reinforcements. If one person has a need to be dominant and the other a need to be submissive, affiliation will lead to need satisfaction for both. The effects of perceived success of the other person, group activities, group goals, and group instrumentality also may be seen as due to the fact that they satisfy individual needs. Thibaut and Kelley's (1959) analysis of attraction in terms of rewards and costs relative to comparison levels also shows how need satisfaction may be related to such factors as personal success of the other and attitude similarity. For example, the successful person is undoubtedly seen as possessing abilities that will help the group achieve its goals or that may be useful in helping the individual achieve individual goals. In either case, the successful person is seen as contributing to the satisfaction of personal needs, if one affiliates with that person. In like manner, the effects of attitude similarity can be shown to be due to the expectation of need satisfaction. One of the rewards or benefits deriving from association with others is the validation of beliefs and attitudes; one may certainly expect validation if the other person holds similar attitudes. Therefore, it appears that interpersonal attraction is a function of the degree to which the person expects affiliation with the other to be rewarding. The difficult task is to identify the many sources of reinforcement in interpersonal relationships.

## PHASES IN GROUP DEVELOPMENT

Group formation does not stop with the affiliation of members. The group develops over a moderately long period and probably never reaches a completely stable state. Development proceeds rapidly at first; much structuring and organization may occur in the first few minutes of interaction and certainly within the first several hours. Much early development is oriented toward the establishment of the social structure of the group: the formation of status and role relations, norms, and power relations. This aspect of the group is discussed in Chapter 8. But there are phases in group development that can be described more or less independently of the particular social structure. It is probable that the kinds and sequences of phases in group development are similar for all groups, although the content and duration of phases vary with the kind of group and with the group task. It is also possible that the sequences of phases may vary, depending upon the characteristics of the group and the situation in which the group develops. Several attempts have been made to identify and describe the phases in group development. We will consider some of these analyses in order to better understand developmental processes.

**Phases in Group Problem Solving**

The examination of phases in group problem solving conducted by Bales and Strodtbeck (1951) was limited to instances in which the groups worked toward a group decision on a specific problem. They defined phases as ". . . qualitatively different subperiods within a total continuous period of interaction in which a group proceeds from initiation to completion of a problem involving group decision" (Bales & Strodtbeck, 1951, p. 485). Their phase hypothesis was that during the problem-solving period groups move from a relative emphasis upon problems of orientation, to problems of evaluation, and finally to problems of control. *Orientation* refers to the process by which the information possessed by the individual members, and which is relevant to the group decision, is made available to the group and coordinated to the group problem. In a sense, it is an exploratory phase during which the members come to understand the problem and the information relevant to it. *Evaluation* occurs in all instances in which there are differences in values and interests regarding judgment of the facts of the situation and proposed courses of action. It is a subperiod during which group members judge the information relative to the problem and alternative solutions of it. *Control* refers to the regulation of members and their common environment. It involves intermember control as well as control over the group's environment, which, of course, includes the task.

The rationale for the phase hypothesis is that orientation is functionally prerequisite to the solution of problems of evaluation and control. Orientation makes it possible to evaluate and eventually to control the situation. Although Bales and Strodtbeck limited their phase hypothesis to problem-solving groups, they believed that it was compatible with processes of social interaction occurring over longer periods.

In order to test the phase hypothesis, Bales and Strodtbeck examined the interaction pattern of twenty-two problem-solving groups, using Bales's (1950) interaction process analysis. The group interactions were divided into thirds and examined for instances of orientation, evaluation, and control. Of all interactions directed toward orientation, approximately

47 percent occurred in the first period; of those directed toward evaluation, approximately 36 percent occurred in the second period; and approximately 40 percent of interactions relative to control occurred in the third period. Furthermore, the greatest frequency of interactions relative to orientation, evaluation, and control occurred in the order predicted. In the problem-solving situation, therefore, the phase hypothesis is supported by the data.

Another analysis of phases of development in task-oriented groups identified four phases: orientation, conflict, emergence, and reinforcement (Fisher, 1970a). Audiotapes of the verbal interactions of groups were analyzed for content, using a category system designed to exclude the socioemotional dimension of group interaction. A consistent four-phase pattern emerged. The *orientation* phase was characterized by clarification and agreement; group members tended to search tentatively for ideas and direction relative to decision making. The second phase, *conflict,* was characterized by disagreement. Group members became more definite in their opinions, attitudes became polarized, and comments became more precise and less ambiguous. The third phase, *emergence,* was characterized by dissipation of conflict and argument, accompanied by a recurrence of ambiguity. Fisher suggested that ambiguity of comments served as a form of modified dissent: group members can change their attitudes gradually by becoming less precise in stating them. In the final phase, *reinforcement,* argument became less important, members became aware that decisions were in the final phase, comments favoring the decision proposals were constantly reinforced, and dissent almost disappeared.

Fisher's analysis has obvious similarities to the Bales and Strodtbeck analysis, despite the difference in number of phases. It appears that Fisher's conflict and emergence phase combined are roughly analogous to Bales and Strodtbeck's evaluation phase. The differences that remain can probably be attributed to the different category systems used for analyzing group interaction. (See also Ellis & Fisher, 1975; Fisher, 1970b).

The decision-making process has also been analyzed with respect to idea development in small groups (Scheidel & Crowell, 1964, 1966). A category system was developed and used in two investigations of idea development in small groups. In the first study, it was found that mutual clarification and verbalizing of ideas (called *anchoring of group thought*) took up almost half of the total interaction time. It was concluded that idea development follows a spiral course: an idea is proposed, followed by much discussion directed toward clarification of the idea and involving much repetition and statements of agreement. When the modified idea is accepted or rejected, the group moves on to the next stage of idea development. Feedback thus becomes an important element in idea development. The second study (Scheidel & Crowell, 1966) revealed that feedback functions to make consensus explicit on one point or idea before the group moves to the next point to be considered. These studies are, of course, limited to one aspect of group development (i.e., idea development) and do not attempt to provide a complete description of group development in problem-solving groups.

### Phases in Sensitivity-Training Groups

Sensitivity-training groups are markedly different from problem-solving groups. Whereas problem-solving groups have a definite goal, the solution of a specific problem or problems, sensitivity-training groups have only vaguely defined goals, at best. The goals are undoubtedly clear to the trainers who assemble the members, but the participants are typically uncertain about what it is the group is trying to accomplish. Bennis and Shepard (1956), who have been intimately involved with sensitivity training at the National Training Laboratory, have described not only the purposes and goals of such training groups, but also the phases of development of the groups. Their analysis reveals a pattern of group development that seems to contrast sharply with that reported by Bales and Strodtbeck for problem-solving groups. Before considering their analysis, however, the nature of the training situation and objectives must be described.

According to Bennis and Shepard, sensitivity training has two major objectives: (1) to help people learn how to behave in groups in such a way that they can solve the problems for which they were assembled and (2) to ensure that individuals have a meaningful and rewarding group experience. The goal of the training group is *valid communication*. That is, members should be able to express freely their own feelings about themselves and others and to accept others as individuals who also have the right to express their feelings, beliefs, and values. It is assumed that a group characterized by valid communication will be a "healthy" group which should function with maximum effectiveness.

Sensitivity-training groups are typically composed of adults who have responsibility for directing the activities of groups as a part of their regular job. School principals, sociologists, business executives, ministers, etc., are examples of the kinds of persons who may participate in training groups. At the time the groups are assembled by the trainers, the participants are likely to be strangers. The trainer ordinarily does not specify the goals of the group, although he or she is available for consultation. Therefore, group members are faced with an ambiguous situation that is undoubtedly unlike any they have experienced before.

Bennis and Shepard identified two major areas of uncertainty that present obstacles for valid communication: dependence (or authority relations) and interdependence (or personal relations). In its development, the group moves from a preoccupation with authority relations to a preoccupation with personal relations. Orientations toward authority are regarded as prior to, and partially determinant of, orientations toward members. The group development thus consists of two phases, the first of which involves problems of authority, and the second problems of personal relations. This pattern appears to be just the reverse of the pattern found in problem-solving groups, but as we shall see, the reversal is more apparent than real.

Within each phase of development there are three subphases. In the authority phase, the members are initially preoccupied with submission (subphase 1). They expect the trainer to establish goals and rules of conduct; when he does not, there is much aimless activity and wonderment about what they are supposed to be doing. After a period of such activity, counter-dependent expressions take over (subphase 2). Typically, two opposed subgroups develop around the problem of leadership and structure. There is disenthrallment with the trainer, and rebellion is the order of the day. Resolution of the dependence problem (subphase 3) occurs rapidly, or there is a long period of vacillation and indecision during which the group is broken into conflicting subgroups. If and when dependence problems are solved, the group moves into the personal phase, starting with a period of preoccupation with intermember identification (subphase 4). During this subphase the group is happy, relaxed, and highly cohesive. All decisions must be unanimous; all members must be happy with whatever the group does. As time goes on, this harmony becomes more and more illusory and the group progresses to subphase 5, a preoccupation with individual identity. Usually the group will separate into two groups, one favoring and one opposed to close interpersonal relations. Those who oppose close interpersonal relations become anxious that their identities as individuals will be destroyed. Eventually, this conflict should be resolved (subphase 6). The resolution of interpersonal problems involves each group member in verbalizing his or her private conceptual scheme for understanding human behavior. When this is possible, the group has achieved its goal of valid communication.

Bennis and Shepard point out that this is not always accomplished. Some groups become fixated at an earlier phase and hence never attain their goal, i.e., the goal established for the group by the trainer.

Another analysis of groups that had self-analysis as the goal has been carried out by Winter (1976). The basis for her formulation was her own experience as co-leader, supervisor, or observer of co-led college self-analytic study groups. The co-leaders were sometimes same-sex and sometimes opposite-sex pairs, and sometimes were matched for experience level and sometimes not. She identified four phases of group development, labeled *encounter; differentiation, conflict, norm-building; production;* and *separation.* Table 4-1 gives an outline description of group members'

| Phase | (a) Group Members' General Concerns | (b) Members' Feelings Toward Co-Leaders | (c) Tendencies in Co-Leader Roles in Group | (d) Co-Leaders' Backstage Concerns |
|---|---|---|---|---|
| I Encounter | Initial uncertainty, fear Concerns with safety, acceptance, inclusion, solidarity | Dependency on, idealization of leaders Group wants leaders in harmony Group wants clear plan | Unity, "united front" Uniformity of role Close monitoring of each others' actions, reactions | Desire to agree; stress on similarity Desire for mutual support Establishment of policies to promote unity and uniformity |
| II Differentiation, Conflict, Norm-Building | Concerns with accommodating individual differences in differentiated roles Intermember leadership struggles | Resentment of leaders and leader solidarity Differentiation of leaders along stereotyped lines (good-bad, strong-weak, etc.) attempts to divide and conquer leaders | Beginning emergence of differences, along stereotyped lines More or less visible strain and conflict | Disagreement, competition, power conflicts, criticism, envy, etc. Development of methods to deal with these issues and feelings |
| III Production | Group norms and roles well established Focus on task | Group looks to leaders for realistic help, direction on group task | Particularized role differentiation, based on the two individuals' real strengths and weaknesses Interaction more spontaneous | Respect for, acceptance of differences Co-leader relationship seems less important than group task |
| IV Separation | Concern with making sense of what happened Reemergence of solidarity concerns, to ward off death of group | Members more dependent again Group wants interpretation of what happened; reassurance re meaningfulness of group Exploration of whether relationships with co-leaders might continue after group ends | Roles in group more uniform again Roles with members outside the group may diverge | Mutual support as group dies Concern about meaning and value of the group and co-leading experience Separation from group and each other |

Source: Sara K. Winter. Developmental stages in the roles and concerns of group co-leaders. Small Group Behavior, Vol. 7, No. 3, August 1976, 349–362. Reprinted by permission of the publisher, Sage Publications, Inc.

general concerns, members' feelings toward co-leaders, tendencies in co-leader roles in the group, and co-leaders' hidden concerns during each phase of the groups' development. The similarity to the phases identified by Bennis and Shepard will be evident from a perusal of this table, although it will also be noted that a fourth phase has been added that relates more directly to the dissolution of the group.

An analysis of the sequential structure of interaction in encounter groups yielded results that are similar to those reported by Bennis and Shepard (Mabry, 1975). Groups of twelve and thirteen members were observed, and three major developmental phases identified: boundary seeking, ambivalence, and actualization. In the *boundary-seeking* phase, group members were concerned with problems of direction and problems related to the roles of group members. The *ambivalence* phase was characterized by tension, vacillation, increased communication among group members, and a decrease in assertiveness by group members. In the third phase, *actualization,* members became less supportive of each other, and aggressive-assertive behavior was more frequent than in earlier phases.

These several studies of group development in experiential groups are thus in general agreement in showing that such groups begin with a period of uncertainty during which group members seek guidance and direction, proceed to a period of conflict, and, if successful, finally achieve a stable state in which group members relate comfortably to each other.

### General Analyses of Group Development

To this point we have reviewed descriptions of group development based upon observations of specific kinds of groups, namely, problem-solving and self-improvement groups. However, a number of persons have attempted descriptions of group development based on observations of several types of groups, suggesting that such descriptions may have more general application than the ones we have discussed so far. Since these are similar, we will describe them briefly and then identify points of agreement and disagreement.

Schutz (1966) suggested a theory of group development that is closely related to his theory of interpersonal relations (FIRO) that was presented in Chapter 2. The theory of development is viewed, first, from the individual needs of group members and, second, with respect to the development of the group as an entity. It will be recalled that individuals have varying needs for inclusion, control, and affection. *Inclusion* concerns the desire to be a part of the group and/or to be involved in group activities; *control* refers to the desire to have power and authority over others or to be controlled by others; and *affection* refers to needs concerning personal and emotional feelings between two persons. The levels of these three needs of group members determine many of the interactions in the group, and the pattern of individual need expression constitutes the pattern of development of the group. That is, members are at first concerned about inclusion, then about control, and finally about affection needs. Therefore, the first phase of group development is inclusion, and members attempt to establish their positions in the group with respect to participation, prominence, etc. The second phase is control, during which members try to negotiate positions of authority and dominance. In the final phase, affection, concern is with satisfaction of emotional and personal needs with respect to others.

Schutz presented reasonable evidence to support his analysis, but at least one attempt to test the theory yielded less than completely supportive results (Near, 1978). Patterns of development were analyzed in a self-analytic and a therapy group. Five developmental stages were discerned: leader abdication, affectivity, control or counterdependence, affectivity *(sic),* and inclusion. The first phase is the result of the trainer's refusal to adopt the traditional leadership role (noted by Bennis and Shepard, but not considered a phase). The second phase, affectivity, involves two aspects: concerns about norm expression (should feelings be expressed spontaneously or within some structure?) and concerns about accepting responsibility for the group. During the third phase some members assume control of the group, leading to discussions of the roles of institutional and peer leaders. The fourth phase, a second phase of affectivity, involves reactions to the peer leadership structure that emerged in the third phase. This is said to be a period of equalization. In the final phase, inclusion, attention is shifted to the role differentiations, followed by some members requesting inclusion in the elite group and some preferring autonomy. It should be noted that this analysis is based upon a small number of groups and that some of the differences between this pattern of development and that proposed by Schutz may be no more than differences in terminology. Accepting Near's phases as valid, one may still observe that the major difference is that the inclusion phase is not first but fifth in sequence. Finally, it can be seen that if one disregards labels, the phases of development correspond quite well to the phases identified by Bennis and Shepard. It is important to note that the types of groups observed by Near and by Bennis and Shepard were essentially the same.

Still another theoretical model of group development was specifically formulated to be applicable to groups in general (Caple, 1978). This model includes five stages of development, each having a central issue. These are:

**1** Orientation stage. In this stage, there is much ambiguity and tentative actions by members. Members' behaviors are uncoordinated, one member may not listen to another, efforts are made to establish traditional structure, the leader's tolerance is tested, etc.

**2** Conflict stage. During this phase, there is much dissension in the group. Members are impatient with each other, disagree over proposed plans, interrupt frequently, attack each other on a personal level, etc.

**3** Integration stage. This is a period of reconciliation. Members begin to listen to one another, consensus-seeking appears, polarization decreases, etc.

**4** Achievement stage. The group has now developed to a functional level. Interpersonal relationships are strong, group norms and roles are well established, problems are attacked rationally, and the group does its work well. This is the ideal stage that every group should reach.

**5** Order stage. In this stage, members are basically satisfied with their group. They do not wish to reassess norms, are less likely to introduce new materials for consideration, etc. Concern is expressed about the future of the group: will it endure?

The pattern of group development proposed by Parsons (1961) may also be regarded as a generalized model. This model was derived empirically from an analysis of small groups, psychotherapy groups, and economic factors in production. Four phases were said to occur in group development, corresponding to four functions that groups must meet in order to be effective. These phases were called latent pattern maintenance, goal attainment, adaptation, and integration. *Latent pattern maintenance* (L) refers to the maintenance of stable patterns of behavior in the group; members make a commitment to act in normative ways. *Goal attainment* (G) is a stage of development or a state of the group in which the group achieves its goal or goals, where a goal is defined as a state of equilibrium and goal attainment as reaching this state. *Adaptation* (A) involves a process of evaluation of the group's "facilities" that are relevant to goal attainment, i.e., the fitting of group resources to task requirements. *Integration* (I) concerns the mutual adjustments of subsystems with respect to the effective functioning of the group as a whole, the establishment of effective relationships among the subsystems of the group. The particular order in which these phases occur is not entirely clear. According to Parsons and his associates (Parsons, Bales, & Shils, 1953), problem-solving groups follow an AGIL order, whereas learning and therapy groups follow a LIGA sequence. However, Hare (1976) maintains that most groups develop in the LAIG sequence, with the AI order being somewhat variable (i.e., some groups may follow a LIAG sequence).

There have, of course, been many other attempts to define phases of group development, but it is neither feasible nor worthwhile to try to present them all. Many of these were reviewed by Tuckman (1965), and he pointed out the similarity of the various analyses. He concluded that the typical sequence of group development can be described by four phases, which he called forming, storming, norming, and performing. In the *forming* phase, groups are concerned with orientation through testing, which serves to define both interpersonal and task behaviors. *Storming* centers around conflict and polarization with respect to interpersonal issues, which is also reflected in task behavior. The third stage, *norming,* is reached when the group begins to resolve conflicts and establishes new standards and roles, cohesiveness, and in-group feelings. Finally, the *performing* stage is one in which the interpersonal structure serves the achievement of group goals. Roles are flexible and energy is devoted to task activities.

It is evident from the many views outlined above that group development is a complex process. The precise nature or sequence of development varies with the kind of group, the situation in which the group must function, the goals of the group, and many other factors. It is not surprising, then, that different observers see varying numbers of stages which sometimes appear in different degrees of clarity, that different labels are attached to basically similar processes, that different events are emphasized, and so on. Despite these differences, there are basic similarities across groups. Most groups require some time for orientation (deciding what the group is all about), experience a period of conflict regarding personal and authority relations among group members, usually resolve these conflicts (or eventually dissolve), and, if effective, achieve a productive state in which the energies of members can be used for goal achievement. Not all groups go through all stages of development (some phases may be attenuated, or the group may break up before the final state is reached), and some phases may recur within the same group. These facts, however, do not negate the fact that most groups develop in the manner described.

## COALITION FORMATION

The preceding discussions have been concerned primarily with processes leading to uniformity and cohesiveness in groups. But the processes of group development often involve divisive forces as well. This is particularly true when the specific outcome of group process is not agreed upon by the group members. In problem-solving groups the goal is to achieve the "correct" solution or at least the best solution to the problem, and the group is unified with respect to the desired outcome. But in some situations, group members are divided with respect to the desired outcome. For example, at a political convention the members of the party may be divided regarding the person who should be nominated for political office. Each subgroup believes that its own interests (and perhaps the interests of the party) will best be served if its candidate is nominated. If one subgroup is powerful enough to obtain the nomination by its efforts alone, divisiveness is minimized. In most such instances, however, no one subgroup has the necessary votes to win; hence two or more subgroups must join together to produce a result that is more satisfactory to both than an outcome that could be achieved by either alone. Such unions are referred to as coalitions; they occur in such diverse situations as children's groups, university committees, and governmental agencies. Subgroups, or coalitions, may even form in problem-solving groups for the purpose of achieving desired structure or procedural arrangements.

## What Is a Coalition?

The term *coalition* has been used in a variety of ways. Sometimes it is applied to mutuality of affective support (Mills, 1953), sometimes to joint activity (M. L. Borgatta, 1961), and sometimes to the joint use of resources to determine the outcome of a decision (Gamson, 1964). The latter usage seems most appropriate for the analysis of formative processes and will be adopted for this discussion. A coalition, defined in this way, is possible only in a certain kind of group situation. The characteristics of such a situation must be examined before a more precise definition of coalition can be stated.

In attempting to describe the type of situation in which true coalitions are possible, Gamson (1964) appealed to Schelling's (1958) classification of two-person games. Three kinds of games were identified: pure conflict games, pure coordination games, and mixed-motive games. According to Gamson, we would expect coalitions to occur only in the mixed-motive situation. In such a situation, there is an element of both conflict and coordination. Conflict exists in the sense that there is no outcome which maximizes rewards for every group member; coordination is involved in that there exists for at least two persons the possibility that they can do better by coordinating their efforts than they can by acting alone. For example, consider a small group that is holding an election for the chairmanship. The chairman has control of desirable appointments, such as high-paying positions in the community. There are three candidates, each of whom has substantial support but no one of whom has sufficient support to win the election. Thus, there exists the possibility that if one candidate withdraws and throws his support to one of the others, the latter can win the election. Furthermore, the winner can reward the candidate who withdraws by appointing him to a lucrative position. Clearly, there exists the possibility of a coalition which will yield a result for two of the candidates that is better than either could achieve acting alone.

Given these considerations, Gamson defined a coalition as . . . the joint use of resources to determine the outcome of a decision in a mixed-motive situation involving more than two units" (Gamson, 1964, p. 85). Thibaut and Kelley offered a similar definition: "By coalition we mean two or more persons who act jointly to affect the outcomes of one or more other persons" (Thibaut & Kelley, 1959, p. 205). These definitions make it clear that coalitions occur only when (1) three or more persons are involved, (2) two or more act as a unit against at least one other, and (3) the joint action produces a result superior to any result possible by individual action.

### Theory and Research on Coalitions

For the most part, research has been directed toward the identification of factors determining coalitions and the prediction of types of coalitions that will be formed under specified conditions. The most common experimental paradigm involves three persons, A, B, and C, each of whom controls resources needed to achieve a desirable outcome. Resources are distributed so that A>B>C, A<(B + C); that is, A controls more resources than B, who controls more resources than C, but B and C together control more resources than A alone. The common finding is that, under these conditions, B and C will form a coalition (Caplow, 1959; Kelley & Arrowood, 1960; Vinacke & Arkoff, 1957). However, this outcome does not always obtain, for example, when subjects are female (Uesugi & Vinacke, 1963). Furthermore, the results of the early studies could be accounted for by a variety of theoretical formulations. Gamson (1964) identified four theories that had been proposed as explanations of coalition formations: (1) minimum resource theory, (2) minimum power theory, (3) anticompetitive theory, and (4) utter confusion theory. In addition, at least two other proposals have been advanced as explanations of coalition formation: (1) minimal range theory and (2) bargaining theory. The utter confusion theory is really not a theory at all, but rather an assertion that coalitions are unpredictable. It states that coalitions are determined by chance events, such as a missed telephone call. Since evidence for this "theory" consists of failures to understand what determined observed coalitions, it cannot be taken seriously by the student of group processes. The other five theories, however, merit consideration. We will outline each one briefly and review some of the relevant evidence.

**The Minimum Resource Theory**   According to the minimum resource theory (Gamson, 1961b), a coalition will form in which the total resources are as small as possible while still being sufficient to determine the outcome of the decision. For example, if person A controls 48 percent of the resources, person B 30 percent, and person C 22 percent, B and C should join together to control the outcome. This prediction is based upon the parity norm, i.e., the expectation that each participant in a coalition is likely to demand a share of the spoils that is proportional to the amount of resources contributed to the coalition. In the above example, if B and C joined together, B could expect approximately 58 percent of the rewards and C 42 percent; if either joined with A, the corresponding proportions would be approximately 38 percent for B and 31 percent for C. According to the parity norm, it is clearly to the advantage of both B and C to form a coalition between themselves instead of either of them joining A.

Empirical evidence from early research supports the minimum resource theory. The study by Vinacke and Arkoff (1957) tested this theory under three distributions of resources; the predicted coalitions occurred far more frequently than any other coalition. Gamson (1961a) tested the theory in a simulated convention situation. Five-person groups were used (in contrast to the three-person groups in Vinacke and Arkoff's study) with resources (votes) distributed 25-25-17-17-17. Minimum resource theory, of course, predicts a 17-17-17 coalition. Although the probability of this particular coalition occurring by chance is only one in ten, Gamson found that it actually occurred 33 percent of the time. Furthermore, he found that the distribution of rewards corresponded to the parity norm. Players with 17 votes averaged 31 percent of the rewards, whereas players with 25 votes averaged 38 percent. Other investigations have also yielded findings consistent with this theory (Chaney & Vinacke, 1960; Vinacke, 1959). However, some research data suggest that the bargaining theory (to be discussed later) is at least equally good for predicting coalition formation (Michener, Fleishman, & Vaske, 1976; Komorita & Brinberg, 1977).

**The Minimum Power Theory**   The origin of the minimum power theory is not entirely clear, although Gamson (1964) attributes it to game theory. According to the minimum power theory, each person is expected to demand a share of the rewards proportional to his or her pivotal power; hence, the coalition will form which has the minimum pivotal power that is sufficient to determine the outcome of the decision. The pivotal power of a given person is the proportion of times he or she can, through personal resources, change a losing coalition into a winning one. For example, suppose A controls 10 percent, B controls 50 percent, and C controls 40 percent of the resources relevant to a given decision, There are three possible coalitions: A + B, A + C, and B + C. The A + C coalition cannot win; hence both A and C have pivotal power in only one winning coalition, whereas B has pivotal power in two. In this instance, the two winning coalitions each has a total of three units of pivotal power. The minimum power theory would predict that one of these would form, but it could not predict which. Minimum resource theory, on the other hand, would predict an A + B coalition.

There is little direct support for the minimum power theory, although one study (R. H. Willis, 1962) provided results consistent with it. This study involved four group members, with a 5-3-3-2 distribution of resources. There are four winning coalitions that might be formed: two 5 + 3 coalitions, one 5 + 2 coalition, and one 3 + 3 + 2 coalition.* If members of the winning coalition are to share in the rewards in proportion to their pivotal power, the 3 + 3 + 2 coalition would be predicted by the minimum power theory. This occurred about 31 percent of the time, whereas the 5 + 2 coalition (predicted by the minimum resource theory) occurred almost exactly 25 percent of the time.

This level of support is not very convincing, although there is some controversy about the reasons for this low level of support. For example, Kelley and Arrowood (1960) argued that the failure to find support for the theory is due to a lack of understanding of power relations by group members. They tried to simplify the experimental conditions and to extend trials over a period long enough to allow participants an adequate opportunity to learn about the illusory nature of the power of the person controlling the largest number of resources. Under these conditions, the weak coalition was markedly less frequent than in previous studies. More extensive studies of the effects of understanding (Vinacke, Crowell, Dien, & Young, 1966) indicate that this explanation is not sufficient to account for the failure to find support for the minimum power theory. Vinacke et al. assigned members of triads weights according to four power patterns— all equal (1-1-1), one stronger (3-2-2), all different (4-3-2), and all powerful (4-2-1).† In each of two sessions six successive games were played in each of the four power patterns, with order of patterns randomized. At first, games were played according to the usual instructions. Then the experimenter took aside designated persons and gave them special information about the minimum resources and the minimum power strategies. In one set of triads information was given to one member, in a second set to two members, and in a third set to all three members. In the two critical power patterns (one stronger and all different) there was little evidence of a significant shift to an equal incidence of the three possible coalitions, as would be required by the "understanding" hypothesis. Under information conditions, weak alliances continued to occur above chance levels. Furthermore, there was no evidence that informed persons differed from uninformed persons in their ability to enter into coalitions. There was some evidence that those persons who displayed the best understanding of correct power relationships arrived at fewer weak alliances than those who had the least understanding, but this was shown to be the result of stronger motivations to win on the part of more understanding persons. Other

---

*Of course, other three-person coalitions could form but these would include an unnecessary third member.

†The 4-2-1 pattern was labeled "all powerful" presumably because one person could determine the outcome without forming a coalition with anyone.

studies (e.g., Michener et al., 1976; Komorita & Brinberg, 1977) also find little support for the minimum power theory.

In summary, there is little empirical support for the minimum power theory and this lack of support does not appear to be the consequence of individuals' lack of understanding of the true nature of power relations among persons having unequal resources.

**The Anticompetitive Theory**   This theory holds that coalitions will form along the lines of least resistance. This is based upon the presumed existence of an anticompetitive norm against efforts to make the best deal possible. That is, group members are more concerned about interpersonal relations that about other kinds of rewards. Therefore, coalitions will form in which the distribution of rewards is obvious and relatively equal. Such a coalition, of course, is one in which resources and pivotal power of participants are about equal. For example, if the resources of a group are distributed 4-4-2, the 4 + 4 coalition is predicted. Evidence for this theory comes primarily from studies using females (Bond & Vinacke, 1961; Uesugi & Vinacke, 1963). It is probable, therefore, that females tend to adopt an anticompetitive norm, whereas males adopt the parity norm.

**The Minimal Range Theory**   This theory is based upon the proposition that those people or parties will coalesce who have the least differences in political opinions. Thus the theory predicts that the coalition which results in minimal differences among members of the coalition with respect to their political orientations will be the one to be formed (de Swaan, 1970; Leierson, 1970). Observations of political coalitions give some credence to the theory. However, evidence from one experimental investigation suggests that political differences are important only in the early stages of coalition formation (Wilke, Pruyn, & De Vries, 1978). These investigators induced three different political orientations (left, center, and right) and three degrees of power (control of 40, 30, and 30 seats in parliament). During the early stages of negotiations, people communicated primarily about the composition of the coalition "programme," and decisions were based upon political orientations. In later stages, however, they bargained about the division of outcomes, and the minimum resource theory was most predictive.

At least one other study yielded some support for the mimimal range theory (Lawler & Youngs, 1975). This study evaluated the effects of probability of success, payoff, and attitudinal agreement. All three variables were found to have some effect on coalition formation, but attitudinal agreement had a much greater effect than the other two variables. Furthermore, the mediation processes were found to be different for these variables. Both probability of success and payoff were mediated by utility, whereas attitudinal agreement was mediated primarily by anticipated conflict. (The alert reader will also have noted that the latter finding is in accord with the anticompetitive theory.)

**The Bargaining Theory** The bargaining theory of coalition formation (Komorita & Chertkoff, 1973) assumes that for any winning coalition, each potential coalition member has a maximum expected payoff, a minimum expected payoff, and a most probable payoff. The maximum outcome or payoff for the potential member with resources below the average for that coalition is equality (rewards divided equally), the minimum payoff is parity (rewards shared in proportion to resources), and the most probable payoff is halfway between equality and parity (Chertkoff & Esser, 1977). For a potential member having more resources than the average for that coalition, the maximum payoff is parity, the minimum is equality, and the most probable halfway between equality and parity. Thus, a person who is above average in resources will expect and demand a share of rewards based on the parity norm, but those that are below average will demand equality. Initially, the theory predicts that reward allocation will be the average of those that are prescribed by the parity and equality norms. Later, however, the rewards will be divided in direct proportion to each member's maximum expectation in alternative coalitions. Consequently, the theory predicts that the most likely coalition is one that minimizes members' temptations to defect, i.e., to leave the coalition in order to gain greater rewards by participating in one of the alternative coalitions.

Much of the research conducted by Komorita and Chertkoff supports the theory. For example, in one study (Chertkoff & Esser, 1977), subjects were asked to participate in a simulated stockholder's meeting. The purpose of the meeting was to determine who would control the company and thereby decide how the company's profits would be divided. Each person played the role of a stockholder who controlled a specific number of shares, each share representing one vote. Three "stockholders" attended each meeting. Two distributions of shares were investigated: a 40-30-20 distribution and a 10-20-20 distribution. Bargaining theory predicts a 30-20 coalition in the first instance and a 10-20 coalition in the second one. These were the coalitions that were most frequently formed.

In another experiment (Murnighan, Komorita, & Szwajkowski, 1977), four persons participated in one of three games or coalition situations. In each game, resources were varied by assigning each person a certain number of votes. The distributions were 8-3-3-3, where a total of nine votes was needed to win; 8-7-1-1 (9 votes needed to win); and 8-7-7-7 (15 votes needed to win). Players were identified by the letters A, B, C, and D, in order of resources. When this is done, it can be seen that the same four winning coalitions are possible in each of the three games, namely, AB,

AC, AD, and BCD. Bargaining theory predicts that the most likely coalitions will be 8-3 (i.e., either an AB, AC, or AD coalition), 8-1, and 8-7, in the three games, respectively. Predicted coalitions formed approximately 78 percent of the time in the 8-3-3-3 game, 56 percent of the time in the 8-7-1-1 game, and 83 percent of the time in the 8-7-7-7 game.

The two investigations that we have described are representative of the research relevant to the bargaining theory, but several other studies also provided generally supportive data (e.g., Komorita & Moore, 1976; Komorita & Meek, 1978; Komorita & Kravitz, 1979; Rapoport & Kahan, 1976). Although research evidence is generally in accord with bargaining theory, most of it has been conducted by proponents of the theory.

Each of the several theories that we have considered has some evidence supporting it, and none is so clearly superior to others that it must be accepted without reservation. It is evident, however, that coalitions often form during the process of group development. They are influenced by the initial resources of group members, by the attitudes and expectations of group members, by norms of the group, by the probability of success in achieving goals, by the alternatives that are available to group members, and similar conditions. Once formed, coalitions exert an important influence on group process. It should be remembered that coalitions are usually not permanent and may be expected to shift from time to time with changing circumstances.

## PLAUSIBLE HYPOTHESES ABOUT GROUP FORMATION AND DEVELOPMENT

The investigations of group formation and development have not answered all the questions about these processes, but they have reduced the number of plausible hypotheses. Again, the reader should recognize that these propositions are the most reasonable interpretations that can be made at this time, but some or all of them may be rejected as new evidence becomes available.

*Hypothesis 1    People join groups in order to satisfy some individual need.* This is the most general proposition that we can derive from the empirical data concerning group formation. To a large extent, Hypotheses 3 through 8 are specifications of the sources of need satisfaction that inhere in groups.

*Hypothesis 2    Proximity, contact, and interaction provide an opportunity for individuals to discover the need satisfactions that can be attained through affiliation with others.* Studies by Festinger, Schachter, and Back (1950), Maissonneuve, Palmade, and Fourment (1952), and Byrne and Buehler (1955) show the effects of proximity upon the formation of friendships in a variety of environmental settings. The effects of contact and interaction upon interpersonal attraction have been shown by Stouffer et al. (1949), Deutsch and Collins (1951), Jahoda (1961), Harding and Hogrefe (1952), and Tyler and Sears (1977), among others. The interpretation of these findings as showing that proximity, contact, and interaction merely provide the opportunity for persons to learn about sources of satisfaction is further supported by the finding that interaction does not always lead to liking (e.g., Stotland & Cottrell, 1962; Stotland, Cottrell, & Laing, 1960) and by evidence that attraction is reduced if contact fails to induce the belief that affiliation will be satisfying (e.g., Festinger, 1953a; Gundlach, 1956).

*Hypothesis 3    Interpersonal attraction is a positive function of physical attractiveness, attitude similarity, personality similarity, economic similarity, racial similarity, perceived ability of the other person (his or her success or failure), and need compatibility.*

Substantial empirical support has been reported for each of the factors listed in Hypothesis 3, but attitude similarity has been studied most extensively, with the generally consistent finding that interpersonal attraction is a positive function of degree of attitude similarity (Byrne, 1961; Byrne & Nelson, 1964; Byrne & Nelson 1965a; Byrne & Nelson, 1965b; Newcomb, 1961; and many others). Studies supporting the other factors listed in Hypothesis 3 are as follows: physical attractiveness (Walster et al., 1966; Kleck & Rubenstein, 1975; Krebs & Adinolfi, 1975); personality similarity (Byrne et al., 1967; Griffitt, 1966; Izard, 1960b); economic similarity (Byrne, Clore, & Worchel, 1966); racial similarity (Kandel, 1978; Smith et al., 1967); need compatibility (Rychlak, 1965); and a variety of demographic variables (Kandel, 1978).

*Hypothesis 4    Individuals desire to affiliate with others whose abilities are equal to or greater than their own.*

Evidence for this hypothesis comes from several experiments showing that successful persons are preferred as groupmates over failing persons (e.g., Blanchard, Adelman, & Cook, 1975; Gilchrist, 1952; Shaw & Gilchrist, 1955). This relationship between perceived ability and attraction is complicated by a number of other variables which may override it (e.g., Blanchard, Weigel, & Cook, 1975; Worchel, Andreoli, & Floger, 1977). More direct evidence, however, suggests that these other variables may be influencing the mediation of perception of ability as a consequence of success-failure (e.g., Wilke et al., 1978; Suls & Miller, 1978); personality similarity (Byrne et al., 1967; Griffitt, 1966; Izard, 1960b); economic similarity (Byrne, Clore, & Worchel, 1966); racial similarity (Smith et al.,

1967); success-failure (Gilchrist, 1952; Shaw & Gilchrist, 1955); and need compatibility (Rychlak, 1965).

*Hypothesis 5    An individual will join a group if he or she finds the activities of the group attractive or rewarding.*
Evidence for this hypothesis is not as strong as the evidence for Hypothesis 3, but it is moderately convincing (Sherif & Sherif, 1953; Thibaut, 1950). Furthermore, it is intuitively plausible.

*Hypothesis 6    An individual will join a group if he or she values the goals of the group.*
Again, the empirical support for this hypothesis is less than adequate, probably because it does not seem to require empirical demonstration. However, results of the studies of Sherif and Sherif (1953), Latane et al. (1966), and Reckman and Goethals (1973) are consistent with the hypothesis.

*Hypothesis 7    There exists a need for affiliation which renders group membership rewarding.*
Empirical evidence consistent with this hypothesis has been reported by a number of investigators (e.g., Gewirtz & Baer, 1958a; Gewirtz & Baer, 1958b; McClelland et al., 1953; Pepitone & Kleiner, 1957; Schachter, 1959; Singer & Shockley, 1965; Stevenson & Odom, 1962).

*Hypothesis 8    An individual will join a group if he or she perceives it to be instrumental in satisfying needs outside the group.*
The basis for this hypothesis is primarily self-reports by members of existing groups (e.g., Rose, 1952; Ross & Zander, 1957; Willerman & Swanson, 1953). As in the case of Hypotheses 5 and 6, Hypothesis 8 seems so obviously true that few investigations have been made to test its validity.

*Hypothesis 9    Group development follows a reasonably consistent pattern that involves a period of orientation, resolution of conflicts about authority and personal relations, and a productive period.*
The data supporting this hypothesis derive primarily from observations of laboratory and natural groups (e.g., Bales & Strodtbeck, 1951; Bennis & Shepard, 1956; Near, 1978; Schutz, 1966; Winter, 1976; and Tuckman, 1965). Although different analysts observed various types of groups and labeled the observed developmental processes differently, there is a basic similarity across descriptions. Not all groups go through all phases, and the duration of each phase varies widely from group to group.

*Hypothesis 10   Coalitions form in situations in which two or more persons can achieve greater rewards through joint action than can either acting alone.*

This hypothesis may appear so self-evident as not to require documentation. If documentation is required, it has been abundantly supplied (e.g., Bond & Vinacke, 1961; Caplow, 1959; Gamson, 1961a,b, 1964; Komorita & Brinberg, 1977; Komorita & Kravitz, 1979; Lawler & Youngs, 1975; Vinacke, 1959; Vinacke & Arkoff, 1957; and many others). The determinants and processes of coalition formation are still not entirely clear and require further research.

## SUGGESTED READINGS

Bennis, W. G., & Shepard, H. A. A theory of group development. *Human Relations,* 1956, **9,** 415–427.

Byrne, D., & Rhamey, R. Magnitude of positive and negative reinforcements as a determinant of attraction. *Journal of Personality and Social Psychology,* 1965, **2,** 884–889.

Deutsch, M., & Collins, M. E. *Interracial housing: A psychological evaluation of a social experiment.* Minneapolis: University of Minnesota Press, 1951.

Gamson, W. A. Experimental studies of coalition formation. In L. Berkowitz (ed.), *Advances in experimental social psychology.* Vol 1. New York: Academic, 1964, Pp. 82–110.

Gilchrist, J. C. The formation of social groups under conditions of success and failure. *Journal of Abnormal and Social Psychology,* 1952, **47,** 174–187.

Kandel, D. B. Similarity in real-life adolescent friendship pairs. *Journal of Personality and Social Psychology,* 1978, **36,** 306–312.

Komorita, S. S., & Brinberg, D. The effects of equity norms in coalition formation. *Sociometry,* 1977, **40,** 351–361.

Near, J. P. Comparison of developmental patterns in groups. *Small Group Behavior,* 1978, **9,** 493–506.

Newcomb, T. M. The prediction of interpersonal attraction. *American Psychologist,* 1956, **11,** 575–586.

Sherif, M., & Sherif, C. W. *Groups in harmony and tension.* New York: Harper & Row, 1953.

Stevenson, H. W., & Odom, R. D. The effectiveness of social reinforcement following two conditions of social deprivation. *Journal of Abnormal and Social Psychology,* 1962, **65,** 429–431.

# Chapter 5

# The Physical Environment of Groups

Groups are embedded in a complex environmental setting that exerts a strong influence on almost every aspect of group process. Because of its complexity, this setting should be regarded as several environments rather than a single one. Obviously, the group must exist in a *physical environment.* The buildings, rooms, chair and table arrangements, communication channels, and the like are different for different groups, and such factors affect the functioning of the group in several important ways. There are other environments that are less obvious, perhaps, but nevertheless are significant factors with respect to group process. The personal characteristics that group members individually bring to the group may be considered one aspect of the environmental setting (*personal environment*), since they may be an important determinant of the group's operational characteristics. Once the members have assembled and begun interaction, a whole set of interpersonal relationships become established; this *social environment* exerts a strong influence upon the group. And finally, the group is usually formed for a purpose. Its task or set of tasks constitutes the *task environment,* which is an important factor in shaping group behavior. This chapter is concerned with the physical or material aspects of the environment. In subsequent chapters we will examine the effects of the personal characteristics of group members, group composition, group structure, leadership, and group goals and tasks—the nonmaterial elements that affect group process.

Although many aspects of the physical environment are potential determinants of group behavior, relatively few of them have been examined systematically. Consideration is restricted to those aspects which have been studied extensively enough to permit sound conclusions about their effects on group process. Particular attention is devoted to territoriality, personal space, spatial arrangements, and patterns of communication channels. Studies of territoriality and personal space reveal the psychological significance of the physical environment for the individual; studies of spatial arrangements and patterns of communication reveal how elements of the physical environment can influence group interaction along a variety of dimensions.

## MATERIAL ASPECTS OF THE PHYSICAL ENVIRONMENT

Among the many aspects of the physical environment that influence group process, perhaps the material components are the most obvious ones: the shape and size of the room, lighting, furniture, color of the walls, and the like. For example, it has been shown in industrial work groups that optimum light intensity varies from 20 to 100 footcandles, depending upon the task (Luckiesh, 1931), and that workers are more efficient when the lighting is evenly distributed in the work area (Tinker, 1939). In one work situation, it was observed that when the walls were painted a "cool blue," working women complained of being cold with the temperature set at 70 degrees; when the thermostat was raised to 75 degrees, they still complained of the cold. The color was then changed to "warm yellows and restful greens"; at 75 degrees the women complained of being too warm (Seghers, 1948). It has been noted that sound conditioning of workrooms reduced workers' negative reactions (expressions of discomfort and annoyance) but had no effect on productivity (Sleight & Tiffin, 1948).

Many of these effects of the material aspects of the environment, however, seem to depend upon the attitude of the group members. The famous Western Electric studies (Roethlisberger & Dickson, 1939) provide an excellent example of this effect. Initial studies were concerned with the effects of lighting intensity upon productivity; it was found that both increasing the light intensity and decreasing the light intensity were followed by increasing productivity. Further investigation revealed that the primary variable was the workers' perception of the situation: they believed that someone was concerned about their welfare and responded by working harder and/or more efficiently than when they believed that no one cared about them. A similar effect was demonstrated in a more highly controlled situation by Baker (1937). Playing music in the workroom increased productivity when workers believed that the purpose of the music was to facilitate productivity and decreased productivity when they believed that interference was the purpose of the music.

Whether the room is brightly or dimly lit influences several aspects of group interaction (Carr & Dabbs, 1974). Female subjects interviewed by female interviewers rated dimly lit rooms as more intimate and less appropriate for the interview situation than brightly lit rooms. Subjects in the dimly lit room, as compared with those in a brightly lit room, decreased eye contact and increased latency to talk.

Some attention has also been given to other aspects of rooms in which group interaction occurs and their effects on group process. For example, Mintz (1956) studied the effects of the esthetic qualities of the room on certain aspects of dyadic interaction. Two examiners (who did not know that they were being studied) tested subjects in either a "beautiful" room or an "ugly" room. The beautiful room was pleasantly decorated and furnished to give it the appearance of an attractive, comfortable study; the ugly room was arranged to appear as an unsightly storeroom in a disheveled, unkempt state. Noise, odors, time of day, lighting, and similar variables were controlled. Each examiner tested thirty-two subjects over a two-week period, alternating so that examiner A was testing in the beautiful room while at the same time examiner B was testing in the ugly room and vice versa. Examiners' ratings of photographs on "well-being" and "energy" were consistently higher in the beautiful room than in the ugly room. Furthermore, examiners reported more fatigue, monontony, headaches, discontent, hostility, irritability, and room avoidance and usually finished the testing more quickly in the ugly room than in the beautiful room.

Room size is another aspect of the physical environment that influences group behavior. For instance, Lecuyer (1975) observed four-person groups in either a large room or a small room. The large room was 12 by 15 meters and seated 250 persons; the small room was 6 by 6 meters and usually held 30 persons. Groups sat at a table in the front of the room. The task was the choice-dilemma questionnaire (see Chapter 3), but a scale of recommendations to the central person substituted for the usual chances of success scale. Subjects responded first individually, then as a group, and finally individually a second time. Greater polarization occurred in the small room, and a significant risky shift was found in the small room but not in the large room. In other words, the effects of group interaction on this task were intensified in the small room relative to the large room. Somewhat similarly, Mehrabian and Diamond (1971a) reported that the presence of props (a puzzle poster and a sculpture) affected dyadic interaction; preoccupation with the puzzle poster reduced affiliative behavior (as revealed by indicators of amount of conversation and cues communicating positive effect, such as head nodding, eye contact, and verbal reinforcers), whereas preoccupation with the sculpture facilitated interaction, but only between persons who were sensitive to rejection.

The current social concern with environmental pollution has led to some findings that are relevant to effects of the material aspects of the environment. For example, Glass, Singer, and Friedman (1969) found that unpredictable noise induces frustration and leads to decrements in performance. However, these effects are reduced if the person believes he or she has control over the termination of the noise, even if the control is indirect (Glass, Reim, & Singer, 1971).

These several investigations, spanning a period of some forty years, are generally consistent in showing that the material aspects of the environment are important factors in determining individual and group behavior. As shall be seen later in this chapter and in later chapters, these variables are interrelated with other physical and psychological determinants of group behavior. These other variables modify the effects of the kinds of variables that have been discussed above and may even lead to a change in the material components themselves. For instance, the personal characteristics of group members may "cause" them to repaint the walls of the room, rearrange the furniture, or even knock down some walls in order to enlarge the size of the room. The reader should remember that what is viewed as "cause" from one perspective may become "effect" when considered from a different point of view.

## TERRITORIALITY

It is a common observation that individuals tend to appropriate space and assume proprietary rights to it in almost all situations in which several people come together over a period of time. For example, when seats are not assigned in the classroom, each student typically selects a particular chair or desk which he or she occupies day after day. If another student sits in the chosen chair, the "proprietor" usually does not hesitate to point out that the other student is occupying his or her seat. Furthermore, the other student ordinarily recognizes the proprietary rights of the first student and moves to another chair without argument. Territoriality, therefore, means the assumption of a proprietary orientation toward a geographical area by a person or group. This proprietary orientation is distinguished from ownership in that the individual or group has no legal right to the geographical area in question. The territory is simply occupied, either permanently or intermittently, by an individual (or group) who then acts as if the property belongs to him or her. That is, individuals use the "territory" for their own purposes and defend it from invasion by others.

The orientations that individuals adopt toward geographical areas and objects in these areas have highly significant implications for small group behavior. When a group member assumes a proprietary right to a particular object, the smooth functioning of the group depends upon the degree to which other group members respect that person's assumed territorial right. For example, if one member adopts a particular chair as his or her own and another sits in it and refuses to move, intragroup conflict is inevitable. Even if the offended member yields to the new occupant, ill feelings are likely to develop between the two members to the detriment of good interpersonal relations. Similarly, when one group assumes territorial rights to a given geographical area, good intergroup relations depend upon other groups respecting that assumed right. Evidence concerning these orientations derives primarily from investigations that focus upon individual territoriality. However, in the following discussions, the reader should keep clearly in mind the consequences of these individual orientations for group behavior.

## Individual Territoriality

Individuals typically assume territorial rights over spatial objects, such as tables, chairs, and beds, as well as over large spatial areas, such as rooms. This has been well documented in a number of carefully controlled observational studies. W. F. Whyte (1949) conducted an extensive study of the social structure of restaurants and found, among other things, that kitchen workers held proprietary attitudes toward the kitchen area. When other workers entered the kitchen, the normal pattern of interaction was disrupted. If the "invaders" had lower status, the kitchen workers openly attempted to block their participation in the work they normally carried out. Higher-status persons were not openly resisted, but their presence typically disrupted relations in the kitchen.

Altman and Haythorn (1967a) studied the interactions of isolated dyads. During the period of isolation the members of the dyad gradually withdrew from one another and established strong preferences for a particular chair, table, and/or bed. These preferences were rigidly respected by both members of the dyad. The degree to which this occurred varied with need compatibility; when both members were either very high or very low on need for dominance, the "territorializing" was much more marked than when dominance needs were more compatible (i.e., one member high and the other low on need for dominance).

The tendency to assume a proprietary orientation toward public geographical areas has been explored by Lyman and Scott (1967). They called attention to public areas that are taken over by groups or individuals for their own purposes. Examples included children's clubhouses, tree houses, coffeehouses, and similar territories appropriated for individual or group activities. These territories become the "property" of the occupants, who resent any implication that they have no right to occupy the area and will defend it against intruders. The recently popular fad of establishing "people's parks" is an example of this kind of behavior. Similar proprietary orientations were observed in seventeen British old folks' homes (Lipman, 1968). Most of the residents had chairs that they regarded as their property. If a newcomer sat in a chair claimed by a resident, he or she was asked in a preemptory manner to move. Others usually respected a particular person's right to the chair and often defended it for him or her. New residents sometimes had difficulty finding a seat that did not "belong" to someone, and various initiation rites were sometimes required to teach the new resident the norms of the home.

As indicated above, the occupants of a territory will ordinarily defend it against invasion by outsiders. Sommer (1969) described a series of studies designed to examine the ways individuals defend their territory against intruders. In one study, twenty-four students were shown diagrams of a rectangular table with three, four, or five chairs per side. They were asked to show where they would sit if they wanted to be as far as possible from the distraction of other people. By a large majority, they chose end positions. Another twenty-one students were shown the same diagrams and asked where they would sit to discourage anyone else from sitting at the table. These students almost unanimously chose the middle chair. Thus different types of territories were defended by different techniques. In another study, an attractive young lady attempted to maintain privacy in a room which was a part of a soda fountain. For twenty-minute periods, on various days, she sat facing the door and gave the appearance of studying. On other days, she watched the room from a distance, in both instances keeping records of the number of people entering, where they sat, and how long they stayed in the room. She was able to keep the room completely to herself on only one of ten occasions; however, she was successful in keeping her table private on nine of ten occasions. This one unwanted visitor compared with thirteen who sat at that table during control sessions.

On the basis of these findings, Sommer concluded that territorial defense is not an all-or-none proposition, and further studies supported this conclusion. For example, one young lady attempted to assert her right to a table in a soda fountain even when she was not physically occupying it. After a person had sat at the table for varying lengths of time, she would approach and inform him that he was occupying her table. If the occupant had been there only a short time, he typically moved to another table without question. But if he had been there for a longer time, he suggested she must be mistaken—that he had been there for a long time. Similar studies in a busy library revealed that territory can be "reserved" by tokens (coats, books, etc.) for long periods.

When a territory is marked, others respect the markers (Becker, 1973; Becker & Mayo, 1971; Shaffer & Sadowski, 1975). For example, Shaffer and Sadowski (1975) assessed the effectiveness of spatial markers in reserving spaces in an overcrowded public facility. Masculine markers (a man's jacket and a small briefcase) and feminine markers (a flowered bookbag and a woman's jacket trimmed with lace) were used in areas that were considered either high or low in potential for promoting social interaction. Markers were effective in delaying invasion of the marked space by others regardless of gender of the marker, although masculine markers were more effective than feminine markers. It was also found that markers were less effective in reserving space when the area had high potential for encouraging social interaction.

Although markers are frequently respected by others, the persons marking the space often do not defend it against invasion (Becker, 1973; Becker & Mayo, 1971). The degree to which persons attempt to exert control over "their" territories probably depends upon situational factors, such as whether the claim to the territory is temporary or relatively permanent. For example, in a study of territoriality and control, Edney (1975) compared the behavior of college students in their own dormitory rooms with the behavior of visitors to those rooms. Control was varied by asking either the resident or the visitor to assist the experimenter, noting that the other person would be expected to cooperate with the assistant. Residents employed more passive types of control than did visitors, regardless of who was in control. Residents also saw the rooms as more pleasant and more private than visitors. Finally, residents tended to attribute their behavior more to the room than to personality factors. In a somewhat similar study, Edney and Uhlig (1977) induced subjects to territorialize laboratory rooms by telling them to make themselves "at home in your room here" and indicating that they would need to return to the room at a later date. They were also asked to draw floor plans of the room and personalize it by decorating it however they wished. Again, subjects attributed their behavior more to the room itself than did subjects who were not on their "own territory," and their own territory was seen as more pleasant. They also reported feeling more stimulated, more aroused, and more happy in their own room, although they unexpectedly reported a lesser feeling of safety than subjects off home territory.

It is clear, then, that individuals assume territorial rights over physical space and objects in space and that they will often defend this territory against intruders. Their "ownership" of the territory may be communicated to others by markers, i.e., signs and symbols on or around the territory.

This proprietary orientation toward physical space and/or objects influences the feelings and actions of those individuals. We will see that groups also assume territorial rights and act upon them.

### Group Territoriality

Group territoriality differs from individual territoriality in a number of ways. First, and most importantly, it is the group qua group that establishes territorial rights and defends against invasions. Second, the areas are usually larger and sometimes less clearly delimited than in the case of individual territoriality. Whereas the individual occupies a chair, a room, or perhaps a vacant lot, the group frequently occupies a much larger geographical area, such as a city subdivision or sometimes a whole town. In the well-known studies of street-corner gangs (W. F. Whyte, 1943) it was found that gangs typically establish a territory that they defend to the death against rival gangs. Mack (1954) and Marine (1966) have also reported evidence of group territoriality. Mack described a residential situation in which Swedes and Italians lived in adjacent areas, but in almost complete social segregation. This separation apparently served the function of reducing conflict. Marine described a number of cities in which racial segregation produced similar effects. Although no one required that certain groups reside in certain areas, the separation into territories was nevertheless rigid and precise.

The "permanence" of a person's or group's occupancy of a territory influences the degree to which it will be defended. For example, Edney (1972) found that persons who were more permanent residents in a suburban setting (i.e., had resided in a given place longer and anticipated future residence) had more visible territorial displays (a verbal sign or a barrier such as a fence or hedge) than less permanent residents. Furthermore, the more permanent residents responded more rapidly to the presence of an outsider on their property.

The size of territories established may be influenced by a number of factors. In one study (Edney & Jordan-Edney, 1974), the use of space on a beach by groups of differing size and composition was examined. It was observed that group territories do not grow in proportion to group size; instead, the amount of space per person decreased with increasing group size. It was also found that males typically claimed more territory than females and that the characteristics of territories (such as size and markers) varied over time. One variable that appeared to be important in determining the size of territories at any given time was the density of the local population; the more people on the beach, the smaller the group territories. Another study of the effects of group size found that group space boundaries increased with group size if group members were strangers, but not if group members were friends (Edney & Grundmann, 1979). However, in this study only groups of two and four persons were observed.

As we noted earlier, group territories are related to the behaviors of group members. For example, Sundstrom and Altman (1974) observed the use of space in cottage groups of boys (12 to 15 years of age) for a period of ten weeks. The study was divided into three periods, the first period involving a relatively stable population, the second a turnover of two highly dominant persons, and the third relatively minor changes in group composition. Territorial behavior decreased during the second period and increased in the third period, suggesting that membership stability fosters territoriality.

As in the case of individual territoriality, others respect the space boundaries of groups. In one study (Knowles, 1973), the reactions of passersby to persons occupying a hallway were observed. In a hallway that was 295 centimeters in width, either two or four persons were spaced 145 centimeters apart and 75 centimeters from the wall (see Figure 5-1). Only about 24 percent of the passersby passed through the group rather than through the smaller space between the group and the wall. When waste barrels were substituted for people, approximately 75 percent passed between them rather than through the smaller space between barrels and the wall. Similarly, data reported by Cheyne and Efran (1972) revealed that both interperson distance and sex composition of the group were related to the degree of avoidance of group space invasion. They observed the proportion of persons going down a 137-inch-wide balcony-style walkway in a shopping mall who walked between interacting pairs of confederates of the experimenters. The confederates varied in sex compo-

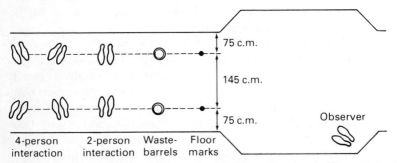

**Figure 5-1** Hallway setting for the stimulus conditions. (Reprinted with permission from E. S. Knowles. Boundaries around group interaction: The effect of group size and member status on boundary permeability. *Journal of Personality and Social Psychology*, 1973, **26**, 327–331. Copyright 1973 by the American Psychological Association. Reprinted by permission.)

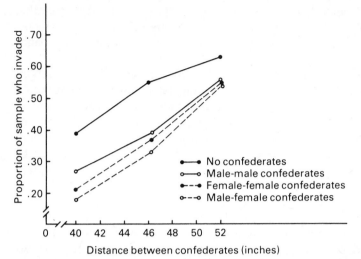

**Figure 5-2** Invasion of controlled territories as a function of sex and distance between interacting persons. (Plotted with permission from data reported by J. A. Cheyne and M. G. Efran. The effect of spatial and interpersonal variables on the invasion of group controlled territories. *Sociometry,* 1972, **35,** 477–489.)

sition (male-male, female-female, or male-female) and in distance between them (40, 46, or 52 inches). Figure 5-2 shows the results of this study.

The proportion of passersby who walked between the interacting confederates was much lower than the proportion who walked through the same space when no confederates were present; the proportion who invaded the territory controlled by the dyad increased with increasing interperson distance; and the proportion who invaded varied with the sex composition of the group.

The effects of degree and type of group interaction on respect for group boundaries were investigated by Lindskold and his associates (Lindskold, Albert, Baer, & Moore, 1976). They arranged situations so that pedestrians encountered four persons who were either (a) apparently unassociated, (b) passively gazing into a store window, (c) calmly conversing among themselves, or (d) conversing in an agitated manner. When the four persons were apparently unassociated, only 22 percent of passersby went around them, as compared with 44.5 percent when they were gazing in a window, 75.8 when they were conversing calmly, and 83.3 percent when the conversation was agitated. Differences in the relative number who avoided walking between persons conversing and those who were not indicates again that interaction increases respect for group space boundaries. It is possible, of course, that group interaction merely increases the perception of entitiativity or "groupness." The fact that persons also avoided walking between persons gazing into a window suggests that common courtesy plays a role in determining avoidance behavior.

In addition to reducing or preventing conflict, group territoriality as well as individual territoriality serves to protect the individual against other people; it provides a bit of privacy that might not otherwise be obtainable. In certain cases, territoriality is a way of asserting the dominance of one group or individual over another group or individual. The close relationship between status and certain ecological factors has been detailed by Sommer (1969) and will be discussed in greater detail later in this chapter.

## INTERPERSON DISTANCE

Persons and groups not only establish territorial orientations, but also appear to have formed personal norms about the appropriate or preferred distance between themselves and others. As we shall see, persons position themselves in relation to others in accordance with these personal standards, if given a choice, or react negatively when these standards are violated. Historically, this phenomenon has been labeled *personal space* because it was viewed as a kind of portable territory that persons carried around with them as they moved from place to place. For example, Little defined personal space as "the area immediately surrounding the individual in which the majority of his interactions with others take place" (Little, 1965, p. 237). According to this conceptualization, personal space has flexible boundaries which vary with the personal and social relationships between the person and others, as well as with the nature and purpose of the interpersonal contact (Sommer, 1959). The area of personal space, as indicated by comfortable approach distances, is smaller in relation to impersonal than to personal objects, and it is smaller in relation to intimate others than to others with whom the person is less intimate. It also varies with the status of the person and with the kind of interaction. Unwanted intrusion evokes negative reactions which vary from subdued expressions of displeasure to strong retaliatory actions, depending upon the characteristics of the intruder and the circumstances in which the invasion occurs.

Although the Little-Sommer concept of personal space has intuitive appeal, it is probably not a valid representation of interperson distance phenomena. Although there is good evidence that persons position themselves in reasonably consistent ways with respect to others, and that they react differentially to varying interperson distances, there is no good reason to believe that persons regard the space around their body as personal and private. In one study (Shaw, Ashton, & Worsham, 1978), persons were asked to tell an approaching other to stop "when you feel you have the right to do so." In most instances, the approaching person was asked to stop only when one more step would have resulted in body contact. Apparently, people believe they have a right to ask that others do not touch their bodies, but they do not believe they own the physical space around their bodies. The traditional conceptualization of personal space also fails to consider positive (favorable) reactions to the proximity of certain others (e.g., loved ones).

Although there are reasons to discredit the common notion of personal space as a portable territory, it is quite clear that persons respond affectively to the distances between themselves and others. This affective response may be highly positive (as when a loved one approaches), highly negative (as when a detestable other approaches), or anywhere between these two extremes. The critical condition is that individuals react to the proximity of others. Like territoriality, interperson distance has important consequences for group process. For example, when one group member approaches another group member more closely than that member desires, negative reactions are inevitable. Groups in which members are insensitive to the space needs of others are likely to experience intragroup conflict and poor interpersonal relations. A consideration of the variables that are related to interperson distance, will contribute to our understanding of these spatial effects upon group behavior.

## Interaction Distances

The preferred interperson distances for social interaction are influenced by many personal, social, and situational variables. These include, at least, the age, sex, and cultural backgrounds of the interacting individuals; the relationships among interactants; the situation in which the interaction occurs; and status differences among interacting persons.

**Age and Interaction Distance**   Feelings about the most desirable or appropriate interpersonal spacings are acquired through socialization processes. Chronological age reflects the amount of socialization that the person has experienced; consequently, it is not surprising that interperson distances vary with age. For example, Meisels and Guardo (1969) examined interperson distances between children in two elementary schools. Pupils in grades three through ten were tested in one school and those in three through eight in the other. Two silhouette figures representing the pupil and another (best friend, acquaintance, stranger, etc.) were presented, and the student was asked to place them in a face-to-face relation. Interfigure distances were assumed to reflect the student's perception of the appropriate distances between persons. It was found that interperson distance decreased with increasing chronological age.

Another study of interperson distance also employed both a simulated and a direct measure of interperson distance (Tennis & Dabbs, 1975). In the simulated situation, subjects of different ages (first-through twelfth-grade students) were told to imagine that they were standing at the end of an 80-millimeter scale and that another person was slowly approaching them. They then were asked to mark the point at which they would want the other person to stop "for a comfortable conversational distance." There was no reliable relationship between age and the distances marked. In the direct part of the study, the same subjects were tested in a behavioral situation. One member of a pair was placed at either the corner or the center of the room. The other member of the pair approached the first (stationary) person along a graded measuring tape, and the stationary member told the approaching person to stop when he or she had reached a "comfortable conversational distance." In this situation, interperson distances *increased* with increasing chronological age. This finding is, of course, the opposite of that reported by Meisels and Guardo (1969). It agrees, however, with data reported by Baxter (1970) from a study of Mexican-Americans, blacks, and whites in natural settings: interaction distances increased with age in all three groups.

Data with respect to age and interperson distances obtained by simulation methods and behavioral methods appear to yield contradictory results. It is clear that age is one factor determining interpersonal spacing, and it is probably the case that, in general, interperson distances increase with increasing age up to some maximum age.

**Interpersonal Relationships and Interperson Distance**    One of the most important determinants of preferred interperson distances is the relationship between the interacting persons. Are they close friends, strangers, lovers, enemies? The most appropriate or the most desirable distance from another depends heavily upon the nature of this relationship. Although this is an important aspect of interpersonal behavior, relatively little careful research has been done to establish the limits of comfortable interaction or the variables related to it. Results of some of the investigations reported in the literature, however, are enlightening. F. N. Willis (1966) recorded the speaking distance between two persons under a wide range of circumstances. Forty investigators obtained data on 755 persons in such diverse places as homes, places of business, and halls of university buildings. Each investigator obtained measures of initial speaking distances in twenty encounters. When an investigator was approached by another person who began a conversation, the investigator remained at a fixed point. At the start of conversation, he measured (with a cloth tape measure) the nose-to-nose distance between himself and the other person and categorized his relationship to the other person according to one of the following definitions: *stranger*—the investigator had never met the other person; *acquaintance*—the investigator had met the other person but did not know him well enough to call him by name; *friend*—the investigator knew the other person well enough to greet him by name; *close friend*—the investigator's best same-sex friend, or person of opposite sex he or she had dated or was married to. There were not enough subjects in some categories to permit meaningful comparisons. However, it was found that women investigators were approached more closely (mean = 21.58 inches) than men (mean = 24.46 inches). Compared with males, female subjects stood very near to "close friends" when speaking, but stood back from "friends." Persons the same age as the investigator stood closer (mean = 23.87 inches) than persons who were older (mean = 26.67 inches), and acquaintances stood closer (mean = 23.80 inches) than strangers (mean = 27.33 inches). On the other hand, parents stood as distant as strangers (median = 27 inches in both instances).

Interaction distances were measured by Little (1965) in a study designed to determine the relationship between such distances as measured by a projective method and by live-person interactions. In one situation, pairs of plexiglass silhouettes were presented to subjects and described as either strangers, acquaintances, or friends. Subjects were asked to place the figures on a blank background (which they were to imagine represented various settings; see page 133) so that they faced each other and to tell what was going on between the figures. A second situation was essentially the same except that live actresses were used instead of plexiglass silhouettes. Subjects were asked to assume the role of theater director and to place the actresses in situations similar to those used in the first part. Considering all conditions, the mean interaction distance was 14.1 inches for the silhouettes (measured in eights of an inch) and 25.6 inches for the actresses. The important finding for the present discussion is that the interaction distance varied with the relationship. The average distance for the actresses was 15.5 inches for friends, 27.2 inches for acquaintances, and 34.3 inches for strangers. The distance scores were similar for the silhouettes: 8.7, 15.0, and 18.5 for friends, acquaintances, and strangers, respectively. There was also some variation as a function of the setting, as already mentioned. Note, however, that this study dealt with perceived interaction distances rather than distances in actual interactions. Little suggested that actual face-to-face interaction distance may be influenced by a variety of factors, such as odor and depth perception, which were not present in his experimental situations.

The study by Meisels and Guardo (1969) found a similar relationship between distance and interpersonal relations among interactants; that is, interperson distances were greater for strangers than for acquaintances, and those for acquaintances were greater than those for friends.

The important point here is that people who have positive feelings for others will usually want to be closer than if their feelings are negative or unfavorable. This conclusion is further supported by a study showing that subjects chose to sit closer to a person who had previously cooperated with them than to a person who had either competed with them or been neutral toward them (Tedesco & Fromme, 1974).

**Gender and Interperson Distance**   In most situations, females prefer closer interperson distances than males. In the study by F. N. Willis (1966) which we described earlier, it will be recalled that women investigators were approached to an average of 21.58 inches as compared with an approach distance of 24.46 inches for men. Observations of different age groups (Tennis & Dabbs, 1975) also revealed that females maintained closer interperson distances than males, although the sex differences were smaller among younger persons. Similar differences between males and females have been reported by a number of other investigators (e.g., Eberts & Lepper, 1975; Patterson & Schaeffer, 1977). These differences are most likely to reflect differences in the socialization process: girls are taught, both by example and explicit instruction, that females are supposed to be warm, cooperative, submissive, nuturant, etc. These "traits" are revealed in many ways, including close physical proximity relative to that regarded as appropriate for males.

**Situational Determinants of Interperson Distance**   It is probably obvious to even the casual observer that the interperson distances which are maintained and regarded as appropriate vary with the circumstances which bring people into close proximity. Closer interperson distances are acceptable in elevators, subways, crowded buses, and similar situations in which the meaning of interperson distance is defined by the situation. For instance, dental patients submit to direct bodily contact with the dentist with no negative reactions to him or her; the physician is permitted unusually intimate contact with the patient. These role relationships define the situation as impersonal, and the dentist and physician may be defined psychologically as nonpersons. The effects of the impersonal-personal dimension on interperson distance have been examined in a number of experimental investigations. For example, Horowitz, Duff, and Stratton (1964) instructed mental patients to walk over to either a person or a hat rack, and measured the distance between their stopping place and the object. They found that each patient tended to establish a characteristic individual distance and that this distance was relatively stable across situations. They also observed that subjects approached the hat rack more closely than they did another person. In a similar study (Argyle & Dean, 1965), subjects were asked to stand as close as comfortable to see well a variety of objects, including two photographs of a person, one with eyes open and one with eyes closed. They found that subjects stood closer to the photograph with the eyes closed. Presumably this photograph represented a more impersonal object than the one with the eyes open.

The effect of impersonality of setting on the perceived interaction distance on line drawings of same-sex figures was investigated by Little (1965). In one study, the figures were said to have been talking for about two minutes, and subjects were asked to arrange the figures on a background setting and to tell what they had been talking about. The settings varied in degree of impersonality: a living room, an office, or a street corner. Little predicted that the interfigure distance would be least in the living room and greatest on the street corner. This prediction was supported when the subjects were female, but not when the subjects were male. A second study in which the settings were an office, a lobby in a public building, an office waiting room, and a scene called "on the campus" revealed that the maximum distances occurred in the office. Thus, the hypothesis that distance should increase with increasing imper- sonality of the settings was only partially verified.

Impersonality is, of course, not the only situational variable that influences interpersonal spacings. It will be recalled from our discussion of group territories (see page 127) that the kind of interactions that group members were engaged in had an effect upon the degree to which others respected group space boundaries. This suggests that the purpose of being in proximity to another will in part determine what is regarded as an appropriate interperson distance. The stimulus intensity of the other person may also act as a situational determinant of interperson distance. In one study (Nesbitt & Steven, 1974), male and female stimulus persons joined lines of persons waiting for attractions at an amusement park. It was found that others in the line maintained greater distances from the stimulus person when he or she was wearing brightly colored clothes than when wearing conservative clothes, and when the stimulus person was using perfume or after-shave lotion. In some situations, interperson distance may serve as a buffer zone to protect the person against unwanted stimulation.

**Cultural Differences in Interperson Distance** Persons who have visited other countries have probably been aware that other cultures are often different from their own with respect to acceptable interperson distances. These cultural differences have been the concern of several investigators. For instance, a study of interactions between male-male, male-female, and female-female pairs in Latin America revealed that interactions were greater in Panama than in Colombia where distances were greater than in Costa Rica (Shuter, 1976). In Columbia and Panama, interaction distances were greatest for male pairs, whereas in Costa Rica the greatest distance was between male-female pairs. Physical contact measures revealed the same pattern.

Baxter (1970) observed Mexican-Americans, blacks, and whites in natural settings. Mexican-Americans were found to stand closest while interacting, blacks stood farthest apart, and whites were intermediate with respect to interaction distance. In contrast, Bauer (1973) reported that whites stood more distant than blacks, when measured in an experimental situation in which individuals were told to stand a comfortable distance from the other. The reversal of the black-white differences may well be due to differences in the procedures followed in the two studies.

Baxter (1970) also noted that interaction distance increased with chronological age in all groups and that differences between cultural groups increased with age. Male-female pairs interacted in closest proximity, female-female pairs were intermediate, and male-male pairs most distant; however, mean differences in sex pairs were very small.

Cultural differences with respect to interperson distance have also been observed in children (Aiello & Jones, 1971; Jones & Aiello, 1973). In the first study, 6- to 8-year-old white children stood farther apart than Puerto Rican children of the same age. In the second study, black and white children were observed in elementary classrooms. Blacks stood closer than whites in first and third grades, but not in the fifth grade. Again, these differences are somewhat similar to the adult pattern, but there are also variations as a function of age.

These several investigations make it abundantly clear that the cultural background of participants is important in determining appropriate interperson distances. These differences are not always consistent across time, however; as cultural experiences change, so do persons' feelings and perceptions about appropriate and acceptable interperson distances for various situations and purposes.

**Social Status and Interperson Distance**   An important function of spatial relations among persons is the establishment and communication of status differences. In general, low-status persons defer to higher-status persons, who in turn behave in ways designed to protect and enhance their high status. Interpersonal spacing is one way that such differential status-related behavior is exemplified. In military establishments, the military ranks of interacting pairs determine, in part, the physical distances that are typically maintained (Dean, Willis, & Hewitt, 1975). Five hundred and sixty-two active-duty officers in the U.S. Navy, ranging in rank from captain to seaman, were observed at the beginning of two-person conversations. The data revealed that interactions directed toward superiors were characterized by greater interperson distances than those directed toward peers. Furthermore, interperson distances were increasingly greater as rank differences increased. This relationship did not hold when the interaction was initiated by a person of higher rank. Presumably, the superior has the option of being formal or informal and thus is free to vary the distance that he or she maintains with respect to subordinates.

The role of interperson distance in the perception and communication of status differences was demonstrated in a study conducted by Hutte and Cohen (cited in Sommer, 1969). They prepared a series of 10 one-minute silent films in which two actors portrayed a simple interaction sequence. In each film, one man is seated at a desk sorting through a card index when he is interrupted by the telephone. The next scene shows the second man, who knocks at the office door, enters, approaches the man at the desk, and discusses something with him. Ratings of the relative status of the two men were obtained from audiences that viewed the films. The caller was rated most subordinate when he stopped just inside the door and least subordinate when he walked directly to the desk. When he walked halfway into the room, he was seen as less subordinate than when he stopped at the door but more subordinate than when he walked all the way to the desk.

It seems clear that interperson distance is related to the perception of the relative statuses of individuals. The distance that a person maintains between himself or herself and another person communicates something about his or her status relative to that other. However, the direction of the difference often depends upon other factors. The study by Lott and Sommer (1967) suggests that individuals tend to place distance between themselves and persons having both higher and lower status; hence interperson distance alone does not indicate which person has the higher status. For example, in the Hutte and Cohen films, the situation in which the interaction occurred provided clues to the direction of the status difference. In most instances, the variations in situation and/or behavior of the persons involved serve as indicators of differences in status level.

### Effects of Interperson Distance

As we have already mentioned, the proximity of others may be expected to have a significant effect on the behavior of group members. The most obvious effect is the negative reaction to unwanted closeness, which has been called "invasion of personal space." In general, when one is nearer another than desired, the person displays signs of discomfort and may take direct action to increase the distance between self and other (e.g., by fleeing or asking the other person to move). Sommer (1969) described a number of investigations of reactions to "invasion." The first study was conducted in a 1500-bed mental institution located in a parklike area. It was easy to find patients seated alone on a bench or knoll. When a male patient was observed alone and not engaged in any definite activity,

Sommer walked over and sat beside him without saying a word. If the patient selected as the victim moved his chair or slid further down on the bench, so did Sommer. Control patients were selected from similar situations but some distance away from the observer. The typical reaction to invasion was simply to leave the scene. During the first nine minutes, half of the victims had departed as compared with only 8 percent of the control subjects. Although flight was the most noticeable reaction to intrusion, Sommer reported other less obvious responses. A typical immediate reaction included facing away, pulling in the shoulders, and placing elbows at the side. Other evidences of discomfort included rubbing the face, breathing heavily, looking at watch, and flexing fingers.

In another study cited by Sommer, Nancy Russo invaded the privacy of students in a college library. She selected female students who were sitting alone with one or more books before them and empty chairs on either side. In any given instance of invasion, one such person was selected as the victim and another in the same kind of situation as a control. The invasion consisted of sitting alongside the victim, directly across from her, or in some other position contrary to seating norms in the library. Again, departure was the most common reaction to intrusion, although this was often preceded by defensive gestures, shifts in posture, and similar behaviors.

In these situations, it is easy for persons to defend their privacy through flight. But many other kinds of behaviors appear to be designed to protect against invasion beforehand. The person may select a position that is as inaccessible as possible, such as an isolated chair or a fenced-in area. Sommer (1969) reported a number of attempts to explore ways in which offensive display and avoidance protect spatial privacy. In one study, subjects were given charts of tables and chairs with instructions to select the position they would want in order to either retreat from others or defend themselves against others. With retreat instructions, 76 percent of the subjects chose a chair with its back to the wall, whereas only 38 percent chose a wall chair under defensive instructions. In other studies, retreat instructions elicited choices of rear seats in preference to front seats, small tables over large tables, and tables against the wall rather than tables with aisles all around. When the room was described as crowded, choices were similar to those produced by retreat instructions.

Reactions to physical nearness were studied experimentally in a shopping mall, with similar results (Harris, Luginbuhl, & Fishbein, 1978). Experimenters waited at the top of an escalator until a person who was alone and not laden with packages boarded the unoccupied escalator. The experimenter then boarded the escalator also and approached to a point approximately 5 to 10 cm from the subject. Observers seated nearby recorded the subject's behavior. Typical responses included spoken comments, glances over shoulder, changes in facial expression, and/or movement to another step on the escalator. Of the 161 persons observed, 71 percent responded in one or more of the above ways. The responses were more frequent when fewer than four other persons were present, a difference that was accounted for by the male subjects. This finding is, of course, in accord with data showing that females typically assume smaller interperson distances than males.

These reactions indicate that people have significant feelings about the physical proximity of others. In one study (Shaw et al., 1978), reports of feelings about the distance between friends and strangers were elicited at several distances. Pairs of friends and pairs of strangers reported to the laboratory where they were asked to stand at specified distances from each other (from 60 to 300 cm). At each distance, the subject rated his or her feelings about the proximity of the other person, using seven-point evaluative scales (good-bad, positive-negative, favorable-unfavorable, pleasant-unpleasant, and fair-unfair). The mean evaluations of interperson distances are shown in Figure 5-3. Positive feelings about the proximity of

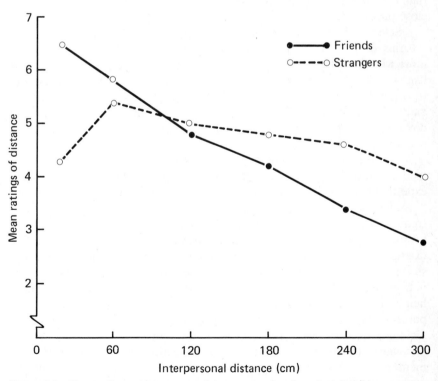

**Figure 5-3** Mean ratings of interperson distances as a function of relationship.

the other person increased as interperson distance decreased for opposite-sex friends; for opposite-sex strangers, positive feelings increased with decreasing distance up to 60 centimeters and then decreased. At least for opposite-sex pairs, friends apparently find no interperson distance too small, but physical nearness elicits less favorable feelings for strangers. This finding is consistent with the data reported earlier showing that friends stand closer than strangers when engaged in interaction.

Not only do persons feel differently about varying distances between themselves and others, but interperson distance also influences their feelings about the other person. For example, Schiffenbauer and Schiavo (1976) asked female subjects to participate in a problem-solving task with another person. The other person was a confederate who made either positive, neutral, or negative statements about the strategy used by the subject. The two persons were seated either 2 or 5 feet apart. At the end of the session, the subject was asked to complete seven-point rating scales which measured how much she liked the confederate. The results showed that when the interaction was positive (the confederate made favorable comments about the subject's strategy), there was more liking for a close than for a more distant partner, but when the interaction was negative, the close partner was liked less than the more distant one.

Several other studies yielded similar results. In a series of three studies (Storms & Thomas, 1977), it was found that males liked another male more when he sat close and was friendly or was perceived as similar; he was liked less when he sat close and was unfriendly or dissimilar. Another study (Murphy-Berman & Berman, 1978) found that as the "invasion of another's personal space" appeared more intentional and personally directed, males were evaluated more negatively and females more positively.

These reactions to others as a function of interperson distance may mediate another interesting effect of interperson distance. In several experiments, it was found that a person who had been approached by an "invader" and then given an opportunity to help the invader, helped more frequently the greater the distance between the two persons when the invader stopped (Konecni, Libuser, Morton, & Ebbesen, 1975). For example, in one experiment the invader approached the subject and stopped within either 1, 2, 5, or 10 feet. The invader then crossed the street in front of the subject and dropped some keys in the street. Only 47 percent helped the invader when he had stood 1 foot away as compared with 80 percent who helped when he stood 10 feet away. Other experiments yielded similar results. The effects of interperson distance on helping behavior was also examined in a different setting (Baron, 1978). Experimenters stood either 12 to 18 inches or 36 to 48 inches from the subject while requesting the subject's assistance on a project that they were doing for fun (low importance) or as a class assignment (high importance). Subjects helped more in the near condition than the far condition when the need of the experimenter was low, but the reverse occurred when the need was high.

Further evidence of the effects of interperson distance on interpersonal behavior was reported by Albert and Dabbs (1970). Friendly or hostile persuaders attempted to change the attitude of another person at 1 to 2 feet, at 4 to 5 feet, or at 14 to 15 feet. Attitude change was found to be linearly related to interperson distance (the greater the distance, the more the attitude changed in the advocated direction), becoming more negative for the hostile persuader at the smaller interperson distances.

The conclusions that may be drawn from these many studies are probably evident to the reader. Individuals devise various techniques to guard against unwanted approaches by others, but if these techniques fail, unwanted proximity of another evokes discomfort, unease, and other negative feelings that are revealed in various defensive responses. In some cases, fight or flight may be elicited by too-small interperson distances. The feelings that people have about interperson distances vary with the nature of the interpersonal relationship and other factors, and may influence the degree to which they are willing to help others. As we shall see, these effects have significant implications for group interaction. Some of these consequences are revealed in crowded situations where insufficient space or other constraints interfere with the maintenance of preferred interperson distances.

## DENSITY AND CROWDING

When many people are in a relatively small space, it often becomes difficult or impossible to maintain desirable interperson distances. When situations of this sort occur, we often say the room is crowded. But, as Stokols (1972) has pointed out, crowding is a psychological variable; the experience of crowding depends not only upon population density (i.e., the number of persons per unit of physical space) but also upon the circumstances under which the population density occurs. For example, a man may feel that he is being "crowded" by another person who approaches too closely if he can see no good reason for the intrusion; a similar invasion would not be viewed as "crowding" if it occurred in an overloaded elevator. A woman may not feel crowded in the back seat of a small foreign car if the other occupant is an attractive man; she probably would experience crowding if the other occupant were an unattractive female. Crowding, then, may be defined as follows: ". . . a state of crowding exists, and is perceived as such by an individual, when the individual's demand for space exceeds the available supply of such space"

(Stokols, 1972, p. 75). Stokols further notes that crowding may be due to *either* nonsocial or social factors. Nonsocial crowding is produced by physical limitations upon the available space, as when a large man must fit into a small cockpit in order to pilot certain kinds of airplanes. We are more interested in social crowding, that is, the individual's awareness that the spatial restriction is the consequence of the presence of others and his or her relationship to them. In short, we are concerned with crowding in groups and the consequences of this crowding for group process.

Investigators of the effects of crowding have typically employed one of two methods of varying the experience of crowding: varying the size of the room or varying the number of people in the room. In either case, variations in population density are presumed to be correlated with variations in the experience of crowding. For example, Freedman, Levy, Buchanan, and Price (1972) observed all-male and all-female groups in a large or a small room. They found that males were more competitive in the small room, whereas females were more competitive in the large room. In a second study, all-male groups serving as members of mock juries gave more severe sentences in a small room; all-female groups gave more severe sentences in a large room. These results are consistent with the findings reported by Ross, Layton, Erickson, and Schopler (1973). Male and female groups were confined in either a large or a small room for five or twenty minutes. Each group discussed a series of choice-dilemma problems (see Chapter 3), after which each group member evaluated himself or herself and others. Males rated themselves more positively in the large room, whereas females rated themselves more positively in the small room.

It is clear from these studies that male and female groups are responding differently to population density, but it is unclear whether this represents a differential response to crowding or a differential experience in the two density conditions. It may be that women can accept greater stimulation than men without feeling crowded, an interpretation that is in accord with Desor's (1972) proposal that being crowded is the reception of excessive stimulation. If this interpretation is valid, the differences between male and female responses to density are essentially differences between feeling crowded and not feeling crowded. This explanation, however, provides no basis for females responding differently to varying room sizes. It is likely that sex differences in response to density reflect both factors, i.e., both the experience of crowding and the reaction to it.

The perception of crowdedness has also been shown to be influenced by interperson distance (Worchel & Teddlie, 1976; Greenberg & Firestone, 1977; Worchel & Yohai, 1979) and by the degree to which persons are under surveillance (Greenberg & Firestone, 1977). It is probable that the feeling of being crowded may be related to many other factors not yet identified. Since we are interested in the consequences for group behavior, it may be more enlightening to examine the effects of density on group performance.

It seems intuitively plausible that when there is high group density (i.e., relatively many persons in a given space) the group process should be affected and group performance impeded. Indeed, there is good evidence that high density can produce negative psychological effects on humans. In one investigation, it was found that all-male groups were more competitive in small rooms than in larger rooms and gave more severe sanctions in the small room (Freedman, Levy, Buchanan, & Price, 1972). Once again, however, all-female groups responded in the opposite manner. In another study (Loo, 1972), 4- and 5-year-olds were observed in a free-play situation of either high or low density. Relative to the low-density situation, the high-density situation resulted in less aggression, more interruptions, and more time spent in solitary play. Negative psychological effects of high density have also been observed in several other studies (e.g., Eoyang, 1974; Paulus, Cox, McCain, & Chandler, 1975; Ross, Layton, Erikson, & Schopler, 1973). On the other hand, several experiments failed to demonstrate a decrement in group performance as a function of high density (Freedman, Klevansky, & Ehrlich, 1971; Kutner, 1973; Sherrod, 1974). These investigations have been criticized on several bases. For instance, it is not clear whether the failure to demonstrate an effect of density on group performance is due to use of an insensitive task, to adaptation to stress during the experimental session, or to use of levels of density that were not sufficiently aversive (Paulus, Annis, Seta, Schkade, & Matthews, 1976). Paulus et al. also noted that density has three primary potential components (group size, room size, and interperson distance) which have often been confounded in previous studies.

In an attempt to resolve the questions raised about attempts to determine the effects of density on group performance, Paulus et al. (1976) designed an experiment that examined the effects of group size, room size, and interperson distance independently of each other. The task was a multiple-U maze that required decisions at each of several choice points. It was found that increasing group size, decreasing room size, and decreasing interperson distance each produced decrements in group performance.

Others have suggested that early failures to find an effect of density on group performance were due to the omission of physical interaction from the experimental paradigms (Heller, Groff, & Solomon, 1977). They manipulated density (high vs. low) and physical interaction (high vs. low). Density was manipulated by varying room size and physical interaction by task requirements. The task involved correctly collating as many eight-page booklets as possible in the allotted time. In the low physical interaction condition subjects were seated and could do the task without moving about, whereas in the high physical interaction condition they were forced to move about in order to complete the task. High density interfered with group performance only in the high physical interaction condition.

Data from a study designed to examine the role of attribution in the experience of crowding appear to reveal a strong negative relationship between the experience of crowding and group performance (Worchel & Yohai, 1979). Groups of subjects were placed so that interpersonal distances were either close or far. Some groups were told that an arousing subliminal noise would be played in the room, some groups that a relaxing subliminal noise would be played, and some were told nothing about subliminal noise. Groups in these six experimental conditions were then asked to derive as many words as possible from the stimulus word "observationally." Measures of the subjects' experiences of crowding (ratings) and of group performance (number of words formed) were then obtained. Although Worchel and Yohai did not relate measures of crowding and group performance scores, a comparison of mean crowding indices with the corresponding mean performance scores yields a correlation of $-.99$. That is, the greater the reported experience of crowding, the lower the mean performance score.

These several studies indicate that many variables are involved in determining the effects of high density on the perception of crowding, on the experiences of people in groups, and on group performance. Interperson distance is one of the more important of these variables, but the goals of the group members may be equally significant.

## SPATIAL ARRANGEMENTS

The preceding pages have been concerned with the orientations that individuals adopt with regard to the space about them and to other persons and impersonal objects in that space. It is now time to consider some of the consequences of certain spatial arrangements in group situations. Although relatively little research has been devoted to this important aspect of group interaction, there is good evidence that spatial arrangements in groups exert significant influences upon the perception of status, the patterns of participation, leadership activities, and the affective reactions of group members. It is not surprising, then, that there are consistent position preferences in group situations; that is, the choices that people make with regard to where they position themselves in the group are consistent with what is known about the effects of spatial arrangements on group process.

## Seating Preferences

When persons are free to choose their position in a group, their choices usually reflect the cultural import of various locations. Persons who perceive themselves to have relatively high status in the group select positions that are in accord with this perception. For example, Strodtbeck and Hook (1961) analyzed data obtained from experimental jury deliberations and found that jurors from professional and managerial classes selected the chair at the head of the table significantly more often than did persons from other classes. Similarly, Hare and Bales (1963) found that subjects who scored high on a pencil-and-paper measure of dominance tended to choose the more central seats in the group situation.

Sommer and his associates examined seating preferences in a number of investigations ranging from questionnaire studies to actual participation in group activities (Sommer, 1969). In one study, subjects were asked to choose from a number of alternatives the seating arrangement at a rectangular table (see Figure 5-4) that they most preferred for four different activities: conversing, cooperating, coacting, and competing. A corner-to-corner or face-to-face arrangement was chosen for casual conversation, whereas cooperating individuals preferred the side-by-side arrangement. Competing pairs tended to choose a face-to-face arrangement, although some chose a more distant setup (e.g., across and at opposite ends of the table). Coacting pairs were consistent in choosing a pattern that minimized intimacy, such as the distant arrangement referred to above. A second questionnaire study using round tables yielded results that were in accord with those found in the first study.

The next step was to try to verify the results of the questionnaire studies by examining seating preferences in real groups. Pairs of children were placed in cooperative, competitive, and coacting activities to see how they would arrange themselves. In general, cooperating pairs sat side by side, competing pairs sat at adjacent corners, and coacting pairs sat at a distance. Very few pairs used the face-to-face arrangement which had been prominent in the questionnaire results. In still another investigation, adult subjects were told that they would be either competing or cooperating with another person who was already seated at a table. In the cooperative situation, thirteen of twenty-four subjects sat on the same side of the table as the decoy, whereas in the competitive situation nineteen of twenty-three subjects sat opposite the decoy. The experimental findings and the questionnaire results are, therefore, consistent in showing that adults prefer the side-by-side arrangement for cooperation and the face-to-face arrangement for competition. These results are also in substantial agreement with findings reported by Myers (1969) in a counseling setting. Counselees overwhelmingly preferred an informal "knee-to-knee" arrangement to a formal face-to-face arrangement.

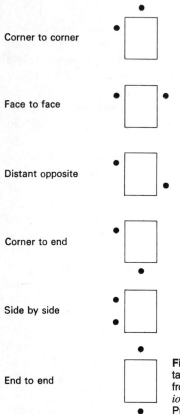

**Figure 5-4** Seating arrangements at rectangular tables. (Adapted with permission from R. Sommer. *Personal space: The behavioral basis of design.* Englewood Cliffs, N.J.: Prentice-Hall, 1969.)

Other investigations have also shown that type of group activity influences preferred seating arrangements. In one study, triads were assigned to one of the following conditions: alone, coacting, cooperating, competing with no feedback or competing with feedback about outcome (Ryen & Kahn, 1975). Following performance of the assigned task, subjects were asked to take seats in another room where members of other groups were also present. The distance others sat from members of their own and from other group members was observed unobtrusively. Members of alone and coacting groups chose random seating patterns. Persons in cooperating groups sat near both ingroup and outgroup members, with a slight preference for owngroup members. Members of competing groups with no feedback sat near ingroup members but far from outgroup members; members of winning competitive groups sat relatively near members of the losing team, but losing group members sat as far from the winning group as possible. In contrast, when groups are to engage in a neutral group discussion, they prefer a circular seating arrangement (Hendrick, Giesen, & Coy, 1974).

The particular kind or pattern of seating arrangement preferred, then, depends largely upon the type of interaction that group members anticipate. It is not possible to determine from these studies whether the preferences for seating arrangements are due to cultural expectations concerning the appropriate spatial relationship in a given setting or to the feelings that various arrangements produce in the individual under certain conditions. Sommer's subjects in the questionnaire studies explained their choices in terms of task efficiency. That is, they suggested that casual conversation is facilitated by both physical proximity and eye contact; hence they chose arrangements that would maximize these factors. It is always possible, however, that explanations of this sort are rationalizations rather than true causes of the observed phenomenon. Evidence reported by Myers (1969) suggests that preferences may be caused by the feelings aroused by the particular seating arrangement. He found that subjects in a formal seating arrangement scored significantly higher on a scale designed to measure situational anxiety than subjects in an informal arrangement. Thus, certain spatial relationships may produce unpleasant affective responses which result in conditioned avoidance reactions. Also, it is not difficult to see that the position-status relationship should make some positions positively rewarding and others negatively rewarding (unpleasant, punishing). Therefore, the most plausible explanation of spatial preferences is in terms of the reinforcement probabilities associated with various spatial positions.

### Seating Arrangement and Interaction

The rewarding values of spatial positions derive in part from their consequences for group interaction. Obviously, it is difficult to interact with another person at a great distance, and certainly interaction with a person one cannot see is less satisfactory than face-to-face interaction. For example, most people find a telephone conversation less satisfactory than a face-to-face conference, largely because the nonverbal parts of communication are not available during a telephone conversation. The significance of eye contact for social interaction has been discussed in some detail by Kendon (1967). His analyses of behavior during dyadic interaction revealed that *where* a person is looking during interaction often functions as a cue to guide the course of the interaction. For example, at points in an interaction when the speaking role shifts from one person to the other, the person who has been speaking typically ends an utterance by looking at the other person with a sustained gaze; when the other person begins to speak, the first usually looks away. Thus, each person can signal to the other his or her intentions and expectations and at the same time can determine whether the other has received and accepted the signals. But there are consequences of spatial arrangement which are not so obvious. For example, the flow of communication in a group is a function of the spatial relationships among group members. When members of a group are seated at a round table, there is a strong tendency for members to communicate with persons across the table and facing them rather than with persons adjacent to them. Steinzor (1950) tabulated the number of times persons removed 5, 4, 3, 2, and 1 seats from others in the group followed each other in making verbal statements. He found no consistent relationship between interperson distance and following, but members across the table followed each other significantly more often than chance. A similar effect was reported by Strodtbeck and Hook (1961) in their study of twelve-person juries seated at rectangular tables. Persons sitting at end positions participated more and were seen as having more influence on the group decision than persons seated at the sides. Similarly, Silverstein and Stang (1976) found that in naturally occurring triads in a field setting, persons with the greatest visual centrality spoke most often.

This so-called "Steinzor effect" was verified in a study in which group members were seated at a square table (Hearn, 1957). Hearn found that, with minimum direction from a designated leader, members of a face-to-face discussion group directed more comments to persons sitting opposite them than to those on either side. However, he found that in groups with a strong directive leader, the opposite occurred; that is, more comments were directed to neighbors than to those sitting opposite. This latter finding does not negate the hypothesis that seating arrangement influences the pattern of communication in the group, but it does specify some of the limiting conditions of the Steinzor effect. Further qualifications are suggested by the work of Mehrabian and Diamond (1971b) who observed that in four-person groups more conversation occurred among persons seated closer together and directly facing one another, but only for those persons who were sensitive to rejection. Gardin, Kaplan, Firestone, and Cowan (1973) reported that more positive cooperation and attitudinal outcomes occurred in a cross-table arrangement, but only when eye-contact was possible. When eye-contact was blocked, a side-by-side arrangement produced the more positive outcomes. Thus, the face-to-face seating arrangement generally facilitates social interaction, but this effect can be altered by the personal qualities of the persons involved in the interaction, the availability of eye-contact, and similar variables.

Seating arrangement also has an effect on the quality of the interaction. Russo (1967) presented diagrams of five seating arrangements at a rectangular table (see Figure 5-5). In each case, two persons were seated on either side of the table and one person at each end. Russo was interested in subjects' perceptions of the social relationships existing

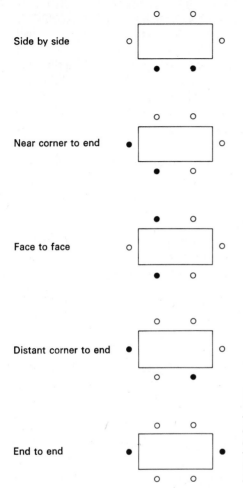

**Figure 5-5** Seating arrangements in Russo's study of perceived social relationships. Filled-in circles represent critical positions and open circles represent empty chairs. (Adapted with permission from N. F. Russo. Connotations of seating arrangements. *Cornell Journal of Social Relations,* 1967, **2,** 37–44.)

between two persons occupying different spatial relationships at the table. The spatial relationships of the two designated persons were: side-by-side, near corner-to-end, on opposite sides and facing, distant corner-to-end, and end-to-end. The two designated persons were identified as members of the same sex. Subjects were asked to rate the couple on four dimensions: intimate-unacquainted, hostile-friendly, talkative-untalkative, and equal-unequal. In general, the more distance there was between the two persons, the less friendly, acquainted, and talkative they were perceived to be. This was qualified by the fact that situations permitting easy eye contact showed less of the interperson distance effect.

The same kind of qualitative effect probably accounts for the relationship between attitude and seating preferences cited by Campbell, Kruskal, and Wallace (1966) in their study of integrated classrooms. They reported that the number of black-white seating adjacencies departed significantly from randomness. An index of aggregation reflecting this lack of randomness in seating arrangements showed the expected differences between two schools selected to represent differing attitudes toward integration.

The effects of seating arrangements on the quality of interaction may also be mediated by the personal feelings, interpersonal reactions, and reactions to the room that are generated differentially by seating arrangements (Patterson, Roth, & Schenk, 1979). For instance, one investigation compared a circle with an L-shaped seating arrangement when either male, female, or mixed-sex groups talked, listened to music, or remained silent. Seating arrangement did not affect self-reports of stress, but the room was seen as more confining with the circle than with the L arrangement. However, other persons were rated as more unfriendly in the L than in the circle arrangement, and most ratings of self and others were more positive in the circle than in the L pattern. There was some evidence that in mixed-sex groups, males were unaffected by arrangement, whereas females reacted more negatively in the circle than in the L arrangement. In a similar study, it was found that the L-shape arrangement produced more self-manipulative behaviors, more postural adjustments, and longer pauses in conversation than the circle arrangement (Patterson, Kelly, Kondracki, & Wulf, 1979).

Finally, seating arrangement has been shown to have an effect on the outcome of bargaining negotiations (Stephenson & Kniveton, 1978). Opposing teams of two-persons each met to negotiate the annual wage agreement and were seated either facing each other across a rectangular table or in a mixed (alternating) pattern around an oval table. The party with the stronger case won more frequently in the mixed arrangement.

In summary, seating arrangements have important effects on the pattern of communication in the group, the quality of the interaction, the nature of the interpersonal reactions to others, and the outcome of certain types of bargaining. As we shall see, these effects may have important consequences for the emergence of leadership and for status in groups.

## Seating Arrangement and Leadership

The relationship between status and interperson distance has already been discussed, and since the leader usually has high status in a group, it is not surprising that there is also a relationship between spatial arrangements and leadership. The leader usually occupies the head of the table, for example, and conversely the person who sits at the head of the table is usually perceived as the leader. These facts mean that the spatial position which a person occupies in the group will have important consequences for his or her chances of emerging as a leader and the amount of influence that he or she exerts on group process.

One of the first demonstrations of the effects of spatial arrangements on leadership status was conducted by Bass and Klubeck (1952). They were interested in the effects of seating position on leadership emergence in a leaderless group discussion situation (Bass, 1949). The leaderless group discussion is a procedure designed to evaluate leadership potential. Small groups are formed and assigned a discussion task, during which observers rate group members on leadership potential. This leadership rating has a moderately high correlation with leadership status attained in natural settings, such as industrial organizations. Bass and Klubeck examined data from 467 participants in sixty-eight half-hour leaderless group discussions involving subjects drawn from such diverse populations as college students and ROTC cadets. Two seating arrangement were involved: a rectangular table with four chairs on either side and an "inverted V" arrangement with three chairs on each side plus a seventh chair at the apex of the V. Two samples drawn from college students had sat at rectangular tables, one sample consisting of three groups and another of four groups. In one of the samples, but not in the other, the person sitting at an end position attained a significantly higher leadership score than persons in middle positions. For groups in the V arrangement, there was little evidence that seating position had a significant influence on leadership status, although one sample did yield significant differences in favor of end positions. It must be remembered, however, that all these studies were conducted for another purpose, and a number of variables, such as participants' own choice of seating position, were confounded with seating arrangement. This fact makes the Bass and Klubeck findings difficult to interpret, to say the least.

A study designed specifically to test the hypothesis that seating arrangement influences leadership emergence (Howells & Becker, 1962) provided more reliable evidence that spatial position in the group is an important determinant of leadership status. The rationale for this hypothesis was that spatial position determines the flow of communication, which in turn determines leadership emergence. The experimental situation involved five-person groups seated at a rectangular table, with three on one side of the table and two on the other. Since interaction is more likely to occur across the table than around it, the investigators expected that each of the two persons on one side would influence three persons on the other, whereas the three could influence only two other persons. Therefore, it was predicted that members from the two-person side of the table would emerge as leaders more frequently than members from the three-person side. The data supported the prediction; fourteen persons emerged as leaders from the two-seat side of the table as compared with six from the three-seat side.

When these findings are related to those concerning spatial position and status and to those concerning spatial position and interaction, it becomes evident that seating arrangement has an important influence upon the interaction process. The physical arrangement of group members determines to a significant degree the flow of communication and interaction in the group, the status assigned to group members, and the emergence of leaders. These effects are caused in part by the cultural patterns of interaction which typically place persons in physical positions that correspond to their leadership or other status positions. It also seems clear that spatial arrangement exerts a more direct influence upon the flow of communication, both verbal and nonverbal, which in turn influences a person's chances to attain status in the group. The many studies of communication networks in small groups provide further evidence of these effects of the physical environment on group process.

## COMMUNICATION NETWORKS

In the preceding pages, we have been concerned primarily with the physical distance between persons and the ways interperson distance affects individual and group behavior. In the discussion of spatial arrangements, it was noted that the particular pattern of physical distance could influence the flow of communication, the perception of status, and the emergence of leadership. In some instances, not only distance but also the particular body orientations among group members determined many facets of group process. In a similar way, the number and arrangement of communication channels among group members exert a powerful influence upon the group. In fact, one may say that communication lies at the heart of group process (M. E. Shaw, 1964). If the group is to function effectively, its members must be able to communicate easily and efficiently. This fact has long been recognized by organizational planners, who try to arrange communication networks in such a manner as to permit the free flow of ideas, knowledge, and other information throughout the organization. Such attempts are exemplified by the military "chain of command," the industrial "table of organization," etc. There can be little doubt that factors affecting communication within the group also influence the efficiency of the group and the satisfaction of its members.

Organizational planners have usually assumed that it is possible to determine logically how the communication channels should be arranged for maximum efficiency, and they have generally concluded that a hierarchical arrangement is most efficient. However, the validity of this assumption is open to question. Years ago Alex Bavelas (1948, 1950) raised several important questions which led to a series of investigations concerning the effect of fixed communication patterns upon group process.

For example, what effects do various patterns of communication have upon leadership emergence? Organizational development? Problem-solving efficiency? The ability of the group to adapt to environmental changes?

It is well to note at this point that we are concerned with the physical *arrangement* of communication channels among group members. In a sense, we are dealing with topological space rather than Euclidean space. It does not matter where the individual group members are located with respect to others. What is important is the distribution of communication channels among them, that is, who can communicate with whom, whether the communication is direct or via another group member, and so on.

Following Bavelas's lead, numerous investigators conducted studies of these questions as well as others that arose during the course of research. The major findings concerned the effects of imposed communication networks upon leadership emergence, organizational development, problem-solving effectiveness, and member reactions.

The usual method of research is to impose various communication networks upon groups in order to determine their consequences for group process. The communication networks that have been investigated are diagramed in Figure 5-6. The circles represent individual group members (or positions in the group), the lines represent channels of communication between positions, and the arrows indicate one-way channels. All lines that do not have arrows represent two-way communication channels. The most common technique for imposing communication networks was first suggested by Bavelas (1948). Group members are placed in cubicles which are connected by slots in the cubicle walls, through which written messages can be passed. When all channels (slots) are open, every group member can communicate directly with every other member. This is the comcon (completely connected) pattern shown in Figure 5-6. Other patterns may be formed merely by closing the appropriate channels. Alternative techniques use telephone lines or messengers as communication channels.

Group members usually are assigned a task to perform working together as a group under conditions which require communication for completion. The kind of task assigned the group varies from simple identification problems to complex sentence-construction and discussion problems. This variation in task characteristics is an important consideration in understanding the effects of communication patterns on group process, a fact which will become evident in the discussion of empirical findings.

### Leadership Emergence

One of the first experimental investigations of communication networks (Leavitt, 1951) compared the five-person wheel, chain, Y, and circle patterns (see Figure 5-6). The task was a symbol-identification task which

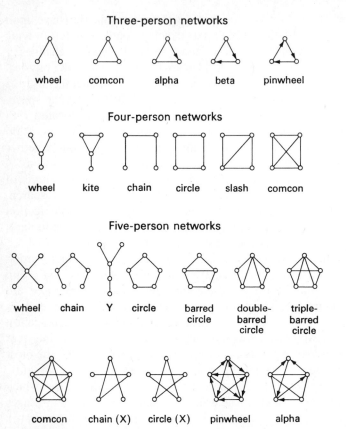

**Figure 5-6** Communication networks used in experimental investigations. Circles represent positions, lines represent communication channels, and arrows indicate one-way channels. [Reprinted with permission from M. E. Shaw. Communication networks. In L. Berkowitz (Ed.), *Advances in experimental social psychology.* Vol. 1, New York: Academic, 1964. Pp. 111–147.]

required that the group identify which of several symbols (stars, triangles, circles, etc.) appeared on each and every card held by group members. This is a relatively simple task involving only the collation of information for solution. Each group was given fifteen trials. When these trials had been completed, each member was asked, "Did your group have a leader? If so, who?" In the wheel pattern the person in the central position was named by twenty-three of twenty-five persons, whereas no one in a peripheral position was named as leader. The persons in the more central positions of the chain and Y patterns were also named considerably more often then peripheral members (seventeen in the Y and twelve in the chain). In the circle, no position was identified as leader significantly more frequently than any other position. Thus it appears that the person who occupies a central position in a communication network has a high probability of emerging as the leader of the group. This finding has been verified in a number of studies. For example, M. E. Shaw (1954b) compared the four-person wheel, slash, and circle patterns shown in Figure 5-6 and found that a leader emerged more frequently in the wheel pattern. Similarly, Shaw and Rothschild (1956) investigated leadership emergence in four-person wheel, slash, and comcon patterns, and found that a leader emerged in only two of eight groups in the comcon and in the slash, whereas a leader emerged in all wheel groups. The criterion of leadership emergence was the naming of an individual as leader by at least three of the four persons in the group, where group members could vote for themselves. The cultural generality of this finding is indicated by the results of a study using Japanese subjects (Hirota, 1953) which replicated Leavitt's findings.

It seems clear, then, that the person who occupies a central position in a communication network has a high probability of emerging as a leader. When the network consists of positions of approximately equal centrality, a leader is less likely to emerge, at least in experimentally assembled groups. The reasons for the centrality-leader-emergence relationship probably are availability of information and the related possibility of coordinating group activities. This interpretation is supported by the fact that this relationship can be modified by giving a member in a peripheral position access to more information initially than a member in the central position (M. E. Shaw, 1954b).

## Organizational Development

The emergence of leadership is, of course, one aspect of organizational development. Another aspect, emphasized by investigators of communication networks, is the mode of operation of the group. That is, the group may develop any one of several alternative methods of attacking the task assigned to them. In general, a group is said to have become organized when it follows a consistent pattern of information exchange during the course of problem solution. In other words, an organizational pattern is the informal communication pattern that the group establishes within the limits imposed by the communication network. There are two basic patterns, each-to-all and centralized. In the each-to-all pattern, all available information is transmitted to all group members, each of whom solves the problem independently. In a centralized organizational pattern, all information is funneled to one person who solves the problem and distributes the answer to other group members. Each of these basic patterns often involves an added checking operation. In the each-to-all plus check pattern, answers are transmitted to other group members for checking before the answer is accepted. The centralized plus check pattern is the same as the centralized except that the central person transmits the solution to at least one other person for checking before it is accepted by the group.

Leavitt (1951) reported that the wheel, Y, and chain networks adopted a centralized organization, However, his definition of organization did not include the each-to-all pattern. M. E. Shaw (1954b) found that all his groups used either the centralized or the each-to-all form of organization. Centralized organization was employed by 73 percent of the wheel groups, 7 percent of the slash groups, and 7 percent of the circle groups, whereas each-to-all organization was used by 27 percent of the wheel groups, 93 percent of the slash, and 93 percent of the circle. Another study in which groups met for an hour per day for ten days (Shaw & Rothschild, 1956) found that all groups in the wheel adopted either a centralized or centralized plus check organization; two groups in the slash developed each-to-all, one used a centralized pattern, and five developed no discernible organization; and two groups in the comcon developed each-to-all, three each-to-all plus check, and three a centralized form of organization. Similar results have been reported by Schein (1958), Guetzkow and Dill (1957), Cohen (1961, 1962), and others.

These experimental findings clearly indicate that the imposition of a centralized communication network predisposes groups to develop a centralized organization. However, when the communication network is unrestricted, as in the comcon, or does not place any person in a highly centralized position, as in the circle, the tendency is to develop an each-to-all organizational pattern. This latter is not merely lack of organization, as might be supposed; it involves a consistent procedure for ensuring that all members receive all available information. As we shall see later, these differences in organizational development are related to differences in group effectiveness but do not seem to be determinants of group efficiency. That is, both forms of organization and group effectiveness are determined by other variables.

### Group Member Reactions

It is inevitable that variations in availability of communication channels will affect the reactions of group members to the group and its activities. In general, a person who occupies a centralized position with its abundance of communication channels is better satisfied with that position than are persons who occupy peripheral positions with limited communication facilities. And since the morale of the group depends upon the satisfaction of its members, group morale (or group satisfaction) is greater in decentralized communication networks (e.g., circle, comcon) than in centralized networks (e.g., wheel, chain). This consequence has been reported by almost all investigators who have examined satisfaction in communication networks. In Leavitt's study, for example, the mean rating of job satisfaction for persons in the most central positions was 7.8 as compared with a mean rating of 4.6 for those occupying peripheral positions. Similarly, the average ratings by networks were 5.4, 5.8, 6.0, and 8.0, for the wheel, chain, Y, and circle networks, respectively. Comparable differences have been reported by M. E. Shaw (1954b), Shaw and Rothschild (1956), Cohen (1961, 1962), Lawson (1965), and others.

### Problem-Solving Efficiency

Although the student of group process is interested in all aspects of group interaction, the emergence of leadership, organizational development, and member reactions are in some ways secondary to the operational efficiency of groups. Certainly the great bulk of research on communication networks has been directed toward the analysis of problem-solving efficiency. This is probably the result of practical considerations, such as how best to organize office committees, work teams, and similar task-oriented groups in order to achieve the group's goal most efficiently. The emergence of a leader and organizational development are often viewed as intervening variables which account for differences in group effectiveness, although there is reason to believe that there is little or no causal relation between these variables and effectiveness (see pages 157–158).

The initial study by Leavitt (1951) indicated that a centralized network was most efficient for problem solution. The circle network was least efficient in terms of time required for solution, number of errors, and number of messages; the wheel and Y patterns were most efficient by these criteria, although the chain was almost as effective. The generality of these findings is limited by the size of the group, the subject population, and the kind of task. Of these, task seems to be the most critical variable. It will be recalled that Leavitt used a simple symbol-identification task which required only that information be collected by at least one position. Such a task makes no demand upon problem-solving ability of group members; it requires no manipulation of information. When the task is more complex, as in the case of mathematical problems, the decentralized network is usually found to be most efficient. For example, M. E. Shaw (1954b) compared the wheel, circle, and slash networks with respect to solution of arithmetic problems. He found that the circle was most efficient and the wheel least efficient in terms of time required for solution. Mean times were 12.3 minutes for the wheel, 12.0 minutes for the slash, and 11.5 minutes for the circle. On the last of three problems attempted, the differences in time required were greater; mean times were 9.7 minutes for the wheel, 8.6 minutes for the slash, and 8.0 for the circle. The circle groups also corrected more errors than did the more centralized groups.

On the other hand, the wheel groups required fewer messages to reach a solution than did the others; however, this difference can be accounted for by the number of communication channels available. Group members tend to use available channels at a relatively constant rate. There were no differences among networks in number of messages per channel.

The differences among networks reported by Shaw are just opposite to those reported by Leavitt, a difference which has been shown to be a consequence of the kind of task (M. E. Shaw, 1954a). When the task is relatively simple and requires only the collation of information, a centralized network is most efficient, but when the task is more complex and requires that operations be performed upon the information (for example, mathematical manipulations), the decentralized networks are more efficient in terms of time and errors. Research by others generally supports these conclusions. For example, on simple identification problems, Hirota (1953), Guetzkow and Simon (1955), Lawson (1964a), and Kano (1971), among others, found centralized networks faster than decentralized networks; on more complex problems, Mulder (1960), Lawson (1964b), and Kano (1971), among others, found the decentralized network faster. M. E. Shaw (1964) examined the findings from eighteen studies in which the assigned task could be classified as either simple or complex. The results of this tabulation are shown in Table 5-1. It is clear that the complexity of the task is a critical factor in determining the relative effectiveness of different communication networks.

The interesting aspect of these findings is that they are contrary to the usual assumptions about the most effective arrangement of communication channels in a group. Since most of the problems that groups are faced with are more complex than the most complex task used in laboratory experiments, it is evident that a decentralized communication network is most likely to be effective in natural group situations. It should be kept in mind, however, that the centralized-decentralized dimension of communication networks does not necessarily correspond to centralized-decentralized decision structures (cf. Mulder, 1960). Therefore one should be cautious about making inferences concerning other kinds of organizational relationships from the data on communication networks.

## Explanatory Concepts

If it be granted that communication networks partially determine group effectiveness, we would like to understand the processes by which this influence occurs. As mentioned earlier, some theorists have sought to explain the effects of communication networks by treating organizational development as an intervening variable. For example, Guetzkow and Simon (1955) and Guetzkow and Dill (1957) proposed that networks affect the efficiency of group interaction only indirectly by governing the group

**Table 5-1   Number of Comparisons Showing Differences between Centralized (Wheel, Chain, Y) and Decentralized (Circle, Comcon) Networks as a Function of Task Complexity**

|                          | Simple problems* | Complex problems† | Total |
|--------------------------|:----------------:|:-----------------:|:-----:|
| **Time**                 |                  |                   |       |
| Centralized faster       | 14               | 0                 | 14    |
| Decentralized faster     | 4                | 18                | 22    |
| **Messages**             |                  |                   |       |
| Centralized sent more    | 0                | 1                 | 1     |
| Decentralized sent more  | 18               | 17                | 35    |
| **Errors**               |                  |                   |       |
| Centralized made more    | 0                | 6                 | 6     |
| Decentralized made more  | 9                | 1                 | 10    |
| No difference            | 1                | 3                 | 4     |
| **Satisfaction**         |                  |                   |       |
| Centralized higher       | 1                | 1                 | 2     |
| Decentralized higher     | 7                | 10                | 17    |

*Simple problems: symbol-, letter-, number-, and color-identification tasks.
†Complex problems: arithmetic, word arrangement, sentence construction, and discussion problems.
*Source*: Reprinted with permission from M. E. Shaw (1964).

members' ability to organize themselves for efficient task performance. In the first test of this hypothesis (Guetzkow & Simon, 1955), five-person groups were tested in the wheel, circle, and comcon networks, using symbol-identification tasks. Groups were given task-free periods between trials for the purpose of organizing themselves for efficient task performance. The results showed that the organizational opportunity did *not* eliminate differences among networks as required by the hypothesis. However, when groups that organized themselves centrally were compared, there was no difference attributable to networks. The investigators believed that this supported their hypothesis. In the second study (Guetzkow & Dill, 1957), groups were allowed time to organize in a comcon network and were then tested in a circle network. The performance of these groups was compared with that of the circle groups in the first experiment. Again, the expected differences did not occur, but when groups were divided into organized and unorganized categories, the organized groups were found to be more effective. Similar findings were reported by Mulder (1959a, 1960), who found that groups with more centralized decision structures performed better than groups with decentralized decision structures.

Unfortunately, the interpretation of these data is not easy. There is a methodological problem that arises whenever comparisons are made between groups that are selected on the basis of some aspect of their behavior during the experimental period. It is always possible that the same, but unnoticed, variable is affecting both the criterion for selection and the criterion for evaluating the differences between the selected groups. This appears to be exactly what happened in the Guetzkow et al. studies and probably in Mulder's experiments as well. In a series of studies reported by Schein (1958), the development of both organization and efficiency was traced over time. Again, it was found that the groups developing a strong organization were the most effective, but efficiency was achieved *before* the organization had developed. It must be concluded, therefore, that the organization could not have caused the efficiency of the groups, even though organization and efficiency were highly correlated.

Two other explanatory concepts have been suggested that are more useful: independence and saturation. The concept of independence was first suggested by Leavitt (1951) to account for differences among network positions. His view was that differences in answer-getting potential would structure group members' perceptions of their roles in the group. For example, group members of a wheel network can readily perceive the degree of information accessibility and the nature of their own roles; the central person is autonomous and controls the group. In a decentralized network, such as the circle, no group member is entirely dependent upon any other member, and any member's role is not clearly different from anyone else's role. Morale is higher because of the greater independence in the decentralized network, which permits the gratification of culturally supported needs for autonomy. Thus, Leavitt concluded that communication networks determine behavior via their effects upon independence of action, which in turn produces differences in activity, accuracy, satisfaction, and other behaviors.

Subsequent research made it clear that Leavitt's original formulation was too limited. Consequently, it has been expanded (M. E. Shaw, 1964) to include freedom from all restrictions on action. As expanded, the term *independence* refers to the degree of freedom with which the individual may function in the group. A group member's independence of action may be influenced not only by accessibility of information but also by situational factors, by the actions of other group members, and by the person's own perceptions of the situation. So defined, independence is related to both group efficiency and member satisfaction, although its strongest effect seems to be on satisfaction (M. E. Shaw, 1955).

The concept of *saturation* was first formulated by Gilchrist, Shaw, and Walker (1954) to refer to the communication overload experienced by group members in centralized positions in communication networks. They observed that when the number of messages which must be handled by a position passed a certain optimal level, the communication requirements began to counteract the effects of the more favorable network position. At this point, the position was said to be "saturated." This suggests that saturation is an all-or-none process, but such is not the case. Positions vary in the degree to which they are overloaded by communication, and so we may speak of degree of saturation. In general, the greater the saturation the less efficient the group and the less satisfied the group members, although saturation probably influences effectiveness to a greater extent than it does satisfaction.

Gilchrist et al. distinguished two kinds of saturation: channel saturation and message unit saturation. Channel saturation refers to the number of channels with which a position must deal, and message unit saturation refers to the number of messages which a position must handle. These two kinds of saturation are correlated and are usually combined to determine the total saturation of a position. Like the concept of independence, the saturation concept, as originally formulated, was too limited. The demands imposed upon an occupant of a position in a communication network call for action, regardless of the source of the demands. Thus, the total saturation of a position derives not only from communication requirements but also from other requirements, such as organizational decisions and data manipulation that may be needed for task completion.

The notion of saturation accounts for most of the effects on group performance that have been observed in communication networks. For example, the central position in a wheel network is more vulnerable to saturation than any position in a decentralized network, such as the circle. When the group is faced with a simple task, the communication requirements are not excessive and the central position does not become saturated. The favorable arrangement of communication channels for information collation in a wheel network thus renders it more effective for simple problems, unhampered by saturation effects. However, when the group is faced with a more complex task, such as a human relations problem or an arithmetic problem, the communication demands upon the central position are great and the position quickly becomes at least partly saturated, thus reducing the efficiency of the group. Decentralized networks, being less subject to saturation, are more effective in solving complex problems.

The negative consequences of saturation can be seen in a variety of other empirical findings. Macy, Christie, and Luce (1953) found that groups were less effective in identifying a "noisy" marble (a marble having many different colors) in a centralized than in a decentralized network. Centralized networks are less effective in dealing with irrelevant information than are decentralized ones (M. E. Shaw, 1958b). In short, anything that increases the demands upon the group is likely to interfere with centralized networks more than with decentralized networks. These effects are, of course, predicted by the saturation hypothesis. In a direct test of the saturation hypothesis, Kano (1977) compared the circle and wheel networks on the common symbol task. For half of the groups in each network the task was to identify one common symbol out of a set of eleven symbols, whereas for the other half the task was to choose the common symbol from a set of six symbols. Thus the task characteristics were identical for all groups, but the amount of information that must be considered varied. As predicted by the saturation hypothesis, amount of information had little effect on the performance of groups in the circle, but groups in the wheel performed much less effectively when required to process additional information.

It has also been shown that it is possible to reduce the saturation effects commonly observed in centralized networks. Moore, Johnson, and Arnold (1972) noted that most network studies involved homogeneous group compositions, that is, all group members were of equal status. They theorized that the differences between centralized and decentralized networks in group effectiveness were due to status incongruence. Individuals typically do not expect equal status persons to occupy different positions in a communication structure, as in the case of homogeneous groups in a centralized network. This lack of status-network congruency leads to tension, lack of cohesiveness, and reduced productivity. Moore and his assoicates conducted an experiment comparing decentralized networks with centralized networks in which the statuses of group members were either equal, unequal and congruent with network positions, or unequal and incongruent with network positions. When the statuses of group members were congruent with their positions in the centralized network, problem-solving efficiency did not differ significantly from the effectiveness of groups in decentralized networks. Furthermore, the experiment demonstrated that status-network congruency reduced saturation effects in the centralized network.

The effects of saturation are not limited to laboratory groups. In a large state university, for example, classrooms traditionally had been assigned to academic departments, which were then free to schedule classes as they chose (a decentralized system). Although a few complications arose at the beginning of each new term, room assignments were handled efficiently. One year, the administration of the university decided that the system was inefficient and could be improved by centralization. All rooms were withdrawn from departments and assigned to a central office. Anyone who needed a room for a new class or for a larger class could, theoretically, obtain one by calling the central office. On the first day of class after the new centralized procedure had been installed, chaos reigned. Requests for room assignments were met with the statement that there were several hundred requests and that things would be straightened out in a few weeks! Although this is anecodotal evidence, it does illustrate the effects of saturation in a natural situation.

In summary, the arrangement of communication channels in the group has been shown to determine leadership emergence, organizational development, member satisfaction, and group efficiency. In general, centralized networks as compared with decentralized networks enhance leadership emergence and organizational development, but impede the efficient solution of complex problems and reduce member satisfaction. These effects are mediated through independence and saturation processes which appear to be operative in both laboratory and natural situations.

## PLAUSIBLE HYPOTHESES ABOUT THE PHYSICAL ENVIRONMENT OF GROUPS

We have seen how individuals and groups are influenced by their physical environment. Personal space and individual territoriality have important consequences for group behavior, and spatial arrangements in groups are important determinants of status, satisfaction, and performance. It is now possible to formulate some more precise plausible hypotheses that have survived the test of empirical data.

*Hypothesis 1 The physical aspects of the environment interact with attitudes and beliefs to help determine group process.*
Several studies have shown that material aspects of the physical environment are related to group process variables. Lighting intensity is related to efficiency (Luckiesh, 1931), but productivity may increase regardless of changes in intensity if the members believe they are being given special attention (Roethlisberger & Dickson, 1939). Dimly lit rooms are seen as more intimate and less appropriate for interviews than brightly lit rooms (Carr & Dabbs, 1974). Playing music increases productivity when group members believe it is supposed to do so but decreases productivity when they believe the music is intended to interfere (Baker, 1937). Noise has negative consequences (frustration and decrements in productivity) when it is unpredictable (Glass et al., 1969), but these effects are reduced when persons believe they have control over the termination of the noise (Glass et al., 1971).

*Hypothesis 2 Individuals and groups typically assume a proprietary orientation toward certain geographical areas which they defend against invasion.*
Individual territoriality has been observed in a variety of situations. Altman and Haythorn (1967a) found that isolated dyads developed strong

preferences for a particular table, chair, and/or bed. Similar evidences of territoriality were reported by Lipman (1968) in his study of old folks' homes. That individuals defend against invasion has also been demonstrated in a number of empirical studies (Sommer, 1969). Similarly, group territoriality has been shown by studies of street-corner gangs (W. F. Whyte, 1943), residential areas (Mack, 1954; Marine, 1966), etc. Territories are often marked with personal items, and these markers are ordinarily respected by others (Becker, 1973; Becker & Mayo, 1971; Shaffer & Sadowski, 1975).

*Hypothesis 3    The size of group territories varies with the density of the locale and the interpersonal relationships among group members.*

Although there is relatively little evidence for this hypothesis from controlled observations, it seems intuitively reasonable and is consistent with available evidence. A study of the boundaries of group territories on a beach revealed that the amount of space per group member decreased with size and that the size of group territories decreased as density increased (Edney & Jordan-Edney, 1974). Another study showed that group territories increased with size if group members were strangers but not if they were friends (Edney & Grundman, 1979).

*Hypothesis 4    Individuals typically have personal standards concerning appropriate interperson distances for various interpersonal relationships and activities.*

There are extensive observational and experimental data supporting this hypothesis (e.g., Sommer, 1959; Little, 1965; Tennis & Dabbs, 1975; Willis, 1966).

*Hypothesis 5    Reactions to unwanted approach by others vary with the personalness of the situation, the intimacy of the person-other relationship, and the status of the person relative to the other.*

Reactions to intrusion vary according to circumstances. For example, Horowitz et al. (1964) observed that patients in a mental hospital approached a hat rack more closely than they approached another individual. The effects of situational impersonality were also observed by Argyle and Dean (1965) in that individuals stood closer to a photograph than to a real person and closer to a photograph of a person with eyes closed than to one with eyes open. The varying effects of intrusion into personal space may be inferred from demonstrations that varying degrees of acquaintanceship result in varying degress of comfortable approach (Little, 1965; F. N. Willis, 1966). Finally, it will be recalled that Lott and

Sommer (1967) found that status was perceived as closely related to spatial position in the group. The high-status person usually occupies the best position, and, conversely, the person who occupies the favored position is seen as having high status.

*Hypothesis 6    Unwanted proximity of another person evokes discomfort and negative feelings which are revealed by various defensive reactions on the part of the victim, the person whose space is invaded.*

This hypothesis has considerable empirical support. Sommer (1969) reported numerous studies of invasion of personal space which revealed the feelings of discomfort produced by such invasion. Typical reactions included change in body orientation, rubbing the face, and similar behaviors. When these defensive responses proved ineffective, the victim usually left the scene. Numerous other studies also support this hypothesis (e.g., Harris et al., 1978; Schiffenbauer & Schiavo, 1976; Murphy-Berman & Berman, 1978).

*Hypothesis 7    Male and female groups react differently to variations in population density.*

Hypothesis 7 cannot be rendered more precisely, given the present state of knowledge about population density and crowding. That male groups react differently to varying number of persons per unit of physical space than do female groups is clearly demonstrated (Freedman et al., 1972; Ross et al., 1973). However, the precise reasons for these differences have not yet been determined.

*Hypothesis 8    High density results in decrements in group performance under some conditions.*

Several studies failed to find an effect of density on group performance (e.g., Freedman et al., 1971; Kutner, 1973; Sherrod, 1974), but decrements have been found when group size, room size, and interperson distance were varied independently (Paulus et al., 1976) and when the group task requires physical interaction (Heller et al., 1977).

*Hypothesis 9    There is a positive relationship between status and the favorability of spatial position in the group.*

There is reliable evidence that not only do high-status individuals prefer certain positions in the group, but occupants of certain positions are accorded higher status than occupants of less favored positions. An analysis of experimental jury deliberations (Strodtbeck & Hook, 1961) revealed that jurists from professional and managerial classes tended to choose the head of the table. Similarly, Hare and Bales (1963) found that persons high on dominance chose central positions in the group. The perception of high status as a function of position was demonstrated clearly by a series of investigations by Lott and Sommer (1967) and Sommer (1969).

**Hypothesis 10**   *Communication patterns in groups are determined, in part, by the seating arrangement in the group.*

Steinzor (1950) analyzed the interaction process of groups seated at round tables and found that group members sitting across the table from each other followed one another in speaking significantly more often than they followed persons in other positions. A similar result was obtained by Strodtbeck and Hook (1961) using rectangular tables. Persons sitting at the ends of the table participated more than others in the group. However, this effect may be altered by personal characteristics (Mehrabian & Diamond, 1971b) or an availability of eye-contact (Gardin et al., 1973). Silverstein and Stang (1976) also found that in naturally occurring triads persons with the greatest visual centrality spoke most often.

**Hypothesis 11**   *Seating arrangement influences the quality of group interaction.*

This general hypothesis summarizes the finding that the relationships of persons seated at a table are perceived as qualitatively different as a function of their relative positions at the table. These interpersonal relationships are undoubtedly reciprocal, since people who are well acquainted tend to sit near each other, etc. However, the research has considered primarily the effects of seating arrangement upon subsequent interaction. Russo (1967) reported that, in general, the more distance between two persons the less well acquainted, the less friendly, and the less talkative the dyad was seen to be. When the relative position permitted eye contact, however, there was less effect of interperson distance on the quality of perceived interaction. Patterson et al. (1979) found that ratings of self and others were generally more positive in a circle arrangement than in an L arrangement.

**Hypothesis 12**   *A leader is more likely to emerge in a centralized communication network than in a decentralized network.*

This finding is well substantiated in a number of investigations. In his initial study, Leavitt (1951) observed that a leader emerged significantly more often in a wheel network than in a chain or Y network, and more frequently in the latter two than in a circle network. In other words, the frequency of leadership emergence varied directly with the degree of network centrality. This finding has been verified in a number of subsequent investigations (for example, Hirota, 1953; M. E. Shaw, 1954b; Shaw & Rothschild, 1956).

*Hypothesis 13    Organizational development occurs more rapidly in a centralized than in a decentralized communication network.*

This hypothesis is supported by Leavitt's research, as well as by that of many others. Leavitt (1951) found that groups in wheel networks organized themselves into centralized patterns, whereas circle groups failed to organize at all. When a different definition of organization is applied, however, organization develops in decentralized as well as in centralized networks (Shaw & Rothschild, 1956). But again, development occurs earlier in the more centralized network. The hypothesis is also supported by the work of Schein (1958), Mulder (1959a), and others. However, there is reason to believe that this organizational development is not causally related to group efficiency.

*Hypothesis 14    Group members have higher morale in decentralized than in centralized communication networks.*

This hypothesis has general support from research on communication networks. Leavitt (1951) found that ratings of satisfaction were negatively correlated with network centralization; the highest ratings occurred in the circle and the lowest in the wheel. Other investigations have verified these results (for example, A. M. Cohen, 1961; Lawson, 1965; M. E. Shaw, 1954b). All these studies used tasks that probably had low relevance for group members, at least outside the experimental situation. It is an open question whether the same relationship would be found with more ego-involving tasks.

*Hypothesis 15    A decentralized communication network is most efficient when the group must solve complex problems, whereas a centralized network is most efficient when the group must solve simple problems.*

In Hypothesis 15, the term *simple problems* refers to tasks that require only the collection of information; when all the information is available in one place, the solution is obvious. Problems of this sort include symbol-, letter-, number-, and color-identification tasks. Many studies have shown that centralized networks are more efficient than decentralized networks with this kind of task (Guetzkow & Simon, 1955; Hirota, 1953; Lawson, 1964a; Leavitt, 1951; and others). The term *complex problems* means that the information must be collected in one place *and* operations must be performed upon it before the solution can be known. Examples of this type of problem are word-arrangement tasks, discussion problems, arithmetic problems, etc. Decentralized communication networks are typically more efficient with this type of task (Lawson, 1964b; Mulder, 1960; M. E. Shaw, 1954b; and others). Table 5-1 shows the frequency with which the empirical data support Hypothesis 15.

*Hypothesis 16    A centralized communication network is more vulnerable to saturation than a decentralized network.*

The term *saturation* refers to the degree to which one or more positions in the group have more requirements placed upon them than can be handled efficiently. It has been demonstrated that a centralized communication network typically places greater demands upon the central position than are placed upon any position in a decentralized network; hence a centralized network becomes saturated more quickly than does the decentralized. For example, groups in centralized networks are impeded more than those in decentralized networks by "noisy" marble-identification tasks (Macy et al., 1953), irrelevant information (M. E. Shaw, 1958a), and similar interferences. These effects are observed in natural situations as well as in the laboratory.

## SUGGESTED READINGS

Bavelas, A. Communication patterns in task-oriented groups. *Journal of the Acoustical Society of America*, 1950, **22**, 725–730.

Hearn, G. Leadership and the spatial factor in small groups. *Journal of Abnormal and Social Psychology*, 1957, **54**, 269–272.

Knowles, E. S. Boundaries around group interaction: The effect of group size and member status on boundary permeability. *Journal of Personality and Social Psychology*, 1973, **26**, 327–331.

Paulus, P. B., Annis, A. B., Seta, J. J., Schkade, J. K., & Matthews, R. W. Density does affect task performance. *Journal of Personality and Social Psychology*, 1976, **34**, 248–253.

Shaw, M. E. Communication networks. In L. Berkowitz (Ed.), *Advances in experimental social psychology.* Vol 1. New York: Academic, 1964. Pp. 111–147.

Sommer, R. *Personal space: The behavioral basis of design.* Englewood Cliffs, N.J.: Prentice-Hall, 1969.

Strodtbeck, F. L., & Hook, L. H. The social dimensions of a twelve man jury table. *Sociometry*, 1961, **24**, 397–415.

Willis, F. N., Jr. Initial speaking distance as a function of the speakers' relationship. *Psychonomic Science*, 1966, **5**, 221–222.

# Chapter 6

# Personal Characteristics of Group Members

Groups are composed of individuals, each of whom has his or her own unique characteristics and idiosyncratic ways of behaving. Within a given group, the personal characteristics of group members may be quite similar, but they often vary widely. Group members' manners of behaving, their typical reactions to others, and their skills and abilities affect not only their own behavior patterns, but also the reactions of others to them. Even the mere fact that they are present influences the behavior of others in the group, as noted earlier in discussions of social facilitation and coaction effects (Chapter 3). One cannot hope to fully understand group behavior without knowing at least some of the ways the personal characteristics of group members affect group processes.

Individual characteristics influence group processes in two ways. First, the characteristics of group members determine to some extent what their own behavior in the group will be and how others will react to them. For example, a person who has special knowledge of the task may be expected to use this knowledge to help the group achieve its goal, and the dominant individual may be expected to enact behaviors designed to give him or her control over others. A second way in which individual characteristics influence the group's behavior is a consequence of the particular combination of individual characteristics. In this case, it is not a question of whether the individual has special knowledge of the task, for example, but whether he or she has more or less knowledge than the others in the group. The relationships among the attributes of group members may be of greater consequence for group action than the attributes as such. For example, the fact that a dyad is composed of one person high on dominance and one low on dominance may be more significant than the absolute degree of dominance exhibited by either member of the dyad. Since this aspect of group composition has to do with relationships among persons, we will consider it in a separate chapter (Chapter 7).

One important variable in group composition is the sheer number of persons in the group. Although mere presence does not, strictly speaking, represent a personal characteristic, it does influence group process, as we demonstrated in Chapter 3. Therefore, it is instructive to begin our discussion with a review of the effects of group size upon various aspects of group functioning. In addition, this chapter will consider three categories or classes of personal attributes of group members: biographical characteristics, abilities, and personality traits. This division is somewhat arbitrary, since the categories are interrelated in several important ways. Biographical characteristics partially determine the personality traits the person reveals by his or her behavior. Special abilities that the individual has developed may also be a consequence of certain background characteristics, such as the amount of education that has been available to him or her. Abilities are sometimes regarded as aspects of the personality, since they reflect unique properties of the individual. Despite these interrelations, it is convenient to discuss these personal factors separately in order to see more clearly their consequences for group behavior.

## GROUP SIZE

The number of persons in a group has several important consequences for group process. The range of abilities, knowledges, and skills that are available to the group increases with increasing group size, as well as the sheer number of "hands" that are available for acquiring and processing information. The advantages of these added resources for problem-solving effectiveness are obvious. The larger group also provides a greater opportunity to meet interesting and attractive others with whom interaction may be rewarding. For shy persons, the larger group provides greater anonymity and so may be more attractive to them. On the other hand, as group size increases, organizational problems become difficult. The potential number of interpersonal relationships between group members increases rapidly with size; subgroups are more likely to form in larger groups and the potential for conflict is correspondingly greater. As size increases, relatively fewer group members participate in the group's activities and members are more likely to conform to normative group pressures. These organizational and interpersonal effects usually interfere with the effective use of resources. Thus group size has both positive and negative influences on group process. Although the optimum group size has been estimated to be approximately five persons (Slater, 1958), this depends upon the group task, group composition, and other factors. In the following sections, some of these effects of group size will be examined in greater detail.

### Group Size and Member Participation

As the size of the group increases, the amount of time available for each member to participate in the group's activities decreases; the larger the group the less opportunity each person has to participate in discussion, to express his or her opinions, etc. Furthermore, group members often feel greater threat and greater inhibition of impulses to participate in larger groups than in smaller groups (Gibb, 1951). As a consequence there is a decrease in the overall amount of participation as the size of the group increases. For example, Dawe (1934) reported that as the size of children's groups increased from 14 to 46, the total amount of discussion in the group decreased. Similarly, Williams and Mattson (1942) reported that more talking occurred in groups of two than in groups of three persons, and Indik (1965) made an intensive study of three organizations and found that as the size of the organization increases the rate of communication decreases. Indik suggested that the larger the organization the lower the probability that communications will be adequate, leading to lower interpersonal attraction, which in turn leads to decreased interpersonal communication.

More significantly, the distribution of participation varies with group size. Group members report that they have fewer chances to speak in larger groups (Hare, 1952), and their feelings are reflected in the pattern of communication in the group. As the size of the group increases, larger and larger proportions of group members participate less than their "fair share." A few members tend to dominate the discussion, with others participating relatively less as size increases. This effect is demonstrated clearly in a study by Bales, Strodtbeck, Mills, and Roseborough (1951). When individuals are ranked in order of amount of participation in group discussion, marked differences are observed among groups of different sizes (see Figure 6-1). Differences in percentage of total acts among members of three or four persons are relatively small; however, with larger groups of five to eight members, the difference between the most active

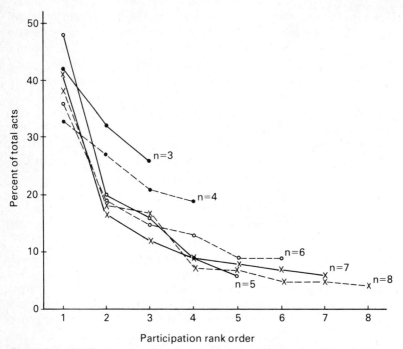

**Figure 6-1** Distribution of participation as a function of group size. (Plotted with permission from data reported by R. F. Bales, F. L. Strodtbeck, T. M. Mills, and M. E. Rosenborough. Channels of communication in small groups. *American Sociological Review,* 1951, **16,** 461–468.)

group member and others in the group increases dramatically. As size increases, there is also an increase in the proportion of communications that are directed toward the group as a whole rather than to specific members of the group. These varying distributions of communication reflect differences in organizational structure which are related to leadership emergence, member reactions to the group, conformity behavior, and group performance.

**Group Size and Leadership**

The data presented in Figure 6-1 reveal that greater differentiation between the most active person in the group and other group members increases with the size of the group. This suggests that the group is becoming more structured and that the leadership role is being increasingly assumed by one person to the exclusion of others. After studying the leadership behavior in groups of varying size, Hemphill (1950) concluded that as the group becomes larger, the demands upon the leader's role become greater and more numerous, and tolerance for leader-centered direction of group activities becomes greater. The tendency for leadership emergence to be more definitive in larger groups is also revealed by a study of leadership ratings in different sized groups (Bass & Norton, 1951). Groups varying in size from two to twelve persons participated in a thirty-minute group discussion, during which two trained observers rated participants on behaviors that reflect leadership potential. It was found that as group size increased, mean leadership scores decreased; however, the relative variance of leadership ratings tended to increase with discussion group size. Although limited, these data support the conclusion that a leader is more likely to emerge in larger groups than in smaller groups.

### Group Size and Member Reactions

The increasing differentiation among group members that occurs with increasing size may be expected to influence the group members' reactions to the group, and indeed there is considerable evidence to support the conclusion that members of larger groups are less attracted to the group, experience greater tension, and are less satisfied than are members of small groups. The lack of time for each member to participate, the increasing domination of the group's activities by one or a few members, and the increased difficulty of maintaining interpersonal relationships in larger groups obviously contribute to negative feelings about the group. These effects of group size have been observed in a variety of situations. An early study of various industrial organizations by Katz (1949) revealed that relative to larger groups, smaller groups were more cohesive,* members were better satisfied, and individual members assumed more importance. Slater (1958) studied laboratory groups of varying size and found that members of smaller groups expressed significantly more positive evaluations of their group. Dissatisfaction with larger groups is also reflected by greater absenteeism and personnel turnover in larger industrial organizations (Cleland, 1955; Baumgartel & Sobol, 1959). Segal (1977) found that ingroup friendship choices made by members of a state police force increased with group size and that the increase was a decreasing function of the initial size of the group. In other words, choices did not increase as much as would have been expected on the basis of the number of potential friends in the group.

The deleterious effects of increasing size of the group are also revealed by the kinds of behaviors enacted by group members during group interaction. O'Dell (1968) studied two-, three-, four-, and five-person groups as they discussed the broad issue of reducing automobile accidents.

---

*Group cohesiveness is usually defined as the resultant of all these forces acting on group members to remain in or to leave the group. (See Chapter 7.)

Analysis of the content of the group's discussion indicated that as size increased group members showed (a) greater disagreement, (b) greater antagonism toward others, (c) less tension, and (d) greater tension release. The finding that larger groups show less tension may appear to be inconsistent with the fact that members of larger groups are less satisfied than members of smaller groups; however, lower tension in larger groups is probably a consequence of the relative anonymity in larger groups which permits greater tension release. When combined, signs of tension and tension release clearly increased with increasing group size. However, an interesting study by Smith and Haythorn (1972) suggests that the effects of group size on member reactions may vary with the circumstances under which the group must function. They observed two- and three-person groups who were confined for twenty-one days with little to do. Among other things, they measured stress, anxiety, hostility, and annoyances experienced by group members over time. Members of the two-person groups reported higher anxiety and more annoyances than did the three-person groups; dyads and triads reported equal amounts of stress and hostility. Furthermore, independent ratings of adaptation to confinement made by a psychiatrist indicated that triads were more adaptable than dyads. It is evident that negative reactions are usually greater in larger groups, but the data reported by Smith and Haythorn suggest that need for the support of other persons may sometimes overcome these negative effects. It may also be noted that larger groups increase the probability that members will find an attractive other and/or someone who satisfies their interpersonal needs.

Finally, it might be noted that several investigations have shown that group members in larger groups are less likely to help a person in need than members of smaller groups (e.g., Darley & Latane, 1968; Latane & Rodin, 1969; Wegner & Schaefer, 1978). Members apparently feel less personal responsibility for helping when more members are present.

### Group Size and Consensus

One of the goals of groups is often the achievement of consensus. For example, a sorority or fraternity committee may be appointed to plan a social affair or to establish the goals that the organization would like to achieve during the coming year. Obviously, such a committee cannot achieve its objective unless the members arrive at a "meeting of minds." In general, the larger the group the greater the difficulty in achieving consensus. Comparing discussion groups of varying size in a Boy Scout camp, Hare (1952) found that in larger groups, as compared with smaller groups, there was less consensus about discussion issues and that group members changed less toward consensus. On the other hand, there are pressures toward uniformity in groups that tend to produce more consensus and conformity to group standards in larger groups. Everyone has observed the similarities of members of the same group: members of athletic teams often wear jackets that are identical, social cliques on the college campus adopt distinctive mannerisms, members of professional groups (such as group dynamicists) use a common jargon, and even groups dedicated to nonconformity (e.g., "hippies" of the 1960s) display strikingly similar hirsute adornments. One might suspect that these pressures toward uniformity vary with group size and perhaps to some extent exert forces counter to those that interfere with the achievement of consensus.

A number of investigators have examined the effects of size on conformity to majority opinion in the group. In a classic study conducted by Asch (1951), a näive person was exposed to obviously incorrect judgments by a unanimous majority. Size of this majority was varied from one (a two-person group) to sixteen (a seventeen-person group). Conformity to the judgments of the majority increased with group size up to a majority of three and remained essentially constant thereafter. Rosenberg (1961) also observed an increase in conformity with increasing size up to four persons, with a slight decrease in five-person groups. However, a replication of the Asch study (Gerard, Wilhelmy, & Conolley, 1968) found a linear increase in conformity with group size. Thus, the relationship between group size and conformity is not clear, although the evidence suggests that under certain circumstances, at least, there is increasing conformity to majority judgments with increasing group size. For instance, one study (Chapko & Revers, 1976) indicates that the effects of group size on conformity is greater when there is greater initial disagreement in the group. There is also some evidence that conformity may be greater in smaller groups when members are trying to win a prize for their group (Feldman, 1974). In groups of boys and girls ranging in age from 9 to 16 years, group size correlated negatively with conformity ($r = -.32$). When increased pressures toward uniformity are operative, however, they counteract to some extent the problems associated with achievement of consensus in larger groups.

## Group Size and Group Performance

As noted earlier, increasing the size of the group introduces opposing forces with respect to group performance and productivity. On the one hand, the added resources that are available in larger groups (abilities, knowledge, range of opinions, etc.) contribute to effective group performance; on the other hand, the increased organizational problems and inhibitions of some members' impulses to contribute tend to decrease the effectiveness of the group. The effect of size on group performance is the resultant of these opposing forces; whether the performance will become more or less effective as size increases will depend upon the degree to which added resources can be utilized and the degree to which group processes exert negative influence on group output. The relative effects of opposing forces depend to a marked degree upon the kind of task adopted by the group.

Group tasks may be classified in many different ways, and several systems will be reviewed and evaluated in Chapter 10. For present purposes, the category system proposed by Steiner (1972) will be convenient. It places tasks in three categories: additive, disjunctive, and conjunctive. An *additive* task is one in which the outcome is the result of some combination of individual products; group performance should, therefore, increase with increasing group size. A *disjunctive* task requires that at least one person in the group be able to perform the task; group performance is expected to increase with increasing group size, since the more persons in the group the higher the probability that at least one will be able to complete the task. A *conjunctive* task is one which requires that everyone in the group accomplish the task; therefore, the group performance is expected to decrease with increasing group size, owing to the increased likelihood that the group will include at least one member who is unable to complete the task.

**Additive Tasks**   If the group task is additive, the more persons who work on the task, the greater the group's output, and/or the more effective the group's performance. Consider, for example, a task that requires pulling a heavy object with a rope; obviously, the more persons who pull on the rope, the more easily the object can be moved. In fact, there must be a sufficiently large number of persons to move the object at all. Documentation for this effect, if it is needed, has been provided by Ringelmann (cited in Steiner, 1972), who had one, two, three, or eight persons pull on a rope attached to a device which measured the amount of force exerted on the rope. One person exerted a force equal to 63 kilograms, two persons exerted a force equal to 118 kilograms, three persons a force equal to 160 kilograms, and eight persons a force equal to 248 kilograms. This shows clearly that the total force exerted by the group increases with size of the group; it may also be observed that the amount of force exerted per person *decreases* with increasing group size. According to Steiner, some individual potential is lost due to faulty group process (e.g., some individuals may have pulled in opposing directions, some may have relied upon others to do more than their share of the work, etc.). The "law of diminishing returns" appears to be operating with additive group tasks.

A partial replication of the Ringelmann experiment was conducted using groups ranging in size from one to six (Ingham, Levinger, Graves, & Peckham, 1974). It was found that increasing size from one to three produced the expected decrement in per person contributions, but the addition of a fourth, fifth, or sixth member produced little effect. However, overall group performance increased with increasing group size as expected. In a second part of the investigation, separation of individual contributions indicated that decreased motivation of group members accounted for most of the performance per person decrement.

**Disjunctive Tasks** When the task is disjunctive, performance is determined by the most competent group member. Therefore, the effect of group size on performance is a function of the proportion of individuals who may be expected to have the ability to perform the task, assuming, of course, that group membership is random with respect to task abilities. Group performance may be expected to be a negatively accelerated function of group size; that is, increasing the size of the group should result in an increase in group performance up to some maximum beyond which additional members have no added effect, either because the most competent cannot be readily recognized or because the group is already large enough to ensure inclusion of at least one member capable of completing the task efficiently. This effect has been observed in a study conducted by Ziller (1957b). He asked groups of two, three, and six persons to estimate the number of dots on a card and to choose from a list of fifteen facts the four that were most critical for solving a complex problem. It was found that groups of three were 74 percent more accurate than two-person groups, and six persons were 83 percent more accurate than two person groups, on the dot task; similarly, on the fact selection task three persons were 51 percent better and six persons only 69 percent better than two persons. A somewhat more extensive examination of the effects of group size on the completion of disjunctive tasks was conducted by Frank and Anderson (1971). Groups of two, three, five, and eight persons worked on production tasks (i.e., tasks that require the generation of images or ideas). Tasks were made either disjunctive or conjunctive by instructions. For the disjunctive tasks, group members were told that as soon as any member completed a task the group could move on to the next one; for the conjunctive tasks, group members were told that each member of the group must complete the task before the group could move on to the next one. The average number of disjunctive tasks completed in a fifteen-minute work period increased with group size, but the increase was not proportional to the number of persons in the group. That is, the number of tasks completed *per person* decreased with increasing group size.

Laughlin, Kerr, Davis, Halff, and Marciniak (1975) compared groups of varying sizes with respect to performance on the Terman Concept Mastery Test, which may be regarded as a series of disjunctive tasks. Performance of high-ability persons increased with group size (means were

59.59, 66.57, 69.10, and 75.88 for groups of 2, 3, 4, and 5 persons, respectively). The mean score for individuals was 52.82. Size had no significant effect on the performance of low-ability groups. Group performance on IQ test items as a function of group size was also examined in two- and three-person groups of fourth- and fifth-grade students (Egerbladh, 1976). Again, performance increased with increasing group size.

Still another type of disjunctive task was employed by Bray, Kerr, and Atkin (1978). This task required that an exact amount of gold dust (e.g., 27 ounces) be removed from a safe using three containers (e.g., containers holding 9 ounces, 42 ounces, and 6 ounces). Tasks were either easy, medium in difficulty, or difficult, and groups were composed of either low-, medium-, or high-ability members. Group size ranged from one to ten. With each level of task difficulty and member ability, group performance increased with increasing group size, although the magnitude of the increase varied with other conditions. Clearly, when the task is disjunctive, increasing the size of the group may be expected to improve the performance of the group.

**Conjunctive Tasks**    When the task is conjunctive, everyone in the group must accomplish the task, and performance depends on the performance of the least competent group member. When the group must complete this kind of task, the probability that the group will have at least one group member who cannot succeed increases with group size; therefore, the larger the group the lower the probability that it will be able to complete the task successfully. For example, consider a group of Boy Scouts who must march 5 miles in the shortest possible time. The speed of the group will be determined by the slowest scout in the group. Data reported by Frank and Anderson (1971) provide some evidence on this hypothesis. Productivity on conjunctive tasks generally decreased with size, but the decrease was less than expected by Steiner's theory.

The task faced by juries may also be considered a conjunctive task, since all members must agree to the verdict. At least two studies have examined the effects of jury size on the decision-making process. The first study found no differences between six- and twelve-person juries with respect to verdict, although the larger groups deliberated longer and took more polls before reaching a decision (Davis, Kerr, Atkin, Holt, & Meek, 1975). In the second study, it was found that jury size had no effect when apparent guilt was low, but six-person juries were significantly more likely to convict than twelve-person juries when apparent guilt was high (Valenti & Downing, 1975). It is somewhat unclear what outcome constitutes effective group performance in these experiments, but it is apparent that size is affecting the group process.

The evidence concerning the effects of group size on group perform-ance of conjunctive tasks is sparse and less consistent than that with respect to additive and disjunctive tasks. This may be because conjunctive tasks are more ambiguously identifiable than other types, or because research has not been adequately designed and carried out. In any case, we will return to this question in Chapter 10.

In summary, the size of the group influences the amount and distribution of participation in the group, the probability that a leader will emerge and be accepted by other group members, the members' reactions to the group, and the probability that the group will achieve consensus. As a partial consequence of these effects, group performance varies with group size. Group effectiveness increases with group size (up to some maximum level) when the group's task is either additive or disjunctive, although the increase is ordinarily not as great as the increase in resources available to the group. Group effectiveness usually decreases with group size when the group's task is conjunctive. All these effects on group process may be modified by other variables, such as the personal characteristics of group members and the structure of the group.

## BIOGRAPHICAL CHARACTERISTICS OF GROUP MEMBERS

This category includes a wide range of background influences, some of which are biological (for example, age and sex) and some are more sociological (for example, education and socioeconomic status). Although the effects of such characteristics upon group process are pervasive, they are often difficult to identify and document. Consequently, there are many unanswered questions concerning them. The evidence available, however, makes it clear that they are important in the determination of group process.

### Chronological Age

It is obvious that persons of different ages behave differently; children do not act like adults, although some adults may behave like children. Nevertheless, it is of interest to see how age differences are reflected in group behavior. Unfortunately, age has been a neglected variable in the study of group behavior, perhaps because its effects are so obvious that controlled studies seem unnecessary. In spite of this neglect, there are some significant studies relative to age effects, and the results of controlled investigations do not always agree with the "obvious."

**Age and Interaction Behaviors**  Age is an important determinant of the kinds of behaviors an individual group member will display in the group. The kinds of contacts individuals make, the friendships resulting from such contacts, and the quality of behavior engaged in during contacts have been shown to vary with the age of group members. As early as 1932 it was noted in an observational study that the number and percentage of social contacts mentioned by individuals increased with chronological age (Beaver, 1932). Social participation in school activities was also found to correlate with age (Parten, 1932), and an observational study by Green (1933b) revealed that the amount of group play activity increased with age. A somewhat more sophisticated motion-picture technique was used to study the behavior of preschool children of three age groups (Bernhardt, Millichamp, Charles, & McFarland, 1937). This investigation failed to show the usual correlation between age and frequency of social contacts, perhaps because of the particular age groups studied. However, qualitative differences as a function of age were observed. With increasing age there was a tendency to restrict contacts to certain individuals and to certain types of contact and to increase the complexity of the interaction pattern.

The increasing complexity of interaction patterns with increasing age has been reported by several other investigators. For example, Dymond, Hughes, and Raabe (1952) measured empathy in two age groups and found that 11-year-olds had greater perceptive ability than 7-year-olds. The older children were more sensitive to the feelings of others than the younger children, a difference which appeared to be related to age differences in popularity. Similarly, Leuba (1933) studied the behavior of children aged 2 to 6 years. Children worked either alone or together on a pegboard task which required that they place pegs in holes as rapidly as possible. Evidences of rivalry did not appear before the age of 5; that is, children did not appear to be sensitive to the behavior of others before that age. Observations of behavior in nursery schools and in kindergarten have revealed that dominating behavior decreases with age, whereas integrative behavior increases with age (Anderson, 1939). This might also be interpreted as showing an increased sensitivity to others and an increased tendency toward more complex behavior patterns with increasing age.

Changing patterns of interaction as a function of age may also be observed with respect to simultaneous talking and interruptions of others. Tabulations of the frequency of simultaneous talking and interruptions in groups ranging in age from 5 to 20 years revealed systematic decreases in both types of verbal behavior (Smith, 1977). Another author (Newman, 1976) analyzed the development of interpersonal skills from infancy through later adolescence and noted that egocentric behavior decreased as the child developed language skills and developed the ability to comprehend rules and to compromise. Later, as the individual begins to try to establish independence from authorities, egocentrism may be heightened. By later adolescence, the person typically consolidates interpersonal style and becomes aware of this style and of his or her own impact on others.

   Differences among older age groups have also been reported. Bass, Wurster, Doll, and Clair (1953) studied behavior in seven sororities and found that older women were more active in extracurricular pursuits than younger women (r = .53 to .60) and were esteemed more highly by their sorority sisters (r = .20 to .28). Although these correlations are low, they indicate that age is a significant variable not only in children's groups but also in adult groups. Finally, Chaubey (1974) found that older adults (45 years of age or older) exemplified less risk-taking than boys (aged 10 to 15 years) or younger adults (20 to 30 years of age). This difference was attributed to the greater achievement motivation of the younger persons.

   **Age and Leadership**   Leadership behavior as a function of age has been studied extensively by investigators using the trait approach to the study of leadership. Unfortunately, the investigations have differed in the way leadership was defined, the kinds of groups studied, and the method of study. The definition of leadership commonly varied with the experimental method. For example, the two most common methods of investigation were (1) the selection of leaders and nonleaders, who were then compared with respect to age (or other characteristic of interest to the investigator), and (2) the correlation of ratings of leadership ability with chronological age (or other trait). When the first method was used, there was a marked tendency to define the leader as the person who occupied a position of leadership, such as the foreman of a factory work group or the president of an organization. When the second method was chosen, there was a strong tendency to define the leader as the person so named by the members of his or her group or by superiors in his or her organization. The groups represented by these studies also varied greatly, ranging from social groups, such as fraternities or sororities, to formal organizations, such as industrial work groups. It is well to keep these differences in mind when considering the data obtained from such studies.

   Stogdill (1948) reviewed trait studies of leadership and found nineteen investigations that had examined the relationship between age and leadership. The findings were quite inconsistent, although more often than not leaders were found to be older than nonleaders. Specifically, ten studies reported that leaders were older than nonleaders, six that leaders were younger than nonleaders, two that there was no age difference between leaders and nonleaders, and one that age differences depended upon the particular situation. Reported correlations between leadership effectiveness and chronological age ranged from −.37 to .71. In view of the large differences in the definition of leader, the kind of group, the measure of leadership effectiveness, etc., it is not surprising that the findings were so inconsistent. Nevertheless, these results fail to support the hypothesis that there is a strong relationship between age and leadership. To the extent that there is such a relationship, it probably means only that an individual must live long enough to achieve his or her leadership potential. Unless one marries the boss's daughter, time is required to attain a position of leadership in most ongoing groups.

**Age and Conformity**   Conformity is one of the most prominent forms of behavior in groups. When individuals interact, pressures toward uniformity are generated and the individual member tends to behave in a manner which conforms to that of the modal group member. Although blind, unreasoning conformity can be debilitating, in most instances conformity serves the useful function of establishing order and stability in our interactions with others. For example, if every automobile driver decided for himself or herself which side of the road to drive on, it would be impossible for anyone to move efficiently from place to place. The fact that most of us conform to normative expectations in our interactions with others means there is order in a world that otherwise would be chaotic, and this order permits us to respond appropriately to the demands of the social situation on most occasions.

Conformity behavior is usually assumed to be the result of developmental processes (Berg & Bass, 1961). At minimum, the individual must learn the norms of the group or groups of which he or she is a member, and presumably this learning occurs as a part of the socialization process; that is, the individual, while growing older, learns more and more about group norms. Hence, it might be expected that conformity would increase with increasing age, at least up to some minimum age level. However, Piaget's extensive research (1954) with children suggests that although social development progresses through an orderly sequence of stages, the consequences for conformity behavior may not be linear. Piaget's analysis of the way the child learns the "rules of the game" indicates that at an early age the child is not influenced by rules, but gradually begins to follow them more and more until about age 11 or 12. At about this age, the child internalizes the rules and recognizes that they are not absolutes, that they are made for convenience, and hence can be broken or modified whenever this appears desirable. This kind of evidence led Costanzo and Shaw (1966) to hypothesize a curvilinear relationship between age and conformity, with conformity increasing to a maximum at about age 12 and decreasing thereafter.

The experimental data reported by other investigators appear to be somewhat less than consistent. For example, Marple (1933) found that high school students conformed more to majority or expert opinion than either college students or adults, and Patel and Gordon (1960) reported that conformity decreased from the tenth to the twelfth grade. Both studies concerned primarily postadolescent age groups. A study by Berenda (1950) conducted in a classroom revealed that subjects in a 7- to 10-year age group conformed more than those in a 10- to 13-year group. This finding would be contrary to the Costanzo-Shaw hypothesis except that social pressure was exerted either by the brightest children in the class or by the teacher. Hence there is some question whether the sources of pressure in these studies can be interpreted as normative.

A more extensive range of ages was studied by Iscoe, Williams, and Harvey (1963). They examined four age groups (7-, 9-, 12-, and 15-year-olds) in a simulated conformity situation. Subjects were asked to count the number of metronome clicks in a series after being confronted by unanimously incorrect judgments by simulated group members. Conformity of females increased up to age 12 followed by a decrease at age 15, whereas that of males increased up to age 12 with no significant change from age 12 to 15.

Costanzo and Shaw (1966) tested their hypothesis by examining conformity behavior in groups ranging in age from 7 to 21 years. Since this is a wider age range than has been examined in other investigations, their procedure will be presented in some detail. The experimental design included both male and female subjects drawn from four age groups. The four age groups were: 7 to 9 years, 11 to 13 years, 15 to 17 years, and 19 to 21 years. They were tested with the Crutchfield apparatus (described in Chapter 8, see page 281) in which subjects are seated in isolated booths, but receive simulated information about the choices of others. The stimuli used were the Asch lines, which require that the subject choose which one of three lines is the same length as the standard. Subjects were tested in four-person groups, each of which was homogeneous with regard to sex. The results of the study, shown in Figure 6-2, indicate that conformity increased with age to a maximum level at age 11 to 13 and decreased thereafter, in close agreement with the hypothesis that age and conformity are curvilinearly related. This conclusion is probably valid only when group pressure is exerted by peers. When pressure is exerted by authority figures, for example, the degree of conformity might be negatively related to age, or the age of maximum conformity might be shifted toward lower age levels. More research is needed before this question can be answered definitely.

In summary, there is good evidence that the chronological age of the group member is related to several aspects of group interaction. With increasing age, the individual has an increasing number of contacts with others, and there is a change toward greater selectivity of contacts and greater complexity of the interaction pattern. Conformity increases to a maximum at about age 12 and decreases thereafter, at least in peer groups. There is little evidence that age and leadership are related in any simple way. To the extent that age is related to behavior in groups, it provides the time required for the individual to learn appropriate social responses. That

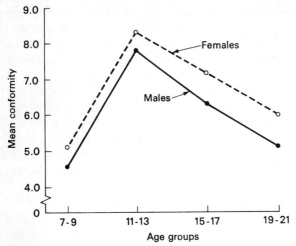

**Figure 6-2** Mean conformity as a function of age. (Reprinted with permission from P. R. Costanzo & M. E. Shaw. Conformity as a function of age level. *Child Development*, 1966, **37**, 967–975.)

is, in most cases it is not the mere fact the individual has aged that is important, but rather that he or she has had greater experience in social situations.

### Sex of Group Members

The sex of the individual group member is another fairly obvious determinant of behavior in groups. Women and men behave differently in groups, and this has important implications for group process. Differences in behavior are usually assumed to be due to role differences imposed upon men and women by the culture in which they live. Traditional sex roles in American society imply that males should be aggressive, assertive, domineering, and task-oriented; females should be passive, submissive, nurturant, and person-oriented (Wiley, 1973). Extensive studies of cultural influences on sex roles (Mead, 1949) strongly indicate that role differences are molded by culture during infancy and childhood. The results of such cultural influences are far-reaching and strongly affect the basic personality characteristics of men and women. For example, a comprehensive study of sex differences in personality (Terman & Miles, 1936) revealed that males are more aggressive, self-assertive, and fearless. They are also likely to display more roughness of manner, language, and sentiments than women. On the other hand, women are likely to express themselves as more compassionate, sympathetic, fastidious, and emotional than men. These findings are of course limited to the American culture in 1936. However, recent findings regarding sex differences in behavior suggest that differences in male and female personalities still exist, despite the changing sex roles of men and women.

As with age differences, relatively little careful research has been directed toward identification of the consequences of sex differences for group interaction. The following discussion indicates some of the differences in the behavior of males and females in groups.

**Sex and Interaction Behaviors**   We have already noted in Chapter 5 that women typically choose closer interperson distances than men. It has also been found that males react more negatively to uninvited face-to-face approach than females (Fisher & Byrne, 1975) and that males respond more quickly to close approach than females (Krail & Leventhal, 1976). The sex differences in personality mentioned above suggest some of the differences that might be expected in interaction behaviors. Since males are generally more aggressive and self-assertive than females, we might expect them to behave more aggressively in groups, and indeed this is the case. McGuire (1973) made time-sampling observations of aggressive behaviors in natural settings and found that males were more aggressive than females, although high aggressive males tended to be unpopular and high aggressive females more popular than their less aggressive counterparts. Among young children, boys are more "quarrelsome" than girls, and the amount of quarreling among girls reaches a peak and declines earlier than among boys (Green, 1933a). A comparable difference has been observed among adults. For example, Ort (1950) observed that females report fewer role conflicts in marriage than do men. Partly because of these sex differences in aggressive-assertive behavior, men are often seen as more influential in a group than are women (Stewart, 1947). The research dealing with coalition formation (see Chapter 4) also reveals sex differences that are consistent with greater ascendancy by men. It will be recalled that women more often than men adopt an anticompetitive norm and attempt to operate so that everyone will benefit. For example, Uesugi and Vinacke (1963) found that women subjects adopted rotation systems and alliances which included everybody, in contrast to men subjects who made the best deals they could under the circumstances. Black and Higbee (1973) reported that males exploited unconditionally cooperative opponents more when the opponent was relatively powerful than when he was relatively weak, whereas females were more exploitative when the opponent had relatively little power. When the opponent could retaliate, males were more exploitative when the opponent had relatively little power, whereas females were less exploitative regardless of the opponent's power position. Men vary their responses to threats of retaliation according to the magnitude of the threat, but females appear to become more submissive regardless of degree of threat.

The general conclusion that women are less aggressive than men has been questioned (de Gloria & de Ridder, 1979). In a study of norm violation versus norm compliance, it was observed that although both men and women aggressed more when the norm was violated than when it was not, men and women differed in the ways they responded to frequency of norm violation. When norm violations were relatively infrequent, men were more aggressive than women, but when norms were violated more frequently, women were more aggressive than men. One might conclude that women are less easily stimulated to aggress than men but they react more strongly than men when they finally decide to respond.

Interaction is frequently mediated through nonverbal communication, such as body orientation and eye contact. Communication through the eyes is especially relevant to interpersonal behavior, as evidenced by the significance placed upon eye contact in different cultures. In the American culture, a man who fails to "look you in the eye" is not to be trusted; what red-blooded American male has not been stirred by the "come-hither look" in the eyes of an attractive female? In other cultures, eye contact may be avoided because of various social taboos. For example, among certain African tribes a man may not look at his mother-in-law. Experimental investigations have revealed the expected sex differences in the frequency of eye contact in social situations. Exline (1963) observed sixteen groups of three men and sixteen groups of three women as they attempted to decide upon the best name for a new soap product. Some of the groups were composed of persons high on need for affiliation, and some of persons low on this need. Also, half of the groups were given instructions designed to arouse competitive motivations, and half were given instructions designed to arouse cooperative motivations. Two observers recorded the frequency of mutual eye contact during the discussions. Females engaged in greater visual interaction than did males under all conditions. However, the effects of sex, affiliation, and competitive-cooperative instructions on mutual visual interaction were interrelated. Competition seemed to inhibit mutual glances among high affiliators and to increase visual interaction among low affiliators. This effect was much stronger in female than in male groups. In a follow-up investigation, Exline, Gray, and Schuette (1965) reported that females look at others more than males, regardless of the sex of the other person.

In contrast to the findings when individuals are engaged in focused interaction, there appear to be no sex differences in mutual eye contact when interaction is unfocused (Coutts & Schneider, 1975). Dyads were observed as they waited to participate in an "audio discrimination acuity" study, during which time they were instructed to neither talk nor walk around the room. Records of eye contact revealed no difference between men and women in amount of looking, although women received more glances than men.

The eye contact studies have been useful in showing a sex difference in the amount of visual interaction, but there is little sound data concerning the meaning of eye contact for men versus women. Undoubtedly the meaning of mutual glances is different for men and women, depending upon the circumstances surrounding the interaction. Studies of these differences are badly needed.

There is a common belief that women talk more than men, and research data provide some support for this belief. For instance, dyads were videotaped as they waited for the experimenter (Ickes & Barnes, 1977). Tapes were then analyzed to obtain behavioral measures of the interaction. There was greater involvement and affiliation in the female dyads than in the male dyads; females talked more frequently (mean = 26.9) than males (mean = 14.7), and their verbalizations were of longer duration (means were 97.1 seconds for females vs. 39.2 seconds for males). However, the degree of verbal interaction by men and women may be influenced by other variables. In self-study groups, males and females appear to be affected differentially by the styles of authority figures (Wright, 1976). When the group leader was relatively responsive to group members (as indicated by eye contact, facial expressions, laughing at jokes, etc.), males were more verbally active than females, speaking an average of 59 percent of the time as compared with approximately 45 percent of the time for females. When the leader was not so responsive, females talked more than males.

Finally, there is evidence that females socialize more intensely in new environments than men (Wheeler & Nezlek, 1977). First-year college students were asked to keep records of their social interactions for two weeks early in the fall semester and for two weeks late in the spring semester. In the fall, females had more interactions per day, but females decreased time per day in interaction more than did males. This decrease was due primarily to reduced length of interaction. Men initiated more interactions with women than vice versa, but females had a higher percentage of their interactions with the opposite sex and they had longer opposite-sex interactions than males.

It is very clear from these several studies that males and females differ in their social interactions. These differences may also be expected to influence other aspects of group behavior, such as conformity behavior and leadership. Since these differences are probably due to different socialization patterns for males and females, they may disappear as differences between expected sex roles narrow.

**Sex and Conformity**     In the previous section it was stated that men are usually more dominant and self-assertive than women. It has also been noted (Reitan & Shaw, 1964) that in the American society females play a relatively submissive role, whereas men play a relatively dominant role.

These considerations suggest that women should conform to the norms of the groups more than men, and experimental evidence supports this expectation (e.g., Beloff, 1958; Costanzo & Shaw, 1966; Reitan & Shaw, 1964; Tuddenham, 1958). The regularity of sex differences in conformity can be seen clearly in Figure 6-2.

Sex differences in conformity behavior may simply reflect cultural differences in sex roles, as suggested above, or they may reflect other cultural influences. For example, it has been suggested that there exists in our society a stereotypical belief that men are superior to women in certain areas of cognitive functioning (Tuddenham, Macbride, & Zahn, 1958). If men are seen as more competent, then it is not surprising that they conform less than women. In line with these expectations, Tuddenham et al. reported that women were more conforming when they were concerned about their answers not appearing peculiar to others, whereas men conformed more when they were concerned about completing the task quickly. This becomes especially significant in explaining sex differences in conformity behavior when the different orientations of men and women are considered. Berg and Bass (1961) cited evidence that college men tend to be task-oriented and concerned with getting the task completed, whereas college women tend to be much more interaction-oriented and concerned with establishing harmonious relations with others. On the other hand, Sistrunk and McDavid (1971) have shown that sex differences in conformity behavior may depend upon the kind of task that the group is trying to complete. They found that when the task was more appropriate for the masculine role, females conformed more than males; but when the task was more appropriate for the feminine role, males conformed more than females. These data suggest that the relation of conformity behavior to role prescriptions may be much more complex than suggested by the male-dominant, female-submissive formulation.

Clearly, in many situations females are more conforming than males. It is probable that these differences are due to the differential cultural influences exerted upon men and women. Regardless of the causes of this sex difference, however, it is a significant factor in the determination of group process.

## Physical Characteristics of Group Members

Physical characteristics, such as size, weight, height, and general health, influence the behavior of the individual group member and the responses of other group members to him or her. Relative to other variables, these factors are generally weak and can be overcome by the effects of more powerful variables such as personality and ability. Nevertheless, it is worthwhile to examine briefly the consequences of physical differences among group members.

**Size of Group Members**   Early studies of leadership indicated quite clearly that physical size is related to the attainment of leadership status. In his review of studies of personal factors in leadership, Stogdill (1948) found a generally positive relationship between leadership and weight, height, and measures of physique. Fourteen studies investigated the relation between height and leadership; nine found leaders taller than nonleaders, two found leaders shorter, two reported no difference, and one reported that differences depended upon the situation. Correlations between leadership status and height ranged from $-.13$ to .71. Eleven studies examined weight in relation to leadership. Seven reported that leaders were heavier than nonleaders, two that leaders were lighter than nonleaders, and two that there was no difference in weight between leaders and nonleaders. Reported correlations averaged .23. Twenty-five investigations dealt with general physical characteristics, with twenty-one reporting a positive relationship between physique and leadership, and four reporting that physique was not a factor. Reported correlations between leadership and measures of physique ranged from .11 to .62. Obviously, all these factors are intercorrelated; tall men tend to be heavier than short men, for example. Nevertheless, these findings indicate that physically superior men have a slightly better chance of *becoming* leaders than others. Exceptions to this general rule come readily to mind. For example, Napoleon, Stalin, and Hitler were all short and relatively small men; however, it is important to note that although size is related to becoming a leader, there is no evidence that size is related to the *performance* of leaders.

Relatively little attention has been devoted to the investigation of the effects of physical size on other aspects of group behavior, although it is evident that size may be a variable in determining acceptability of an individual to others. It is a common observation that the tall, handsome man or the beautiful woman elicits a more favorable response from others than the homely man or ugly woman. The skinny group member or the overweight individual may be less acceptable in groups, and hence less effective as a group member. Indeed, Burgess and Cottrell (1939) found that the wife being overweight correlated negatively with marital adjustment. However this set of variables seems to have been generally neglected by researchers.

**Other Physical Characteristics**   Only a few other physical characteristics have been investigated with respect to interpersonal behavior. Two observational studies were conducted to investigate subcultural differences in the use of gaze direction as a regulatory mechanism in conversations (LaFrance & Mayo, 1976). Blacks as compared with whites revealed less other-directed gaze during listening than during speaking, but the overall amount of looking was the same for blacks and whites. Another study comparing blacks and whites revealed no significant differences on a variety of measures (Edwards, 1974). Although there appear to be some differences between blacks and whites, they are minimal and probably merely the consequence of different cultural backgrounds.

Finally, one study examined differences in social skills of physically attractive and unattractive persons (Goldman & Lewis, 1977). College students engaged in a telephone conversation with an opposite-sex partner and rated them for social skill, anxiety, liking, and desirability for future interaction. Participants were rated for physical attractiveness by three independent judges. The more physically attractive persons were rated by their telephone partners as more socially skillful and more likeable than less attractive participants.

It is obvious that physical characteristics of individuals affect their behaviors when interacting with others. The source of these effects is unclear, but it is likely that physical characteristics influence the behavior of others toward the individual, in turn influencing the person's behavior in interpersonal situations.

## ABILITIES OF GROUP MEMBERS

In the preceding discussions, primary concern has been with the characteristics which determine what the individual may *choose* to do in group situations. But equally important is the question of what the individual *can* do. The abilities of the group member determine how effectively that member can perform the acts that he or she wishes to perform in the group, and this in turn influences how others react to him or her as a group member. Abilities, of course, may be general (intelligence) or they may be specific to the particular situation or task faced by the group.

### Intelligence of Group Members

When we discuss the effects of intelligence upon group process, we are referring to "test intelligence," or the general ability that is measured by intelligence tests. In a sense, this intelligence is an estimate of the individual's ability to deal with a variety of situations and problems. It is presumed to be determined by both innate ability and the experiences that the individual has had during his or her lifetime. The data regarding this general ability and behavior in groups are based upon measures of intelligence obtained by means of standard intelligence tests.

As in the case of biographical characteristics, the most extensive studies involving intelligence and group behavior have been in the field of leadership. Stogdill (1948) identified thirty-two studies dealing with the relationship between intelligence and leadership. Of these, twenty-two found that leaders were brighter than nonleaders, five that leaders and nonleaders were not different in intellectual ability, and five that too great a difference between the leader and other group members was undesirable from the standpoint of effectiveness. All reported correlations between intelligence and leadership ability were positive (average r = .28). Similar results have been reported in studies conducted since that review was completed. For example, Bass and Wurster (1953a, 1953b) examined the correlations between intelligence and leaderless group discussion (LGD) scores of oil refinery supervisors and obtained correlations ranging from .34 to .61. Hollander (1954) found that the American Council on Education (ACE) test scores of 268 naval cadets in preflight school correlated .30 with leader choice scores, i.e., the extent to which the cadet was named as leader by his group. These data make it clear that there is a low positive correlation between tested intelligence and leadership behavior. However, emphasis should be placed upon the word *low* in the above statement. It seems reasonable to conclude that intelligence accounts for approximately 10 percent of the variance among leadership scores.

Intelligence has also been found to be related to general activity, popularity, and conformity of individual group members. Bass et al. (1953) reported low positive correlations between general participation in LGD discussions and ACE scores (r = .21), and Zeleny (1939a) reported similar findings. A positive relationship between intelligence and popularity was found by Mill (1953). Mann (1959), in a review of the literature, reported that of thirteen studies reviewed, 81 percent indicated a positive relationship between intelligence and popularity. However, caution must be used in interpreting these results, first, because Mann included studies using a variety of measures of intelligence, such as scholastic grade-point average, and, second, because the highest correlation reported was only .37, with the median correlation about .10.

Studies of the effects of intelligence on conformity behavior are somewhat more convincing. Crutchfield (1955) reported a correlation of −.63 between the "assessment staff's rating of intellectual competence" and estimates of conformity, and a correlation of −.51 between the Concept Mastery Test (a measure of superior mental ability) and conformity. Nakamura (1958) obtained similar results using the analogies portion of the Concept Mastery Test as the measure of intelligence. Correlations between intelligence and conformity ranged from −.22 to −.44. Results consistent with the hypothesis that conformity and intelligence are negatively correlated have also been reported by Wyer (1967).

In summary, the evidence indicates that the more intelligent individual tends to be more active and less conforming in groups than the less intelligent person. As a partial consequence, he or she is more effective as a leader than the less intelligent group member. These effects are generally weak and probably can be outweighed by other factors.

### Specific Abilities of Group Members

Since intelligence as measured by intelligence tests is a composite of specific abilities, it is not surprising that its effects upon group behavior are somewhat variable and less than robust. Specific abilities are more directly related to behaviors in the group and hence exert a more powerful effect upon group process. The specific abilities that are of interest include not only those which may be reflected in general ability, but also special skills and knowledges. As we shall see, some of these special knowledges are essentially unrelated to general ability, although the use that the individual makes of them may be determined in part by intelligence.

Supervisory aptitude as measured by pencil-and-paper tests was examined by Bass and Wurster (1953b) in their study of oil refinery supervisors. They found correlations between supervisory aptitude scores and LGD scores ranging from .07 to .54, with an average r = .30. The higher correlation was between supervisory aptitude and LGD scores derived from a case history discussion task, whereas the lower correlation was between aptitude scores and LGD scores derived from a group discussion of in-plant leader specifications. General education and LGD scores were also found to be positively related (r = .47 to .63).

The relation between task-specific ability and effective leadership was also investigated by Palmer (1962a, 1962b). Ability with respect to the group task was measured by a multiple-choice test, after which subjects worked at the task in four- or five-person groups. Successful leadership was defined as the degree to which the individual influenced the group's decision, and effective leadership was defined as the exchange of accurate information. Task ability correlated .66 with successful leadership and .83 with effective leadership.

These task-related abilities undoubtedly reflect the possession of special knowledges and skills which enable the individual to aid the group in achieving its goal. This has been demonstrated in a number of studies in which the individual group member was provided with task-relevant information by the experimenter. For example, Maier (1950, 1953) has shown that a leader who knows the correct solution to the group problem is more effective in leading a group to the solution than is a leader who does not know the solution. Similarly, Shevitz (1955) has shown that the exclusive possession of expert knowledge results in more attempts to lead and higher status in the group. A series of investigations have shown that the amount of influence an individual has in the group, the individual's satisfaction with the group, and the amount of effort he or she expends in helping the group achieve its goal—all are related to the probability that the individual's information will lead the group to a valid conclusion if it is accepted by the group (M. E. Shaw, 1961a; Shaw & Penrod, 1962a; Shaw & Penrod, 1962b). The performance of the group also varies directly with the probability that an informed member's information will lead to the correct solution if accepted by the group. However, if there is reason to believe that the informed group member is not to be trusted or that his information is incorrect, he will be unable to use his knowledge to aid the group in achieving its goal (Shaw & Penrod, 1962a; Shaw & Penrod, 1962b).

In general, if an individual has specific abilities that are related to the group task, he or she will be more active in the group, will make more contributions to the group's attempts to complete the task, and will have more influence on the group's decisions. As a consequence of these behavioral effects, the individual is more likely to emerge as a leader and the group's performance is improved. The individual is better satisfied with the group's cooperation and performance, probably because he or she is accorded a special place in the group and because the group is more successful as a result of his or her contributions.

## PERSONALITY CHARACTERISTICS OF GROUP MEMBERS

As Haythorn (1968) noted, to say that personality characteristics are related to behavior is almost a tautology, because a personality trait is usually defined as a tendency or predisposition to behave in a particular manner in differing situations. Hence, to say that a person possesses a particular personality trait is equivalent to saying that we expect the person to behave in a particular way in many different situations. We do not necessarily expect that he or she will behave this way in *all* situations, nor do we always know precisely how the trait will be expressed. But to the extent that the personality characteristic exists, there should be some degree of behavior consistency.

Researchers have not neglected personality variables in the study of group behavior. In reviewing the literature, Mann (1959) found that researchers had used over 500 different measures of personality, and the list has grown since that review was conducted. Unfortunately, fewer than one-quarter of these measures were used in more than one investigation. Mann's findings lead to two possible conclusions: (1) There is a tremendously large number of different personality attributes, or (2) different investigators often use different names and measures for the same attribute. Although personality is exceedingly complex, it is doubtful that meaningful results or theories can be achieved by subdividing personality into so many parts. Furthermore, it is clear that basically the same characteristic is given many names and many different measures have been devised to measure it. Indeed, Mann concluded that empirical work indicates that the multitude of measured personality attributes can be subsumed under seven dimensions of personality. Although his dimensions may not be entirely accurate, it is evident that personality can be represented by fewer characteristics than have been employed in the past.

In the following discussion, the various personality characteristics that have been studied are grouped into five broad categories or classes: interpersonal orientation, social sensitivity, ascendant tendencies, dependability, and emotional stability. These five categories correspond reasonably well to those Mann identified, excluding intelligence and masculinity-femininity. The effects of intelligence have already been discussed; data concerning the effects of masculinity-femininity are sparse and generally contribute very little to our understanding of group process. However, the labels listed above more nearly reflect the kinds of characteristics included in the five categories.

### Interpersonal Orientation and Group Processes

An individual typically adopts a particular way or ways of viewing or reacting to other persons. This interpersonal orientation is reflected in the individual's typical behavior toward others in a variety of situations, although, of course, it does not by itself determine his or her behavior. It is only one of several personality attributes that, along with many nonpersonality factors, influence his or her behavior. Nevertheless, empirical investigations have revealed consistent effects of the group member's interpersonal orientation on group process and on the individual's behavior in the group.

The personality characteristics listed in Table 6-1 are subsumed under the general orientation category, along with some representative findings concerning the relationships among characteristics and behaviors. Whenever available, the correlations between personality measures and behavioral measures are given; in other cases, only the direction of the relationship can be indicated. As might be expected, the magnitudes of the correlations are not great, but the pattern of relationships is quite consistent.

**Authoritarianism**   Authoritarian persons believe that it is right and proper that there should be status and power differences among persons. It is "in the nature of things" that some persons occupy more powerful positions than others. Therefore, when authoritarians are in a position of authority and power, they use their power. They are demanding, directive, and controlling in their relations with those less powerful than themselves.

**Table 6-1    Relationships between Interpersonal Orientation and Group Processes**

| Personality characteristic | Behavior variable | Relationship | Reference |
|---|---|---|---|
| Approval-orientation | Performance | Positive | Sorrentino & Sheppard, 1978 |
| Authoritarianism | Conformity | .39 | Crutchfield, 1955 |
| Authoritarianism | Conformity | Positive | Beloff, 1958 |
| Authoritarianism | Conformity | .48 | Nadler, 1959 |
| Adventurous cyclothymia | Cohesiveness | .29 | Haythorn, 1953 |
| Adventurous cyclothymia | Social interaction | .62 | Haythorn, 1953 |
| Cyclothymia | Cohesiveness | .37 | Haythorn, 1953 |
| Cyclothymia | Competitiveness | −.45 | Haythorn, 1953 |
| Cyclothymia | Morale | .24 | Haythorn, 1953 |
| Expressed inclusion | Verbal participation | Positive | Markel, Bein, Campbell, & Shaw, 1976 |
| Paranoid schizothymia | Cohesiveness | −.69 | Haythorn, 1953 |
| Paranoid schizothymia | Friendliness | −.57 | Haythorn, 1953 |
| Message/source orientation | Conformity source | Message > | McDavid, 1959 |

When they are in a subordinate position, they are submissive and compliant; they accept their subordinate roles as natural and appropriate. Nonauthoritarians (or equalitarians), on the other hand, believe that there should not be status and power differences among individuals; hence they reject both the superior and the subordinate roles. There is some doubt concerning the extent to which true authoritarians or true nonauthoritarians actually exist in the general population. It seems likely that the behavior of individuals varies in the extent to which it reflects authoritarian tendencies.

Authoritarianism is usually measured by the California F-scale or some variation of it (Adorno, Frenkel-Brunswik, Levinson, & Sanford, 1950). This scale has been criticized because agreement with statements in it always reflects authoritarianism, and hence the score may be contaminated by acquiescence, and because it correlates negatively with intelligence. Nevertheless, it has been shown that the scores earned by individuals correlate in the expected way with behavior in groups (Haythorn, Couch, Haefner, Langham, & Carter, 1956a). For example, leaders emerging in groups composed of highly authoritarian persons behaved more autocratically than leaders emerging in groups composed of highly nonauthoritarian individuals. More will be said about this research in Chapter 7.

Also implicit in the concept of authoritarianism is the notion of adherence to rules and norms of the group. Therefore, it follows that the authoritarian should show greater conformity behavior when faced with a unanimous majority judgment. The data cited in Table 6-1 show that this expectation has been verified by research. Furthermore, this correlation cannot be completely accounted for by the common correlation of F-scale scores and intelligence scores with conformity.

In general, there is evidence that the authoritarian behaves differently from the nonauthoritarian in group situations. The authoritarian is autocratic and demanding and tends to conform to the norms of the group more closely than the nonauthoritarian. However, the most significant effects of authoritarianism are consequences of the particular combinations of individuals in the group and the kind of structure the group has established or had imposed upon it. These effects will be discussed in subsequent chapters.

**Approach-Avoidance Tendencies**   The characteristics labeled cyclothymia, adventurous cyclothymia, and paranoid schizothymia in Table 6-1 refer to a person's tendency to approach (like, esteem, trust) or to avoid (dislike, distrust) other people. Persons who score high on measures of cyclothymia tend to be cooperative, trustful, and adaptable; they prefer situations involving interaction with others. Low scorers prefer situations involving inanimate objects. Adventurous cyclothymia describes the extent to which individuals like people. Paranoid schizothymia refers to the avoidance aspect of interpersonal tendencies. Persons who score high on this dimension are said to be suspicious and jealous of others. They are dour and rigid and tend not to accept suggestions from others.

Persons who are highly motivated to gain approval from others behave differently from those who are concerned about rejection. For instance, Sorrentino and Sheppard (1978) found that approval-oriented swimmers had faster swimming speeds in group than in individual competition, but the reverse pattern was observed for rejection-threatened swimmers. Positive motivation appears to enhance performance in the presence of others, whereas negative motivation inhibits performance in the presence of others.

The representative studies cited in Table 6-1 reveal the expected pattern of correlations with respect to behavior in groups. Approach tendencies (cyclothymia, adventurous cyclothymia) enhance social interaction, cohesiveness, and morale in groups and suppress competitiveness. Avoidance tendencies (paranoid schizothymia) suppress friendliness and cohesiveness in groups.

## Social Sensitivity and Group Processes

Social sensitivity refers to the degree to which the individual perceives and responds to the needs, emotions, preferences, etc., of the other person. This sensitivity to others has been labeled empathy, insight, social judgment, and the like. It seems obvious that this personality attribute should lead to positive effects in the group. The representative studies listed in Table 6-2 are entirely consistent with this expectation. Empathy, social insight, social judgment, and similar characteristics are positively correlated with leadership attempts and success, acceptance in the group, amount of participation, and group effectiveness. Independence and resoluteness are essentially opposite to social sensitivity in that the person who possesses these characteristics is unconcerned about others. They correlate negatively with friendliness and social interaction, as expected.

The only trait listed in Table 6-2 that may require further discussion is *parmia*. This term was used by Cattell and Stice (1960) to label a dimension reflecting outgoing sociability and expressed emotional responsiveness. From their description, it seems evident that this personality characteristic is one aspect of social sensitivity; hence it is not surprising that parmia correlates positively with degree of acceptance in the group and amount of participation.

### Ascendant Tendencies and Group Processes

Individuals vary markedly in the extent to which they wish to be prominent in group situations, the degree to which they assert themselves as

**Table 6-2   Relationships between Social Sensitivity and Group Processes**

| Personality characteristic | Behavior variable | Relationship | Reference |
|---|---|---|---|
| Empathy | Leadership | .19 to .25 | Bell & Hall, 1954 |
| Empathy | Learning/self | .59, .90 | Neville, 1978 |
| Empathy | Emotional satisfaction | .64, .81 | Neville, 1978 |
| Empathy | Learning about processes | .51, .70 | Neville, 1978 |
| Independence, resoluteness | Friendliness | −.33 | Haythorn, 1953 |
| Independence, resoluteness | Social interaction | −.42 | Haythorn, 1953 |
| Parmia | Acceptance in group | .27 to .34 | Cattell & Stice, 1960 |
| Parmia | Participation | .16 to .28 | Cattell & Stice, 1960 |
| Sociability | Attempted leadership | .39 | Bass, Wurster, Doll, & Clair, 1953 |
| Sociability | LGD participation | .22 | Bass, McGehee, Hawkins, Young, & Gebel, 1953 |
| Sociability | Group performance | Positive | Bouchard, 1969 |
| Social activeness | Group effectiveness | .23 | Greer, 1955 |
| Social insight | Leadership | Positive | Stogdill, 1948 |
| Social judgment | Leadership success | .36 | Meyer, 1951 |
| Social skills | Leadership | .10 to .98 | Stogdill, 1948 |

individuals, and the extent to which they wish to dominate others. All these tendencies reflect an individualistic orientation, or at least a tendency to emphasize self in contrast to submission to oblivion in the group. This general ascendant tendency is referred to variously by such terms as *ascendancy, assertiveness, dominance,* and *individual prominence.* Although each of these terms refers to a slightly different aspect of the ascendant predisposition, there is enough commonality to consider them as a set.

Table 6-3 lists a number of investigations that have examined the relationships between ascendant tendencies and certain group processes. Persons who possess the personality characteristics associated with ascen-

**Table 6-3   Relationships between Ascendant Tendencies and Group Processes**

| Personality characteristic | Behavior variable | Relationship | Reference |
|---|---|---|---|
| Ascendance | Attempted leadership | .39 | Bass, Wurster, Doll, & Clair, 1953 |
| Ascendance | LGD participation | .37 | Bass, Wurster, Doll, & Clair, 1953 |
| Assertiveness | Assertive behavior | .42 | Borg, 1960 |
| Assertiveness | Popularity | .25 | Borg, 1960 |
| Assertiveness | Good follower role | −.22 | Borg, 1960 |
| Assertiveness | Rigid behavior | .22 | Borg, 1960 |
| Assertiveness | Creativity | .42 | Borg, 1960 |
| Assertiveness | Leadership | .39 | Borg, 1960 |
| Dominance | Conformity | −.23 to −.50 | McDavid & Sistrunk, 1964 |
| Dominance | Cohesiveness | .26 | Haythorn, 1953 |
| Dominance | Social interaction | .33 | Haythorn, 1953 |
| Dominance | Dissatisfaction with leader | −.19 | Cattell & Stice, 1960 |
| Dominance | Leader emergence | .17 to .18 | Cattell & Stice, 1960 |
| Dominance | Negative social-emotional remarks | .35 | Cattell & Stice, 1960 |
| Dominance | Leadership status | .20 to .29 | Stogdill, 1948 |
| Dominance | Choice of leadership role | Positive | Smith & Cook, 1973 |
| Dominance | Leadership emergence | Positive | Scioli, Dyson, & Fleitas, 1974 |
| Dominance | Communication | Positive | Watson, 1971 |
| Individual prominence | Influence on decisions | Positive | Shaw, 1959 |
| Individual prominence | Participation | Positive | Shaw, 1959 |
| Individual prominence | Performance | Positive | Shaw & Harkey, 1976 |

dancy generally behave as one would expect from the description of the dimension. They attempt leadership, participate in group activities, are assertive, and are creative. They tend to emerge as leaders, promote group cohesiveness, influence group decisions, conform to group norms, and are popular. They also tend to be dissatisfied with the leader—when the leader is someone else!

Two relationships shown in Table 6-3 do not appear to be consistent with the general pattern of relationships: Assertiveness was found to correlate positively with rigid behavior (Borg, 1960), and dominance correlated positively with negative social-emotional remarks (Cattell & Stice, 1960). Although Borg stated that the correlation between rigidity and assertiveness was predicted, it nevertheless does not appear to be consistent with a positive correlation between assertiveness and creativity, since rigidity and creativity are usually presumed to be incompatible. Similarly, the positive correlation between dominance and negative social-emotional remarks does not seem in agreement with the positive correlations between dominance and cohesiveness and between assertiveness and popularity. However, these inconsistencies may be due to the particular measures used or to the particular circumstances under which the data were collected.

## Dependability and Group Processes

The average group member is probably attracted to others who are dependable both with regard to personal integrity and ability and with regard to behavioral consistency. A person who is self-reliant and responsible for his or her actions probably will be viewed as a desirable group member and will contribute to the effectiveness of the group. Similarly, an individual who can be expected to behave in conventional ways is unlikely to disrupt the group, whereas an unconventional person is likely to cause disorder and dissatisfaction. These two aspects of personality are placed in a single category, labeled *dependability,* because both aspects seem to predict responsible, dependable behavior. Table 6-4 lists representative studies of this dimension of personality.

**Self-reliance and Responsibility** The tendency toward dependable, responsible behavior is identified by such traits as integrity, self-blame (negatively), self-esteem, responsibility, self-reliance, and will control. Each of these represents a unique aspect of personality, but there is a common core that reflects dependability in the personal area. Self-esteem and self-blame fit the categroy least adequately. Self-esteem refers to the degree to which individuals respect themselves as persons; self-blame refers to the degree to which individuals blame themselves when things go wrong. The persons' self-esteem should lead them to behave in ways which

**Table 6-4   Relationships between Dependability and Group Processes**

| Personality characteristic | Behavior variable | Relationship | Reference |
|---|---|---|---|
| Integrity | Leadership | .32 to .41 | Stogdill, 1948 |
| Introversion | Emotional expression | Negative | Buck, Miller, & Caul, 1974 |
| Original thinking | Change in T-groups | Positive | Mitchell, 1975 |
| Responsibility | Change in T-groups | Positive | Mitchell, 1975 |
| Responsibility | Leadership | .10 to .87 | Stogdill, 1948 |
| Self-blame | Conformity | Positive | Costanzo, 1970 |
| Self-concept | Attraction to others | Positive | Leonard, 1975 |
| Self-esteem | Emotional expression | Positive | Buck, Miller, & Caul, 1974 |
| Self-esteem | Conformity | Curvilinear | Gergen & Bauer, 1967 |
| Self-reliance | Group effectiveness | .23 | Greer, 1955 |
| Sensitization | Emotional expression | Positive | Buck, Miller, & Caul, 1974 |
| Unconventionality, undependability | Group productivity* | −.61 | Haythorn, 1953 |
| Unconventionality, undependability | Interest in job | −.43 | Haythorn, 1953 |
| Will control | Group productivity* | .41 | Haythorn, 1953 |

*Ratings of performance on reasoning, mechanical assembly, and discussion tasks.

would enhance their self-esteem, that is, in a dependable and responsible manner. Self-blame should lead individuals to accept responsibility for negative outcomes and to more readily accept the opinions of others.

The representative findings shown in Table 6-4 suggest that persons who are high with respect to dependability are likely to emerge as leaders and to be successful in helping the group to be effective in accomplishing its task. The finding with respect to self-esteem is unclear, since the curvilinear relationship was observed only when the task was of low or moderate difficulty, and with female subjects. This unusual result may be due to these factors, or it may be that self-esteem is basically different from the other characteristics considered in this category.

It is probable that the dependability of the person has other important effects on behavior vis-à-vis others. The dependable person will probably be more attractive to others, more popular as a group member, more active in the group, and so on. Such effects would have significant consequences for group process.

**Unconventionality**   The unconventional person cannot be depended upon to behave in typical or expected ways in relations with others. Hence, others are always a bit uncertain about his or her behavior in social interaction. This lack of behavioral stability can be expected to reflect a disinterest in the group's task and consequently to lead to lowered group productivity. The data given in Table 6-4 strongly support these expectations. Unconventionality is negatively correlated with interest in the job and with group productivity.

Again, it is expected that unconventionality is related to other behaviors that are important for group interaction. For example, it is a common observation that the deviant who consistently fails to conform to the group norms is rejected by the other group members (Schachter, 1951).

## Emotional Stability and Group Processes

The emotional stability of the individual in relation to group processes has been studied more extensively than any of the other categories that have been examined. And it is reflected by more different labels and measures than any other category. In general, emotional stability refers to a class of personality characteristics that are related to the emotional or mental well-being of the individual. It is reflected by such positive characteristics as adjustment, emotional control, and emotional stability, and by such negative characteristics as anxiety, defensiveness, depressive tendencies, and neuroticism. Representative studies relating emotional stability to group processes are listed in Table 6-5.

**Anxiety**   Anxiety may be defined as a general worry or concern about some uncertain or future event. Although it is not necessarily associated with a definite event, it is often related to a specific kind of situation or event, as in the case of "free-floating anxiety." In any case, the person who experiences anxiety feels a vague unease, a nagging worry and concern, which is psychologically unpleasant and which interferes with responses to the demands of everyday living. Such a state, if chronic, as is suggested by labeling it a personality characteristic, undoubtedly influences interpersonal behavior.

At least three kinds of anxiety have been described and studied in relation to groups: *manifest anxiety* (J. A. Taylor, 1953), *test anxiety* (Mandler & Sarason, 1952), and *state anxiety* (Spielberger, 1966). Manifest anxiety is the level of anxiety that a person reveals (manifests) at any particular time, test anxiety is anxiety associated with test taking or with the evaluation process, and state anxiety is a predisposition for anxiety (i.e., an anxiety trait). Manifest anxiety is measured by the Manifest Anxiety Scale (MAS) developed by Taylor, largely by selecting items from

**Table 6-5  Relationships between Emotional Stability and Group Process**

| Personality characteristic | Behavior variable | Relationship | Reference |
|---|---|---|---|
| Achievement anxiety | Risky shift | Positive | Kogan & Wallach, 1967 |
| Manifest anxiety | Response latency | Negative | Cervin, 1956 |
| Manifest anxiety | Performance variability | Negative | Ryan & Lakie, 1965 |
| Self-consciousness | Reaction to rejection | Negative | Fenigstein, 1979 |
| State Anxiety | Affiliation | Negative when emotionally aroused, positive when not | Teichman, 1974 |
| Test anxiety | Aspiration level | Negative | Beckwith, Iverson, & Render, 1965 |
| Test anxiety | Conformity | Positive | Meunier & Rule, 1967 |
| Test anxiety | Satisfaction with group | Positive | Zander & Wulff, 1966 |
| Adjustment | Group effectiveness | .31 | Greer, 1955 |
| Emotional control | Leadership | .18 to .70 | Stogdill, 1948 |
| Defensiveness | Risky shift | Negative | Kogan & Wallach, 1967 |
| Depressive tendencies | Cohesiveness | −.33 | Haythorn, 1953 |
| Depressive tendencies | Morale | −.49 | Haythorn, 1953 |
| Depressive tendencies | Motivation | −.26 | Haythorn, 1953 |
| Emotional stability | Job interest | .43 | Haythorn, 1953 |
| Emotional stability | Morale | .57 | Haythorn, 1953 |
| Emotional stability | Group productivity* | .47 | Haythorn, 1953 |
| Emotional stability | Leadership status | .21 | Bass, Wurster, Doll, & Clair, 1953 |
| Neuroticism | Opinion change | Negative | Cervin, 1956 |
| Neuroticism | Response latency | Negative | Cervin, 1956 |
| Paranoid tendencies | Group effectiveness | −.32 | Greer, 1955 |
| Peripheral nervousness | Group effectiveness | −.25 | Greer, 1955 |
| Pathology | Communication efficiency | Negative | Bixenstine & Douglas, 1967 |

*Ratings of performance on reasoning, mechanical assembly, and discussion tasks.

the Minnesota Multiphasic Personality Inventory (MMPI). Test anxiety is usually measured by the Test Anxiety Questionnaire (TAQ) developed by Mandler and Sarason. State anxiety may be measured by the State-Trait Anxiety Inventory (Spielberger, Gorsuch, & Lushene, 1969), which is also a pencil-and-paper test. When reviewing the data shown in Table 6-5, the reader should keep in mind that such tests may be less than perfectly reliable and valid. Achievement anxiety may be considered one form of test anxiety, and peripheral nervousness a form of manifest anxiety.

The pattern of relationships between measures of anxiety and measures of group process variables is generally consistent, in spite of the differences in measures and their potential deficiencies. Anxious individuals reveal an overall picture of inadequacy in their relations to others and to the group. They have lower aspirations for the group, their responses are slower and more variable, they conform to the norms more closely, they alter their judgment in response to the group more readily, and they are better satisfied with the group than are nonanxious individuals. Their personal concerns apparently cause them to be unusually dependent upon the group and, at the same time, lead them to expect less from the group. Since they expect little from the group, they are better satisfied with whatever outcome is obtained than are the individuals who set higher group goals. Conformity to norms may be one means of reducing anxiety or at least preventing it from increasing. Such behaviors can scarcely contribute to effective group functioning.

**Adjustment**    All the characteristics in the second set of general tendencies are more or less related to personal adjustment, that is, the degree to which the individual's personality reflects adequate organization relative to his or her environment, including other people. These characteristics are often labeled and measured negatively; they include such traits as depressive tendencies, paranoid tendencies, pathology, and the like. Each trait, whether stated positively or negatively, has to do with the degree to which individuals have adjusted to their world and achieved a personality organization that enables them to function effectively in that world.

Again, the pattern of correlations between adjustment measures and measures of group process is quite consistent, although the size of the correlations is not impressive. Group effectiveness, cohesiveness, morale, group motivation, and communication efficiency are positively related to such attributes as adjustment, emotional control, and emotional stability, and negatively related to such attributes as depressive tendencies, neuroticism, paranoid tendencies, and pathology. In short, the well-adjusted person is an asset to the group and the maladjusted person is a liability.

To summarize the findings relative to personality characteristics and group processes, there is good, though limited, evidence that behaviors in groups are caused, in part, by the personality characteristics of the group members. Personality attributes of leaders exert strong influences on group process, and the personality characteristics of individual members have been found to be both facilitative and inhibitive with respect to group process. The magnitude of these effects is not great, however, and relatively little has been done to reduce the number of plausible hypotheses about the effects of personality on behavior in groups.

## PLAUSIBLE HYPOTHESES ABOUT THE PERSONAL ENVIRONMENT OF GROUPS

Although the effect of any given personality characteristic on behavior in groups is relatively weak, it is clear that such attributes have profound consequences for group process. Many of the following hypotheses are in agreement with "common sense" expectations, and many must be stated in terms of behavioral tendencies. Nevertheless, it is important to state them explicitly so that the effects of personality characteristics upon group process can be examined more completely.

*Hypothesis 1    The total amount of participation in the group decreases with increasing group size.*
That overall participation in the group's activities decreases in larger groups has been observed in a variety of studies, including children's groups (Dawe, 1934), adult groups (Williams & Mattson, 1942), and organizations (Indik, 1965).

*Hypothesis 2    Differences in relative participation by group members increases with increasing group size.*
Hare (1952) noted that group members report that they have fewer opportunities to speak in larger groups. Bales et al. (1951) and others have demonstrated that this feeling is consistent with actual communication in groups: as group size increases, the discrepancy between the most active person and others in the group increases (see Figure 6-1) and a greater proportion of total communications are directed toward the group as a whole.

*Hypothesis 3    The probability that a leader will emerge increases with increasing size of the group.*
The effect of group size on leadership emergence is consistent with the changes in distribution of participation noted in Hypothesis 2. Not only is a leader more likely to emerge in larger groups (Bass & Norton, 1951) but the leader is also more likely to be acceptable to other group members (Hemphill, 1950).

*Hypothesis 4    Smaller groups are usually evaluated more positively than larger groups by group members.*
Generally greater dissatisfaction with larger groups is revealed not only by

the reports of group members (Slater, 1958) but also by greater absentee-ism in industrial groups (Cleland, 1955; Baumgartel & Sobol, 1959) and by signs of tension during group interaction (O'Dell, 1968). However, under special circumstances, having more persons in the group may elicit more positive member reactions (Smith & Haythorn, 1972).

*Hypothesis 5　Conformity to a unanimous majority increases with increas-ing group size, at least up to some maximum.*
Some investigations (Asch, 1951; Rosenberg, 1961) indicated that the effects of increased group size upon conformity probably reaches a maximum in a group of four persons; later evidence (Gerard et al., 1968) raises some question about the upper limits of group size as a determinant of conformity behavior. That the size of the majority influences conformi-ty, however, is not questioned.

*Hypothesis 6　The effects of group size upon group performance are a function of the kind of task that the group must complete.*
Group performance increases with increasing group size when the task is either additive or disjunctive; group performance decreases with increasing group size when the task is conjunctive (Frank & Anderson, 1971; Bray, Kerr, and Atkin, 1978; Egerbladh, 1976; Steiner, 1972; Ziller, 1957b). These size effects are the result of the rules governing the manner in which individual resources can be used by the group and the probability that persons who either can or cannot complete the task successfully will be members of the group.

*Hypothesis 7　Social participation increases with increasing chronological age to some maximum level.*
Numerous observation studies have shown that the number and percent-age of social contacts (Beaver, 1932; Green, 1933b) and the amount of social participation in school activities increase with age. This increase in social participation is presumed to be a consequence of increased opportunity for social contact as well as increased development of cognitive and motor skills.

*Hypothesis 8　Social interaction becomes more highly differentiated and complex with increasing chronological age to some maxi-mum.*
As the child grows older, contacts with others become more complex. As a partial consequence of this increased complexity, the older person often becomes more sensitive to others, more popular, and more highly esteemed by associates than younger persons (Bass et al., 1953; Dymond, Hughes, & Raabe, 1952; Leuba, 1933; Newman, 1976; Smith, 1977).

*Hypothesis 9    There is a tendency for the group leader to be older than other group members.*

Although the older person does not always emerge as the leader, there is a slight trend in this direction (Stogdill, 1948). The low positive correlation between age and leadership status probably means only (or primarily) that a person must live long enough to achieve whatever leadership potential he or she may have. However, this does *not* imply that all persons who live long enough get to be leaders.

*Hypothesis 10    Conformity behavior increases with chronological age to about age 12, and decreases thereafter.*

The empirical evidence for this hypothesis is reasonably good. The clearest support comes from the study by Costanzo and Shaw (1966), which revealed a curvilinear relationship between age and conformity (see Figure 6-1). However, the findings by researchers who observed the influence of nonpeer majorities on conformity at different age levels (Berenda, 1950) suggest that this effect may be limited to pressure from peers.

*Hypothesis 11    Women are less self-assertive and less competitive in groups than are men.*

Sex differences in assertive, competitive behavior were noted by Terman and Miles (1936), and studies of sex differences in group behavior agree with this finding. For example, Ort (1950) found that women reported fewer role conflicts in marriage than men, and the studies of sex differences in coalition formations demonstrate quite clearly that women more frequently than men adopt an anticompetitive attitude toward others (Uesugi & Vinacke, 1963). Similarly, McGuire (1973) found that males were more aggressive than females and Black and Higbee (1973) reported that males are generally more exploitative than females. However, one recent study suggests that women may be more aggressive than men under some circumstances (de Gloria & de Ridder, 1979).

*Hypothesis 12    Women use eye contact as a form of communication more frequently than men.*

The evidence generally supports this hypothesis (Exline, 1963; Exline et al., 1965), although one study found no sex difference in eye contact when members of dyads were engaged in "unfocused interaction" (Coutts & Schneider, 1975). It is probable that women simply did not desire to communicate under the conditions created in this experiment.

*Hypothesis 13    Women usually talk more in groups than men.*

This "conventional wisdom" has direct support from the research on sex differences in interaction, although the number of studies is small (Ickes & Barnes, 1977; Wheeler & Nezlek, 1977). This difference in amount of social interaction by men and women may be reversed if an authority figure is responsive to group members (Wright, 1976).

*Hypothesis 14    Females conform to majority opinion more than males.*
Again, the evidence is unambiguous with respect to a sex difference in conformity (Costanzo & Shaw, 1966; Reitan & Shaw, 1964; Tuddenham, 1958), but the interpretation of this difference is still controversial. The most probable explanations are: (1) The female role in the American culture requires that the woman be more submissive than the man. (2) Men are usually regarded as superior to women on the kinds of tasks used in most conformity studies; hence the sex difference is the result of differences in perceived competence on the task (Sistrunk & McDavid, 1971).

*Hypothesis 15    There is a slight tendency for physically superior individuals to become leaders.*
In his review of the literature, Stogdill (1948) found leadership status to be positively correlated with height, weight, and physique, although a few negative correlations were reported. The correlations were generally low and may only reflect the fact that physically superior persons are usually more energetic and active than physically inferior persons.

*Hypothesis 16    Leaders are usually more intelligent than nonleaders.*
The studies comparing leaders and nonleaders reviewed by Stogdill (1948) overwhelmingly indicated that the leader was, on the average, more intelligent than the average nonleader. However, the correlations between intelligence and leadership status were generally low and averaged only .28. Studies of leadership behavior in leaderless group discussions (Bass & Wurster, 1953a; Bass & Wurster, 1953b) also revealed a positive correlation between intelligence and leadership scores. Thus it is clear that intelligence contributes to leadership potential, but the size of the contribution is small. Also, there is some reason to believe that too great a difference between the intelligence of the leader and that of other group members may be detrimental to group effectiveness.

*Hypothesis 17    The more intelligent group member is usually more active in the group than less intelligent group members.*
A number of investigators (e.g., Bass et al., 1953; Zeleny, 1939a) have reported a positive correlation between general activity in the group and intelligence.

*Hypothesis 18    The more intelligent group member is usually more popular than less intelligent group members.*
Mann (1959) reported thirteen studies dealing with the relationship

between intelligence and popularity, most of which showed a positive correlation. The correlations were very low, however, and averaged only .10. Therefore, intelligence does not appear to play an important role in determining popularity in groups.

*Hypothesis 19    More intelligent persons are less conforming than less intelligent persons.*

Again this evidence is consistent and unambiguous in supporting this hypothesis (Crutchfield, 1955; Nakamura, 1958), but the correlations between conformity and intelligence are only moderately high, ranging from $-.22$ to $-.63$. The more intelligent person apparently feels more confident that his or her judgment is accurate, and perhaps does not feel the need to have the support of others in the group.

*Hypothesis 20    The individual who possesses special skills (abilities, knowledges, information) relative to the group task usually is more active in the group, makes more contributions toward task completion, and has more influence on the group decision.*

Activity in the group, contributions to the task, and influence on group decision have been grouped together in Hypothesis 20 because all these behaviors seem to be related to task-oriented activity in the group. Several studies have contributed to the support of this hypothesis (for example, Bass & Wurster, 1953b; Palmer, 1962a; Palmer 1962b; Shaw & Penrod, 1962b; Shevitz, 1955); however, it must be limited to the situation in which the other group members have reason to believe that the informed person's knowledge is accurate. The informed person must be accepted and trusted by other group members if he or she is to use his or her special skills effectively.

*Hypothesis 21    The authoritarian is autocratic and demanding of others in the group.*

Hypothesis 21 is basically a statement that the concept of the authoritarian personality is validated by the behavior of individuals in groups (Haythorn et al., 1956a).

*Hypothesis 22    The authoritarian conforms to the majority opinion more than does the nonauthoritarian.*

Evidence from experimental investigations reveals low positive correlations between authoritarianism (as measured by the F-scale) and conformity behavior. These correlations are on the order of .40, and hence authoritarianism accounts for only a small percentage of the variance among individual conformity scores.

*Hypothesis 23     Individuals who are positively oriented toward other people enhance social interaction, cohesiveness, and morale in groups, whereas individuals who are positively oriented toward things inhibit social interaction, cohesiveness, and morale.*

A number of personality characteristics reflect general approach-avoidance tendencies with respect to other people. The person who tends to like others, trusts them, wishes to cooperate with them, etc., produces favorable group atmospheres; the one who tends to prefer things to people, who is suspicious and jealous of others, etc., produces undesirable group atmospheres such as low cohesiveness and low morale (Haythorn, 1953).

*Hypothesis 24     Socially sensitive persons behave in ways which enhance their acceptance in the group and group effectiveness.*

This hypothesis is a brief summary of the pattern of relationships revealed in Table 6-2. For example, persons who score high on measures of empathy are more likely to emerge as leaders (Bell & Hall, 1954); sociability and social insight correlate positively with group effectiveness (Bouchard, 1969; Greer, 1955); and parmia (outgoing sociability and emotional responsiveness) correlates positively with acceptance in the group and with participation (Cattell & Stice, 1960).

*Hypothesis 25     Ascendant individuals are dominating and self-assertive in groups and generally facilitate group functioning.*

In general, the empirical evidence cited in Table 6-3 indicates that the ascendant, dominant individual, to a greater extent than others, attempts leadership, participates in group activities, asserts himself or herself in the group, and conforms to group norms. Partly as a consequence of these behaviors, dominant individuals promote group cohesiveness, are popular, and influence group decisions. It seems probable, however, that extremely assertive-dominant persons would have an adverse effect upon group functioning.

*Hypothesis 26     The more dependable the group member, the more probable it is that he or she will emerge as a leader and will be successful in helping the group achieve its goal.*

Dependability is reflected by such personality characteristics as integrity, responsibility, and self-reliance. Table 6-4 shows clearly that attributes of this sort are related to leadership emergence and group effectiveness (Greer, 1955; Haythorn, 1953; Stogdill, 1948). This research merely verifies commonsense expectations, and Hypothesis 26 makes explicit the relationships between dependability and group process.

*Hypothesis 27    The unconventional group member inhibits group functioning.*

Unconventional behavior means that the person's actions cannot be predicted with any degree of accuracy, and hence the unconventional person cannot be relied upon to behave in socially acceptable ways. This behavior disrupts group functioning (Haythorn, 1953).

*Hypothesis 28    The anxious group member inhibits effective group functioning.*

The person who scores high on tests of anxiety tends to set relatively low goals for the group (Beckwith, Iversion, & Render, 1965), responds more slowly and less consistently than low scorers (Cervin, 1956), shifts his or her opinion more readily than others (Kogan & Wallach, 1964a; Meunier & Rule, 1967), and is better satisfied with the group's performance than nonanxious group members (Zander & Wulff, 1966). All these response patterns may be expected to interfere with group efficiency.

*Hypothesis 29    The well-adjusted group member contributes to effective group functioning.*

Hypothesis 29 appears obvious, and indeed it is almost a tautology. Nevertheless, it is important that personal adjustment be recognized and made explicit in the study of group process. To summarize, adjustment indicators (for example, emotional stability and emotional control) are positively correlated with cohesiveness, morale, and group effectiveness (Greer, 1955; Haythorn, 1953), whereas indicators of maladjustment (for example, depressive tendencies and neuroticism) are negatively correlated with these group processes (Cervin, 1956; Greer, 1955; Haythorn, 1953).

In conclusion, it is clear that the personality characteristics of group members play an important role in determining their behavior in groups. The magnitude of the effect of any given characteristic is small, but taken together the consequences for group process are of major significance.

**SUGGESTED READINGS**

Asch, S. E. *Social psychology.* Englewood Cliffs, N.J.: Prentice-Hall, 1952. Chap. 16.

Bass, B. M., McGehee, C. R., Hawkins, W. C., Young, P. C., & Gebel, A. S. Personality variables related to leaderless group discussion. *Journal of Abnormal and Social Psychology,* 1953, **48,** 120–128.

Borg, W. R. Prediction of small group role behavior from personality variables. *Journal of Abnormal and Social Psychology,* 1960, **60,** 112–116.

Costanzo, P. R., & Shaw, M. E. Conformity as a function of age level. *Child Development*, 1966, **37**, 967–975.

Exline, R. V., Gray, D., & Schuette, D. Visual behavior in a dyad as affected by interview content and sex of respondent. *Journal of Personality and Social Psychology*, 1965, **1**, 201–209.

Ickes, W., & Barnes, R. D. The role of sex and self-monitoring in unstructured dyadic interactions. *Journal of Personality and Social Psychology*, 1977, **35**, 315–330.

Smith, H. W. Small group interaction at various ages: Simultaneous talking and interruptions of others. *Small Group Behavior*, 1977, **8**, 65–74.

Chapter 7

# Group Composition

Ample evidence has already been presented showing that the individuals who compose a group are highly significant determinants of group process. The mere presence of others is sufficient to alter the behavior of individuals (Chapter 3); the formation of groups depends, in part, upon the attractions among individuals and the rewards they provide one another (Chapter 4); the spatial relations among individuals contribute to the interactions among them and the kinds of relationships they establish (Chapter 5); and legions of personal characteristics are correlated with almost all aspects of group functioning, as well as with many individual behaviors in the group (Chapter 6). There can be no doubt that the kinds of individuals who make up a group constitute a set of powerful determinants of group behavior.

In the preceding chapter, attention was given to the consequences of the individual's characteristics upon group process without regard to the characteristics of others in the group. The correlations between personal attributes and behavior in groups were considered under conditions of random or undetermined group composition in an attempt to establish general effects of personal characteristics upon group process. In a sense, these correlations reflect consequences when other members in the group are average or typical with respect to personal attributes, that is, the effects of personal characteristics in the modal group. In this chapter, we are concerned with the *relationships* among the personal characteristics of group members and the consequences of these relationships for group functioning. It is not the particular characteristics of an individual group member that are of interest, but rather the *relative* characteristics of the various persons who compose the group. For example, when we discuss intelligence, we will be concerned with the differences in the intelligence of the various individuals in the group, rather than with the group's "mean intelligence" or the intellectual level of individual members in the group.

The first question the investigator should raise in connection with group composition effects is: Does the particular composition make *any* difference, or can differences among groups treated alike be explained on the basis of individual characteristics alone? For example, suppose that fifty persons are available for assignment to ten groups of five persons each. Does it make any difference how these fifty persons are distributed among the groups? Or can they be assigned at random with no gain or loss in group achievement? The answer, as we shall see, is that it does make a difference how the groups are formed.

The next questions concern the particular combinations of individuals and the effects of these combinations on group process. Investigators have employed various approaches in studying these aspects of group composition. Some were concerned with interpersonal attraction (cohesiveness) and similarity versus complementarity of personal characteristics; others were concerned with compatibility of needs; and still others with the heterogeneity-homogeneity dimension of group composition. These approaches have much in common, but the interests and techniques of the investigators vary considerably. For example, Winch (1955) was interested primarily in need complementarity in mate selection and, therefore, limited his investigations to dating and married couples. Students of cohesiveness have been interested in group problem solving and small group interaction, and hence have concentrated on the small group. In the following sections, we will first consider the empirical evidence supporting the conclusion that the particular combination of individual characteristics does produce a significant effect upon group process. Subsequent sections consider the effects of cohesiveness, compatibility, and heterogeneity-homogeneity of group membership upon group behavior.

## THE ASSEMBLY EFFECT

The term *assembly effect* refers to variations in group behavior that are a consequence of the particular combination of persons in the group, apart from the effects produced by the specific characteristics of group members. Consider an instance in which four persons are to be assigned to two dyads. Two of the four persons tend to dominate others and two tend to be submissive toward others. It seems obvious that a better overall result will be obtained by pairing each dominant person with a submissive person than by pairing the two dominant persons and the two submissive persons. This may seem so obvious as not to require verification. Indeed, Haythorn (1953), in the extensive study of the effects of personality characteristics on group process discussed in Chapter 6, assumed that such effects must be eliminated from the data in order to identify personality effects per se. He therefore designed his experiment so that each subject worked in five unique four-person groups, and no other subject was a member of more than one of them.

Serious students of small group behavior, however, are careful not to make many assumptions; they therefore want verification of all hypotheses, even those which appear obvious. It was probably this concern with verification of the apparently obvious proposition that stimulated a study by Rosenberg, Erlick, and Berkowitz (1955) which contributed the most convincing evidence that assembly is indeed a determinant of group behavior. Two samples of nine persons each were drawn from a large pool of Air Force enlisted men. Each sample of nine was subdivided into three groups of three persons each. The membership of these groups was shifted from trial to trial so that each individual in the sample worked with every other individual in that sample. Hence, every triad differed in composition from every other triad, although any given arrangement included the same individuals as any other arrangement. Therefore, any differences in the functioning of triads could not be accounted for by differences in the resources and attributes of the individuals who composed the groups. That is, when different arrangements or assemblies of the same individuals are compared, any nonchance differences may be attributed to the effects of group composition.

The task assigned these differently assembled groups required a group version of the ball and spiral apparatus. This apparatus consisted of a hexagonal base from which a track or channel spiraled upward through five levels to a circular receptacle at the top of the channel. Six handles were attached to the base, so that it could be manipulated by the three members of the group. A golf ball was placed at the bottom of the channel, and the group's task on each trial was to manipulate the spiral in such a way as to move the golf ball to the receptacle at the top. An error was recorded for the group each time the ball fell off the track, and a performance score was recorded as the average height attained before the ball fell. The effectiveness of the triads differed on both measures, although the difference in performance scores was minimally reliable. The results of this investigation thus verified the hypothesis that individuals contribute differently to the group product, depending upon the particular other individuals with whom they are grouped.

The effects of group composition may also be noted in a study of peer learning groups (Shaw, Ackerman, McCown, Worsham, Haugh, Gebhardt, & Small, 1979). Clinically relevant problems were presented to four-person groups of students in a course on immunology. The objective was to have students apply their knowledge of basic science to solutions of clinical problems. Each student participated in eight different groups, each group working on one of eight problems. Students were assigned to groups by a computer program that ensured that no one worked with a particular other student more than once. Among other things, it was found that the performance of students varied depending upon which other students were members of the group.

There is good evidence, then, that the way groups are assembled from a given set of persons is an important determinant of group process. It is, therefore, important to examine some of the kinds of assemblies that may occur and to evaluate some of their consequences for group behavior.

## GROUP COHESIVENESS

Now that it is clearly established that group composition is a significant variable in group process, we must turn to an examination of the specific interpersonal relationships that contribute to this effect. One such interpersonal relationship is the degree to which the members of the group are attracted to each other, or the degree to which the group coheres or "hangs together." This aspect of the group is usually referred to as *group cohesiveness*. Unfortunately, at least three different meanings have been attached to the term *cohesiveness:* (1) attraction to the group, including resistance to leaving it, (2) morale, or the level of motivation evidenced by group members, and (3) coordination of efforts of group members. Most persons who use the term, however, agree that it refers to the degree to which members are motivated to remain in the group. Members of highly cohesive groups are more energetic in group activities, they are less likely to be absent from group meetings, they are happy when the group succeeds and sad when it fails, etc., whereas members of less cohesive groups are less concerned about the group's activities. The following discussion adopts the definition advanced by Festinger: Group cohesiveness is "the resultant of all the forces acting on the members to remain in the group" (Festinger, 1950, p. 274). According to this definition, all those factors contributing to interpersonal attraction which were discussed in Chapter 4 also contribute to group cohesiveness. The chief difference between the study of interpersonal attraction and group cohesiveness is that the former emphasizes individual attractions, whereas the latter emphasizes the number, strength, and pattern of attractions within the group. This difference is illustrated by data provided by Good and Nelson (1971). They varied both the proportion of person-group attitude similarity (i.e., the similarity of each group member to others in the group) and the proportion of intragroup similarity (i.e., the similarity of group members to one another). The attractiveness of the group was positively related to the person's similarity to the group, whereas group cohesiveness was a function of degree of intragroup similarity.

### Measuring Group Cohesiveness

Group cohesiveness is reflected by many different behaviors of group members; hence, it is not surprising that the operational measures of cohesiveness vary considerably from investigation to investigation. The most common technique for assessing cohesiveness is sociometric choice. Group members are asked to name the person or persons they would most prefer as associates for various activities, and the number of ingroup choices is presumed to reflect the degree of cohesiveness of that group. This measure is based upon the attraction of group members and disregards other forces that may be acting on a person to remain in or to leave the group. Variations in the application of this technique may also be important in understanding the relationship of cohesiveness to other aspects of group process. For example, some investigators count only positive choices, whereas others may ask individuals to name the least preferred as well as the most preferred, and then subtract the negative choices from the positive to estimate cohesiveness. Still others may take into account mutual choices. In addition, cohesiveness has been estimated by the relative frequency with which group members use "we" and "I" in their discussions, by the regularity of attendance at group meetings, and by direct questions about members' desires to remain in the group. These different measures of cohesiveness reflect different aspects of group cohesiveness, and none takes into account all aspects of group spirit. These variations in measurement techniques should be kept in mind as one attempts to evaluate research findings relative to cohesiveness.

### Determinants of Cohesiveness

Group cohesiveness is a complex phenomenon that is determined by many factors. We have already noted many of the variables that attract individuals to a group, such as other persons in the group, group activities, the goals of the group, the need for affiliation, and the like. For instance, it has been demonstrated that groups composed of persons having similar attitudes are more cohesive than groups composed of persons having less similar attitudes (Terborg, Castore, & DeNinno, 1976). These groups worked on six projects spanning a period of three months. Measures of cohesiveness obtained at different points in time revealed that the influence of attitude similarity on cohesiveness was not immediate but developed over time. Presumably, time is required for persons to learn about each other's attitudes; the knowledge that others hold similar attitudes is important for group cohesiveness.

Several other variables have been shown to influence group cohesiveness, such as the success or failure of the group, the clarity of the path to the group goal, the outcome of conflict, and the nature and timing of feedback. It probably seems obvious that successful groups should be more cohesive than unsuccessful groups, and that is what research shows (e.g., Blanchard, Weigel, & Cook, 1975). It may also appear reasonable that when the path to the goal is clear (procedures for achieving the goal are evident), group members find the group more attractive than when the path to the goal is not so clear, and, again, that is the finding (e.g., Anderson, 1975). On the other hand, it may not be so obvious that conflict in a group can sometimes result in increased cohesiveness, but this has been shown to occur (Wheaton, 1974). Whether conflict in the group will have positive or negative consequences for group cohesiveness depends upon the nature of the conflict. When there is conflict over principles, the conflict has negative effects on group cohesiveness; however, when the group members agree on principles but are in disagreement over matters that assume adherence to those principles, the conflict enhances cohesiveness.

Group cohesiveness may also be influenced by the nature and timing of feedback to group members. After reviewing research on group cohesiveness, Deutsch (1968) noted that cohesiveness is associated with communication among group members, the readiness of group members to be influenced by others in the group, and the tendency to respond positively to the actions of other group members. For example, if a group leader provides both positive and negative feedback to group members about their behaviors, it is important that initial feedback be positive (Schaible & Jacobs, 1975). When positive feedback is followed by negative feedback, cohesiveness is higher than when the negative feedback is given first.

The evidence cited above makes it quite clear that group cohesiveness varies with many aspects of the group process and the characteristics of group members. The important thing for group behavior, however, is the degree of cohesiveness, regardless of how this state was created. It is, therefore, important to examine the effects of group cohesiveness on group interaction, group performance, and member satisfaction.

### Consequences of Group Cohesiveness

The cohesiveness of the group has been supposed to influence a wide range of group activities, but perhaps its most significant influence is on group maintenance. According to most theories (cf. Cattell's syntality theory [Chapter 2] and Bennis and Shepard's theory of group development [Chapter 4]), the first demand that must be met by a group is the resolution of internal problems. Indeed, unless it solves these problems the group will cease to exist. Therefore, there must be some minimum degree of cohesiveness if the group is to continue to function as a group. To the extent that this minimum requirement is exceeded, one may expect that the degree of cohesiveness will be related to other aspects of group process.

Although group cohesiveness has been related both theoretically and empirically to numerous process variables, the major ones are interaction, social influence, group productivity, and satisfaction. It will be instructive to consider the relationship of cohesiveness to each of these processes.

**Cohesiveness and Interaction**   We interact, both verbally and nonverbally, with those others who are attractive to us. However, this relationship between interaction and interpersonal attraction is usually associated with opportunity for interaction, since we choose to join groups composed of attractive persons and to live and work in social environments composed of others who are attractive to us. It is theoretically possible that interaction is merely a by-product of affiliation and is only indirectly influenced by attraction or cohesiveness. There is good evidence, however, that both the quantity and quality of interaction are related to the cohesiveness of the group. Lott and Lott (1961) obtained groups of six to ten friends from student organizations at the University of Kentucky and Kentucky State College, representing religious, academic, athletic, and social activities. Groups of strangers were also obtained from introductory psychology courses. At the beginning of each group meeting, each person was asked to indicate, on a 9-point rating scale, how much he liked each other individual present.

Each member was paired with every other member and the difference in each pair's ratings of each other was averaged. A group cohesiveness index was then computed as the average of the scores earned by each pair. Each group then discussed a topic concerning student attitudes while an observer tallied the frequency of member communication. These procedures resulted in an estimate of group cohesiveness and a measure of quantity of communication activity for each of the fifteen groups. A rank difference correlation of .42 was obtained between cohesiveness and communication level. Although not exceedingly high, this correlation is statistically reliable and indicates that cohesiveness and amount of communication are related, even when opportunity for interaction is the same for all groups.

Behavior in accord with the findings reported by Lott and Lott has also been observed in a radically different setting (Moran, 1966). The subjects for Moran's study were 233 dyads obtained from nine Dutch industrial training groups. High- and low-cohesive dyads were identified on the basis of expressed ability to work together. Amount of communication between members of each dyad was obtained by asking each person to mark 70-millimeter rating scales showing how often he communicated with every other member in his training group. The communication level of each dyad was computed as the sum of the two members' perceptions of the amount of communication each had received from the other. The relationship between quantity of communication and cohesiveness was determined by comparing the relative number of high- and low-cohesive dyads that were above and below the median communication level for all dyads. There were 112 high-cohesive dyads above the median as compared with four low-cohesive dyads above the median. Clearly, then, cohesiveness facilitates verbal interaction.

Differences in the pattern of communication within groups as a function of cohesiveness were also noted by Back (1951) in a study designed to measure the effects of cohesiveness on pressures toward uniformity. Each member of each dyad was given a set of three pictures believing the two sets were identical, although in fact there were slight differences. They were asked to discuss the sequences of pictures and to write a story about them. Two observers recorded the discussion using a twenty-category recording system. High- and low-cohesive dyads were created through instructions, based upon either attraction to the partner, attraction to the task, or attraction to the group itself (prestige). A subsequent check revealed that the experimental inductions produced the wanted differences in cohesiveness. In general, members of low-cohesive groups tended to act independently, with little consideration for the other member of the dyad, whereas the cohesive group members were active in seeking facts and in reaching agreement. Also, within the high-cohesive groups the interaction patterns were quite different for different kinds of cohesivenss. When cohesiveness was based upon interpersonal attraction, members of the dyad wanted to prolong the discussion and to engage in pleasant conversation; when cohesiveness was based upon task performance, they wanted to complete the task quickly and efficiently; and when cohesiveness was based upon group prestige, members of the dyad acted cautiously and attempted to avoid any actions that might endanger their status.

Differential patterns of interaction as a function of cohesiveness have also been observed in children's groups (Shaw & Shaw, 1962). Three-person groups varying in degree of cohesiveness were formed on the basis of choice preferences for work partners in a classroom situation. The groups were then assigned the task of learning to spell lists of words, working together in groups. The teacher, who did not know the cohesiveness scores, observed and recorded the behavior of each group. Differences between high- and low-cohesive groups were observed in four categories: group atmosphere, method of study, leadership behavior, and nontask behavior. High-cohesive groups were cooperative and friendly, and the members praised one another for accomplishments; low-cohesive groups were hostile and aggressive, and members were delighted when others made errors. High-cohesive groups initially devoted time to planning their method of study, and all group members followed the agreed-upon plan; low-cohesive groups usually began immediately to test each other, with no preliminary planning. A strong leader emerged in both high- and low-cohesive groups, but in high-cohesive groups the leader behaved in a democratic manner, whereas in the low-cohesive groups the leader was "bossy" and autocratic. Initially, both high- and low-cohesive groups devoted most of their time to the assigned task, but by the third task period the high-cohesive groups engaged in much more nontask (social) activity, whereas the low-cohesive groups developed interpersonal conflicts and tended to break up and study as individuals.

In summary, it is clear that cohesiveness is related to both quantity and quality of group interaction. Members of high-cohesive groups communicate with each other to a greater extent, and the content of group interaction is positively oriented, whereas members of low-cohesive groups are less communicative and the content of their interactions is more negatively oriented. Members of high-cohesive groups are cooperative, friendly, and generally behave in ways designed to promote group integration, whereas low-cohesive group members behave much more independently, with little concern for others in the group.

**Cohesiveness and Social Influence**   Groups characterized by friendliness, cooperation, interpersonal attraction, and similar indications of group cohesiveness exert strong influences upon members to behave in accordance with group expectations. Members of cohesive groups are motivated to respond positively to others in the group, and their behavior should reflect this motivation. For example, French (1941) found that organized groups were more highly motivated than unorganized groups, as indicated both by observers' ratings and by group member questionnaire responses. Hence, members of cohesive groups theoretically should conform to group norms and respond positively to attempted influence by others in the group. Empirical observations generally support these theoretical expectations. Festinger, Schachter, and Back (1950) found that members of cohesive groups in university housing units held uniform opinions and usually acted in conformity with group standards. Thus, pressures toward uniformity increased with increasing group cohesiveness. In the laboratory study described in the preceding section, Back (1951) found that members of highly cohesive dyads changed their opinions more toward their partner's position than did members of the less cohesive dyads. Back interpreted this as showing that influence through social communication was greater in cohesive than in noncohesive groups.

The greater effectiveness of attempted influence in cohesive than noncohesive groups under certain conditions was also demonstrated in an investigation by Schachter, Ellertson, McBride, and Gregory (1951). These investigators examined the effects of positive and negative inductions in high- and low-cohesive groups. Cohesiveness was manipulated by telling the members of some groups that their responses to questionnaires indicated that they were members of extremely congenial groups (high cohesiveness); members of other groups were told that, owing to scheduling difficulties, it was impossible to assemble congenial groups and hence there was no reason to think that others in the group would like them. Each group member was assigned to a different room and given the task of cutting cardboard parts which ostensibly were to be used by the other group members to make checkerboards. Influence attempts were introduced by written notes which the subject believed came from other group members, although in fact they were prepared by the experimenter. During the first sixteen minutes of the work period each group member received five notes that made no attempt to influence productivity. During the final sixteen minutes, each group member received six notes that attempted to either increase or decrease productivity. Positive influence attempts were equally successful in both high- and low-cohesive groups, but the negative induction was much more effective in the high-cohesive than in the low-cohesive groups. Schachter et al. theorized that two forces were acting upon the subject, a force to please the experimenter and do well on the assigned task and a force to be accepted in the group. In the positive induction condition both forces were acting in the same direction, whereas in the negative induction condition they were operating in opposite directions. This would explain the overall greater effect of the positive induction, but the reason for the failure to find differences between high- and low-cohesive groups in the positive induction condition is not clear.

Somewhat different results were reported by Berkowitz (1954), although the procedure was essentially the same as that followed by Schachter et al. The subjects were male ROTC students and students in economics who were told either that they would be in congenial groups or that they would not find others congenial. The task was to assemble ashtrays, although each member actually cut out disks from desk blotters. In some groups, a high productivity standard was established through experimenter-controlled communications, whereas in others a low standard was established. In this experiment, however, members of high-cohesive groups were influenced more than the low-cohesive groups by both the positive and the negative inductions. The reasons for this difference with respect to positive inductions in high-cohesive groups are not immediately evident, but it may be due to subject differences. The Schachter et al. subjects were female and might have been more positively oriented toward the task than the male subjects used by Berkowitz. If so, the positive induction in the low-cohesive female groups may have produced maximum productivity, in which case the high-cohesive subjects could do no better even if they were more strongly influenced by the requests from fellow group members.

The differential effects of social influence as a function of cohesiveness are shown most clearly in studies of conformity. An early study by Festinger, Gerard, Hymovitch, Kelley, and Raven (1952) found that groups who were told that they would find each other congenial and interesting exerted greater pressures toward uniformity of opinion than did groups that had been given no such instructions. In the Lott and Lott (1961) study cited earlier, the group cohesiveness index correlated .54 with a measure of conformity to contrived group opinion. Using a more traditional approach to conformity, Wyer (1966) found that group members conformed more to a contrived group majority judgment of the number of dots on a card in high-cohesive than in low-cohesive groups, although the magnitude of the cohesive effect varied with other conditions. A positive relationship between cohesiveness and conformity was also reported by Bovard (1951), but in another study (1953) he found no difference in conformity as a function of cohesiveness. Failure to find positive results was also reported by Downing (1958), using the autokinetic task (judgment of movement of a stationary light in a dark room), and by Seashore (1954), using agreement of members of industrial groups regarding production standards as the measure of conformity. In both of the latter studies, however, other factors were so strong that the effects of cohesiveness were undoubtedly suppressed.

The general conclusion from these studies is that cohesiveness leads to increased social influence, which in most cases produces greater conformity to group standards. However, other variables may be sufficiently strong to negate the effects of cohesiveness. Some of these other variables have been identified by Thibaut and Strickland (1956) in an experiment involving two levels of cohesiveness (high and low), three levels of confidence (high, medium, and low), and two psychological sets (task set and group set). High-cohesive groups were made up of freshman pledges from social fraternities on a college campus; low-cohesive groups were composed of male strangers. The different levels of confidence were created in connection with the group task. Each member was seated in a cubicle facing a square board divided into four quadrants, each of which contained twenty-four thumbtacks arranged in different ways. The tacks were arranged so that quadrants could be rank-ordered according to any one of four criteria. Subjects were instructed to imagine that the tacks in each quadrant represented four groups of people and were told to rank-order the groups on the basis of friendliness. Ten simulated balloting trials were given, during which each subject circled one of four alternative orders and indicated his degree of confidence in his judgment on each of five cards to be transmitted to other group members. The ballots were intercepted by the experimenter, who replaced them with premarked ones which varied the level of confidence and communicated a majority decision different from that of the subject. Psychological set was manipulated through instructions. Task set instructions emphasized the importance of problem solution, whereas group set instructions were designed to make social evaluation within the group as salient as possible.

Across all experimental conditions, the high-cohesive groups conformed approximately 51 percent of the time as compared with 41 percent for the low-cohesive groups. However, the amount of conformity varied systematically with other variables in the situation. Figure 7-1 provides a graphic representation of the amount of conformity under the various conditions. It can be seen that when the majority expresses low confidence in its judgment, there is little difference in conformity as a function of

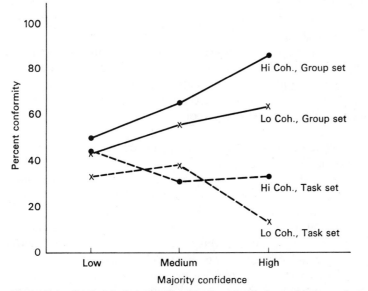

**Figure 7-1**  Conformity behavior as a function of majority confidence and psychological set. (Plotted with permission from data reported by J. W. Thibaut & L. Strickland. Psychological set and social conformity. *Journal of Personality*, 1956, **25**, 115–129.)

cohesiveness. When the majority's confidence is high, however, the high-cohesive groups conformed more than the low-cohesive groups under both psychological sets. It is also interesting that high-cohesive groups conformed more than low-cohesive groups at all levels of confidence under group set conditions, although the difference in the low majority confidence condition is probably not reliable.

As we shall see in Chapter 8, conformity may have either positive or negative consequences for the group. An important question, therefore, is whether the influence of cohesiveness on conformity occurs under all conditions or is a function of the degree to which conformity promotes group welfare. There is limited evidence that the answer to this question depends upon the source of group cohesiveness (Sakurai, 1975). In one condition, cohesiveness was manipulated by emphasizing the need for interpersonal compatibility, whereas in another condition cohesiveness was established by making group members interdependent with respect to outcomes. For both types of cohesiveness, conformity either facilitated or impeded group effectiveness. It was found that when cohesiveness was based upon interpersonal attraction, group members conformed whether or not conformity promoted or impeded group performance, but when cohesiveness was based on interdependence, group members conformed only when it promoted group welfare.

In summary, there is good evidence that group cohesiveness is related to social influence in the group. When group members are attracted to the group, they are motivated to behave in accordance with the wishes of other group members and in ways that facilitate group functioning. These motivations are reflected in greater responsiveness to group inductions and in greater conformity to group norms and standards. It must be recognized, however, that many other variables are related to social influence processes, and under some circumstances these other variables may be strong enough to negate the effects of cohesiveness.

**Cohesiveness and Productivity**   Group members who are attracted to the group presumably want the group to succeed and so work harder to achieve the goals of the group. It seems obvious, therefore, that the more cohesive the group, the higher its productivity. Despite the apparently obvious nature of this conclusion about cohesiveness and productivity, a considerable amount of research has been devoted to determining whether it is valid. After reviewing some of this research, more can be said about the validity of the expected relationship of cohesiveness to productivity. To anticipate, it appears that the cohesive group can achieve goals that it accepts more efficiently than the noncohesive group. The problem often is that groups do not set the same goals for themselves that outside agencies (experimenters, boards of directors, etc.) set for them. Hence a cohesive group may achieve its own goals but be relatively unproductive with regard to the goals of the researcher. But let us examine some of these studies.

Relatively few laboratory studies have been designed for the primary purpose of examining the relationship between cohesiveness and productivity, although there is some evidence on this issue from studies designed for other purposes. In the studies concerned with the effects of cohesiveness on social influence, for example, base-line measures of productivity were obtained before the influence attempts were introduced. These data showed no differences between the high- and low-cohesive groups in the Schachter et al. (1951) experiment and only small increments in favor of the high-cohesive groups in the Berkowitz (1954) study. Since the group members were working in separate rooms with no knowledge about the expectations of other group members, it is perhaps not too surprising that the group atmosphere had little effect on group productivity.

A study of the effects of cohesiveness on the performance of individual and group tasks yielded more positive results (Hoogstraten & Vorst, 1978). Four-person groups of college freshmen served in either high- or low-cohesive groups, where cohesiveness was varied via instructions and reports on test performance. Group performance comparisons favored the high-cohesive groups in each of eight comparisons, four of which were statistically reliable.

More acceptable evidence derives from field studies and field experiments. A field study of 12 six-man squads in the United States Army was conducted by Goodacre (1951). Prior to participation in a military problem conducted in the field, squad members were asked to indicate their choices of buddies in various social and tactical situations. These choices were used to compute measures of cohesiveness for each group. The correlation between the measures of group cohesiveness and the scores earned on the military problem ranged from .61 to .78. An overall group cohesion score correlated .77 with the field score. Hemphill and Sechrest (1952) also studied military personnel. They tested ninety-four B-29 bomber crews in combat in the Pacific area. Each person was asked to select an air crew from the squadron by naming one man for each crew position. They then computed an "on-crew" versus "off-crew" index of cohesiveness for each air crew; this index was correlated with bombing accuracy scores obtained from official records. The correlation was positive ($r = .36$) but was not as high as those obtained by Goodacre. Strupp and Hausman (1953) also reported a positive relationship between cohesiveness and productivity for aircraft maintenance crews, but a study by Roby (1952) yielded equivocal results. Nevertheless, evidence from field studies in military situations generally supports the proposition that cohesiveness and productivity are positively correlated.

Evidence from studies in industrial settings is also generally in accord with the hypothesis. In a series of studies, Van Zelst (1952a, 1952b) reported positive relationships between measures of cohesiveness and productivity indices. In the first study, carpenters and bricklayers were asked to list three choices for teammates. Voluntary regrouping was permitted on the basis of these choices, after which the men worked together for five months on a construction job. Compared with a nine-month period prior to regrouping, the rate of turnover dropped and there was a 5 percent savings in total production costs. In a second study, sociometrically constructed work groups of carpenters and bricklayers were compared with control groups during a three-month work period. Experimental groups were superior to control groups with respect to turnover rate, an index of labor cost, and an index of materials cost. Similar results were reported by Speroff and Kerr (1952) in a study of accident reduction through sociometric grouping. Negro and Spanish-speaking manual workers in a steel mill were asked to name the person they would most like to work with and the person they would least like to work with. An index of desirability was computed by subtracting the square of number of least-like choices from the square of number of most-like choices. This index correlated $-.54$ with the number of accidents during the three previous years. Thus, cohesiveness is demonstrably related to behavior in the industrial realm.

Finally, there is evidence that cohesiveness is related to group effectiveness in the classroom. In the study by Shaw and Shaw (1962) cited earlier, second graders were grouped according to sociometric choices in such a way as to form groups varying in cohesiveness. Each pupil was asked to name the three persons he would most like to study with and the three he would least like to study with. A cohesiveness index was computed for each three-person group by assigning a weight of 1 for a rejection, a weight of 2 for no choice, and a weight of 3 for a positive choice. For example, consider a group composed of persons A, B, and C, in which A had chosen B as most preferred and B had rejected C. The cohesiveness index would, therefore, be 12, since there were four possible choices that were not made, plus one rejection and one positive choice. Each group was tested on two word lists, with group effectiveness being measured by the number of words that the group could spell which it could not spell before the study period; that is, the sum of individual gains over pretest scores. Altogether, four sets of groups were tested, resulting in four correlations for each test period. In the initial test period correlations between cohesiveness and performance were all positive, ranging from .16 to .56 and averaging .47. In the second test period, however, the correlations ranged from $-.56$ to .47 and averaged only $-.01$.

This study is presented in some detail because it makes a point about the experimental study of cohesiveness and productivity. It will be recalled that the interaction patterns were different in the high- and low-cohesive groups and that this pattern changed during the course of the study. In the second test period the more highly cohesive groups engaged in much more social activity and devoted less time to the assigned task, whereas the less cohesive groups broke down and studied individually. This differential pattern of interaction during the second test period effectively destroyed any relationship between cohesiveness and performance. In other words, the more cohesive groups set social activity as their goal, and they apparently achieved this goal!

In spite of some equivocal evidence, it seems evident that the empirical data support the hypothesis that high-cohesive groups are more effective than low-cohesive groups in achieving their goals. The cohesive group does whatever it tries to do better than the noncohesive group. Indeed, Seashore (1954) reported that among industrial groups cohesiveness was related to either high or low productivity, depending upon the production standards established by the group.

The effect of cohesiveness upon the performance of the group is undoubtedly mediated by motivational factors. According to Cattell's syntality theory (see Chapter 2), it might be inferred that cohesiveness increases the effective synergy in the group in two ways: It increases the total synergy of the group by producing more favorable attitudes toward the group on the part of its members, and it reduces the amount of synergy that is needed to maintain the group. The resulting increase in effective synergy enables the group to attain its goal or goals more efficiently. Data concerning the relationship between cohesiveness and member satisfaction (reported in the next section) are generally in accord with this interpretation (cf. Lott & Lott, 1961).

**Cohesiveness and Satisfaction**    As we suggested in the preceding section, cohesive group members are usually better satisfied with the group than members of noncohesive groups. Indeed, the concept of cohesiveness almost demands that this be the case, for it is highly unlikely that an individual will experience forces to remain in a group that he or she is dissatisfied with. Of course, it is possible that a person will be attracted to some aspects of a group, such as group goals, without being satisfied with the group as a whole. Nevertheless, the general theoretical expectation is greater satisfaction with increasing cohesiveness.

The empirical data are entirely consistent with this proposition. In the study of carpenters and bricklayers cited earlier, Van Zelst (1952b) found that members of groups formed on the basis of sociometric choice had higher job satisfaction than members of control groups. Similar findings were reported by Marquis, Guetzkow, and Heyns (1951) in a field study of decision-making conferences. The participation in seventy-two conferences in business and government were observed at the University of Michigan, and a cohesiveness index was computed for each group determined from observer ratings of liking among group members. Group members rated their satisfaction with several aspects of the conference. The cohesiveness index correlated positively with members' satisfaction with the group process and with the meeting. Gross (1954) reported a positive relationship between cohesiveness of Air Force groups and their satisfaction with the Air Force and its goals.

The findings from field studies have also been supported by data from more traditional laboratory studies. Exline (1957) told some participants that they were in groups that were well matched and congenial, and told others that it was not possible to arrange a congenial group for them. Persons assigned to presumably congenial groups expressed greater satisfaction with their group's progress than did those given the opposite orientation.

The general findings with respect to group cohesiveness and group process are, therefore, reasonably consistent, despite the many inadequacies in the operationalizing of cohesiveness. Relative to low-cohesive groups, high-cohesive groups engage in more social interaction, engage in more positve interactions (friendly, cooperative, democratic, etc.), exert greater influence over their members, are more effective in achieving goals they set for themselves, and have higher member satisfaction.

## GROUP COMPATIBILITY

It should be clear from the preceding discussions that high-cohesive groups are composed of members who are in some ways compatible; hence, group cohesiveness is one form of group compatibility. The questions asked about the behavior of cohesive groups, however, are not based upon the proposition that they are either compatible or incompatible, at least not beyond the compatibility implied by interpersonal attraction. But a number of theorists and researchers have been interested in the consequences of compatibility per se. These scholars have generally attempted to formulate theoretical propositions about the characteristics of individuals that make them compatible or incompatible with particular other individuals. Groups varying in degree of compatibility are then formed and studied under controlled conditions. In this way, the theoretical hypotheses can be tested and empirical relationships between compatibility indices and group process variables can be established.

Although approaches to the analysis and study of compatibility are varied, they can be classified into two general categories: need compatibility and response compatibility. These two approaches are basically similar in that both are concerned with personal characteristics of group members which reflect response tendencies that are either compatible or incompatible. They differ in the kinds of characteristics that are considered important.

**Need Compatibility**

The satisfaction of individual needs may be either facilitated or interfered with through group interaction. When the needs of two or more persons can be mutually satisfied through interpersonal activities, they are compatible in terms of needs; when their needs cannot be satisfied through interaction or when the satisfaction of their needs is interfered with through the interaction process, they are incompatible. Obviously, groups whose members are incompatible are likely to be unhappy and the effectiveness of group members will be adversely affected; when member needs are met (i.e., when the group is compatible), the opposite effects should occur.

This simple notion of compatibility was applied to mate selection by Winch (1955) in his theory of complementarity of needs. Basically, Winch theorized that individuals choose mates whose personal characteristics complement their own characteristics. For example, assertive persons should marry receptive or submissive persons, since the need to assert oneself can be satisfied through interaction with a person who needs to be submissive. To test this theory, Winch conducted "need interviews" with twenty-five married couples. On the basis of these interviews, he identified the needs of each person and correlated them to determine whether the expected relationships occurred. The correlations were generally in the predicted direction, and thus tended to support Winch's theory. However. data from case history interviews and from the analysis of responses to Thematic Apperception Test cards failed to support the hypothesis. Winch discounted these data because the need scores were unreliable. He therefore concluded that his data supported the hypothesis that marriage partners choose each other to satisfy complementary needs.

Need compatibility was also found to be related to marital adjustment in a study of thirty-six married couples (Meyer & Pepper, 1977). Need compatibility was defined as similarity of responses to a test (called the Personality Research Form, or PRF) designed to measure needs such as affiliation, aggression, dominance, and nurturance. Marital adjustment was also measured by a scale (called the Locke-Wallace Marital Adjustment Scale). The results showed that well-adjusted spouses were more similar than poorly adjusted spouses in their self and spouse need ratings, especially with respect to needs for affiliation, aggression, autonomy, and nurturance.

Other investigators have not been so successful in obtaining support for the Winch hypothesis. Kelly (1955) studied 300 engaged couples to test the hypothesis that "opposites attract." He administered a battery of tests designed to measure attitude, interest, and social values, and computed correlations between the scores of the engaged couples. Since these correlations ranged from −.02 to .58, he concluded that there is no evidence that opposites attract. However, the characteristics studied did not include the kinds of needs investigated by Winch. Inconclusive evidence was also reported by Gross (1956) from a study of groups at Air Defense Command bases. Groups were analyzed for composition with regard to seventeen variables, such as marital status, religion, education, and source of income. He found that some groups were composed of men having dissimilar or contrasting characteristics, whereas others were composed of men having similar characteristics. Again, it is questionable whether these findings are relevant to the need complementarity hypothesis.

More interesting data relevant to the similarity-dissimilarity question derive from studies of changes in relationships over time. For example, one study attempted to discover whether value consensus or need complementarity of seriously attached couples would better predict their relationship from one point of time to another point of time six months later (Kerckhoff & Davis, 1962). Value consensus was found to be the better predictor among couples with relatively short relationships, whereas need complementarity was the better predictor among couples with longer relationships. They proposed that relationships are influenced by different variables at different points in time. Initially, similarity of backgrounds and interests encourage persons to get to know each other; somewhat later similarity of values and attitudes contribute to development of the attachment to each other; and still later need complementarity determines the further progress of the relationship. This theory received marginal support from a later study that attempted to replicate and extend the Kerckhoff and Davis investigation (Levinger, Senn, & Jorgensen, 1970). They found that although need complementarity and value consensus had some effect on progress toward permanence of relationships, the length of the couples' relationship did not interact with these variables as predicted by Kerckhoff and Davis. These findings make it clear that the effects of value consensus and need complementarity on interpersonal relationships are complex and probably depend upon other variables.

The most ambitious attempt to analyze need compatibility in groups is Schutz's three-dimensional theory of interpersonal behavior (also called FIRO), which was outlined briefly in Chapter 2 (Schutz, 1955, 1958). It will be recalled that Schutz proposed three interpersonal needs—inclusion, control, and affection—which he believed were necessary and sufficient to explain interpersonal behavior. Certain combinations of needs were presumed to produce group compatibility and others incompatibility. In general, the more compatible a group the more it would approximate goal achievement.

In the early states of theory development, Schutz (1955) attempted to construct compatible and incompatible groups on the basis of three individual characteristics of group members: dependence, assertiveness, and personalness. These three attributes were measured by specially constructed scales, and groups were composed according to the pattern shown in Table 7-1. Intelligence was used as a control variable. According to the theory, compatible groups can be constructed by selecting as group members persons who favor the personal orientation and who disfavor the dependent orientation, like those shown in Table 7-1. In addition, Schutz assumed that the group would need a focal person to initiate the appropriate atmosphere. Thus, in Table 7-1, the person identified by the symbol $FP_p$ should play this role, since he is high on assertiveness and all other members are low to medium on assertiveness. An incompatible group can be formed by establishing two opposing subgroups. Thus, the group shown in Table 7-1 includes one compatible subgroup made up of a focal person and a compatible member, and a second subgroup which favors the power orientation over the personal orientation. This subgroup also has a focal person, $FP_c$, who initiates the power-oriented atmosphere

**Table 7-1   Characteristics of Members Used in Constructing Compatible and Incompatible Groups**

| Variables | Compatible group members | | | | |
| | FPp | MSp | Mp | Mp | Mp |
| --- | --- | --- | --- | --- | --- |
| Personalness | H* | H | H | H | H |
| Dependence | L,M | L,M | L,M | L,M | L,M |
| Assertiveness | H | L,M | L,M | L,M | L,M |
| Intelligence | H | H | L,M | L,M | L,M |

| Variables | Incompatible group members | | | | |
| | FPp | Sp | FPc | Sc | N |
| --- | --- | --- | --- | --- | --- |
| Personalness | H | H | L | L | M |
| Dependence | L,M | L,M | H | H | M |
| Assertiveness | H | L,M | H | L,M | L |
| Intelligence | H | L,M | H | L,M | L,M |

Personal subgroup   Counterpersonal dependent subgroup

Antagonistic subgroups

*H—roughly highest quartile; M—roughly second or third quartile; L—roughly lowest quartile.
Source: Reproduced with permission from W. C. Schutz, What makes groups productive? *Human Relations,* 1955, **8**, 429–465.

for his subgroup. Therefore, the incompatible group is composed of a personal subgroup and a counterpersonal subgroup which are antagonistic. The compatible groups were expected to be more productive than the incompatible groups when the group task was a complex one requiring cooperation among group members. Groups were required to solve three problems, varying in complexity. The most complex task was a plotting problem designed to require cooperation through a division of labor. Essentially, the group was required to plot the track of many planes on a large plotting board, with the planes arranged in such a way that different group members had different tasks to complete at the same time. The second most complex problem, the intercept problem, required agreement among group members for each decision made by the group. The final problem, and the least complex, involved two intellectual problems, a decoding exercise and a logical exercise, neither of which required a great deal of group cooperation. The results showed clearly that the compatible groups were more productive than the incompatible ones, and this effect was greater as task complexity increased. Evidence from questionnaire results also indicated that the group members felt more positive toward the compatible groups and that the focal person emerged as a leader more frequently than others. Since the groups were matched with respect to intelligence, these differences in productivity must be attributed to differences in compatibility. The results of this initial study thus generally supported Schutz's hypotheses regarding the differences between compatible and incompatible groups.

As the theory was developed more fully, Schutz (1958) identified three types of compatibility: interchange compatibilty, originator compatibility, and reciprocal compatibility. These types of compatibility are described in more detail in Chapter 2. A compatibility index can be computed for each of these types within each of the three need areas; indices for the three types can be computed by summing the appropriate index for the three need areas; inclusion, control, and affection indices can be computed by summing the indices for the three types within the appropriate need area; and an overall compatibility index can be computed by summing the three type indices or the three need indices. Thus, it is possible to compute sixteen different compatibility indices. Schutz cited a number of studies relating the various types of compatibility to group productivity and group cohesiveness. These studies generally supported the view that compatibility is positively related to these group processes, although in some cases the results were equivocal. In a later study, Schutz (1961) found that members of compatible groups are more aware of the interactional characteristics of their group than are members of incompatible groups.

Positive results supporting the hypothesis of a relationship between compatibility and productivity were also reported by Reddy and Byrnes

(1972). Groups were randomly composed of ten to twelve middle managers employed by a large food merchandising company and were required to construct a model of a man from blocks. Using the FIRO-B scales, an index of interchange compatibility was computed for each group in each of the three need areas. Each of these indices of compatibility was correlated with the time required to construct the model. The more compatible the groups were in control and in affection, the faster they assembled the model ($r = .53$ for control and $r = .42$ for affection compatibility). Compatibility in the area of inclusion was not significantly related to time scores. On the other hand, Moos and Speisman (1962) failed to find a relationship between compatibility and time required to transfer rings from one set of pegs to another following certain rules of transfer, although they did find that compatibility was positively related to the number of moves made by the group. Failure to find a significant relationship between compatibility and group functioning was also reported by Shaw and Nickols (1964). They administered the Schutz scales to a large population of subjects, formed groups at random, and observed them in problem-solving situations. All possible compatibility indices and all possible correlations between these indices and measures of group productivity and group satisfaction were computed. Only a few of the correlations were significant, and these could have been due to chance factors. However, it was noted that the range of compatibility scores was not great, which might have accounted for the low correlations. It appears from these results that extremely compatible or extremely incompatible groups probably do not often occur naturally.

Investigations of compatibility in sensitivity training groups have also yielded contradictory results. In one study (Lundgren, 1975), compatibility of trainer and group member was found to be significantly related to the member's attitude toward the trainer and the group. The most important form of compatibility was interchange compatibility. (It will be recalled from Chapter 2 that interchange compatibility exists when two interacting persons are similar with respect to the amount of exchange desired.) In the Lundgren study, group members were most comfortable and most satisfied when the trainer had the same kind of interpersonal orientation that they themselves possessed. However, in a later study (Lundgren & Knight, 1977), no evidence was found that compatibility of needs between members and trainers had an effect on members' attitudes toward either the trainer or the group.

Altman and Haythorn (1967b) also investigated compatibility-incompatibility based upon need achievement, need affiliation, and need dominance, and found the expected compatibility effects only with respect to need affiliation. They predicted that dyads homogeneous with respect to need achievement or need affiliation would be more compatible than dyads heterogeneous with respect to these needs, and therefore that homogeneous groups should perform more effectively than heterogeneous dyads. Homogeneous need-affiliation dyads performed better than heterogeneous need-affiliation dyads, as expected, but heterogeneous need-achievement dyads performed better than homogeneous need-achievement dyads, contrary to expectation. On the other hand, *heterogeneous* need-dominance dyads were expected to be more compatible and hence to perform better than homogeneous need-dominance dyads, but the opposite effect was observed. Altman and Haythorn noted that their experimental design did not permit the assessment of interactions among need variables; hence some of the observed effects may be the result of such interactions rather than of compatibility-incompatibility. It is also possible that the particular needs in question, especially need achievement, are related to effective performance quite independently of group composition; hence, compatibility-incompatibility effects are at least partially confounded with such individual effects. It is also possible, of course, that Altman and Haythorn's assumptions regarding need compatibility were incorrect, although this would be difficult to explain with respect to need dominance, particularly. Despite these possible flaws in design and prediction, the results of this study raise questions about the generality of need compatibility-incompatibility effects on group effectiveness.

A somewhat different approach was taken by Sapolsky (1960). He investigated the effects of verbal reinforcement on acquisition and extinction as a function of the compatibility-incompatibility of experimenter and subject. He selected five female experimenters on the basis of their scores on the Schutz scales, such that all were high on need for control but varied with respect to need for inclusion and affection. Subjects were then selected to be either compatible or incompatible with the experimenter with whom they worked. Each subject was asked to make up sentences using words presented on cards. During this procedure, E verbally reinforced the use of first-person pronouns by saying "mmm-hmmm" at the end of any sentence that began with either "I" or "We." The acquisition period was followed by an extinction period during which no reinforcement was given. The results are shown in Figure 7-2. It is clear that the subjects in the compatible dyads responded to verbal reinforcement more than subjects in incompatible dyads, and that this effect continued for some time after reinforcement was discontinued. This may be a partial explanation of the greater productivity and satisfaction of compatible groups; reinforcements provided by compatible others enhance the motivation and efforts of individual group members.

### Response Compatibility

Another group of investigators has been interested in patterns of behavior predicted from personality characteristics. The basic assumption is that

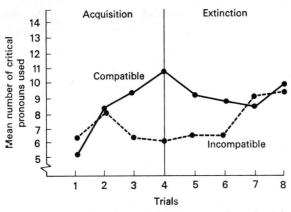

**Figure 7-2** Curves showing the mean number of reinforced pronouns used by the compatible and incompatible groups. (Reprinted with permission from A. Sapolsky. Effect of interpersonal relationships upon verbal conditioning. *Journal of Abnormal and Social Psychology,* 1960, **60,** 241–246. Copyright 1960 by the American Psychological Association. Reprinted by permission.)

certain personality attributes predispose the individual to behave in typical ways and that these ways of behaving may produce either group compatibility or group incompatibility. Some of these considerations were noted in Chapter 6 and in the first part of this chapter. It will be recalled, for example, that the authoritarian person is autocratic and demanding, ascendant individuals are assertive and dominating, etc. (see Table 6-3). A person who is autocratic would probably be compatible with a person who is submissive but would be incompatible with a person who behaves in a dominating manner. It is, therefore, important to know how the various combinations of personality characteristics are related to compatibility-incompatibility and hence how they influence the performance and satisfaction of groups. Unfortunately, relatively little work has been done on the effects of response compatibility as determined by personality characteristics. What has been done is limited almost entirely to studies of authoritarianism and dominance.

Perhaps the most extensive examination of response compatibility based upon authoritarianism was made by Haythorn, Couch, Haefner, Langham, and Carter (1956b). The California F-scale was used as the measure of member authoritarianism, and groups were composed of various leader-follower combinations: leader high on authoritarianism, followers high (Ff groups); leader high, followers low (Fd groups); leader low, followers high (Df groups); and leader low, followers low (Dd groups). Although Haythorn et al. discussed their predictions in terms of similarity-dissimilarity of leaders and followers, their hypotheses were based upon the assumption that the same individuals would behave differently depending upon the characteristics of others in the group. For example, they expected that leaders would be less directive and autocratic with democratic followers (low scorers on the authoritarianism scale) than with autocratic followers (high scorers). With authoritarian followers, leaders were predicted to be more decisive and directive because these kinds of followers expected the leader to behave this way. In general, similar group members should be compatible, and dissimilar group members should be incompatible.

The four-person groups formed according to the above design were required to perform a task which called for discussion of a human relations problem presented by film, after which they composed and recorded dialogue for similar problems. Observers recorded the interaction, and postexperimental questionnaires were administered to obtain reactions to the group. The results revealed the usual differences between the behavior of authoritarian and democratic leaders, with the authoritarian leaders less concerned with group approval, less sensitive to others, and more autocratic than the democratic leaders. There were also differences that depended upon the particular combinations of leader-follower personality. Leaders with authoritarian followers were rated by observers as higher on autocratic behavior, and their groups were rated as more dominated by the leader than the groups with democratic followers. Under democratic leadership, followers were rated by observers as having more influence, more effective influence, and equal participation in group activities. Compatible groups revealed less personality conflict than the less compatible groups. Furthermore, followers in the compatible groups were rated as more secure and as striving for goal achievement more than those in the less compatible groups.

A somewhat similar study was conducted by M. E. Shaw (1959b), although he was concerned primarily with compatibility of group membership with respect to the structure of the group. As in the Haythorn et al. study, groups were composed of varying combinations of leader-follower authoritarianism; however, the measure of authoritarianism was the acceptance of authority scale devised by Bales (1956). Groups of four persons each were assigned to either a centralized communication structure or a decentralized communication structure. In the centralized structure, one person in the group could communicate with all other members, but these other members could not communicate with each other. In the decentralized structure, everyone could communicate with everyone else in the group. Groups were required to solve a series of three arithmetic problems requiring written communication among group members. It was expected that groups composed of authoritarian members would perform better and be better satisfied in the centralized than in the decentralized structure, whereas groups composed of nonauthoritarian members would be more effective in decentralized networks. Theoretically, then, the most efficient combinations should be authoritarian leaders and followers in a centralized structure and nonauthoritarian leaders and followers in a decentralized structure. Unfortunately, measures of authoritarianism are negatively correlated with intelligence, so that a direct test of these expectations is not valid. Therefore, correlations were computed between the leader's authoritarianism score and the performance of the group, with the effects of intelligence partialed out (i.e., controlled) and between the average authoritarianism score for all group members and the group's performance score, with intelligence partialed out. The partial correlations between group authoritarianism and performance (time to solve) were $-.18$ in the centralized structure and $.22$ in the decentralized structure. This difference was in the predicted direction, but was not statistically reliable. The partial correlations between leader authoritarianism score and group performance were $-.29$ in the centralized and $.38$ in the decentralized structure, a highly significant difference. This finding is important because it suggests that the effects of group member characteristics may depend upon the roles that group members are expected to play in the group.

In summary, the evidence concerning response compatibility predicted from authoritarianism is disappointing, not so much because it is negative, but because of its paucity. The very limited amount of evidence available indicates that certain combinations should be more effective than others, at least under certain circumstances, but considerably more work is required before definitive statements can be made about the most effective combinations under specified circumstances. This research probably must await the development of more adequate measures of authoritarianism.

Investigators in the area of dominance have had better success in showing that compatible groupings lead to more effective group action. Smelser (1961) theorized that different combinations of dominant-submissive individuals would determine the extent to which such individuals can use salient interpersonal techniques, and that the use of such techniques is related to anxiety reduction. When the situation, including the other person in the group, permits the use of techniques consistent with the person's predispositions, anxiety is reduced and the performance of the group is enhanced. If the individual cannot use habitual modes of response, anxiety is likely to occur and group performance will be inhibited or interfered with. Compatible or incompatible dyads were formed by pairing individuals who were either similar or dissimilar with respect to dominance-submission, based upon scores on a scale designed to measure dominance. Some of the pairs were assigned roles (one dominant, the other submissive) and some were not; within pairs that were assigned roles, personality and roles were congruent for some subjects and not for others.

Each dyad was given the task of simultaneously operating two trains on a common set of tracks. Switches controlling trains, crossovers, sidings, etc., were controlled by each person; hence, carelessness of either could interfere with the performance of the other. Group scores were based upon mutual round trips, so achievement scores depended upon cooperation.

Smelser was primarily interested in the congruency of personality and role, but his data also provide evidence concerning the compatibility of group composition. Other things equal, a pair consisting of one dominant and one submissive member should be compatible, whereas pairs composed of either two dominant or two submissive individuals should be incompatible. When dominant-submissive pairs were compared with the other two combinations in the no-role-assignment condition, they were found to be more effective (mean performance score = 141.2) than submissive-submissive pairs (mean = 130.2) but approximately equal to the dominant-dominant pairs (mean = 142.0). Under conditions of role assignment, personality and role could be completely congruent only in dominant-submissive pairs; that is, in both dominant-dominant and submissive-submissive pairs, one of the two members was assigned a congruent role and the other an incongruent role. When the dominant-submissive congruent-role pairs were compared with the other two, the dominant-submissive were clearly more effective (mean = 160.4 versus means of 153.3 and 142.9). The dominant-submissive pairs assigned to incongruent roles were least efficient (mean = 116.4).

Essentially similar results were obtained by Fry (1965) in a study of various combinations of ascendant group members. In the first study reported, subjects were divided into quartiles according to scores on a scale designed to measure ascendance, matched for intelligence and authoritarianism. Groups of four persons, one from each level of ascendancy, reported to the laboratory for each experimental session. Each person played a game requiring coordination with each of the other three persons on three successive trials. The results showed that individuals with discrepant ascendance scores performed better than did those with similar ascendance scores. In a second experiment, individuals were paired as similar if they came from adjacent quartiles and as dissimilar if they came from more remote quartiles. The differences were the same, although not as great as in the first study, a variation that may have been due to the grouping procedure. Considering the results from the investigations of both Smelser and Fry, it is clear that compatible groups with respect to dominance-ascendance are more effective than groups that are incompatible in this respect.

Compatibility based upon ego-defense preference has also been shown to influence interpersonal relations (A. R. Cohen, 1956). Cohen hypothesized that when two persons have a similar type of psychosexual disturbance and this disturbance is aroused, they react to each other in terms of their defenses against the disturbance. Using the Blacky Pictures Test and its auxiliary Defense Preference Inquiry, he identified the following defenses against psychosexual disturbances; projection, avoidance, regression, reaction formation, and intellectualization. Individuals were paired according to type of disturbance and preferred defense against it so that three kinds of pairs were formed: pairs of projectors, pairs with similar defenses other than projection, and pairs with dissimilar defenses. Each pair then discussed material related to their psychosexual disturbance, after which they rated various aspects of the group process. The results revealed that members of projector pairs experienced their interaction as more negative than other pairs, and the more intense the disturbance the greater was the group composition effect. Since this negative reaction occurred only when projectors were paired with each other, it appears that it is due to composition of the group rather than to member projection per se. Cohen interpreted this effect in terms of the anxiety aroused through the projection process.

A somewhat different approach to the study of compatible groups was adopted by Thelen (1966). He recognized that each teacher teaches some children more effectively than others, and consequently attempted to group teachers and children who would be compatible. He asked thirteen teachers to list the names of students they thought "got a lot out of class" and those who "got very little out of class." Nominees were then tested on a multidimensional inventory designed to measure attitudes, preferences, semantic projections, and similar characteristics. Using this information, "teachable" classes were composed for each teacher; i.e., the pupils in the class were chosen to be like those that the teacher had nominated as "getting a lot out of class." From the remaining students, thirteen control groups were composed by the usual administrative procedures. The teachables presumably were more compatible, at least with the teacher, than were the controls. Comparison of the two kinds of groups indicated that (1) eleven of the thirteen teachable classes received higher marks, one received the same, and one received lower marks from their teachers than did the corresponding control classes, and (2) five of the thirteen teachables showed superior gains on achievement tests and eight showed inferior gains as compared with the corresponding controls. In short, the teachers apparently perceived that pupils did better in the more compatible groups, but the objective data failed to verify this perception. It is unclear, however, whether the procedure followed by Thelen actually resulted in more compatible groups.

In summary, the evidence is moderately supportive of the compatibility-productivity hypothesis. Some studies have failed to find the expected relationship between compatibility measures and measures of group performance, but in most instances it is unclear whether there were differences in compatibility and/or whether other variables were adequately controlled. It is probably accurate to say that when group members have personality attributes which predispose them to behave in compatible ways, the group atmosphere is congenial, the members are relaxed, and group functioning is more effective. On the other hand, when member attributes lead to incompatible behaviors, members are anxious, tense, and/or dissatisfied, and group functioning is less effective.

## HOMOGENEITY-HETEROGENEITY OF GROUP MEMBERSHIP

It is evident from the preceding discussions that in many studies the incompatible groups were heterogeneous with respect to needs and personality attributes and the compatible groups were homogeneous with respect to these characteristics. Examination of Table 7-1 reveals that the compatible groups composed by Schutz were much more homogeneous than the incompatible ones. Similarly, the groups formed upon the basis of authoritarianism and of dominance also varied with respect to homogeneity-heterogeneity. These types of composition can be distinguished from those we are about to discuss primarily because compatibility theorists assumed that certain homogeneous groups might be compatible and others incompatible; the emphasis was thus placed upon the relationships among particular characteristics rather than upon the mere fact that group member characteristics were homogeneous or heterogeneous. On the other hand, many theorists believe that the homogeneous-heterogeneous dimension is the most important one and so have concentrated their research upon this aspect of group composition. The general assumption is that most group activities require a variety of skills and knowledges; hence, the more heterogeneous the group, the more likely the necessary abilities and information will be available and the more effective the group is likely to be. Indeed, some investigators (for example, Hoffman, 1959; Hoffman & Maier, 1961) assert that heterogeneous groups are generally more effective than homogeneous groups. However, the reader should keep in mind that the distinction between compatibility and homogeneity-heterogeneity is somewhat arbitrary. It should also be remembered that groups are homogeneous or heterogeneous with respect to specific characteristics, not all of which are relevant to the group's activities.

The most common approach to homogeneity-heterogeneity of group composition is a simple comparison of homogeneous and heterogeneous groups, where homogeneity is defined in terms of a single characteristic. For example, groups composed of persons of the same sex are compared with mixed-sex groups, or groups composed of members having similar abilities are compared with groups composed of members having diverse abilities. This has been referred to elsewhere as *trait homogeneity* (M. E. Shaw, 1966). In contrast, some studies have considered several characteristics of group members in defining homogeneity and heterogeneity. In these studies, personality profiles are usually compared to determine degree of correspondence of member characteristics. *Profile homogeneity* may be considered a more powerful determinant of group process than trait homogeneity because of the greater number of characteristics used in the identification of group differences. It is obvious that the effects of one variable can be obscured by uncontrolled variables. On the other hand, different variables reflected in the personality profiles of group members may have opposite effects, and thus some will cancel out others. That is, homogeneity of some traits may facilitate group functioning whereas heterogeneity of other traits may be desirable. These effects cannot be ascertained if the investigator considers only profile homogeneity. The best approach is the simultaneous investigation of both profile and trait homogeneity. Unfortunately, this approach is rarely used, as we shall see in the following discussions.

## Trait Homogeneity

Trait homogeneity may be measured in several ways, all of which are based upon variability of scores earned by group members on some standard measure. In some cases, such as sex composition, the measure may be only visual inspection and the degrees of homogeneity-heterogeneity limited by the number of persons in the group. That is, a two-person group is either homogeneous or heterogeneous; a four-person group may be homogeneous, or it may vary in degree of heterogeneity since there may be three of one sex and one of the other or two of each sex, etc. In the case of personality characteristics, however, the degree of heterogeneity is limited only by the characteristics of the personality measure and the method of computing variability among members' scores. Any standard measure of variability may be used, such as range, standard deviation, or average deviation, or an average of the discrepancy between the scores of each pair of group members may be used. All measures should yield comparable scores, although they would not be perfectly correlated.

The number of characteristics that have been investigated is not great, despite the obvious significance of this aspect of group composition. A review of the literature reveals studies dealing with ability, sex, race, conceptual systems, authoritarianism, individual prominence, and "interpersonal comparability." However, there is sufficient evidence to draw conclusions only with regard to ability, sex, race, and conceptual systems.

**Ability Homogeneity-Heterogeneity**   One early investigation of ability composition was reported by M. E. Shaw (1960), with largely negative results. In an experiment designed for another purpose, four-person groups solved problems in either a centralized or a decentralized power structure, or in either a centralized or a decentralized communication network. Homogeneity-heterogeneity scores were computed for each group as the average deviation among member scores on the Scholastic Aptitude Test. These scores were then correlated with achievement scores and ratings of member satisfaction. Correlations between homogeneity-heterogeneity and performance ranged from $-.07$ to $.38$; none was statistically reliable. The correlations of homogeneity scores with ratings of satisfaction ranged from $-.49$ to $.30$. The $-.49$ correlation was statistically reliable and occurred in the centralized power structure. Considering the number of correlations computed, this one reliable correlation could have been due to chance factors.

A different approach was taken by Goldman (1965), who was interested in the relative performance of individuals and two-person groups. Subjects from a college population were given the Wonderlic Intelligence Test and divided into high (H), medium (M), and low (L) intelligence levels on the basis of their test scores. Subjects were paired in the following combinations: HH, MM, LL, HM, HL, and ML. The pairs were given a different form of the same intelligence test and instructed to work together on the test, discuss each item, and reach consensus regarding the correct answer. Although Goldman was interested in differences between the performance of pairs and that of individuals, we are interested here primarily in the differences between the homogeneous and the heterogeneous pairs. An examination of Goldman's data reveals that the heterogeneous pairs did slightly better than the homogeneous; however, the HH, HM, and HL pairs did not differ significantly from one another, and the ML and LL did not differ, although the MM was significantly better than either the ML or the LL pair. If one combines all homogeneous pairs (i.e., the HH, MM, and LL pairs) and compares the performance of these with the combined heterogeneous pairs (i.e., the HM, HL, and ML pairs), one finds that the average gain over individual performance was 4.37 in the homogeneous pairs as compared with a gain of 6.58 in the heterogeneous pairs. Since this study was not designed to examine the effects of homogeneity-heterogeneity, the results are not entirely unambiguous. However, improvement on intelligence test scores is a rigorous test of group effectiveness, and the data suggest that heterogeneous ability groups are more effective than homogeneous groups.

A very similar study was conducted by Laughlin, Branch, and Johnson (1969), again for the primary purpose of comparing individual and group performance. Subjects were administered the first part of the Concept Mastery Test (Terman, 1956) and divided into high (H), medium (M), and low (L) intelligence categories. Triads of the following combinations were formed: HHH, HHM, HHL, HML, HMM, HLL, MMM, MLL, and LLL. Again, performance of triads on a second administration of the test was taken as the measure of group effectiveness. This means that there is a problem in comparing homogeneous and heterogeneous triads, because a part of the differences among triads can obviously be attributed to differences in the abilities of members of triads. However, if one compares the average score of HHH, MMM, and LLL groups with that of HML groups, the overall level of ability should be the same for homogeneous and heterogeneous groups. Examination of data presented by Laughlin et al. reveals that the heterogeneous groups were clearly superior to the homogeneous groups (means = 63.75 and 49.83 respectively). Of the three types of homogeneous groups, only the HHH group (mean = 79.94) performed better than the HML group.

Further evidence concerning the relative effects of homogeneous and heterogeneous ability grouping derives from studies of such groups in elementary and secondary schools. This is a controversial issue in the education world, and there is little agreement among teachers as to the best way to group pupils for academic achievement. Ability or homogeneous grouping has a long history, dating back at least to 1867 when systematic attempts at homogeneous grouping were initiated in St. Louis elementary schools. However, it was not until about 1920 that serious attempts were made to evaluate the effectiveness of this procedure for academic achievement. Many of the problems in conducting research that have been noted elsewhere are found in the evaluation of ability grouping: definitions of ability are varied and often ambiguous, measures of achievement are often of questionable reliability and validity (e.g., measures of "ability" usually reflect some combination of ability and application), uncontrolled variables make it difficult to interpret findings, and so on. We will not elaborate further here, but the reader should remember these difficulties when interpreting the evidence.

Numerous studies have been conducted in the past fifty years for the purpose of exploring the relative effectiveness of homogeneous and heterogeneous ability groupings. For example, an extensive study covering a two-year period was carried out by Goldberg, Passow, and Justman (1966). The study was designed to examine differences in achievement, social and personal relations, interests, and attitudes among intermediate-grade children when placed in groups with various ranges of intellectual ability. Children were first categorized according to IQ: Those with IQs of 130 and higher were identified as gifted, those with IQs between 120 and 129 as very bright, those with IQs from 110 to 119 as bright, those with IQs of 100 to 109 as high average, and those having IQs of 99 and lower as low and below average. Fifteen patterns of grouping were established to allow for each ability level to be studied either alone or in combination with one or more other levels. Principals of the schools involved were required not only to form the special classes, but also to keep these special classes intact for two years and to provide adequate time for pre- and post-testing. No attempt was made to select teachers or to instruct them regarding method of instruction. The intent was to vary only the pattern of ability grouping. Altogether, 86 groups were studied, involving 2,219 pupils. Measures of achievement, attitudes, and interest were administered at the beginning of grade five and again at the end of grade six.

The findings reported by Goldberg et al. may be summarized as follows:

**1** Significantly greater achievement in social studies, reading comprehension, vocabulary, arithmetic, and total average occurred in the more heterogeneous groups. Science, language arts, and work-study skills were not significantly affected by the grouping patterns.
**2** Pupils in the more heterogeneous groups raised their self-esteem to a greater extent than did pupils in the more homogeneous groups, except for the low and below-average students who showed lowered self-esteem during the two-year period.
**3** Grouping elementary pupils by ability had no consistent effects on their interests and attitudes toward the school.*

In general, these findings provide little support for the thesis that homogeneous ability grouping facilitates academic achievement or raises the self-esteem of pupils (except for the low and below average). One further study may be cited as representative of research on the effects of ability grouping. This study (Daniels, 1961) was conducted in England where the equivalent term for homogeneous ability grouping is *streaming*. Between 1953 and 1960, Daniels investigated the effects of streaming in primary schools. Two groups of schools were selected to be as similar as possible with repsect to size, social background of pupils, efficiency of teachers, etc., differing only in that one group practiced streaming and the other group did not. Comparison of the progress of pupils in the two types of schools led to the following conclusions:

**1** Average performances on tests of English, reading, mathematics, and intelligence in the streamed schools was lower than in the unstreamed schools.

---

*Goldberg et al. reported numerous other data, but the findings given here are the most important ones for present purposes.

**2**   Both the more able and the less able children performed better in the unstreamed than in the streamed schools, with the less able children making far better progress in the unstreamed schools.

These findings are in accord with those reported by Goldberg et al. (1966) and once again indicate that heterogeneous ability grouping, rather than homogeneous ability grouping, tends to facilitate academic achievement. Reviews of the many studies reported in the literature also reveal data that are consistent with this conclusion. For example, Eash (1961) examined the research on ability grouping and concluded that ability grouping may actually be detrimental to children in the average and lower ability groups because they are deprived of the intellectual stimulation provided by the presence of brighter children. On the other hand, Eash noted that the evidence is "fairly conclusive" that homogeneous ability grouping influences the student's self-perception, sense of dignity and worth, and attitudes toward other children. Furthermore, the research shows that teachers tend to react more favorably to teaching homogeneous ability groups (Goodlad, 1960).

In short, the belief that homogeneous ability grouping generally facilitates academic achievement appears to be erroneous; as in other situations, heterogeneous ability groups make as great or greater progress than homogeneous ability groups. Ability grouping apparently has desirable effects upon the student's self-esteem and the teacher's attitudes toward teaching, but these are attained at the expense of lowered academic achievement.

If homogeneous ability grouping has been unsuccessful, how can we explain its widespread appeal? The usual explanation is that in a homogeneous class the teacher would have fewer individual differences to contend with (Thelen, 1949). It may also satisfy the need to stratify society and to segregate persons (Bettelheim, 1958). Whatever the reason, homogeneous grouping apparently still enjoys popularity among some educators, despite the fact that other forms of grouping may be more effective. For example, Thelen (1949) suggested the principle of least group size, which holds that each subgroup should be the smallest group in which it is possible to have represented all the social and achievement skills that are needed for the particular activity or task of the group. This form of grouping has been labeled *complementation;* the resources of each group member complement the resources of other members so that the group as a whole has the needed resources to complete the activity in question. This is, of course, a form of heterogeneous grouping which considers the abilities, skills, etc., of each member relative to other members of the group. Complementation is probably the most effective grouping procedure, but it is also the most difficult to achieve.

In summary, the empirical evidence regarding ability homogeneity-heterogeneity and the effectiveness of adult groups is not extensive, and many of the comparisons were not as well controlled as would be desirable. The evidence concerning ability grouping in the schools is much more extensive, but again control of unwanted variables is a problem. On the other hand, data from both adult and children's groups support the hypothesis that, other things equal, groups composed of members having diverse abilities perform more effectively than groups composed of members having similar abilities.

**Sex Homogeneity-Heterogeneity**   It is a common observation that women's groups behave differently from men's. Groups of men are commonly believed to be task-oriented and businesslike, and women's groups social-oriented and interested more in gossip than in getting the job done. Despite these stereotyped beliefs, comparatively little research has been done to determine how sex composition actually is related to group processes. In general, the research has elected to study either all-male or all-female groups so that the effects of the gender of group members are presumably the same for all experimental conditions. Although limited, there is some evidence that the sex composition of the group is related to interaction styles, leadership behavior, bargaining processes, conformity, and group performance.

The effects of group sex composition on interaction styles have been observed in several studies. For example, Wyer and Malinowski (1972) found that same-sex pairs engaged in more individualistic and more competitive behavior than mixed-sex pairs. Kent and McGrath (1969) observed that group products of same-sex groups were more action-oriented and revealed greater originality and optimisim than the products of mixed-sex groups. Another study (Aries, 1976) found that men were more personally oriented in mixed-sex groups, addressed individuals (as opposed to the group as a whole) more often, and spoke about themselves and their feelings more often in mixed-sex groups. By contrast, in all-male groups they were more concerned with status and competition. Women in mixed-sex groups, as compared with women in same-sex groups, were less dominant; they tended to let men dominate them.

Further research is needed before we can fully understand the implications of these effects of sex homogeneity-heterogeneity, but they probably influence many other aspects of group process. Differences in male-female behavior and interaction styles may account for other effects of group composition on behavior in groups. For instance, females (but not males) preferred large groups to small groups when in mixed-sex groups, but they preferred small groups to large when in same-sex groups (Marshall & Heslin, 1975). In another study (Vallacher, Callahan-Levy, & Messe,

1979), it was found that mixed-sex dyads reached agreement more quickly when they bargained face-to-face than when apart, whereas same-sex dyads reached agreement as quickly when face-to-face as when apart. Unfortunately, neither of these studies provided much evidence concerning the kinds of behaviors that might have produced these effects.

Given that sex composition affects the behavior of group members, the question of effects on group performance naturally arises. When members of a group have differing perspectives, the quality of the group's problem solving is likely to be higher than when group members are homogeneous in this regard. We have already seen that males and females have differing viewpoints and behaviors in social situations; hence, mixed-sex groups should be more effective problem solvers than same-sex groups. Hoffman and Maier (1961) compared same-sex and mixed-sex groups as they interacted in case discussions, problem solving, and role playing. Three problems that the groups attempted could be scored quantitatively for quality of solution: the mined road problem, the student assistance fund problem, and the painter-inspector argument problem. The mined road problem required the group to devise a plan for getting five men across a heavily mined road; the student assistance fund problem was a role-playing task requiring that group members decide how to distribute a $3,000 student assistance fund among five students (the group members), each of whom needed and qualified for $1,500 for the next academic year; and the painter-inspector argument task required the group to settle an argument between a painter and an inspector, both of whom were members of the group. Three sex compositions were studied: all-male groups, groups composed of three males and one female, and groups composed of two or three females and one or two males. Mixed-sex groups generally performed more efficiently on all three problems than did same-sex groups. Unfortunately this study was concerned primarily with homogeneity-heterogeneity of personality, and it was not always clear which effects were due to that variable and which to sex composition. The fact that no all-female groups were included also clouds the interpretation of these findings, since it is unclear to what extent the differences may have been due to sex differences per se.

On some kinds of tasks, mixed-sex groups have been found to perform less efficiently than same-sex groups. Clement and Schiereck (1973) compared all-male (MMMM), all-female (FFFF), mixed-adjacent (same sex members seated next to each other, MMFF), and mixed-alternate (members seated alternately by sex, MFMF) groups on a signal detection task. The task was to find the location of a target object when projected on a screen. The MMMM and FFFF groups did not differ in efficiency, and both performed better than the mixed-sex groups. The mixed-adjacent groups performed better than the mixed-alternate groups, an outcome which Clement and Schiereck attributed to the greater probability that same-sex coalitions will occur in the MMFF seating arrangement. It seems more likely that the presence of members of the opposite sex may be distracting, an event which would explain both the generally better performance of the same-sex groups and the difference between the two mixed-sex groups.

When the sex composition of the group is skewed (i.e., the group contains a relatively large proportion of one sex relative to the other), some interesting effects are observed. For instance, in a field study of industrial groups containing relatively few women (Kanter, 1977), three perceptual phenomena were noted: (1) The "token" women became more visible than in more balanced groups; (2) the differences between men and women were exaggerated (i.e., polarization occurred); and (3) perceptions of women were distorted to fit the preexisting generalization about women (a process called *assimilation*). Analysis of group process suggested that visibility generated pressures for women to perform, polarization induced men to heighten their group boundaries (i.e., men formed stronger subgroups that excluded women), and assimilation led to "role entrapment" of women (i.e., women found it difficult to change the role that men in the group perceived to be appropriate for them).

Effects of group composition on group performance may also depend upon the roles enacted by males and females in the group. Ruhe (1978) employed three-member groups (a leader and two followers) in a management task that required group members to work together to deduce the correct placement of six trainees. Male and female leaders worked with both same-sex and mixed-sex dyads (followers). Group performance was measured by time required to complete the task. The results are depicted in Figure 7-3. It can be seen that heterogeneous groups performed better than homogeneous groups with both male and female leaders. It is also interesting to note that the poorest performance was by all-male groups; all-female groups performed no worse than male-led heterogeneous dyads. Again, these differences may be the result of differential behavior of leaders in homogeneous and heterogeneous groups. For instance, it has been observed that leaders of both sexes address more directive behavior toward own-sex groups (Eskilson & Wiley, 1976).

Group performance may also be mediated by leadership emergence. In one investigation (Dyson, Godwin, & Hazlewood, 1976), it was found that a leader was less likely to emerge in homogeneous than in heterogeneous groups and that groups with a leader were more likely to reach consensus regarding decisions. This finding may, of course, be related to conformity behavior, which has also been shown to vary with sex composition. An examination of these effects may be enlightening.

Conformity behavior as a function of sex composition has been

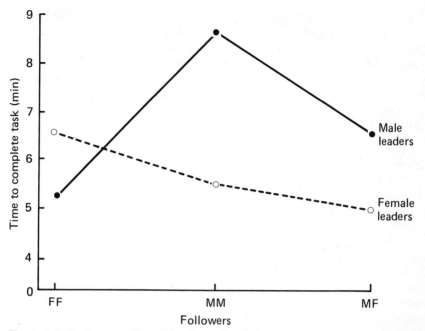

**Figure 7-3** Performance time of female- and male-led groups in a management training task. (Plotted with permission using data reported by J. A. Ruhe, Effect of leader sex and leader behavior on group problem solving. *Proceedings of the American Institute for Decision Sciences*, Northeast Division, May 1978, pp. 123–127.)

studied more extensively than other aspects of group behavior. However, there is a methodological problem which complicates the study of sex homogeneity-heterogeneity as it affects conformity behavior: Females typically conform more than males, at least on most tasks used in studies of conformity (see Chapter 6), and a heterogeneous group should, therefore, conform more than a homogeneous male group but less than a homogeneous female group, assuming that there are no composition effects. Any comparison of homogeneous and heterogeneous groups based on sex must take this factor into account. The most common way of doing this is to compare the amount of conformity of members of a given sex in same-sex and mixed-sex groups. In studies using this approach, the results are somewhat conflicting, although the general conclusion that both males and females conform more in mixed-sex than in same-sex groups seems justified. Luchins and Luchins (1955) found that men conformed more to erroneous judgments of a female partner than to those of a male partner. However, from the data obtained in a more complicated experimental situation, Tuddenham, MacBride, and Zahn (1958) concluded that men conformed more in same-sex groups than in mixed-sex groups. Several sex compositions were examined: five men; three men and two women; two men and three women; and five women. These groups were asked to make judgments of visual stimuli (e.g., which line was the same length as a comparison line), information problems (e.g., percentages of persons in the United States over age 65), and opinions (e.g., that most people would be better off if they had never gone to school), after being exposed to unanimously incorrect judgments (or discrepant opinion judgments) by other group members. Although there were some variations in conformity as a function of kind of judgment, the best evidence is probably the total conformity score for all tasks. These data showed that men conformed less in the two-men–three-women groups (mean = 2.12) than in either the all-male groups (mean = 3.80) or the three-men–two-women groups (mean = 4.00). On the other hand, women conformed more in the three-women–two-men groups (mean = 6.60) or in the all-female groups (mean = 5.81), although none of these differences was statistically reliable.

The relationship between sex composition and conformity behavior was also studied by Reitan and Shaw (1964). Groups composed of four men, four women, or two men and two women were tested in an apparatus which exposed them to unanimously wrong judgments by other group members. The results of this study clearly revealed that all group members, regardless of sex, conformed more in the mixed-sex groups than in the same-sex groups (medians = 2.5 and 2.1, respectively). The interpretation of these results is bolstered by questionnaire responses of group members which showed that members of mixed-sex groups were more concerned about disagreements and were more doubtful of their accuracy than were members of same-sex groups. Reitan and Shaw interpreted these findings as showing a greater concern for interpersonal relations in the mixed-sex groups; men may not wish to be in a position of disagreeing with a woman, or the distracting influences of members of the other sex may reduce an individual's confidence in his judgments.

Although there are some inconsistent findings, the empirical data generally support the hypothesis that individuals conform more in mixed-sex than in same-sex groups, and this effect applies to both men and women. When the group is homogeneous with respect to the sex of its members, group members are task-oriented and hence are more concerned with effective performance than with social-emotional problems. The judgments of others in the group, therefore, serve as a source of information to be considered along with other relevant information about the task. When there is a conflict between social information and objective information about the task, objective information is weighted more heavily, and less conformity occurs. On the other hand, members of mixed-sex groups are more concerned with social-emotional activity and with a desire to conform to the expectations of others in the group. The majority opinion thus becomes of greater importance than objective information, and greater conformity occurs.

It is evident that the sex composition of groups exerts a strong influence on group processes. The interaction styles of both men and women vary with sex composition, conformity behavior is affected, leadership emergence is greater in heterogeneous than in homogeneous groups, and heterogeneous groups usually perform more effectively than homogeneous groups. It should be remembered, however, that sex-related patterns of behavior are greatly influenced by the norms of society, which are prone to change over time. It is probable that many of the effects attributable to sex composition may change as societal forces deemphasize sex differences and related normative behaviors.

**Race Homogeneity-Heterogeneity**   Relations among members of different racial groups have long been a concern of social scientists and are probably of even greater concern today than in the past. In particular, black-white groupings have become more common with the advent of school desegregation, affirmative action programs, and other social reforms. Perhaps because of these changes, several investigators have examined the effects of black-white interactions. Many of these studies have been limited to observations of differences in the feelings and behavior of black and white leaders in various settings (e.g., Battle & Rotter, 1963; Delbecq & Kaplan, 1968; Katz, Roberts, & Robinson, 1965; Lefcourt & Ladwig, 1965). The results of these studies generally show that in black-white interactions the black is more anxious, shows less self-assertion, has a higher expectancy of failure, and is less efficient than when interacting with other blacks. Blacks also tend to talk to whites more than to other blacks. These differences in black-white behaviors are similar to differences in behaviors of high-low status persons (see Chapter 8). It is probable that status differences between blacks and whites account for differences in their behaviors when they interact. Whatever the reasons for them may be, these differential responses to the racial composition of the group may be expected to influence the relative effectiveness of racially homogeneous and heterogeneous groups.

In some instances, racially mixed groups perform less efficiently than racially homogeneous groups. Fenelon and Megargee (1971) selected black and white college women who scored either high or low on a dominance scale, and paired high- and low-dominant persons. Four types of pairs were formed: two blacks, two whites, a high-dominant black paired with a low-dominant white, and a high-dominant white paired with a low-dominant black. Each pair was then assigned clerical tasks that required a group decision. The average time to reach a decision in the homogeneous groups was 5.8 seconds as compared with 9.8 seconds in the heterogeneous groups. Apparently the tension created in the racially mixed groups inhibited effective group interaction. It was also observed that the high-dominant person most frequently assumed the leadership role in all compositions except the high-dominant white paired with a low-dominant black. This was attributed to the white member not wanting to assert authority over the black, plus increased assertiveness of the low-dominant black.

Less effective performance by racially mixed groups was also found in an investigation by Ruhe and Allen (1977). Groups were composed of all white members, 25 percent black, 50 percent black, 75 percent black, or all black members. All groups worked on two tasks: a knot-tying task and a ship-routing task. The first task required each group member to tie an unusual knot and required little group interaction. As might have been anticipated, group composition did not affect performance on this task. On the second task, each group was asked to work together quickly in order to find the shortest route for a ship that had to touch five ports. The mean times to complete this task were 439.15, 820.50, 798.81, 1355.75, and 461.93 seconds for the all white, 25 percent black, 50 percent black, 75 percent black, and all black groups, respectively. It is obvious that the racially homogeneous groups (all white and all black) completed the task much more quickly than the racially heterogeneous groups.

On the other hand, racially mixed groups are not necessarily less efficient than racially homogeneous groups. For instance, Ruhe (1972) studied three-person groups consisting of either a black or a white supervisor and either two black, two white, or one black and one white subordinate. Two trained judges observed the groups through a one-way mirror and coded group interactions. Black supervisors exhibited less asking for opinion and gave fewer suggestions than white supervisors regardless of the racial composition of the subordinates. In the heterogeneous subordinate groups, the black subordinate talked less, gave fewer suggestions and less information, and expressed greater satisfaction with work on the assigned tasks than did the white subordinate. When the supervisor was white, black subordinates were less agreeable and accepting than the white subordinates. Despite these behavioral differences, the racial composition of the groups did not affect group productivity.

Finally, at least one study showed that blacks, but not whites, were advantageously affected by racially heterogeneous groups (Ruhe & Eatman, 1977). Blacks in integrated groups performed better on the ship-routing task (described above) and on a letter-writing task and had higher self-esteem than blacks in segregated groups. These results refer to the productivity of individual group members rather than to group productivity, but group productivity is ordinarily presumed to be the resultant of individual contributions by group members.

In summary, the racial composition of the group clearly influences the feelings and behaviors of group members, particularly of the black group members. In some cases, these behavioral differences interfere with group performance, but this is not invariably true. With increasing equal-status association among blacks and whites, the effects of racial composition may be expected to decrease and perhaps disappear.

**Homogeneity-Heterogeneity of Conceptual Systems** In a careful analysis of personality, Harvey, Hunt, and Schroder (1961) identified four conceptual systems which reflect the individual's level of cognitive functioning. System I individuals are said to function at the lower level of abstractness or integrative complexity, whereas System IV individuals, at the other extreme, function at the highest level of integrative complexity. System I individuals find ambiguity threatening; hence, they invoke authority and normative standards to avoid ambiguity. They tend to use a few dimensions or categories in organizing information about their world. System IV individuals, on the other hand, perceive many dimensions of information and use several ways of organizing their world. Their processing of information is flexible and permits many alternative interpretations.

Groups composed of individuals who function at the same conceptual level (homogeneous groups) may be expected to behave in similar ways and thus to perform more effectively on tasks requiring uniformity and less effectively on tasks requiring diversity of opinion than groups composed of individuals differing in level of conceptual functioning (heterogeneous groups). Unfortunately, few researchers have examined this particular aspect of group composition. Studies regarding conceptual system composition have based their analyses upon the relative effectiveness of individuals, largely irrespective of others in the group. In general, predictions have been based upon the relative number of System I and System IV individuals in the group; the more System IV individuals in the group, the better the performance is expected to be. For example, Tuckman (1967) examined the performance of three-person groups of homogeneous System IV's, homogeneous System I's, heterogeneous System IV's composed of one System I and two System IV individuals, and heterogeneous System I's composed of two I's and one IV. He predicted that the groups having the greatest number of System IV members, the homogeneous IV's and the heterogeneous IV's, would perform more effectively than homogeneous I's and heterogeneous I's on "abstract" tasks, but not on "concrete" tasks. The abstract task required the group to make a number of decisions about the best way to take an island held by an enemy. It was described as a task that imposed no structural limitations and permitted multiple solutions and multiple routes to those solutions. The concrete task was the Combat

Information Center Task used by Altman and Haythorn (1967b), which required group members to plot inputs from a sonar scope (presumably) on a vertical plotting board. It was said to require single solutions and single routes to those solutions. In general, homogeneous groups performed slightly better than heterogeneous groups, although this was accounted for by the relatively better performance of the homogeneous System IV groups. The homogeneous System I groups performed more poorly than any other composition. The interpretation of these results is complicated by the fact that System IV individuals are more successful than System I individuals, and this effect is confounded with the group composition variable. This study was also complicated by the fact that dominance of group members was also varied in a complex manner, making it difficult to isolate conceptual system composition effects. However, the results generally supported Tuckman's hypothesis that groups in which abstract group members (System IV's) predominate outperform groups in which concrete group members (System I's) predominate, at least when the task is unstructured. No differences were observed on a concrete, structured task.

A more easily interpreted experiment was conducted by Stager (1967). As in Tuckman's study, the relative number of System I–System IV group members constituted the major composition variable. Four-person groups were composed to represent four levels of homogeneity-heterogeneity: 100 percent System IV members; 75 percent System IV and 25 percent System I members; 50 percent System IV and 50 percent System I members; and 25 percent System IV and 75 percent System I members. The groups were equated across composition conditions for intelligence and for dominance tendencies. The task used was the island problem (abstract task), which required that the group plan the capture of the island from the enemy. The group was instructed to act as an equal-status military field staff and was required to make a series of decisions during seven half-hour periods. Observers coded the interaction of the group members and rated their performance. It was predicted that the amount of search for new information, the number of alternatives suggested, the use of conflict in synthesizing and evaluating alternatives, and role differentiation would increase with increasing percentage of group members of a high conceptual level. The results generally supported predictions, as shown in Figure 7-4. Complexity of communications and evaluations of alternatives increased with increased percentage of members of a high conceptual level, as expected. The generation of alternatives (suggestions) did not vary with group composition, but the ratio of suggestions to evaluations (S/E ratio) decreased with increasing high-conceptual membership. Role flexibility also increased with increased proportion of highs in the group.

The research data are consistent in showing that the conceptual

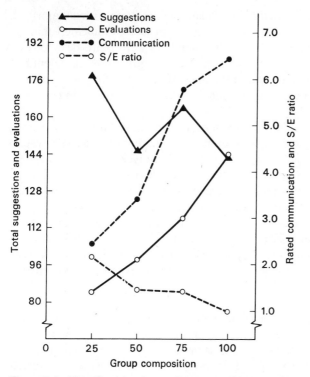

**Figure 7-4**   The effect of an increasing percentage of members of a high conceptual level in the group on the generation of alternatives, communication complexity, and S/E ratio. (Reprinted with permission from P. Stager. Conceptual levels as a composition variable in small-group decision making. *Journal of Personality and Social Psychology,* 1967, **5,** 152–161. Copyright 1967 by the American Psychological Association. Reprinted by permission.)

systems of group members are related to group function, although it is evident that much of this effect can be accounted for by the additivity of individual contributions to the group. That is, the group composition effects are produced by behavior attributable to the individual in any situation and do not depend upon the particular other person with whom the individual is grouped. Presumably, a four-person group composed of three high-conceptual level persons and one intermediate would be as effective as one with three highs and one low, or even with two or more lows.

Although not based upon the Harvey et al. analysis of conceptual systems, a study of group composition based on cognitive complexity may be relevant (Turney, 1970). Four- and five-person groups, varying in number of cognitively complex group members, worked on a complex information processing task. Groups having a majority of cognitively complex members performed more efficiently than those with a majority of concrete group members. Analysis of group processes indicated that the groups with more cognitively complex members were more flexible, they developed a stronger leadership structure, and a more interdependent role structure emerged. It is likely that the ineffectiveness of the more concrete groups was due to their relative ineffectiveness in developing a group structure.

In summary, the limited evidence concerning trait homogeneity suggests that (1) groups composed of members heterogeneous with respect to abilities are more effective than those homogeneous in ability, (2) members of mixed-sex groups conform more than members of same-sex groups, (3) racial homogeneity-heterogeneity influences the feelings and behaviors of group members and sometimes, but not always, negatively influences group productivity, and (4) heterogeneity of conceptual systems probably is not a determinant of group functioning, since such functioning is a result of the proportion of System IV individuals in the group. Studies utilizing profile homogeneity-heterogeneity measures are more promising.

## Profile Homogeneity

As noted earlier, group problem solving requires a variety of skills, abilities, and perspectives; hence, a group that is heterogeneous on a number of member characteristics is more likely to contain members having the needed attributes and, therefore, is more likely to be effective than a homogeneous group. The profile approach to the study of homogeneity-heterogeneity considers several individual attributes rather than a single characteristic as in the trait approach; this enhances the probability that heterogeneous groups will perform more effectively than homogeneous groups. This effect has been demonstrated clearly by Hoffman (1959) and Hoffman and Maier (1961). In the first study, Hoffman composed groups upon the basis of personality profiles obtained by administering the Guilford-Zimmerman Temperament Survey (GZTS) (Guilford & Zimmerman, 1949). This survey measures ten personality traits that are relatively independent dimensions of the personality. Homogeneous groups were made up of individuals who had similar GZTS profiles and heterogeneous groups of individuals who had dissimilar GZTS profiles. Each group solved two problems: the mined road problem (already described) and the change of work problem (CWP). The CWP is a role-playing situation in which three workers report to a supervisor, who is the fourth man in the group. The supervisor requests, at the suggestion of a time-study man, that the three workers work at fixed positions instead of rotating as they have been doing in the past. The group must decide what to do about this request, since the workers would prefer to rotate to relieve monotony. When the group had finished the problem, they responded to a questionnaire designed to measure satisfaction with the solution reached by the group.

The heterogeneous groups performed better on both tasks. On the mined road problem, the heterogeneous groups earned a mean score of 63.1 compared with a mean score of 44.5 earned by the homogeneous groups. The solutions produced on the CWP were scored in terms of old solutions (the group continues rotation), new solutions (acceptance of the supervisor's suggestion), or inventive solutions (attempts to compromise between the old and the new). The heterogeneous groups produced more inventive solutions, although there was no difference between types of groups in satisfaction with the solution achieved.

The Hoffman and Maier (1961) study extended this approach to a variety of tasks in an attempt to determine whether heterogeneous groups would produce higher quality solutions on tasks involving conflicts in values and personal conflicts. The three problems that could be scored objectively were described on page 245. The results of this study were consistent with those reported by Hoffman. Heterogeneous groups produced a higher proportion of "good" solutions on most tasks and equally good solutions on others. The conclusion that high-quality solutions can be obtained more readily from heterogeneous than from homogeneous groups appears justified.

Two other studies may be considered to have adopted the profile approach in the sense that more than one personal attribute was considered in the determination of homogeneity-heterogeneity. Triandis, Hall, and Ewen (1965) conducted three experiments to investigate the relationship between group member heterogeneity and dyadic creativity. In the first experiment, subjects were given eighteen semantic differential scales concerning such issues as war, socialized medicine, and immortality. Dyads were then formed (on the basis of responses to these scales) that were high, medium, or low on cognitive similarity. The dyads were asked to consider social problems, such as how to reduce unemployment in the United States. Half of the dyads had had previous experience with such tasks and half had not. Group products were scored for originality, practicality, and quality. Heterogeneous dyads performed better when they had had experience, but were less effective when they were untrained. In the other two experiments, group composition was based upon attitudinal measures and measures of creativity. Dyads were formed that were (1) homogeneous on both attitudes and creative ability, (2) heterogeneous on both attitudes and creative ability, (3) homogeneous on attitudes but heterogeneous on ability, or (4) heterogeneous on attitudes but homogeneous on ability. The problems were similar to those used in Experiment I; dyads responded to such questions as "How can a person of average ability achieve fame, though he does not possess any particular talents?" Results showed that dyads that are heterogeneous in attitudes and homogeneous in abilities are more creative than other group compositions. The relatively complex manner in which the attitudes and creative abilities were measured and in which groups were formed makes these results difficult to interpret.

A study by Fiedler (1966) also may be considered a study of profile homogeneity, since he investigated groups differing in homogeneity of cultural background. Half of the groups were "homocultural" groups composed of either three French-speaking men or three Dutch-speaking men in the Belgian Navy. The other half were "heterocultural" groups composed of either a French-speaking leader and two Dutch-speaking followers or a Dutch-speaking leader and two French-speaking followers. Since the language difference correlated with wide cultural differences in the men's backgrounds, homogeneity-heterogeneity was actually based upon many personal attributes. Also, it should be evident that language heterogeneity would be expected to inhibit effective group performance, whereas heterogeneity of opinions and perspectives might be expected to enhance performance. This particular way of forming groups, therefore, produces two opposed forces relative to group effectiveness. This fact probably accounts for the "strikingly small" differences in performance by homogeneous and heterogeneous groups. However, Fiedler, Meuwese, and Oonk (1961) also failed to find a difference in the performance of Dutch groups differing in religious and subcultural homogeneity. It is possible that the characteristics studied by Fiedler and his associates were not relevant to the tasks the groups were assigned to complete.

In summary, groups that are heterogeneous in terms of personality profile usually perform more effectively than groups that are homogeneous in this respect. When the group members have a variety of opinions, abilities, skills, and perspectives, the probability is increased that the group as a whole will possess the characteristics necessary for efficient group performance. Obviously, there are some personal attributes on which group members should be similar for effective group functioning. For example, language homogeneity clearly facilitates group communication, which in turn facilitates group functioning. Heterogeneity on such characteristics can counteract the desirable effects of other types of member heterogeneity, a fact which reinforces the earlier assertion that the best approach to the study of homogeneity-heterogeneity of group membership involves both trait and profile analyses.

## PLAUSIBLE HYPOTHESES ABOUT GROUP COMPOSITION

This rather brief review of studies dealing with group composition effects makes it evident that the research in this area has only begun to reduce the number of plausible hypotheses concerning relations among group member characteristics and group processes. Nevertheless, several hypotheses have tentative support. Each of the following should be considered a plausible hypothesis, but further research is required before some of them can be regarded as *probably* valid.

*Hypothesis 1    Individuals contribute differently to the group product, depending upon the particular other individuals in the group.*

Although the evidence for Hypothesis 1 is limited largely to a single study (Rosenberg et al., 1955), the hypothesis gains strength from the fact that it is intuitively plausible. A given individual may be active and outspoken when in a group of friends or with submissive strangers, but be very inactive and uncommunicative when in a group of aggressive strangers. Such variations in behavior obviously mean differences in the amount of contribution to the group's products.

*Hypothesis 2    Members of high-cohesive groups communicate with each other to a greater extent than members of low-cohesive groups.*

Numerous studies have shown that the amount of interaction is greater in groups composed of members who are highly attracted to the group than in groups composed of members who are less attracted to or are repelled by the group (Back, 1951; French, 1941; Lott & Lott, 1961). Persons who like each other talk with each other more than do individuals who dislike each other. This obvious fact has important implications for group behavior.

*Hypothesis 3    The pattern and content of interaction are more positively oriented in high-cohesive than in low-cohesive groups.*

When the group is highly cohesive, members tend to be friendly and cooperative and to engage in behaviors which facilitate group integration. Members of low-cohesive groups tend to function as individuals rather than as group members; their group-oriented behavior tends to be aggressive and uncooperative (Back, 1951; Shaw & Shaw, 1962).

*Hypothesis 4    High-cohesive groups exert greater influence over their members than do low-cohesive groups.*

One source of social power is interpersonal attraction; hence, it is reasonable to suppose that members of high-cohesive groups should have more power and, therefore, more influence over each other. This expectation is supported by studies showing that members of high-cohesive groups respond to attempted influence by other group members more than do members of low-cohesive groups (Berkowitz, 1954; Schachter et al., 1951), that members of high-cohesive dyads change their opinions in the direction of their partner's opinion more than members of low-cohesive dyads (Back, 1951), and that members of high-cohesive groups conform to majority judgments more than do members of low-cohesive groups (Bovard, 1951; Lott & Lott, 1961; Wyer, 1966). However, there is some evidence that cohesive groups conform more only when conformity facilitates group effectiveness, at least under some conditions (Sakurai, 1975).

**Hypothesis 5**   *High-cohesive groups are more effective than low-cohesive groups in achieving their respective goals.*

Evidence concerning the relationship between group cohesiveness and group effectiveness is not altogether consistent. Laboratory studies have shown only small increments in favor of the high-cohesive group (Schachter et al., 1951) or no difference in the productivity of high- and low-cohesive groups (Berkowitz, 1954). However, such failures to support Hypothesis 5 are probably due to the fact that groups do not always accept the goal specified by the experimenter. Results of field studies and field experiments generally support the hypothesis (Goodacre, 1951; Shaw & Shaw, 1962; Van Zelst, 1952a; Van Zelst, 1952b). The results of these studies suggest that the high-cohesive group is effective in achieving whatever goals its members establish, although these may not always be the ones of interest to the investigator.

**Hypothesis 6**   *Members of high-cohesive groups are generally better satisfied than members of low-cohesive groups.*

Results from both field studies (Gross, 1954; Marquis et al., 1951; Van Zelst, 1952b) and laboratory experiments (Exline, 1957) support the proposition that members of high-cohesive groups are better satisfied with the group and with its products than are members of low-cohesive groups. Members of high-cohesive groups are motivated to interact with others in their group and to achieve group goals; this motivation leads to effective group functioning and to high member satisfaction.

**Hypothesis 7**   *Compatible groups are more effective in achieving group goals than are incompatible groups.*

Although there are some negative results, the bulk of the evidence suggests that groups that are compatible with respect to needs and personality characteristics are able to function more smoothly, devote less of their energy to group maintenance, and thus achieve their goals more effectively than groups whose members are incompatible with respect to needs and personality characteristics (Haythorn et al., 1956b; Sapolsky, 1960; Schutz, 1955; Schutz, 1958; M. E. Shaw, 1959b). However, much more theoretical work is required to determine which individual characteristics may be expected to be compatible and which incompatible; only then can empirical work establish valid hypotheses about specific aspects of group compatibility and group process. For example, studies of the effects of compatibility in sensitivity training groups yielded contradictory results (Lundgren, 1975; Lundgren & Knight, 1977).

*Hypothesis 8    Members of compatible groups are better satisfied than members of incompatible groups.*

The studies cited in connection with Hypothesis 7 also provide some support for Hypothesis 8. In addition, studies by Smelser (1961), Fry (1965), and A. R. Cohen (1956) indicate that members of incompatible groups experience anxiety and general dissatisfaction with the group. It seems inevitable that such factors will eventually interfere with effective group functioning.

*Hypothesis 9    Other things being equal, groups composed of members having diverse, relevant abilities perform more effectively than groups composed of members having similar abilities.*

This hypothesis has a firm theoretical foundation as well as adequate empirical support. Group performance usually calls for diverse skills, and these are more likely to be found in groups whose members have diverse abilities than in groups whose members have similar abilities. Work by a number of researchers verifies this expectation (Goldman, 1965; Laughlin et al., 1969).

*Hypothesis 10    The interaction styles of men and women are affected differently by the sex composition of the group.*

This hypothesis is supported by research showing that men are more personally oriented, address individuals more often, and speak about themselves more frequently in mixed-sex than in same-sex groups, whereas women become less dominant in mixed-sex groups (Aries, 1976). Indirect support also comes from a study showing that same-sex and mixed-sex dyads are affected differently by social context (face-to-face versus apart) in bargaining situations (Vallacher et al., 1979).

*Hypothesis 11    Sexually heterogeneous groups are more effective than sexually homogeneous groups.*

Evidence for this hypothesis is very limited, having been investigated in only one study (Ruhe, 1978). However, it has indirect support from at least two studies that show that sex composition influences other aspects of the group process which may be expected to affect group performance. For instance, Eskilson and Wiley (1976) found that leaders of both sexes address more directive behavior toward members of their own sex, and

Dyson et al. (1976) found that a leader is more likely to emerge in sexually heterogeneous groups than in sexually homogeneous groups.

*Hypothesis 12   Members conform more in mixed-sex groups than in same-sex groups.*
The best evidence suggests that members of mixed-sex groups are more concerned about interpersonal relations and hence conform more than members of same-sex groups, who are more concerned with the task at hand. Despite some inconsistent results (Tuddenham et al., 1958) the empirical data generally support the above hypothesis (Reitan & Shaw, 1964).

*Hypothesis 13   Racial heterogeneity tends to create interpersonal tension which is reflected in the feelings and behaviors of group members.*
Evidence concerning the effects of racial composition upon group behavior is very limited. However, several studies reveal black-white differences in racially heterogeneous groups that do not appear in racially homogeneous groups. In racially mixed groups, blacks talk less than whites, they often show less self-assertion and greater expectancy of failure, and often are less efficient than whites (Delbecq & Kaplan, 1968; Katz, Roberts, & Robinson, 1965; Lefcourt & Ladwig, 1965; Ruhe, 1972). These effects may or may not adversely affect group performance (cf. Ruhe, 1972; Ruhe & Allen, 1977).

*Hypothesis 14   Groups whose members are heterogeneous with respect to personality profiles perform more effectively than groups whose members are homogeneous with respect to personality profiles.*
Although the evidence supporting this hypothesis is relatively good (Hoffman, 1959; Hoffman & Maier, 1961), there is also some reason to believe that certain composition effects may be obscured by limiting attention to profiles. For example, Fiedler (1966) found little difference between the performance of homocultural and heterocultural groups, a finding which probably resulted from the combination of attributes which should be homogeneous (language) with those which should be heterogeneous (opinions, perspectives) for effective group functioning.

In brief smmary: We have just begun the analysis of group composition effects. It is already clear that such effects are far more complex than they appeared to be initially. We may hazard a guess that interpersonal compatibility is the basic variable in group composition; the large task facing group dynamicists is the theoretical analysis of interpersonal relations so that the compatibility-incompatibility of individual characteristics can be identified.

## SUGGESTED READINGS

Altman, I., & Haythorn, W. W. The effects of social isolation and group composition on performance. *Human Relations,* 1967, **20,** 313–340.

Fenelon, J. R., & Megargee, E. I. Influence of race on the manifestation of leadership. *Journal of Applied Psychology,* 1971, **55,** 353–358.

Good, L. R., & Nelson, D. A. Effects of person-group and intragroup attitude similarity on perceived group attractiveness and cohesiveness. *Psychonomic Science,* 1971, **25,** 215–217.

Goodacre, D. M., III. The use of a sociometric test as a predictor of combat unit effectiveness. *Sociometry,* 1951, **14,** 148–152.

Hoffman, L. R., & Maier, N. R. F. Quality and acceptance of problem solutions by members of homogeneous and heterogeneous groups. *Journal of Abnormal and Social Psychology,* 1961, **62,** 401–407.

Hoogstraten, J., & Vorst, H. C. M. Group cohesion, task performance, and the experimenter expectancy effect. *Human Relations,* 1978, **31,** 939–956.

Laughlin, P. R., Branch, L. G., & Johnson, H. H. Individual versus triadic performance on a unidimensional complementary task as a function of initial ability level. *Journal of Personality and Social Psychology,* 1969, **12,** 144–150.

Rosenberg, S., Erlick, D. E., & Berkowitz, L. Some effects of varying combinations of group members on group performance measures and leadership behaviors. *Journal of Abnormal and Social Psychology,* 1955, **51.** 195–203.

Ruhe, J. A., & Eatman, J. Effects of racial composition on small work groups. *Small Group Behavior,* 1977, **8,** 479–486.

# Chapter 8

# Group Structure

Everyone has been impressed at one time or another by the very different behaviors enacted by an individual in different situations. The agressive boss greets the demands of his wife with a meek "Yes, dear." The young man who is outspoken and witty when with other young men becomes a confused imcompetent in mixed-sex social groups. The young woman who confidently and accurately makes judgments alone often errs when faced with the unanimous wrong judgments of her fellow group members. It may be noted, upon closer examination, that these variations are associated with particular group memberships. A person's behavior is a function of his or her relationships to others in the group.

When several individuals come together for the first time and begin to interact, consistent individual differences begin to appear. Some persons talk more than others; some exert more influence upon the group's decisions; some are generally more active than others; some appear to elicit greater respect from other group members; and so on. Differentiations occur among the members of the group such that inequalities exist among them along a variety of dimensions. These differentiations are the basis for the formation of group structure. As differentiations occur, relationships are established among the separate parts so that there exists a pattern of relationships in the group. This pattern of relationships among the differentiated parts of the group is often referred to as group structure (Cartwright & Zander, 1953). However, since the group may become differentiated along a variety of dimensions, this conception of group structure means that there is not a single group structure but rather many group structures—in fact, as many structures as there are dimensions along which the group may be differentiated (M.E. Shaw, 1961b). But in reality, the structure of a group is not merely a set of separate, albeit interrelated, patterns of relationships among diverse units; it is an integrated organizational pattern that reflects the totality of the separate parts that inhere in each individual group member. An adequate conception of group structure must recognize this complexity.

## NATURE OF GROUP STRUCTURE

Within any given group, the various differentiations result in parts of the group that reside in individual group members. That is, it is the group member who is differentiated from other group members with respect to the particular dimension under consideration. Hence, a given group member may simultaneously be the person who talks most, the person who is most active, the person who has least influence in the group, and so on. The total characterization of the differentiated parts associated with an individual group member may be referred to as the person's *position* in the group. Thus, each group member occupies a position in the group, and the pattern of relationships among the positions in the group constitutes a *group structure.*

Each position is evaluated by the members of the group, including the occupant, in terms of its prestige, importance, or value to the group. This evaluation is referred to as *social status,* or simply *status.* Although several positions may enjoy equal status, there almost always exist status differences such that the group structure is hierarchical. The occupant of each position is expected to carry out certain functions (enact certain behaviors) during group interaction. The set of expected behaviors associated with a position within the group constitutes the *social role* or, more briefly, *role* of the occupant of that position. These aspects of group structure are shown graphically in Figure 8–1. This diagram depicts the structure of a sales department in a small business. The sales manager occupies the highest status position, exerts the greatest influence on the group, has the most power, is the most respected group member, etc. The sales manager is expected to lead the group, to set policy, to decide group goals, to serve as the final arbiter of disputes, and to perform similar group funtions. The

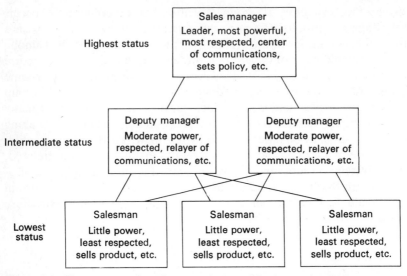

**Figure 8-1**  The structure of a sales group in a small business organization.

deputy sales managers have equal status, but it is lower than that of the sales manager; they have some power in the group, have an intermediate amount of influence on the group, enjoy less respect than the sales manager, but more than others in the group, etc. They are expected to advise the sales manager regarding policy matters, to lead others in the group in the performance of their duties, and to perform similar functions for the group. The three salesmen are at the bottom of the status hierarchy and are of equal status. They have little power, exert little influence on others in the group, and are generally less respected than the sales manager and the deputies. Their role requires that they carry out the instructions of the managers; that is, their primary function is to sell the product produced by the small business.

The example in Figure 8–1 represents a formal group structure. The positions, roles, and statuses are made explicit by the larger organization of which the group is a part. But the structure need not be explicit, and indeed is not in many informal groups. For example, the participants in a game of bridge may constitute an informal group in which each member has a definite position, and each position may be evaluated differently by the group members. There is a pattern of relationships among positions which constitutes the group structure, and the occupant of each position is expected to engage in certain kinds of behavior which constitute the role associated with that position. Each group member is more or less aware of this group structure and often can verbalize it quite clearly; yet there is no explicit statement concerning the organization of the group. Group structure may, therefore, be either formal or informal; it may be explicitly recognized and stated or merely implicit in the functioning of the group. In either case, the group structure exerts a pervasive influence upon the behavior of the members of that group.

In addition to the status accorded each position, the group establishes rules which specify acceptable behavior in the group. These "rules of conduct" are called *social norms* or, more simply, *norms*. Norms specify acceptable behavior in the group; they may apply to all members of the group or only to the occupants of certain positions in the group. Role specifications are norms that apply to positions, but not all norms are role specifications. Furthermore, there are wide variations in the degree to which group members may disobey norms without sanctions being administered. The many ramifications of group norms will be explored later.

The structure of the group, once established, is largely independent of the particular individuals who compose the group. A given position is accorded a given status regardless of the person who happens to occupy it, and the occupant is expected to carry out certain behaviors. For example, the president of a company is expected to set broad policy, to plan the goals for the organization, etc. However, what policies and goals are set may depend heavily upon the characteristics of the particular person who occupies the position. Thus, role enactment is a function of the structural aspects of the group (i.e., the expected behaviors associated with a position) *and* the personal characteristics of the occupant. Although the occupant of a position may alter the role associated with the position and the status ascribed to it, group structure tends to be stable over time even when group membership changes.

The stability of group structure has been demonstrated experimentally by Jacobs and Campbell (1961). After a cultural norm had been established with the help of confederates, confederates and old members were removed from the group one at a time as new members replaced them. The arbitrary norm persisted for four or five generations after the last confederate had been removed, after which it decayed. This study shows that at least one aspect of group structure does not depend solely on the particular individuals who compose the group. Perpetuation of arbitrary norms with changing group membership was also observed in a study that partially replicated the Jacobs and Campbell study (Montgomery, Hinkle, & Enzie, 1976). Again, it was found that the norm persisted after all original group members had left the group, but the arbitrary norm declined more rapidly when the group was composed of less authoritarian persons. The latter finding suggests that the stability of group structure is a joint function of inertia and member characteristics. A third study of the persistence of norms revealed that conformity to imposed arbitrary norms was an inverse function of degree of arbitrariness (MacNeil & Sherif, 1976). The results of these studies also suggest that purely arbitrary aspects of group structure are not likely to be perpetuated indefinitely with changing group membership. Indeed, it has been shown that some aspects of group structure can be altered by reward distribution in the group (Bevelas, Hastorf, Gross, & Kite, 1965). Members of four-person groups were reinforced differentially by means of colored lights: a green light indicated that the member was making positive contributions to the group and red lights indicated negative contributions. The group member who was chosen to receive high positive reinforcement (relatively many green lights) was ranked higher by fellow group members following reinforcement than prior to the reinforcement period. In short, positive reinforcements administered by a source outside the group can change the relative statuses of group members, a finding that has been verified by Smith (1972).

## Status, Positions, and Differentiated Parts

The status assigned to a given position is a consequence of other characteristics which lead to the differentiation of that position from other positions in the group. The leadership position is ordinarily evaluated more highly than nonleadership positions; the position with the greatest amount of power is accorded higher status than less powerful positions; the position with the greatest communication potential is perceived as more important than other positions; and so on. Thus, the status attributed to a given position is a function of the differentiations that occur in the group and subsumes the various aspects of group structure that are commonly referred to as leadership structure, power structure, sociometric structure, communication structure, and the like. These different aspects of group structure are intercorrelated such that the leader is usually the most powerful person in the group and has the greatest communication potential (that is, he or she is the center of the communication network). For instance, Freese and Cohen (1973) observed that status differences among group members that were not group-related (e.g., high status in the community) produced differences among group members with respect to power and prestige, although this effect did not occur if the performance attributes of members did not coincide with status. In other words, the various aspects of group structure, although correlated, are independent in the sense that one aspect (e.g., power) may vary while another (e.g., leadership) remains unchanged. Each dimension may be varied independently for experimental purposes, and a number of studies have examined the effects of "single structures." Some of these studies have already been discussed; others will be presented in later sections of this chapter.

It should now be evident that our analysis of group structure and the way we are using the terms *position, status, role,* and *group structure* are different from some other analyses and usages. For example, status has been given a variety of conceptual meanings by group theorists, and it is often confused with position and/or with role. Discussion of these differing viewpoints has been reserved for a later part of this chapter.

## ORIGINS OF GROUP STRUCTURE

The formation of group structure is one of the basic aspects of group development; hence, the emergence of positions, statuses, roles, and norms occurs during the process of group formation and development. It is not possible to consider the process of group formation without simultaneously considering the origins of group structure. In Chapter 4, some of the phases in group development that have been observed in various kinds of groups were described (e.g., in problem-solving groups, Bales & Strodtbeck, 1951; sensitivity training groups, Bennis & Shepard, 1956; self-analytic groups, Winter, 1976; and others, Caple, 1978; Near, 1978; Tuckman, 1965). It will be recalled that in all those groups, members were concerned with problems of interpersonal relations within the group and with the locus of control. These are important aspects of group structure. We also noted instances of coalition formation and the ways subgroups are formed. In subsequent chapters, we observed the effects of the physical environment, the personal attributes of group members, and the composition of the group on such aspects of the group as the development of leadership, status, and power relations. Consequently, much has already been said about the origins of group structure. Therefore, the present discussion will be restricted to a review of these earlier considerations and an attempt to show how they are interrelated.

According to Cartwright and Zander (1968), the factors that determine group structure can be classified into three major categories: (1) the requirements for efficient group performance; (2) the abilities and motivations of group members; and (3) the physical and social environments of the group. We have seen how each of these sets of variables influences various aspects of group structure, but we have also seen how one aspect of group structure may influence another aspect and thereby the nature of the structure as a whole. Thus, a fourth category must be considered: the "single structures" of the group.

### Requirements for Efficient Group Performance

Groups usually assemble for a purpose, be it to solve a problem of great magnitude or merely to engage in friendly social interaction. The kind of task that the group establishes or accepts as its goal becomes important to group members, who usually consider the best ways of organizing themselves to achieve the goal. This tendency was brought into sharp focus in a study of communication and leader choice in small groups (Shaw & Gilchrist, 1956). Groups of five subjects each were observed in an experiment requiring that group members select problems and solve them via written communication. Each group member was assigned a mailbox, and the only way the group members could interact was by writing letters to each other. In eight of ten groups, one or more group members suggested early in the interaction period that the group needed to organize itself for efficient performance. In various ways, members suggested that the group needed a leader, a coordinator, etc., who would direct the activities of others. These suggestions were acted upon in every instance, and the group organized itself in a way that group members believed would help them perform efficiently.

In Chapter 4, considerable evidence was cited to show that coalitions form in situations in which greater rewards can be achieved by subgroups than by individuals acting alone. Clearly, concern for outcomes influences the kinds of subgroupings that develop, although the overall efficiency of the group may sometimes be impaired.

## Characteristics of Group Members

The kinds of differentiations that are likely to develop in neonate groups are also influenced by the attributes of individuals who compose them.

The individual who likes to dominate others will try to establish a centralized power structure with himself or herself at the center; the person who enjoys social interaction will seek to establish an equalitarian structure that permits easy interpersonal exchange; the knowledgeable group member is likely to emerge as the task leader; and so on. In some individuals, a need for structure exists; the individual needs to structure relevant situations in meaningful and integrated ways (Cohen, Stotland, & Wolfe, 1955). When persons having such needs are in group situations, they attempt to structure the group to satisfy their needs. For example, Aronoff and Messé (1971) found that five-person groups composed of members having high safety needs were likely to develop a hierarchical structure, whereas groups composed of persons having high esteem needs tended to develop more equalitarian structures. In other words, groups tended to develop structures that were in accord with the motivations of their members. Another study of groups composed of one male and two females who were homogeneously high on either esteem or safety needs also revealed the influence of individual characteristics on group structure (Messé, Aronoff, & Wilson, 1972). As predicted, males became leaders more frequently in the safety groups than in the esteem groups. Presumably, safety-oriented persons focus on an easily identifiable quality, "maleness," and use this quality as a basis for role assignment.

The role of member characteristics on the emergence of group structure was further explicated by a study of abstract and concrete groups (Tuckman, 1964). Group members were assembled on the basis of scores on tests designed to identify the extent to which persons engage in categorical thinking (concrete) versus more complex, differentiated thinking (abstract). Four types of relatively homogeneous groups were formed, corresponding to the four conceptual types identified by Harvey et al. (1961) (see pp. 251–254). More abstract groups, relative to more concrete groups, adopted a group structure that was flexible and open. These findings are consistent with those reported by Turney (1970) which we cited in Chapter 7. It will be remembered that groups having a majority of cognitively complex members were more likely to develop a group structure characterized by flexibility, strong leadership, and interdependent roles.

In Chapter 6, it was noted that characteristics of individual group members contribute to group structure in several important ways. Physical superiority, intelligence, and task-related skills were shown to be positively related to leadership emergence. Persons who are positively oriented toward others contribute to the development of group cohesiveness. The individual who is dependable contributes to goal achievement and is more likely to emerge as the leader. These member characteristics, and undoubtedly many other aspects of the group members which have not yet been carefully studied, contribute greatly to the development of group structure.

### Environment of the Group

That the environment of the group plays a highly significant role in group process has been emphasized throughout this book. The physical surroundings provide the opportunity for other variables to influence group structure and also exert a direct effect upon the development of structure through the cultural connotations of spatial positions. For example, the well-known study of student housing (Festinger, Schachter, & Back, 1950) revealed clearly that the physical location of living quarters determined the sociometric structure of groups. In Chapter 5, we found that the status of group members was intimately related to their physical position in the group. Persons sitting at the head of the table, for instance, are typically accorded higher status than individuals who sit at the sides. Conversely, an individual who has high status in the group usually chooses to sit at the head of the table. Similarly, an individual who is arbitrarily assigned a central position in a communication network has a high probablility of emerging as a leader. The pattern of communication also influences the sociometric structure of the group and the degree to which the occupant of any specific position in the communication network is perceived as having prestige in the group.

## Single Structures as Factors in the Origins of Group Structure

Interaction among the various aspects of group structure also contributes to the development of structure. As noted earlier in this chapter, the group becomes differentiated along a variety of dimensions; hence one can view the group as having several structures—one for each dimension on which the group becomes differentiated. We have designated these structurings with respect to single dimensions as "single structures." Each single structure has an effect upon other such structures. A person who achieves a position of leadership in the group is usually accorded high status; the individual who is attractive to others in the group (a high sociometric status) is more likely to be given a high-status position and to become the leader; sociometric status is one source of power, as we shall see later; and so on. Each single structure is thus a factor in the development of other single structures and, ultimately the overall structure of the group. In other words, differentiation along one dimension often is a determinant of differentiations along other group dimensions, each of which influences the total group structure.

In summary: numerous factors influence the development of group structure. These range from the characteristics of members who compose the group to the effects of one aspect of the structuring process on others. Although the general nature of these effects is known, few have been studied in careful detail. Perhaps more can be said about the effects of group structure upon group process.

## STATUSES, ROLES, AND NORMS

*Status, role,* and *norm* are significant concepts for the description and analysis of group structure, and they are interrelated in a variety of ways. Furthermore, these terms have been used with a variety of meanings and have been qualified by various prefixes which give them different connotations. This section will explore the different meanings of status, role, and norm, and attempt to show some of their consequences for group behavior.

### Status and Position

Status and position are so closely interrelated that the two terms are often used interchangeably (Davis, 1940; Linton, 1936), but they are basically different aspects of group structure. A person's position in a group is the total characterization of the differentiated parts of the group associated with that person; it is his or her place in the social system. When one identifies a person's position in the group, one is at the same time identifying his relative standing with respect to such dimensions as power, leadership, and attractiveness. Status, on the other hand, refers to the evaluation of that position. It is the rank accorded the position by group members—the prestige of the position.

Some authors have made a distinction between *ascribed status* and *achieved status* (Davis, 1940; Linton, 1936). Ascribed status is attributed to individuals through no fault or merit of their own; it is based on such arbitrary characteristics as sex, age, wealth, and kinship. The individual's personal qualities, possessions, and relationships are the bases for attribution of ascribed status. For example, it is evident that a person "born to the color" has higher ascribed status than a person who has the misfortune to be born "on the wrong side of the tracks." The person's own achievements or qualifications have little to do with this kind of status. On the other hand, achieved status is based on individual accomplishments. Persons born into undistinguished families can achieve high status if they have the necessary abilities and motivations. Abraham Lincoln reportedly was born in a log cabin, yet he achieved high status in our society. When such a distinction is made, however, it is clear that status is being used in essentially the same way that we have used the term *position,* although prestige rank is also implied. Hence, in the following discussions, the reader should keep in mind that the term *position* refers to a person's place in the social structure and *status* refers to the group members's evaluation of that position.

## Status Effects

When two persons meet for the first time, each seeks to acquire as much information as possible about the other person, e.g., information about competence, trustworthiness, self-conception, and, of course, status. Some of this information is sought for its own sake, but usually there is a practical reason for wanting to know about the other person. Such information helps the person define the situation so that he or she can determine in advance what to expect of the other person and what the other person is likely to expect. The importance of status as a cue to appropriate interaction probably cannot be overemphasized, but of course it is the *perceived* status that influences behavior. Status perception is necessary for defining the social situation because it is through this process that an individual relates to others. The perception of status plays a significant role in social organization and social adjustment, as well as in social disorganization and social maladjustment (Lasswell, 1961). Since it is the perception of status that is important for social interaction, it is fortunate that the perception of status usually agrees with objective measures of status (Harms, 1961; Forgas, 1978).

In earlier discussions it was noted that status contributes to a number of group processes and member behaviors. The high-status person selects a culturally valued spatial position in the group, conforms to group norms both more and less than the low-status group member, depending upon the situation, and is likely to have greater influence upon the group's products than lower-status group members. For instance, several studies have shown that the high-status person tends to conform more than the low-status group member (Berg & Bass, 1961), and Homans (1950) suggested that a person must live up to all the norms of the group if he or she desires high status in the group. On the other hand, Harvey and Consalvi (1960) reported that under financial reward conditions the second-highest-status person in the group was found to conform more than either the highest- or the lowest-status person. Similarly, Hollander (1958) noted that a group member may be permitted deviation from group norms to the extent that he or she has contributed to the group's goals in the past and has thus built up "idiosyncrasy credit." The conclusion to be drawn from these findings is that the high-status person, to a greater extent than the low-status person, is permitted to deviate from group norms in an attempt to aid in goal achievement, although he or she usually conforms more than low-status members.

Gergen and Taylor (1969) have identified another source of variation in conformity as a function of status: the degree to which the context emphasizes productivity or solidarity. When the situation stresses productivity, the high-status person is reluctant to conform to the expectations of low-status persons. According to Gergen and Taylor, this reluctance derives from the fact that success in achieving the goal depends upon the high-status person's freedom to marshal resources for goal attainment; however, conformity to the expectations of the low-status person may be seen as an erosion of the high-status person's standing in the group. Under conditions which emphasize solidarity, this effect does not occur, since conformity does not represent a threat to either goal achievement or status.

The reactions of group members to failure to conform (deviation) are also influenced by the status of the deviator. In one study (Wahrman, 1977), members of fraternities and sororities were given a list of eighteen behaviors and a list of eleven potential responses to these behaviors. First, they were asked to rate the behaviors for seriousness and to indicate how harsh or mild they considered each of the potential responses to be. Behaviors that were described as mild were such things as "Lies to protect a friend," "Speaks in a dictatorial manner." Serious behaviors were things like "Embezzles funds from group treasury." Potential sanctions (responses) ranged from friendly criticism to being asked to resign from the group. After ratings had been obtained, high and low status were discussed, and subjects were asked to identify either a high- or low-status person in their group (i.e., half were asked to name a high- and half a low-status person all agreed on). Next, they were told to imagine that, rather than the abstract person rated earlier, the person just named had performed the behaviors, and to again rate them for seriousness. Half of the subjects were also asked to indicate the rsponse (sanction) that they believed appropriate for each action. Finally, they were asked to discuss the behaviors and responses as a group and agree on one seriousness rating and one sanction for each behavior, still imagining that the high- or low-status person had enacted the behaviors. When evaluating seriousness and identifying the appropriate response after the high- and low-status persons had been identified, the behavior was judged to be more serious and the selected sanction more severe for the low- than for the high-status person, an effect that was especially pronounced when the deviation was mild rather than severe.

On the other hand, high status does not always protect a person from severe sanctions relative to the low-status person. For instance, in a study of destructive obediance (a military officer carries out orders from a superior officer that has disastrous consequences, as in the Lt. Calley affair) it was found that the superior officer who gave the order was held more responsible than the person who carried out the order (Hamilton, 1978). Furthermore, increasing the rank (status) of the defendant's superior officer from sergeant to captain increased the gap between the responsibility attributed to defendant and superior. These findings, to some extent, reflect conformity to group norms; it is well known that a military officer is supposed to accept responsibility for the behavior of those under his or her command.

Probably one of the more pervasive influences of status differences is on the pattern and content of communications in groups. The relative statuses of group members influence the amount of communication that he or she initiates, the amount of communication he or she receives from others in the group, and the particular other group member(s) that he or she communicates with most frequently. In general, more communications are both initiated and received by the high-status person than by the low-status person, and the content of such messages tends to be more positive than messages directed downward in the status hierarchy. It is also more likely that a given group member will receive communications from others having a status equal to his or her own (Barnlund & Harland, 1963). These effects of status upon communication processes have been demonstrated in a number of laboratory and field studies. Thibaut (1950) varied status differences in groups composed of ten to twelve boys between the ages of 10 and 12. Some of the boys were assigned a menial task (so described by the experimenter to the boys) and the others an attractive task that was described in prestige terms. In some of the groups, it was indicated that perhaps statuses could be changed, whereas in others no such manipulation was introduced. With increasing status differences, the lows increased in total amount of communication addressed to the highs but decreased in the proportion which was aggressively toned. In a study having a very similar design, Kelley (1951) observed a number of interesting effects of status upon communication: (1) Low-status group members communicated more task-irrelevant information than the high-status group members. (2) High-status persons appeared to be restrained from communicating criticisms of their own jobs to those of lower status; for example, their communications to low-status members contained relatively few expressions of negative attitudes or confusions about their own jobs. (3) Communication with high-status persons apparently served as a substitute for real upward locomotion for low-status persons who had little or no possibility of real upward locomotion.

The effect of status on message content was also demonstrated in a rather different experimental situation by Worchel (1957). Students were frustrated either by a high-status faculty member or by a low-status student, after which they were given an opportunity to communicate with the frustration agent. A common outcome of frustration is aggression, usually directed toward the person responsible for the frustration. Worchel found that the amount of verbal aggression directed toward the agent decreased with the increasing status of the agent.

Further evidence of the tendency for communications to be directed upward in the status hierarchy has been provided by an ingenious field experiment conducted by Back, Festinger, Hymovitch, Kelley, Schachter, and Thibaut (1950). Rumors were planted in an industrial organization containing five levels of status, and selected members of the organization cooperated in reporting from whom they first heard one of the rumors. Of seventeen communications, eleven were upward in the status hierarchy, four were at the same level, and two were downward. There also appeared to be restraining forces against the communication of rumors that were critical of high-status persons.

The relative status of interacting persons has been shown to affect a variety of other behaviors. We noted in Chapter 5 that interperson distances are related to status differences and suggested that high-status persons may feel free to approach a low-status person closely or stand far away when interacting, whereas a low-status person is restricted to an "appropriate distance." This effect was shown clearly in a study of interaction of persons of equal and unequal military rank (Dean, Willis, & Hewitt, 1975). Interactions initiated by persons of lower rank occurred at interperson distances that increased with increasing discrepancies in the rank of the persons interacting, whereas interactions initiated by persons of higher rank occurred at interperson distances that were unrelated to rank discrepancies. It is probable that such interperson distances are related to attempted self-presentation. For instance, one study found that students who were asked to state performance expectancies to either a teacher, fellow students, or a graduate student researcher displayed greater self-enhancement to the teacher than to the students (Hendricks & Brickman, 1974).

These several studies appear to demonstrate clearly that communication is influenced by the status hierarchy. However, there is a problem of interpretation, since status and power often vary together. For instance, Bradley (1978) attempted to vary power and status independently and assess their effects on the content of communications. The status of group members was assessed by questionnaire, and power was manipulted by giving one person authority to make decisions about group activities. In this study, power, but not status, was related to the content of the communications in the group.

Status differences also influence perceptions and attributions in groups. For example, the skill attributed to high- and low-status persons does not differ when they attempt difficult tasks, but high-status persons are seen as having greater skill than low-status persons when the task is easy (Zimmer & Sheposh, 1975). Persons are more likely to help another person who asks a favor if they have similar status than if they have dissimilar status, but only if there is some likelihood that future reciprocation and interaction will occur (Romer, Bontemps, Flynn, McGuire, & Gruder, 1977). This effect may be due to lack of positive evaluation of persons at different status levels. In one study (Dion, 1979) it was found that status differences in a group may inhibit favoritism toward one's own group (ingroup). That is, group members usually evaluate their own group products and group members more highly than the products and members of other groups (outgroups), but status differences within a group reduced this tendency toward ingroup favoritism. Finally, the person's expectations about status placement in a group influence satisfaction with the position. Placement in an unexpectedly high status position results in satisfaction with the position, whereas unexpectedly low status placement results in dissatisfaction with the position (Smith & Bordnaro, 1975). Self-esteem was lowered by unexpected placement in either high- or low-status positions, but placement in the low-status position resulted in lowered self-esteem only when the placing agent was attitudinally similar.

The status associated with the individual's position in the group thus has extensive consequences for the person's behavior toward others, the behavior of others toward the person, evaluations of performance, communications within the group, and a number of other group processes. As we noted earlier, status is ordinarily coextensive or highly correlated with other group aspects, such as leadership, power, role, etc. It is not always easy to determine whether the status effects that we have noted are "caused" by status or by one or more of these correlated variables.

## Role and Role Effects

Each position in the group structure has an associated role which consists of the behaviors expected of the occupant of that position. The principal of a school is expected to supervise the teachers of the school, to plan and organize the school's program, to assist teachers with tutorial and disciplinary problems, to deal with parent-teacher relations, and to engage in many other school-related activities. The school custodian, on the other hand, is expected to maintain the building and grounds but has no responsibility for the school's educational program. The head of a city fire department is expected to carry out whatever behaviors are generally agreed upon not only by the occupant of the position but also by other members of the group and often by members of other groups and of the larger society in which the group is embedded.

As in the case of status, the term *role* may be viewed in several ways. In addition to the definition used in this discussion, which might be designated the *expected role,* some writers have identified a *perceived role* and an *enacted role* The perceived role is the set of behaviors that the occupant of the position believes he or she should enact. This may or may not correspond to the expected role, since the latter depends upon the perceptions of others. The enacted role is the set of behaviors an occupant actually carries out. Again, the enacted role may be different from the expected role and/or the perceived role. To the extent that there are differences among these different aspects of role, the probability of conflict and group dysfunction is increased. In most instances, however, there is relatively good agreement between expected and perceived roles; when the enacted role departs too much from the expected role, the role will change or the occupant will be evicted. In the following discussions, role is used in the sense of expected behaviors of a position occupant.

The role that a person chooses to enact is, in part, a function of the impression he or she wants to make on other people. For instance, one study showed that males who anticipated interaction with an attractive female chose to enact a role that reflected relatively high status as compared with choices by males who anticipated interaction with an unattractive female (Shaw & Wagner, 1975).

The effects of roles upon behavior and group process have not been studied extensively, perhaps because the definition of role specifies the kinds of behaviors that are expected. Furthermore, studies are difficult to interpret because the definition of role is confused with other aspects of the group structure. For example, Slater (1955) conducted a study of role differentiations in groups of high and low status-consensus. He studied twenty groups, varying in size from three to seven persons, as they discussed an administrative case for forty minutes. He found that three types of role structures emerged: (1) The rare case in which the leader performs all functions and essentially no differentiation occurs. This is found only in high-consensus groups. (2) Moderate specialization occurs in high-consensus groups when the specialists do not have the exceptional talent required to establish the first type of role structure. (3) Extreme specialization occurs when the individual performs a specialty because he or she *must* rather than because it is good for the group. This is a low-consensus phenomenon. As can be seen, this study dealt primarily with the development of role differentiations rather than with the effects of roles. However, it was observed that the extreme form of role differentiation disrupted the group, an effect which may be due to low status-consensus rather than to the form of role differentiation.

A study by Torrance (1954) gives some evidence of the consequences of role for influence on the group, although again there is confusion with other aspects of the group's structure. Torrance studied sixty-two permanent and thirty-two temporary air crews consisting of pilot, navigator, and gunner. The roles of these positions are clearly different: The pilot is supposed to fly the plane, the navigator to direct it to its destination, and the gunner to protect it. But there are also other differences: The pilot has the highest status (he is the commander of the ship and usually has the highest military rank), the navigator has the second highest status, and the gunner the lowest status. The Torrance study revealed that the amount of influence on the group's decisions was generally correlated with role, with the pilot having the greatest influence and the gunner least, an effect which was more pronounced in the permanent than in the temporary groups. As we have seen, however, this could be caused by status differences rather than role differences.

Roles also exert a pervasive influence on the perceptions and evaluations of role occupants by others. Roles specify the kinds of behaviors that the occupant is expected to display, and these specifications may (and often do) bias the perceptions and judgments concerning the role occupant. For instance, in interpersonal encounters roles often specify unequal control over the style, content, and duration of the encounter, which in turn permits some role occupants to reveal much more about his or her knowledge, wit, sensitivity, etc., and/or to conceal deficiencies (Ross, Amabile, & Steinmetz, 1977). This was demonstrated in a quiz game in which one person was assigned the role of questioner and the other the role of answerer. The role of questioner made it possible for the person to choose questions reflecting his or her own esoteric knowledge, whereas the answerer had no such advantage. Although this was quite evident, both participants and observers rated the questioner more highly on general knowledge than the answerer. In short, they did not take into account the great advantage conferred by the questioner role when evaluating the occupant's store of knowledge.

**Role Conflicts**   A given individual occupies many different roles in many different groups. In most instances, the behaviors specified by the different roles are not incompatible (for example, the physician usually is not also an undertaker) so long as different roles are not made salient at the same time. The policeman may be expected to protect the property and lives of members of the community, but in the role of father he is expected to protect his family. Under normal circumstances, there is no role conflict since enactment of the policeman role is not required at the same time as enactment of the father role. Under unusual circumstances, however, the occupant of positions in different groups may be called upon to enact both roles simultaneously, when this happens, the individual will resolve the conflict in the direction of greatest group attraction; he or she will elect to enact the role required by the group which has the greatest importance for him or her. This form of resolution was revealed in a disastrous Texas City fire (Killian, 1952). When oil refineries caught fire and endangered the entire city, policemen were faced with role requirements that were obviously conflicting: each had to decide whether to enact the policeman role and help protect the community or to enact the father role and look to the needs of their families. In every case except one the conflict was resolved in favor of the father role; in the one exception it turned out that there was no conflict at all—the policeman knew that his family was safe in another town visiting friends. A similar conflict has been observed in a strike by telephone operators in a small town. As a member of the telephone union, the operator role required staying off the job for the duration of the strike, whereas the role associated with community membership required the operator to return to the job when failure to do so would be greatly detrimental to the community. In this instance, the direction of the resolution was not so consistent. Some of the operators remained away from the job throughout the strike despite sanctions by their community group; others returned to the job when the consequences for the community became serious. Apparently, there was no clear difference in role importance for these operators.

An interesting case of role conflict was also observed among Roman Catholic priests (Reilly, 1978). This study investigated seventeen sources of role conflict and the level of agreement on eight current issues within the church. Role conflict occurred most frequently among younger priests, based on differing expectations of the younger and older segments of persons served. These conflicts were usually resolved by attaching greater significance to the younger people in the church.

## Norms and Behavior

Norms are rules of conduct established by the members of the group to maintain behavioral consistency. If each member of the group decided individually how to behave in each interaction, no one would be able to predict the behavior of any other member, and chaos would reign. Norms provide a basis for predicting the behavior of others and thus enable the individual to anticipate the others' actions and to prepare an appropriate response. Such rules also serve as a guide for the group member's own behavior and thus reduce ambiguity, which many persons find intolerable.

Social norms represent standardized generalizations concerning expected behavior in matters that are of some importance to the group. Thus, they are concepts, albeit special kinds of concepts, and, like all concepts, refer to classes or groupings of items. That is, a norm usually does not identify a specific behavior, such as saying "Good morning" when one encounters an acquaintance; rather, the norm specifies that one should greet an acquaintance pleasantly with some acceptable form of address. Norms are distinguished from concepts in general by their evaluative nature; norms refer to what *should* be done. Norms thus represent value judgments with respect to modes of behavior in social situations.

Norms are social products which are formed during the course of social interaction. A standard may be imposed from without (for example, the school board may require that pupils dress in a certain way), but such imposed standards do not become norms unless they are accepted as right and proper by the pupils. This fact, of course, raises an important question that has not been answered satisfactorily: How many group members must accept a standard of conduct in order for it to become a norm? Everyone? A majority? It is clear that one cannot point to an exact proportion of group members that must accept a rule before it becomes a norm, but it is also clear that a norm is rarely accepted by all members of the group. Most students of group dynamics regard a standard as a norm if more than half of the group members agree that it is a norm.

We can now identify some of the characteristics of norms that are important for understanding how norms develop and how they influence behavior in groups. First, a group does not establish norms about every conceivable situation; norms are formed only with respect to things that have some significance for the group. Second, norms may apply to every member of the group, or they may apply only to certain members. For example, all members of a bridge team are expected to follow suit whenever possible; however, only dummy is expected to display the faces of his or her cards. Those norms which apply to particular group members are usually norms which specify the role of the occupant of a position in the group structure. Third, norms vary in the degree to which they are accepted by the group; some norms are accepted by almost everyone (for instance, that an automobile driver should stop the vehicle for a red light), whereas others are accepted by some group members and not by others (for instance, that the driver of a slow-moving vehicle should drive in the outside lane). Fourth, norms vary in range of permissible deviation. When a person deviates from a norm, some form of sanction is usually directed toward the deviant (Schachter, 1951). Sanctions vary from mild disapproval to the death penalty, depending upon the severity of the outcome of the deviation and the circumstances under which it occurs (see Shaw & Reitan, 1969). But norms differ with respect to the amount of deviation that is tolerable. Some norms require strict adherence to the rule (for example, thou shalt not kill), whereas others permit a wide range of behavior that is regarded as acceptable (for example, persons should not be impolite to others).

**Conformity to Norm Requirements**    Not only do norms vary in the degree to which conformity is required, but there are also variations in the degree of conformity to a particular norm under differing conditions. Many variables that influence degree of conformity have already been noted, but the concept of "conformity" and the methods that have been used to study it in the laboratory have not been considered in detail. The everyday conception of conformity is that it consists of blind, unreasoning, slavish adherence to the patterns of behavior established by others or to the demands of authority. Even among social psychologists there is the pervasive conception of conformity as agreement with the majority only for the sake of agreement. Fortunately, some investigators (for example, Deutsch & Gerard, 1955) have begun to make a distinction between this kind of conformity (based upon normative social influence) and other kinds of conformity (for example, that based upon informational social influence). Whereas normative social influence results from a desire to conform to the expectations of the group, informational social influence is the result of the value that conformity may have for the individual. The group member uses the majority's behavior as a source of information to help make the best response in that particular situation. Although this conceptual distinction between types of conformity is logical and undoubtedly significant for the interpretation of conformity behavior, most investigators have not made the distinction. Nor have they adopted the common conception of conformity. In fact, they have simply ignored the person's reasons for the behavior and have defined conformity as the agreement of the individual's response with that of the majority of the group.

The methods of study vary greatly in details, but most investigators adopt one or the other of two basic procedures. The first experimental paradigm is exemplified by the classic study of conformity conducted by Solomon Asch (1952). A person is exposed to obviously incorrect judgments of a unanimous majority in a face-to-face group. This is accomplished by means of confederates who have been instructed by the experimenter to make incorrect responses. In the Asch study, individuals were shown slides containing four lines, including a standard and three stimulus lines. The person's task was to select the stimulus line which was the same length as the standard. (Other kinds of tasks have been used, of course, such as judgments of the area of geometric figures, counting the number of metronome clicks in a series, estimates of the movement of a stationary light in a dark room, etc.) Conformity was measured by the frequency with which the person's choice agrees with that of the unanimous majority. Since few errors in judgment occur when the individual faces the task alone, such agreement is presumed to be due to the influence of the majority.

The other method is a simulated group, of sorts, first suggested by Crutchfield (1955). Each group member is seated in an isolated cubicle from which judgments are signaled to the experimenter by throwing an electric switch. Each person has a response panel on which the choices of others in the group presumably are shown. Several persons may be present at a given session, but each person is designated as the last person to make a judgment; hence all other choices are "known" to individuals at the time they respond. Obviously, the "judgments" of the other group members are determined by the experimenter. Stimuli and methods of estimating conformity are the same as in the Asch paradigm.

Although one may raise grave questions about this definition of conformity and these methods of studying the factors determining conformity, much has been learned by these procedures. Also, there is evidence that the results obtained agree very well with results obtained in natural settings, as we shall see later. It is now possible to consider the classes of variables that influence conformity behavior and to try to show how the forces toward uniformity combine to produce a given level of conformity behavior.

Four general classes of variables influence conformity to group norms: (1) personality characteristics of group members; (2) the kinds of stimuli evoking the response reflecting conformity; (3) situational factors; and (4) intragroup relationships (Reitan & Shaw, 1964). *Personality* factors refer to the characteristics of the individual group member that predispose the person to conform to group norms. In Chapter 6 it was noted that more intelligent persons are less likely to conform than less intelligent persons; there is a curvilinear relationship between age and conformity; persons who generally blame themselves for what happens to them conform more than those low on self-blame; authoritarians conform more than non-authoritarians; and women usually conform more than men. The conclusion that women conform more than men has been challenged more than the others listed above. For instance, Sistrunk and McDavid (1971) found that women conform *less* than men on tasks that are more familiar to women than to men. On the other hand, a statistical analysis of the many studies of conformity by men and women revealed that, taken as a whole, the body of evidence supports the conclusion that females conform more than males (Cooper, 1979).

It has also been shown that there is a general predisposition to acquiesce, which is positively related to conformity (Frye & Bass, 1963). In addition, Crutchfield (1955) reported negative correlations between conformity and measures of leadership ability ($r = -.30$), tolerance ($r = -.30$), social participation ($r = -.36$), and responsibility ($r = -.41$). All these correlations are relatively low, a result attributable in part to the unreliability of the personality measures, but due largely to the fact that personality factors are relatively less powerful in determining conformity behavior than other classes of variables listed above.

Finally, it appears that some persons not only conform to normative expectations, but actually exceed them in the socially desirable direction (Myers, 1978). Presumably, by exceeding the modal expected behavior in the preferred direction, such persons may present themselves favorably relative to others who merely conform to the norm. For instance, if the norm is to be pleasant, such persons may be overly cordial; if the norm is to share rewards equally, the person may insist on a smaller share; etc.

*Stimulus* factors include all those aspects of the problem faced by the individual, that is, the stimuli that are related to the norm to which the individual is presumably conforming. It will be recalled that, in the typical laboratory experiment on conformity behavior, the norm is established by exposing the person to unanimously false (incorrect) responses to a stimulus by other group members (real or simulated). Conformity to this arbitrarily established "group norm" is measured by the extent of agreement of the person's response to the stimulus with that reportedly made by other group members. Such stimuli include the autokinetic phenomenon (judgment of perceived movement of a stationary pinpoint of light in a dark room), counting a series of metronome clicks, estimating areas of geometric figures, judging the length of lines, and so on. In general, the more ambiguous the stimulus situation, the greater will be the conformity behavior. Consider the four stimuli mentioned above. The autokinetic situation requires the individual to judge the movement of a light that is really stationary, although it appears to move; hence, the individual is faced with a very ambiguous situation and is very uncertain about the actual amount of perceived movement. Under these conditions, about eight of every ten persons yield to unanimous group pressure (Sherif & Sherif, 1956). The ambiguity of metronome clicks can be varied greatly, but in the typical situation the stimulus is moderately ambiguous and the person is uncertain about the accuracy of his or her count. About six of every ten persons conform to the perceived group norm with this kind of stimulus (Shaw, Rothschild, & Strickland, 1957). When geometric figures are used as stimuli, the task is to judge the relative areas of circles, squares, triangles, etc. In this instance, there is an objectively correct answer, but the individual would probably have to be a mathematical genius to compute the areas in the time allotted and under the conditions of stimulus presentation. Typically, about half of the persons conform at least some of the time to unanimous group pressure (Nickols, 1964). The least ambiguous stimuli listed above are the lines originally used by Asch (1951) and later by many other investigators. The person is asked to judge which of three vertical lines is the same length as a standard line which is presented at the same time. Typically, there is little doubt about the correct answer; when individuals respond in isolation, few errors of judgment are made. Nevertheless, about one-third of all persons tested show some degree of conformity to unanimous group pressure in the form of a false norm. These four types of stimuli vary in degree of ambiguity roughly in the order presented here, and it is evident that the degree of conformity corresponds very closely to the degree of ambiguity. Clearly, then, the stimulus situation exerts a powerful influence upon conformity behavior; it appears to be the most powerful set of variables that has been identified.

*Situational* factors include all aspects of the group context except the stimulus situation; it refers to such variables as size of the group, unanimity of the majority, structure of the group, and so on. In his early studies, Asch (1951) found that conformity to unanimous false judgments increased with group size up to size four, and was essentially constant thereafter. Although this precise effect has been questioned (Gerard, Wilhelmy, & Conolley, 1968), it is evident that the size of the group is an important determinant of conformity. For example, it has been found that the size of a stimulus queue influenced the behavior of others, even in a setting where it is not customary to queue. Two, four, six, or eight persons lined up at a bus stop in Jerusalem, and the number of commuters joining the line was observed (Mann, 1977). The percentages of first arrivers joining the queue were 17, 17, 58, and 83, for the two-, four-, six-, and eight-person queues, respectively. It is clear that conformity increases with group size up to some maximum, but the maximum number for producing an increase in conformity undoubtedly depends upon the setting and other variables that influence conformity. The increase in conformity with increasing size of the majority probably occurs because the larger number of group members who give the same response or behave in the same way weakens the person's confidence in own judgment and strengthens his or her belief in the group norm. Indirect evidence for this assumption derives from an experiment concerning the relative novelty of an individual's attitude

(Duval, 1976). Subjects were led to believe that either 95, 50, or 5 percent of the population of 10,000 held the same position they did on ten important attitudinal issues. They were then exposed to a consistent majority of two persons who disagreed with their positions. The amount of attitudinal change in the direction of the two-person majority varied directly with the perceived novelty of the person's own position (means were 2.9, 4.6, and 5.3 for the 95, 50, and 5 percent agreement conditions, respectively).

Asch (1951) also found that conformity was greater when the majority was unanimous than when one or more other group members (confederates) gave the correct response. For example, when one member was instructed to respond correctly to the lines stimulus, the percentage of conformity decreased from the usual 33 percent with a unanimous majority to 5.5 percent. This finding has been verified by others in quite different settings (Morris & Miller, 1975). However, Shaw et al. (1957) demonstrated that this effect was due to lack of unanimity rather than to the support given by the instructed confederate. A group member who merely said that he was unable to make a judgment had essentially the same effects on conformity behavior as a person who gave the correct response.

The complexity of situational influences on conformity behavior is further revealed by a study by Goldberg (1955). He found greater conformity in a decentralized communication network than in a centralized one, a finding confirmed by Shaw et al. (1957). The lack of direct communication among peripheral members of a group with a centralized communication pattern presumably reduces the impact of disagreement by those persons. These several studies show clearly that the social context in which group interaction occurs has a marked effect on the conformity behavior of group members.

The term *intragroup relationships* refers to the relations among the members of the group. This category includes such variables as the kind of pressure exerted, the composition of the group, how successful the group has been in achieving past goals, the degree to which the person identifies with the group, and so on. All these variables have been shown to be related to conformity. Kelley (1952) suggested that the group serves both a normative function and comparative function, a distinction which is similar to the Deutsch and Gerard (1955) distinction between normative and informational social influence. Normative social influence was defined as pressure to conform to the positive expectations of group members, whereas informational social influence was based upon the individual's use of others' responses as a source of information about the external world. Deutsch and Gerard were able to show that subjects respond differentially to these different kinds of pressure. It has already been noted in Chapter 7 that conformity increases with identification with the group (cohesiveness) and that mixed-sex groups generally produce greater conformity than same-sex groups. Group composition effects were also revealed in a study by Costanzo, Reitan, and Shaw (1968), which found that conformity is influenced by both the perceived competence of the majority and the individual's perception of his or her own competence relative to the task. Figure 8-2 illustrates these effects. Perceived competence was manipulated by the experimenter reporting performance scores on nonpressure trials to the group members. When the person (minority) has high confidence in own ability, he or she conforms less than when own competence is perceived to be low, regardless of the competence of the majority. However, a person in the minority conforms more when the perceived competence of the majority is high than when it is low, regardless of level of competence. This effect has also been demonstrated by several other investigators (Hollander, 1960). Kidd and Campbell (1955) have shown that the past success of the group also contributes to conformity behavior, and Schneider (1968) reported that both whites and blacks conformed more to a white majority than to a black majority.

When the individual anticipates that his or her relationship will be more or less permanent, he or she is more likely to be concerned about

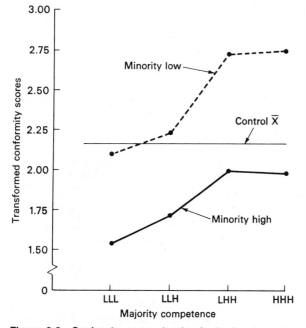

**Figure 8-2** Conformity at two levels of minority competence as a function of majority competence. (Reprinted with permission from P. R. Costanzo, H. T. Reitan, & M. E. Shaw Conformity as a function of experimentally induced minority and majority competence *Psychonomic Science*, 1968, **10**, 327–330.)

conforming to the norms of the group. This effect was demonstrated by Lewis, Langan, and Hollander (1972) in a study involving problems dealing with population, pollution, international relations, and urban affairs. Some individuals were led to believe that they would be discussing the problems with other group members in the future, whereas some were not given this information. Individuals who anticipated future interaction conformed more to majority opinion than those who did not anticipate future interaction. Incidentally, this finding also suggests that conformity to group norms is greater in ongoing groups than in temporary groups.

The effects of prior experiences in a group on later conformity was shown clearly in a study of conformity of a fellow deviant as a function of prior deviation (Darley, Moriarty, Darley, & Berscheid, 1974). A subject was induced to state his or her opinion on a variety of issues. Then a group of confederates disagreed with the subject, but one confederate agreed. Each subject was then paired with one individual from the previous group and subjected to a constant amount of conformity pressure from the confederate on a new set of judgments. Subjects conformed more to the confederate who had previously given them support than to the confederate who had previuusly been a member of the disagreeing majority.

In summary, it is evident that conformity to group norms is influenced by a variety of factors that can be classified into the four sets of variables outlined above. But an important question is raised by these findings: Are the effects of these variables independent and additive, or do they operate as alternative forces toward conformity? For example, if a given stimulus elicits 50 percent conformity behavior with a randomly selected population, can this degree of conformity be increased or decreased by varying the size of the group or by selecting more or less conformity-prone subjects? Or stated another way, if a given stimulus situation produces 50 percent conformity across a variety of group sizes and a unanimous majority of three produces 30 percent conformity (across a variety of stimulus situations), will the same stimulus plus a majority of three produce 80 percent conformity, or perhaps only 50 percent? This question was attacked experimentally by Nickols (1964). She systematically varied a personality variable (acquiescence), a stimulus variable (ambiguity), and a situational variable (size of the group). Acquiescence was varied by selecting subjects who scored either high or low on the Bass (1956) Social Acquiescence Scale; stimulus ambiguity was varied by using the Asch lines task (an unambiguous stimulus) and the autokinetic light (an ambiguous stimulus); and size of group was varied from two to four persons (a "majority" of one versus a majority of three). Since prior experimental evidence had indicated that stimulus factors have the greatest influence on conformity and personality factors the least effect, Nickols weighted the three variables in the following way: stimulus—3; group size—2; and personality of group member—1. She then arbitrarily assumed that the difference between the high and low level of each variable should be weighted by a factor of 2. Using these weights, she was able to compute a conformity index for purposes of predicting amount of conformity in each of the several experimental conditions. For example, if a given individual scored low on the acquiescence scale, was exposed to the unambiguous stimuli, and was a member of a two-person group, his or her conformity index would be $1 + 2 + 3 = 6$. If an individual happened to be at the other extreme (high on acquiescence, exposed to an ambiguous stimulus situation, and a member of a four-person group), each weight would be doubled and his or her conformity index would be 12. Figure 8-3 shows the relationship between this index and mean conformity under the various experimental conditions. It can be seen that the index predicted the amount of conformity extremely well, thus supporting the proposition that the effects of the variables influencing conformity behavior are additive. The curve shown in Figure 8-3 is slightly ogival. This probably reflects the fact that some minimal amount of pressure is required to elicit any conformity behavior, on the one hand, and the fact that when the forces are strong enough to elicit maximum conformity, additional force has no further effect, on the other hand.

The interested reader will probably ask at this point whether these laboratory findings have any relationship to behavior in natural situations. Fortunately, several field studies have shown that such behavior does indeed occur in natural settings. Lefkowitz, Blake, and Mouton (1955)

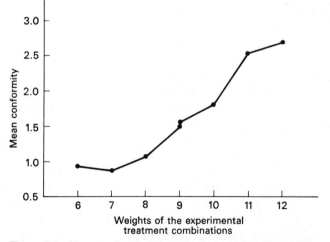

**Figure 8-3**  Mean conformity scores for the experimental treatment combinations, ordered in terms of weights assigned to the combinations of the variables. (Reprinted with permission from S. A. Nickols. A study of the additivity of variables influencing conformity. Unpublished doctoral dissertation, University of Florida, Gainesville, 1964.)

observed obedience and violations of traffic signals as a function of a model who either obeyed or violated the signal. Observations were made at three different street corners in Austin, Texas, on three afternoons during the hours of 12:00 to 1:00, 2:00 to 3:00, and 4:00 to 5:00. No policeman was on duty, although the study had the approval of the police department. The traffic lights at the experimental corners had a forty-second "wait" signal, followed by a fifteen-second "walk" signal. Observations were made during the "wait" period. The 2,103 pedestrians who happened by during the observation periods unknowingly served as subjects. Observations were made under five conditions: (1) a control (violations were merely recorded); (2) a high-status conformer (a well-dressed person approached the corner and waited for the walk signal); (3) a high-status violator (a well-dressed confederate violated the signal); (4) a low-status conformer (a poorly dressed confederate waited for the walk signal); and (5) a low-status violator (a poorly dressed confederate walked against the light). In the control condition subjects violated the signal only 8 times in 742 instances; in the conformer conditions subjects violated the signal only 4 times in 771 instances; but in the violator conditions the signal was violated 52 times in 526 instances. Clearly, the confederate who violated the traffic signal influenced others to do likewise. Of the 52 violations, 40 occurred with the high-status violator. A conforming confederate had little effect, probably because there were few violators in the control condition.

A somewhat similar study was conducted by Barch, Trumbo, and Nangle (1957) in Greater Lansing, Michigan. They observed the signaling behavior of automobile drivers for a period of sixty-one hours over a four-week period. Pairs of cars were selected according to the following criteria: Both cars were turning, there was no car between them, and the second car was 100 feet or less behind the lead car. Altogether, 1,195 pairs were observed, of which 723 lead drivers signaled and 472 did not. Conformity was recorded if the follower either signaled when the lead car did or did not signal when the lead car did not. When the leader signaled, the follower signaled 432 times and failed to signal only 291 times; when the leader did not signal, the follower signaled only 226 times and failed to signal 246 times. Again, the effect of the behavior of others was demonstrated in a natural situation.

Similar effects have been observed by Freed, Chandler, Mouton, and Blake (1955) with respect to conformity to "do not enter" signs on doors, and by Rosenbaum and Blake (1955) with respect to volunteering behavior. The study of the effects of number of persons in a queue on new arrivals at a bus stop also demonstrates conformity behavior in a natural setting (Mann, 1977). There can be little doubt that conformity occurs not only in the laboratory but in "real-life" situations as well. In fact, the principles illustrated by these investigations have been put to practical, if somewhat questionable, use by organizations soliciting funds by mail. The target of the fund-raising scheme receives a request for money, along with a list of persons who reportedly have donated specified amounts of money to the cause. Presumably, this creates the perception of a social norm which influences the target person to donate to the fund.

**Consequences of Conformity**   Conformity is generally rewarded by the group; deviancy is punished, or at least not rewarded. Thus, it is not surprising that there is general conformity to group norms. To many observers, conformity is an undersirable outcome of group interaction. It is seen as leading to loss of individuality, restriction of creativity, and reduction of all group members to the level of mediocrity (cf. Asch, 1951; Milgram, 1964; W. H. Whyte, 1957). These undesirable consequences undoubtedly would follow from a blind, unreasoning "follow the crowd" type of conformity. Fortunately, there is no evidence that behaving in accordance with group norms *necessarily,* or even usually, results from such unthinking compliance. In many, perhaps most, instances, there are good and sufficient reasons for conforming to group norms. Conformity introduces order into the group process and provides for the coordination of individual behaviors. If no one conformed, group members would not know what behavior to expect from others in the group and so would have no basis for determining appropriate courses of action for effective group funtioning. Consider a society in which each automobile driver decided individually which side of the road to drive on at any given moment, or a bridge game in which each player decided the meaning of a particular bid or the value of each contract. It is clear that effective group interaction would be impossible under such circumstances.

Although most studies have emphasized the negative consequences of conformity, some investigators have examined its positive effects. Berkowitz and Daniels (1963) have shown that conformity to a social norm can lead to desirable outcomes even when there are few or no social or material rewards to be gained by conforming to the norm. In their experiments each person played the role of "worker," supposedly under the direct supervision of a peer (a stranger) who played the role of "supervisor." In one experimental condition, the individuals were told that the evaluation of the supervisor would depend upon the worker's productivity (high dependency), and in another condition that the evaluation would not be affected by his or her performance (low dependency). Berkowitz and Daniels postulated a social responsibility norm that should cause the worker to try to help the supervisor reach his or her goal even though there were no rewards for doing so. The results of this study supported the hypothesis: The workers produced significantly more in the high-dependency condition than in the low-dependency condition.

A somewhat different approach was used by Milgram to show that in some situations conformity frees the individual to behave in accordance with his or her own standards of conduct rather than in accordance with authoritative coercion. In one study (1963), he demonstrated that persons in an experimental situation would administer exceedingly strong electric shock to another person when instructed to do so by the experimenter. In a later series of studies, Milgram (1965) observed similar effects, but the introduction of confederates who defied the experimenter's authority changed the individual's behavior. In Experiment I, individuals were instructed to give five increasingly strong shocks to a victim, despite the victim's protests and cries of anguish. Most persons complied with the experimenter's commands, even though this behavior was incompatible with normal standards of conduct. In Experiment II, two confederates were instructed to defy the experimenter's authority when the shock to be administered reached the "very strong" level (about midway in the range, which went from "slight shock" to "danger: severe shock"). Under these conditions, only four of forty persons continued to obey the experimenter. In a third experiment, the procedure was the same as in Experiment II except that the two confederates followed the experimenter's orders without question. The results were essentially the same as in Experiment I; the obedience of the confederates had little effect on the behavior of the individuals. Thus, it can be seen that conformity to an experimentally established norm can sometimes free the individual from the pressures of authority and enable the individual to follow his or her own standards.

In conclusion, conformity to group norms can be either positive or negative. Some agreed-upon standards of conduct are essential for effective group action, and sometimes conformity can result in altruistic behavior or behavior that agrees with the individual's own moral or ethical standards. Conformity produces the undesirable negative effects so frequently attributed to it when the group member conforms only for the sake of conformity.

**Deviation from Norm Requirements**  Obviously, not every group member conforms to the norms of the group, and deviancy usually brings some sanctions to the deviant. Many years ago, observers in industrial organizations noted that members of male work groups typically established production standards (norms) which were adhered to by most group members (Homans, 1950; Roethlisberger & Dickson, 1939). When a worker deviated too much from the standard, he was subjected to ridicule and various other forms of sanction. If the worker produced too much, he was referred to as a "speed king" or "ratebuster"; if he produced too little, he was called a "chiseler." One especially interesting means of controlling the overproducer was referred to as "binging," a game in which one man hit another on the arm, whereupon the second man had the right to retaliate. The alleged object was to see who could hit the harder, but this game was often used to interfere with productivity.

These kinds of sanctions have also been demonstrated in the laboratory. Schachter (1951) conducted a study designed to reveal some of the processes related to reactions to deviancy from an experimentally created group norm. Four types of clubs were established, each representing a different degree and combination of cohesiveness and relevance (importance of the discussion topic to the members of the club). Each club consisted of five to seven members, all of whom were male college students. Each member of the group read a case history of a juvenile delinquent and then indicated on a 7-point scale what he thought should be done with the delinquent. The opinion of each group member was then announced to the group, followed by the opinion of each of three paid participants. The paid participants (confederates) were assigned three different roles: (1) The *deviate* chose an extreme position and maintained it throughout the subsequent group discussion; (2) the *mode* chose the modal opinion of the group and maintained it throughout the discussion; and (3) the *slider* chose an extreme position but allowed himself to be influenced so that by the end of the discussion he was at the modal position. The case was then discussed for forty-five minutes, during which time an observer recorded selected aspects of the group interaction. Postexperimental questionnaires were also used to obtain measures of the group members' reactions to the confederates. The results indicated clearly that initially communications were directed primarily toward the deviates (the deviate and slider). Communications to the slider decreased as he approached the modal group opinion. Communications to the deviate increased up to a point and then decreased, but this effect was limited to group members who rejected the deviate. The magnitude of these effects varied with cohesiveness and relevance, but the general picture that emerged was one of increasing attempts to get the deviate to conform, followed by acceptance if the deviate succumbed or rejection if he maintained the deviant position.

Another investigation of the effects of changing position with respect to group norms generally supported Schachter's findings, with some exceptions (Levine, Saxe, & Harris, 1976). Male undergraduates, in groups of four, saw three members of a simulated group vote several times on appropriate treatment for a delinquent. Two members consistently agreed with subjects' initial opinion, but the third member varied his responses according to one of six patterns: consistent agreement, consistent disagreement, agreement followed by disagreement, neutrality followed by disagreement, disagreement followed by agreement, or neutrality followed by agreement. Following the viewing of the simulated group, subjects were asked to vote five times on whether the delinquent would benefit more from psychological help than from imprisonment, with person four following one of the above patterns of response. After each set of votes, each subject was permitted to write a short note to one other member. Actually, all subjects communicated with person four, whose notes had been prewritten to restate and defend his most recent vote. After the session was completed, subjects responded to a questionnaire designed to measure attraction to others and attributions of the importance of several possible reasons for other subjects' votes. The mean attraction scores for person four are depicted in Figure 8-4, with response patterns arranged in decreasing order of person four's agreement with the group norm (modal position). It is interesting to note that the attractiveness of the deviate (person four) was a function of the overall amount of agreement with the group norm, with final position having the greatest effect. These findings are generally in accord with those reported by Schachter. However, Schachter's finding that more communications were

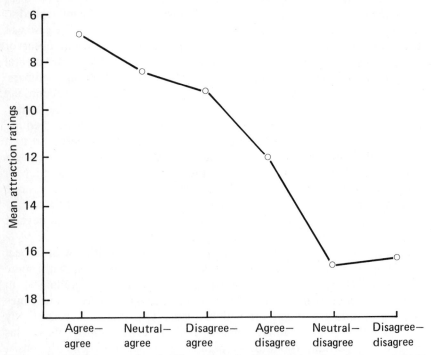

**Figure 8-4** Mean composite attraction ratings for person four, where low scores mean higher attraction. (Plotted with permission from data reported by J. M. Levine, L. Saxe, and H. J. Harris. Reaction to attitudinal deviance: Impact on deviate's direction and distance of movement. *Sociometry,* 1976, **39,** 97–107.)

directed toward the deviate early rather than late was not replicated, perhaps because the group situations were so different in the two studies. In addition, Levine et al. found that attributions of importance of possible determinants of person four's final position differed with pattern of response. Belief in opinion correctness and desire to demonstrate assertiveness were seen as important determinants for those whose final position deviated from the group modal position, whereas belief in opinion correctness and influence of others were seen as determinants for those who changed toward agreement with the majority.

The effects of timing on the consequences of deviation have also been observed in other studies. For instance, one study found that the earlier a female violated norms, the less her influence, the more she was disliked, and the less desirable she became as a coworker (Wahrman & Pugh, 1974). It should be noted that in this study violation of norms was not "corrected" by later conformity. Perhaps the conclusion to be drawn from these studies is that deviation leads to undesirable consequences, but these consequences are less severe if the deviation occurs late in the interaction or, better, if the deviator alters his or her behavior to conform to the norm.

Finally, reactions to deviators may be evidenced in more subtle ways than those we have been discussing. People usually expect some attention from others in their group, and violation of this implicit norm often leads to a devaluation of the person ignored both by the other group members and by the person himself or herself (Geller, Goodstein, Silver, & Sternberg, 1974). Furthermore, rejection of a deviant may be reflected in the "collective projections" of group members (Farrell, 1979). Groups with or without a deviant member wrote stories based on TAT cards, which were later analyzed for content. Groups with a deviant member, relative to those without a deviant member, revealed their concern and feelings toward the deviant as well as their anxiety that someone would get hurt by the deviant or by the negative feelings generated in the group.

In the preceding pages we have seen how group structure is an inevitable consequence of group interaction, and we have noted some of the many ways various aspects of group structure influence the behavior of group members. In the following section, we will consider an especially important element of group structure, *social power,* and in the final section of this chapter we will review some of the more general effects of group structure on group process.

## SOCIAL POWER

There is usually some variation in the power associated with different positions in the group structure. Most group dynamicists would agree with this statement, but different persons would probably interpret its meaning differently. Everyone believes that there is something that can be called power, but there is little agreement about its characteristics. Social power is also sometimes confused with other aspects of group structure. For example, Emerson (1964) and Alkire, Collum, Kaswan, and Love (1968) appear to use *status* and *power* interchangeably; and in their analysis of authority relationships Adams and Romney (1950) use the term *authority* to mean the same thing that others label *power* (Bass, 1960; Mulder, 1959b). Despite these diverse uses of the term, it is possible to define power in a consistent manner and to study its consequences for group functioning.

## Nature of Social Power

The various conceptions of social power have in common the view that power involves at minimum the ability of one person to control or influence another person in some way. Lewin (1951) defined the power of person A over person B as the quotient of the maximum force which A can induce on B and the maximum resistance which B can mobilize against A. French (1956) modified this definition somewhat, although he also defined power in terms of force; the power of person A over person B was defined as the maximum force which A can induce on B *minus* the maximum force which B can mobilize to resist A. In both these definitions, power is a joint function of the forces controlled by A and B. The definitions were derived from field theory, but in many ways they are similar to definitions of power derived from reinforcement theory. For example, Bass (1960) defined power as control over others through the use of rewards and punishments, a definition which is not unlike that formulated by Thibaut and Kelley (1959) in their exchange theory. If one substitutes *power* for *authority,* the Bass definition also agrees with that of Adams and Romney (1959).

In general, it appears appropriate to define power as the *control of reinforcers.* Thus, person A has power over person B to the extent that he or she controls reinforcers for B. For instance, in an all-male industrial work group, the foreman has power over his men because he controls reinforcers for them, such as pay, work schedules, promotions, etc. The men also have some power over the foreman, since they control productivity, to some extent, and the foreman's reinforcements are closely related to the productivity of his work group. However, the foreman has greater power over his men than they have over him because he controls more reinforcers, and he controls them more directly.

This conception of social power permits a meaningful distinction among similar concepts, such as power, social influence, authority, and leadership. Thus, authority may be defined as legitimate power, or the control of reinforcers that is approved by members of the group. Social influence may be defined as the exercise of power or the use of reinforcers to control another person's behavior. Social influence is sometimes used to refer to a process, as in the definition given here, and sometimes to an outcome or end result of a social process. When social influence is used in the latter sense, it is defined as the consequence of the exercise of social power. Leadership is a special case of social influence; that is, leadership is the exercise of power in particular situations, as by the occupant of a particular position in the group structure.

The main problem with the conceptual scheme outlined above is the identification of reinforcers, since a reinforcer for one person is not necessarily a reinforcer for another. Nevertheless, it is generally the case that certain things, for example, money, are reinforcing for most persons in a given group. Also, it is no more difficult to identify reinforcers than it is to identify the forces that one person can mobilize for or against another person, and it may be that "reinforcers" and "forces" are merely different labels for the same phenomenon. Consider, for example, the bases of social power identified by French and Raven (1959), which apply equally well to power defined by the field theory orientation and by the reinforcement orientation. They distinguished five bases or kinds of social power: attraction power, reward power, coercive power, legitimate power, and expert power. Attraction power is based upon identification or a liking relationship: A person who is liked by another person has more power over the other person than one who is disliked. Reward power is based upon the ability to mediate rewards for the other person, and coercive power is based upon the ability to mediate punishments for the other person. Thus, reward power and coercive power, taken together, constitute the definition of power as control of reinforcers. Legitimate power is based upon the belief that one person has the right to prescribe the behavior of another person, and expert power is based upon the less powerful person's belief that the powerful person has greater resources with respect to a given area. It should be evident from an analysis of these bases of power that all represent some form of control over reinforcers. The attractive person can bestow favors that are reinforcing for the person who is attracted to him or her; the expert can reinforce the other person by providing resources that are unavailable to the other person; and legitimate power merely describes the group members' attitude toward the power held by the powerful group member. Thus, these three kinds of power reduce to reward power and coercive power, and we have already noted that these agree closely with the view of power as control of reinforcers. The distinction among types of power is nevertheless useful, since it is quite possible that the effects of power upon group process vary with the sources of power.

Variations among group members with respect to power are likely to influence group process in several ways. The powerful group member elicits reactions from other group members that are different from those elicited by less powerful group members; the behavior of the individual group member is influenced by the relative amount of power that he or she possesses; and the power structure of the group determines to some extent the kinds of products produced by the group.

## Reactions to the Powerful Group Member

The way individual group members are perceived varies with their power position in the group, and the reactions of others to a particular group member are in part consequences of his or her relative power in the group. In general, the powerful group member is seen as more likable than the less powerful group member, is treated deferentially, is the target of a disproportionate share of intragroup communications, and others are more likely to comply with his or her wishes.* These effects may be seen in field studies conducted by Hurwitz, Zander, and Hymovitch (1953) and by Lippitt, Polansky, Redl, and Rosen (1952). Hurwitz et al. selected forty-two workers in the general area of mental hygiene on the basis of prestige rankings by two qualified persons. These rankings were assumed to reflect power differences among mental hygiene workers, and subsequent ratings of perceived power to influence others supported this assumption. The workers were subdivided into groups of six persons each, such that the groups varied in degree of power distribution. All members subsequently rated the extent to which they liked each of the other group members, their perceptions of how well others liked them and their perceptions of the amount of verbal participation of each group member. Observers kept a record of the pattern of participation. High-power members communicated more frequently and received more communications than low-power members. Powerful group members were also better liked than low-power members. The finding that low-power persons send most of their communications to high-power persons was verified in groups with both centralized and decentralized communication networks (Watson, 1965).

   Similar effects were observed by Lippitt et al. in two studies of attributed power among members of fresh-air camps in Michigan and Wisconsin. The person with high attributed power was the target of more deferential, approval-seeking behavior than were the low-power members. Others also tended to accept influence attempts from high-power persons to a greater extent. These reactions suggest that powerful group members are seen as able to either help or hurt others with respect to their goals; such behaviors are thus designed to reduce the uneasiness aroused by this perception. This aspect is supported by a laboratory study by Butler and

---

*It may be noted that these behaviors are very similar to behaviors toward high-status persons, as described earlier. This similarity probably reflects the high correlation between power and status.

Miller (1965) which revealed that more rewards and fewer punishments were directed to subjects with higher power to reward others in the group.

The reactions of group members to a group leader as a function of his power have been investigated by Mulder, Van Dijk, SoutenDijk, Stelwagen, and Verhagen (1964). Power was manipulated by varying the magnitude of rewards or fines that the leader could administer to group members. Three levels of power were created: (1) High power—the leader could administer rewards or punishments equal to 190 cents (where 250 cents was roughly equal to one American dollar); (2) medium power—the leader controlled rewards and punishments of 100 cents; and (3) low power—the leader controlled rewards and punishments equaling only 10 cents. After group interaction, members rated the leader on a number of attributes. The greater the leader's power, the greater the self-confidence and satisfaction with self attributed to the leader. Two ratings, however, correlated negatively with leader power: ratings of the leader as "a nice fellow" and degree of preference as an associate in a social situation.

Similar reactions of the less powerful to the more powerful person were observed by Johnson and Ewens (1971). This study examined a worker's perceptions of a supervisor who either controlled the worker's outcomes, believed he controlled the worker's outcomes (although he actually could not), or had no control over the worker's outcomes. During the course of dyadic interaction, the supervisor either harmed the worker (i.e., used his power to produce unfavorable outcomes for the worker), believed he was harming the worker, or did not harm the worker. When the supervisor harmed the worker, he was seen as unfriendly and self-assured—even if he was unaware of the consequences of his behavior. Furthermore, the workers expressed much greater confidence in their impressions of the powerful supervisor than in their impressions of the nonpowerful supervisor.

Our everyday experiences lead us to expect that the powerful person will be able to get other persons to comply with his or her "requests." In particular, if the person controls reinforcers (i.e., can administer rewards or punishments), we expect others to respond to these attempts to influence their behavior. Our everyday experiences, however, are not always an adequate basis for understanding complex behavior, and research reveals that the reactions of others to the powerful person depend, in part, upon the kind of power resources that the person has and how he or she attempts to use them. A study of the effects of threats by a powerful person upon the compliance of others (Schlenker, Bonoma, Tedeschi, & Pivnick, 1970) shows that the degree of compliance is a function of the powerful person's behavior after he sends the threat. When the threat is followed by accommodative behavior (i.e., behavior that benefits both the powerful and the less powerful group members), the target of the threat is more compliant than when the powerful person is exploitative (i.e., behaves in a manner that benefits himself at the expense of the other person). Similarly, Tedeschi, Lindskold, Horai, and Gahagan (1969) found that powerful group members more often ignored other members' statements of intent to be cooperative and were themselves less cooperative than less powerful group members.

In summary: The studies of member reactions to a powerful group member show that he or she is seen as capable of helping or hindering others in the achievement of their goals; hence he or she is the target of communications and deferential behavior. The powerful person is better liked than the low-power group members, but he or she is not seen as an attractive person for social interaction—at least, not as attractive as less powerful group members. When the powerful person uses his or her power to produce negative outcomes for the less powerful group member, he or she is seen as unfriendly and self-assured, and the group members are more confident that their impressions are correct when the other group member has power over them than when he or she does not.

## Reactions of the Powerful Group Member

The power possessed by a group member affects not only the reactions of others in the group, but also the powerful person's own behavior. Compared with other group members, the more powerful member is more highly attracted to the group, perceives that he or she has greater influence on it, is better satisfied with own position, etc. Some of these reactions of the powerful member can be demonstrated quite easily in a laboratory or classroom setting. In Zander and Cohen's experimental demonstration (1955), groups of seven persons each were formed in a classroom. The groups were told to assume that their "committee" had been appointed by the vice president of the university to advise him on the use of a large sum of money that had been donated anonymously. Then two of the members were asked to leave the room for a time so that they could experience the feelings of a new member in a previously organized group. While they were out of the room, the remaining five members were told that one of the new members was to play the role of dean and the other the role of freshman; however, the members were to make no mention of the positions held by the new members. The assumption was that the dean would have greater power in an academic community, although it is evident that other differences might also exist. After the new members rejoined the group, the problem was discussed for a short time, and then members filled out questionnaires about their reactions to the group. The results showed that, relative to the freshman, the dean (1) was more attracted to the group (means = 6.2 versus 4.1), (2) believed that he or she had made a better first impression on the group (means = 5.0 versus 3.9), (3) believed that the group gave greater "social validity" to his or her opinions (means = 5.4 versus 3.9), and (4) believed that he or she had more influence on the group (means = 6.8 versus 4.4).

These findings are consistent with those reported by Lippitt et al. (1952) in the study cited earlier. Similar results were also reported by Watson and Bromberg (1965). Power was manipulated in laboratory groups by appointing one member "coordinator" and giving him the power to issue commands which the other group members were required to obey. Each group solved a series of problems in which interaction was limited to written communications. Under these conditions, the high-power member indicated that he or she had greater opportunity to influence the group and to be helpful in the attainment of group goals than did low-power members. The powerful person also expressed greater enjoyment of position than did low-power persons, a finding that was verified by Watson (1965).

The relatively more favorable self-perceptions of powerful persons is revealed in a study of bargaining (Stolte, 1978). Four-person groups engaged in an interpersonal bargaining situation in social exchange networks varying in centrality. Persons randomly assigned to central positions in the network (the more powerful positions) not only saw themselves as more powerful than others but also rated themselves as being more capable than others in the group. Similarly, subjects given absolute power over the outcomes of others were found to be less interested in understanding the other person's intentions and plans for future action, but more interested in learning the other person's feelings than persons with less power (Tjosvold & Sagaria, 1978). Conversely, those persons with no power were more suspicious that others would compete rather than cooperate.

Although the powerful member's feelings about the group undoubtedly have some effect on group interaction, when and how power is used probably exert a more pervasive influence on group process. Throughout history, social philosophers have been concerned about power and its use in the larger society, although there has been little agreement among them. Many have feared that power corrupts the person who has it so that the power will be used for despotic purposes, and, indeed, evidences of such outcomes come readily to mind. Hitler used his power to dominate nations; the tsars of Russia ruled with an iron hand. Today, many believe that our own political leaders use their power in dictatorial fashions. On the other hand, some persons believe that power may induce the holder to behave compassionately and to use his or her power for the benefit of less powerful associates. It is probable that either outcome may occur, depending upon the characteristics of the powerful person and the circumstances at the time. However, it is not obvious that the effects of power which are observed in the larger society also occur in small groups. The many differences between a small group and a society probably make meaningless any attempt to learn about one from a consideration of events in the other. Fortunately, we have direct evidence about the use of power in small groups.

Consider, for example, a study by Kipnis (1972). College students majoring in business were recruited to act as manager in a simulated industrial situation. Each manager was told that he or she would be supervising four high school students located in an adjacent building. Actually, the "workers" were simulated and their output was preprogrammed. Managers were also told that their job was to operate the company at a profitable level by maintaining the efficiency of the workers. Half of the managers were given control of reinforcers (promising or awarding pay increases, threatening or actually transferring workers to another job, giving the workers additional instructions, threatening or actually reducing the worker's pay, and threatening or actually firing the worker); the other half of the managers had no such control. There were several significant differences between the behaviors of the powerful and less powerful managers. Relative to the less powerful managers, powerful managers (1) made more attempts to influence the behavior of the workers, (2) devalued the performance of the workers, (3) attributed the efforts of the workers to their own control of power rather than to the workers' motivations to do well, (4) viewed the workers as objects of manipulation, and (5) expressed a preference for the maintenance of psychological distance from the worker. These findings show clearly how the possession of power influences the perception of less powerful others. The less powerful are seen as less motivated to achieve, as objects to be used by the powerful person, and as less effective. Furthermore, it is clear that the more powerful person is likely to use his or her power to get others to abide by his or her wishes.

The tendency for the more powerful persons to use their power has also been observed in other small groups (Smith, 1967). Seventy-two individuals were told that they must work through an intermediary in order to affect their own rewards from another person. They were also told that they had either high or low power over the intermediary and that the intermediary had either high or low power over the source of the rewards. Individuals used their power more when they thought that they had high power and also when they thought the intermediary had high power. The empirical evidence thus reveals that more powerful group members not only enjoy their positions more and perceive that they have greater influence on the group, but they also tend to use their power in direct proportion to the amount of power they believe they possess.

The degree to which persons use the power they possess and the kind of reinforcers they use vary with the characteristics of the powerful persons, the characteristics of less powerful persons, the kind and amount of power they have, and the circumstances in which the interaction occurs. It has already been noted that males and females differ in their use of power: males are more likely to exploit cooperative opponents when they are powerful, whereas women are more exploitative when they are relatively weak (Black & Higbee, 1973). Similarly, Bedell and Sistrunk (1973) observed that males used power to reward more than females; however, males and females did not differ in their use of punishment.

In general, the more power a person has, the greater the probability that he or she will use it. However, the specific effects of magnitude upon the powerful person's behavior are influenced by how precisely he or she can control the reinforcers available to him or her. For instance, Smith and Leginski (1970) made it possible for males to threaten or fine a bargaining opponent a maximum of either 20, 50, 90, or 140 points under either precise power (magnitude of threats or fines could be below the maximum if the person wished) or imprecise power (threat or fines could be only maximum or none). The frequency with which the person used his power varied with the amount of power he had only when the power was precise; however, resistance to compromise increased with power in both precision conditions.

In addition, the particular relation between the powerful and the less powerful person affects the actions of the powerful group member. For instance, Kipnis and Vanderveer (1971) found that an ingratiating subordinate received more than his share of rewards from an appointed leader, whereas a hostile subordinate caused the leader to dispense more rewards to all compliant subordinates. There is reason to believe, however, that certain characteristics of the power holder determine how he or she responds to problem subordinates. In a recent study, Goodstadt and Hjelle (1973) studied supervisors who were either externally oriented (i.e., believed that their outcomes were controlled by forces outside themselves) or internally oriented (i.e., believed that they controlled their own "destiny"). In dealing with a problem worker, externals used more coercive power and internals used more persuasive power.

These findings show that, although the more powerful person tends to use his or her power, the kinds of reinforcers he or she chooses to use are determined by a number of other factors. We are just beginning to learn what some of these other factors are and how they influence the use of power.

### Effects of Power Differences on the Group's Products

The behaviors of the powerful group member and the reactions of others to him or her inevitably influence the functioning of the group. It is curious that few studies have been directed toward an analysis of this effect. Most investigators have been interested in the effects of other variables upon the consequences of power differences among group members. For example, it seems obvious that greater conformity should be observed in a group characterized by a power hierarchy than in an equal-power structure, at least on the part of low-power group members. Studies in this area have been largely limited to comparisons of reward and coercive power, with special reference to other variables. Kipnis (1958) exposed grammar school children to propaganda regarding comic books, administered by an adult who could either reward or punish the children for conformity. In some cases the propaganda was presented in a group discussion and in others via lecture. Initial compliance was equal for all conditions, but a check one week later revealed that in the group discussion reward power was more effective in maintaining conformity than coercive power, whereas in the lecture sections the opposite was true. Kipnis suggested that group discussion made the coercive forces more salient and thus reduced their long-range effects on conformity.

The relative ineffectiveness of power to punish versus power to reward has also been observed in adult groups of males (Miller, Butler, & McMartin, 1969). The results of this study showed that greater reward power facilitates a person's attempts to induce others to be rewarding, whereas greater punishment power has the opposite effect. This finding is of course contrary to "common sense" expectations that one who can administer punishments can induce others to obey his or her commands. Miller et al. suggested that the effectiveness of punishment power rests on its nonuse. When a person punishes another person, he or she not only produces negative consequences for that person, but also arouses negative feelings toward the person who administered the punishment. The victim may get satisfaction from *not* complying with the desires of a person who has used punishment power. These findings suggest that coercion is an ineffective means of controlling the behavior of others, except perhaps in the case of disliked or hostile opponents whose behavior cannot be influenced by other methods (Schlenker & Tedeschi, 1973; Schlenker, Nacci, Helm, & Tedeschi, 1976).

The undesirable consequences of using coercive power have been demonstrated in a study of the leader's influence on followers' productivity (Sheley & Shaw, 1979). Group leaders were given control over either rewards (additional points for good performance) or punishments (fewer points for poor performance) for followers. Followers attempted to solve sets of anagrams, and leaders either used or did not use their power following each of several trials. Just before the final trial, the leader made a special appeal to followers to exert more effort to solve as many of the next set of anagrams as possible. The results are shown in Figure 8-5. Followers

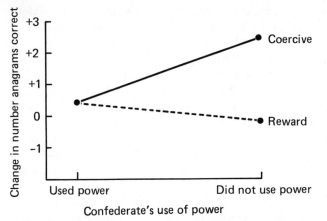

**Figure 8-5** Change in number of anagrams completed as a function of type and use of power. (Reprinted with permission from K. Sheley and M. E. Shaw, Social power: To use or not to use. *Bulletin of the Psychonomic Society,* 1979, **13**, 257–260.)

performed equally well whether the leader did or did not use reward power, but use of coercive power caused followers to *decrease* their performance level following the leader's appeal for *greater* effort.

It is interesting that the effects of power derived from different sources are perceived differently by observers (Litman-Adizes, Fontaine, & Raven, 1978). Subjects read six scenarios in which a supervisor used different bases of power to successfully influence a worker to change work methods. Information power was perceived as most effective in inducing private acceptance of the change, whereas subjects were more likely to attribute compliance to the worker's will when referent, information, or reward power was used.

Empirical investigations concerning group productivity are also limited in number and tend to be concerned with the effects of other variables relative to power. For instance, G. B. Cohen (1968) examined the effects of power as a function of communication network and "weight" of the group member in the determination of group output. In each three-person group, member A was given the greatest amount of power in that his decisions limited the alternatives available to member B, whose decisions in turn limited the alternatives of member C. The power structure was, therefore, always hierarchical, with member A having the greatest restriction power and member C the least. In the first experiment, two communication networks were imposed: B-A-C and A-B-C. Thus the two networks were chains, with member A in the central position in one and member B in the central position in the other. In the second experiment, a third chain was introduced (A-C-B), with member C in the central position. The "weight" of each member was determined by formulas which gave the greatest weight either to A's yield or to C's yield in determining the value of the final group product. In a sense, then, two aspects of power were varied: restriction power and influence power. A prediction that the communication network with member A in the central position would be more effective was not supported. However, the results of both experiments supported the prediction that group productivity would be higher when member A, who had the most restriction power, also had the greatest weight relative to the group's output. The finding that giving the greatest weight to the inputs of the member having the most influence over the group's alternatives produces higher productivity scores is probably not too surprising, but it does show that power differences are determinants of group productivity.

The emphasis upon other variables relative to the effects of power differences is also noticeable in studies of bargaining behavior. Komorita, Sheposh, and Braver (1968) investigated the effects of different perceptions of the more powerful member of a dyad on the level of cooperation of the less powerful member. Subjects were asked to play the prisoner's dilemma game in which the best outcomes for both members can be obtained only through cooperation in response choices. The low-power member was led to believe that the high-power member intended to use his or her power either benevolently, malevolently, or passively (nonuse of power). The benevolent condition elicited the greatest amount of cooperation (and hence the greatest rewards for both members), and the malevolent condition the least amount of cooperation. The consequences of power differences in this situation are thus seen to be a function of the group member's perceptions of the powerful member's intentions. In a somewhat similar situation, Thibaut and Gruder (1969) noted that groups with an attractive alternative to interdependent negotiation formed agreements regulating their bargaining behavior; however, groups with an unattractive alternative formed such agreements only if the low-power member could in some way compensate the high-power member for his loss of power. Swingle (1968) also found that an equal power structure produced greater cooperation than an unequal power structure, even when the unequal power was illusory. The undesirable effects of power inequality were reduced, however, when the group members discovered that they actually had equal power.

In brief summary, the power differences among group members influence the reactions of other group members to the powerful member, the powerful member's reactions to the group, and the group's products. The particular effects of power differences upon the group's products are determined by a number of other variables, such as the weight given to the outputs of group members, the perceptions of the intentions of the powerful group member, and the kinds of alternatives that are available to the group.

## GENERAL EFFECTS OF GROUP STRUCTURE

In the preceding pages we have discussed many facets of group structure and their effects upon the behavior of group members and on group process. A further question of interest concerns the more general effects of group structure, i.e., the functioning of groups with a well-defined group structure relative to groups with no clearly delineated structure. Unfortunately, few studies have been designed to examine this question. Those that have been conducted reveal some interesting effects of structure on group process and outcome. For instance, the study of permanent and temporary Air Force flight crews by Torrance (1954) cited earlier may be considered as a comparison of groups with a well-defined structure (the permanent flight crews) and groups with poorly developed structures (the temporary flight crews). It may be recalled that the behavior and influence of group members was a function of their roles in the group, and that the impact of roles was much stronger in the permanent than in the temporary groups.

In another experiment, Torrance (1971b) tested the hypothesis that increasing group structure increases cooperative behavior in children's groups. Six-person groups were assembled and assigned the task of building a dream castle. Structure was varied by assigning a leader in some groups but no leader in others. Observers recorded five categories of behavior: planning, cooperating, verbal aggression, physical aggression, and leaving the field (i.e., not working on the task). More planning occurred in the structured groups, but more cooperative behavior was observed in the unstructured groups.

Comparisons of established and ad hoc groups in a management training situation yielded somewhat different results (Hall & Williams, 1966). Twenty established groups (members had worked together for several weeks, at minimum, and presumably had developed a clear group structure) were compared with twenty groups whose members had not worked together before (and presumably had developed little or no group structure). Group size ranged from six to nine persons, with average size approximately the same for the two kinds of groups. Each group was shown the beginning of the film *12 Angry Men* in which twelve jurors attempt to reach a unanimous verdict of guilty or innocent concerning a defendant accused of murder. On a preliminary ballot, eleven voted guilty and one not guilty. After 38 minutes of discussion, a second ballot was taken, and one of those voting guilty had changed to not guilty. The film was stopped at this point and the group was told that all jurors eventually voted not guilty. The group's task was to predict the order in which jurors changed their votes. Group performance was measured by agreement of the group's ranking with the order jurors actually changed their votes. According to this criterion, established groups performed significantly better than the less structured groups. It was also observed that ad hoc groups were likely to resolve differences through compromise, whereas established groups responded to conflict with increased creativity. However, in a later study they found no performance differences between established and ad hoc groups (Hall & Williams, 1970). To complicate things further, a comparison of groups composed of individuals who had worked together for several weeks (and presumably had a well-established group structure) with ad hoc groups showed that the less structured groups performed better (made fewer errors and required less time to complete the task) than the more well-established groups (Ford, Nemiroff, & Pasmore, 1977).

The effects of power structure versus no structure on group effectiveness have been investigated in at least two studies (Shaw, 1959b). In the first experiment, groups of four male students attempted to earn as many points as possible by locating a target on a diagram somewhat like a bulls-eye, but with the location of the target hidden from view. Location of the target could be inferred from the pattern of rewards given for each successive trial. Structure was varied by giving one person in the group complete power to make unilateral decisions, whereas in other groups no such power difference was made. Subjects in the no-power structures were better satisfied than those in the power structures, but there was no difference in group effectiveness. However, the average authoritarianism of group members (measured by a pencil-and-paper test) correlated positively with time required to complete trials on the task ($+.42$) and with number of suggestions made by group members ($+.56$). These correlations were negative ($-.25$ and $-.13$, respectively) in the no-power condition and differed significantly from those in the power structure. It appears that at least some of the effects of structure are mediated by group member characteristics.

The second experiment also revealed that group structure and member characteristics jointly influence group behavior. Individual prominence tendencies of group members were measured by a scale (the IP scale), and power structure was varied as in the first experiment. The task was the same target-location task used earlier. Again, differences in the relationship between member characteristics (IP scores) and behavior in the group were dissimilar for the structured and unstructured situations. Number of suggestions made, number of suggestions accepted by the group, and perceived influence on the group decision all correlated positively with the group member's IP score in the no-power structure but were unrelated to IP score in the structured groups. Measures of performance also correlated negatively with average IP scores in the unstructured groups but not in the structured groups.

Thus the limited evidence concerning the effects of a relatively well-developed group structure indicates that structure does have an effect on group performance and the behavior of group members, but this effect depends upon the kind of structure and the characteristics of group members. It is also probable that other variables, such as the group task, determine the effects of structure. Because of these interrelated effects, the influence of structure on group process and group effectiveness is better understood via status, roles, norms, etc.

## PLAUSIBLE HYPOTHESES ABOUT GROUP STRUCTURE

The discussions of group structure have considered many aspects of this feature of groups. They have shown that there has been no concerted attack on the variables determining the development of group structure or its effects on group behavior. The many individual bits of research nevertheless suggest a number of plausible hypotheses that merit further consideration.

*Hypothesis 1    The perception that organization facilitates goal achievement is a determinant of group structure.*
Many group members believe that some form of organization is necessary if the group is to attain its goals. A study by Shaw and Gilchrist (1956) revealed that one or more members of problem-solving groups suggested some form of organization in eight of ten groups studied. This belief in the efficacy of structure with respect to goal achievement leads group members to establish structural relations among parts of the group.

*Hypothesis 2    The formation of group structure is facilitated to the extent that group members have a need for structure.*
This hypothesis concerns a different determinant of group structure from that referred to in Hypothesis 1. The need of group members for structure is a general need rather than a belief concerning the efficacy of structure for goal attainment. Cohen, Stotland, and Wolfe (1955) have demonstrated that certain individuals need to structure relevant situations in meaningful and integrated ways. To the extent that the group is relevant, such persons also experience a need to structure the group. Hence, the more group members who have such a need and the greater the strengths of their needs for structure, the greater will be the tendency for them to structure the group. The observations of Bennis and Shepard (1956) are also in accord with this hypothesis.

*Hypothesis 3    The kind of structure that the group develops is influenced by the particular needs of the group members.*
Aronoff and Messé (1971) reported that groups composed of persons high on safety needs tended to develop hierarchical structures; groups com-

posed of persons high on esteem needs tended to develop equalitarian structures. Evidence for this hypothesis also derives from another study which found that males became leaders more frequently in groups high on safety needs (Messé, Aronoff, & Wilson, 1972). The finding that the abstract-concrete dimension of personality influences the kind of structure that groups develop (Tuckman, 1964) is also consistent with Hypothesis 3.

*Hypothesis 4   The kind of structure that the group develops is influenced by the physical environment of the group.*

The effects of the physical environment are pervasive and relate to so many specific aspects of group structure that it is difficult to formulate a general hypothesis concerning them. Festinger et al. (1950) noted the effects of physical arrangements of housing units upon friendship formations (an aspect of structure), and Chapter 5 noted many instances of the culturally mediated influences of spatial arrangements on group differentiation. The close relationship between spatial position and perceived status of the group member is an outstanding example of this effect (Lott & Sommer, 1967; Sommer, 1969).

*Hypothesis 5   A high-status group member may deviate from group norms without being sanctioned if his or her deviancy contributes to goal attainment.*

The high-status person generally conforms to the norms of the group more than most other group members; however, if such a person has contributed to goal attainment in the past, he or she may build up idiosyncrasy credit (Hollander, 1958) which permits greater deviancy under certain circumstances. Studies by Gergen and Taylor (1969) suggest that this effect is especially strong when the group is concerned primarily with productivity. The study by Wahrman (1977) provides further support for this proposal. On the other hand, high status may actually increase sanctions for deviation if the norms of the group specify that high-status persons accept greater responsibility for their actions, as in the military (e.g., Hamilton, 1978).

*Hypothesis 6   The high-status person both initiates and receives more communications than the low-status person.*

Numerous studies have shown that more communications tend to be directed toward the high-status than toward the low-status person (Kelley, 1951; Thibaut, 1950). Such upward communication has been interpreted as a substitute for real upward locomotion. It may also reflect an attempt to attain vicarious rewards through interaction with the high-status persons.

*Hypothesis 7   Communications directed upward in the status hierarchy have more positive content than communications directed downward.*

This effect is reflected in the communications of both high- and low-status group members. In the studies by Thibaut and by Kelley cited above, it was observed that communications directed to high-status persons contained fewer aggressive comments and more task-irrelevant information than did communications directed to peers; on the other hand, high-status persons refrained from communicating negative attitudes or confusion concerning their own jobs. Worchel (1957) also noted that the amount of verbal aggression directed toward a high-status person following frustration was less than that directed toward a low-status person under similar circumstances. The low-status person is probably restrained from aggressive communication by fear of punishment, whereas the high-status person may fear a loss of status for expressing any concern about his or her own effectiveness.

*Hypothesis 8   Role specifications may bias the perceptions and judgments of the role occupant by others.*

The evidence for this hypothesis comes from a single study; therefore, the hypothesis is more questionable than those with greater empirical support. However, the hypothesis is reasonable, and the data reported by Ross et al. (1977) are strongly supportive.

*Hypothesis 9   Role conflicts will ordinarily be resolved in favor of the group that is most important to the role occupant.*

In addition to the validity indicated by the logic of common sense, the studies of disasters reported by Killian (1952) clearly support this hypothesis. Faced with role requirements from two different roles that cannot be met simultaneously, the group member responds to the requirements of the role associated with the group that he or she is most attracted to.

*Hypothesis 10   Individuals differ in their predisposition toward conformity to group norms.*

There is good evidence that there are individual differences in susceptibility to social influence. Although there are many factors related to these differences (such as intelligence and social responsibility), Frye and Bass (1963) have shown that there is a general tendency to agree with diverse propositions, and that this general tendency toward acquiescence is correlated with conformity behavior. This tendency appears to be real, but its effect is relatively weak.

*Hypothesis 11    The more ambiguous the stimulus situation, the greater the probability that a group member will conform to the perceived norms of the group.*

Numerous studies have demonstrated that ambiguous stimuli, such as judging movement of the autokinetic light (Sherif & Sherif, 1956), produce greater conformity than unambiguous stimuli, such as judging the length of lines (Asch, 1951). The individual who has little objective evidence about reality must rely upon others to validate his opinions. On the other hand, if the objective evidence is clear, that person does not need to rely upon normative standards. This is probably the most powerful set of variables with respect to conformity behavior.

*Hypothesis 12    A group member is more likely to conform to group judgment when other members are in unanimous agreement than when they are not.*

Asch (1951) demonstrated conclusively that introducing a confederate who agreed with the näive group member reduced conformity dramatically and that the inclusion of two or more uninstructed group members resulted in a significant decrease in conformity. This finding has been verified by Morris and Miller (1975). However, these results could have been due to the fact that the subject had support or to the mere fact that the majority was not unanimous. Shaw, Rothschild, and Strickland (1957) found that even a subject who declined to make a judgment led to reduced conformity by the naïve group member. Hence, it appears that the critical variable is the unanimity or nonunanimity of the opinions of other group members.

*Hypothesis 13    Greater conformity occurs in groups with decentralized communication networks than in groups with centralized communication networks.*

In a decentralized network all group members can exert direct pressure on each other member in the group, whereas in a centralized network pressure can be exerted by some members on some others only through intermediaries. Direct contact should be more influential than contact via another person. At least four separate studies have demonstrated this effect. Goldberg (1955) found greater group influence on the group member's estimation of the number of dots on a card in a decentralized than in a centralized network. Shaw et al. (1957) conducted three experiments using human relations discussion tasks and counting metronome clicks, again finding greater conformity in the decentralized network.

*Hypothesis 14   Conformity varies positively with the perceived competence on the majority relative to the individual's perception of his or her own competence.*

The effects on conformity of the competence of the group member relative to that of others in the group are shown most clearly in Figure 8-2. It can be seen that conformity is influenced by both the perceived competence of the majority and the individual's perception of his or her own competence. The member who believes that he or she is more competent than others in the group, is less inclined to conform to their standards. This effect is probably the result of a number of intervening variables: (1) Competent persons feel more confident of their own judgments; (2) the member of a group composed of a majority of relatively incompetent members will not be as attractive to a person as a group composed of relatively competent others; (3) the judgments of a competent majority are seen as more valid representations of reality than the judgments of a less competent majority; etc.

*Hypothesis 15   The effects of personality, situational, and stimulus variables are additive within the normal ranges of conformity behavior.*

The general import of this hypothesis is that the effects of several variables summate in the production of conformity behavior up to some maximum level. For example, if the personality factor "acquiescence" elicits 10 percent conformity, an ambiguous stimulus 40 percent conformity, and a given majority size 20 percent conformity, the three variables operating together should elicit approximately 70 percent conformity. The additivity of conformity variables is illustrated in Figure 8-3.

*Hypothesis 16   Conformity introduces order into the group process and provides for the coordination of individual behavior.*

There are only observational data available to support this hypothesis, but the data are so logically imperative that the validity of Hypothesis 16 can scarcely be doubted.

*Hypothesis 17   Under certain circumstances, conformity frees the individual from the coercive influence of authority.*

It is an unfortunate fact of social life that the individual is sometimes the victim of coercive forces which elicit behaviors that are not in accord with the individual's own standards of conduct. Milgram (1963) demonstrated the extreme consequences of such forces and later demonstrated that conformity can operate to liberate the individual so that he or she can resist authority (Milgram, 1965). The desirable consequences of conformity under some conditions have also been revealed by the Berkowitz and Daniels (1963) experiment which showed that conformity to a norm of social responsibility often leads to helping a dependent other.

*Hypothesis 18   Deviation from group norms usually elicits sanctioning behavior by other group members. Continued or habitual deviation may lead to rejection by other group members.*

Many observations of work groups reveal that such groups typically establish norms concerning a proper day's output (e.g., Homans, 1950; Roethlisberger & Dickson, 1939) and that deviation from these norms elicits various forms of sanction. Laboratory studies indicate a similar effect. Schachter (1951) found that deviation from normative group opinion initially elicited many communications directed toward the deviate. If the deviate continued to maintain a divergent opinion, communications decreased, and the deviate was apparently rejected as an acceptable group member. Levine et al. (1976) failed to find the decrease in communications to the deviate but also found that attraction to the deviate was a function of agreement-disagreement with the majority (see Figure 8-4). Further evidence consistent with this hypothesis was reported by Geller et al. (1974) and Farrell (1979).

*Hypothesis 19   High-power group members are usually better liked than low-power group members.*

Field studies with young people (boys and girls in fresh-air camps) and with older people (mental hygiene workers) indicate that group members express greater liking for high-power than for low-power group members (Hurwitz et al., 1953; Lippitt et al., 1952). The high-power person is seen as the source of rewards and punishments; a liked other is perceived as more likely to reward and less likely to punish than a disliked other.

*Hypothesis 20   The high-power group member is the target of more deferential, approval-seeking behavior than low-power group members.*

The basis for the effects referred to in Hypothesis 20 is probably the same as for the effects specified by Hypothesis 19: The high-power person is potentially threatening because of being capable of hurting the weaker group member. Deferential, approval-seeking behavior reduces the uneasiness aroused by this potential threat (Lippitt et al., 1952). This interpretation is also supported by the findings of Butler and Miller (1965) that more rewards and fewer punishments are directed toward the high-power group member than toward low-power group members.

*Hypothesis 21    The high-power person has greater influence upon the group than low-power group members.*

This very reasonable hypothesis is also supported by studies reported by Lippitt et al. (1952) and Hurwitz et al. (1953). The person who controls more reinforcements obviously should be able to influence others more than the one who controls fewer reinforcements. This hypothesis must be qualified somewhat, however, because the degree to which the high-power person can influence other group members varies with the kind of power he or she tries to use. Miller, Butler, and McMartin (1969) observed that use of coercive power was less effective than use of reward power; the effectiveness of threats has been shown to be a function of the threatener's behavior following the threat (Schlenker et al., 1970).

*Hypothesis 22    The high-power group member is more highly attracted to the group than are low-power group members.*

A group member who is highly accepted by the group, who is the target of deferential treatment from others, who has great influence upon the group process, etc., undoubtedly finds the group more attractive than a member who is not treated so favorably. That the above hypothesis is valid one is supported by the results of several empirical investigations. For instance, Zander and Cohen (1955) demonstrated this phenomenon clearly in their classroom exercise: The person whom the group identified as a dean was much more highly attracted to the group than a member identified as a freshman, although neither knew that these role identifications had been made. Results reported by Lippitt et al. (1952) and by Watson and Bromberg (1965) are also consistent with Hypothesis 22.

*Hypothesis 23    The more power a group member has, the greater the probability that he or she will use it.*

This interesting hypothesis does not have a great deal of supporting evidence, but the two studies reporting this effect are reasonably convincing (Kipnis, 1972; W. P. Smith, 1967).

## SUGGESTED READINGS

Farrell, M. P. Collective projection and group structure: The relationship between deviance and projection in groups. *Small Group Behavior,* 1979, **10,** 81–100.

Gerard, H. B., Wilhelmy, R. A., & Conolley, E. S. Conformity and group size. *Journal of Personality and Social Psychology,* 1968, **8,** 79–82.

Kipnis, D. Does power corrupt? *Journal of Personality and Social Psychology,* 1972, **24,** 33–41.

Levine, J. M., Saxe, L., & Harris, H. J. Reaction to attitudinal deviance: Impact of deviate's direction and distance of movement. *Sociometry,* 1976, **39,** 97–107.

Montgomery, R. L., Hinkle, S. W., & Enzie, R. F. Arbitrary norms and social change in high- and low-authoritarian societies. *Journal of Personality and Social Psychology,* 1976, **33,** 698–708.

Ross, L. D., Amabile, T. M., & Steinmetz, J. L. Social roles, social control, and biases in social-perception processes. *Journal of Personality and Social Psychology,* 1977, **35,** 485–494.

Wahrman, R. Status, deviance, sanctions, and group discussion. *Small Group Behavior,* 1977, **8,** 147–168.

# Leadership

The leadership role is one of the most important roles associated with positions in the group structure. The effective functioning of the group depends in large part on the degree to which the activities of group members are coordinated and directed toward achievement of group goals. Although such coordination is possible without a formal group leader, it is probable that effective group action seldom occurs unless someone in the group directs the various activities of group members. It is not surprising, therefore, that leadership has been a concern of social scientists throughout recorded history. For instance, Rousseau (1772) noted that the problem of social entities is to find a form of association that permits common effort for the good of all and at the same time permits individual freedom. Much of leadership behavior is still directed to this age-old problem.

Interest in leaders and leadership is as strong today as in the past, and researchers continue to try to adequately define and analyze these concepts. Historically, the study of leadership has been influenced by the dominant philosophical orientations in the larger society. The philosophy of the Western world at the beginning of the twentieth century emphasized individualism, based upon the views of Spencer, Mills, and others. Consequently, it is understandable that early attempts to study leadership emphasized individual characteristics, leading to the trait approach to leadership. The goal of this approach was to identify leadership traits that distinguished leaders from nonleaders, "good" leaders from "bad" leaders, etc. It was reasoned that once leadership traits were identified, they could be measured, and persons assigned to leadership positions on the basis of this measure. It soon became clear that leadership was much more complex than implied by the trait conceptualization, and the emphasis shifted to the study of leadership styles, situational factors, and other aspects of group process. As we shall see, current approaches view leadership as a process involving the interaction of many factors relevant to group behavior.

The study of leadership has been further complicated by lack of agreement about the nature of the process and the definition of leader. Everyone "knows" what a leader is, but if asked to give a definition, each person is likely to state his or her own unique notion of leaders and leadership behaviors. Those who devote their research efforts to understanding leadership are little closer to agreement on these concepts than naïve persons. Numerous definitions have been proposed and used as guides for research. Obviously, different conceptions of leadership may induce different conclusions concerning this important process.

Much of the research and theory concerning leadership has been in organizations and societies. Consequently, it is questionable whether principles established in those settings also apply to small groups. In the remainder of this chapter we will consider the various definitions and conceptualizations of leader and leadership, the various approaches to the study of leadership, and some of the conclusions that may be drawn from those studies. As far as possible, we will limit our discussion to those aspects that seem relevant to small group behavior. However, the reader should be aware that the literature on leadership in small groups is almost inextricably interrelated with the literature on leadership in larger social units.

## WHAT IS LEADERSHIP?

In Chapter 8 we stated that leadership is a special case of social influence, namely, the exercise of power by the occupant of a particular position in the group structure. This way of describing leadership is adequate for distinguishing among such interrelated concepts as power, social influence, authority, and leadership but is not sufficiently precise to serve as a definition of leadership. As a beginning, it is important to distinguish between *leader* and *leadership*. Although these two terms are often used interchangeably, they refer to different aspects of group process. *Leadership* refers to a process, whereas *leader* refers to a position within the group structure or to a person who occupies such a position. It will be recalled from Chapter 8 that positions in the group structure, including the leader position, are not necessarily formally established but often emerge through group interaction. Perhaps the various interpretations of leadership and leaders may be clarified by comparing some of the definitions proposed by others:

> Leadership is the process of influencing group activities toward goal setting and goal achievement (Stogdill, 1950).

> We define leadership as *interpersonal influence, exercised in situation and directed, through the communication process, toward the attainment of a specified goal or goals* (Tannenbaum & Massarik, 1957).

> Leadership constitutes an influence relationship between two, or usually more, persons who depend upon one another for the attainment of certain mutual goals within a group situation (Hollander & Julian, 1969).

> By *leadership behavior* we generally mean the particular acts in which a leader engages in the course of directing and coordinating the work of his group members (Fiedler, 1967).

Although these definitions of leadership are stated differently all have in common, explicitly or implicitly, the notion that leadership is an influence process which is directed toward goal achievement.* Despite the coalescence of viewpoints concerning leadership, there has not been a corresponding convergence of definitions of leader. At least five distinctly different conceptions of leader have appeared in the literature (Carter, 1953) and continue to be used at present. First, a leader may be defined as a person who is the focus of group behaviors. This definition emphasizes the polarization of group members around the leader. As noted earlier, the leader is likely to receive more communications than others, have more influence on the group's decisions, etc. Hence, the leader usually is the center of attention in the group. As Carter noted, however, there are many situations in which an individual who is the focus of attention is not the person most researchers would identify as the leader. He cited the example of an obnoxious drunk at a social gathering. The behavior of all members of the group might be centered around the drunk, but few would be willing

---

*In his massive review of the literature on leadership, Stogdill (1974) identified no fewer than eleven definitions of leadership that were basically different. However, many of these definitions are of historical interest only, and a number of them incorporate the idea of influence and goal achievement.

to call him the leader. In the studies of deviancy cited earlier in this chapter, the deviant was initially the center of group interaction, but, again, few would call that person the leader.

A second approach defines leadership in terms of group goals. Thus, the leader is the person who is able to lead the group toward its goals. Most people would probably agree with this definition, although Carter found it unsatisfactory because of the difficulty of identifying group goals. This is indeed a problem, as we shall see in the next chapter; however, it is probably not an impossible task. Carter also noted that such a definition would exclude persons who lead the group away from its goals, as in the case of leaders like Hitler.

A third approach defines the leader as the person so named by the members of the group. This definition of leadership is thus based upon sociometric choice. Carter objected that this definition only points to a person who occupies the leadership role but says nothing about the characteristics of leadership. This is obviously true, but the views of group members may, nevertheless, be useful in identifying the group leader.

A fourth approach was proposed by Cattell (1951b) in connection with his theory of group syntality (see Chapter 2). Accordingly, a leader is defined as a person who has demonstrable influence upon group syntality, that is, a person who causes syntality change. It will be recalled that syntality was said to be for the group what personality is for the individual and also that it could be thought of as the measured performance of the group. In terms of the latter interpretation of syntality, the definition of leader as one who produces syntality change would mean that the leader is one who changes the level of group performance. Unfortunately, Cattell did not provide precise methods for determining when a given person has produced such a change, and Carter rejected this definition as impractical. However, another assumption implicit in Cattell's definition is worthy of note, namely, that any group member is a leader to the extent that he or she influences group syntality. Thus, there is not a single group leader; instead, each member is a leader to some degree, depending upon the amount of influence he or she has upon syntality change. This is undoubtedly true; when we speak of *the leader* we mean the group member who has exerted the *greatest* influence upon the group's performance.

The fifth definition of leadership cited by Carter is the one that he preferred: the leader is a person who engages in leadership behaviors. This is an operational definition that is pragmatic with respect to research. That is, the researcher can identify the specific kinds of behaviors that he or she calls leadership behaviors; others can accept or reject them as evidences of leadership, but at least it is clear what is being discussed. Nevertheless, this approach leads to a heterogeneous mass of specific acts that supposedly identify leadership in the group. What constitutes leadership depends upon the view of the person who is listing leadership behaviors.

There are other definitions that Carter did not mention. For example, many investigators have defined the leader as the person who occupies a position of leadership in a group. The president of a company, the foreman of a work group, the platoon sergeant in military organizations, the chairperson of the student honors committee, etc., are, therefore, leaders by virtue of the positions they hold. This definition really refers to headship rather than leadership. That is, this kind of role occupant is supported by forces outside the group and may or may not be able to function as a leader of the group. Psychologically, a leader is a person who has the support of the members of his or her group and is able to influence their behavior without invoking external authority. Therefore, we prefer to define the *leader* as the group member who exerts positive influence over other group members, or as the member who exerts more positive influence over others than they exert over him or her. The term *positive* indicates that the direction of the influence is that desired by the leader. This definition permits the inclusion of leaders who lead the group away from the group goal, so long as that is the direction the leader intends to go—whether or not he or she believes the outcome will be goal achievement. It excludes the person who exerts negative influence on the group, that is, the group member who always manages to get the group to do just the opposite of what he or she desires them to do.

## LEADERSHIP ATTAINMENT

Whether a given group member attains a position of leadership in the group is not merely a matter of chance but is a function of numerous personal, situational, and group variables. We have already seen that the probability that a particular person will become the leader in a group is related to spatial position (a spatial location providing maximum eye contact increases the likelihood that the person will emerge as the leader), location in the communication pattern (central positions enhance leadership selection and emergence), and numerous personal characteristics (Chapter 6). The relationship of personal characteristics will be considered in some detail in the section on the trait approach, but it is necessary at this time to indicate some of the more important behavior patterns that influence leadership attainment. Rate of participation is one kind of behavior which has been examined extensively, with the most common finding being that the person who participates most has the highest probability of becoming the leader (Stogdill, 1974). For example, in one study of four-man problem-solving groups, a trained confederate served as a group member and systematically varied his quality and quantity of interaction (Sorrentino & Boutillier, 1975). Although quality of verbal interaction affected perceptions of competence, influence, and contribution to the group's goal, only quantity of verbal interaction affected perception of leadership. Similarly, it has been found that selection of a group representative depends heavily upon participation rate (Buban, 1976). Conversely, leaders who participate are readily identified by outside observers (Stein, 1975). Furthermore, the effect of participation on leadership attainment is not limited to verbal participation; nonverbal participation, such as "gesticulation of the shoulders and arms," contributes to leadership emergence (Baird, 1977).

The participation–leadership attainment relationship has also been observed in female groups (Gintner & Lindskold, 1975) but only when the talkative confederate was identified as inexpert. This finding is consistent with another factor that contributes to leadership attainment, namely, abilities (intelligence, knowledge, skill, etc.) of group members. It will come as no surprise that group members who possess task-relevant knowledge and abilities are more likely to emerge or be selected as group leaders. Such persons are in a better position to assist the group in achieving its goal, they can more effectively direct the application of the resources possessed by others, and they are generally better qualified to occupy the leader position. On the other hand, it may not be obvious that persons' perceptions of their own abilities also influence their chances of becoming leaders. For example, Stires (1970) told some members that they differed in ability, but not others. Persons with confidence in their ability attempted to gain leadership through modesty whereas others attempted to gain respect through self-enhancement.

An early study of task ability and leadership (Carter & Nixon, 1949) found that kind of ability and kind of task determined leadership emergence: word fluency and clerical aptitude were related to leadership attainment when the task was clerical, whereas mechanical aptitude was related to leadership emergence when the task was a mechanical one.

When a group member does not possess certain characteristics, that person may be eliminated from consideration for the leadership position. In one study of leadership emergence in leaderless groups, sixteen groups were observed as they discussed a problem and prepared a document presenting suggested solutions (Geier, 1967). It was found that almost all group members wanted to be the leader, but those who were perceived as uninformed, authoritative, or rigid were eliminated from the competition. Also, those who either participated relatively little in the group discussion or used offensive language seldom emerged as leaders.

It is clear that who becomes the leader in a group depends upon many factors, including personal characteristics, individual behaviors, spatial relations, task characteristics, and numerous situational and group variables. But the *source* of the leader's authority, i.e., the way that the person became the group leader, has important consequences for the group's functioning. For instance, whether the leader emerges via group interaction or is appointed by some outside authority affects the behavior of the leader, the reactions of others, and the effectiveness of the group. In an early study of the behavior of leaders and other group members (Carter, Haythorn, Shriver, & Lanzetta, 1951), it was found that emergent leaders behaved in a more authoritarian manner than appointed leaders, especially in discussion tasks. Similarly, in a study of decision-making conferences in government and business, it was found that emergent leaders were more highly motivated and expressed more self-oriented needs than other group members (Crockett, 1955).

The source of the leader's authority also influences the degree of legitimacy attributed to the leader and hence his or her effectiveness (Hollander & Julian, 1970). Legitimacy may derive from the willingness of followers to support the leader, or it may be based upon the manner in which the person attained the leadership position. Hollander and his associates have conducted several studies relating the source of the leader's authority to several aspects of group functioning. In general, it is found that source of leader's authority (e.g., appointment or election) interacts with a leader's perceived motivation, competence, and the degree to which the group is successful (Hollander, 1978). For example, one study involved the division of a group's winnings under rules that gave the leader authority to make the decision about that division (Hollander, Julian, & Perry, 1966). Members were more willing to accept a selfish action (the leader gave the greatest share to himself) by an elected leader than by an appointed one. They also indicated that they had been influenced more by an elected leader than by an appointed one. In another experiment (Julian, Hollander, & Regula, 1969), legitimacy of the leader's position was varied by perceived leader competence (high or low), task success (versus failure), and source of authority (appointment or election). Four-person groups of men participated in discussions under varying combinations of legitimacy variables. Reactions to the "spokesman" varied with all three conditions, as may be seen in Figure 9-1. As might be expected, the more competent and successful spokesman was endorsed more strongly than the less competent and unsuccessful one. Importantly, the competent elected leader was endorsed more strongly than the incompetent elected leader only when the group was successful, whereas the appointed leader was endorsed more strongly when the group succeeded than when it failed whether competent or incompetent, but relatively more strongly when

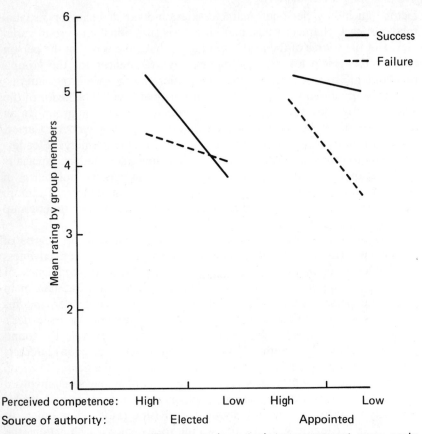

**Figure 9-1** Mean member willingness to have spokesman represent group again, presented for each condition. (Reprinted with permission from J. W. Julian, E. P. Hollander, & C. R. Regula. Endorsement of the group spokesman as a function of his source of authority, competence, and success. *Journal of Personality and Social Psychology,* 1969, **11,** 42–49. Copyright 1969 by the American Psychological Association. Reprinted by permission.)

incompetent. In short, the elected spokesman was more likely to be rejected than the appointed one if he was either perceived to be incompetent or failed to produce a successful outcome; the appointed leader apparently satisfied group members if he was either competent or produced a favorable group outcome.

Several other investigations have shown that the source of the leader's authority influences group behavior. One important study examined four types of leadership attainment on problem-solving effectiveness by laboratory groups (Goldman & Fraas, 1965). Groups with no assigned leader were compared with groups having a leader who was either arbitrarily appointed, appointed on the basis of merit, or selected by group members. Groups were more effective on problem-solving tasks when the leader was either selected by the group or appointed on the basis of merit. Groups with no leader or an arbitrarily appointed leader performed relatively poorly on these tasks. The relatively better performance of groups with a selected leader as compared with groups with an arbitrarily appointed leader has also been observed in natural settings (Walker, 1976). The groups in this study were judicial tribunals consisting of three to nine judges sitting as courts of last resort. Some of these groups employed an arbitrary method of selecting the formally designated leader (known as a *chief justice*), and others employed systems of selection that involved merit. Performance was measured by level of dissent on the cases that came before the tribunals. The mean index of dissent for groups with merit leaders was 8.18 as compared with 14.13 for those groups with arbitrarily selected leaders. If level of dissent is indeed an index of performance, merit leaders performed better than arbitrary leaders, in accord with the findings of Goldman and Fraas. Source of leader authority has also been shown to predict evaluation of the leader and tenure in office (Read, 1974).

An implicit assumption in these investigations is that the leaders wanted to be leaders and viewed themselves positively with regard to leadership ability. Furthermore, even the appointed leaders were allowed to enact the role to which they had been assigned. But what happens if a person is placed in a position that does not "fit" his or her self-concept or if the other group members demand behavior that is not in accord with the assigned role? According to group congruency theory (see Chapter 2), such circumstances should produce incongruency, which results in reduced group efficiency. An interesting study of three-man groups investigated the effects of such incongruence on leader behavior (Beckhouse, Tanur, Weiler, & Weinstein, 1975). Sixty-four subjects were selected for study, one-half of whom were high and one-half low on a measure of leadership self-concept. Each subject was appointed leader of a three-man group on two occasions, once exposed to followers who pushed him to lead and once to followers who pushed him to follow. When pushed to lead, they led whether high or low on leadership self-concept; but when pushed to follow, they increased behavior of a socioemotional nature, an effect that was greater for leaders having more favorable leadership self-concepts. Unfortunately, no measure of task performance was obtained.

In brief summary, individuals may attain a position of leadership in the group as a consequence of many personal, situational, and group variables. Having become a leader, the way the position was attained often has important consequences for the leader's own behavior, the reactions of others, and group process. The nature of these effects is highly complex and inadequately understood at present.

## THE TRAIT APPROACH TO THE STUDY OF LEADERSHIP

The trait approach to the study of leadership was based on the belief that leaders have personal characteristics which set them apart from nonleaders and make them leaders. The goal, then, was simply to identify those unique leadership characteristics, devise techniques for measuring them, and use these techniques for the selection of leaders. As we mentioned earlier, this orientation probably derived from the dominant philosophical positions of the time. In the Western world, it was believed that a man could become whatever he wished to become, so long as he had the ability and persevered. Thus, leaders became leaders because of their own personal efforts and attributes. This view of leaders was reflected in many aspects of the academic literature and other public proclamations. For example, Thomas Carlyle, the Scottish historian and essayist, gave a series of lectures in 1840 in which he eulogized "Great Men." He asserted that ". . . the history of what man has accomplished in this world, is at bottom, the History of the Great Men who have worked here. They were the leaders of men, these great ones; the modelers, patterns, and in a wide sense creators of whatsoever the general mass of men contrived to do or to attain."

Thus, it is not surprising that students of leadership looked first to individual characteristics as the major determinants of leadership. In the early part of this century, hundreds of empirical studies attempted to identify the personal attributes or traits of leaders. These studies employed one of two major methodologies: (1) Leaders and nonleaders were identified, their personal characteristics measured, and differences between leaders and nonleaders obtained, or (2) leadership ability of individuals was estimated in some manner, the personal attributes measured, and correlations between measures of ability and traits computed. In the first case, any trait possessed to a greater extent by leaders than nonleaders was assumed to be a leadership trait; in the second case, traits that correlated highly with measures of leadership ability were assumed to be leadership traits. Methods of identifying leaders, estimating leadership ability, and even the kinds of traits that were studied varied widely. In a review of trait studies, Stogdill (1948) found no fewer than twenty-nine different characteristics that had been examined in one or more investigations, including "traits" ranging from chronological age and physical size to more psychological attributes such as initiative, self-confidence, and emotional control. The most obvious result of this review of trait studies was that the various findings were highly inconsistent. For instance, correlations between chronological age and leadership status ranged from $-.37$ to $+.71$; between appearance and leadership, from $-.20$ to $+.81$; emotional control, from $.18$ to $.70$. However, more careful examination also revealed several consistent findings. Uniformly positive correlations reported in at least fifteen separate studies indicated that the average person who occupies a position of leadership exceeds the average group member with respect to intelligence, scholarship, dependability in exercising responsibilities, participation, and socioeconomic status. Ten or more studies reported consistent evidence indicating that the average leader exceeds the average group member on sociability, initiative, persistence, knowing how to get things done, self-confidence, insight, cooperativeness, popularity, and adaptability. Although many of these correlations and leader-nonleader differences were small, they do indicate that personal characteristics contribute to leadership. At the same time, several studies suggested that situational factors determine which traits are important for leadership.

The characteristics that appear to be related to leadership fall neatly into the three clusters or factors identified by Carter (1954):

*Group goal facilitation,* which includes those abilities that are necessary to help the group attain its goal (e.g., insight, intelligence, knowing how to get things done).
*Group sociability,* which includes those factors that are necessary to keep the group functioning smoothly (e.g., sociability, cooperativeness, popularity).
*Individual prominence,* which includes factors related to the person's desire for group recognition (e.g., initiative, self-confidence, persistence).

In short, the findings from the trait approach suggest that in order for a person to be a leader, he or she needs the necessary goal-related abilities and skills, must be able to relate effectively to others, and must *want* to be a leader. At the same time, it becomes evident that the particular abilities needed and the particular social skills required depend upon the situation in which the group interaction occurs. The trait approach yielded interesting theoretical data, but dependence on situational factors makes these data of only minor *practical* use. Thus, many researchers and theorists turned to the situational approach. At the same time, others emphasized leadership behavior and were concerned with leadership styles. We will examine first the leadership style approach and then the situational approaches to leadership.

## LEADERSHIP STYLES*

Since characteristics of individuals presumably reflect behavioral tendencies, it has seemed to many students of leadership that investigations should deal with behavior directly. Even casual observation of leaders at work reveals tremendous differences in leadership style. Some leaders give orders, demand obedience, make all decisions without regard to the opinions of others, etc., whereas other leaders are considerate, request the cooperation of others, ask their opinions before making decisions, etc. Such differences in leadership style obviously should affect group process, and a number of studies have been conducted to determine the exact nature of the effects.

The pioneering study of leadership styles was conducted by Lewin and his associates (Lewin, Lippitt, & White, 1939; Lippitt & White, 1943). Four comparable groups of 10-year-old boys were observed as they successively experienced autocratic, democratic, and "laissez-faire" adult leadership. The leadership styles were experienced in different orders by different groups. The group task was to engage in hobby activities, such as making paper masks. Each group met after school for 3 six-week periods, with a different adult leader and a different leadership style for each period. Four adult leaders were trained to play each of the three leadership roles. The autocratic leader determined all policy for the group, dictated techniques and actions—one at a time to ensure that future actions would always be uncertain, usually dictated the particular work task and work companions, and was subjective in praise and criticism of the work of group members. His attitude was impersonal and aloof, but not openly hostile. The democratic leader allowed the group to determine matters of policy, the general steps to the goal were sketched and alternative procedures suggested when appropriate, the members were free to work with whomever they chose, and the leader was objective in his praise and criticism of group members. The laissez-faire leader was essentially a nonparticipant in group activities. The group was given complete freedom to make its own decisions, materials and information were supplied when asked for, and comments on members' activities were very infrequent.

Relatively complete records were kept of group behavior and included observations, structure analysis, interpretation of significant member actions, stenographic records of all conversation, interpretation of member relationships, movies of several parts of group interaction, and comments by the leader and by visitors. The results showed markedly different patterns of interaction as a function of leadership style. Hostility was thirty

*Leadership style is used here to refer to a set of behaviors that characterize the leader's activities during the time of investigation. This set of behaviors may or may not reflect a personality attribute of the leader (cf. Fiedler, 1967).

times as great in the autocratic as in the democratic groups, and aggression was eight times as great in the autocratic as in the democratic. There was more scapegoating in the autocratic groups than in either of the other two; one group member was frequently made the target of hostility and aggression until he left the group, and then another boy would be chosen for this honor. Nineteen of twenty boys liked the democratic leader better than the autocrat, and seven of ten liked the laissez-faire leader better than the autocrat. There was no reliable difference in the number of products produced, but the products of the democratic groups were judged to be qualitatively superior to those of the other groups.

There were some very interesting sequential effects associated with the change in leadership style, although, unfortunately, the design did not permit their precise interpretation. The most interesting effects occured when the group experienced the autocratic leader first in the sequence, followed by the laissez-faire leader in the second period. The rise in aggression under laissez-faire leadership can be seen in Figure 9-2. This was attributed to repressed aggression during the autocratic period. Under the freer group atmosphere, the boys expressed the pent-up aggressive tendencies that they had not been able to express under the autocratic leader. Sequential effects of this kind are probably very important for interaction in natural groups and merit further study. For instance,

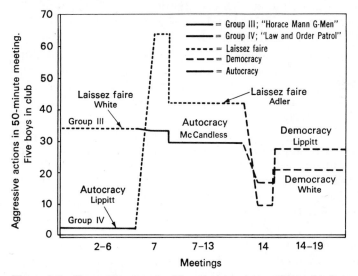

**Figure 9-2** The same group in different atmospheres. Group IV shows changes to the levels typical for each atmosphere. It shows also the "release of tension" on the first day of freedom (7) after apathetic autocracy. Group III seemed resistant to change; it was relatively aggressive even in democracy. (Reprinted with permission from K. Lewin, R. Lippitt, & R. K. White. Patterns of aggressive behavior in experimentally created "social climates." *Journal of Social Psychology*, 1939, **10**, 271–299.)

consider the reaction of a worker who has been a member of a work group led by an autocratic foreman, who now finds himself in a group with a democratic leader. Perhaps he will be ineffective in such a group because his aggressive responses now dominate his behavior.

Many of the findings reported by Lewin et al. have been replicated in widely divergent settings. Preston and Heintz (1949) asked members of several laboratory classes to rank twelve potential presidential candidates in order of individual preference. Class members were then divided into groups of four or five members each and asked to rank the candidates, working as a group. Assigned leaders were instructed to play either a participatory or a supervisory role. The participatory leader was told to be sure that each name was considered, to encourage all members to take part in the discussions, to discourage chance methods of deciding doubtful cases, and to complete the work in half an hour. The supervisory leaders were instructed not to participate in the discussion and to limit their responsibility to seeing that the work was done in the allotted time. The results showed that participatory leadership was more effective in changing attitudes than was supervisory leadership. Participatory group members also were better satisfied with the group's ranking, found the task more interesting and meaningful, and rated their group discussions as more friendly and enjoyable than did members of supervisory groups.

The effects of authoritarian and nonauthoritarian leadership were also examined in a laboratory setting by M. E. Shaw (1955). Groups of four college males were assembled and assigned instructed leaders who played either an authoritarian or a nonauthoritarian leadership role. The authoritarian leader was asked to issue orders, to accept no suggestion uncritically, and to make it clear that he was boss of the group. The nonauthoritarian leader was instructed to solicit suggestions, make requests instead of issuing orders, and make it clear that he wanted the group to function democratically. Each group solved three arithmetic problems via written communication. The authoritarian groups made fewer errors, required fewer messages for problem solution, and required less time than did the nonauthoritarian groups; however, the ratings of satisfaction with the group were higher in nonauthoritarian groups.

In another study (Rosenbaum & Rosenbaum, 1971), groups of four males worked on structured and unstructured tasks under stressful or nonstressful conditions. Groups were more productive with an autocratic leader under stress conditions, but democratic leaders had more productive groups under nonstressful conditions. Ratings of satisfaction were slightly higher for democratic- than for autocratic-led groups, but this difference was not statistically reliable.

Similar effects have been reported from studies conducted in natural settings. Morse and Reimer (1956) selected four work groups from a nonunionized industrial organization. The four groups were matched as closely as possible with respect to satisfaction and productivity measures taken before the study began. Two of the four groups were assigned to an autonomy condition in which they were given greater control over all aspects of the work situation except their salary. The others were assigned to a hierarchically controlled situation in which greater control was given to the supervisor. The task was clerical work which required that the groups process whatever material came to them. Hence, productivity was measured by the number of workers required to handle a given number of units. After the groups had spent one year under the experimental conditions, measures of satisfaction and productivity were again obtained. As in laboratory experiments, satisfaction increased in the autonomy groups but decreased in the hierarchically controlled groups. Productivity increased in both groups, but the increase was greater in the hierarchically controlled groups ($+14.1$) than in the autonomy groups ($+10$). In interpreting this difference in productivity, we must remember the restriction that no worker could be fired because he was not needed. However, a worker who resigned did not have to be replaced, and a worker could be transferred to another department in the company. It is possible that members of the autonomy work group were more reluctant to transfer a worker who was no longer needed than was the supervisor in the hierarchically controlled groups.

It is evident that, although different terms are used, these several researchers are dealing with similar leadership variables. In each instance, a directive leader is compared with a nondirective one. The results concerning the group members' reactions to the group are entirely consistent across a wide range of situations and groups: Members of groups with nondirective leaders react more positively to the group than do members of groups led by directive leaders. The evidence concerning productivity is inconsistent; however, it appears that either the directive-led groups are usually more productive than the nondirective-led groups or there is no difference in productivity.

Laboratory studies have indicated one other interesting aspect of autocratic versus democratic leadership: It is apparently much easier to be a good autocratic leader than a good democratic leader. For example, in the study by M. E. Shaw (1955) both the most and least effective groups had democratic leaders; there was relatively little variance among autocratic groups. It is easy to issue orders, but difficult to utilize effectively the abilities of group members. A leader who doubts his or her ability to be an effective democratic leader probably is well advised to play the autocratic role.

Several other investigations have varied leader behavior in ways that are related to the autocratic-democratic dimension, with similar results.

For instance, one study found that confederates trained to exhibit different levels of "opinionatedness" had different effects on the group (Hill, 1976). Groups with unopinionated leaders came closer to consensus, and the leaders were seen as more competent and more objective than opinionated leaders. Structuring and unstructuring leaders were observed in another study (Jurma, 1978). Structuring leaders directed the group discussion, gave guiding suggestions, helped the group budget time, established group goals, ensured that all opinions were considered, and acted in a friendly manner, whereas the unstructuring leader enacted these behaviors to a much lesser degree. Members of groups with structuring leaders rated their task as more interesting, valuable, and important, and were more satisfied than members of groups with unstructuring leaders. Furthermore, structuring leaders were rated by their followers as significantly stronger, more competent, more enthusiastic, more active, and more positive than were unstructuring leaders. Still another study found that groups with directive leaders engaged in less group interaction than groups with nondirective leaders (Gilstein, Wright, & Stone, 1977).

The Ohio State University studies of leadership (Stogdill, 1974) identified two aspects of leadership that are in many ways similar to leadership styles. These dimensions are called *consideration* and *initiating structure* (Halpin, 1957). Consideration reflects the extent to which a leader is concerned about the feelings of followers; initiating structure represents the extent to which the leader defines the leader-follower roles in relation to group goals. It can be seen that a leader who emphasizes consideration is similar to a democratic leader, whereas a leader high on initiating structure is similar to an autocratic leader. Not surprisingly, research findings regarding these types of leaders (considerate versus structuring) are similar to those regarding democratic versus autocratic leaders. After reviewing the literature, Stogdill (1974) concluded that group productivity is somewhat more highly related to structure than to consideration, whereas member satisfaction is somewhat more highly related to consideration than to structure.

In general, it appears that group productivity may be facilitated by a leader who provides direction and structure, but whether and to what extent this is true depends upon situational and task variables. Member satisfaction, however, is almost always facilitated by a leader who is considerate and relation-oriented.

Finally, it is of some interest that the style of leadership adopted by the occupant of the leader position in the group is influenced by situational factors. For instance, in one study, foremen assumed the role of supervisor in simulated industrial work crews (Fodor, 1978). In one condition the members of the work crew they directed exhibited characteristics of group stress, and in another condition they did not. The "supervisors" adopted a more authoritarian style in the group stress condition than in the neutral condition. In another study of "revolutionary leaders" (Suedfeld & Rank, 1976), it was found that such leaders exemplified a categorical, single-minded approach to problems. However, after the revolution, those leaders who retained power became more flexible, whereas those that did not retain power maintained their original leadership style.

These several studies which we have reviewed show clearly that leadership styles are related to productivity, member satisfaction, and other aspects of group process. But they also show the importance of situational factors, which we will examine more closely in the next section.

## SITUATIONAL APPROACHES TO LEADERSHIP

In the preceding discussions we have seen that the personal characteristics of leaders are related to leadership attainment and effectiveness, although the results may be inconsistent across situations (at least with respect to specific traits). Leadership styles or patterns of behavior also exert strong influences on group process and effectiveness, but, again, the effects of a particular leadership style often depend upon other variables. It was probably these interaction effects of leadership variables that induced many researchers and theoreticians to emphasize situational factors. The view that leadership depends heavily on the situation is not a new idea, of course. As early as 1931 Emory Bogardus strongly endorsed the situational approach:

> Consistency of behavior is doubtless a leadership trait, but behavior may vary according to situations, even on the part of any person. A person may be generally consistent in some situations and inconsistent in others. It is apparently necessary, therefore, to study situations in relation to personality reactions in order to account for ability, or for failure, to lead (Bogardus, 1931-32, p. 165).

Similarly, Murphy (1941) argued that leadership traits are fluid and that individual characteristics may change with the situation. For example, a person who is usually dominant may become shy if placed in an unfamiliar situation. Consequently, a trait that is positively related to leadership in one situation may be unrelated or even negatively related in another. Leaders must have those characteristics that are relevant to the situations in which they find themselves. A person who has great ability with respect to building bridges has a better chance of becoming an effective leader of a bridge-building crew than a person without such skills, but his or her chances of becoming the leader of a chemical research team might be very low indeed.

The situational approach was undoubtedly encouraged by experiences of the Office of Strategic Services (OSS)* during World War II. The OSS staff was charged with training persons who would be capable of carrying out secret missions, often in enemy territory. The method they adopted was basically situational in nature. For three and one-half days, candidates were tested, interviewed, and observed in a series of problem situations. These included discussions, debates, performance in leaderless groups, serving as appointed group leader, and working with helpers who were either overly aggressive or listless. The assessment staff assigned each candidate a leadership score, which was later correlated with appraisals by area commanders and with ratings by fellow returnees. The two correlations were identical (+.11) and most discouraging. According to the assessment staff, these low correlations were due, at least in part, to the fact that the persons who were evaluated and went overseas were not called upon to deal with many general situations, as had been anticipated, but with a limited number of more specific situations (OSS Assessment Staff, 1948).

These considerations lead us to suspect that situational factors influence both the emergence of leaders and their behavior in groups. Research findings verify this expectation. We have already noted many of these effects (e.g., the effects of tasks on leadership behavior, the effects of source of leader authority on group performance and leader evaluation), but many other effects have been reported in the leadership literature. For instance, Miller (1966) reported that officials of craft unions expressed a greater need for other-directed behavior than officials of industrial unions. It was also found that other-directed behavior varied with type of organization and with the levels of positions within the organizational structure. An investigation of navy officers who transferred to new positions revealed that, although patterns of interpersonal behavior did not change, patterns of work performance changed in accordance with the requirements of the situation (Stogdill, Shartle, Scott, Coons, & Jaynes, 1956).

Several studies have shown that the followers in a group exert a strong influence on the leader's behavior. For instance, Morris and Hackman (1969) observed that persons who are perceived to be leaders of a group participate more than nonleaders, although high participation was not sufficient for leadership emergence. Nonleaders who were high participators emphasized activities that were detrimental to group creativity and deemphasized facilitative activities. Low participators who were seen as leaders were usually persons who had been named as the leader by the investigator. Similarly, Michener and Tausig (1971) found that a formal

*Known today as the Central Intelligence Agency (CIA).

leader who usurped control was endorsed for leadership (i.e., seen as having legitimate power) by group members to a lesser extent than a formal leader who did not usurp control. Furthermore, a group member who perceived that other group members uniformly supported a specific leader endorsed the leader to a greater extent than a group member who perceived that the leader did not have such general support. This latter finding, of course, could merely reflect conformity to majority opinion. The degree to which the leader is endorsed by group members may also depend on situational variables such as group success and distribution of rewards in the group (Michener & Lawler, 1975). Endorsement of the leader was found to be greater when the group was successful, when reward distribution was hierarchical (the leader received a larger share of rewards than lower-status members), and when the leader was not vulnerable to removal from office.

Threat of removal from office has other important consequences for leader behavior, as shown in a study of intergroup cooperation-competition (Rabbie & Bekkers, 1978). Group leaders were given the choice of engaging in either intergroup cooperation or intergroup competition under threat of being deposed by followers or under no threat. Threatened leaders were more likely to choose competition when the group was internally divided and had a strong bargaining position relative to the other group. It is probable that leaders believe group cohesiveness can be facilitated by having a "common enemy," a state that can be achieved by choosing to compete rather than cooperate with another group. Threat of being removed from the leader position may well be stressful, a situational factor that also influences reactions to the leader. For example, a study of "panic behavior" compared reactions to elected and appointed leaders under stressful or nonstressful conditions (Klein, 1976). The task in this experiment involved removal of cones from a container through a small opening that would permit removal of only one cone at a time. For some of the groups, members received shock for failure to remove cones quickly (the stressful or "panic" condition), whereas others only forfeited a small amount of money for failure to remove the cone quickly enough. Elected leaders were seen as more competent and were given more responsibility than appointed leaders, but only when stress was low (monetary loss for failure).

It has also been shown that emergent leaders who are given recognition and support show more attempted leadership than leaders who are not reinforced by group members (Mortensen, 1966). Clearly, situational factors affect the perceptions of leadership and the behaviors of leaders in group interaction.

By this point it should be clear to the reader that leadership behavior is a complex phenomenon which is influenced by a vast array of factors.

The personal characteristics of group members (both leaders and follow-ers), styles or patterns of leadership behavior, and numerous situational variables affect leadership emergence, behavior, and effectiveness. Fur-thermore, these factors interact in complicated ways to determine group outcomes and member reactions. The recognition of these complexities led to the formulation of "contingency models" of leadership behavior that attempt to explain the interrelationships of personal, situational, and group variables. Collectively, these attempts represent an approach that may·be called interactionism.

## INTERACTIONISM

The term *interactionism* is employed here to denote a wide range of approaches to the study of leadership that emphasize the joint effects of the many factors known to be related to leadership emergence, group behavior, and group outcomes. According to this general view, leadership is a phenomenon that arises when group formation takes place (Gibb, 1969). As outlined in Chapter 8, a group structure emerges through the interaction process; positions and roles appear, norms are established, and relative statuses are assigned. These aspects of group structure are determined in part by the needs of the group and in part by the personal attributes of group members. Thus, the position that a person occupies in the group and the role that is associated with that position derive from *interactions* among personal qualities of group members, their relationship to others in the group, the needs of the group, group goals, and other group-related variables. The leader position and the leadership role represent only one position and role among the many that emerge during group formation and development.

There are many theoretical "models" of leadership that reflect interactionism, so many, in fact, that it would serve no useful purpose to review them all. We will, however, consider three approaches that represent rather different views of the interaction of variables: (1) the transactional approach, (2) the vertical dyad approach, and (3) a contin-gency model of leadership effectiveness.

### The Transactional Approach

Although the idea of leadership as a transaction is evident in the work of many writers, this approach has been explicated most clearly by Hollander (1978). His analysis emphasizes that leadership is a two-way influence process which involves a social exchange relationship between the leader and his or her followers. That is, leaders and followers engage in a process of social exchange in which each both gives and receives rewards or benefits. For example, the leader provides direction toward successful goal achievement, acts as a buffer against conflicting demands, helps reduce uncertainty associated with ambiguity, and in many other ways provides benefits for others in the group. In exchange, followers accord the leader greater esteem, higher status, and similar social rewards.

In order for the transaction process to function effectively, the exchange of benefits must be perceived as equitable. Thus, for the leader to be supported by the followers, some minimum degree of success is necessary. Otherwise, providing the leader with social benefits such as esteem and status would appear unfair and inequitable. A fair exchange is one in which the leader performs efficiently, deserves the advantages of status, and has status accorded to him or her by followers.

In general, the transactional approach to leadership involves three complex elements: the leader, the followers, and the situation. The relationships among these three elements are depicted in Figure 9-3. The

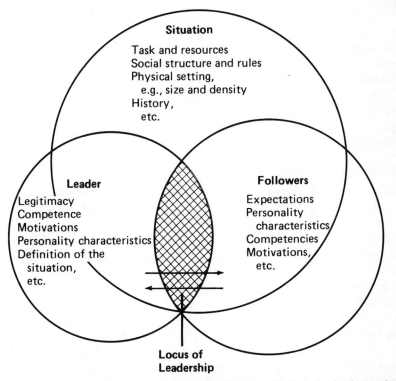

**Figure 9-3** Three elements involved in leadership—the situation, the leader, and the followers—with some of their relevant attributes. The crosshatched area represents their intersection, which is the locus of leadership. The arrows indicate the social exchange which occurs there between the leader and the followers. (Reprinted with permission from E. P. Hollander. *Leadership dynamics: A practical guide to effective relationships.* New York: The Free Press, 1978, p. 8.)

area in this figure where the three elements overlap represents the "locus of leadership," which Hollander described as the place where a leader and his or her followers are bound together in a relationship within a situation. Both leaders and followers are placed largely in the situation to indicate that this situation is the one they are primarily involved in. They are not entirely within the situation to show that they do have other roles in other groups and situations.

An important aspect of the transaction approach is that leaders and followers are not greatly different. It is assumed that all group members are leaders to some extent and that all leaders are sometimes followers. There is no sharp dichotomy between the two roles and types of persons. This view is based, in part, on an early study of leaders and followers which showed that persons who were chosen as qualified to lead were also named as persons one would like to have as followers (Hollander & Webb, 1955).

Much of the research on leadership is at least consistent with the transactional view. The research on appointed versus elected leaders, leadership style, and several insights derived from the trait approach support the transactional approach. This research has already been discussed and will not be reviewed again. The reader may have observed by this point in our presentation that, although the analysis is interesting and plausible, it does not allow easy and specific predictions about leadership behavior and group outcome. It does provide guidance for the person in a leadership role.

### Vertical Dyad Linkages

The vertical dyad approach to leadership assumes that a unique interactional relationship develops between the leader and each member of the group (Caine, 1976). This relationship derives both from the characteristics of group members and from environmental factors. The basic elements of the theory were worked out by Graen and his associates (e.g., Graen & Cashman, 1975). The approach considers the development of these leader-follower relationships as well as their outcomes. The basic propositions of the approach concern the role-making process that occurs during group development, the outcome of this process, and the consequences for leadership effectiveness.

According to Graen and Cashman, role making is a set of processes through which an actor and a functionally interdependent other work out how they will behave in specified situations and reach agreement concerning the general nature of their relationship. For instance, they must agree about the degree of dominance each will have vis-a-vis the other, the degree of involvement that will be expected and/or tolerated, and the level of interpersonal intimacy that will exist. In the process of role making, it is assumed that each person will have some influence on the perceptions of the other concerning actions that are appropriate, i.e., that constitute an appropriate role or set of behaviors for an occupant of the person's position in the group. In other words, the roles associated with the leader-follower positions are developed through the interactions of occupants of those positions.

The leader-follower relationship is, therefore, a special case of role making, leading to the establishment of vertical dyad linkages. Vertical dyad linkages must be shaped (at least sometimes) and in some instances must be carefully developed over time. Leadership is simply a process of vertical exchange. Unfortunately, Graen and Cashman did not clearly identify the nature of vertical exchange, nor did they specify whether it is the degree of exchange or the content (quality) of the exchange that is important for effective leadership. Presumably, both quality and quantity of exchange are important. Caine (1976) suggested that in-group linkages "are characterized by open, two-way communication, mutual trust and respect, and the exercise of influence without resort to threat or coercion" (p. 365), where *in-group* refers to a select subgroup within the larger unit. For other subordinates, the linkages are more formal and involve one-way downward communications.

The vertical dyad approach to leadership has some interesting implications for the person who aspires to leadership or who occupies a leadership position. At the present time, it has not greatly inspired researchers, and empirical evidence is sparse.

## A Contingency Model of Leadership Effectiveness

One of the most promising analyses of leadership was proposed by Fiedler (1964, 1967), who attempted to integrate the effects of leadership style and situational variables. In this model of leadership effectiveness, leadership styles are identified by the ASo/LPC scores of the leaders. The method is simple. ASo and LPC scores are obtained from responses to a questionnaire which requires that the respondent rate his or her most preferred and least preferred coworkers on a number of characteristics. The ASo (assumed similarity of opposites) score is derived from a comparison of most and least preferred coworker ratings: the greater the difference between the two sets of ratings the higher the ASo score. The LPC score is based on the ratings of least preferred coworker and correlates highly with the ASo score. Hence, the two scores are used interchangeably; currently only the LPC score is used by most investigators. The high-LPC person perceives his or her least preferred coworker in a relatively favorable manner. Fiedler (1967) describes this person as one who derives major satisfaction from successful interpersonal relationships. The low-LPC person perceives his or her least preferred coworker in very unfavorable terms and is described as a person who derives major satisfaction from task performance.

Thus, high-LPC leaders are concerned with having good interpersonal relations and with gaining prominence and self-esteem through these interpersonal relations. Low-LPC leaders are concerned with achieving success on assigned tasks, even at the risk of having poor interpersonal relations with fellow workers. The behaviors of high- and low-LPC leaders will thus be quite different if the situation is such that the satisfaction of their respective needs is threatened. Under these conditions the high-LPC leader will increase his interpersonal interaction in order to cement his relations with other group members while the low-LPC leader will interact in order to complete the task successfully. The high-LPC person is concerned with gaining self-esteem through recognition by others, the low-LPC person is concerned with gaining self-esteem through the successful performance of the task. Both types of leaders may thus be concerned with the task and both will use interpersonal relationships, although the high-LPC leader will concern himself with the task in order to have successful interpersonal relationships, while the low-LPC leader will concern himself with interpersonal relations in order to achieve task success (Fiedler, 1967, pp. 45–46.).

The relationship between LPC score and effectiveness as a group leader was examined in numerous investigations, with varying results. Correlations between leader LPC scores and measures of group effectiveness ranged from $-.67$ to $.69$. Since these correlations were obtained from a variety of groups operating in widely different settings, the interpretation of LPC scores described above suggests that the effects of leadership styles on group effectiveness can be understood only by considering situational variables. In other words, some system of classifying group situations is required. Fiedler's proposed classification system was based on the belief that the leader's style of interacting with followers is affected by the degree to which the leader can wield power and influence over them. His proposed system postulated three major factors: (1) the leader's position power, (2) the structure of the task, and (3) the personal relationships between leader and members.

Position power was defined as the degree to which the position itself enables the leader to get followers to comply with his or her wishes and to accept his or her leadership. This conception of position power is closely related to French and Raven's (1959) concepts of legitimate power, reward power, and coercive power, which were discussed earlier (see page 295). It is also related to Adams and Romney's (1959) conception of authority as control of reinforcers. In general, the situation is more favorable for the leader when occupying a strong power position. Fiedler assessed position power by means of an eighteen-item checklist which contains various indices of position power.

The structure of the task refers to the degree to which the task requirements are clearly specified, that is, the degree to which the task is capable of being programmed. Fiedler defined task structure operationally in terms of four task dimensions: decision verifiability, goal clarity, goal-path multiplicity, and solution specificity. Briefly, decision verifiability is the degree to which the correctness of a decision can be verified by appeal to authority, by logical procedures, or by feedback; goal clarity is the degree to which the requirements of the task are known to group members; goal-path multiplicity refers to the degree to which the task can be completed by a variety of procedures; and solution specificity (or more appropriately, solution multiplicity) is the degree to which there is more than one correct solution or decision. (Task dimensions are discussed in greater detail in Chapter 10.) The task is structured to the extent that the goal is clear, there is a single path to the goal, there is only one correct solution or decision, and the decision is easily verified. In general, the more structured the task, the more favorable the situation is for the leader.

The personal relationship between leader and followers depends upon the leader's affective relations with group members, the acceptance the leader is able to obtain, and the loyalty he or she is able to elicit. When the leader has good personal relations with fellow group members, the situation is more favorable for the leader than when relations are poor. Leader-member relations are assessed by sociometric ratings and/or ratings of group atmosphere.

Leader-member relations presumably exert the strongest effect on the favorability dimension, followed by task structure, and finally position power of the leader. By taking into account these differences, one can order group situations according to degree of favorability to the leader. For example, the most favorable situation for the leader is one in which leader-member relations are good, the task is highly structured, and the leader's position power is strong; the most unfavorable situation is one in which leader-member relations are poor, the task is unstructured, and the leader's position power is weak. According to Fiedler's theory, the low-LPC leader is more effective when the situation is either highly favorable or unfavorable to the leader, whereas the high-LPC leader is more effective when the situation is moderately favorable. That is, when the situation is very favorable, the leader can be managing and controlling without arousing negative responses by group members; because things are going well, there is no reason to reject the directive behaviors of the leader. On the other hand, when the situation is highly unfavorable, things are going badly, and the group is in danger of falling apart, then directive leadership is required and again the low-LPC leader is more effective. But if the situation is only moderately favorable, the group expects to be treated with consideration, and the permissive, high-LPC leader is more effective. The data presented by Fiedler and reproduced in Figure 9-4 reveal that these expectations are supported by empirical findings.

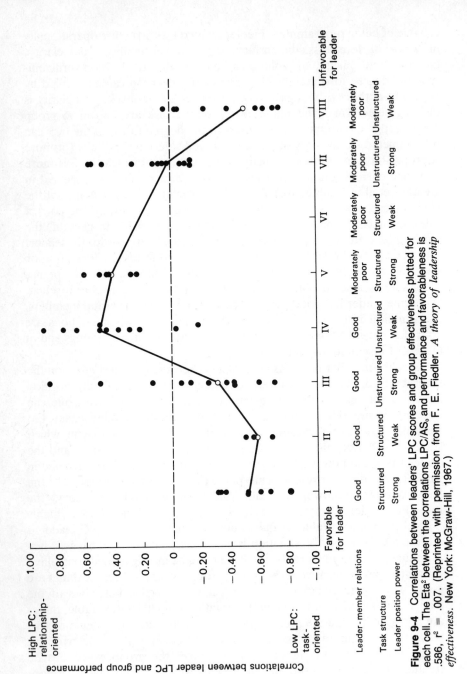

**Figure 9-4** Correlations between leaders' LPC scores and group effectiveness plotted for each cell. The Eta$^2$ between the correlations LPC/AS$_0$ and performance and favorableness is .586, $r^2$ = .007. (Reprinted with permission from F. E. Fiedler. *A theory of leadership effectiveness.* New York: McGraw-Hill, 1967.)

Although the data presented in Figure 9-4 are post hoc, Fiedler and others later conducted research that supports the model (Fiedler, 1967).

More recent research also tends to support the theory, although in some cases not as strongly as might be desired. For instance, one study examined two types of leaders (task-oriented and both task- and relation-oriented) and a no-leader condition in conjunction with three levels of interchange compatibility (underpersonal, incompatible, and overpersonal) that were defined by Schutz's (1958) formulas (Downs & Pickett, 1977). It may be recalled from Chapter 2 that underpersonal people desire relatively little behavior exchange, whereas overpersonal types desire a great deal of behavior exchange with others. In the present experiment, both the underpersonal and overpersonal groups were compatible in that the members agreed on the appropriate amount of behavior exchange but differed in the level of exchange desired. The incompatible groups included both underpersonal and overpersonal members. The two types of assigned leaders performed differently with different groups. The task-oriented leader had more effective groups when group members were either overpersonal or incompatible, whereas the leader who was both task- and person-oriented had groups that performed slightly better when group members were underspersonal. The no-leader groups performed better than incompatible groups with either of the two kinds of leaders, much worse than overpersonal groups with leaders, and about the same as underpersonal groups with task-oriented leaders. These data partially support Fiedler's theory.

Another study compared the performance of groups at four points on the favorability continuum (I, IV, and VIII in Figure 9-4). Group performance was measured in terms of speed and quality of solution (Saha, 1979). According to the contingency model, the correlations between group performance and leader LPC should be negative at I and VIII and positive at IV, and this was what was found. Speed of solving problems correlated $-.69$, $+.48$, and $-.51$ for I, IV, and VIII, respectively. The corresponding correlations for quality of solution were $-.10$, $+.34$, and $-.10$. Although both sets of correlations are in the direction predicted by the theory, only those for speed are strongly supportive. A field study of the consequences of shifts in leadership style yielded results that were also interpreted as supporting Fielder's theory (Koch, 1978). In situations where the favorability for the leader was judged to be low, shifting from a leader who was high on consideration to a leader who was high on initiating structure disrupted peer leadership processes of immediate subordinates.

The data from research generally support the contingency model of leadership as proposed by Fiedler, although the agreement between predicted effectiveness and actual performance is not always precise. There appear to be two major problems with the model: (1) too much reliance on the LPC questionnaire as a measure of leadership behavior and (2) oversimplification of the favorability continuum. With regard to the first, there is some evidence that manipulating or measuring leader behavior in other ways yields results that support the theory (e.g., Koch, 1978; Shaw & Blum, 1966). With regard to the second, there appear to have been no attempts to more precisely delimit the favorability continuum. Despite these limitations, the model is probably the most useful one that has been proposed to date.

It is now evident that the behavior of the leader depends not only upon personality attributes but also upon the characteristics of the situation. In moderately favorable group situations, the needs of the relationship-oriented (high-LPC) leader are gratified by good interpersonal relations and the favorable power position he or she occupies; therefore such a leader devotes more energy to the task. In the same situation, the task-oriented (low-LPC) leader becomes more concerned with building good interpersonal relationships. In general, high-LPC persons behave in a relationship-relevant manner in situations that are unfavorable for them, and low-LPC leaders act in a task-relevant manner in situations that are unfavorable to them. These patterns of behavior determine the relative effectiveness of leaders in various situations. The task-oriented leader tends to be more effective when the situation is either highly favorable or highly unfavorable for the leader, whereas the relationship-oriented leader tends to be more effective in situations that are only moderately favorable or moderately unfavorable.

In a recent discussion of the theory, Fiedler (1978) stated that it makes important contributions to problems involving organizational change, leadership training, and job rotation. But he also noted that there is need for a cleaner definition of the situational control dimension and a better method of measuring it. In addition, he suggested that there is need for more research on the personality and behavioral correlates of the LPC score. Similar problems with the model have been mentioned by others (e.g., Shaw & Costanzo, 1970). However, despite some problems and unanswered questions, the contingency model is a promising start toward the integration of leadership styles and situational factors as determinants of group effectiveness. The model is important in that it not only asserts that the kind of leadership behavior which is most effective depends upon the situation, but it also attempts to specify what behaviors are likely to be most effective in which situations.

## PLAUSIBLE HYPOTHESES ABOUT LEADERSHIP

In this chapter we have considered several conceptualizations of leadership and definitions of leader. We have attempted to trace the historical development of theory and research on leadership, beginning with the trait approach and ending with the current view of leadership as a complex phenomenon resulting from the interaction of personal characteristics of group members, situational variables, tasks and goals of the group, and other group-related factors. Despite the plethora of investigations of leaders and leadership processes, few hypotheses are sufficiently supported by empirical data to be accepted as plausible. The following are offered for the reader's consideration and evaluation.

*Hypothesis 1    Persons who actively participate in the group are more likely to attain a position of leadership than those who participate less in the group's activities.*

Several studies have shown that participation in the group's activities is related to leadership emergence (Sorrentino & Boutillier, 1975; Buban, 1976; Baird, 1977). However, there is some evidence that this relationship does not hold when the expertise of group members is made evident (Gintner & Lindskold, 1975). It may be that an expert in the area of interest to the group does not need to be overly participative in order to achieve a position of leadership, as suggested by the next hypothesis.

*Hypothesis 2    Possession of task-related abilities and skills enhances attainment of a position of leadership.*

Evidence for this hypothesis derives from many studies of leadership traits (Stogdill, 1948, 1974). This hypothesis may appear to be self-evident to many readers.

*Hypothesis 3    Emergent leaders tend to behave in a more authoritarian manner than elected or appointed leaders.*

This difference in the behavior of leaders as a consequence of the way the leadership position was attained was observed in an early study of leaders and other group members (Carter et al., 1951). It is possible that emergent leaders believe (or discover) that they must behave autocratically in order to maintain their position in the group, or this difference in behavior may be the result of their relatively strong motivation and self-oriented needs (Crockett, 1955).

*Hypothesis 4    The source of the leader's authority influences both the leader's behavior and the reactions of other group members.*

This hypothesis is supported by data from many studies (e.g., Hollander & Julian, 1970; Hollander, Julian, & Perry, 1966; Goldman & Fraas, 1965; Read, 1974; Walker, 1976). However, there is also evidence that source of the leader's authority interacts with such other variables as the perceived competence of the leader, perceived motivation of the leader, and the success of the group (Hollander, 1978; Julian, Hollander, & Regula, 1969). The complexity of some of these interrelationships can be seen in Figure 9-1.

*Hypothesis 5   Effective leaders are characterized by task-related abilities, sociability, and motivation to be a leader.*

To be effective, leaders must have knowledge and skills related to the group's task so that they may guide members toward their goal. Leaders must also have interpersonal skills (sociability) in order to deal effectively with the inevitable friction and conflict among group members. But possession of these necessary abilities and skills will not guarantee that an individual will become an effective leader. In addition, a person must *want* to be a leader or at least want the group to achieve its goals badly enough to be willing to serve as leader in order to help achieve those goals. Evidence from numerous studies supports this conclusion (Stogdill, 1948, 1974).

*Hypothesis 6   Democratic leadership results in greater member satisfaction than autocratic leadership.*

Initial evidence for this hypothesis derives from the classic study of "social climates" by Lewin, Lippitt, and White (1939), but many subsequent studies provide almost unanimous support for it (e.g., Preston & Heintz, 1949; Shaw, 1955; Rosenbaum & Rosenbaum, 1971; Morse & Reimer, 1956).

*Hypothesis 7   Leaders tend to behave in a more authoritarian manner in stressful than in nonstressful situations.*

This hypothesis may appear intuitively plausible, but it also has empirical support. Fodor (1978) found that when group members exhibited the characteristics of group stress, leaders adopted a more authoritarian style of leadership than when group members did not exhibit this characteristic. This aspect of leadership behavior is also related to Hypothesis 3.

*Hypothesis 8   The degree to which the leader is endorsed by group members depends upon the success of the group in achieving its goals.*

It is not surprising that group members endorse leaders who are successful, and the limited available evidence is supportive (Michener & Lawler, 1975). However, additional data are needed for more than the most tentative acceptance of this hypothesis.

*Hypothesis 9   A task-oriented leader is more effective when the group-task situation is either very favorable or very unfavorable for the leader, whereas a relationship-oriented leader is more effective when the group-task situation is only moderately favorable or unfavorable for the leader.*

Fiedler (1964, 1967) has provided a substantial amount of empirical evidence to support this hypothesis, which is central to his contingency model of leadership effectiveness (see also Chemers & Skrzpek, 1972). Additional evidence has been obtained in laboratory studies using procedures that differ greatly from those used by Fiedler and his associates (Koch, 1978; Shaw & Blum, 1966). Although the definition and measurement of favorability for the leader may require further consideration, the hypothesis is supported reasonably well by data available at this time.

## SUGGESTED READINGS

Fiedler, R. E. The effects of leadership training and experience: A contingency model interpretation. *Administrative Science Quarterly,* 1972 **17,** 453–470.

Fodor, E. M. Simulated work climate as an influence on choice of leadership style. *Personality and Social Psychology Bulletin,* 1978, **4,** 111–114.

Hollander, E. P., & Julian, J. W. Contemporary trends in the analysis of leadership processes. *Psychological Bulletin,* 1969, **71,** 387–397.

Lewin, K., Lippitt, R., & White, R. K. Patterns of aggressive behavior in experimentally created "social climates." *Journal of Social Psychology,* 1939, **10,** 271–299.

Morse, N. C., & Reimer, E. The experimental change of a major organizational variable. *Journal of Abnormal and Social Psychology,* 1956, **52,** 120–129.

Saha, S. K. Contingency theories of leadership: A study. *Human Relations,* 1979, **32,** 313–322.

Chapter 10

# Group Tasks and
# Group Goals

A group forms and continues its existence for some purpose; when this purpose no longer exists, the group disintegrates unless a new purpose can be established. There may, of course, be more than one group purpose. The purpose is usually labeled *group goal,* but sometimes it is referred to as *group task.* Group goal and group task are not necessarily coextensive, although they are interrelated and may in some instances be identical. That is, the task faced by the group may constitute its goal, and when that task is completed, the group will have no further basis for existence. An example of this is a committee appointed for the purpose of making recommendations concerning the disposition of money available for student support. The task of the group is to prepare a statement of recommendations, and completion of such a statement is its goal. But in many instances, the task may be only to achieve a subgoal that must be attained in order to reach the ultimate goal of the group. For instance, a group may have as its goal the improvement of the educational system in a particular community. In attempting to realize this goal, the group may have to complete a number of tasks, such as raising money for library books, recruiting highly qualified teachers, etc. Whether the task faced by the group at any particular moment is direct achievement of its ultimate goal, as in the example of the committee making recommendations, or whether it is merely to achieve a subgoal, as in the example of the educational improvement group, the characteristics of the task may be expected to exert a strong influence upon group process.

Throughout this book the effects of variables upon group productivity and task solution have been discussed, and the dependence of particular effects of variables upon the task of the group has been noted. Although it would have been helpful to consider task characteristics before taking up other aspects of the group such as member characteristics, group composition, and group structure, it would have been exceedingly difficult to analyze the task environment without the background information provided in earlier portions of this book. And the *task* of analyzing task characteristics and their effects will not be an easy one even at this stage in our discussion. We must begin by asking what is meant by the term *group goal* so that we may relate it properly to group tasks. Next, we must inquire whether and to what extent group members establish goals for the group and whether they react to group goals as they do to individual goals. Finally, we need to consider the analysis of group tasks and the relationships of group tasks to group functioning.

## NATURE OF GROUP GOALS

Everyone seems to agree that groups have goals, and almost all authors and researchers appear to assume that everyone knows what is meant by the term *group goal*. In any event, group goal usually is not defined beyond the identification of a particular goal for a particular group. For example, a researcher may state that the goal of the group was to solve an assigned problem in the shortest possible time, when, in fact, although the group has been instructed to adopt such a goal, there is no reliable evidence that the group members accepted problem solution as their goal. Thus, both the definition of group goal and the identification of the goal for a particular group are based upon unverified assumptions by the investigator. However, these is one noteworthy exception; Cartwright and Zander (1953, 1960, 1968) have made heroic attempts to deal with this knotty problem. The difficulties involved in formulating an acceptable definition of group goal are reflected in the changing views of these writers. In the first edition of their book, an entire section was devoted to "Group Goals and Group Locomotion," and four conceptions of group goals were presented. When the book was revised in 1960, the section heading was changed to "Individual Motives and Group Goals," and the four conceptions, although still presented, were embedded in a general discussion of motivational influences. By the third edition (1968), the section on goals had been eliminated altogether, and the discussion of group goals appeared in a section dealing with motivational processes in groups. Since Cartwright and Zander's analysis represents the most extensive attempt to deal with the conceptualization of group goals, it will be helpful to consider their treatment.

Cartwright and Zander (1953) began their analysis by assuming that the formal properties of group goals do not differ in essentials from the properties of individual goals. Thus, the activities of group members with respect to group goals are similar to the activities of individuals with respect to individual goals. (We will see later that this assumption has a firm empirical basis.) Hence, they regarded the major problem as how to link individual goals with group goals. Their four conceptions represent different attempts to solve this problem.

The first conception proposes that a group goal is merely the composite of similar individual goals. Cartwright and Zander found this definition most unsatisfactory. They cited the example of two young men who want to marry the same girl. Although the individual goals of the men are indeed similar, few would agree that they have established a group goal. Even the qualification that the individual goals must be shared was rejected in view of the above example. On closer examination, however, it becomes clear that the two young men have very different end results in mind; young man A desires a goal of "A married to young lady C," whereas young man B desires a goal of "B married to C." Although the two goals are similar in that C is involved in both, they are quite dissimilar in all other respects. Furthermore, it is questionable that the two young men constitute a psychological group. However, there are other problems associated with this conception of group goal. First, how are the individual goals to be "composited." Are they additive? Or should more weight be given to some individual goals than to others? Second, how is similarity to be determined, and just how similar must the individual goals be before they constitute a group goal. Third, Cartwright and Zander noted that sometimes a group goal exists even when the goals of individual group members are not at all similar. They cited the example of three boys who joined forces to build a lemonade stand, although A's goal was to make enough money to buy a baseball glove, B's goal was to use carpenter tools that he had received for his birthday, and C's goal was merely to join in the others' activities. Again, the objection disappears if one considers the entire situation. It is evident that a distinction must be made between immediate and long-range goals. A shared immediate goal of each of the three boys can be identified: the construction of a lemonade stand. True, this is merely a means to an end which is different for each of the three boys, and as such might be considered a subgoal. For A, the desired end constitutes a long-range goal, whereas for B and C, the desired ends are also immediate goals since they can be achieved simultaneously with the achievement of the goal "completed lemonade stand." Whether or not a group goal can appear to exist when individual goals are different thus depends upon whether immediate or long-range goals are considered.

The second conception of goal discussed by Cartwright and Zander holds that the group goal consists of individual goals for the group. This approach begins with a phenomenological point of view and asks how the group members see the situation. Accordingly, this definition provides an operational procedure for identifying group goals: Ask the group members to specify the group goal; the degree of consensus reflects the degree to which the group has a unitary goal. It also meets Cartwright and Zander's criterion of linking individual and group goals. On the other hand, they objected that it is limited to consciously reportable goals and does not reveal hidden agenda. Also, it does not tell how the individual goals are to be combined.

The third conception views the group goal as depending upon a particular interrelation among motivational systems of group members. This formulation is not at all clear, either conceptually or operationally. Presumably, when the relations between two or more persons are such that the actions of any one satisfy the needs or reduce the need tensions of others, a group goal exists. The major problems with this conception are: (1) There is no easy way to determine when such a relationship exists; the group members must engage in goal-directed activities before the goal can be identified with confidence. (2) It does not identify what the group goal is but merely asserts the existence of some goal.

The fourth and final conception identifies the group goal as an inducing agent. This view takes into account the fact that the group goal can influence group members to engage in goal-directed activities. Group members are expected to work toward the achievement of the group goal. Although it is true that the group goal can induce motivational forces upon group members, this cannot be seriously considered a *definition* of group goal.

The reader will undoubtedly find himself or herself experiencing a strong feeling of dissatisfaction with these attempts to define group goals. Apparently Cartwright and Zander were also less than happy with their analysis; in their third edition (1968) they defined group goal simply as a preferred location of the group in its environment. That is, a group occupies some location in its environment which can be changed by certain activities of group members. When the group engages in such activities, the assumption is that another location is preferred by all or some of the group members. The location of the group when these activities terminate is regarded as the preferred one and, therefore, the group's goal. It, therefore, provides no basis for identifying group goals prior to goal attainment. Furthermore, it makes no distinction between achievement of the end state *desired* by group members and the end state *attained* by group action. Conceivably a group could engage in activities designed to reach location A but actually arrive at B, at which time the activities ceased because locomotion to A appeared impossible.

Group goals probably are best regarded as some composite of individual goals, despite the difficulties associated with such a conception. It is obvious that whatever goals can be attributed to the group must be held by the members of the group. It also seems clear that groups whose members all agree upon a single goal to the exclusion of all other goals, both individual and group, are extremely rare. In the typical group, there exists at least one goal which is acceptable to a majority of the group and which can properly be identified as a group goal. Group members who accept this goal are motivated to enact activities that are expected to aid in the achievement of this goal, and they are pleased (experience tension reduction?) when there is movement toward the goal or when the goal is achieved. Even those members who are not enthusiastic about this goal may, nevertheless, work toward it for a variety of individual goals or subgoals. Thus, a *group goal is an end state desired by a majority of the group members.* It can be identified by observing the activities of group members or, usually, by asking the members of the group to specify it.

In defining group goal in this way, one should take care to avoid the assumption that the group must have only one goal. A group may indeed have a single goal, but it is also common for a group to have several goals. A city planning committee may at one and the same time have the goals of paving city streets, obtaining federal funds for a control tower for the municipal airport, and building city parks. All these goals might be subsumed under the more general goal of city improvement. This consideration again raises the question concerning immediate and long-range goals. The achievement of city improvement constitutes a long-range goal, whereas paving city streets is a more immediate goal. In attempting to understand the behavior of group members, one must remember that it is usually the immediate goal that is of greatest significance. The activities of the group members are directly related to immediate goals, but are only indirectly related to a long-range goals. As indicated earlier, the immediate goal or subgoal is often identical with the task of the group.

Finally, it is important to recognize that individual goals which are not a part of the group goal do not cease to influence an individual's behavior just because he or she becomes a member of a group and accepts the goal or goals of that group. The group member may be trying to achieve only individual goals, only group goals, or both individual and group goals when he or she engages in a particular set of activities. Usually, he or she is attempting to achieve both simultaneously. The relative strengths of individual and group goals, and the degree to which both can be achieved by the same activities, help to determine how effective the group will be in achieving its goal.

## DO INDIVIDUALS SET GOALS FOR THE GROUP?

It is now time to return to the assumption that is implicit in earlier discussions of the task environment, namely, that individuals establish goals for the group and respond to those goals in essentially the same way that they respond to individual goals. If this is a valid assumption, then it should be possible to demonstrate that group members do set goals for the group which have predictable consequences for behavior in the group. An early study by Shelley (1954) approached this problem by means of the level of aspiration paradigm. The level of aspiration is defined as the level of difficulty of that task chosen as the goal for the next action. In the typical experiment, the individual attempts a particular task and achieves some level of success or failure; that is, a particular score is earned. The person is then asked to state the score expected on the next trial. This projected score is the level of aspiration. Although it is influenced by many factors, such as intelligence, knowledge of others' performance, etc., empirical findings generally show that the level of aspiration is raised following success and lowered following failure, where success is defined as a performance equaling or exceeding the previous level or aspiration (Lewin, Dembo, Festinger, & Sears, 1944). In an experiment conducted for another purpose, Shelley (1954) elicited levels of aspiration for the group from members of four-person groups that had experienced varying degrees of success and failure. Success was manipulated through a trained assistant who served as a fifth group member. During the solution of five problems, the assistant guided certain groups to success, and the experimenter assured failure for others by presenting them with unsolvable tasks. Some of the groups were led to succeed on the first four problems (success groups); some were made to fail on the first four problems (failure groups); some succeeded on the first problem, failed on the second, succeeded on the third, and failed on the fourth (SFSF groups); and some failed on the first, succeeded on the second, failed on the third, and succeeded on the fourth (FSFS groups). After the third problem and again after the fourth, each group member was asked to rate how well he or she thought the group would do on the next problem, using an 11-point rating scale. The ratings were used as a measure of level of aspiration for the group. The mean levels of aspiration for the fourth problem were 7.1 for the success groups, 2.3 for the failure groups, 6.0 for the SFSF groups, and 4.5 for the FSFS groups. The pattern thus corresponded closely to the degree of success and failure experienced by the groups on the problems previously attempted. The mean levels of aspiration for problem 5 were 7.2, 1.9, 4.9, and 5.6, respectively. Again, the pattern corresponded to degree of success and failure; the level of aspiration increased for those groups experiencing success on problem 4 and decreased for those experiencing failure on problem 4. Members of Shelley's experimental groups thus established goals for their group and responded to success or failure of the group in much the same way that individuals respond to individual success or failure.

Zander and his associates (Zander, 1968; Zander & Medow, 1963; Zander & Newcomb, 1967) also adopted the level of aspiration procedure for the study of group goal setting. However, these investigators' approach was somewhat different from Shelley's procedure. Instead of asking each group member to set a level of aspiration for the group, Zander et al. required that group members agree upon a joint level of aspiration, which they called the group's level of aspiration. Zander and Medow (1963) used a group ball-propelling task which requires all group members to stand in single file, to grasp a long pole, and to swing it collectively so that the end of the pole strikes a wooden ball and drives it down a channel. Numbers are painted on the side of the channel; the group's score is the number nearest the ball when it stops. Each group is given five shots per trial and may earn a maximum of 50 on each trial. When groups performed this task, the group level of aspiration was raised following a success and lowered following a failure. Thus group members set goals for the group very much as they do individual goals, whether asked to do so as individuals or as a group.

Zander and Medow also noted that the group level of aspiration was more often raised following success than it was lowered following failure, as asymmetry that has also been observed in some studies of individual levels of aspiration (Lewin et al., 1944). This finding was interpreted as reflecting both the percieved probability of succeeding and the attractiveness of doing so. It was assumed that when people must decide whether to engage in solitary activities, they do so on the basis of satisfactions which may be obtained from those activities. In a similar fashion, when group members must choose a level of aspiration for the group, they do so on the basis of expected satisfaction, which in turn derives from both potential satisfaction and the probability that this possible satisfaction actually will be attained by the group's action relative to that task. It is interesting to note that the stronger tendency to raise the group level of aspiration following success than to lower it following failure has also been observed in natural situations. Zander and Newcomb (1967) studied changes in the official goals of United Fund campaigns in 149 cities over a four-year period. A successful campaign was almost always followed by the setting of a higher goal the next year, whereas a failing campaign was rarely followed by a lowered goal the next year.

The studies of levels of aspiration in groups reveal that individuals establish goals for the group and respond to goal achievement in essentially the same way that they respond to personal goal achievement. Group goals serve as an inducing agent in that they motivate group members to work toward their attainment. Thus, it appears that many of the motivational concepts which apply to individuals working toward their own goals also apply to individuals working toward group goals. A further test of this expectation was reported by Horwitz (1954). He began with the assumption that no individual group member can achieve the group goal acting alone, although each group member may contribute in some degree to the movement of the group toward its goal. A group goal is like an individual goal in that it terminates a sequence of group activities. Since individual goals usually presuppose the existence of an internal system of tension, such as a need, then it follows that the existence of a group goal should also be based upon tension systems. Following Lewin (1951), Horwitz adopted the "interrupted task" experimental paradigm to test his hypothesis that tension systems can be aroused for goals which the individual holds for the group. Lewin and his associates have shown that when an individual works on a series of tasks, some of which are completed and some of which are interrupted, the individual tends to recall more of the incompleted tasks than the completed ones. This greater recall of the interrupted tasks is interpreted as reflecting unreduced tension associated with the goal of task completion.

Horwitz recruited 18 five-person groups from sororities at the University of Michigan. Each group was exposed to several experiences designed to arouse a feeling of group solidarity among its members. First, the groups were told that they were engaged in a contest in which each team represented its sorority and that each group would be judged by the quality of its cooperative performance on jigsaw puzzles. Next, group members were involved in a group discussion designed to increase their awareness as group members. Finally, they were given a questionnaire entitled "Test on Group Loyalty" which included items dealing with team spirit, willingness to go along with the group, etc. Following these procedures, each group worked on seventeen jigsaw puzzles. A 14- by 14-inch cardboard poster was exposed to the group. The group's task was to direct the experimenter in filling in the parts of the figure one piece at a time. Each group member was seated in a separate booth so that she could see the poster and the experimenter but could not see the other group members. Each person had four differently shaped cardboard pieces, each corresponding to a section of the figure. On each trial, each group member indicated which piece the experimenter should fill in by holding up the corresponding piece. According to the rules, if a specified number of group members—and no more—held up a given piece, then the experimenter placed the piece in the figure. This procedure permitted those who did not hold up the piece to take credit for successful task completion, since their *not* holding up the piece resulted in the correct number. The actual determination of whether the correct number of subjects had held up a piece was, of course, made by the experimenter. At the midpoint of each task, the experimenter explained that he had the basic score, and asked if the group wanted to stop or to complete the puzzle. Group members voted by holding up the right hand for completion and the left hand for stopping. The experimenter then announced the majority vote; if the vote was "yes," work was continued, if "no," the puzzle was set aside and work was started on the next one. The first two puzzles were practice. On the last fifteen trials, the announced majority vote was "no" on five and "yes" on ten puzzles. Group members were allowed to continue five of the "yes" puzzles to completion, whereas the other five "yes" puzzles were interrupted by the experimenter midway in the work on the third piece, with the explanation that they would return to it later. Thus, there were three experimental conditions: a "no" vote followed by work stoppage (N); a "yes" vote followed by task completion (Y-C); and a "yes" vote followed by task interruption (Y-I).

According to Horwitz's analysis, the psychological situation for the "yes" conditions is very different from that of the "no" condition. These differences are shown graphically in Figure 10-1. The group goal was characterized as earning as many points as possible, which is represented in Figure 10-1a as a region toward which the group is locomoting. If the group votes "yes," this region has a positive valence; that is, the group is motivated to move toward that region, thus reducing tension. If the group votes "no," then the region representing task completion has a negative valence, as shown in Figure 10-1b, and the goal is to avoid completion; that is, tension will be increased if the group locomotes toward task completion. These considerations suggest that task completion should lead to tension reduction in the Y-C condition, whereas tension reduction should occur in the N condition when the task is not completed. Tension reduction should not occur in the Y-I condition, since the group did not achieve its goal. Therefore, Horwitz predicted that the Y-I condition should result in the greatest recall of interrupted tasks, with the N and Y-C conditions equal in this respect. The results verified this predicition: The Y-I condition resulted in 55.9 percent recall of interrupted tasks as compared with 44.4 percent and 46.0 percent in the Y-C and N conditions, respectively.

This investigation has been outlined in detail because it represents a particular orientation to group goal and reveals so clearly some of the consequences of group goals for the individual group member. The results

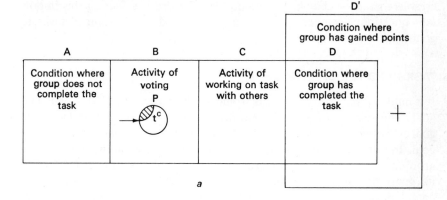

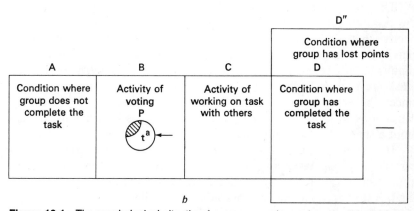

**Figure 10-1** The psychological situation for group members who vote "Yes" (*a*) and for group members who vote "no" (*b*). (Reprinted with permission from M. Horwitz. The recall of interrupted group tasks: An experimental study of individual motivation in relation to group goals. *Human Relations,* 1954, **7,** 3–38.

show that tension systems can be aroused for goals which the individual holds for the group and that tension is reduced by task completion but is not reduced when the task is interrupted—at least not to the same extent. The findings also suggest that tension may be aroused for avoidances which the individual holds for the group and that the tension will be reduced if the possibility of the group moving into the avoidance region is removed. Taken together with the results from the level of aspiration studies, these findings leave little doubt that individuals do establish goals for the group and that such goals arouse motivational forces in group members that are similar to those aroused by individual goals.

The next important question that may be asked is how group members establish goals or choose a common task. Before considering this important question, however, we need to understand the relation of tasks to goals.

## TASKS AND GROUP GOALS

It is unlikely that group members would attempt a group task if they had no goal. The reason for attempting a task is that task completion facilitates goal achievement. Task completion may be either a subgoal or the ultimate goal. In any case, the task faced by the group is intimately related to the group goal; to the extent that task completion will move the group toward its goal, the group members will be motivated to work toward task completion. The *task,* then, is what must be done in order for the group to achieve its goal or subgoal.

This formulation of task is similar to that proposed by Hackman: "It (the task) consists of a stimulus complex and a set of instructions which specify what is to be done vis-à-vis the stimuli. The instructions indicate what operations are to be performed by the subject(s) with respect to the stimuli and/or what goal is to be achieved" (Hackman, 1969, p. 113). Thus, a task must always include identifiable stimulus material and instructions concerning what to do about this material. According to Hackman, instructions to think would not be a task, whereas instructions to think about a specific picture and relate its meaning would be.

In the following pages, we will be concerned primarily with the analysis of group tasks and the consequences of task environment for group process. However, the reader should keep one thing firmly in mind: The fact that group members work at a task implies that some goal is held for the group. The ultimate goal of each group member might be no more than a desire to escape from an unpleasant experimental situation; but for the group collectively, there must be at least a subgoal which can be attained through task completion.

## SELECTION OF GROUP TASKS

Groups sometimes have tasks assigned to them, and there is no problem of task selection. It is probably more common, however, for group members to choose which task out of a set of possible tasks they will work on at any given time. That is, even when the final group goal is clearly established, it is often the case that many tasks must be completed in order that the goal be attained. Furthermore, it often appears that the goal can be achieved through the completion of any one of several possible sets of tasks. For example, consider a group whose goal is to build a recreation hall for disadvantaged children. The goal could be accomplished by many different means: the members could (1) conduct a series of fund-raising activities, (2) solicit donations from wealthy members of the community, (3) try to convince the city commission to provide funds for the hall, (4) submit a proposal to a benevolent tax-exempt foundation, or engage in any one of a number of other procedures. How groups choose which task or tasks to work on at any particular time may be an important factor with respect to group effectiveness. Relatively little is known about this important aspect of group behavior, although some theoretical and empirical work has been undertaken by Zander (1971).

Zander's work is based upon the level of aspiration phenomena and achievement motivation theory. We have already discussed some of his research which shows that group members apparently establish goals for the group in much the same way as individuals establish goals for themselves. It will be recalled that the level of aspiration is defined as the level of difficulty chosen as the goal for the next action. Thus the level of aspiration is the goal that the individual or group hopes to achieve in the immediate future. Zander suggests that in many groups the aspiration choice does not describe the outcome the group is expected to achieve among an array of possible scores, but instead indicates which task is selected from a set of tasks that the group might undertake with some probability of success. When this is the case, the level of aspiration or aspiration choice is the choice of a group task.

According to Zander's analysis, the member's aspiration for the group is one which either maximizes the expected satisfaction from success or minimizes the expected dissatisfaction from failure, or both. In general, the task chosen by a member for the group will be the one with the greatest perceived probability of success times the incentive value of that success (i.e., the amount of satisfaction with the group that a member experiences following successful task completion) minus the perceived probability of failure times the repulsiveness of that failure. In other words, the chosen task is the one "that best resolves the conflict between the attractiveness of success, the repulsiveness of failure, and the perceived probabilities of success and failure" (Zander, 1971, pp. 179–180). This analysis leads to some interesting hypotheses about the selection of group tasks. For example, Zander suggested that when the quality of past performance is unknown or ambiguous, group members cannot adequately estimate the probability of success and failure; hence, their choice of a task will be influenced primarily by incentive values. Therefore, the level of aspiration should be higher when past performance on similar tasks is not known than when it is known. In the former instance, the relatively greater attractiveness of success on a difficult task will lead to the selection of that task.

This expectation was tested in an experiment which required group members to perform a card-marking task. The group could choose how many sets of cards it wanted to process within a standard time period. The number of sets chosen of course reflected the difficulty of the task. On a series of trials, some of the groups were told, after each trial, how well their group had performed, whereas others were given no information about their performance. It can be seen in Figure 10-2 that the groups who did not know how well they performed chose more difficult tasks than the groups with knowledge of past performance. This kind of effect may explain why some groups choose unrealistic but attractive tasks.

### Effects of Success and Failure

The selection of a group task is influenced by a variety of factors, but perhaps the most powerful one is the degree of past success or failure by the group. In general, both individuals and groups tend to choose tasks that are slightly more difficult than tasks that they have successfully completed in the past. A general rule might be that success is followed by selection of a more difficult task; failure is followed by selection of a less difficult task for future action. The shift to more difficult tasks following success is usually greater than the shift to less difficult tasks following failure. In fact, as noted earlier, there may be no change in task selection following failure, especially if achievement of the more difficult tasks is highly attractive. Presumably, group members are usually influenced more by the attractiveness of task completion than by the repulsiveness of task failure.

Some support for this view is provided by a study of task selection by

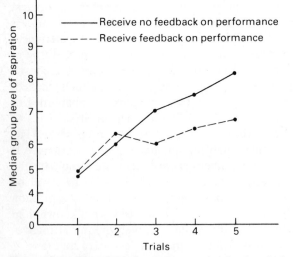

**Figure 10-2** Effect of feedback on group levels of aspiration. (Reprinted with permission from A. Zander. *Motives and goals in groups.* New York: Academic Press, 1971, p. 15.)

subjects differing in level of motivation (Kukla, 1975). Subjects were given a choice between tasks that varied in difficulty but on which their own success or failure was certain. They consistently preferred the more difficult of two impossibly difficult tasks (thus making it easier to attribute failure to the task rather than self, or to enhance credit when successful). There was no difference between motive levels, probably because both types of subjects were motivated to achieve success. Although this study did not involve group choices, the findings are consistent with Zander's theory.

## Effects of External Pressures

Individuals often rely upon others for information about appropriate behavior, the validity of their judgments and opinions, their task abilities, and so on, whether they are functioning as individuals or as members of a group. It is not surprising that group members respond to social pressures arising outside the group when selecting a group task. For instance, group members select relatively more difficult tasks if they learn that their past performance is worse than the average performance of groups like their own; they choose relatively less difficult tasks if they learn that their past performance is better than the average for groups like their own. Presumably, the relatively better or worse performance by others causes group members to view their own past performance as a less valid indicator of potential future performance than when such information is not available. Similarly, the group's choice of a group task is influenced by observers' predictions about the group's future performance, the awareness of needs of the larger organization of which the group is a part, and other external pressures to choose particular tasks. According to Zander, these various influences operate more or less independently and generate additive effects on task selection.

## Effects of Group-Oriented Motives

During the process of group interaction the group member becomes aware of the attractiveness of group success and the unattractiveness of group failure. This awareness leads him or her to seek group success and to try to avoid group failure, tendencies which are supported by forces both from within and without the group. Accordingly, Zander posited two group-oriented motives: the desire for group success and the desire to avoid group failure. These group-oriented motives are reflected in tendencies on the part of the group member to engage in activities that he or she perceives will enhance group success and/or will increase the probability that the group will not fail. These group-oriented motives and related action tendencies have predictable effects on task selection. For example, the greater the members' desire for group success, the greater the preference for tasks perceived to be in the intermediate range of difficulty; conversely, the stronger the desire to avoid group failure, the greater will be the tendency to choose tasks at the extremes of the difficulty range.

For persons having a strong desire to achieve group success, the maximum "payoff" occurs when the probability of success is .50, since the incentive value is inversely proportional to the probability of success and these persons are influenced primarily by the attractiveness of success. When the group member is motivated primarily by the desire to avoid group failure, he or she would prefer to choose no task at all, thereby avoiding any possiblilty of failure. Usually, however, some choice is necessary and the least unattractive alternatives are tasks at the extremes of the difficulty range. If a very easy task is chosen, the probability of success is high and the probability of failure is low; if a very difficult task is chosen, the probability of failure is high, but failure can be attributed to task difficulty rather than to the group's performance.

Other effects upon task selection may also be expected from a consideration of group-oriented motives: A group of high unity and high cohesiveness (a strong group) is more likely to select tasks in the intermediate difficulty range, a group member in a central position is more likely to select tasks of intermediate difficulty than peripheral members, and a task is more often selected in the intermediate difficulty range when a successful outcome is expected to be rewarding than when a successful outcome merely avoids costs. These effects are predicted because group strength, position centrality, and reward conditions each invoke high desires for group success. Zander reports evidence supporting each of these hypotheses.

### Effects of Person-Oriented Motives

Individuals typically have some degree of motivation to achieve success and to avoid failure, and they bring these needs with them when they join groups. These person-oriented motives influence task selection in much the same manner as group-oriented motives, although the two sets of motives are independent and each may either supplement or weaken the effects of the other. In general, groups composed wholly of persons with desires to achieve success stronger than their desires to avoid failure more often select tasks of intermediate difficulty than groups composed wholly of persons whose desires to avoid failure exceed their desires to achieve success.

Some investigators have noted that choice of intermediate tasks can maximize both the motivational value of success and the informational value of the outcome (Trope & Brickman, 1975; Trope, 1975). They reasoned that if people are primarily interested in maximizing the information they gain about themselves, they should prefer easy or difficult tasks over moderately difficult tasks when the easy or difficult ones provide more information about their true ability. On the other hand, if they are primarily motivated to achieve success, they should choose tasks of intermediate difficulty regardless of their informational value about own ability. They found that informational value was the primary determinant of task choice. At first glance, these findings appear to be inconsistent with Zander's theory. However, in these studies, motivation to avoid failure was not considered. Consequently, the data are not directly relevant to motives concerning success versus failure, but they do demonstrate another personal motive that influences task selection, namely, motivation to evaluate own ability.

In brief summary, groups select tasks that maximize the expected satisfaction from group success and minimize the expected dissatisfaction from failure. The choice of a task for any given time period is influenced by (1) past success or failure of the group, (2) external pressures arising outside the group, (3) group-oriented motives, and (4) person-oriented motives. Task selection is probably influenced by many other variables that we have not mentioned, but additional research is needed before these can be specified with any confidence.

## PROBLEM OF TASK ANALYSIS

For many years, most group dynamicists commented upon the importance of the task for group functioning but continued to use a wide variety of unanalyzed tasks in their empirical investigations. The result was an almost complete lack of systematization of task-related information about group behavior. This made it very difficult to establish general principles that could be applied to specific task situations. In recent years, however, a number of theorists and researchers have attempted to introduce some order into the task environment. Although the attempts have taken many forms, they can be represented by three general approaches: (1) the development of a standard group task; (2) the classification of tasks into specific categories (a typology of tasks); and (3) the dimensional analysis of group tasks.

### Standard Group Tasks

A standard group task is a task with known characteristics that is adaptable to the study of a variety of problems relative to small group behavior. That is, the inputs can be described, the operations required of group members for successful task completion can be specified, and the outputs (group products or performance measures) can be observed and quantified. For the standard task to be generally useful, it should be possible to study different kinds of questions about group behavior by suitably modifying elements of the task. For example, a standard task might be equally useful for the study of leadership, of social facilitation, or of conformity behavior.

The design of a standard group task usually arises from a consideration of the great difficulty of comparing experimental results derived from heterogeneous group tasks. The need for some systematic assessment becomes obvious, and the adoption of a standard task is a relatively easy way of making a minimal response to this need. The term *minimal* is used deliberately, since the problems created by the use of a standard task are almost as great as those resulting from task heterogeneity. Nevertheless, standard tasks are useful for certain purposes and should not be dismissed summarily. Examples of standard tasks include a group maze (McCurdy & Lambert, 1952), a mechanical switch-setting task (Lanzetta & Roby, 1957), and a group reaction-time apparatus (Zajonc, 1965b).

### Task Typologies

A task typology consists of a set of categories or classes into which group tasks can be sorted, more or less exclusively. In the simplest typology, tasks are classified into two mutually exclusive categories, such as simple and complex (M. E. Shaw, 1954) or easy and difficult (Bass, Pryer, Gaier, & Flint, 1958). More complex typologies can be formulated, of course, by increasing the number of categories, or by classifying the same set of tasks in several different ways. The first of these is exemplified by Carter, Haythorn, and Howell (1950), who classified tasks into six categories: clerical, discussion, intellectual construction, mechanical assembly, motor coordination, and reasoning. The second procedure is represented by Steiner's (1972) "partial typology of tasks." According to this analysis, tasks may be either divisible or unitary, maximizing or optimizing, and may involve permitted process or prescribed process. A task is *divisible* if it can readily be divided into subtasks, each of which may be performed by a different person. For example, if the task is to build a house, some persons may lay the foundations, others install the plumbing, and still others put on the roof. Other tasks, called *unitary* tasks, cannot be divided into parts or subtasks that can be performed efficiently by different individuals. For example, if two persons are assigned to read the evidence and draw conclusions about a proper course of action, it is conceivable that one person could read the evidence and the other draw conclusions, but no one would expect this to be a reasonable course of action.

A task sometimes requires that the group should do as much as possible of something or do it as quickly as possible. Such tasks are called *maximizing* tasks. An example of this type of task is an assignment that must be completed in the shortest possible time, as when the task is to produce 10 billion barrels of crude oil as soon as possible, or an assignment to produce as much oil as possible by the end of the year. On the other hand, the goal may be the production of some specific or preferred outcome. If the task is to predict how many barrels of crude oil will be available at the end of the year, the goal is to make a prediction that agrees with the amount of oil actually available at year's end. Tasks of this type are called *optimizing* tasks.

Finally, Steiner notes that when a task is unitary, a group's product must be the outcome produced by a group member or by some combination of the outcomes produced by different group members. Tasks differ with respect to the ways members are *permitted* to combine their individual products and with respect to the *prescribed* process that must be used if maximum success is to be achieved. Although Steiner stated that it is possible to classify tasks on the basis of both permitted process and prescribed process, he elected to simplify the typology by classifying tasks only on the basis of permitted process. On this basis, tasks may be disjunctive, conjunctive, additive, or discretionary.

A *disjunctive* task is one that requires an "either-or" decision. That is, the group must accept only one of two or more available alternatives. A *conjunctive* task is one that requires each group member to perform the task. The task is said to be *additive* when the requirements of the task are such that the success of the group depends upon the summation of individual products. Finally, there are some tasks that permit the members of a group to combine their individual contributions in any way that they wish. Tasks of this type are called *discretionary* tasks. Presumably, when the task is of this type, the decisions of the group could make the task either disjunctive (by assigning total weight to the contributions of the most capable group member), conjunctive (by requiring that everyone complete the task), additive (by assigning equal weight to each group member), or some unique type (for example, by multiplying the contributions of the most capable member by the contributions of the least capable one). Thus when the task is discretionary, "anything goes" and the nature of the task can be determined only by analyzing the group's behavior. Apparently, there has been no research on this kind of task, perhaps because of its unstable characteristics.

It should be obvious that typologies can have many different bases and the complexity of the system depends upon the purposes and/or the ingenuity of the person who formulates the typology.

## Dimensional Analysis of Group Tasks

Dimensional analysis represents an attempt to specify task differences along a variety of relatively independent dimensions or continua. It differs from the typology approach primarily in degree of differentiation. That is, each task is assigned a position on each task dimension under consideration. The nature of dimensional analysis will become clear if we consider some procedures for analyzing tasks in this way. One technique (M. E. Shaw, 1973a) is an adaptation of the Thurstone and Chave (1929) method for the construction of attitude scales. This procedure involves several steps: (1) a number of potential task dimensions are identified and defined; (2) a large sample of group tasks is assembled and each task described as clearly as possible; (3) a sizable number of judges who are familiar with the field of psychology sort the set of tasks into eight categories on each potential task dimension; (4) the median of the distribution of judgments by the judges for each task and on each dimension is taken as the scale value (i.e., a score which indicates the placement of the task on the dimension being considered); (5) the interquartile range (i.e., the distance between the upper and lower one-fourths of the distribution of judgments) is computed and used as a basis for accepting or rejecting potential dimensions as valid—if the interquartile range indicates great inconsistency of judgments, the dimension is considered invalid; and (6) intercorrelations among dimensions are computed and highly correlated dimensions combined into a single dimension. By use of this procedure, a set of 104 tasks were analyzed, resulting in 6 task dimensions. These dimensions may be described briefly as follows:

*Difficulty* may be defined as the amount of effort required to complete the task. Tasks vary on the difficulty dimension from easy (requiring few operations, skills, and knowledges, and/or having a clear goal) to difficult (requiring many operations, skills, and knowledges, and/or having no clear goal).

*Solution multiplicity* is the degree to which there is more than one correct solution to the task. A task that has a high scale value on this dimension is one that has many acceptable solutions, many alternatives for attaining those solutions, and no solution that can be easily verified; a task that has a low scale value has a single acceptable solution that can be easily demonstrated to be correct and has a single path to this goal.

*Intrinsic interest* is defined as the degree to which the task in and of itself is interesting, motivating, or attractive to the group members. Tasks vary from dull to extremely interesting.

*Cooperation requirements* may be defined as the degree to which integrated action of group members is required to complete the task. Tasks at the upper end of this dimensional continuum require that group members coordinate their actions so that each member is performing the appropriate function at the right time relative to the actions of other members, whereas a task at the other extreme could be completed by each group member working independently and at his or her own speed.

*Intellectual-manipulative requirements* is defined as the ratio of mental requirements to motor requirements of the group task. Tasks at the upper end of this dimension require only mental activities (reasoning, thinking, etc.) for task completion; those at the low end of the continuum require only motor activities (manipulating levers, turning cranks, etc.) for successful completion.

*Population familiarity* is defined as the degree to which members of the larger society have had experience with the task. Tasks may vary from highly familiar (encountered by everyone in the population) to very unfamiliar (encountered by no one in the population).

The six dimensions are representative of the kinds of tasks characteristics that may be identified by the method of dimensional analysis; the list is not exhaustive. In the following section we will examine how these and other aspects of the task influence group process.

## TASK CHARACTERISTICS AND GROUP PROCESS

Standard tasks have been used in research with some success. However, when standard tasks have been used, other task parameters have been varied also. For instance, Zajonc and Taylor (1963) used the Group Reaction Time Apparatus to investigate the effects of task difficulty; in a similar way, Lanzetta and Roby (1956, 1957) used their dial-setting task to study the consequences of task demands. In the discussion of task characteristics and group process we will examine the effects of task characteristics as identified and measured by the persons conducting the research, more or less independently of the method used for analysis.

### Task Difficulty

Task difficulty refers to the amount of effort required for task completion. This aspect of task has probably been studied more extensively than any other task characteristic. Many of the studies of task difficulty merely demonstrate that the more difficult the task, the more time the group requires for solution and the greater the probability that the group product will be inferior. These findings are certainly not astounding, although they may be significant for methodological purposes. That is, it may be necessary to demonstrate that tasks do indeed differ in difficulty, or that a particular method of measuring task difficulty is valid, before one can investigate other effects of task difficulty. An interesting variation in the study of the effects of task difficulty on group performance was reported by Zajonc and Taylor (1963). Using the Group Reaction Time Apparatus, they varied difficulty either by varying the time permitted for reaction before failure or by varying the number of group members required to make the response before failure time elapsed. The probability of success under each level of difficulty was computed, and performance was evaluated relative to the probability of success. The results showed that both individual and group reaction times decreased with increasing difficulty for both manipulations of task difficulty. Thus, task difficulty does not inevitably impair group performance; the relationship between difficulty and performance depends upon the nature of the task and the performance measure. In the Zajonc and Taylor study, the effects were probably mediated by motivation; that is, increasing difficulty may increase the motivation of group members, thus increasing speed of reaction.

However, task difficulty affects other aspects of group process as well as group performance. Bass, Pryer, Gaier, and Flint (1958) studied 51 five-person groups as they solved easy and difficult tasks. The task required that group members rank-order lists of words in terms of familiarity. Easy tasks were lists of familiar words and difficult tasks were lists of less familiar words. They found that less leadership was attempted by group members when the task was easy than when it was difficult.

Task difficulty in relation to self-esteem of group members and conformity behavior was investigated by Gergen and Bauer (1967). They speculated that the relationship between self-esteem and conformity should vary with the difficulty of the task, since the relevance of self-confidence to conformity should become greater with increasing task difficulty. The conformity behavior of persons having low, medium, or high self-esteem was measured, using tasks that were low, medium, or high with respect to difficulty. The task involved comparisons of pairs of paintings on criteria of varying clarity, e.g., amount of color when one painting clearly had more color than the other (low difficulty), degree of creativeness (moderate difficulty), and degree of aesthetic goodness (high difficulty). The results are depicted in Figure 10-3. It can be seen that conformity was curvilinearly related to self-esteem when task difficulty was either low or medium, whereas it was essentially unrelated to self-esteem when task difficulty was high. When the task becomes very difficult, one might suppose that self-esteem would not be threatened by failure in any case; hence degree of conformity would not be influenced by the person's general attitude toward himself or herself.

The various studies by Lanzetta and Roby (1956, 1957) on task demands are closely related to the studies of task difficulty. When the information-processing demands upon the group are increased, it is plausible to suspect that the difficulty of the task also increases. In approaching the question of how task demands influence group process, Lanzetta and Roby used a standard task which required changing control settings in response to changes in instrument readings. In the first study (Lanzetta & Roby, 1956), task demands were varied in three ways. First, the location of controls relative to instruments was varied so that two different amounts of information transmission were required. Second, the

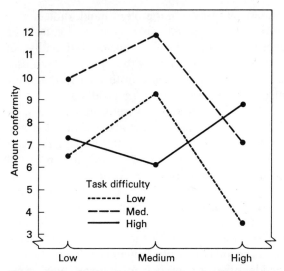

**Figure 10-3** Conformity as a function of self-esteem level and task difficulty. (Reprinted with permission from K. J. Gergen & R. A. Bauer. Interactive effects of self-esteem and task difficulty on social conformity. *Journal of Personality and Social Psychology,* 1967, **6,** 16–22. Copyright 1967 by the American Psychological Association. Reprinted by permission.)

rate of change of instrument readings was varied, and, third, the predictability and sequence of instrument changes were varied. Two 3-person groups performed under each combination of "work group structures" created by the task variations. Performance was measured by the number of times each control was incorrectly set. Errors increased linearly with amount of information transmission required, increasing rate of change of instrument readings, and decreasing predictability of changes of instrument readings. The second study (Lanzetta & Roby, 1957) verified these findings and also demonstrated that the proportion of time spent in communication varied with input load.

In Hackman's study (1968) cited earlier, difficulty was one of several dimensions evaluated by the scaling technique and related to dimensions of group products. Task difficulty was found to be related to action orientation, originality, optimism, quality of presentation, issue involvement, and adequacy. Products from more difficult tasks were generally more original and issue-involved, whereas products from easier tasks met specific task requirements more adequately and the quality of presentatiion was higher. The relationships between difficulty and action orientation and between difficulty and optimism depended upon the general type of the task. For example, products from medium-difficulty production tasks showed more action orientation than did other difficulty levels of that type of task, whereas difficulty level and action orientation were essentially unrelated for problem-solving and discussion tasks. On the other hand, difficulty of production tasks had little effect on optimism, whereas discussion tasks of medium difficulty produced relatively low optimism. Difficulty of problem-solving tasks was positively correlated with degree of optimism reflected in group products. These data demonstrate clearly that task characteristics exert an important influence on group products.

Difficulty was also manipulated through task selection based upon scale analysis in a study of group awareness of member satisfaction and group performance (Shaw & Blum, 1965). This study used three tasks varying in level of difficulty (scale values were 2.5, 4.2, and 6.1) but approximately equal on other task dimensions (i.e., cooperation requirements, solution multiplicity, population familiarity, intrinsic interest, and intellectual-manipulative requirements). Five-person groups completed each of the three tasks, under three feedback conditions. In one condition, group members indicated their satisfaction with the group by identifiable signals (overt feedback); in a second condition, they indicated satisfaction by signals that could not be identified as coming from any particular group member (covert feedback); and in the third condition, no feedback was permitted. The results showed the expected differences in time to solve, with the easy tasks requiring less time than the difficult tasks (means =7.7, 18.4, and 29.2 minutes). Much more interesting is the fact that the effects of satisfaction feedback varied with the difficulty of the task. It can be seen in Table 10-1 that group performance was higher under feedback conditions than under no-feedback conditions for all tasks, but the effect was most pronounced for the most difficult task. These findings were interpreted in terms of "pluralistic ignorance." When the task is being solved, one group member may be dissatisfied with the proposed solution but believe that he or she is the only dissatisfied member—so remains silent. Or more than one member may react this way. A solution or decision may be accepted that most members find unsatisfactory. This result is most likely to occur with difficult tasks where the correct solution or procedure is not

**Table 10-1  Mean Performance Scores for Task and Satisfaction Feedback Conditions**

| Condition | Easy | Medium | Difficult |
|---|---|---|---|
| No feedback | .66 | 3.02 | .89 |
| Overt feedback | .83 | 3.65 | 1.11 |
| Covert feedback | .88 | 3.39 | 2.44 |

NOTE: Scores are not comparable across tasks.
*Source:* Reprinted with permission from M. E. Shaw and J. M. Blum, Group performance as a function of task difficulty and the group's awareness of member satisfaction. *Journal of Applied Psychology*, 1965, **49**, 151–154. Copyright 1965 by the American Psychological Association. Reprinted by permission.

so readily discovered by the group. When a member can signal his or her feelings about proposed solutions without disrupting group interaction, he or she presumably feels freer to do so, and this information leads the group to reconsider faulty decisions, thus resulting in better group performance.

Studies of task difficulty reveal the expected effects upon time to complete the task, number of errors, and similar performance measures. Task difficulty also increases speed of reaction and attempted leadership, and it is complexly related to conformity behavior and self-esteem. Although measurement of task difficulty was far from precise, these findings are sufficiently intriguing to suggest that other aspects of group process are undoubtedly related to the difficulty of the group task and that studies of these effects should yield rich rewards in the understanding of group behavior.

## Task Complexity

Task complexity refers to the extent to which operations must be performed upon the resources available to the group for successful task completion. For example, a task that requires only that information be collected in one place is a simple task; one that requires not only information collection but also manipulations of the information (such as addition, multiplication, etc.) is a complex one. This is a gross classification, at least as it has been used in small group research. Relatively little attention has been given to this task characteristic, and we have already presented most of the data relevant to its effects on group process (see Chapter 5). The reader will recall that one major consequence of this gross indifference in type of task is in conjunction with the group's communication pattern: Centralized networks are more effective only when the task is simple. [As an interesting aside, Faucheux and Moscovici (1960) found that the group spontaneously adopts the communication structure which allows it to carry out its assigned task in the optimum manner.]

## Qualitative Aspects of Group Tasks

Some researchers classify tasks according to their global or qualitative characteristics, including such categories as reasoning tasks, mechanical assembly tasks, production tasks, etc. One of the earliest studies of the effects of these aspects of task on group behavior was conducted by Carter, Haythorn, and Howell (1950). They were interested in the degree to which different kinds of tasks call for different leadership abilities. The six kinds of tasks mentioned earlier were used: reasoning, intellectual construction, clerical, discussion, motor coordination, and mechanical assembly tasks. The *reasoning task* was a true-false form of syllogistic reasoning which required group members to determine the correct conclusion from four "given statements." The *intellectual construction task* required that group members plot a field, such as a basketball court, on the floor, using strings and cellophane tape. They were given some dimensions, but had to determine others from those given. The *clerical tasks* required that group members sort a large number of cards according to several dimensions. This task demanded considerable coordination of efforts. *Discussion tasks* required that group members discuss an issue to consensus and write a statement of their conclusions. The *motor coordination task* was the ball and spiral task that we have encountered in other research. The *mechanical assembly tasks* required construction of simple objects, such as goalposts, using precut lumber. Leadership ratings of group members were obtained by five different methods: the leaderless group discussion technique, nominations, ratings by faculty members, ratings by friends, and assessment of leadership in other activities. Correlations of leadership ratings across tasks indicated a certain degree of generality of leadership ability, but they also revealed wide variations from task to task. A factor analysis suggested that there were two different kinds of tasks requiring different kinds of leadership abilities: intellectual tasks and manipulative tasks. The dichotomy is very similar to 'the intellectual-manipulative requirements dimension derived from the scale analysis of group tasks.

Hackman (1968) classified tasks into three types: production tasks, discussion tasks, and problem-solving tasks. *Production tasks* require the production and presentation of ideas, images, or arrangements (e.g., write a story about a mountain scene). *Discussion tasks* call for the evaluation of issues (e.g., write a defense of the proposition that the President of the United States should have broad executive privilege). This type of task usually requires group consensus. *Problem-solving tasks* require the group to determine a course of action to be followed to resolve some specific problem (e.g., how can a delicate instrument be transported across a river using only certain limited materials?). A study was conducted which involved 108 three-person groups and 108 different tasks, 12 for each combination of the 3 types of tasks with 3 levels of difficulty. Groups produced written products in response to questionnaires, which were then analyzed according to six general dimensions: action orientation, length, originality, optimism, quality of presentation, and issue involvement. In addition, group products were evaluated on two "task-dependent dimensions": adequacy and creativity. Type of task was shown to be systematically related to all these dimensions except adequacy. "In general, problem-solving tasks were characterized by high action orientation, production tasks by high originality, and discussion tasks by high issue involvement" (Hackman, 1968, p. 169). A somewhat similar study was conducted by Hackman and Vidmar (1970) to determine whether the effects of production, discussion, and problem-solving tasks would influence group behavior differently in different size groups. They failed to find the expected interaction between type of task and group size, but their findings revealed several significant effects on group performance and member reactions. The findings are given in Table 10-2. These data support earlier findings and also show that type of task influences members' reactions to the group in several important ways. A study by Morris (1965) used the same three types of tasks and found that leaders were more active on problem-solving tasks than on production tasks or on discussion tasks. In general, discussion tasks and problem-solving tasks produced similar effects upon group process and contrasted with production tasks. However, production tasks seemed to lead to an emphasis by the group on getting the job done, whereas discussion tasks produced more process-oriented activity, such as clarifying, explaining, and defending. Problem-solving tasks combined both output-oriented activity and process-oriented activities. Morris concluded that about 60 percent of a group's or a leader's behavior is highly sensitive to type of task. A similar classification was used by O'Neill

**Table 10-2  Task Effects on Performance and Member Reactions**

| | Task type | | | |
|---|---|---|---|---|
| Group product characteristics | Production | Discussion | Problem solving | F-ratio* |
| Action orientation | 2.96 | 3.17 | 6.22 | 102.69§ |
| Length | 4.42 | 3.31 | 3.77 | 10.71§ |
| Originality | 4.87 | 3.24 | 2.62 | 58.83§ |
| Optimism | 3.49 | 3.77 | 5.06 | 45.36§ |
| Quality of presentation | 4.34 | 4.26 | 3.61 | 5.53§ |
| Issue involvement | 2.39 | 5.20 | 4.44 | 98.65§ |
| Creativity | 4.35 | 3.85 | 3.88 | 4.03§ |
| Member reactions† | | | | |
| 1  Group too small | 2.13 | 2.44 | 2.37 | 3.30‡ |
| 2  Group too large | 3.23 | 2.90 | 2.66 | 8.80§ |
| 3  Made best use of time | 4.34 | 4.36 | 4.79 | 4.95§ |
| 5  Too much competition | 2.62 | 2.43 | 2.29 | 3.43‡ |
| 12  Group *needed* strong leader | 3.56 | 3.21 | 2.98 | 7.90§ |
| 13  Group was creative | 4.94 | 4.05 | 4.26 | 15.81§ |
| 14  I was inhibited | 2.26 | 2.20 | 2.03 | 3.23‡ |
| 15  Was sufficient time | 3.79 | 4.47 | 4.30 | 4.31‡ |
| 18  Not unified: subgroups | 3.17 | 3.02 | 2.72 | 5.04§ |
| 20  Group influenced me | 2.90 | 2.62 | 2.65 | 7.17§ |

*df = 5, 60.
†Only items relating significantly to task type are included.
‡$p < .05$
§$p < .01$.
*Source:* Reprinted with permission from J. R. Hackman and N. Vidmar. Effects of size and task on group performance and member reactions. *Sociometry*, 1970, **33**, 37–54.

and Alexander (1971) in a study of family process. The relative dominance of husbands and wives was observed as they performed discussion, decision, and performance tasks. *Discussion tasks* were essentially the same as in Hackman's system; husband-wife pairs were asked to discuss a topic such as: What brought you together in the first place? *Decision tasks* required that a joint decision be reached regarding some issue, such as: Decide which partner each of several blame labels fits better. *Performance tasks* required some operation performed jointly, such as a Chinese block puzzle to be assembled cooperatively. The husband dominated the interaction on the performance task; the wife more often dominated on the discussion tasks; and the the husband and wife dominated equally often on the decision tasks. More recent reviews of the research on types of tasks have provided additional evidence that the interaction process and the group's products vary significantly with the type of task (Hackman & Morris, 1975, 1978). These reviewers concluded that variations in group performance on "intellective" tasks are controlled by the nature of the group interaction process; that is, task characteristics affect the kinds of interactions that occur in the group which, in turn, influence the kinds of products the group will produce.

These several studies make it abundantly clear that the general type of task faced by the group will have important consequences for group interaction. It has been shown that the type of task, grossly determined, influences the kinds of leadership abilities which are required for successful task completion (e.g., see the contingency model of leadership effectiveness described in Chapter 9), the amount of leader activity, and the particular kinds of interactions that occur during the process of task completion.

### Disjunctive, Conjunctive, and Additive Tasks

As we noted earlier, the classification of tasks as disjunctive, conjunctive, or additive is based on the requirements for task completion (Steiner, 1972). A disjunctive task requires a choice among alternatives. The choice may be either "yes" or "no," or it may require the selection of the correct alternative among several possible ones. On this type of task, if one person in the group can complete the task, the group can complete it. Therefore, the group's potential performance should be determined by the most competent group member and by the probability that the group will contain at least one member capable of completing the task. One would predict, then, that the performance of randomly formed groups would increase with increasing group size (because the more persons in the group, the greater the probability that at least one of them can complete the task). If one knows the proportion of persons in the population that are capable of completing the task, the potential performance of a group of a given size can be predicted from the following formula: $100(1 - Q^n)$, where Q is the proportion of individuals in the population who cannot complete the task and $n$ is the number of persons in the group. Consider a task that can be completed by only 20 percent of the population. Then $Q = .80$ and, for a group of four persons, $Q^n = .4096$; the percentage of four-person groups that should be able to do the task is, therefore, $100(1 - .4096) = 59.04$. In other words, for this relatively difficult task, we would expect approximately 59 percent of randomly formed four-person groups to perform the task successfully. This prediction assumes, of course, that group interaction neither contributes to nor detracts from group performance. Steiner (1972) proposed that actual group performance will be potential group performance minus losses due to faulty group process.

The prediction that group performance on a disjunctive task of a given level of difficulty should increase with increasing group size is generally well supported by empirical evidence (Marquart, 1955; Lorge & Solomon, 1955; Maier & Solem, 1952; Laughlin & Bitz, 1975; Bray, Kerr, & Atkin, 1978). For instance, Bray et al. compared the performance of individuals and groups of two, three, six, and ten members. The proportion of correct solutions increased with increasing group size. Furthermore, the increases were not always as great as predicted from Steiner's formula, suggesting that there were, indeed, some losses due to faulty group processes. On the other hand, one study found that at least on one task groups performed significantly better than predicted by Steiner's formula (Shaw & Ashton, 1976). It is likely that group interaction can both interfere with and enhance group performance. Faulty group processes, such as lack of coordination among members, may impede progress, but the impetus provided by contributions of others may elicit behaviors that would not otherwise occur and that facilitate group functioning. This latter process has been called an "assembly effect bonus" (Collins & Guetzkow, 1964).

A *conjunctive task* is one that requires each member of the group to perform essentially the same function, and the success of the group is determined by the effectiveness of the least proficient member. With tasks of this sort, Steiner suggested that the group's potential productivity cannot exceed the productivity of the least competent member, although it may be less if group process is faulty. Following the same logic as applied to disjunctive tasks, if groups of $n$ size are randomly composed from a given population, the probability of a group having at least one member who cannot perform the task is $1 - P^n$, where P is the proportion of persons who can perform the task. For example, if we consider groups of four persons and a relatively difficult conjunctive task that can be performed by only 20 percent of the population, then the percentage of groups that would not be able to perform the task should be $100(1 - .20^4) = 100(1 - .0016) = 99.84$. In other words, very few groups would be expected to be able to perform the task, even if there were no losses due to faulty group process. It is clear, then, that groups should vary considerably in productivity as a function of type of task, even when the tasks are equally difficult for individuals.

There is little direct evidence concerning the effects of conjunctive tasks on group proformance. Steiner and Rajaratnam (1961) analyzed data from an earlier experiment (McCurdy & Lambert, 1952) for the purpose of comparing the performance of groups with that of their least competent members. Individuals who had worked alone on a conjunctive task (operating switches on an electrical panel) were randomly assigned to three-person "nominal" groups, and each was awarded the score earned by the least successful member. It was found that the scores of these nominal groups were almost identical to those earned by real groups. In addition, there is at least one study that compared disjunctive and conjunctive tasks. The study cited earlier by Frank and Anderson (1971) used production tasks such as "Write three points pro and con on the issue of legalized gambling." Tasks were made either conjunctive or disjunctive by altering the instructions to the groups. The disjunctive instructions stated that the group was to work on nine tasks in sequence, and as soon as any member had completed the task the group could move on to the next task. For the conjunctive tasks, the instructions were similar except that the group was not permitted to move on to the next task in the sequence until all members of the group had completed the task. Productivity was measured by the number of tasks completed in a fifteen-minute work period. The results are shown in Figure 10-4. Clearly, groups performed better on the disjunctive tasks.

The type of task also influenced the group members' reactions to the group. Group members rated their group as more pleasant, friendly, warm, and cooperative when the task was disjunctive than when it was conjunctive. Group members also expressed greater satisfaction with the group's performance on disjunctive than on conjunctive tasks.

*Additive* tasks are those that permit combination of contributions of individual group members to yield a group outcome or product. Thus, the more persons in the group, the better the group performance should be. As we discussed in Chapter 6, empirical data agree with this expectation, although the increment added by each additional member usually decreases with increasing group size (Ingham et al., 1974).

## Solution Multiplicity

Tasks vary in the degree to which there is a single acceptable outcome that can be easily demonstrated to be correct. Although it seems apparent that this aspect of task should have a significant effect on group process, the research on this task dimension is scarce. In the one study known to the

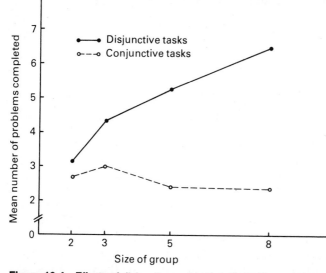

**Figure 10-4** Effects of disjunctive and conjunctive tasks upon group productivity. (Plotted with permission from data reported by F. Frank and L. R. Anderson. Effects of task and group size upon group productivity and member satisfaction. *Sociometry,* 1971, **34,** 135–149.)

author (Shaw & Blum, 1966) five-person groups attempted three tasks varying on the dimension of solution multiplicity, working under either directive or nondirective leadership. Task A required group members to list the five most important traits needed for success in our culture; hence, solution multiplicity was high (scale value =7.4). Task B was intermediate with respect to solution multiplicity (scale value =4.1); it required subjects to decide which of five alternatives was best for a young politician burdened with an alcoholic wife. Task C was similar to the parlor game "twenty questions" and was very low on solution multiplicity (scale value =.9). The three tasks were approximately equal on other task dimensions. Findings were in general agreement with Fiedler's theory: Directive leadership was more effective on the low solution multiplicity task, whereas nondirective leadership was more effective on the other two (see Table 10-3).

**Cooperation Requirements**

Tasks vary in the degree to which they require interrelated and coordinated actions by group members. Some tasks require much coordination of effort for successful completion, whereas others can be completed with little concern for this aspect of group process. Obviously, the cooperation requirements imposed by the group task should influence the performance of the group. What is not so obvious, perhaps, is that the magnitude of this

**Table 10-3  Mean Time Scores (Minutes) for Leadership and Task Conditions**

|  | Task | | |
| Leadership style | A | B | C |
| --- | --- | --- | --- |
| Directive | 23.42 | 13.36 | 24.67 |
| Nondirective | 16.76 | 5.29 | 34.73 |

Source: Reprinted with permission from M. E. Shaw and J. M. Blum, Effects of leadership style upon group performance as a function of task structure. Journal of Personality and Social Psychology, 1966, 3, 238–242. Slightly adapted. Copyright 1966 by the American Psychological Association. Reprinted by permission.

effect is determined by other characteristics of the group and the situation in which it must function. Empirical evidence concerning these effects is extremely limited. In Chapter 7 we discussed a study by Schutz (1955) which was designed to test his theory of interpersonal relations (FIRO). It will be recalled that the three problems attempted by the compatible and incompatible groups varied in the degree to which they required cooperation among group members, although Schutz referred to these differences as task complexity. Nevertheless, the results from this study provide good evidence that the better performance of the compatible groups relative to the incompatible groups varied with the cooperation requirements of the task: the greater the cooperation requirements of the task the greater the difference between the performance levels of the compatible and the incompatible groups.

One other study examined the effects of cooperation requirements on performance in relation to other aspects of the group situation. In this study (Shaw & Briscoe, 1966), two tasks varying in degree of cooperation requirements (scale values =2.04 and 6.25) were attempted by three-, four-, and five-person groups. It was predicted that the larger groups would be relatively less effective in dealing with the task having high cooperation requirements, because the difficulty of coordinating activities increases with size of group. The hypothesis was not supported by the data. However, the high-cooperation-requirements task required more time than did the low-cooperation-requirements task (means =1.5 versus .3). Since the difficulty of the two tasks was approximately equal, these differences may be attributed to the fact that the tasks differed in the amount of intermember coordination required for successful completion.

The available evidence, although limited, is sufficient to demonstrate that the cooperation requirements of the task are an important determinant of group effectiveness and that its effects may be modified by other influences upon group process. More definitive conclusions must await the outcome of future research.

### Goal Clarity and Goal-Path Clarity

We have all observed groups that have clearly established goals and clearly specified ways of achieving those goals, and we have noticed other groups that seem to be confused and disorganized with no clear idea about what they want to do or how to do it. When the task of the group is clearly identified, it is an example of *goal clarity,* and when the manner of completing the task is clearly defined, we refer to this situation as *goal-path clarity.* Clearly, tasks may vary with respect to their degree of clarity, and these variations influence group effectiveness. When the goal of the group is not clearly specified and/or the path to the goal is not clear, the resulting confusion about what the group is supposed to be doing can scarcely be conducive to effective group action. For example, A. R. Cohen (1959) examined the effects of goal-path clarity upon certain individual behaviors. He studied telephone operators who were being evaluated by a supervisor. From the standpoint of the telephone operators, the goal was clear: to get a good rating from the supervisor. The way to achieve this desirable outcome, i.e., the path to the goal, was not always clear. For some of the operators, the supervisor gave a single clue that presumably would help them get a good rating; for others, various inconsistent clues were given throughout the test session. Thus, the path to the goal was considerably less clear under the second set of conditions than under the first. Under the low goal-path clarity conditions, operators were less motivated, less secure, evaluated themselves lower, and worked less efficiently than operators in the higher condition.

Goal-path clarity has also been shown to affect interpersonal attraction and cohesiveness of the group. For example, in one study forty all-female triads attempted a task that could be varied with respect to goal-path clarity by varying the amount of information given to individual group members (Anderson, 1975). The task was to rate dormitory rooms in terms of desirability, using information provided each group member. The goal was to win a $15 prize by performing better than other groups. Group activities were disrupted more frequently when the path to the goal was unclear than when it was clear, and questionnaire data indicated that both cohesiveness and interpersonal liking were greater when goal-path clarity was high.

The effects of goal clarity were examined in a laboratory study conducted by Raven and Rietsema (1957). Through tape recordings, some group members were given a clear picture of the goal, whereas others received only vague and ambiguous information about it. Members of high-clarity groups were more attracted to the task, showed less nontask-directed tension, were more involved with the group, and conformed more to group expectations than low-clarity group members.

It will be remembered that goal clarity was revealed to be an aspect of difficulty in the dimensional study cited earlier. Furthermore, it is questionable whether goal clarity and goal-path clarity represent two aspects of the task situation or only one. Therefore, it is probable that the findings of A. R. Cohen and Raven and Rietsema can be validly interpreted as further evidence concerning the effects of task difficulty on group process.

In brief summary, the empirical investigations of the effects of task characteristics upon group process are unsystematic, loosely controlled, and restricted to relatively few task dimensions and group situations. The identification and measurement of task dimensions have been haphazard, for the most part, and only recently has there been some promise of advances in research sophistication. Nevertheless, the evidence amassed thus far provides strong support for those who expect significant benefits to derive from detailed analysis of task characteristics and group process.

## HETEROGENEITY-HOMOGENEITY OF GROUP GOALS

To this point, we have tacitly assumed that the group goal is known to group members and that all accept it and work toward its attainment. Although this situation undoubtedly does occur, group members commonly differ, to some extent, in their perceptions of the group goal and, especially, in the degree to which they are committed to achieving it. In some instances, group members hold different goals for the group, or they hold different individual goals that can be achieved only through group action. These differing individual orientations have powerful effects upon the behaviors of group members and upon the products of the group.

Perhaps the most extensive studies of heterogeneity of group goals are those dealing with "cooperation and competition." It requires only a brief consideration of the definitions of cooperation and competition to observe that in a cooperative situation group goals are homogeneous (i.e., members hold the same goal for the group) and in a competitive situation group goals are heterogeneous (i.e., group members hold differing goals for the group). This conclusion is illustrated by the definitions offered by M. Deutsch (1949a). A competitive social situation was defined as one in which the goal regions of each group member are such that if the goal region is entered by any individual group member, other group members will, to some degree, be unable to reach their respective goal regions. A cooperative social situation was defined as one in which the goal regions of individual group members are such that if a goal region is entered by any given individual, all other group members are facilitated in reaching their respective regions. In other words, in a competitive situation, goal achievement by one group member to some extent hinders the goal achievement of other members, whereas in a cooperative situation, goal achievement by one member facilitates goal achievement by all others. A competitive situation clearly cannot exist if group goals are homogeneous; it is theoretically possible for a cooperative situation to exist without homogeneous group goals, but this situation is relatively rare.

Relative to individual orientations, cooperation and competition influence a wide range of group processes, including preferences, attitudes and reactions toward others in the group, cohesiveness, and group effectiveness. We will examine the way these aspects of the group's goal affect intragroup processes and group effectiveness.

### Homogeneity-Heterogeneity of Goals and Intragroup Processes

When the group members are agreed upon a goal and work cooperatively to achieve it, they are more likely to be attracted to each other, to be less hostile and display more friendliness toward others, to be more cooperative in group discussions, to react more favorably to the contributions of others, and generally behave positively toward the group. Many of these effects were revealed in a study conducted at the Massachusetts Institute of Technology (Deutsch, 1949b). There were 10 five-person groups, five groups working in a cooperative situation and five in a ·competitive situation. Each group met once a week for five weeks, to work on puzzles and human relations problems. Competitive groups were told that individual contributions to the puzzle solutions would be ranked from 1 to 5, with 5 being assigned to the person who contributed the most. The individual who received the highest average was excused from one term paper and given an automatic H (the highest grade awarded at MIT). The five cooperative groups were told that they would be ranked and that all members of the group with the highest rank would be excused from a term paper and given an automatic H. Similar instructions were given with respect to the human relations problems, except that the ranks were to be used in determining the final grade in the course. Observers recorded selected portions of the group interaction and rated certain aspects of the group process at the conclusion of each task. Group members completed questionnaires designed to provide data on a wide range of group perceptions and products. It was found that cooperation and competition affected many aspects of the group process. Relative to the competitive situation, cooperation increased diversity of member contributions, subdivision of activities, achievement pressure, attentiveness to fellow members, friendliness during discussions, favorable evaluations of the group and its products, and similar interpersonal processes. In short, the cooperative groups engaged in more specialized activities, displayed more positive interpersonal relations, and had higher morale than competitive groups.

Other research has yielded results which generally support the hypothesis that members of cooperative groups are more favorably disposed toward the group and their fellow members, although there are some exceptions. In a study of intragroup and intergroup cooperation and competition, it was found that in cooperative groups the atmosphere was more relaxed and members felt greater freedom to contribute than in competitive groups (Rabbie, Benoist, Oosterbaan, & Visser, 1974). On the other hand, cordiality of group atmosphere and cohesiveness were greater in cooperative groups only when bargaining position was weak, and pressures toward conformity were greater in the competitive groups. In another study it was found that members of competitive groups reported higher levels of arousal and less interpersonal attraction than members of cooperative groups (Scott & Cherrington, 1974). The higher arousal produced by competition is consistent with the results of another study to be reported later (Shaw, 1958a).

Despite the few inconsistent findings, it is reasonably clear that interpersonal relations are generally more positive in cooperative than in competitive situations. Members are more attracted to each other, react more favorably to their contributions, make more diverse contributions, display greater friendliness, and so on.

### Homogeneity-Heterogeneity of Goals and Group Effectiveness

Given the more favorable interpersonal relations in cooperative groups, one might expect that those groups would be more effective than competitive groups. When group members coordinate their efforts toward achievement of a common goal, the outcome should be superior to the outcomes produced by groups whose members are competing. The empirical evidence generally agrees with this expectation. In the study by Deutsch (1949b) cited earlier, productivity per unit time was greater in the cooperative than in the competitive groups, and the quality of products and group discussions was rated higher in the cooperative groups.

Several other studies of the relative effectiveness of cooperation and competition yielded findings that are in general agreement with those reported by Deutsch. For instance, the author (M. E. Shaw, 1958a) attempted to separate the effects of task requirements and motivational requirements in cooperative and competitive situations. Members of dyads were led to believe they were cooperating, competing, or working individually, whereas their performance score actually depended upon their own efforts. In one task situation, two hand cranks controlled a pointer which was to be kept in alignment with a moving target. Performance was measured by time on target during fifteen-second test periods. The results are shown graphically in Figure 10-5. Clearly, the cooperative situation resulted in the most proficient tracking behavior, whereas the competitive situation was least effective. Contrary to Deutsch's findings, satisfaction was rated higher in the competitive than in the cooperative situation. These results were replicated using a task requiring less eye-hand coordination and greater mental activity. Results reported by Clifford (1972) are in agreement with these latter findings. Competitive situations in fifth grade classrooms significantly increased interest in the subject being studied relative to a noncompetitive control situation; however, competition had no effect on performance. In a very different situation, Willis and Joseph (1959) observed that cooperative instructions to dyads playing nonzero sum games* resulted in more agreements (and greater mutual rewards) than did competitive instructions.

Cooperation has also been observed to be more effective than competition in natural situations. Blau (1954) compared two groups of interviewers in a public employment agency whose task was to place as many job applicants as possible, as quickly as possible. In one group, a

---

*A zero sum game is one in which the gains of group members sum to some specified value so that a gain by one person must be compensated for by a loss on the part of another group member or members. A nonzero sum game is one in which gain by one member is not necessarily at the expense of others in the group.

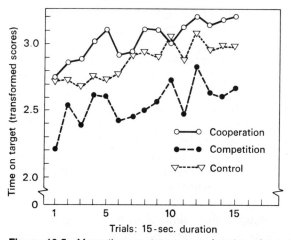

**Figure 10-5** Mean time on target as a function of practice in the three motivational conditions. (Reprinted with permission from M. E. Shaw. Some motivational factors in cooperation and competiion. *Journal of Personality*, 1958, **26**, 155–169.)

cooperative atmosphere existed such that each member helped others to place an applicant that he had interviewed. In the other, a competitive atmosphere emerged such that each member attempted to place as many applicants as he could on an individual basis. Job openings were hoarded rather than distributed among the group in accordance with approved practices. The result was reduced productivity by the competitive group. According to Blau, anxiety over productivity led to behaviors which interfered with group effectiveness.

There is some research, however, which indicates that under some conditions competitive situations may result in more effective group outcomes. In one study, it was found that cooperation led to more efficient problem-solving activity than competition only when group members were engaged in a high-task-interdependent situation (Okun & Di Vesta, 1975). A similar finding was reported by Goldman, Stockbauer, and McAuliffe (1977). Perhaps these findings are not too surprising when one remembers that one of the major differences between the two goal orientations is that cooperation facilitates intermember coordination and diversity of activities relative to the task. It is probable that the influence of cooperation can be eliminated by lack of interdependence among group members.

Heterogeneity of group goals not only influences group productivity and member satisfaction but also affects group members' attributions of responsibility for group outputs. In one study (Wolosin, Sherman, & Till, 1973) male pairs performed a cooperative or a competitive task and either exceeded, met, or failed to meet a predetermined outcome level. Following task completion, they were asked to attribute responsibility for their outcomes. Under both cooperation and competition, exceeding the standard tended to produce attribution to self (i.e., each member saw himself as having been more responsible for the success than his partner); meeting the standard tended to produce attribution to the situation. However, failure to meet the standard resulted in attribution to the other person (more than to self) in the cooperative situation, but relatively greater attribution to the situation in the competitive condition. The attribution of responsibility for failure to the other group member in the cooperative situation is of particular interest, since such attribution has negative consequences for group action. For example, it has been shown that attribution for negative events to a group member results in that member being viewed unfavorably and rejected by others in the group (Shaw & Breed, 1970) and to interfere with efficient group decisions (Shaw & Tremble, 1971).

These empirical studies make it abundantly clear that homogeneity of group goals facilitates group functioning, whereas heterogeneity of group goals interferes with group functioning. This effect is produced by the specialization of task behaviors and helpful actions of group members in the cooperative situation. Members of groups with homogeneous group goals are usually happier than members of groups with heterogeneous goals. Homogeneity of goals generally has positive effects upon group functioning, both in the laboratory and in natural situations, but may lead to ego-defensive interpretation of some group-related events.

## PLAUSIBLE HYPOTHESES ABOUT GROUP GOALS AND TASKS

In the preceding pages the various conceptions of group task in relation to group goals have been reviewed, and it has been shown that individuals establish group goals which function in much the same way as individual goals. Empirical evidence of the effects of tasks and goals has been presented. Although research on tasks and goals is limited, some general conclusions about their effects can be drawn. Some conclusions are intuitively obvious but have relatively little empirical support; some are less obvious but have strong support from empirical investigations; and most have significant implications for group process.

*Hypothesis 1  Individuals establish goals for their groups which influence their behavior in ways similar to the influence of personal goals.*

The evidence for this hypothesis is reasonably extensive and is quite consistent. The work of Shelley (1954) on the establishment of individual levels of aspiration for the group and that of Zander and his associates (Zander, 1968; Zander & Medow, 1963; Zander & Newcomb, 1967) on the setting of group levels of aspiration demonstrate conclusively that group members set goals for the group and that these goals exert a measurable influence upon behavior in the group.

*Hypothesis 2  Tension systems can be aroused for goals which the individual holds for the group.*

*Hypothesis 3  Tension systems can be aroused for avoidances which the individual holds for the group.*

These two interrelated hypotheses are derived from the work by Horwitz (1954) on incompleted group tasks. His work revealed that once a group goal is established, group members experience task-related tension which is reduced by task completion. Group members recalled more incompleted tasks than completed ones in situations where the majority of group members had voted to complete the task, but they recalled no more incompleted tasks than completed ones in situations where the majority of group members had voted to discontinue working toward completion. Whether group members hold goals for task completion or goals for task incompletion, tension systems are aroused which influence the members' reactions to movement relative to the group goal.

Hypothesis 4    *Group success is followed by choice of a more difficult task; failure is followed by selection of an easier task.*

Hypothesis 5    *Group members select relatively more difficult tasks if they learn that their past performance is worse than the average for groups like their own; they choose relatively less difficult tasks if they learn that their past performance is better than the average of groups like their own.*

Hypothesis 6    *The greater the group members' desires for group success the greater the preference for tasks perceived to be in the intermediate range of difficulty; the stronger the desires to avoid group failure the greater the preference for tasks at the extremes of the difficulty range.*

Hypothesis 7    *Groups composed wholly of persons with desires to achieve success stronger than their desires to avoid failure more often select tasks in the intermediate range of difficulty than groups composed wholly of persons whose desires to avoid failure exceed their desires to achieve success.*

Hypotheses 4 to 7 are supported primarily by the work of Zander (1971). The evidence that he presents, however, is sufficiently convincing to permit their acceptance as plausible hypotheses. Data reported by Kukla (1975) are also consistent with these hypotheses.

Hypothesis 8    *The quality of group performance, as measured by time and errors, decreases with increasing task difficulty.*

This hypothesis is supported not only by logical considerations but also by a large amount of empirical evidence. Various studies of task difficulty measured by scale analysis provided uniform data supporting this proposition (e.g., M. E. Shaw, 1963; Shaw & Blum, 1965). Studies of the effects of task demands upon group performance also are in agreement with Hypothesis 8 (Lanzetta & Roby, 1956, 1957). However, all these studies used tasks requiring some degree of problem solving; there is some doubt regarding the validity of this hypothesis when the task requires only a motor response.

Hypothesis 9    *Reaction time decreases with increased task difficulty.*

Zajonc and Taylor (1963) found that increasing the difficulty of a task requiring rapid reaction time led to increased group effectiveness. This contrasts sharply with the findings cited above when the task requires problem-solving activities. Probably Hypothesis 8 should be qualified to apply to problem-solving tasks, and Hypothesis 9 to apply only to motor-reaction tasks.

*Hypothesis 10    Group members attempt leadership more frequently when the task is difficult than when it is easy.*

Again, the evidence is limited to a single investigation (Bass et al., 1958), although the hypothesis appears eminently reasonable. The question of the adaptiveness of the response, however, has not been answered; hence, the meaning of this relationship for group functioning is unclear.

*Hypothesis 11    When task difficulty is low or moderate, conformity is curvilinearly related to the self-esteem of the group member.*

When the task is not too difficult, failure may be attributed to personal deficiencies and, hence, is ego-threatening to some individuals. Persons who have low self-esteem are not concerned about their performance because they expect to fail regardless of the difficulty of the task, whereas persons with high self-esteem do not anticipate failure. Hence neither of these types of group members conforms excessively to the standards of the majority. Group members of intermediate self-esteem experience some doubt about their effectiveness and feel threatened by failure; hence, they tend to conform to group norms more closely than either low or high self-esteem members. When the task is difficult, failure may be attributed to the task rather than to the person and so is not ego-threatening to anyone. The group member need not conform regardless of self-esteem. Gergen and Bauer (1967) demonstrated these effects quite clearly, although the interpretation given above is somewhat different from their proposals.

*Hypothesis 12    The quality of group performance decreases with increasing task demands.*

This is another fairly obvious hypothesis which nevertheless has important consequences for group behavior. When the demands of the task are increased, group members must distribute their activities more broadly and thus cannot give the same amount of attention to each aspect of the task as they can when demands are fewer. The work of Lanzetta and Roby (1956, 1957) illustrates these effects.

*Hypothesis 13    The characteristics of group products vary with the difficulty of the group task.*

In the study of group products as a function of type of task and task characteristics, Hackman (1968) also examined the effects of task difficulty as measured by the scale analysis procedure. He found that products from more difficult tasks were generally more original and issue-involved, whereas products from easier tasks met specific task requirements more adequately. Quality of presentation was also higher for easy tasks than for difficult ones.

*Hypothesis 14    On difficult tasks, group performance is facilitated to the extent that group members can freely communicate their feelings of satisfaction with the group's progress toward goal achievement.*

A group member often disagrees with a proposed decision or action of the group but believes incorrectly that he or she is the only group member who is dissatisfied. Such members are reluctant to express their views, lest they be considered disruptive or nonconformists. When members are encouraged to express disagreement (Maier, 1950) or when they can do so without disrupting the group (Shaw & Blum, 1965), the group's performance is superior. Effective group functioning can be facilitated by providing an opportunity for group members to express their feelings and opinions in an uninhibited manner. This opportunity can be provided either through a leader who encourages the expression of minority opinion or by some device which permits an indication of satisfaction or dissatisfaction without focusing attention on the group member.

*Hypothesis 15    The kinds of leadership abilities that are required for effective group action vary with type of task.*

Although Hypothesis 15 appears obvious in light of present knowledge, this was not always so. Early studies of leadership traits implicitly assumed that the kind of task faced by the group was irrelevant, and the failure of these studies to predict leadership effectiveness accurately can be attributed in large measure to this neglect of task environment. Studies by Carter et al. (1950) provided strong empirical support for this hypothesis.

*Hypothesis 16    The characteristics of group products are a function of the kind of task faced by the group.*

The phrase "kind of task" in Hypothesis 16 refers to the global classification of tasks into such categories as discussion tasks, problem-solving tasks, and production tasks. Hypothesis 16 is based primarily upon the work of Hackman (1968) and Hackman and Vidmar (1970) which found that the products of groups working on discussion tasks are characterized by high issue involvement, those of groups working on problem-solving tasks are characterized by high action orientation, and those of groups working on production tasks by high originality. The results of the study by Morris (1965) are consistent with Hackman's result, although the two investigators did not use the same dimensions in their analyses of group products. (See also Hackman & Morris, 1975, 1978.)

*Hypothesis 17    The activity of group leaders varies with the kind of task faced by the group.*
This hypothesis also has minimal empirical support. Morris (1965) found that leaders were more active on problem-solving tasks than on production tasks or on discussion tasks. More data are required to determine whether this represents a realistic response of the leader to the requirements of the task or whether such a response is maladaptive with respect to at least some aspects of the task environment.

*Hypothesis 18    Group performance is better when the task is disjunctive than when it is conjunctive.*
Evidence for this hypothesis is sparse, but data reported by Frank and Anderson (1971) suggest that this is a plausible conclusion about the effects of this type of task upon group performance.

*Hypothesis 19    The style of leadership that is most effective varies with task solution multiplicity.*
Hypothesis 19 may be taken as a more specific instance of the functional relationship stated in Hypothesis 9 in Chapter 9, which asserted that a directive leader is more effective when the group-task situation is either very favorable or very unfavorable for the leader, whereas a nondirective leader is more effective when the situation is moderately favorable. Given that leader-member affective relations are at least moderately good and that the power position of the leader is at least moderately strong, then a task with low solution multiplicity should constitute a favorable group-task situation for the leader, and directive leadership should be more effective. On the other hand, a task high on solution multiplicity should create a group-task situation of intermediate favorability, and nondirective leadership should be more effective. These effects were domonstrated clearly in the study reported by Shaw and Blum (1966). Thus one must conclude that the kind of behavior which a leader should enact for efficient group performance depends in part upon the degree to which the group task has one or many acceptable outcomes; or, conversely, the kind of leader selected for a group should be determined in part by the solution-multiplicity characteristics of the task.

*Hypothesis 20    The quality of group performance, as measured by time and errors, is negatively correlated with the cooperation requirements of the group task.*
The evidence for this hypothesis is limited to a single study (Shaw &

Briscoe, 1966) but is strongly supportive. A task having high cooperation requirements required approximately four times as long as a similar task having lower cooperation requirements. Groups made approximately five times as many errors on the high than on the low cooperation requirements task. Increasing the requirements for cooperation among group members also increases coordination problems and, hence, reduces the quality of group performance.

*Hypothesis 21    Goal clarity and goal-path clarity are positively related to motivational characteristics of group members.*

*Hypothesis 22    Goal clarity and goal-path clarity are positively correlated with the efficiency of group members.*

These two related hypotheses are bases upon findings from a field study (A. R. Cohen, 1959) and from a laboratory study (Raven & Rietsema, 1957). The field study showed that telephone operators were more highly motivated, felt more secure, and worked more efficiently when the path to the goal was relatively clear than when it was ambiguous. The laboratory study generally agreed with those findings and also reported similar effects with respect to goal clarity. Although it seems obvious that group members are more highly motivated and perform more efficiently when they know what is expected of them, it is important to remember this obvious fact when attempting to understand group processes.

*Hypothesis 23    Interpersonal relations are generally more positive in cooperative than in competitive situations.*

This hypothesis is supported by the findings from several studies. The early study by Deutsch (1949b) revealed many evidences of more favorable interpersonal relations in cooperative than in competitive groups, findings that were generally supported by Rabbie et al. (1974) and by Scott and Cherrington (1974). However, there is some evidence that these differences may be attenuated by other variables, such as bargaining position (Rabbie et al., 1974).

*Hypothesis 24    Homogeneous group goals facilitate effective group functioning, whereas heterogeneous group goals hinder effective group functioning.*

Numerous studies of cooperation and competition have shown that groups perform more efficiently when the situation is cooperative than when it is competitive (Blau, 1954; M. Deutsch, 1949b; M. E. Shaw, 1958a). Since cooperation is defined as a situation in which the goals of the group are homogeneous, and competition as a situation in which the goals are heterogeneous, these studies support Hypothesis 24. This effect is produced largely through the specialization of individual contributions and through helpful actions of each member vis-à-vis other members in the cooperative situation. Motivational factors also play a role; the competitive situation may arouse greater motivation than the cooperative situation, but this increased motivation does not always improve group performance (M. E. Shaw, 1958a). Planners for group action are well advised to provide homogeneous group goals if efficient group performance is the desired outcome of group process.

In brief summary, a multitude of factors related to task environment influence group interaction, group effectiveness, and group products. Empirical data relative to these factors and their effects are sparse indeed, and much remains to be done before one can confidently predict the consequences of task environment for many aspects of group behavior. Even at this early stage, however, it is clear that the characteristics of a task cannot be ignored in the analysis of group process.

## SUGGESTED READINGS

Deutsch, M. An experimental study of the effects of co-operation and competition upon group process. *Human Relations,* 1949, **2,** 199–232.

Goldman, M., Stockbauer, J. W., & McAuliffe, T. G. Intergroup and intragroup competition and cooperation. *Journal of Experimental Social Psychology,* 1977, **13,** 81–88.

Hackman, J. R., & Vidmar, N. Effects of size and task type on group performance and member reactions. *Sociometry,* 1970, **33,** 37–54.

Horwitz, M. The recall of interrupted group tasks: An experimental study of individual motivation in relation to group goals. *Human Relations,* 1954, **7,** 3–38.

Shaw, M. E., & Tremble, T. R., Jr. Effects of attribution of responsibility for a negative event to a group member upon group process as a function of the structure of the event. *Sociometry,* 1971, **34,** 504–514.

Wolosin, R. J., Sherman, S. J., & Till, A. Effects of cooperation and competition on responsibility attribution after success and failure. *Journal of Experimental Social Psychology,* 1973, **9,** 220–235.

Zander, A., & Medow, H. Individual and group levels of aspiration. *Human Relations,* 1963, **16,** 89–105.

# Chapter 11

# Groups in Action

In the preceding chapters the concern has been with *understanding* group behavior. This analysis of group process relied upon both theoretical and empirical data. An attempt was made to present what is *known* about group behavior, what we *believe* is known, and what we *suspect* may be true about group behavior. Much of this information about groups is of interest for its own sake; i.e., individuals are curious about human behavior and especially about the behavior of people vis-à-vis one another. But of even greater interest are the uses that can be made of knowledge about group behavior. Most persons want to know how the various principles of group behavior affect their own experiences in groups and how group principles may be applied for special purposes.

In this section of the book the intent is to illustrate some of the principles of group behavior in groups created for special purposes. This chapter considers some specialized groups that are designed for achieving more or less specific kinds of goals. Although groups may be, and often are, used for many special purposes, we will be concerned with three of the more common types of groups that function in our society, namely, *problem-solving groups, educational groups,* and *experiential groups.* Our aim is to illustrate how the principles of group behavior are exemplified in action groups.

## PROBLEM-SOLVING GROUPS

Situations constantly arise that call for the solution of some difficulty, or a decision about some issue or an appropriate course of action. The college administrator must decide how to handle student complaints; the president of the student body must determine the best way to use available funds; the business man or woman must formulate the most appropriate procedures for running the business; political leaders must decide how to handle the energy crisis. All these problems could be handled by a single person (e.g., the leader), but for a variety of reasons they are often assigned to groups (committees, task forces, etc.). For instance, in Chapter 2 we described a series of studies which suggest that people accept, and work harder to implement decisions they help make (Lewin, 1953). In Chapter 3, we reviewed research comparing individual versus group problem solving and noted some of the advantages of groups over individuals. It may be recalled that groups usually produce more and better solutions than individuals. Groups typically possess a greater diversity of resources, recognize and correct errors more frequently, and increase the motivation of group members above that of individuals. Many apparently believe that these advantages outweigh the disadvantages of groups, such as pressures toward uniformity, slowness, and diffusion of responsibility.

In our earlier discussions of group processes we noted many factors that either facilitated or interfered with effective problem solving. The effects of these factors are often complex, and a given factor may either enhance or impede progress as a function of other variables. A brief review of the factors influencing group problem solving may be instructive.

### Factors That Facilitate Group Problem Solving

Effective group problem solving consists of a series of steps or stages: (1) recognizing the problem, (2) diagnosing the problem, (3) decision making, and (4) accepting and carrying out decisions. The need for these steps is probably obvious. Unless someone in the group recognizes that a problem exists, it is unlikely that any action will be taken to solve the problem. Of course, someone outside the group may point out the problem, but even then group members must accept the view that a problem exists which merits attention. Once the problem has been identified, some groups proceed immediately to try to solve it, and many random solutions are proposed. However, the more effective groups analyze the problem before attempting solution. Knowing the various ramifications of the problem usually promotes more adequate solutions. Sometimes the solution to a problem is a decision, but in many instances a definite decision must be made to accept one of several possible solutions. The decision must be made by someone, but it may be the group itself or the leader of the group; *how* the decision is made has important implications for acceptance and implementation.

Little evidence is available concerning the *identification* of problems by groups, but many factors are known to influence *diagnosis, decision making,* and *acceptance-implementation.* Diagnosis or identification of problem requirements is a critical step in the problem-solving process. If a group begins attempted solution with incomplete or faulty evidence concerning problem requirements, it may take an initial direction that prevents adequate solution. Maier and Solem (1962) observed that effective groups typically followed a three-step procedure: a brief statement of each member's view, a listing of important factors in the problem by the group, and use of the list as the basis for the final solution. Groups that followed these procedures produced significantly more creative solutions than groups that began to offer solutions without exploring the facts relevant to the problem. Similarly, it has been shown that if groups are given the opportunity to plan for problem solving, they perform better than groups which do not have this opportunity (Shure, Rogers, Larsen, & Tassone, 1962). One of the reasons planning opportunity promotes effective problem solution is that it permits groups to decide in advance that attention should be devoted to problem diagnosis.

The problem-solving process is influenced by a multitude of variables, including at least the physical environment, group size, member characteristics, group structure, leadership behavior, task characteristics, and group process variables.

**The Physical Environment**   The setting in which the group interaction occurs often exerts an important influence on the problem-solving process (see Chapter 5). The performance of groups may be promoted by such mundane aspects of the environment as proper lighting (Luckiesh, 1931; Tinker, 1939), pleasant wall colors (Seghers, 1948), soundproof walls (Sleight & Tiffin, 1948), and esthetically pleasing environments (Mintz, 1956). Less obvious, perhaps, are the indirect effects of the environment on group problem solving. For instance, interperson distances affect the perception of status differences, which in turn affect group process and hence problem-solving effectiveness (Dean et al., 1975; Sommer, 1969). Seating arrangements affect leadership emergence (Steinzor, 1950; Strodtbeck & Hook, 1961), amount of interaction between specific group members (Mehrabian & Diamond, 1971b; Silverstein & Stang, 1976), quality of interaction (Campbell, Kruskal, & Wallace, 1966; Russo, 1967), positive cooperation (Gardin et al., 1973), and personal feelings of group members (Patterson et al., 1979). All these variables that are related to seating arrangements are known to influence group problem solving. Therefore, group problem-solving effectiveness can be facilitated by proper seating arrangements in the group. For instance, if the person most qualified to serve as leader is seated at the head of the table, he or she will have a greater than chance probability of emerging as leader. Communication among group members is encouraged by seating arrangement that permits easy eye contact, and interpersonal communication generally improves decision making and problem solving, at least when the measure is the quantity produced (Cohen, 1968; Thibaut, Strickland, Mundy, & Goding, 1960; Shaw & Blum, 1965).

The arrangement of communication channels among group members (communication networks) may be viewed as one aspect of the physical environment. It may be recalled that centralized communication networks contribute to problem-solving effectiveness when the task is very simple (Leavitt, 1951), whereas decentralized networks promote problem-solving effectiveness when the task or problem is more complex (Shaw, 1964). Most of the problems faced by groups are relatively complex; therefore, decentralized communication networks are more likely to facilitate problem solving than centralized ones. This effect is largely a consequence of the distribution of task-related functions that is possible in the decentralized network.

**Group Size**   The sheer number of persons in the group has also been shown to influence group performance, although whether increasing group size facilitates or interferes with group problem solving depends on the kind of problem the group is trying to solve (see Chapters 6 and 10). When the task or problem is one that permits the addition of individual member contributions (additive) or can be solved if a single group member can solve it (disjunctive), increasing the size of the group facilitates group performance. On such tasks, the unique abilities and resources of individual group members can be used to improve problem-solving effectiveness. The exception to this general principle occurs when the performance of larger groups is impaired by faulty group processes. When the task or problem is one that can be solved only if each and every group member can solve it (conjunctive), group performance is enhanced by decreasing the size of the group. This effect is the consequence of the relatively poor performance of the least capable member in the group (Steiner, 1972). The exception to this general rule occurs when the positive effects of group interaction (assembly effects bonus) are great enough to counteract the task effects (Shaw & Ashton, 1976).

The size of the group also affects other aspects of group process that may be expected to influence group problem solving. As the size of the group increases, the distribution of participation among group members becomes more unequal: a relatively small proportion of the group's membership contributes most of the total participation (Bales et al., 1951). A further consequence of this is that many good ideas may not be expressed by minority group members. Smaller groups are less likely to exemplify this unequal participation and hence should be more effective than larger groups, unless other factors counteract its effect. A leader is more likely to emerge in larger groups, and this fact may contribute to group effectiveness in many situations. Thus it is clear that group size influences group performance, but the direction of the effect (i.e., whether large or small groups are more effective problem solvers) depends upon other factors.

**Member Characteristics**   As described in Chapter 6, the personal attributes that individual members bring with them when they join a group contribute to the group's effectiveness or lack of it. Obviously, group members possessing the knowledge, skills, and abilities that are relevant to the problem promote the effective solution of that problem. What is not so obvious, perhaps, is that the degree to which the effects of these personal characteristics are evident often depends upon other factors. For example, it has been shown that the person who possesses more task-relevant information than others has a greater influence on the group decision than those having less information (Shaw, 1963), but only if other group members perceive the information as valid (Shaw & Penrod, 1962a). The personality characteristics of members may also influence the degree to which the abilities and skills of group members can be employed to facilitate group problem solving. For example, sociability and social activeness are positively related to group performance (Bouchard, 1969; Greer, 1955). Group problem solving is also facilitated if group members display individual prominence tendencies (Shaw & Harkey, 1976), self-reliance (Greer, 1955), dependability and/or emotional stability (Haythron, 1953), and personal adjustment (Greer, 1955). In short, those member characteristics that are generally viewed favorably and that may be expected to contribute to effective interpersonal relations in the group are also related to effective group problem solving.

**Group Composition**   Not only do member characteristics influence group problem solving, but also the particular combination of personal characteristics is important (see Chapter 7). The assembly factors that are of special significance for group problem solving are group cohesiveness, compatibility, and heterogeneity of group membership. Although these aspects of group composition are not independent, the specific relationships among group-member characteristics that are considered vary with the type of assembly factor.

Group cohesiveness, it may be recalled, refers to the degree to which group members are attracted to each other and to the group, or, more precisely, the resultant of all those forces acting on the person to remain in or to leave the group. Group members who are attracted to the group presumably want the group to succeed and, therefore, work harder to help the group achieve its goals. It follows that group problem solving should be facilitated by group cohesiveness. Despite some negative findings (Palmer & Myers, 1955; Stogdill, 1968), the empirical evidence generally supports this expectation (Goodacre, 1951; Berkowitz, 1954; Hemphill & Sechrest, 1952; Hoogstraten & Vorst, 1978; Van Zelst, 1952a, 1952b). In evaluating the relationship of group cohesiveness to group effectiveness, it is important to determine whether the group members accept problem solution as the group goal. The evidence suggests that cohesive groups are more effective than noncohesive groups in achieving those goals accepted for the group (Seashore, 1954; Shaw & Shaw, 1962).

Group compatibility may be considered a more general assembly characteristic than cohesiveness, although both factors refer to harmonious relations among group members. The study of compatibility and its effects on group problem solving has been limited almost entirely to need compatibility, and most investigations have derived from Schutz's (1955, 1958) theory of interpersonal relations. The general findings from these studies indicate that compatible groups are more effective than incompatible groups (Schutz, 1955, 1958; Reddy & Byrnes, 1972).

Another aspect of group composition that influences group performance is the degree to which the personal characteristics of group members are similar or dissimilar. It should be obvious that most problem solving requires a variety of abilities, skills, and knowledge: therefore, heterogeneous group composition should facilitate group problem solving. Much of the research in this area has been devoted to ability heterogeneity-homogeneity. Again, some studies failed to find the expected relationship (Shaw, 1960), but the majority of studies find that heterogeneous ability groups are more effective than homogeneous ability groups (Goldman, 1965; Laughlin, Branch, & Johnson, 1969). Heterogeneity with respect to personality characteristics also appears to facilitate group problem solving (Hoffman, 1959; Hoffman & Maier, 1961).

The relationship of other kinds of homogeneity-heterogeneity of group composition on problem solving is not so clear. For example, mixed-sex groups have been found to perform both more efficiently (Hoffman & Maier, 1961) and less effectively (Clement & Schiereck, 1973) than same-sex groups. It is likely that the effects of this kind of group composition may depend upon other factors, such as type of task and leadership behavior. Similarly, investigations of racially heterogeneous-homogeneous groups have yielded conflicting results. Racially mixed groups (black and white college students) were found to be more effective (Fenelon & Megargee, 1971; Ruhe & Allen, 1977), less effective (Ruhe & Eatman, 1977), and equally as effective (Ruhe, 1972) in comparison with racially homogeneous groups.

In summary, ability heterogeneity clearly promotes effective group problem solving, personality heterogeneity appears to facilitate group problem solving, and the effects of other types of heterogeneity are apparently dependent upon other factors.

**Group Structure**   The kind of structure the group develops or has imposed upon it influences several aspects of group process, such as conformity behavior, member reactions, and degree of cooperation among group members. Thus one might expect that group structure would also be related to problem-solving effectiveness. The limited research that has been conducted to examine this expected relationship has yielded inconsistent results. No differences in performance between structured and unstructured groups were found in three studies (Hall & Williams, 1966; Shaw, 1959a, 1959b), whereas unstructured groups performed better than structured groups in two studies (Hall & Williams, 1970; Ford, Nemiroff, & Pasmore, 1977). It appears that group structure interferes with group problem solving under some conditions but has little or no effect in other circumstances.

**Leader Behavior**   One of the most pervasive beliefs in our society is that "good" leadership promotes effective group action. Empirical evidence on group problem solving generally supports this belief, although what constitutes "good" leadership is often controversial. Groups with leaders, in comparison with leaderless groups, usually are more effective problem solvers, although the degree to which this is so depends upon the source of the leader's authority (Goldman & Fraas, 1965; Walker, 1976).

More importantly, the kind of behavior exemplified by the leader influences group effectiveness. In general, a leader who provides direction and structure for the group facilitates group problem solving (Morse & Reimer, 1956; Shaw, 1955; Stogdill, 1974), but whether and to what extent this is true depends upon situational and task variables. As revealed in Fiedler's theory and related research (see Chapter 9), a directive, controlling, managing leader facilitates group performance when the situation is either highly favorable (leader-member relations good, the task is structured, and the leader's power position is strong) or highly unfavorable (leader-member relations poor, task unstructured, and leader's power position weak), whereas a leader who is relationship-oriented will have more effective groups when the situation is moderately favorable to the leader.

## Factors that Inhibit Effective Group Problem Solving

Most of the variables that facilitate effective group problem solving are also related to poor group performance, but of course in the opposite direction. That is, conditions like lack of cohesiveness, incompatibility, and inappropriate leader behavior inhibit effective group problem solving. These effects will not be reiterated here; instead, we will examine some aspects of groups and group process that are especially detrimental to effective group performance. Many things may impede effective group action, but we will limit our discussion here to three aspects that appear to be especially disadvantageous for group problem solving, namely, pressures toward uniformity, participation biases, and status and power differences.

**Pressure toward Uniformity** One of the most notable processes that occurs in groups is conformity behavior (see Chapter 8). When a group member deviates from group norms or behaves in ways that are different from the behaviors of most group members, he or she is subjected to a variety of pressures from others to alter the behavior to agree with that of the majority. Although conformity is necessary to some extent to bring some order into group interaction, undue pressures toward uniformity can have serious consequences for effective group problem solving. The desire for unanimity, for example, can lead to premature decisions by the group—decisions that are made before enough information has been acquired to permit the best or perhaps even an adequate decision. Group members who disagree with the majority view may withhold their opinions because they do not wish to be different or because they believe that everyone else in the group agrees with the majority (Schanck, 1932). Furthermore, the pressures toward uniformity may prevent members of the group from seeking additional information or consulting outside experts (Janis, 1972).

The detrimental effects of pressures toward uniformity have been observed in several studies (Hoffman, 1978). For example, in one study groups ranging in size from two to five persons were asked to solve Maier's Horse-Trading problem* (Thomas & Fink, 1961). Almost 64 percent of the groups gave unanimous answers after group discussion, despite instructions that group members could disregard the discussion if they wished. Furthermore, almost half of the groups giving unanimous answers were

*Maier's Horse-Trading Problem is as follows: A man buys a horse for $60 and sells it for $70. He then buys the same horse again for $80 and sells it for $90. How much money did he make in the horse-trading business?

incorrect. Pressures toward uniformity obviously led to poor decisions in many groups, even on a very simple arithmetic problem. Evidence that this effect is indeed a consequence of pressures toward uniformity may be derived from a study by Maier and Solem (1952), again using the horse-trading problem. When the majority initially gave the correct answer, 60 percent of the group members who were incorrect initially accepted the correct answer after group discussion. But when the majority was initially incorrect, only 46 percent of those who were incorrect adopted the correct answer after group discussion. (This effect occurred only in groups that did not have an appointed leader. A leader who ensured that minority opinion could be heard eliminated this effect.)

The deleterious effects of pressures toward uniformity are likely to be exacerbated if group members have low confidence in their ability to solve the problem (Hochbaum, 1954), if they are highly attracted to the group (Jackson & Saltzstein, 1958), when the majority is relatively large (Asch, 1951; Gerard, Wilhelmy, & Conolley, 1968), or when other factors that encourage conformity are operating in the group.

**Participation Biases**   The degree to which group members participate in group discussion and other group activities varies with a number of factors. We noted earlier (see Figure 6-1) that distribution of participation in a group is unequal (Bales et al., 1951). Typically, a few group members account for a majority of the total participation in group activities, and this unequal distribution of participation increases with increasing group size. The potentially detrimental consequences of this aspect of group process are shown by a study of the impact of the talkative member on group problem solving (Riecken, 1958). The most talkative and the least talkative group members were identified in groups that had solved two previous problems. Then either the most or the least talkative group member was given a hint about the best solution to a third problem. When the most talkative member was given the hint, the solution was accepted by most groups, but when the least talkative member had this information, the solution was usually rejected by the group. Furthermore, it has been shown that the solution receiving the largest number of favorable comments is usually adopted and that most of the comments come from a single member (Hoffman & Maier, 1964). These findings do not "prove" that unequal distribution of participation necessarily impedes effective group problem solving, but they do suggest that it will be detrimental to effective problem solution when the high participators have incorrect information or do not have the best solution. It has been shown that the relationship between participation and influence on group decision holds regardless of the quality of solutions attained by the group (Mann, 1961).

Other aspects of intragroup communication may also interfere with group performance. For example, the expression of self-oriented needs appears to be related to ineffective group performance (Fouriezos, Hutt, & Guetzkow, 1950), and the degree of self-confidnece exemplified by group members may determine whether their ideas and information are accepted by the group, even when the information is accurate and task-relevant (Shaw, 1963; Shaw & Penrod, 1962a). It is probable that the more self-confident group members sometimes prevent a group from utilizing all the task-relevant information available to it (Hoffman, 1978).

**Status and Power Differences**    Status and power, although conceptually independent, often covary in groups and have similar effects on group process. For example, both high-status persons and powerful group members have more influence on the group and its decisions than group members of lower status and less power (see Chapter 8). Studies of Air Force crews indicate that the lowest-ranked member had little influence on group decisions, even when that member had the correct solution to the problem (Torrance, 1954). Similarly, Maier and Hoffman (1960) have found that the group typically spends much of its time either supporting or rejecting the ideas of the high-status person rather than searching for alternative solutions to the problem. Furthermore, persons who are strongly identified with the group, and presumably are willing to work hard to help the group achieve its goals, are the ones most likely to accept the suggestions of the authority in the group (Maier & Hoffman, 1961).

It has been demonstrated that one of the reasons group members accede to the wishes of the more powerful group member is the potential threat of such members to others in the group (Mellinger, 1956; Read, 1962). Even implied threats can produce harmful effects on group process (Deutsch & Krauss, 1962; Stolte, 1978, Tjosvold & Sagaria, 1978). When power to punish others is actually used, the effects are even more severe (Hoffman, 1978; Sheley & Shaw, 1979). And when group members have power, they are likely to use it (Kipnis, 1972).

This brief consideration of problem-solving groups reveals that groups may be used effectively to solve a variety of problems, but it also shows that groups are not a panacea for all problem-solving difficulties. Group problem solving is complex and influenced by a multitude of variables. Many aspects of group process facilitate problem solving, but many others interfere with effective group problem solving.

## EDUCATIONAL GROUPS

Another kind of specialized group is one created to facilitate learning by group members. These groups are designed to help the members achieve academically, rather than to learn about group processes.* Groups have been used in many ways in educational settings, but procedures have not always been based upon known principles of group behavior. For example, ability grouping or "streaming," which we discussed in Chapter 7, is an example of a procedure based more on untested beliefs than on empirical evidence. It will be recalled that heterogeneous grouping generally promotes academic achievement to a greater extent than homogeneous ability grouping. Some grouping procedures are facilitative, however, and we will examine three of these for purposes of illustration.

### Sociometric Groups

Many group theorists believe that good interpersonal relations may be more important for effective group action than abilities and skills possessed by members of the group. The underlying assumption is that a group has only a finite amount of energy available to it and any energy expended in alleviating interpersonal conflicts will detract from the energy available for the group task (e.g., Cattell's syntality theory described in Chapter 2). Several approaches to grouping for good interpersonal relations have been proposed (e.g., complementarity, compatibility, etc.), but the most common procedure used with educational groups is sociometric choice. In this procedure, students are grouped according to their stated preferences; i.e., the reported attractions and repulsions they feel for one another (Moreno, 1934). A typical sociometric test asks students to list the persons they would most like to work with and those they would least like to work with. It is assumed that when individuals are grouped with those persons that they prefer, the group will be compatible, cohesive, and characterized by few interpersonal conflicts as compared with groups composed of persons who reject each other. For example, Moreno regrouped residents in an institution for delinquent girls and found that morale and discipline improved. Similarly, Zeleny (1939b) reported than when pupils in school were regrouped according to their sociometric choices to maximize mutual acceptance, morale rose.

Since the morale of groups is increased by appropriate sociometric grouping, it might be expected that members of such groups would learn more efficiently than members of less cohesive groups. Only a few experiments have been conducted to test the proposition that sociometrically cohesive groups result in greater academic achievement. One of these studies (Shaw & Shaw, 1962) was described in Chapter 7. It will be recalled that more cohesive groups initially performed better (i.e., learned to spell more words) than less cohesive groups, but became less efficient in the later parts of the study. Observations reported by the teacher suggested

*Groups that are designed to help the person via the group process itself are called *experiential groups* and will be discussed later in this chapter.

that this decrease in academic achievement by the more cohesive groups was caused by the greater social activities engaged in by the members of the cohesive groups. The energy that might have been devoted to the task of learning to spell the assigned words was actually expended in social behavior. By contrast, the lower cohesive groups engaged in greater individual study which led to greater achievement gains.

A somewhat similar study was conducted by Lott and Lott (1966). They suggested that groups composed of individuals who state a preference for each other (i.e., sociometrically cohesive groups) have drive arousal consequences for the group members. This increased drive was expected to lead to more learning and better retention than in less cohesive groups. Two hundred and six students in each of the fourth and fifth grades were grouped according to IQs and sociometric choices, forming four kinds of groups: high cohesive, high IQ; high cohesive, low IQ; low cohesive, high IQ; and low cohesive, low IQ. Members of each group were tested on two verbal learning tasks, followed by tests for retention and relearning. The high-IQ groups learned significantly more in the high-cohesive groups; there was no significant difference between the high- and low-cohesive groups composed of low-IQ members, although there was a tendency for the low-cohesive groups to perform better than the high-cohesive groups. This finding suggests that the effects of sociometric grouping on academic achievement are complex and probably vary with the kinds of individuals who compose the group.

A somewhat different approach to the study of compatible groups was adopted by Thelen (1966). He recognized that each teacher teaches some children more effectively than others, and consequently attempted to group teachers and children who would be compatible. He asked thirteen teachers to list the names of students they thought "got a lot out of class" and those who "got very little out of class." Nominees were then tested on a multidimensional inventory designed to measure attitudes, preferences, semantic projections, and similar characteristics. By use of this information, "teachable" classes were composed for each teacher; i.e., the pupils in the class were chosen to be like those that the teacher had nominated as "getting a lot out of class." From the remaining students, thirteen control groups were composed by the usual administrative procedures. The teachables presumably were more compatible, at least with the teacher, than were the controls. Comparison of the two kinds of groups indicated that (1) eleven of the thirteen teachable classes received higher marks, one received the same, and one received lower marks from their teachers than did the corresponding control classes, and (2) five of the thirteen teachables showed superior gains on achievement tests and eight showed inferior gains as compared with the corresponding controls. In short, the teachers apparently perceived that pupils did better in the more compatible groups, but the objective data failed to verify this perception. It is unclear, however, whether the procedure followed by Thelen actually resulted in more compatible groups.

In summary, the evidence concerning the effects of sociometric and related types of groupings on academic achievement is only moderately consistent. In general, the data suggest that groups composed to be compatible or cohesive in terms of sociometric choices learn more than less cohesive groups when they want to learn; however, this effect operates more strongly (or perhaps only) for individuals having greater abilities.

**Peer Learning Groups**

In some academic situations learning groups are formed on bases other than interpersonal relationships among group members, either randomly or for some theoretical or practical reason. The underlying assumption is that members of peer groups contribute to each other's academic achievement; working together facilitates learning. That students are capable of helping each other in the learning process is not a new idea, of course, and there have been many programs employing cross-age helping, tutoring by more advanced or more capable students, and the like. However, procedures using the group process itself as a means of facilitating learning is of relatively recent origin.

One attempt to employ groups to facilitate learning is called the teams-games-tournament (TGT) technique (DeVries, Edwards, & Fennessey, 1973). As the label implies, the technique involves three parts—teams, games, and a tournament. The *teams* are composed of elementary or high school students who vary in achievement levels. Typically, a team consists of one high achiever, one low achiever, and two average achievers. The purpose of this grouping procedure is to equalize teams with respect to achievement level; i.e., the desire is to have all teams about average in achievement level. The *games* used for instructional purposes are quite varied. They have in common that they can be played by a small group of individuals in a short period of time so that several games can be played per class period. Each student's performance on the game can be scored, and team scores are created by summing individual member scores. Teams are competitively compared on the basis of their total or average scores in a weekly *tournament.*

The TGT technique has been employed in a number of courses and grade levels. For example, TGT has enhanced the development of skills in mathematics in junior high school students (Edwards, DeVries, & Snyder, 1972), and in social studies in seventh grade students (Edwards & DeVries, 1974) and in tenth to twelfth graders (DeVries, Edwards, & Wells, 1974). The technique was also successfully used in teaching language arts skills in a third grade class (DeVries & Mescon, 1975). TGT pupils showed a significant increase in performance on both general elementary English tests and a treatment-specific test of language arts skills. In all these studies, students taught by the TGT technique apparently learned more than students taught by more traditional methods that were essentially individual instructional procedures.

Another peer group learning procedure has been developed for teaching medical and dental students (Small, 1975). The method of teaching immunology presents clinically relevant problems to randomly assembled groups of four persons each. Each group member is given part of the information needed to complete the program, and group members must share their knowledge during the process of problem solution. The objective is to have students apply their knowledge of basic science to clinical problems, thus learning more about the field of immunology. For example, one problem is entitled "Is Stud Smith the Father?" and involves a fictitious paternity case. Solution requires a knowledge of the genetics of immunoglobin allotypes, blood types, and similar information. Typically, eight problems are attempted, with group membership being shifted following completion of each problem.

Following an individually administered pretest on the problem content, each group meets and members work cooperatively on the task. The group activity is divided into two parts: discussion of the pretest and problem solution. During the first part, each person shares the correct answers and explanations he or she has been given by the professor. Problem-solving activity immediately follows the pretest discussion. After the group has arrived at a solution and recorded it, members are given the correct answer and encouraged to discuss any mistakes they may have made. The whole process requires from two to three hours per problem. This procedure is reported to be an effective teaching model (Small, 1974, 1975).

The employment of peer groups to facilitate academic achievement is not extensive, but the evidence to date suggests that groups may be used effectively for this purpose.

### Team Teaching and Academic Achievement

Still another attempt to apply the principles of group behavior to the educational process is team teaching. In this procedure, a group of teachers is assigned responsibility for a large group of children, in contrast to the more common procedure of one teacher with a smaller group of children in a self-contained classroom. In theory, teaching teams are composed in such a way that all the necessary resources are available in each team. In teaching the children, each teacher contributes his or her particular expertise to the total team effort. Actual teaching often occurs in small subgroups with one or more of the team members participating in the educational process. The added resourses available to each group of students is expected to lead to greater academic achievement.

Evaluation of this educational approach is difficult, and relatively few well-controlled studies have been reported in the literature. One study conducted by the author will be described briefly to indicate the kinds of effects that team teaching may have upon academic achievement. This study compared the academic progress of pupils in three elementary schools that employed the team teaching approach with three control schools that used the more traditional self-contained classroom approach. The study covered a two-year period, beginning with the first full-year operation of the three team teaching schools. The Stanford Achievement Tests were administered to all pupils in the second, fourth, and sixth grades near the beginning of the school year and again near the end of the school year. The results from the first year of this study are shown in Figure 11-1. It can be seen that the pupils in the team-teaching schools showed greater achievement gains than those in control schools for the second and fourth grades, but lesser gains in the sixth grade. In the second year, pupils in the second grade maintained their advantage in the team-teaching schools, those in the fourth grade again made significantly greater gains in the team-teaching schools than in the control schools, and the sixth-grade pupils in the control schools maintained their advantage over those in the team-teaching schools (although there were some reversals in specific areas of learning). In short, the differences observed in the first year generally endured at least until the end of the second year.

The effects of team teaching on pupil achievement in the second and fourth grades is consistent with our knowledge of effects in adult groups. The diversity of ideas, opinions, abilities, etc., that is available in a group usually leads to more effective group decisions than either individual

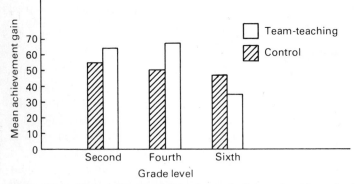

**Figure 11-1**   Mean achievement gains by pupils in team-teaching schools and in control schools.

decisions (Barnlund, 1959; Husband, 1940; Marjorie E. Shaw, 1932) or decisions by groups that are either homogeneous or do not permit minority opinion to be heard (Hoffman, 1959; Hoffman & Maier, 1961). Team teaching not only increases the range of abilities and information available in the team but also ensures that each team member will be exposed to ideas, knowledge, and opinions of other team members. Decisions of teams should, therefore, be more effective then the decisions of individual teachers in the control schools, which in turn would be expected to produce greater achievement by their pupils. Furthermore, the pupils will be exposed to the greater range of abilities represented in the team, and the probability that a given child in the class will find a teacher with whom he or she is compatible is greatly increased. All these factors probably contribute to the greater academic achievement of children in the team-teaching schools.

The failure to observe a similar effect in the sixth grade is not consistent with this interpretation, but other considerations may account for the differences between the younger and older pupils. First, the sixth-grade pupils had a longer history of experience in the more traditional self-contained classroom situation which may have created problems of adjusting to the new situation in the team-teaching schools. Second, it is possible that differences in developmental levels of pupils may have produced the grade level differences in response to the team-teaching classes. Pupils in the sixth grade have reached the stage of self-assertion; they are concerned with establishing independence, etc., and may therefore respond more effectively to the relatively structured situation in more traditional settings. Whatever the reason, teaching teams appear to be more effective than single teachers for pupils in the lower grade levels.

To summarize, principles of group behavior may be applied in the classroom to facilitate academic achievement (although of course group process is only one of the many factors influencing academic achievement). In general, academic achievement is facilitated by (1) heterogeneous ability grouping, (2) sociometric grouping for mutual attraction, and (3) team-teaching methods of instruction. Application of these procedures does not invariably lead to greater academic achievement, however, since other factors may interfere with effective learning. Some attempt to combine complementary heterogeneous grouping of pupils in conjunction with team-teaching methods of instruction may be the most effective way of facilitating academic achievement.

## EXPERIENTIAL GROUPS

An experiential group is a special kind of group ordinarily formed for some explicit purpose that presumably can be achieved through participation in groups. The essential characteristic of the experiential group is that group members hope to benefit from the group experience itself (Lakin, 1972).* In everyday life, everyone experiences many role relationships that are governed by social norms and that imply fairly specific status relationships. These role relationships occur in many settings such as family (mother, father, son, daughter, brother, sister, etc.), the work environment (boss, coworker, subordinate, etc.), social situations (friend, foe, rival, etc.), and many others. Although there are norms concerning appropriate role behavior, these are often implicit rather than explicit, and many role occupants discover that their relationships with others are often not as harmonious as they would like them to be. These group members want to establish good interpersonal relationships in their groups but are unaware of the reasons for being unable to do so. Individuals rarely give conscious thought to their role relationships, and when they do, it is often difficult to accept the negative consequences of their own behavior. For example, few persons can easily accept that they are aggressive, snobbish, insulting, or defensive in their interactions with others. Theoretically, by becoming aware of how one relates to others and why one acts that way, one should become more effective in interpersonal relationships. Again theoretically, participation in an experiential group should help an individual become aware of the nature and consequences of his or her behavior in groups.

Experiential groups occur in many forms and for many different reasons. They are variously labeled as T-groups, sensitivity training groups, therapy groups, encounter groups, authentic encounter groups, personal growth groups, human relations groups, experiential groups, and perhaps by other terms. Although all such groups have in common the general purpose of benefitting from the experience itself, they differ in the particular kinds of benefits that are emphasized and desired by group members. Lakin (1972) identified three types of experiential groups, based primarily upon the motivations of participants: learning, therapeutic, and expressive. The purposes of *learning* groups are to gain understanding of group influences on the individual group member's responses, to obtain feedback concerning the effects of the member's own behavior on others, and to facilitate group communication. Sensitivity training groups, T-groups, and human relations groups are examples of learning groups.

*Therapeutic* groups represent one of the earliest attempts to use group processes for changing individual functioning. Individuals participate in therapeutic groups to repair something in themselves, to correct emotional experiences, to eliminate disvalued aspects of the personality, to change

---

*The benefits that group members hope to attain through participation may take many forms, including the correction of some disvalued aspect of self, achievement of greater emotional expressiveness, learning about one's own and others' behavior in groups, and/or learning about groups.

personality style, etc. Persons who enter into a therapeutic experiential group are concerned with changing their perceived selves so that they become more congruent with their ideal selves. They want to improve their own psychological functioning. Consider, for example, a therapist who has several clients each of whom expresses dissatisfaction with some aspect of his or her personality. In all probability, the various complaints will be poorly articulated; the clients will have only vague notions of the true source of their dissatisfaction and may be unable or unwilling to perceive or accept many aspects of their personality. In attempting to help these clients, the therapist may elect to bring them together in an "encounter" group. During the group sessions the therapist serves as leader and encourages participants to freely express their feelings about themselves—their anxieties and concerns, frustrations and emotional reactions in interpersonal relations. Participants are encouraged to tell others in the group how they are perceived and what feelings their behavior evokes in others. In short, the therapist tries to help each individual to work through personal problems by encouraging open discussion and confrontation. The particular ways that group interaction is guided may depend upon many aspects of the group situation, including the therapist's own beliefs and skills as a facilitator of the therapeutic group process.*

*Expressive* groups are based upon the motivations of participants to achieve greater emotional expressiveness for its own sake. Persons who join expressive groups believe that a happier life is associated with greater emotional expressiveness and that participation in experiential groups can help them learn to express their emotions more freely and completely than they have been able to in the past. Those who seek such an experience often believe that their emotional feelings have been suppressed by the strictures of society; they feel unable to exhibit their passions with the fervor that is required for the enjoyment of life to its fullest extent. Relative to learning and therapeutic groups, expressive groups often emphasize the hedonistic aspect of social interaction. Expressive groups are a relatively recent phenomenon which has many of the characteristics of a fad.

### Historical Antecedents of Experiential Groups

The use of group action as an end in itself is a process that grew out of many diverse disciplines. Harbingers of experiential groups can be detected in the history of social psychology, psychotherapy, and industrial psychology, and perhaps in other disciplines as well. In the last several years, the use of experiential groups by industry, education, religion, clinical psychology, and similar interest collectivities has grown so precipi-

---

*Excellent descriptions of the various models of group psychotherapy may be found in Shaffer and Galinsky (1974).

tiously that some writers view this phenomenon as a social movement (e.g., Back, 1973; Lakin, 1972), and indeed the experiential group phenomenon does have many characteristics of a social movement. A social movement is a form of collective behavior which is relatively long-lasting and has a clear program or purpose (Toch, 1965). It is an attempt by a large number of persons to solve collectively a problem they have or believe they have in common. The sine qua non of a social movement is that it is aimed at promoting or resisting change in society at large. The widespread use of experiential groups involves collective behavior, and it has been long-lasting (at least, from the early 1930s to the present); however, it cannot be said to have a clear program or purpose, and in many cases it has nothing to do with changes in the society at large. Instead, the purposes of involvement in experiential groups vary greatly (e.g., to change personality style, to gain understanding of group processes, to improve emotional expressiveness, etc.), and there is no evidence that the many different organizations using group action as an end in itself are working collectively to solve a common problem. Historically, the experiential group phenomenon is best described as the emergence of a popularized technique for improving some aspect or aspects of personal or interpersonal functioning.

The precursors of the experiential group procedure growing out of psychotherapy have been noted in the work of Freud, Reich, Klein, Bion, Moreno, Foulkes, and others (Back, 1973; Lakin, 1972). The precursors of experiential groups are seen clearly in group psychotherapy, which is designed to aid the therapist in treating psychological disorders in the individual patient. Consider a situation in which the therapist is trying to help neurotic individuals. The number of persons in the group is eight, and meetings are held twice a week with the therapist-leader and the group members sitting informally around a table. At first, the group members direct their comments and questions to the "leader" and expect him or her to respond with authoritative statements. Instead, the therapist-leader responds by asking the group member what he or she thinks about the question. Group members usually find this frustrating, but eventually this procedure forces them out of their dependency orientation, and they begin to talk with each other rather than to the therapist, who now functions as an interpreter, catalyst, and source of information (Foulkes & Anthony, 1957). The reader will undoubtedly be impressed by the similarity of this description to the description of group formation in sensitivity groups by Bennis and Shepard (see Chapter 4).

Another direct precursor of experiential group phenomena may be observed in Moreno's (1946) psychodrama. This approach is a variant of group psychotherapy and is used for psychotherapeutic purposes. Basically, Moreno created dramatic plays in which patients acted out their feelings toward significant others in their lives (e.g., mother, father, love object), represented in the drama by other persons who role-played the characters (i.e., the significant others in the life of a given patient). Theoretically, patients are able to express feelings toward the surrogate significant others that they are unable to express in real life. Through these expressions they become aware of feelings and attitudes that have been suppressed because they are socially unacceptable or personally painful. Although Moreno developed this procedure for use with hospitalized patients, he sometimes used it with others as a short-term training experience. The similarity of psychodrama and certain aspects of modern-day experiential groups is obvious.

Signs of the experiential group phenomenon are equally apparent in the history of social psychology, most notably in the work of Kurt Lewin (1936, 1948, 1951). Lewin was one of the prime movers in the development of the National Training Laboratory (NTL), which was one of the first units organized for sensitivity training groups. The establishment of this laboratory was the outgrowth of a serendipitous event which occurred at a summer workshop designed to explore the use of small groups as a means of personal and social change. The research team came from the Research Center for Group Dynamics at the Massachusetts Institute of Technology which had been created by Lewin for the purpose of integrating research and theory on groups. The participants in the workshop were educators, public officials, and representatives of intergroup organizations. The participants were divided into three groups, each with its own trainers, researchers, and observers. Trainers and researchers of the three groups met each evening to review the events within the groups and to assess their progress. At one of these meetings, three participants appeared and asked permission to listen to the discussion (Back, 1973). Permission was granted, and during the discussion one participant mentioned that her experience did not agree with what the trainers were saying. A lively discussion followed, and the participants were invited to return the next night. The contributions of participants thus became an integral part of the review process.

This event probably represents the starting point of the development of the many laboratories, training programs, workshops, and other group intervention procedures that appeared later. The trainers and researchers involved were significant contributors to theory, research, and practice relative to experiential groups.

Finally, events in the field of industrial psychology involved elements of the experiential group process. In Chapter 5 we discussed the Westinghouse studies in which it was discovered that interpersonal factors were more important determinants of group performance than lighting. As a consequence, investigators directed their attention toward informal interactions in small work groups. At about the same time a counseling program was started at Westinghouse which was designed to resolve personal problems and conflicts within the group. Group orientation programs were also established in other industries. These programs probably were not as significant in the history of experiential groups as those in psychotherapy and social psychology, but they, too, contained aspects that influenced later developments.

## Experiential Group Processes

The preceding brief historical account perhaps provides some basis for understanding the great variety of experiential groups that are observed today. With such a heterogeneous background, it is not surprising that there is little coherent theory about current practices in experiential groups. Nevertheless, there is general agreement concerning the importance of the small group as a vehicle for change and about its influence on the individual and on the organization in which the group is embedded. There are also certain processes that are common to all experiential groups. For example, Lakin (1972) identified the most common processes as:

1   Facilitating emotional expressiveness
2   Generating feelings of belongingness
3   Fostering a norm of self-disclosure as a condition of group membership
4   Sampling personal behaviors
5   Making sanctioned interpersonal comparison
6   Sharing responsibility for leadership and direction with the appointed leader

All the variables influencing group behavior that have been discussed in this book may be expected to influence experiential group processes, although not all these effects have been systematically observed and described. It may seem obvious that the personal characteristics of participants are related to experiential group processes. For example, Lakin (1972) notes that some members are avidly listened to and their opinions highly valued whereas others are generally ignored; some are assertive and exert much influence upon the activities of the group while others sit passively and accept events as they occur; some members are defensive and try to protect their "ego," but some reveal their innermost feelings; and some participants are happy to be a group member whereas others strive to establish their individuality. The nature of these individual characteristics should have a predictable influence upon the *content* of group interactions, but experiences in the group permit each participant to become aware of his or her own characteristics and the effects they are having on others.

In general, it may be expected that the many personal characteristics examined in Chapter 6 (e.g., age, sex, individual needs, personality characteristics, etc.) will also influence behavior in experiential groups. Unfortunately, little attention has been devoted to this important factor in experiential group process. The few studies that have been conducted have been concerned primarily with the question of whether and to what extent the outcomes of group experiences are different for different kinds of persons. For example, Bennis, Burke, Cutter, Harrington, and Hoffman (1957) studied twelve business administration students in a semester-long T-group. They attempted to make differential predictions about changes in the participant's perceptions of self and ideal self on the basis of standardized measures of personality. Relationships between personality characteristics and perceptual changes were negligible. Failure to find major differences as a function of personality variations was also reported by Steele (1968). On the other hand, Mathis (1958) and Harrison and Lubin (1965) reported data supporting the proposition that individual differences are related to the effects of participation in experiential groups. Mathis reasoned that tendencies toward open communication of both affection and agression and the existence of intrapersonal conflicts would increase receptivity to training. He administered a sentence-completion scale which was designed to measure these factors. At the conlcusion of T-group training, the ten highest scorers and the ten lowest scorers (of fifty participants) were interviewed. The high scorers were rated higher on sensitivity, sophistication, and productivity. In a somewhat similar study, Harrison and Lubin (1965) divided participants into person-oriented/work-oriented categories on the basis of questionnaire responses. Trainers made judgments of learning during training and concluded that person-oriented participants were more warm, expressive, and comfortable, whereas the work-oriented participants learned more during the training period. Unfortunately, the conclusions from both the Mathis and the Harrison and Lubin studies are based upon highly subjective data obtained at the conclusion or during training sessions.

The particular combination of personal characteristics may be a more important factor in experiential groups than the particular attributes of group members per se. For instance, if all members are combative, mutual defensiveness may preclude effective interaction (Lakin, 1972). Despite the importance of group composition, little attention has been devoted to its effects in experiential groups. Available evidence, however, reveals the need to learn more about group composition effects in order to create more effective experiential groups. For example, Harrison and Lubin

(1965) studied the effects of homogeneity-heterogeneity of group membership upon learning in T-groups. Four group compositions were formed with
respect to group members' preferences for structure: (1) homogeneous—
all preferred high structure; (2) homogeneous—all preferred moderate
structure; (3) homogeneous—all preferred low structure; (4)
heterogeneous—half preferred high structure and half preferred low
structure. Participants rated each other's behavior, and staff interviews
were conducted during the third, tenth, and fourteenth weeks after
training ended. Although differences between groups were not great, the
effects were sufficiently strong to suggest that more learning occurred in
the heterogeneous groups. The authors concluded that homogeneous
groups do not provide the confrontation needed for optimal learning. They
also suggested that feelings of completion, cohesion, and emotional
satisfaction of members may be inappropriate criteria for evaluating the
impact of training groups. These data are subjective and desirable controls
were absent. Nevertheless, it is interesting to note that they agree with data
obtained from problem-solving groups. The fact that both heterogeneous
problem-solving groups and heterogeneous experiential groups are found
to be more effective than their homogeneous counterparts makes the
Harrison-Lubin conclusions more credible.

Some of the effects of member compatibility have also been observed
(Reddy, 1972a, 1972b). In the first study, forty interdenominational
missionaries participated in a human relations sensitivity training program.
Participants were divided into four groups, two compatible and two
incompatible in the area of affection. Affection compatibility was predetermined according to participants' responses to the FIRO-B scales and the
formulas developed by Schutz (see Chapter 7). An inventory designed to
measure self-actualization (roughly, the degree to which an individual
approximates maximum realization of his or her potential) was completed
by group members one week before training began and again two days
after training ended. Members of the two incompatible groups gained
significantly more on the measure of self-actualization than did compatible
groups. In the second study (Reddy, 1972b), each participant's compatibility with each other member in the group was computed, and the mean of
his or her dyadic compatibility scores was correlated with pre/post
differences in measures of self-actualization. Significant correlations
ranged from −.66 to +.73. In this instance, whether compatibility or
incompatibility was more effective in changing self-actualization depended
upon the overall compatibility of the group. If the group mean compatibility indicated that members were mutually exchanging affection, members
whose dyadic compatibility deviated toward avoidance of affection made
more progress; in groups where overall compatibility indicated that

members were avoiding the exchange of affection, members whose compatibility score deviated toward mutual expression of affection gained more on self-actualization measures.*

The structural aspects of experiential groups also influence the interaction process. According to Lakin (1972) the roles that emerge in experiential groups are central elements in group functioning and include, at minimum, leader, initiator, clarifier, and harmonizer. The roles that are specified at the beginning of a typical experiential group interaction are leader (trainer) and group members. However, as we have seen, neither of these general roles is correctly perceived by group members. The leader is expected to behave in a much more authoritative manner than he or she actually does, and there are no indications of how members are expected to behave. Therefore, the true roles emerge from group interaction. It seems intuitively evident that the kinds of roles which emerge in the group affect the functioning of the group and its effect on group members. Unfortunately, almost no research has been done on this aspect of experiential group process. A study by Culbert (1968), however, suggests that investigation of role effects would increase our understanding of experiential group process. In the Culbert study, the effects of more and less self-disclosing trainers (i.e., trainers who did or did not reveal much about themselves to others) were examined. Group members were divided into dyads which met once a week with the trainer for one semester. Group interactions were tape-recorded, and randomly selected segments of the content were analyzed. Participants also completed an inventory that was designed to measure the degree to which one person perceives another as having positive regard, empathy, congruence, and unconditionality of regard toward him or her. The content analysis revealed that less self-disclosing trainers intervened more but spoke for a shorter time than more self-disclosing trainers. In addition, two experienced clinicians gave their impressions of the trainers' performances as revealed by the transcripts of the taped group interactions; the more self-disclosing trainer was judged to be more genuine, more involved, and more personal than the less self-disclosing trainer. Contrary to the author's hypothesis, participants viewed their relationships with the less self-disclosing trainer as more "therapeutic" than their relationships with the more self-disclosing trainer. Finally, participants with the more self-disclosing trainer achieved self-awareness more quickly than participants with the less self-disclosing trainer.

This very limited evidence does not permit firm conclusions about the

---

*These effects may have been an artifact of the method of analysis. That is, those persons who deviate away from the group mean have more room to change, on the average, than those who deviate in the same direction as the group tendency.

effects of role differences upon experiential group process, but it does indicate that trainer roles affect experiential group outcomes and suggests that further research would yield useful data.

The norms governing behavior in experiential groups are also different from those typically observed in more conventional groups. In most experiential groups explicit norms require frankness, expressiveness, warmth, and the like (Lakin, 1972) to a much greater extent than in other groups. Furthermore, it is expected that norms are less fixed than in conventional groups and hence can be revised or rejected as necessary to promote the aims of the group. Nevertheless, once the norm is established, it exerts pressures toward conformity just as norms in other kinds of groups. Pressures toward agreement are especially strong in experiential groups, perhaps because members of these groups must depend upon others for "social reality" (Sherif, 1936; Festinger, 1954). Since the situation is initially unstructured, each group member must validate his own perceptions and behavior by comparing them with the perceptions and behaviors of others.

It should be clear from this brief review that group processes in experiential groups are complex and many of the principles which apply to task-oriented groups also hold for experiential groups. The particular effects of variables influencing experiential group process are still understood only imperfectly and require further research.

### Effectiveness of Experiential Groups

An important question is whether and to what extent experiential groups are effective tools for achieving the goals for which they are designed. Attempts to answer this question are many and varied, but all suffer from theoretical and technical problems. An awareness of these problems will facilitate the evaluation of research findings concerning the effectiveness of experiential groups.

**Problems in Research**   As we noted above, the problems associated with research on the effectiveness of experiential groups are both theoretical and practical. The major theoretical problem is that there *is* no generally accepted theory about the experiences which a participant has in the group and the expected outcomes from those experiences (Schein & Bennis, 1965). This lack of theory is probably the result of the widely diverse uses of the group experience. There are at least three major applications of experiential groups (learning, therapeutic, and expressive; see pages 406–407), even if we ignore the many minor variations within each of the major classes. The basic problem is that a wide range of outcomes is expected by various practitioners, such as changes in attitude, in awareness, in motivation, in sensitivity to the feelings of others, in understanding of group process, in behavior in other groups, and so on. It is too much to expect that a single theory or a single set of specific procedures could be made relevant to all these different possible outcomes, but even in a specific setting with a more or less definite purpose there seems to be no clear statement about the relationship between the group experience and the expected outcome. For example, there is no precise explication of what is meant by such terms as "sensitivity to the feelings of others" nor about the kinds of group experiences that are expected to produce this desirable outcome. This problem must be dealt with before effective research can be carried out.

The practical problems are extensive and just as difficult to solve as the theoretical ones. In fact, the first practical problem derives, in part, from a theoretical problem, namely, that it is difficult to measure an outcome which is not clearly defined. But inadequate definition is only one of the problems involved in measuring group outcomes. Even if such expected outcomes as "increased self-awareness" or "increased understanding of group process" were clearly defined, at least two important problems would remain: (1) the problem of reliable and valid techniques for measuring whatever is supposed to change (e.g., awareness, understanding, etc.) and (2) the detection of change in awareness or understanding (or whatever is supposed to change). Change scores are notoriously unreliable because they are affected by events that have nothing to do with true change in the thing being measured.*

A second practical problem concerns the comparability of experimental and control groups. Individuals who participate in experiential groups are usually volunteers and consequently may differ in important ways from those who do not volunteer to participate in experiential groups. This lack of randomization in the assignment of individuals to experimental and control groups makes it very difficult to interpret any observed differences in the outcome of group process. Any change that appears to be the result of the group experience may really be the result of initial differences in group composition. Perhaps it is this problem that has led many investigators to forego the use of control groups and simply examine relationships between events occurring in the group and observed outcomes of the group experience. Unfortunately, this procedure creates more problems than it solves because the meaning of observed outcomes becomes highly ambiguous.

Research related to the effectiveness of experiential groups varies in

---

*The statistical complexities of change scores cannot be adequately delineated here. The interested reader may wish to consult Harris (1967) and/or Cronbach and Furby (1970) for excellent discussions of the problems of measuring change.

the degree to which these difficulties have been resolved, but no research study has overcome all of them. The reader should be alert to these issues when considering the evidence from research on experiential groups.

**Evaluative Research**  Various techniques have been used in attempting to evaluate the effects of experiential groups. The major ones are (1) self-report by participants, (2) reports by associates, and (3) behavioral measures. Perhaps the most widely used procedure (and the one most open to criticism) is to ask participants about their reactions to the group experience. In the typical study, participants are tested before and after the group experience, using either standard psychological tests, specially devised questionnaires, or interviews. Pre/post differences are attributed to the group experience, although, as we have seen, this attribution may not be correct. A consideration of some of the studies will be instructive.

*Personality change* has been investigated by a number of researchers, with generally mixed results. For example, Baumgartel and Goldstein (1967) administered the FIRO-B scales and the Allport-Vernon-Lindzey Study of Values to participants in a human relations training program before and after training. It was predicted that the FIRO-B scales would show positive changes in the expressed control area; results showed no change in expressed control but increased wanted control and decreased wanted affection. The Allport-Vernon-Lindzey Study of Values measures six value areas: theoretical, economic, aesthetic, social, political, and religious. It was predicted that after training participants would express less religious value and more political value than before training; the only change was toward greater aesthetic value. Since there was no control group, even the changes that were observed cannot be unequivocally attributed to the training experience. FIRO-B was also administered before and after training in a sensitivity program (Schutz & Allen, 1966). Thirty students in an education class at the University of California at Berkeley were used as controls. Schutz and Allen reported that pre/post correlations were lower in the sensitivity group than in the control group, but there was no specific statement of nature and direction of change. Similarly, Smith (1964) reported that members of human relations training groups showed a convergence toward median scores on the FIRO-B scales measuring needs for control and affection, whereas control group members did not. Thus the evidence concerning personality change as measured by the FIRO-B scales is mixed and generally not strongly supportive of the proposition that group experiences alter participants' personalities.

Research using other measures of personality yielded equally unclear results. In a study of the effects of nine weeks' experience in personal growth groups (Ware & Barr, 1977) pre and post measures were obtained using the Personal Orientation Inventory (POI), the Tennessee Self Concept Scale (TSCS), the Marlowe-Crowne Social Desirability Scale, and a Locus of Control (IE) Scale. Significant change as a function of the group experience was found for only three of the twelve dimensions measured by the POI; the participants in the personal growth groups increased in self-actualization, self-regard, and synergy. There was no overall change in self-concept, although there appeared to be change on the self-criticism subscale. Social desirability increased in some groups but not in others, and there was no effect on locus of control. Another study of T-groups found no difference between pre and post measures of self-concept (White, 1974). Similarly, a study of the effects of experiences in marathon groups by heroin abusers revealed no difference between experimental and control groups in locus of control (IE) and significant differences on only three of twenty semantic differential scales designed to measure attitudes toward self (Page & Kubiak, 1978).

Two studies designed to detect personality change on several personality dimensions yielded negative results. McLeish and Park (1972) examined a wide range of experiential groups, including a self-analytic group, a direct communications group, a Bales training group observing a self-analytic group, a Bales training group observing a direct communications group, a clinical group observing a self-analytic group, and a clinical group observing a direct communications group. In each case, the sixteen factor personality inventory (16-PF) was administered before and after the group experience. None of the sixteen personality characteristics supposedly measured by the 16-PF inventory showed any change as a result of the group experience. Negative findings were also noted by Massarik and Carlson in a study described by Dunnette (1962). The California Personality Inventory, which is designed to measure eighteen personality characteristics, was administered before and after participation in a sensitivity training course. No changes were observed.

Changes in "democratic attitudes" as a result of group experiences have been reported by at least two investigators. Haiman (1963) administered the California F-scale, which is supposed to measure authoritarianism, before and after discussion courses that were devoted to training in sensitivity and skills in group process. After the group experience, group members were less authoritarian (as measured by changes in F-scale scores) than before training. Individuals who participated in courses in public speaking and interpretation showed no change. Similarly, Nadler and Fink (1970) reported changes in the direction of more democratic attitudes (again as measured by the F-scale) after taking part in a college training laboratory. On the other hand, Kernan (1964) found no change in F-scale scores after a three-day T-group laboratory experience. A basic question in all these studies is whether real attitude change occurred or whether the participants merely learned the appropriate responses to the test items.

Attempts to demonstrate that participation in experiential groups reduces dogmatism have also yielded mixed results. For example, the Dogmatism Scale (Rokeach, 1960) was administered before and after participation in either twenty-four hour marathon groups or control groups (Foulds, Guinan, & Warehime, 1974). Significant change toward less dogmatic responses was found for the marathon groups but not for the control groups. The Dogmatism Scale presumably measures openminded-ness or individual differences in openness or closedness of belief systems. Therefore, these results suggest that participation in marathon groups increases openmindedness. However, another study found that participation in group-centered counseling classes had no effect on dogmatism (Goodman, Randolph, & Brown, 1978).

Finally, Harrison (1966) reported positive findings concerning the impact of group experiences upon cognitive processes. One hundred fifteen participants described a coworker before and after group participation, using Kelly's Repertory Test (Rep Test). The Rep Test supposedly measures the cognitive complexity of the person, i.e., the degree to which the person organizes concepts in a complex or simple fashion. Harrison found that participants changed toward a greater proportion of inferential-expressive concepts (i.e., concepts that deal with feelings, attitudes, emotions, and perceptions) as compared with concrete instrumental concepts (i.e., concepts related to good, bad, etc.). Again, it is uncertain whether this represents an actual change or merely learning to respond to the test in an approved manner.

To summarize, the evidence concerning personality change as a result of group experiences is inconsistent, and those data that reflect change are open to conflicting interpretations. On the other hand, it may be too much to expect change in deep-rooted personal dispositions as a consequence of relatively short group experiences.

*Self-perceptions* have been regarded as evidence of the impact of group experiences upon participants by several investigators, so many in fact that a review of all would serve no useful purpose. Examination of a few of these investigations will suffice for our purposes. Some studies tested the degree to which group experiences facilitated movement toward the ideal self, presumably on the assumption that such movement represents a desirable change. In one study (Burke & Bennis, 1961), six T-groups composed of thirteen to fifteen members were tested at the National Training Laboratory. There were eighty-four participants in these groups, consisting of both males and females. Each participant completed a questionnaire midway in the first week of training and again in the latter part of the third and final week of training. The questionnaire asked for ratings on a seven-point scale regarding: (1) The way I actually am in this T-group; (2) the way I would like to be in this T-group; and (3) person concepts (i.e., evaluations of each of the other group members). Each item was rated on nineteen bipolar scales. The results showed that participants rated the way they were as more similar to the way they would like to be at the end of the session than at the beginning; i.e., the actual self was seen as more similar to the ideal self after the T-group experience. This result was produced by changes in the ratings of actual self. It was also found that self-other ratings became more similar after the group experience. Since there was no control group, it is uncertain whether these changes can be attributed to the impact of the group training. However, Gassner, Gold, and Snadowsky (1964) reported that human relations training reduced the discrepancy between the person's self-concept and ideal self, and that the phenomenal self changed more for participants in the training groups than in a control group.

Other investigators have noted self-reported changes in feelings and behavior. For example, Bass (1962) had thirty trainees in a ten-day sensitivity training laboratory complete an adjective check list at five points in the training period. He found that skepticism and anxiety decreased during training, and other mood shifts occurred that were related to particular experiences in the group, as shown in Figure 11-2. Bolman (1970) asked 463 teen-agers who had participated in a sensitivity training program at the YMCA to respond to a questionnaire about the effects of their experience, and received 420 completed questionnaires. These participants reported that they gained in understanding, increased in self-identity, improved in ability to make new friends, and were better able to express themselves than before the group experience. These must be considered as opinions about the benefits of training, since there was no pretest and no control group.

A relatively well-designed self-report study was conducted by Friedlander (1967). Using interview data and other sources of information about group process, he devised a questionnaire to measure several dimensions of group interaction:

**1** *Group effectiveness* in solving problems and formulating policy
**2** *Approach to vs. withdrawal from leader,* or the degree to which the leader is approachable by group members
**3** *Mutual influence,* or the degree to which members see themselves as having influence with other group members and with the leader
**4** *Personal involvement and participation* in group meetings
**5** *Intragroup trust vs. intragroup competitiveness,* or the degree to which members have confidence in each other
**6** *General evaluation of meetings*

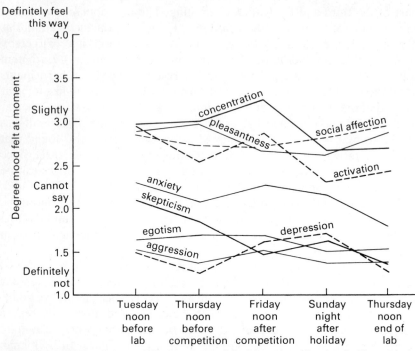

**Figure 11-2** Changes in mood during course of the laboratory. (Reprinted with permission from B. M. Bass. Mood changes during a management training laboratory. *Journal of Applied Psychology,* 1962, **46,** 361–364. Copyright 1962 by the American Psychological Association. Reprinted by permission.)

The questionnaire was administered to twelve task-oriented work groups composed of from five to fifteen members; four groups participated in organizational training laboratories and eight served as comparison groups. The questionnaire was given to members of the training groups before training and again six months after training; it was given to members of the comparison groups on two occasions six months apart. Relative to the control groups, members of the training groups showed greater change in group effectiveness, mutual influence, and personal involvement and participation.

One investigation failed to find significant changes in self-report as a result of participation in experiential groups (O'Dell & Seiler, 1975). An anxiety questionnaire and a self-perception semantic differential instrument were administered to individuals before and after participation in encounter groups, Gestalt groups, or self-discovery groups. No change was observed. In general, however, the data from these various studies are consistent in showing that participants *say* (and presumably believe) that they have made important gains from participation in experiential groups. Whether these self-perceptions are valid is an open question.

*Reports by associates,* another way of assessing the impact of experiential groups, are based upon judgments about each participant's behavior by other persons who work with him or her. Miles (1965) conducted an extensive study using both self-report and reports by associates. Experimental groups consisted of thirty-four high school principals who were members of T-groups in National Training Laboratory programs. Two control groups were used, one randomly chosen (N = 148) and one chosen by asking each person in the T-groups to nominate a control person who was in a similar organizational position and had not participated in experiential groups (N = 29). Responses to perceived change measures were obtained from six to eight associates for each T-group member and from the member himself or herself. The observers reported perceived behavioral changes for 30 percent of the T-group members, 10 percent of the matched controls, and 12 percent of the random controls. Comparable percentages for self-reports were 82 percent, 33 percent, and 21 percent, suggesting that participants see much more change than observers. Several other measures failed to show any change.

Somewhat similar studies were conducted by Boyd and Elliss (1962), Bunker (1965), and Valiquet (1968). In the Boyd and Elliss study, the experimental group consisted of forty-two business managers who had participated in T-groups, and controls consisted of twelve persons who had had no training and ten managers who had had more conventional training in human relations. A mailed questionnaire asked associates of each person to report any changes they had observed in the person's behavior during the past year. Data were collected several months after T-group training. Sixty-five percent of the observers reported perceived changes for the laboratory-trained group, fifty-one percent for the conventional trained group, and thirty-four percent for the no-training group. Bunker (1965) used a very similar questionnaire approach; however, he content-analyzed questionnaire responses to obtain perceived change scores in three major classes: overt operational changes, such as communication, risk-taking, and self-control; inferred changes in insight and attitudes; and global judgments, i.e., changes with no specific referent. Several changes were observed, but Bunker emphasized that changes differed greatly from person to person. Again using the questionnaire approach, Valiquet (1968) reported that T-group participants were seen by coworkers as increasing more than controls in effective initiation and assertiveness, in capacity for collaboration and operational skills in interpersonal relations, and in diagnostic awareness of self and the ability to fulfill perceived needs.

An extensive study of the effects of encounter groups that employed self-reports, reports by participant-nominated others, and reports by associates was conducted by Lieberman, Yalom, and Miles (1973). The groups studied included T-groups, Gestalt groups, psychodrama groups, psychoanalytic groups, transactional groups, eclectic groups, marathon groups, personal growth groups, and "tape-led" groups. One interesting finding was that the label given groups was not related to outcome. On the other hand, the results were not encouraging. Of the 179 participants who completed the group experience, 78 percent indicated that they thought the experience had been constructive, and 64 percent still believed it had been constructive six months later. However, only 56 percent of associates stated that they perceived some change in participants' behavior following the group experience, and much of that perceived change was in a negative direction. Furthermore, there was much inconsistency across participants and associates concerning the amount and kind of change. The investigators then computed a 'yield score" that was a composite of all the outcome measures available. This score indicated that 33 percent improved, 38 percent were unchanged, and 29 percent changed in the negative direction (including dropouts). On the positive side, it was found that outcomes could be predicted from a knowledge of participants' values and their conceptions of others. Those who improved following group participation valued experiencing and changing and saw others positively.

These several studies are in agreement in showing that observers report changes in the behaviors of persons who have participated in experiential groups, but they differ in the specific kinds of behavior changes that reportedly occur.

*Objective behavioral change* would be the most convincing evidence that participation in experiential groups has positive consequences for those who participate. However, in a search of the literature, only two research reports (Cooper, 1972a, 1972b) were found that employed an objective behavioral measure to assess the impact of participation in experiential groups. Both of these studies attempted to assess the psychologically disturbing effects of T-group training. On the assumption that such disturbances would be reflected in visits to the health center, number of such visits by students who had participated in T-groups was compared with number of visits by a control group of students who had not experienced T-group training. Data were obtained immediately following the T-group training and again one year later. No significant difference between training and control groups was observed.

In summary, the evidence concerning the effectiveness of experiential groups is of questionable reliability because of the theoretical and practical problems in research on such groups. To the degree that research data can be accepted as reliable and valid, the evidence indicates that (1) personality changes are small and inconsistent, (2) participants perceive that their behavior and psychological functioning have changed as a result of group experiences, (3) observers report perceived changes in behavior, although the kinds of perceived changes vary considerably, and (4) very limited objective measures of behavior change show no effect of T-group experiences.

Overall, then the evidence that experiential groups are effective tools for personal growth is not strongly supportive. Evidence is beginning to appear, however, indicating that participation in such groups may be beneficial for some people but not for others. In addition to the data reported by Lieberman et al. (1973), another study revealed that some personal characteristics promote and others hinder individual positive behavior change in sensitivity-training groups (Mitchell, 1975). Persons that benefitted most from the training were high with respect to perseverance and reliability, need to be successful, vigor, flexibility, and enjoyment of challenging tasks. Positive behavior change was hindered by need to help others, need to have help and understanding from others, and need to be independent of others. In another study, persons classified as internalizers, as compared with externalizers, reported greater benefit from sensitivity training after five months (Smith, 1976). Psychologically healthy participants also appear to make greater gains in self-acutalization than those who identify themselves as less healthy (Reddy & Beers, 1977).

## Dangers in Experiential Groups

Participation in experiential groups is an intensely emotional experience, and almost everyone involved in experiential group training warns against the casual application of this technique. It is suggested that trainers should be highly skilled, not only in group psychology, but also in recognizing serious emotional reactions and in dealing with them in an appropriate manner; participants should be screened to eliminate those candidates who appear to be emotionally unstable; and so on. It is also emphasized that the crucial aspect of experiential groups is the provision for open expression of feelings in a "psychologically safe" environment. Schein and Bennis (1965) suggested that the conditions facilitating this kind of environment are: (1) a group which meets for a relatively long time in an isolated place; (2) a low probability that the group will meet again; (3) continual assurance by the training staff that the situation is supportive, nonevaluative, and nonthreatening; and (4) an attitude on the part of participants that the group is temporary and gamelike. Failure to create these conditions increases the risk that the group experience will produce undesirable consequences.

The evidence concerning the possible harms from participation in experiential groups is sparse, but it is apparent that severely negative effects sometimes occur. Lakin (1972) noted that damaging incidents associated with group experiences include incapacitating anxiety, depression, suicide, and hospitalization for emotional breakdown. Official data given by the National Training Laboratory lists 25 serious psychiatric problems among 11,000 participants in industrial laboratory programs (cited in Back, 1973). An intensive study by Lieberman, Yalom, and Miles (1971) found an overall casualty rate of 9.6 percent, compared with none in control groups. (Casualties were defined as definite evidence of harm occurring as a result of the training sessions.) The study of encounter groups cited earlier (Lieberman et al., 1973) found that 16 participants (7.8 percent of the 206 who started or 9.1 percent of those who completed 50 percent of the group meetings) suffered significant psychological injury. Although these data are not conclusive, they are sufficient to indicate a real danger in experiential group participation.

Psychotic breakdowns and severe emotional disturbances are the problems that are given the most attention, but minor damages also occur, ranging from invasion of privacy to the agony experienced by the person who is unable or unwilling to conform to the norms of spontaneity and self-disclosure in the group. These potential harms do not necessarily indicate that experiential groups should not be exploited; instead, they stand as reminders that extreme care should be taken in using this potentially powerful psychological tool.

## PLAUSIBLE HYPOTHESES ABOUT GROUPS IN ACTION

In this chapter we have considered somewhat briefly the processes of groups in action. The intent was to provide illustrative examples of the ways that principles of group behavior operate in "real" groups. The discussions often revealed not only what is known about groups in action but also what is not known. The following hypotheses are, as in other chapters, tentative and subject to change when new data are available. In particular, few definitive conclusions can be drawn about experiential groups. In stating hypotheses that appear to be plausible with respect to problem-solving groups, educational groups, and experiential groups, those hypotheses that have already been stated in other chapters are usually omitted.

*Hypothesis 1   Heterogeneous ability grouping facilitates academic achievement to a greater extent than homogeneous ability grouping.*
This conclusion is contrary to a widespread belief among educators that homogeneous ability grouping facilitates academic achievement. However, the data are reasonably consistent in showing the opposite result (Goldberg et al., 1966; Daniels, 1961; Eash, 1961). It appears that the less

capable children benefit from interaction with the more capable children, while the latter are not harmed by their association with the slower pupils. This conclusion is, of course, in agreement with findings regarding ability grouping and problem-solving effectiveness of adult groups.

**Hypothesis 2**    *Teachers react more favorably to teaching homogeneous ability groups than to teaching heterogeneous groups.*
This hypothesis is supported by data from several studies (Goodlad, 1960). Teachers find it easier to meet the demands of individual pupils that are similar in ability than of those that are dissimilar in ability. The latter requires more diverse teaching skills, planning, and learning activities.

**Hypothesis 3**    *Homogeneous ability grouping tends to raise the self-esteem of the less capable group members, whereas heterogeneous grouping tends to raise the self-esteem of the more capable individuals.*
Presumably, the effect of grouping upon self-esteem is mediated by social comparison processes. In heterogeneous groups, less capable individuals compare themselves unfavorably with the more capable and hence evaluate themselves less favorably than in the homogeneous groups in which the comparison is more favorable for them. The opposite effects occur for the more capable individuals. Evidence for this hypothesis derives from numerous studies (e.g., Goldberg et al., 1966; Eash, 1961).

**Hypothesis 4**    *Members of sociometrically cohesive groups learn more than members of less cohesive groups when they want to learn. (cf. Hypothesis 5 in Chapter 7)*
The findings with respect to this hypothesis are not entirely consistent, but the available data suggest that the hypothesis is valid (Lott & Lott, 1966; Shaw & Shaw, 1962; Thelen, 1966). This hypothesis is also strengthened by the fact that it is congruent with data relative to cohesiveness and problem solving in adult groups.

**Hypothesis 5**    *Peer learning groups facilitate academic achievement.*
The evidence for this hypothesis derives from several sources. Research by Edwards, DeVries, and their associates (e.g., Edwards, DeVries, & Snyder, 1972; Edwards & DeVries, 1974; DeVries & Mescon, 1975) indicates that elementary and high school students working in teams learn more than students in more traditional settings. The work reported by Small (1974, 1975) shows that groups may also facilitate learning in medical and dental students.

*Hypothesis 6   Team teaching facilitates academic achievement in the lower grades but impedes academic achievement in higher elementary grades.*

The additional skills and abilities available in teaching teams contributes to achievement in grades two and four (at least) relative to achievement in traditional classrooms; traditional classroom procedures appear to be more effective in grade six (unpublished study by the author). The failure of team teaching to produce greater academic achievement in grade six may be due to the developmental stage of the pupils or to their previous experiences in more traditional classrooms.

*Hypothesis 7   The discrepancy between the perceived self and the ideal self decreases as a function of participation in experiential groups.*

This hypothesis is supported by data from at least two investigations (Burke & Bennis, 1961; Gassner et al., 1964). It is unclear, however, whether this represents a real change in self-concept or merely learning to respond in an approved fashion.

*Hypothesis 8   Participants in experiential groups perceive changes in their feelings and behavior as a consequence of the group experience.*

This hypothesis is supported by data from several self-report studies (e.g., Bass, 1962; Bolman, 1970; Himber, 1970; Friedlander, 1967). These studies vary in the degree to which extraneous variables were controlled, but they are consistent in showing that individuals report changes in their feelings and behavior following participation in experiental groups. However, at least one study failed to find significant changes in self-reports as a function of participation in various personal growth groups (O'Dell & Seiler, 1975).

*Hypothesis 9   Observers report perceived changes in participants' behavior following participation in experiential groups.*

Several studies have demonstrated this effect (Miles, 1965; Boyd & Elliss, 1962; Bunker, 1965; Valiquet, 1968). Associates of experiential group participants report changes in their behavior both during and after the group experience.

*Hypothesis 10   Under some conditions, participation in experiential groups results in severe psychological disturbances.*

The evidence for this hypothesis is imprecise and fragmentary, although it is sufficient to demonstrate that this kind of harmful effect sometimes occurs (Lakin, 1972; Lieberman et al., 1971). There seems to be little question that participation in experiential groups can result in either beneficial or harmful outcomes, although the frequency of neither is clearly established.

## SUGGESTED READINGS

Back, K. W. *Beyond words: The story of sensitivity training and the encounter movement.* Baltimore: Penguin Books, 1973.

Campbell, J. P., & Dunnette, M. D. Effectiveness of T-group experiences in managerial training and development. In D. W. Johnson (Ed.), *Contemporary social psychology.* Philadelphia: J. B. Lippincott, 1973. Pp. 247–279.

Hoffman, L. R. Group problem solving. In L. Berkowitz (Ed.), *Group Processes.* New York: Academic Press, 1978. Pp. 67–100.

Lakin, M. *Experiential groups: The uses of interpersonal encounter, psychotherapy groups, and sensitivity training.* Morristown, N.J.: General Learning Press, 1972.

Ware, J. R., & Barr, J. E. Effects of a nine-week structured and unstructured group experience on measures of self-concept and self-actualization. *Small Group Behavior,* 1977, **8,** 93–100.

Chapter 12

# Issues and Problems

Our explorations of the many facets of groups, the variables that influence group behaviors, and the relationships among these variables reveal the great complexity of group processes. It was shown clearly that the characteristics of individuals who compose the group influence group performance both directly and indirectly via group structure and that the physical environment may influence group structure as well as behavior. Group composition and task effects were delineated and related to various group processes and outcomes. But it also became evident that much is not known about groups and that many controversial issues and problems are yet to be resolved. Although we were able to formulate 141 plausible hypotheses about group behavior, in many instances it was necessary to warn the reader that the validity of these hypotheses has not been established beyond the specific situations in which the data were collected.

The student may justly ask about the significance of the "scientific" study of group dynamics. Can one expect principles established in the laboratory to generalize to natural situations? A partial answer to the first question may be obtained from a comparison of the findings of investigations conducted in the laboratory with those of studies conducted in natural situations. Whether laboratory findings can be generalized to more naturally occurring situations is an empirical question. If it can be shown that similar data are usually obtained from both laboratory and field investigations, some of the uneasiness aroused by the lack of control in natural situations and by the presumed artificiality of the laboratory should be allayed.

With regard to the second question, some applications of group principles in problem-solving groups, educational groups, and experiential groups have already been discussed (Chapter 11). In this chapter we will try to show how an individual can be a more effective participant in groups by using his or her knowledge of group process. However, there are also some negative consequences of group action, and we will try to delineate some of these undesirable effects. A final section deals with past mistakes and suggestions for the future.

## LABORATORY AND NATURAL SITUATIONS

Questions concerning the relevance of laboratory findings for natural situations revolve about two major issues:

**1** Does the psychology of the college sophomore correspond to the psychology of human beings in general? This puts it strongly, but fairly represents the position taken by many critics. Somehow, it is assumed that the college student—and the college sophomore in particular—cannot be taken as representative of the human race. It is believed that his or her behavior is governed by a set of psychological laws that do not apply to others and particularly to those others who are engaged in "real" activities in "real life." It is true that college students differ in certain significant ways from the general population. On the average, they are more intelligent, better educated, and younger than the general population of adults. These differences may, indeed, result in behavioral differences of significance for group behavior. Whether these differences exist, and to what extent they invalidate conclusions drawn from the study of groups of college students, can be determined empirically. An armchair answer is no more likely to be correct here than armchair answers to other questions about psychological events.

**2** Do the results obtained from "artificial" groups functioning in a laboratory have any relevance for natural groups functioning "out there" in the "real world"? The argument of critics is that laboratory groups cannot hope to re-create the richness of groups in natural situations; and, hence, a principle that operates in such ad hoc groups cannot be expected to operate in ongoing groups exposed to the complex pattern of variables that exists in the larger society. Furthermore, it is asserted that members of such groups are probably not motivated, that the whole situation is regarded as a game, that the typical "subject" is motivated to please the experimenter, or, conversely, to deliberately foul up the experiment, and so on. It is certainly true that laboratory groups differ in many ways from natural groups, although it is not at all certain that the differences are those pointed to by critics. For example, it is only necessary to observe the involvement of group members in the assigned task to become convinced that the question of motivation is not always a legitimate one.

On the other hand, research in natural settings is criticized for the lack of control of relevant variables. Natural groups are clearly exposed to more variables than laboratory groups, and the identification of causal relationships is more difficult than in laboratory situations. Indeed, Festinger (1953b) noted many years ago that the great advantage of studying laboratory groups is that the number of variables influencing group behavior at any one time can be reduced to manageable proportions. Only by controlling some variables while allowing others to operate can the effects of such variables be identified. But once again, these are empirical questions that cannot be resolved by polemics. The basic question is: Do laboratory studies and field studies yield similar results?

In practice, the two questions raised above resolve to a single issue. The great bulk of laboratory investigations involve college students as group members, whereas the majority of field studies involve noncollege personnel. However, it can be shown that investigations of similar problems often lead to similar conclusions, whether the subjects be college students or members of the larger population and whether the groups are ad hoc laboratory groups or natural groups functioning in the "real world." Comparison of laboratory and field studies dealing with several aspects of group behavior will illustrate this point.

### Alone versus Together

The comparability of results from laboratory and field studies was demonstrated as early as 1897 in the studies by Triplett dealing with behavior of the individual acting alone and in the presence of others. The initial studies were based upon data taken from official records of bicycle races and compared unpaced, paced, and competitive situations. In the unpaced situation, the bicyclist rode against an established time; in the paced, he rode against time but with another cycle setting the pace; and in the competitive situation, several riders competed, as in an ordinary race. Triplett found that the competitive situation produced the fastest time and the unpaced the slowest time. He then conducted a laboratory study in which forty children, working alone or in pairs, operated a gadget constructed of fishing reels. As in the initial study, the together situation produced the faster performance rates. These studies differed not only in setting (laboratory versus field) but also in kind of task and subject population. Nevertheless, the results agreed perfectly.

## Interpersonal Attraction

Studies of interpersonal attraction provide evidence of the comparability of laboratory and natural group studies with respect to at least two variables: similarity and physical attractiveness. A long-range study of the acquaintance process (Newcomb, 1961) revealed that perceived similarity of attitudes was an important determinant of attraction. Students were invited to live in a house rent-free in exchange for participating in the research project. The students were initially unacquainted; hence, it was possible to study the variables related to friendship formation. Newcomb concluded that ". . . as individuals acquired more information about each others' attitudes, their high attraction preferences tended to change in favor of individuals with whom they were more closely in agreement" (Newcomb, 1961, p. 254). Certainly these students were members of "real groups" living in the "real world." The same conclusions may be drawn from the many studies reported by Byrne and his associates, using strictly laboratory groups. The basic procedure required subjects to respond to attitude scales, after which fake conditions were established which led them to believe that their attitudes agreed with those of another to varying degrees. Subsequent measures of attraction correlated highly with degree of perceived similarity of attitudes (see, for example, Byrne, 1961; Byrne & Nelson, 1964; Byrne & Nelson, 1965b; Byrne & Rhamey, 1965). Attitude similarity has thus been demonstrated to be an important determinant of attraction, both in the laboratory and in natural situations.

Physical attractiveness of the other person has also been shown to be a determinant of interpersonal attraction. Walster, Aronson, Abrahams, and Rottman (1966) conducted a field study utilizing a procedure they called a "computer dance." Ostensibly, males and females were paired by a computer for a dance, after which the investigators obtained measures of the degree to which a person was attracted to his partner. The results showed that how much the male liked his partner, how much he wanted to see her again, and how often he actually asked her out again were a function of his date's physical attractiveness. Similar effects were observed for females. A laboratory study by Schlosser (1969) revealed the same results. A female confederate was made up to be either attractive or unattractive and paired with a naïve male to work on a laboratory task. The physical attractive confederate was rated more highly than the less attractive version, even when she behaved in a manner that interfered with task completion. The effects of physical attractiveness on interpersonal attraction have been found in several other laboratory investigations (e.g., Kleck & Rubenstein, 1975; Krebs & Adinolfi, 1975).

The empirical evidence thus yields consistent results with respect to both attitude similarity and physical attractiveness as determinants of interpersonal attraction, whether the studies are conducted in natural situations or in the laboratory.

## Conformity Behavior

The numerous studies conducted in the laboratory demonstrating that individual group members tend to conform to a perceived group standard scarcely need mentioning (see, for example, Asch, 1951; Berg & Bass, 1961). Conformity also has been demonstrated in many field studies. For example, Freed, Chandler, Mouton, and Blake (1955) observed considerable conformity behavior among automobile drivers: Signaling before making a turn depended to a marked extent upon the behavior of the driver in the car immediately ahead of the driver being observed. The reader may have viewed the behavior of elevator occupants on the television show "Candid Camera." Confederates of the program director deliberately turned to face in a particular direction after entering the elevator; other passengers obediently turned to face in the same direction. This show may have been "rigged," but the behavior of the elevator passengers corresponded closely to behavior demonstrated in the laboratory and in other field situations. The study by Rosenbaum and Blake (1955) concerning volunteer behavior also demonstrated conformity in a non-laboratory situation. An investigator entered the reading room of a college library, approached a confederate already seated there, and invited him to participate in an experiment. The confederate either agreed or refused. Others seated at the table were approached with the same request. Considerably more naïve students volunteered following the confederate's agreement than following his refusal. Similarly, the number of persons who, for a study, joined a queue at a bus stop where it was not customary to queue increased the number of persons voluntarily joining the line (Mann, 1977). These data are, of course, consistent with those obtained in laboratory studies (e.g., Asch, 1951; Gerard, Wilhelmy, & Conolley, 1968).

Much more interesting, however, is that the amount of conformity has been shown to vary with the status of the other person, both in the laboratory and in natural settings. Mausner (1953) tested individuals alone or with a partner who was introduced as either a fellow student or an "art authority." The task was the Meier Art Judgment Test. The partner, who was a confederate of the experimenter, made choices that were incorrect according to the scoring key for the art test. Significantly greater conformity to the partner's erroneous choices occurred when the partner was introduced as an art authority than when he was introduced as a fellow student. The study by Lefkowitz et al. (1955) dealing with pedestrian violation of traffic signals also demonstrated greater conformity to a high-status person. A confederate dressed either as a high-status or as a low-status person violated a "don't walk" signal. Other persons waiting to cross the street violated the signal considerably more frequently when the confederate-violator was dressed as a high-status person than when he was dressed as a low-status person.

In summary, there is strong evidence that the effects of others on an individual's behavior are essentially the same in both laboratory and natural situations.

## Leadership Styles

The correspondence between laboratory and field data is shown most clearly in the many studies of the effects of leadership style upon group behavior. The initial study by Lewin, Lippitt, and White (1939) might be considered a field study, since it was conducted in a laboratory school. It was experimental, however, in that the behavior of the leaders was systematically varied. It will be recalled that the morale of the autocratic groups was considerably lower than that of the democratic groups; there was more scapegoating, more aggression and hostility, and less liking for the autocratic leader. The productivity of the autocratic groups was slightly higher than that of the democratic groups, although the difference was not statistically reliable. Similar results have been obtained in a number of studies employing ad hoc laboratory groups. For instance, Preston and Heintz (1949) compared participatory and supervisory leadership in groups composed of four or five students. The assigned task was to rank potential presidential candidates in order of merit. The results showed that participatory leadership resulted in higher group morale (satisfaction) than did supervisory leadership. Supervisory leadership revealed less influence on the final product than participatory leadership, but the meaning of this result with respect to productivity is difficult to interpret. M. E. Shaw (1955) conducted a laboratory study of four-person ad hoc groups solving problems under either autocratic or democratic leadership. The instructions to the leaders attempted to stimulate behaviors similar to those displayed by the autocratic and democratic leaders in the Lewin et al. study. The subjects were college students who worked in the groups for approximately fifty minutes. Thus, the experimental situation differed considerably from that of the Lewin et al. study; it differed, in fact, in just about all respects except that the leaders behaved either autocratically or democratically. And yet the results of the two studies were in close agreement. Morale was considerably higher in the democratic than in the autocratic groups, whereas the quality of group performance was higher in the autocratic groups. The autocratic groups required less time and made fewer errors than the democratic groups.

Although the correspondence between the Lewin et al. study and the Shaw study suggests that similar conclusions may be drawn from both laboratory and natural group data, there is one other study that reveals this fact even more clearly. Morse and Reimer (1956) conducted a study in an industrial organization in which changes were made that corresponded to a change in the direction of either greater autocratic behavior on the part of the leader or greater democratic behavior. Four groups were selected by pretest to be as nearly alike as possible. In two of the groups, a change was introduced which led to greater "hierarchical control"; that is, the change led to greater control by upper management of decisions affecting group members. In the other two groups, members were given greater autonomy with respect to matters affecting their work. After six months of training to create the experimental conditions, the groups functioned for one year under the autonomy or hierarchically controlled conditions. Then morale and productivity were measured a second time. Differences between initial and final measures were taken as evidence of the effects of the experimentally introduced changes. Several measures of satisfaction were obtained, with the general finding that satisfaction increased under the autonomy conditions and decreased under the hierarchically controlled conditions. For example, one question asked for a global estimate of how well the worker liked working for the company. Ratings increased in the autonomy condition (+.17) and decreased in the hierarchical condition (−.27), a highly reliable difference. Other indices of job satisfaction and satisfaction with supervision revealed a similar pattern. The measure of productivity was indirect, since group members were required to process whatever materials were assigned to them. Thus, productivity was measured in terms of the cost of doing a given volume of work. The results showed an increase in productivity in both situations, but the increase was greater in the hierarchically controlled groups. The results of this long-range field study are, therefore, in close agreement with findings of studies conducted in other settings.

It is very interesting that investigations conducted under such diverse conditions should yield essentially the same results. It may be noted that (1) the group members differed in age, experience, and familiarity with the group, (2) the leaders were either highly trained or untrained with respect to their role, and were either peers of group members or of higher status, (3) the groups were either traditioned or ad hoc, (4) the settings were either field or laboratory, and (5) the tasks differed widely from study to study. Despite these many differences, the conclusions that may be drawn are basically identical. Regardless of the circumstances, autocratic leadership leads to reduced group morale or satisfaction, whereas democratic leadership leads to improved morale; the productivity of autocratic groups is either equal or superior to that of democratic groups.

## Setting of Group Goals

The study by Shelley (1954) revealed that members of laboratory groups set levels of aspiration (goals) for their groups and react to achievement or nonachievement of the goals in much the same way that individuals react relative to personal goals. That is, levels of aspiration are raised after success and lowered after failure, whether these are personal or group levels of aspiration. Zander (1968) and Zander and Medow (1963) reported similar results when group members were asked to arrive at group consensus concerning a level of aspiration for the group. The one difference was that groups lowered the level of aspiration for the group less after failure than they raised it after success. These studies were conducted in the laboratory with ad hoc groups composed of college students. Essentially the same effects were observed by Zander and Newcomb (1967) in their study of fund-raising campaigns. Over a period of several years, it was found that United Fund groups in charge of fund-raising activities almost always raised their goal after a successful campaign but were much less likely to lower it after a failing campaign.

In the preceding discussions, we have shown that the findings of laboratory studies using ad hoc groups suggest conclusions about many aspects of group behavior that are the same as the conclusions suggested by the findings of field studies using natural groups. These investigations included the following areas: (1) behaviors in alone situations compared with behaviors in the presence of others, (2) variables influencing interpersonal attraction, (3) conformity behavior, (4) the effects of leadership styles, and (5) the setting of group goals. These are diverse forms of behavior, indeed, and the demonstration that principles identified in the laboratory also operate in natural settings reduces the force both of critics who argue that the results of studies of artificial groups in an artificial atmosphere have no relevance to natural groups in natural social situations and of those who argue that lack of control in natural settings invalidates the findings of field studies. It has been shown that in many instances the same functional relationships apply to both situations.

However, let the reader beware. These findings *do not* mean that there is no difference between laboratory and natural groups or situations, nor do they imply that the findings of laboratory investigations can be generalized automatically to the field situation. On the contrary, principles established in the laboratory must be tested in the field before we can know whether they can be generalized to natural groups. By the same token, principles derived from observations of groups functioning in natural settings, with the lack of control of variables inherent in such situations, cannot be accepted as valid until they are tested under controlled conditions. For example, several investigations have shown that longevity (the length of time that groups have been in existence) is related to various aspects of group behavior (e.g., member satisfaction: Katz, 1978; evaluation of own group products: Worchel, Lind, & Kaufman, 1975; reward allocation: Shapiro, 1975). Although expectations of future interaction may be created in the laboratory, as in some of the studies just cited, it is difficult to simulate a history of group interaction. The important point is that many of the findings from controlled studies of ad hoc groups also apply to natural groups, but the only way this can be known is through similar studies in *both* settings. It cannot be asserted without examination either that the results of laboratory studies are irrelevant to "real life" or that they can be generalized directly to natural situations or that field studies always yield valid data.

## EFFECTIVE PARTICIPATION IN GROUPS

Evidence concerning the many variables which determine group process provides many guidelines for the individual who wishes to become a more effective group member. The purpose is not to engage in an extended discussion of the application of the principles of group dynamics to effective participation in groups; instead, a limited number of practical implications will be considered to suggest how knowledge about group process can be used to improve one's effectivenes as a group member. Let us examine some data concerning each of the several environments of the group.

### Physical Environment and Effective Participation

To be an effective group member, one must recognize that each individual is responsive to the distance between self and others. Feelings about interperson distances may be positive or negative and vary with personal, situational, and other factors. In particular, reactions to interperson distances vary with the relationships between interacting individuals. To the extent that group members are sensitive to the feelings of others about interperson distances, and respect these feelings, their chances of being effective in the group are increased. For example, attempting to maintain an interaction distance other than that desired by another group member will arouse negative reactions which interfere with effective interaction. In a similar way, group members establish territorial rights that must be respected by the individual who wishes to be accepted and admired by other persons in the group. Recognition and respect of territorial rights of others will increase the group member's chances of being an effective group member.

Spatial arrangements must also be considered by the aspiring effective group member. Spatial positions are associated with status in the group, and the group member must behave accordingly. For example, suppose that a member of low status sits at the head of the table, a high-status seating position. Other group members will regard him or her as unduly arrogant or impolite or perhaps a bit stupid. On the other hand, suppose he or she is high status, say the leader of the group, but sits at the side of the table. Others will probably regard that person as trying to show that he or she does not take the position too seriously. Especially in neonate groups, behavior that is inconsistent with norms relative to spatial position may produce undesirable consequences for effective group participation.

Conversely, suppose that the group is so new that structural differentiations have not occurred. The group member may enhance opportunities for a position of leadership or high status in the group simply by choosing a favorable spatial position. Insofar as there is no basis for judging the selection of a particular position as inappropriate, the position that a person occupies at the initial meeting of a group probably determines to some extent the social position (role, status) he or she will have in the established group.

## Personal Characteristics and Effective Participation

It is difficult for people to change their personalities when they become members of groups, but it is not too difficult to become aware of the characteristics of other group members and to adjust one's own behavior accordingly. For example, a man who is a member of a mixed-sex group may discover that others in the group lack certain abilities which appear to be necessary for task completion. He might fail to act on this information for fear of appearing aggressive or supercilious; such a response would reduce his effectiveness as a group member. On the other hand, he could offer his suggestions in a way that would aid the group in achieving its objectives and hence increase his own effectiveness as a member of the group. In a similar way, a group member might adjust his behavior to other attributes of his fellow group members. For instance, it is known that women are less assertive and less competitive in groups than are men. When the group is composed of women, therefore, the individual group member might become more effective by behaving in a less self-assertive, ascendant fashion than might be necessary in all-male groups. Also, a recognition that assertiveness and competitiveness are characteristic of men should serve as an aid in determining the appropriate responses to such behavior by other group members.

When a group member is also the leader of the group, it is important to evaluate the favorability of the group-task situation. When the group-task situation is either very favorable or very unfavorable, the leader will probably be more effective by adopting a directive leadership style. On the other hand, when the group-task situation is only moderately favorable or unfavorable for the leader, the nondirective leadership style is likely to be more effective (Chapter 9). The leader often errs in this respect, especially when the group-task situation becomes highly unfavorable. The leader often changes to less directive behavior when interacting with other group members, whereas research and theory suggest that a more directive leadership style should be adopted.

The socially sensitive group member is more effective than the less sensitive member. It is at least theoretically possible for an individual to deliberately attend to the moods, feelings, and emotions of others and therefore become more sensitve to them. When this is done, the probability is increased that the group member will behave in ways that enhance acceptance in the group and also the effectiveness of the group.

Finally, it is evident that a member who behaves either in an unconventional manner or in an unusually conforming manner is likely to interfere with effective group action. Hence, effective group members will be alert to the problems of conformity-nonconformity: They will conform when it appears that conformity is desirable for effective group performance but will also recognize the occasions on which nonconformity is the better course.

## Group Composition and Effective Participation

As in the case of the personal environment, group composition depends upon the characteristics of group members or, more specifically, upon the relationships among the characteristics of group members. Since it is difficult to change one's characteristics, improvement in effectiveness of group membership can be achieved primarily through a modification of behavior, which usually requires that the person behave in uncharacteristic ways. For example, suppose a woman finds herself in a noncohesive group. Her natural reaction probably would involve behaviors that reveal her disenchantment with the group. However, if she is seriously interested in becoming a more effective group member and in making the group more effective, she can modify her behaviors so as to communicate a more favorable orientation toward the group or at least to conceal her lack of enthusiasm for it.

In a similar way, a group member may increase effectiveness in incompatible groups by attending to the interpersonal needs of other group members. If another group member expresses a need for affection, one might satisfy this need by showing affection even though such behavior is contrary to one's own desires or typical ways of reacting to others. Or if others in the group indicate a need for dominance, one might become more submissive in the interests of effective group action.

Heterogeneity of abilities and opinions probably cannot be increased at will, but it is possible for the group member to encourage the use of available abilities and the expression of diverse opinions. This is especially important when the group member is in a position of leadership. The degree to which he or she encourages the expression of minority opinion is an important determinant of group effectiveness. The follower may also improve his or her effectiveness as a group member by encouraging others to contribute to the group process.

## Group Structure and Effective Participation

Behaviors that contribute to effective group membership are obviously related to group structure. The position an individual occupies in a group specifies the behaviors expected of him or her and the reactions of others to the person's actions. This expectation is stated explicitly in the case of social roles; the role is the set of behaviors expected of an individual who occupies a particular position in the group. To be an effective group member, therefore, one must be fully aware of the role specifications associated with one's position in the group. In general, the more nearly the occupant's behavior coincides with role requirements, the more effective the person is likely to be as a member of his group.

But there are also some implicit expectations associated with the individual's position that may be equally important for effective group participation. For example, the high-status group member is usually accorded greater latitude with respect to degree of conformity to group norms. Hence, a high-status group member may be more effective under certain circimstances by *not* conforming to group norms, whereas a low-status group member may be more effective by conforming to group norms. This means that the group member who aspires to be effective in the group must consider his or her status and what this means with respect to others' reactions to deviation from group standards. Either conformity or nonconformity may be indicated, depending on the person's status in the group and the requirements of the situation.

The pattern of communication in the group is also related to status structure. Communications tend to be directed upward in the status hierarchy, and the communications directed upward have more positive content than those directed downward. These facts mean (1) that the individual who is in a low-status position must recognize that his or her source of information is relatively limited and (2) that the high-status person must be aware of the potentially distorted nature of the information received. The low-status person can enhance his or her effectiveness in the group by making a special effort to learn about those things that are of importance to the group and to his or her own effectiveness as a group member. The high-status person, on the other hand, must be alert to the possibility that things are not as rosy as implied by the communications directed toward his or her position in the status hierarchy. To be most effective as a group member, he or she must make a special effort to determine the validity of the information received.

Since conformity is sometimes desirable and sometimes undesirable with regard to group effectiveness, it is important for the group member not only to ascertain when conformity is indicated and when it is contraindicated, but also to recognize the factors that determine conformity behavior. For instance, when one is faced with an ambiguous stimulus situation and there is unanimous agreement among other group members, effectiveness in the group may be improved by considering the consequences of conformity and nonconformity. If nonconformity is judged to be the better course, effectiveness may be improved by resisting pressures toward uniformity.

Finally, if the group member has power in the group, it is important to remember that others may be responding in ways designed to maximize their own reinforcements, rather than in ways designed to ensure the achievement of group goals. When another group member enacts deferential, approval-seeking behavior, this may be entirely unrelated to the effectiveness of the powerful group member. To be effective, the powerful group member must use his or her power to enhance group effectiveness, and this usually means arranging the situation in such a way that individual group member reinforcement and goal achievement are congruent.

## Tasks, Goals, and Effective Participation

It is obvious that the effective group member is responsive to the demands of the task faced by the group. Effective behaviors with respect to one task may be completely ineffective with a task having different characteristics. It is important, therefore, for the group member to become thoroughly familiar with the group task and to adjust his or her behaviors to its demands.

It is also important for the group member to recognize that other members set goals for the group which arouse tension systems influencing behavior in much the same way as tensions associated with personal goals. The behaviors of others may become more understandable, and sometimes less irritating, when it is evident that these behaviors are related to goals held for the group. The effective group member will behave in ways designed to reduce these tensions through goal achievement.

Most significant, perhaps, is the fact that goals held for the group may be heterogeneous; not every group member perceives the goals of the group in the same way. When this is the case, the group is likely to be ineffective in achieving its goals. A group member may improve effectiveness by working toward goal clarification and unification. If the person is successful in identifying differences among group members with respect to the goals they have established for the group, many of the difficulties associated with heterogeneity of goals may be solved. And if the person is successful in bringing about goal unification so that all or most group members are working toward the same goal, he or she will have increased not only his or her own effectiveness as a group member but the effectiveness of the group as well.

## SOME NEGATIVE ASPECTS OF GROUPS

Consider the following statements attributed to well-known persons. "Judged by ordinary standards, the group is almost devoid of intellectual content" (Bion). "Madness is the exception in individuals but the rule in groups" (Nietzsche). "A committee is the organized result of a group of the incompetent who have been appointed by the uninformed to accomplish the unnecessary" (Churchill). Although the positive aspects of groups have been emphasized, the foregoing quotations attest to the fact that not everyone is enthusiastic about them. Many persons are impressed, not by the successes of groups, but by their shortcomings and failures and by the spectacularly erroneous decisions that sometimes emerge from group discussions. Indeed, it is easy to identify defective decisions made by groups and to point to disastrous results produced by decisions made by groups. Group decisions are often superior to individual decisions, but there are obvious and noteworthy exceptions. There are many forces operating in groups which, if not counteracted by other group processes, contribute to inefficient group action. The reader may recall from Chapter 1 that one social psychologist went so far as to suggest that we would be better off without groups (Buys, 1978). Although few persons would agree with this extreme position, there are negative aspects of groups that need to be made explicit and examined in some detail. In the following sections of this chapter some of the more common negative consequences of group process will be considered.

### Problems of Coordination

Groups are faced with a number of problems that do not arise when individuals work alone. As mentioned several times in this book, group products are the result of the behaviors of individuals who compose the group. Efficient group action, therefore, requires coordination of individual effort. Attempts to provide for adequate coordination lead to the formation of group structure, in the form of roles, statuses, norms, power differentials, and more or less fixed patterns of communication (see Chapter 8). When the group is unsuccessful in attempting to establish a group structure that is appropriate for the group's task, the group is inefficient with respect to task completion. But even if the group succeeds in establishing an adequate structure, time and energy are required for this purpose. One consequence of the necessity to devote time and energy to problems of organization and coordination is that groups are slow relative to individuals. It will be recalled from Chapter 3 that, although groups sometimes complete a task in less elapsed time than individuals, they almost always require more man-hours than individuals. This unfavorable aspect of group action is further complicated when interpersonal conflicts emerge in the group. Again, time and energy are required to solve these conflicts and thus contribute to group inefficiency.

Although groups are relatively slow, group action is sometimes preferable to individual action because (1) there are some tasks that cannot be carried out by individuals. (2) the group product may be superior to the individual product (e.g., when accuracy is more important than speed), and (3) group decisions are often more readily accepted and implemented by group members than are decisions made by a single person (e.g., by the leader of the group).

### Deindividuation in Groups

In some situations, individuals in groups behave as if they were "submerged in the group" (Festinger, Pepitone, and Newcomb, 1952, p. 382). Group members do not pay attention to other individuals as individuals, and the members do not feel that they are being singled out by others in the group. The state of affairs, which Festinger et al. termed "deindividuation," results in a reduction of inner restraints, and group members feel free to engage in behavior that they would not display under more usual circumstances. This "liberating" effect of groups was observed many years ago in lynch mobs, in which ordinarily intelligent persons temporarily resign their personal standards and join others in committing atrocities (see Raper, 1933).

The phenomenon of deindividuation is probably the resultant of several related group processes, including at least anonymity, diffusion of responsibility, social facilitation, and shifting norms. It is generally agreed that individuals in groups, as well as individuals alone, behave in ways that are expected to increase the probability of positive outcomes and decrease the probability of negative outcomes. As a general rule, individuals refrain from enacting certain behaviors which they might want to enact because they believe that others in the group will disapprove and possibly sanction them. In the state of deindividuation, however, anonymity greatly reduces the possibility that individuals will experience negative consequences as a result of their behavior. Even if there are negative outcomes, they believe that responsibility will be distributed among the group members (diffusion of responsibility) so that each member's own negative outcomes are greatly reduced. Social facilitation effects may also occur. If others are behaving in ways that are normally socially unacceptable, this helps remove restraints on one's own behavior.* Such observations also contribute to shifts in the perceived norms of the group: behavior that had previously appeared to be

---

*Perhaps even the mere presence of others releases the individual from some inhibitions against the performance of otherwise socially unacceptable behavior (see Chapter 3 for a discussion of social facilitation effects).

counter-normative is now perceived to be in accord with the group norms. All these processes probably contribute to the occasional appearance of behavior in groups that is inconsistent with the individual's usual mode of behavior.

Festinger, Pepitone, and Newcomb (1952) noted the positive consequences of deindividuation, namely, that the lessening of inner restraints permits individual group members to satisfy certain needs which they cannot satisfy otherwise. But deindividuation may also produce negative group effects, as evidenced by the behavior of lynch mobs. More recently, Zimbardo (1970) has documented negative outcomes attributable to deindividuation. In the laboratory, he found that the duration of electric shocks delivered to others by girls who were made to feel anonymous was twice as great as the duration of shocks delivered by girls who were made aware of their individuality. Similar effects were observed in field settings. Automobiles that were ostensibly abandoned in the anonymity of New York City were quickly destroyed by vandals, whereas similar cars abandoned in smaller communities were left untouched.

Deindividuation may also permit group members to avoid enacting certain behaviors that are necessary for, or contribute to, effective group action. These effects have not been adequately documented but are strongly suggested by studies of helping behavior which generally show that individuals in groups are less likely to help a person in need than individuals who are alone (Bryan & Test, 1967; Darley & Latane, 1968; Latane & Rodin, 1969).

Finally, deindividuation may account in part for the fact that group decisions are sometimes overly risky or overly conservative for optimum group productivity (see pages 68–76).

### Pressures toward Uniformity

Earlier discussions noted the strong pressures toward uniformity of opinion and behavior in groups and some of the ways that the resulting conformity affected group process and performance. It was also noted that such pressures are greater in certain groups than in others. In many instances, such pressures interfere with efficient group action and in extreme cases may lead to disastrous group decisions. When group members experience strong feelings of solidarity and loyalty to the group, the desire for unanimity may override the motivation to logically and realistically evaluate alternative courses of action. Janis used the invidious term "groupthink" to refer to the "deterioriation of mental efficiency, reality testing, and moral judgment that results from in-group pressures" (Janis, 1972, p. 9).

According to Janis's analysis, groupthink is characterized by (1) the illusion that the group is invulnerable, (2) collective efforts to rationalize and discount negative information, (3) a tendency to ignore ethical or moral consequences of group decision, (4) stereotyped views of other groups, (5) active pressure to change the views of any deviate member, (6) self-censorship of deviations from apparent group consensus, (7) a shared illusion of unanimity, and (8) the emergence of "mindguards" who take it upon themselves to guard the group against information not in accord with the group consensus. When a group exemplifies these characteristics, processes contributing to efficient decision making are interfered with. The group tends to limit discussion to relatively few alternatives of action, it often fails to reexamine the initially preferred course of action, there are relatively few attempts to obtain information from outside critics or knowledgeable persons, and little consideration is given to things that might cause the failure of the preferred course of action. Defective group decisions are likely to result from these procedures.

The limited experimental data concerning Janis's hypotheses are only partially supportive. For instance, in one study college students were assigned to four-person groups and given a crisis problem to solve (Flowers, 1977). Half of the groups were formed to be highly cohesive and half noncohesive, and the assigned leaders used either a nondirective (open) or directive (closed) leadership style. The open leader did not state his or her opinion until other group members had stated their views, encouraged discussion, etc., whereas closed leaders stated their own preferred solution at once, did not encourage discussion, etc. According to Janis's hypotheses high-cohesive groups and groups with closed leaders should show evidences of groupthink and thus perform less efficiently than low-cohesive groups and groups with open leaders. The results showed that groups with open leaders produced significantly more suggested solutions and made better use of available information regardless of level of cohesiveness, but high- and low-cohesive groups did not differ. Similar results were reported by Cartwright (1978). It appears that some of the deleterious effects of group process identified by Janis occur for the reasons he described but other factors are also operative.

Although cohesiveness and conformity may be factors in the production of groupthink, many other group processes also contribute to this mode of thinking. The failure of group members to hear minority opinions in the group is facilitated by "pluralistic ignorance" (Schanck, 1932). Each group member who disagrees with the initially preferred decision often believes that he or she is the only person in the group who does not agree with the decision and, therefore, that expressing his or her disagreement would serve no useful purpose. Unless the leader of the group makes a special effort to elicit minority views, the illusion of unanimity will remain unchallenged. And this is a vicious circle, since the illusion of unanimity will make it less likely that the leader will encourage the expression of minority views: He or she sees no evidence that there *is* a minority opinion. Pluralistic ignorance is, therefore, an aspect of group process that leads to restriction of the range of alternatives considered by the group and thereby contributes to the occurrence of groupthink.

Another factor contributing to groupthink comes into play when one group member has special knowledge about the problem being considered by the group, or when one person is aware of several alternatives to the initially preferred solution. Although one may overcome the inhibitions resulting from pluralistic ignorance and offer the information to the group, it is often rejected. This effect is due in part to the selective perception created by the desire for consensus, but it may also be the result of the perceived validity of the information offered by the knowledgeable group member (Shaw, 1961b, 1963; Shaw & Penrod, 1962a, 1962b, 1964). When one member of a group is provided with additional information that is relevant to the group's task, his or her influence on the group's decision depends on the extent to which the information is accepted as valid by other group members. For example, if a member has much information that could be obtained from public documents (e.g., the population of major U.S. cities), that person has more influence in the group than other group members, and the quality of the group decision varies with the amount of information possessed by the informed member. However, if other members of the group can see no reason why the informed member should have valid information about the task (e.g., special knowledge about a human relations problem), attempts to help the group are rebuffed, and the group decision is sometimes inferior to the decisions of groups in which the informed member has less information. Thus in highly cohesive groups, a member who has special information may find it difficult to get the other group members to accept it—unless, of course, the informed member can demonstrate its validity and is permitted to do so.

## FACTORS THAT IMPEDE ADVANCES IN GROUP DYNAMICS

The history of science is to large extent the history of the mistakes of humans, and the history of group dynamics is no exception to this general rule. It is inevitable that researchers who seek to push back the frontiers of knowledge will make many false starts, that they will do some things they should not do (because those things fail to accomplish their purpose) and leave undone some things that should be accomplished. To some extent, these statements are clichés—mere assertions of the obvious. But is is important to keep them in mind, lest we become unduly critical of those who have preceded us. The discussion that follows is not intended as an indictment of group dynamics and/or those who have attempted to solve the riddles of small group behavior; instead, it is *intended* as an unbiased analysis of the field as it has developed over the past several years.

From this point in time, it seems evident that students of small group behavior have allowed themselves to be overly influenced by certain viewpoints and orientations and that they have failed to deal with certain significant issues. The field of group dynamics has been characterized by (1) an overemphasis on laboratory research and a corresponding lack of emphasis on research in natural settings, (2) an overemphasis on ad hoc groups, with a corresponding lack of concern for traditioned groups, (3) a tendency toward the elegant treatment of trivial problems, (4) an overdependence on arbitrary statistical standards, (5) a lack of application of research findings to current social problems, (6) a restriction of research to intragroup processes, and (7) a failure to develop integrative theories. These aspects of group dynamics are not independent, of course, and several of them probably reflect a single orientation. For example, the first four are probably consequences of the emphasis upon the rigorous control of variables that has characterized general psychology throughout the twentieth century. Therefore, the major shortcomings of group dynamics may be subsumed under four major headings: preference for rigor, restriction of the scope of research, lack of a theory, and failure to apply research findings.

## Preference for Rigor

Several years ago, Seeman and Marks (1962) wrote an amusing article about a white rat that wanted to be a psychologist. This white rat, after much "soul-searching" activity, chose as his dissertation topic a comparison of the rigor with which a problem could be attacked and the interest value of the problem. After constructing reliable measures of rigor (RIGS) and interest (INTS), he was able to demonstrate a strong inverse relationship between RIGS and INTS: the greater the rigor that could be applied to the problem, the lower its interest value. This little story illustrates a not-so-amusing aspect of research in group dynamics. There has been an overconcern for rigorous research methods, and this has often led to concern for trivial, uninteresting problems.

The preference for rigor over problem significance is reflected in a variety of ways in research. In the first place, it has led to an overemphasis on laboratory studies. In general, laboratory studies can be conducted with a great deal more rigor than field studies. Variables can be controlled, manipulated, etc., to a much greater extent in the laboratory than in natural settings. It is not surprising, then, that those who place greater emphasis upon rigor than upon problem significance should also emphasize laboratory research. The problem is not that there has been too much laboratory research, but rather that there has been too little research in the field. As noted in Chapter 2, both laboratory and field studies are needed to completely understand small group phenomena. Field studies help in the identification of significant problems; laboratory studies permit a more precise determination of functional relationships; and, finally, field studies are again necessary to determine whether laboratory-established principles can be generalized to natural situations. There is a need for constant interchange between the laboratory and the field; group dynamicists have tended to neglect the field, although there has been some shifting to field studies in recent years.

The overemphasis upon laboratory research probably accounts for another mistake, namely, the tendency to study ad hoc groups of short duration and to avoid studies of extant groups over long periods. There are two undesirable consequences of this limited approach. First, newly formed groups do not have a set of traditions, nor do they have expectations about future interactions. In some instances, these factors may not be important; that is, the same principles may operate in both ad hoc and traditioned groups. On the other hand, these variables may be extremely important in some cases, and this can be determined only by studying both kinds of groups. Second, the study of fifty-minute groups does not permit the observation of long-term changes. Although it is possible to conduct longitudinal studies in the laboratory, this is difficult to do and it is rare for a laboratory study to span even a week.

We have already mentioned that there is evidence that longevity and the anticipation of future interaction influence group processes (Katz, 1978; Shapiro, 1975; Worchel et al., 1975). Although comparable data often derive from short-term and long-term groups, there can be no doubt that some variables are present in groups with a tradition which are absent from ad hoc groups.

Finally, the emphasis upon rigor has led to an almost servile dependence upon arbitrary statistical standards; $p < .05$ has become a cruel master. Consider for a moment the meaning of statistical probabilities. When a difference between two experimental treatments is found to be significant at the 5 percent level of confidence ($p = .05$), this means that the chances that the observed difference is due to uncontrolled factors are only 5 in 100. Since .05 is an arbitrary standard that, by convention, allows the rejection of the null hypothesis (the hypothesis that there is no difference between the treatments except that caused by uncontrolled variables), it is then inferred that the observed difference was due to the experimental treatments. But if the probability value is greater than .05, convention holds that the difference is not significant; hence the null hypothesis is accepted. But suppose the significance level is $p = .10$. This means that the chances are only 10 in 100 that the observed difference was due to chance factors, or, conversely, that the chances are 90 in 100 that the observed difference is *not* due to chance factors. When the null hypothesis is accepted, the researcher is putting faith in the lower probability. In effect, the person is betting on an event that has only 10 chances in 100 of occurring in preference to one that has 90 chances in 100. The argument here is not that researchers should accept probabilities higher than .05 for establishing truth, but rather that they should *not* accept even much higher probabilities for this purpose. In far too many instances, the group dynamicist has interpreted a failure to establish a relationship as a demonstration that the relationship does not exist. Everyone who has had an elementary course in statistics knows that this conclusion is not valid, but it appears to be one of the undesirable consequences of the demand for rigorous experimental procedures.

### Restriction of the Scope of Research

The complete analysis of group behavior must include not only the investigation of intragroup processes, but also the behavior of groups vis-à-vis other groups. Research on group dynamics, however, has emphasized the study of intragroup effects. If we are to make a contribution to the solution of the vexing problems of society, attention must be given to intergroup processes. Failure to do so means that group dynamics can say little about such significant issues as international relations, industrial negotiations, peace talks, political machinations, interracial conferences, and the like. Studies of interpersonal bargaining (e.g., Deutsch & Krauss, 1962; McGrath & Julian, 1963), international relations (e.g., Guetzkow et al., 1963), and coalition formation (see Chapter 4) represent the kind of research that needs to be done. Unfortunately, such investigations are rare.

In evaluating research relevant to experiential groups, Weigel and Corazzini (1978) noted that the quality of research has been notoriously poor. They suggested that much of the problem involves the attitudes of potential researchers. For instance, many group practitioners believe that one cannot engage in well-controlled research without infringing upon the rights of group members. Whether this attitude or belief is correct obviously depends upon the particular conditions under which the research is conducted. An even greater barrier to quality research is the attitude that any research which is not perfect is not worth doing. Since no research design is perfect, it follows that no research will be done. Weigel and Corazzini argue correctly that this is an unreasonable view. They urged a balance between the extremes of perfectionism and ill-conceived or poorly executed research. Modification of some of these barriers to research should lead to an extension of the kinds of groups and group processes that are investigated.

## Lack of a Theory

In the first few chapters of this book, it was argued that research data are unlikely to be very useful if they are not organized in a theoretically meaningful way. Theory is a convenient way of organizing experiences so that a large amount of empirical data can be treated with relatively few propositions. Theoretical organization of data also allows us to discover implications and relationships that are not evident from isolated bits of information. Thus, any discipline must provide for the integration of its data by the development of adequate theoretical formulations. Group dynamics has largely failed in this respect. As noted in Chapter 2, a few attempts have been made, with varying degrees of success. But for the most part, these theories are capable of encompassing only limited amounts of the information gleaned from small group research. One can appeal to the complexity of the phenomena as a reason for the failure of group dynamicists to devise an adequate theory, but the fact remains that no existing theory can adequately organize the empirical data of group dynamics (cf. Kaul & Bednar, 1978; Ruzicka, Palisi, & Berven, 1979). Such a theory is sorely needed.

## Failure to Apply Research Findings

Historically, scientists have maintained a position of aloofness with regard to the use of research findings. The "pure" scientist has not been concerned with the application of findings to events outside the laboratory. If a lifesaving drug is discovered, it is not the discoverer's responsibility to see that it is used by physicians; or if a device that could destroy the world is created, the fact that it can be used by some maniac is not the scientist's concern. Application simply has not been viewed as a proper function of the scientist. This view is being seriously questioned today. No longer can researchers remain in their ivory towers and ignore the consequences of their work. With an ever-increasing demand for "relevance" and "account-ability," those who support research expect the researcher to aid in relating his or her work to the problems of society. And this expectation applies especially to the social scientist, including group dynamicists.

Students of group behavior have not been noted for their overwhelming responsiveness to the needs of society. With the exceptions of concern for sensitivity training and applications to industrial work groups, little attention has been given in the past to the possible application of research findings to small groups in everyday life. This lack of responsiveness is beginning to be overcome, and attention is being directed toward more effective use of our knowledge about small groups. Some evidences of this were cited in our discussions of action groups (Chapter 11).

## SOME CONCLUSIONS

The field of group dynamics is still in its infancy, but even so, a tremendous amount of information has been amassed through empirical investigations. Much of this information is unreliable and lacking in validation; theoretical integration is practically nonexistent. Nevertheless, a beginning has been made, and available data reveal the great complexity of small group behavior. The interrelations among the many parts of the group and the variables that influence group process almost defy comprehension. But hope springs eternal; we are beginning to gain some understanding of this multiplex phenomenon.

In the preceding pages, we have examined many facets of small group behavior, explored the many variables that influence group processes, and noted the way variables interact to determine group functioning. The complexities of group processes make it extremely difficult to unravel the consequences of these interactive factors. Nevertheless, data obtained from empirical studies permit the formulation of relatively precise plausible hypotheses. These hypotheses have been shown to be useful not only for the understanding of group process, but also for practical purposes. Given the data at hand, an effective group can be described; the formation of effective groups then becomes limited by lack of control over variables rather than by lack of knowledge about the characteristics of an effective group. The knowledge that is available concerning group behavior is also useful for persons who wish to improve their effectiveness as group members. By being aware of the internal functioning of small groups, the individual can adjust his or her own behavior to improve the effectiveness of the group.

Group dynamicists have thus made progress in the analysis of group interaction and group functioning. But much remains to be done before group process can be completely understood. The greatest need today is an adequate theory for the organization of data, so that the implications of the data at hand can be spelled out more definitively and deficiencies revealed more clearly. When this is done, we may learn much more about small group behavior.

With some trepidation, one may offer some suggestions for future activities in group dynamics. Most of these suggestions are found in preceding discussions. First, there is a need to place greater emphasis upon the significance of the research problem than has been done in the past. This is not to say that there should be a decreased concern for rigorous research procedures. On the contrary, the most rigorous research methods available must be adopted. But significant problems must not be avoided simply because elegant research techniques are not available to study them, nor are sophisticated research methods sufficient justification for investigating meaningless problems. Significant problems must be attacked even if this means using less than perfect research procedures. This "mandate" probably means that there must be an increase in experimentation in natural settings, an increase in the study of traditioned groups, an increase in longitudinal studies, and a greater concern for the logic of statistical analysis.

Second, future researchers should be willing to expand their outlook with respect to both appropriate areas of research and possible application of their findings to the problems of society. In particular, there is a need to enlarge the scope of research to include many aspects of intergroup relations that have been all but neglected in the past.

Finally, there must be a greater concern for theory. Theory and research are equal partners in the advancement of knowledge. One without the other can only be a sterile exercise of the intellect. In far too many instances the two endeavors have traveled different roads, with few interconnecting pathways. Let researchers give heed to theory and theorists take account of research data. By this cooperative endeavor, perhaps an adequate theoretical integration of empirical data can be accomplished.

## SUGGESTED READINGS

Fisher, B. A. Communication research and the task-oriented group. *The Journal of Communication*, 1971, **21,** 136–149.

Flowers, M. L. A laboratory test of some implications of Janis' groupthink hypothesis. *Journal of Personality and Social Psychology*, 1977, **35,** 888–896.

Janis, I. L. *Victims of groupthink*. Boston: Houghton Mifflin, 1972.

Kaul, T. J., & Bednar, R. L. Conceptualizing group research: A preliminary analysis. *Small Group Behavior*, 1978, **9,** 173–191.

Ruzicka, M. F., Palisi, A. T., & Berven, N. L. Use of Cattell's three panel model: Remedying problems in small group research. *Small Group Behavior*, 1979, **10,** 40–48.

Schlenker, B. R. Social psychology and science. *Journal of Personality and Social Psychology*, 1974, **29,** 1–15.

# Glossary

**achieved status**   Status attributed to an individual on the basis of his or her own performance.

**additive task**   A task in which the outcome is the result of some combination of individual products.

**affection need**   A need for close personal and emotional relations with others.

**anxiety**   A general worry or concern about some uncertain or future event.

**ascribed status**   Status attributed to an individual on the basis of arbitrary characteristics, such as age, sex, and kinship.

**assembly effect**   Variations in group behavior that are a consequence of the particular combinations of persons in the group, excluding the effects of specific characteristics of group members.

**behavior repertoire**   All the possible behavior sequences that a person might enact during interaction with another person, including all possible combinations of possible behavior sequences.

**behavior sequence**   A number of specific motor and verbal acts that are sequentially organized and directed toward some immediate goal.

**coaction**   Two or more persons working individually on the same task, but in the presence of each other.

**coalition**  The joint use of resources by a subgroup to determine the outcome of a group decision.

**communication network**  The arrangement (or pattern) of communication channels among the members of a group.

**comparison level (CL)**  The standard against which an individual evaluates the attractiveness of an interpersonal relationship.

**comparison level for alternatives (CL$_{alt}$)**  The standard that an individual uses to decide whether to remain in or to leave an interpersonal relationship.

**competitive social situation**  A situation in which the goal of each group member is such that if any individual group member achieves his or her goal, other group members will, to some degree, be unable to achieve their respective goals.

**computer simulation study**  A research technique in which the variables are programmed and behavior is "enacted" by the computer rather than by groups of real persons.

**conceptual system**  The individual's characteristic ways of conceptualizing and organizing his or her world.

**conformity**  The degree to which an individual's behavior corresponds to the norms of his or her group.

**conjunctive task**  A task that requires completion by each and every group member.

**control need**  A need to dominate others and to have power and authority over them.

**cooperative social situation**  A situation in which the goals of individuals are such that if any group member achieves his or her goal, all other group members, to some extent, achieve their respective goals.

**crowding**  A psychological experience that occurs when an individual's demand for space exceeds the space available to the individual.

**decision structure**  Defined by Mulder as "who takes decisions for whom" in the group; the pattern of decision making in the group.

**deindividuation**  A presumed state of the group in which group members lose their identity and are not attended to as individuals.

**descriptive exploratory study**  A research technique for describing small groups, often for the purpose of identifying relationships among variables.

**dimensional analysis**  A form of analysis designed to identify dimensions of group tasks and to assign tasks to appropriate positions with respect to those dimensions.

**disjunctive task**  A task which requires that at least one member of the group be able to complete it in order for the group to be able to complete it.

**educational groups**  Groups that are designed to help group members improve their academic achievement.

**effective synergy**  The amount of energy available to the group after it has satisfied its maintenance requirements; total synergy minus maintenance synergy.

**entitativity**  The degree of having real existence; the degree of being an entity.

**exchange theory**  A theory which attempts to explain interpersonal behavior in terms of the exchange of rewards and costs.

**experiential group**  A group formed for the explicit purpose of helping group members via group participation.

**expressive group**   A group based upon the motivations of group members to achieve greater emotional expressiveness for its own sake.

**facilitation of peer learning (FPL)**   A process by which one group member contributes to learning by other group members.

**favorability continuum**   The range of group situations with respect to leader advantages.

**field experiment**   A study conducted in a natural setting in which the investigator deliberately produces variations in the natural situation in order to examine their effects upon group behavior.

**FIRO (fundamental interpersonal relations orientation)**   A theory of interpersonal behavior based upon three interpersonal needs: inclusion, control, and affection needs.

**goal clarity**   The degree to which the requirements of the task are clearly stated or known to the group members.

**goal-path multiplicity**   The degree to which the task can be completed by a number of alternative procedures.

**group**   Two or more persons who are interacting with one another in such a manner that each person influences and is influenced by each other person.

**group cohesiveness**   The resultant of all those forces acting upon group members to remain in or to leave the group.

**group compatibility**   The extent to which the needs and behaviors of group members are mutually satisfying.

**group composition**   The relationships among the characteristics of individuals who compose the group.

**group congruency**   A state of the group that results when the relationships among group elements are nonconflicting and harmonious.

**group elements**   Those aspects of the group and the group situation that influence or may be expected to influence group processes.

**group goal**   An end state desired by a majority of the members of a group. The group may have a single goal or multiple goals.

**group goal facilitation**   A leadership factor that includes those abilities which are necessary to help the group attain its goal.

**group polarization**   Changes of attitudes, opinions, beliefs, or decisions toward a more extreme position following group discussion.

**group sociability**   A leadership factor that includes those skills and abilities which are needed to keep the group functioning smoothly (i.e., without undue intermember conflict).

**group structure**   The pattern of relationships among the differentiated parts of the group. The group may be differentiated along a variety of dimensions; hence, the group structure consists of a set of separate, highly interrelated relationships among diverse units of the group.

**group syntality**   The personality of the group; any effect that the group has as a totality.

**group task**   That which must be done in order for the group to achieve its goal or subgoal. It consists of a stimulus complex and a set of "instructions" concerning what is to be done with respect to the stimuli.

**groupthink** Defective group processes resulting from pressures toward uniformity in highly cohesive groups.

**inclusion need** The need for togetherness; the need to associate with others, to be a member of a group.

**independence** The degree of freedom with which an individual may function as a member of a group.

**individual prominence** A leadership factor that includes characteristics related to a person's desire for group recognition.

**informational social influence** Influence exerted upon a group member which is based upon the value that conformity may have for the individual. The majority opinion serves as a source of information.

**interaction** An interpersonal exchange in which each person emits behavior in the presence of the other, with at least the possibility that the behaviors of each person affect the other person.

**interactionism** A term that denotes a wide range of approaches to the study of leadership which emphasize the joint effects of the many factors known to influence leadership emergence, group behavior, and group outcomes.

**interchange compatibility** Compatibility based upon the mutual expression of inclusion, control, or affection needs. Interchange compatibility exists when two persons are similar with respect to the amount of exchange desired.

**interperson distance** The physical distance between two persons; applied especially to interpersonal proximity that affects interpersonal behavior.

**interpersonal orientation** The particular way or ways that an individual views or reacts to other persons.

**interpersonal relationship** A relationship between two or more persons developed through interaction on a number of specific occasions.

**leader** The group member who exerts more positive influence on others in the group than they exert on him or her.

**leadership** A process in which one group member exerts positive influence over other group members.

**leadership style** The pattern of behaviors adopted by the leader of a group; the leader's orientation toward the group.

**learning group** A group formed to help group members gain an understanding of group processes.

**level of aspiration** The level of difficulty of that task chosen as the goal for the next action.

**maintenance synergy** That portion of the total energy available to the group that must be devoted to the establishment of cohesion and harmony in the group.

**natural experiment** An investigation that capitalizes upon naturally occurring changes in variables in order to examine their effects upon group process.

**nominal group** A group composed by pooling the outputs of randomly chosen individuals who have worked alone.

**normative social influence** The influence of the group upon a group member which is based upon his or her desire to conform to the normative expectations of other group members.

**norms** Rules of conduct; standards which specify appropriate behavior in the group.

**originator compatibility**   Compatibility based upon the originator-receiver dimension of interaction. Two persons are compatible to the degree that the expression of inclusion, control, or affection needs corresponds to that which the other person wishes to receive in each of the three need areas.

**peer learning groups**   Groups established to encourage facilitation of peer learning.

**population density**   The number of persons per unit of physical space; the average area available to each person in the group.

**position**   The person's standing in the group; the total characterization of the differentiated parts of the group that are associated with a given member of the group.

**profile homogeneity**   The degree to which the members of a group are similar on a variety of individual characteristics, considered collectively; for example, the similarity of the personality profiles of group members.

**reciprocal compatibility**   The degree to which two persons satisfy each other's behavior preferences.

**response compatibility**   The extent to which the behaviors of two or more persons are mutually agreeable, i.e., can coexist without conflict.

**risky shift**   The tendency of decisions made in groups to be less conservative than the decision of the average group member.

**role**   The behaviors expected of the occupant of a given position in a group by other group members.

**role conflict**   Conflict which results when the expectations associated with two or more positions in different groups that an individual occupies are incompatible, or when the various expectations associated with a single position that a person occupies are incompatible.

**role enactment**   An experimental procedure that manipulates role playing in order to study the effects of role-related behavior on group processes and outcomes.

**role playing**   Assumption of a particular role that may or may not be the role associated with the person's actual position in a natural group.

**role visualization**   An experimental approach that requires the subject to passively imagine (visualize) another person's role and to predict that person's behavior.

**saturation**   The degree to which a communication network is overloaded by the total requirements imposed upon the group by such aspects of group process as communication demands, organizational decisions, and data manipulations.

**social facilitation**   The effect that the mere presence of others has upon the behavior of individuals. At one time, this effect was believed to be facilitative, but it is now known that the presence of others may either facilitate or impede individual performance, depending upon other factors.

**social power**   The control of reinforcers for other members of one's group. Person A has power over person B to the extent that he or she controls reinforcers for B.

**social sensitivity**   The ability to perceive and respond to the needs, emotions, and preferences of others.

**solution multiplicity** The degree to which there is more than one "correct" solution to a problem or task.

**standard group task** A task with known characteristics that is adaptable to a variety of problem situations relative to small group behavior.

**status** The evaluation of a position in a group; the prestige of a position in a group.

**synergy** The vectorial resultant of the attitudes of members toward the group; the total amount of energy that is available to the group.

**team-games-tournament (TGT)** A technique in which teams play a series of games following a tournament format for the purpose of facilitating learning by participants.

**tension system** A psychological state produced by opposing forces in the life space; for example, an internal state created by the establishment of a personal or group goal.

**territoriality** The assumption of a proprietary orientation toward a geographical area by a person or by a group, either legitimately (as by purchase) or illegitimately (as by "squatting").

**theory** A set of interrelated hypotheses or propositions concerning a phenomenon or set of phenomena.

**therapeutic group** A group designed to help individuals to repair something in themselves (e.g., change a personality style, correct emotional experiences).

**trait homogeneity** The degree to which the members of a group are similar with respect to a single individual characteristic.

**transactional approach** An approach that attempts to explain group behavior as an interchange of inputs and outputs.

**valid communication** A stage in group development in which each group member is able to freely express his or her true feelings about himself or herself and about others in the group, and can accept other group members as individuals who have the right to express their feelings, their beliefs, and their values.

**vertical dyad linkage** A relationship that develops between the leader and each member of the group, deriving from both environmental factors and the personal characteristics of group members.

# References

Adams, J. S., & Romney, A. K. A functional analysis of authority. *Psychological Review,* 1959, **66,** 234–251.

Adams, S. Status congruency as a variable in small group performance. *Social Forces,* 1953, **32,** 16–22.

Adorno, T. W., Frenkel-Brunswik, E., Levinson, D. J., & Sanford, R. N. *The authoritarian personality.* New York: Harper, 1950.

Aiello, J. R., & Jones, S. E. Field study of the proxemic behavior of young school children in three subcultural groups. *Journal of Personality and Social Psychology,* 1971, **19,** 351–356.

Albert, S., & Dabbs, J. M., Jr. Physical distance and persuasion. *Journal of Personality and Social Psychology,* 1970, **15,** 265–270.

Alexander, C. N., Jr., & Scriven, G. D. Role playing: An essential component of experimentation. *Personality and Social Psychology Bulletin,* 1977, **3,** 455–466.

Alkire, A. A., Collum, M. E., Kaswan, J., & Love, L. R. Information exchange and accuracy of verbal communication under social power conditions. *Journal of Personality and Social Psychology,* 1968, **9,** 301–308.

Allport, F. H. The influence of the group upon association and thought. *Journal of Experimental Psychology.* 1920, **3,** 159–182.

Allport, F. H. *Social psychology*. Boston: Houghton Mifflin, 1924.

Altman, I., & Haythorn, W. W. The ecology of isolated groups. *Behavioral Science*, 1967a, **12**, 169–182.

Altman, I., & Haythorn, W. W. The effects of social isolation and group composition on performance. *Human Relations*, 1967b, **20**, 313–340.

Anderson, A. B. Combined effects of interpersonal attraction and goal-path clarity on the cohesiveness of task oriented groups. *Journal of Personality and Social Psychology*, 1975, **31**, 68–75.

Anderson, H. H. Domination and social integration in the behavior of kindergarten children and teachers. *Genetic Psychology Monographs*, 1939, **21**, 287–385.

Anderson, L. R. Groups would do better without humans. *Personality and Social Psychology Bulletin*, 1978, **4**, 557–558.

Argyle, M., & Dean, J. Eye contact, distance, and affiliation. *Sociometry*, 1965, **28**, 289–304.

Aries, E. Interaction patterns and themes of male, female, and mixed groups. *Small Group Behavior*, 1976, **7**, 7–18.

Armstrong, S., & Roback, H. An empirical test of Schutz' three-dimensional theory of group process in adolescent dyads. *Small Group Behavior*, 1977, **8**, 443–456.

Aronoff, J., & Messé, L. A. Motivational determinants of small-group structure. *Journal of Personality and Social Psychology*, 1971, **17**, 319–324.

Aronson, E., & Carlsmith, J. M. Experimentation in social psychology. In G. Lindzey & E. Aronson (Eds.), *The handbook of social psychology* (Vol. 2). Reading, Mass.: Addison-Wesley, 1968. Pp. 1–79.

Asch, S. E. Effects of group pressure upon the modification and distortion of judgments. In H. Guetzkow (Ed.), *Groups, leadership and men*. Pittsburgh: Carnegie Press, 1951. Pp. 177–190.

Asch, S. E. *Social psychology*. Englewood Cliffs, N.J.: Prentice-Hall, 1952.

Asch, S. E. Studies of independence and a minority of one against a unanimous majority. *Psychological Monographs*, 1956, **70**, No. 9 (Whole No. 416).

Atkinson, J. W. Strength of motivation and efficiency of performance. In J. W. Atkinson & J. O. Raynor (Eds.), *Motivation and achievement*. New York: Wiley, 1974.

Back, K. W. Influence through social communication. *Journal of Abnormal and Social Psychology*, 1951, **46**, 9–23.

Back, K. W. *Beyond words: The story of sensitivity training and the encounter movement*. Baltimore: Penguin Books, 1973.

Back, K. W., Festinger, L., Hymovitch, B., Kelley, H. H., Schachter, S., & Thibaut, J. W. The methodology of studying rumor transmission. *Human Relations*, 1950, **3**, 307–312.

Baird, J. E., Jr. Some nonverbal elements of leadership emergence. *The Southern Speech Communication Journal*, 1977, **42**, 352–361.

Baker, K. H. Pre-experimental set in distraction experiments. *Journal of General Psychology*, 1937, **16**, 471–486.

Bales, R. F. *Interaction process analysis: A method for the study of small groups*. Cambridge, Mass.: Addison-Wesley, 1950.

Bales, R. F. Factor analysis of the domain of values in the value profile test. Mimeographed report, Laboratory of Social Relations, Harvard University, 1956.

Bales, R. F., & Strodtbeck, F. L. Phases in group problem solving. *Journal of Abnormal and Social Psychology,* 1951, **46**, 485–495.

Bales, R. F., Strodtbeck, F. L., Mills, T. M., & Roseborough, M. E. Channels of communication in small groups. *American Sociological Review,* 1951, **16**, 461–468.

Barch, A. M., Trumbo, D., & Nangle, J. Social setting and conformity to a legal requirement. *Journal of Abnormal and Social Psychology,* 1957, **55**, 396–398.

Barnlund, D. C. A comparative study of individual majority, and group judgment. *Journal of Abnormal and Social Psychology,* 1959, **58**, 55–60.

Barnlund, D. C., & Harland, C. Propinquity and prestige as determinants of communication networks. *Sociometry,* 1963, **26**, 467–479.

Baron, R. A. Invasions of personal space and helping: Mediating effects of invader's apparent need. *Journal of Experimental Social Psychology,* 1978, **14**, 304–312.

Baron, R. S., Moore, D., & Sanders, G. S. Distraction as a source of drive in social facilitation research. *Journal of Personality and Social Psychology,* 1978, **36**, 816–824.

Baron, R. S., & Roper, G. Reaffirmation of social comparison views of choice shifts: Averaging and extremity effects in an autokinetic situation. *Journal of Personality and Social Psychology,* 1976, **33**, 521–530.

Barton, W. A., Jr. The effect of group activity and individual effort in developing ability to solve problems in first-year algebra. *Journal of Educational Administration and Supervision,* 1926, **12**, 512–518.

Bass, B. M. An analysis of the leaderless group discussion. *Journal of Applied Psychology,* 1949, **33**, 527–533.

Bass, B. M. Development and evaluation of a social acquiescence scale. *Journal of Abnormal and Social Psychology,* 1956, **53**, 296–299.

Bass, B. M. *Leadership, psychology, and organizational behavior.* New York: Harper & Row, 1960.

Bass, B. M. Mood changes during a management training laboratory. *Journal of Applied Psychology,* 1962, **46**, 361–364.

Bass, B. M., & Klubeck, S. Effects of seating arrangement on leaderless group discussions. *Journal of Abnormal and Social Psychology,* 1952, **47**, 724–727.

Bass, B. M., McGehee, C. R., Hawkins, W. C., Young, P. C., & Gebel, A. S. Personality variables related to leaderless group discussion. *Journal of Abnormal and Social Psychology,* 1953, **48**, 120–128.

Bass, B. M., & Norton, F-T. M. Group size and leaderless discussions. *Journal of Applied Psychology,* 1951, **35**, 397–400.

Bass, B. M., Pryer, M. W., Gaier, E. L., & Flint, A. W. Interacting effects of control motivation, group practice and problems difficulty on attempted leadership. *Journal of Abnormal and Social Psychology,* 1958, **56**, 352–358.

Bass, B. M., & Wurster, C. R. Effects of company rank on LGD performance of oil refinery supervisors. *Journal of Applied Psychology,* 1953a, **37**, 100–104.

Bass, B. M., & Wurster, C. R. Effects of the nature of the problem on LGD performance. *Journal of Applied Psychology,* 1953b, **37,** 96–99.

Bass, B. M., Wurster, C. R., Doll, P. A., & Clair, D. J. Situational and personality factors in leadership among sorority women. *Psychological Monographs,* 1953, **67,** No. 16 (Whole No. 366).

Bateson, N. Familiarization, group discussion, and risk-taking. *Journal of Experimental Social Psychology,* 1966, **2,** 119–129.

Battle, E. S., & Rotter, J. B. Children's feelings of personal control as related to social class and ethnic group. *Journal of Personality,* 1963, **31,** 482–490.

Bauer, E. A. Personal space: A study of blacks and whites. *Sociometry,* 1973, **36,** 402–408.

Baumgartel, H., & Goldstein, J. W. Need and value shifts in college training groups. *Journal of Applied Behavioral Science,* 1967, **3,** 87–101.

Baumgartel, H., & Sobol, R. Background and organizational factors in absenteeism. *Personnel Psychology,* 1959, **12,** 431–443.

Bavelas, A. A mathematical model for group structures. *Applied Anthropology,* 1948, **7,** 16–30.

Bavelas, A. Communication patterns in task-oriented groups. *Journal of the Acoustical Society of America,* 1950, **22,** 725–730.

Bavelas, A., Hastorf, A. H., Gross, A. E., & Kite, W. R. Experiments on the alteration of group structure. *Journal of Experimental Social Psychology,* 1965, **1,** 55–70.

Baxter, J. C. Interpersonal spacing in natural settings. *Sociometry,* 1970, **33,** 444–456.

Beaty, W. E., & Shaw, M. E. Some effects of social interaction on probability learning. *Journal of Psychology,* 1965, **59,** 299–306.

Beaver, A. P. The initiation of social contacts by pre-school children. *Child Development Monographs,* 1932, No. 7.

Becker, F. D. A study of spatial markers. *Journal of Personality and Social Psychology,* 1973, **26,** 439–445.

Becker, F. D., & Mayo, C. Delineating personal distance and territory. *Environment and Behavior,* 1971, **3,** 375–382.

Beckhouse, L., Tanur, J., Weiler, J., & Weinstein, E. And some men have leadership thrust upon them. *Journal of Personality and Social Psychology,* 1975, **31,** 557–566.

Beckwith, J., Iverson, M. A., & Render, M. E. Test anxiety, task relevance of group experience, and change in level of aspiration. *Journal of Personality and Social Psychology,* 1965, **1,** 579–588.

Bedell, J., & Sistrunk, F. Power, opportunity costs, and sex in a mixed-motive game. *Journal of Personality and Social Psychology,* 1973, **25,** 219–226.

Begum, B. O., & Lehr, D. J. Effects of authoritarianism on vigilance performance. *Journal of Applied Psychology,* 1963, **47,** 75–77.

Bell, G. B., & Hall, H. E., Jr. The relationship between leadership and empathy. *Journal of Abnormal and Social Psychology,* 1954, **49,** 156–157.

Beloff, H. Two forms of social conformity: Acquiescence and conventionality. *Journal of Abnormal and Social Psychology,* 1958, **56,** 99–104.

Bem, D. J. Self perception: An alternative interpretation of cognitive dissonance phenomena. *Psychological Review,* 1967, **74,** 183–200.

Bem, D. J., Wallach, M. A., & Kogan, N. Group decision making under risk of aversive consequences. *Journal of Personality and Social Psychology,* 1965, **1,** 453–460.

Bennis, W. G., & Shepard, H. A. A theory of group development. *Human Relations,* 1956, **9,** 415–437.

Bennis, W., Burke, R., Cutter, H., Harrington, H., & Hoffman, J. A note on some problems of measurement and prediction in a training group. *Group Psychotherapy,* 1957, **10,** 328–341.

Benoit-Smullyan, E. Status, status types, and status interrelations. *American Sociological Review,* 1944, **9,** 151–161.

Berenda, R. W. *The influence of the group on the judgments of children.* New York: King's Crown, 1950.

Berg, I. A., & Bass, B. M. (Eds.) *Conformity and deviation.* New York: Harper, 1961.

Berger, E. The relation between expressed acceptance of self and expressed acceptance of others. *Journal of Abnormal and Social Psychology,* 1952, **47,** 778–782.

Berkowitz, L. Group standards, cohesiveness, and productivity. *Human Relations,* 1954, **7,** 509–519.

Berkowitz, L., & Daniels, L. R. Responsibility and dependency. *Journal of Abnormal and Social Psychology,* 1963, **66,** 429–436.

Bernhardt, K. S., Millichamp, D. A., Charles, M. W., & McFarland, M. P. An analysis of the social contacts of pre-school children with the aid of motion pictures. *University of Toronto Studies of Child Development,* 1937, No. 10.

Berrien, F. K. A general systems approach to organizations. In M. D. Dunnette (Ed.), *Handbook of industrial and organizational psychology.* Chicago: Rand McNally, 1976. Pp. 41–62.

Bettelheim, B. Segregation: New style. *School Review,* 1958, **66,** 251–272.

Bixenstine, V. E., & Douglas, J. Effects of psychopathology on group consensus and cooperative choice in a six-person game. *Journal of Personality and Social Psychology,* 1967, **5,** 32–37.

Bixenstine, V. E., Potash, H. M., & Wilson, K. V. Effects of level of cooperative choice by the other player on choices in a prisoner's dilemma game. Part I. *Journal of Abnormal and Social Psychology,* 1963, **66,** 308–313.

Black, T. E., & Higbee, K. L. Effects of power, threat, and sex on exploitation. *Journal of Personality and Social Psychology,* 1973, **27,** 382–388.

Blanchard, F. A., Adelman, L., & Cook, S. W. Effect of group success and failure upon interpersonal attraction in cooperating interracial groups. *Journal of Personality and Social Psychology,* 1975, **31,** 1020–1030.

Blanchard, F. A., Weigel, R. H., & Cook, S. W. The effect of relative competence of group members upon interpersonal attraction in cooperating interracial groups. *Journal of Personality and Social Psychology,* 1975, **32,** 519–530.

Blank, T. O., Staff, I., & Shaver, P. Social facilitation of word associations:

Further questions. *Journal of Personality and Social Psychology,* 1976, **34,** 725–733.

Blascovich, J., & Ginsburg, G. P. Emergent norms and choice shifts involving risks. *Sociometry,* 1974, **37,** 205–218.

Blascovich, J., Ginsburg, G. P., & Howe, R. C. Blackjack, choice shifts in the field. *Sociometry,* 1976, **39,** 274–276.

Blau, P. M. Co-operation and competition in a bureaucracy. *American Journal of Sociology,* 1954, **59,** 530–535.

Blau, P. M. Social integration, social rank, and the process of interaction. *Human Relations,* 1959–1960, **18,** 152–157.

Bogardus, E. S. Leadership and social situations. *Sociology and Social Research,* 1931-32, **16,** 164–170.

Bolman, L. Laboratory versus lecture in training executives. *Journal of Applied Behavioral Science,* 1970, **6,** 323–335.

Bond, J. R., & Vinacke, W. E. Coalitions in mixed-sex triads. *Sociometry,* 1961, **24,** 61–75.

Bonner, H. *Group dynamics: Principles and applications.* New York: Ronald, 1959.

Borg, W. R. Prediction of small group role behavior from personality variables. *Journal of Abnormal and Social Psychology,* 1960, **60,** 112–116.

Borgatta, E. F. Sidesteps toward a nonspecial theory. *Psychological Review,* 1954, **61,** 343–352.

Borgatta, M. L. Power structure and coalitions in three person groups. *Journal of Social Psychology,* 1961, **55,** 287–300.

Borko, H. (Ed.) *Computer applications in the behavioral sciences.* Englewood Cliffs, N.J.: Prentice-Hall, 1962.

Bouchard, T. J., Jr. Personality, problem-solving procedure, and performance in small groups. *Journal of Applied Psychology,* 1969, **53,** 1–29.

Bovard, E. W. Group structure and perception. *Journal of Abnormal and Social Psychology,* 1951, **46,** 398–405.

Bovard, E. W. Conformity to social norms and attraction to the group. *Science,* 1953, **118,** 598–599.

Bovard, E. W. Interaction and attraction to the group. *Human Relations,* 1956, **9,** 481–489.

Bowen, A. J., Jr. Coalition patterns in three-person family and non-family groups. Unpublished doctoral dissertation, University of Florida, Gainesville, 1966.

Boyd, J. B., & Elliss, J. D. *Findings of research into senior management seminars.* Toronto: The Hydro-Electric Power Commission of Ontario, 1962.

Bradley, P. H. Power, status, and upward communication in small decision-making groups. *Communication Monographs,* 1978, **45,** 33–43.

Brandon, A. C. Status congruence and expectations. *Sociometry,* 1965, **28,** 272–288.

Bray, R. M., Kerr, N. L., & Atkin, R. S. Effects of group size, problem difficulty, and sex on group performance and member reactions. *Journal of Personality and Social Psychology,* 1978, **36,** 1224–1240.

Brown, R. *Social psychology.* New York: Free Press, 1965.

Brown, R. Further comment on the risky shift. *American Psychologist*, 1974, **29**, 468–470.

Bryan, J. H., & Test, M. A. Models and helping: Naturalistic studies in aiding behavior. *Journal of Personality and Social Psychology*, 1967, **6**, 400–407.

Buban, S. L. Focus control and prominence in triads. *Sociometry*, 1976, **39**, 281–288.

Buck, R., Miller, R. E., & Caul, W. F. Sex, personality, and physiological variables in the communication of affect via facial expression. *Journal of Personality and Social Psychology*, 1974, **30**, 587–596.

Bunker, D. R. Individual applications of laboratory training. *Journal of Applied Behavioral Science*, 1965, **1**, 131–148.

Burgess, E. W., & Cottrell, L. S. *Predicting success or failure in marriage.* Englewood Cliffs, N.J.: Prentice-Hall, 1939.

Burke, R. L., & Bennis, W. G. Changes in perception of self and others during human relations training. *Human Relations*, 1961, **14**, 165–182.

Burnstein, E., & Vinokur, A. What a person thinks upon learning that he has chosen differently from others: Nice evidence for the persuasive-arguments explanation of choice shifts. *Journal of Experimental Social Psychology*, 1975, **11**, 412–426.

Burnstein, E., Vinokur, A., & Pichevin, M-F. What do differences between own, admired, and attributed choices have to do with group induced shifts in choice. *Journal of Experimental Social Psychology*, 1974, **10**, 428–443.

Burnstein, E., Vinokur, A., & Trope, Y. Interpersonal comparison versus persuasive argumentation: A more direct test of alternative explanations for group induced shifts in individual choice. *Journal of Experimental Social Psychology*, 1973, **9**, 236–245.

Burton, A. The influence of social factors upon the persistence of satiation in school children. *Child Development*, 1941, **12**, 121–129.

Burtt, H. E. Sex differences in the effect of discussion. *Journal of Experimental Psychology*, 1920, **3**, 390–395.

Butler, D. C., & Miller, N. Power to reward and punish in social interaction. *Journal of Experimental Social Psychology*, 1965, **1**, 311–322.

Buys, C. J. Humans would do better without groups. *Personality and Social Psychology Bulletin*, 1978, **4**, 123–125.

Byrne, D. Interpersonal attraction and attitudes similarity. *Journal of Abnormal and Social Psychology*, 1961, **62**, 713–715.

Byrne, D., & Buehler, J. A. A note on the influence of propinquity upon acquaintanceships. *Journal of Abnormal and Social Psychology*, 1955, **51**, 147–148.

Byrne, D., Clore, J. L., Jr., & Worchel, P. Effect of economic similarity-dissimilarity on interpersonal attraction. *Journal of Personality and Social Psychology*, 1966, **4**, 220–224.

Byrne, D., & Griffitt, W. A developmental investigation of the law of attraction. *Journal of Personality and Social Psychology*, 1966, **4**, 699–702.

Byrne, D., Griffitt, W., & Stefaniak, D. Attraction and similarity of personality characteristics. *Journal of Personality and Social Psychology*, 1967, **5**, 82–90.

Byrne, D., London, O., & Griffitt, W. The effect of topic importance and attitude similarity-dissimilarity on attraction in an intra-stranger design. *Psychonomic Science,* 1968, **11,** 303–304.

Byrne, D., & Nelson, D. Attraction as a function of attitude similarity-dissimilarity: The effect of topic importance. *Psychonomic Science,* 1964, **1,** 93–94.

Byrne, D., & Nelson, D. Attraction as a linear function of proportion of positive reinforcements. *Journal of Personality and Social Psychology,* 1965a, **1,** 659–663.

Byrne, D., & Nelson, D. The effect of topic importance and attitude similarity-dissimilarity on attraction in a multi-stranger design. *Psychonomic Science,* 1965b, **3,** 449–450.

Byrne, D., Nelson, D., & Reeves, K. Effects of consensual validation and invalidation on attraction as a function of verifiability. *Journal of Experimental Social Psychology,* 1966, **2,** 98–107.

Byrne, D., & Rhamey, R. Magnitude of positive and negative reinforcements as a determinant of attraction. *Journal of Personality and Social Psychology,* 1965, **2,** 884–889.

Caine, B. T. Role making and the assumption of leadership. In Associates, Office of Military Leadership (Eds.), *A Study of Organizational Leadership.* Harrisburg, Pa.: Stackpole Books, 1976. Pp. 362–372.

Campbell, D. T. Common fate, similarity, and other indices of the status of aggregates of persons as social entities. *Behavioral Science,* 1958, **3,** 14-25.

Campbell, D. T., Kruskal, W. H., & Wallace, W. P. Seating aggregation as an index of attitude. *Sociometry,* 1966, **29,** 1–15.

Campbell, D. T., & Stanley, J. C. Experimental and quasi-experimental designs for research on teaching. In N. L. Gage (Ed.), *Handbook of research on teaching.* Chicago: Rand McNally, 1963. Pp. 171–246.

Caple, R. B. The sequential stages of group development. *Small Group Behavior,* 1978, **9,** 470–476.

Caplow, T. Further development of a theory of coalitions in the triad. *American Journal of Sociology,* 1959, **64,** 488–493.

Carr, S. J., & Dabbs, J. M., Jr. The effects of lighting, distance and intimacy of topic on verbal and visual behavior. *Sociometry,* 1974, **37,** 592–600.

Carter, L. F. On defining leadership. In M. Sherif & M. O. Wilson (Eds.), *Group relations at the crossroads.* New York: Harper & Row, 1953. Pp. 262–265.

Carter, L. F. Recording and evaluating the performance of individuals as members of small groups. *Personnel Psychology,* 1954, **7,** 477–484.

Carter, L. F., Haythorn, W. W., & Howell, M. A. A further investigation of the criteria of leadership. *Journal of Abnormal and Social Psychology,* 1950, **45,** 350–358.

Carter, L., Haythorn, W. W., Shriver, B., & Lanzetta, J. The behavior of leaders and other group members. *Journal of Abnormal and Social Psychology,* 1951, **46,** 589–595.

Carter, L. F., & Nixon, M. An investigation of the relationship between four criteria of leadership ability for three different tasks. *Journal of Psychology,* 1949, **27,** 245–261.

Cartwright, D., & Zander, A. (Eds.) *Group dynamics: Research and theory.* Evanston, Ill.: Row, Peterson, 1953.

Cartwright, D., & Zander, A. (Eds.) *Group dynamics: Research and theory.* (2d ed.) Evanston, Ill.: Row, Peterson, 1960.

Cartwright, D., & Zander, A. (Eds.) *Group dynamics: Research and theory.* (3d ed.) New York: Harper & Row, 1968.

Cartwright, J. A. A laboratory investigation of groupthink. *Communication Monographs,* 1978, **45,** 229–246.

Cattell, R. B. Concepts and methods in the measurement of group syntality. *Psychological Review,* 1948, **55,** 48–63.

Cattell, R. B. Determining syntality dimension as a basis for morale and leadership measurement. In H. Guetzkow (Ed.), *Groups, leadership and men.* Pittsburgh: Carnegie Press, 1951a. Pp. 16–27.

Cattell, R. B. New concepts for measuring leadership, in terms of group syntality. *Human Relations,* 1951b, **4,** 161–184.

Cattell, R. B., Saunders, D. R., & Stice, G. F. The dimensions of syntality in small groups. *Human Relations,* 1953, **6,** 331–356.

Cattell, R. B., & Stice, G. F. The dimensions of groups and their relations to the behavior of members. Champaign, Ill.: Institute for Personality and Ability Testing, 1960.

Cattell, R. B., & Wispe, L. G. The dimensions of syntality in small groups. *Journal of Social Psychology,* 1948, **28,** 57–78.

Cervin, V. Individual behavior in social situations: Its relation to anxiety, neuroticism, and group solidarity. *Journal of Experimental Psychology,* 1956, **51,** 161–168.

Chaney, M. V., & Vinacke, W. E. Achievement and nurturance in triads varying in power distribution. *Journal of Abnormal and Social Psychology,* 1960, **60,** 175–181.

Chapko, M. K., & Revers, R. R. Contagion in a crowd: The effects of crowd size and initial discrepancy from unanimity. *Journal of Personality and Social Psychology,* 1976, **33,** 382–386.

Chaubey, N. P. Effect of age on expectancy of success and on risk-taking behavior. *Journal of Personality and Social Psychology,* 1974, **29,** 774–778.

Chemers, M. M., & Skrzypek, G. J. Experimental test of the contingency model of leadership effectiveness. *Journal of Personality and Social Psychology,* 1972, **24,** 172–177.

Chertkoff, J. M., & Esser, J. K. A test of three theories of coalition formation when agreements can be short-term or long-term. *Journal of Personality and Social Psychology,* 1977, **35,** 237–249.

Cheyne, J. A., & Efran, M. G. The effects of spatial and interpersonal variables on the invasion of group controlled territories. *Sociometry,* 1972, **35,** 477–489.

Clark, R. D. III, Crockett, W. H., & Archer, R. L. Risk-as-value hypothesis: The relationship between perception of self, others, and the risky shift. *Journal of Personality and Social Psychology,* 1971, **20,** 425–429.

Cleland, S. *Influence of plant size on industrial relations.* Princeton University Press, 1955.

Clement, D. E., & Schiereck, J. J., Jr. Sex composition and group performance in a visual signal detection task. *Memory and Cognition*, 1973, **1**, 251–255.

Clifford, M. M. Effects of competition as a motivational technique in the classroom. *American Educational Research Journal*, 1972, **9**, 123–137.

Coch, L., & French, J. R. P., Jr. Overcoming resistance to change. *Human Relations*, 1948, **1**, 512–532.

Cohen, A. M. Changing small group communication networks. *Journal of Communication*, 1961, **11**, 116–124 and 128.

Cohen, A. M. Changing small group communication networks. *Administrative Science Quarterly*, 1962, **6**, 443–462.

Cohen, A. R. Experimental effects of ego-defense preference on interpersonal relations. *Journal of Abnormal and Social Psychology*, 1956, **52**, 19–27.

Cohen, A. R. Situational structure, self-esteem, and threat-oriented reactions to power. In D. Cartwright (Ed.), *Studies in social power*. Ann Arbor, Mich.: Institute for Social Research, 1959.

Cohen, A. R., Stotland, E., & Wolfe, D. M. An experimental investigation of need for cognition. *Journal of Abnormal and Social Psychology*, 1955, **51**, 291–294.

Cohen, G. B. Communication network and distribution of "weight" of group members as determinants of group effectiveness. *Journal of Experimental Social Psychology*, 1968, **4**, 302–314.

Collins, E. B., & Guetzkow, H. *A social psychology of group processes for decision-making*. New York: Wiley, 1964.

Cook, S. W., Havel, J., & Christ, J. R. The effects of an orientation program for foreign students. Mimeographed report, Research Center for Human Relations, New York University, 1957. (Cited in Selltiz, C., Jahoda, M., Deutsch, M., & Cook, S. W. *Research methods in social relations*. New York: Holt, Rinehart and Winston, 1961. Pp. 128–129.)

Cook, T. D., & Campbell, D. T. *Quasi-experimentation: Design and analysis for field settings*. Chicago: Rand McNally, 1979.

Cooper, C. L. An attempt to assess the psychologically disturbing effects of T-group training. *British Journal of Social and Clinical Psychology*, 1972a, **11**, 342–345.

Cooper, C. L. Coping with life stress after sensitivity training. *Psychological Reports*, 1972b, **31**, 602.

Cooper, H. M. Statistically combining independent studies: A meta-analysis of sex differences in conformity research. *Journal of Personality and Social Psychology*, 1979, **37**, 131–146.

Cooper, J. Deception and role-playing: On telling the good guys from the bad guys. *American Psychologist*, 1976, **31**, 605–610.

Costanzo, P. R. Conformity development as a function of self-blame. *Journal of Personality and Social Psychology*, 1970, **14**, 366–374.

Costanzo, P. R., Reitan, H. T., & Shaw, M. E. Conformity as a function of experimentally induced minority and majority competence. *Psychonomic Science*, 1968, **10**, 329–330.

Costanzo, P. R., & Shaw, M. E. Conformity as a function of age level. *Child Development*, 1966, **37**, 967–975.

Cottrell, N. B. Social facilitation. In C. G. McClintock (Ed.), *Experimental social psychology*. New York: Holt, 1972. Pp. 185–236.

Cottrell, N. B., Wack, D. L., Sekerak, G. J., & Rittle, R. H. Social facilitation of dominant and subordinate responses by the presence of an audience and the mere presence of others. *Journal of Personality and Social Psychology*, 1968, **9**, 245–250.

Coutts, L. M., & Schneider, F. W. Verbal behavior in an unfocused interaction as a function of sex and distance. *Journal of Experimental Social Psychology*, 1975, **11**, 64–77.

Coutu, W. Role-playing vs. role-taking: An appeal for clarification. *American Sociological Review*, 1951, **16**, 180–187.

Cronbach, L. J., & Furby, L. How should we measure change—or should we? *Psychological Bulletin*, 1970, **74**, 68–80.

Cronbach, L. J., & Gleser, G. C. Assessing similarity between profiles. *Psychological Bulletin*, 1953, **50**, 456–473.

Crockett, W. H. Emergent leadership in small decision-making groups. *Journal of Abnormal and Social Psychology*, 1955, **51**, 378–383.

Crutchfield, R. S. Conformity and character. *American Psychologist*, 1955, **10**, 191–198.

Culbert, S. A. Trainer self-disclosure and member growth in two T-groups. *Journal of Applied Behavioral Science*, 1968, **4**, 47–73.

Daniels, J. C. The effects of streaming in the primary school: 2. Comparison of streamed and unstreamed schools. *British Journal of Educational Psychology*, 1961, **31**, 119–127.

Darley, J. M., & Latane, B. Bystander intervention in emergencies: Diffusion of responsibility. *Journal of Personality and Social Psychology*, 1968, **8**, 377–383.

Darley, J. M., Moriarty, T., Darley, S., & Berscheid, E. Increased conformity to a fellow deviant as a function of prior deviation. *Journal of Experimental Social Psychology*, 1974, **10**, 211–223.

Dashiell, J. F. An experimental analysis of some group effects. *Journal of Abnormal and Social Psychology*, 1930, **25**, 190–199.

Davis, J. H., Kerr, N. L., Atkin, R. S., Hold, R., & Meek, D. The decision processes of 6- and 12-person mock juries assigned unanimous and two-thirds majority rules. *Journal of Personality and Social Psychology*, 1975, **32**, 1–14.

Davis, J. H., & Restle, F. The analysis of problems and prediction of group problem solving. *Journal of Abnormal and Social Psychology*, 1963, **66**, 103–116.

Davis, K. The child and the social structure. *Journal of Educational Sociology*, 1940, **14**, 217–229.

Dawe, H. C. The influence of size of kindergarten group upon performance. *Child Development*, 1934, **5**, 295–303.

Dean, L. M., Willis, F. N., & Hewitt, J. Initial interaction distance among individuals equal and unequal in military rank. *Journal of Personality and Social Psychology*, 1975, **32**, 294–299.

de Gloria, J., & de Ridder, R. Sex differences in aggression: Are current notions misleading? *European Journal of Social Psychology*, 1979, **9**, 49–66.

DeLamater, J. A definition of "group". *Small Group Behavior*, 1974, **5**, 30–44.

Delbecq, A. L., & Kaplan, S. J. The myth of the indigenous community leader within the war on poverty. *Academy of Management Journal*, 1968, **11**, 11–25.

Desor, J. A. Toward a psychological theory of crowding. *Journal of Personality and Social Psychology*, 1972, **21**, 79–83.

de Swaan, A. An empirical model of coalition formation as an n-person game of policy distance minimization. In S. Groenings (Ed.), *The Study of Coalition Behavior*. New York: Holt, Rinehart and Winston, 1970.

Deutsch, K. W. *Political community at the international level*. Garden City, N.Y.: Doubleday, 1954.

Deutsch, M. An experimental study of the effects of co-operation and competition upon group process. *Human Relations*, 1949a, **2**, 199–232.

Deutsch, M. A theory of co-operation and competition. *Human Relations*, 1949b, **2**, 129–152.

Deutsch, M. Field theory in social psychology. In G. Lindzey & E. Aronson (Eds.), *The Handbook of Social Psychology*, 2d ed. Reading, Mass: Addison-Wesley, 1968. Pp. 412–487.

Deutsch, M., & Collins, M. E. *Interracial housing: A psychological evaluation of a social experiment*. Minneapolis: The University of Minnesota Press, 1951.

Deutsch, M., & Gerard, H. B. A study of normative and informational social influences upon individual judgment. *Journal of Abnormal and Social Psychology*, 1955, **51**, 629–636.

Deutsch, M., & Krauss, R. Studies of interpersonal bargaining. *Conflict Resolution*, 1962, **1**, 52–76.

DeVries, D. L., Edwards, K. J., & Fennessey, G. M. Using Teams-Games-Tournament (TGT) in the classroom. Center for Social Organization in Schools, Johns Hopkins University, June, 1973.

DeVries, D. L., Edwards, K. J., & Wells, E. H. Team competition effects on classroom process. Report No. 174, Center for Social Organization of Schools, Johns Hopkins University, 1974.

DeVries, D. L., & Mescon, I. T. Teams-Games-Tournament: An effective task and reward structure in the elementary grades. Report No 189, Center for Social Organization of Schools, Johns Hopkins University, January, 1975.

Diener, E., Dineen, J., Endresen, K., Beaman, A. L., & Fraser, S. C. Effects of altered responsibility, cognitive set, and modeling on physical aggression and deindividuation. *Journal of Personality and Social Psychology*, 1975, **31**, 328–337.

Diener, E., Westford, K. L., Dineen, J., & Fraser, S. C. Beat the pacificist: The deindividuating effects of anonymity and group presence. *Proceedings of the 81st Annual Convention of the American Psychological Association*, 1973, **8**, 221–222.

Dion, K. L. Status equity, sex composition of group, and intergroup bias. *Personality and Social Psychology Bulletin*, 1979, **5**, 240–244.

Downing, J. Cohesiveness, perception, and values. *Human Relations*, 1958, **11**, 157–166.

Downs, C. W., & Pickett, T. An analysis of the effects of nine leader-group compatibility contingencies upon productivity and member satisfaction. *Communication Monographs*, 1977, **44**, 220–230.

Drews, E. M. Recent findings about gifted adolescents. In E. P. Torrance (Ed.), *New ideas: Third Minnesota conference on gifted children.* Minneapolis: Center for Continuing Studies, University of Minnesota, 1961.

Dunnette, M. D. Personnel management. *Annual Review of Psychology,* 1962, **13,** 285–314.

Durkheim, E. Représentations individuelles et représentations collectives. *Revue de Métaphysique,* 1898, **6,** 274–302. (Translated by D. F. Pocock, *Sociology and philosophy.* New York: Free Press, 1953.)

Duval, S. Conformity on a visual task as a function of personal novelty on attitudinal dimensions and being reminded of the object status of self. *Journal of Experimental Social Psychology,* 1976, **12,** 87–98.

Dymond, R. S., Hughes, A. S., & Raabe, V. L. Measurable changes in empathy with age. *Journal of Consulting Psychology,* 1952, **16,** 202–206.

Dyson, J. W., Godwin, P. H. B., & Hazlewood, L. A. Group composition, leadership orientation, and decisional outcomes. *Small Group Behavior,* 1976, **7,** 114–128.

Eash, M. J. Grouping: What have we learned: *Educational Leadership,* 1961, **18,** 429–434.

Ebbesen, E. B., & Bowers, R. J. Proportion of risky to conservative arguments in a group discussion and choice shifts. *Journal of Personality and Social Psychology,* 1974, **29,** 316–327.

Eberts, E. H., & Lepper, M. R. Individual consistency in the proxemic behavior of preschool children. *Journal of Personality and Social Psychology,* 1975, **32,** 841–849.

Edney, J. J. Property, possession and permanence: A field study in human territoriality. *Journal of Applied Social Psychology,* 1972, **2,** 275–282.

Edney, J. J. Territoriality and control: A field experiment. *Journal of Personality and Social Psychology,* 1975, **31,** 1108–1115.

Edney, J. J., & Grundmann, M. J. Friendship, group size and boundary size: Small group spaces. *Small Group Behavior,* 1979, **10,** 124–135.

Edney, J. J., & Jordan-Edney, N. L. Territorial spacing on a beach. *Sociometry,* 1974, **37,** 92–104.

Edney, J. J., & Uhlig, S. R. Individual and small group territories. *Small Group Behavior,* 1977, **8,** 457–468.

Edwards, D. W. Blacks versus whites: When is race a relevant variable? *Journal of Personality and Social Psychology,* 1974, **29,** 39–49.

Edwards, K. J., & DeVries, D. L. The effects of Teams-Games-Tournament and two instructional variations on classroom process, student attitudes and student achievement. Report No. 172, Center for Social Organization of Schools, Johns Hopkins University, April, 1974.

Edwards, K. J., DeVries, D. L., & Snyder, J. P. Games and teams: A winning combination. *Simulation and Games,* 1972, **3,** 247–269.

Egerbladh, T. The function of group size and ability level on solving a multidimensional complementary task. *Journal of Personality and Social Psychology,* 1976, **34,** 805–808.

Ellis, D. G., & Fisher, B. A. Phases of conflict in small group development: A Markov analysis. *Human Communication Research,* 1975, **1,** 195–212.

Emerson, R. M. Power-dependence relations: Two experiments. *Sociometry,* 1964, **27,** 282–298.

Eoyang, C. K. Effects of group size and privacy in residential crowding. *Journal of Personality and Social Psychology,* 1974, **30,** 389–392.

Eskilson, A., & Wiley, M. G. Sex composition and leadership in small groups. *Sociometry,* 1976, **39,** 183–194.

Exline, R. V. Group climate as a factor in the relevance and accuracy of social perception. *Journal of Abnormal and Social Psychology,* 1957, **55,** 382–388.

Exline, R. V. Explorations in the process of person perception: Visual interaction in relation to competition, sex, and need for affiliation. *Journal of Personality,* 1963, **31,** 1–20.

Exline, R. V., Gray, D., & Schuette, D. Visual behavior in a dyad as affected by interview content and sex of respondent. *Journal of Personality and Social Psychology,* 1965, **1,** 201–209.

Farnsworth, P. R. Concerning so-called group effects. *Journal of Genetic Psychology,* 1928, **35,** 587–594.

Farrell, M. P. Collective projection and group structure: The relationship between deviance and projection in groups. *Small Group Behavior,* 1979, **10,** 81-100.

Faucheux, C., & Moscovici, S. Etude de sur la créativité des groups. Tâche, structure des communications et réussite. *Bulletin d'Etudes et Recherches Psychologiques,* 1960, **9,** 11–12.

Feldman, R. A. An experimental study of conformity behavior as small group phenomenon. *Small Group Behavior,* 1974, **5,** 404–426.

Fenelon, J. R., & Megargee, E. I. Influence of race on the manifestation of leadership. *Journal of Applied Psychology,* 1971, **55,** 353–358.

Fenigstein, A. Self-consciousness, self-attention, and social interaction. *Journal of Personality and Social Psychology,* 1979, **37,** 75–86.

Festinger, L. Informal social communication. *Psychological Review,* 1950, **57,** 271–282.

Festinger, L. A theory of social comparison processes. *Human Relations,* 1954, **7,** 117–140.

Festinger, L. Group attraction and membership. In D. Cartwright and A. Zander (Eds.), *Group dynamics: Research and theory.* Evanston, Ill.: Row, Peterson, 1953a. Pp. 92–101.

Festinger, L. Laboratory experiments. In L. Festinger & D. Katz (Eds.), *Research methods in the behavioral sciences.* New York: The Dryden Press, Inc., 1953b. Pp. 136–172.

Festinger, L., Gerard, H., Hymovitch, B., Kelley, H. H., & Raven, B. The influence process in the presence of extreme deviates. *Human Relations,* 1952, **5,** 327–346.

Festinger, L., Pepitone, A., & Newcomb, T. Some consequences of deindividuation in a group. *Journal of Abnormal and Social Psychology,* 1952, **47,** 382–389.

Festinger, L., Schachter, S., & Back, K. W. *Social pressure in informal groups.* New York: Harper, 1950.

Fiedler, F. E. A contingency model of leadership effectiveness. In L. Berkowitz

(Ed.), *Advances in experimental social psychology.* Vol. 1. New York: Academic Press, 1964. Pp. 149–190.

Fiedler, F. E. The effect of leadership and cultural heterogeneity on group performance: A test of the contingency model. *Journal of Experimental Social Psychology,* 1966, **2,** 237–264.

Fiedler, F. E. *A theory of leadership effectiveness.* New York: McGraw-Hill, 1967.

Fiedler, F. E. The effects of leadership training and experience: A contingency model interpretation. *Administrative Science Quarterly,* 1972, **17,** 453–470.

Fiedler, F. E. The contingency model and the dynamics of the leadership process. In L. Berkowitz (Ed.), *Advances in experimental social psychology.* Vol. 11. New York: Academic Press, 1978. Pp. 59–112.

Fiedler, F. E., Hutchins, E. B., & Dodge, J. S. Quasi-therapeutic relations in small college and military groups. *Psychological Monographs,* 1959, **73,** No. 473.

Fiedler, F. E., Meuwese, W. A. T., & Oonk, S. Performance of laboratory tasks requiring group creativity. *Acta Psychologica,* 1961, **18,** 100–119.

Fiedler, F. E., Warrington, W. G., & Blaisdell, F. J. Unconscious attitudes as correlates of sociometric choice in a social group. *Journal of Abnormal and Social Psychology,* 1952, **47,** 790–796.

Fisher, B. A. Decision emergence: Phases in group decision-making. *Speech Monographs,* 1970a, **37,** 53–66.

Fisher, B. A. The process of decision modification in small discussion groups. *Journal of Communication,* 1970b, **20,** 51–64.

Fisher, B. A. Communication research and the task-oriented group. *Journal of Communication,* 1971, **21,** 136–149.

Fisher, J. D., & Byrne, D. Too close for comfort: Sex differences in response to invasions of personal space. *Journal of Personality and Social Psychology,* 1975, **32,** 15–21.

Flanders, J. P., & Thistlethwaite, D. L. Effects of familiarization and group discussion upon risk taking. *Journal of Personality and Social Psychology,* 1967, **5,** 91–97.

Flowers, M. L. A laboratory test of some implications of Janis's groupthink hypothesis. *Journal of Personality and Social Psychology,* 1977, **35,** 888–896.

Fodor, E. M. Stimulated work climate as an influence on choice of leadership style. *Personality and Social Psychology Bulletin,* 1978, **4,** 111–114.

Ford, D. L., Jr., Nemiroff, P. M., & Pasmore, W. A. Group decision-making performance as influenced by group tradition. *Small Group Behavior,* 1977, **8,** 223–228.

Forgas, J. P. Social episodes and social structure in an academic setting: The social environment of an intact group. *Journal of Experimental Social Psychology,* 1978, **14,** 434–448.

Foulds, M. L., Guinan, J. F., & Warehime, R. G. Marathon group: Changes in a measure of dogmatism. *Small Group Behavior,* 1974, **5,** 387–392.

Foulkes, S. H., & Anthony, E. J. *Group psychotherapy: The psychoanalytic approach.* London: Penguin Books, 1957.

Fouriezos, N. T., Hutt, M. L., & Guetzkow, H. Measurement of self-oriented needs in discussion groups. *Journal of Abnormal and Social Psychology,* 1950, **45,** 682–690.

Frank, F., & Anderson, L. R. Effects of task and group size upon group productivity and member satisfaction. *Sociometry,* 1971, **34,** 135–149.

Fraser, S. C., Kelem, R. T., Diener, E., & Beaman, A. L. The effects of deindividuation variables on stealing among Holloween trick-or-treaters. *Journal of Personality and Social Psychology,* 1975, **33,** 178–183.

Freed, A. M., Chandler, P. J., Mouton, J. S., & Blake, R. R. Stimulus background factors in sign violation. *Journal of Personality,* 1955, **23,** 499.

Freedman, J. L. Role playing: Psychology by consensus. *Journal of Personality and Social Psychology,* 1969, **13,** 107–114.

Freedman, J. L., Carlsmith, J. M., & Sears, D. O. *Social Psychology* (2d ed.). Englewood Cliffs, N.J.: Prentice-Hall, 1974.

Freedman, J. L., Klevansky, S., & Ehrlich, P. The effect of crowding on human task performance. *Journal of Applied Social Psychology,* 1971, **1,** 7–25.

Freedman, J. L., Levy, A. S., Buchanan, R. W., & Price, J. Crowding and human aggressiveness. *Journal of Experimental Social Psychology,* 1972, **8,** 528–548.

Freeman, S., Walker, M. R., Borden, R., & Latane, B. Diffusion of responsibility and restaurant tipping: Cheaper by the bunch. *Personality and Social Psychology Bulletin,* 1975, **1,** 584–587.

Freese, L., & Cohen, B. P. Eliminating status generalization. *Sociometry,* 1973, **36,** 177–193.

French, J. R. P., Jr. The disruption and cohesion of groups. *Journal of Abnormal and Social Psychology,* 1941, **36,** 361–377.

French, J. R. P., Jr. A formal theory of social power. *Psychological Review,* 1956, **63,** 181–194.

French, J. R. P., Jr., & Raven, B. The bases of social power. In D. Cartwright (Ed.), *Studies in social power.* Ann Arbor, Mich.: Institute for Social Research, 1959. Pp. 150–167.

Friedland, N., Arnold, S. E., & Thibaut, J. Motivational bases in mixed-motive interactions: The effects of comparison levels. *Journal of Experimental Social Psychology,* 1974, **10,** 188–199.

Freidlander, F. The impact of organizational training upon the effectiveness and interaction of ongoing work groups. *Personnel Psychology,* 1967, **20,** 289-309.

Fry, C. L. Personality and acquisition factors in the development of coordination strategy. *Journal of Personality and Social Psychology,* 1965, **2,** 403–407.

Frye, R. L., & Bass, B. M. Behavior in a group related to tested social acquiescence. *Journal of Social Psychology,* 1963, **61,** 263–266.

Gamson, W. A. An experimental test of a theory of coalition formation. *American Sociological Review,* 1961a, **26,** 565–573.

Gamson, W. A. A theory of coalition formation. *American Sociological Review,* 1961b, **26,** 373–382.

Gamson, W. A. Experimental studies of coalition formation. In L. Berkowitz (Ed.), *Advances in experimental social psychology.* Vol. 1. New York: Academic Press, 1964. Pp. 82–110.

Gardin, H., Kaplan, K. J., Firestone, I. J., & Cowan, G. A. Proxemic effects on cooperation, attitude, and approach-avoidance in a prisoner's dilemma game. *Journal of Personality and Social Psychology,* 1973, **27,** 13–18.

Gardner, R. A. Probability-learning with two and three choices. *American Journal of Psychology,* 1957, **70,** 174–185.

Gardner, R. A. Multiple-choice decision-behavior. *American Journal of Psychology,* 1958, **71,** 710–717.

Garner, W. R., Hake, H. W., & Eriksen, C. W. Operationism and the concept of perception. *Psychological Review,* 1956, **63,** 149–159.

Gassner, S. M., Gold, J., & Snadowsky, A. M. Changes in the phenomenal field as a result of human relations training. *Journal of Psychology,* 1964, **58,** 33–41.

Geier, J. G. A trait approach to the study of leadership in small groups. *Journal of Communication,* 1967, **17,** 316–323.

Geller, D. M., Goodstein, L., Silver, M., & Sternberg, W. C. On being ignored: The effects of the violation of implicit rules of social interaction. *Sociometry,* 1974, **37,** 541–556.

Gerard, H. B., Wilhelmy, R. A., & Conolley, E. S. Conformity and group size. *Journal of Personality and Social Psychology,* 1968, **8,** 79–82.

Gergen, K. J., & Bauer, R. A. Interaction effects of self-esteem and task difficulty on social conformity. *Journal of Personality and Social Psychology,* 1967, **6,** 16–22.

Gergen, K. J., & Taylor, M. G. Social expectancy and self-presentation in a status hierarchy. *Journal of Experimental Social Psychology,* 1969, **5,** 79–92.

Gewirtz, J. L., & Baer, D. M. Deprivation and satiation of social reinforcers as drive conditions. *Journal of Abnormal and Social Psychology,* 1958a, **57,** 165–172.

Gewirtz, J. L., & Baer, D. M. The effect of brief social deprivation on behaviors for a social reinforcer. *Journal of Abnormal and Social Psychology,* 1958b, **56,** 49–56.

Gibb, C. A. Leadership. In G. Lindzey & E. Aronson (Eds.), *The handbook of social psychology* (2d ed.) Vol. 4. Reading, Mass.: Addison-Wesley, 1969. Pp. 205–282.

Gibb, J. R. The effects of group size and of threat upon certainty in a problem-solving situation. *American Psychologist,* 1951, **6,** 324.

Gilchrist, J. C. The formation of social groups under conditions of success and failure. *Journal of Abnormal and Social Psychology,* 1952, **47,** 174–187.

Gilchrist, J. C., Shaw, M. E., & Walker, L. C. Some effects of unequal distribution of information in a wheel group structure. *Journal of Abnormal and Social Psychology,* 1954, **49,** 554–556.

Gilstein, K. W., Wright, E. W., & Stone, D. R. The effects of leadership style on group interactions in differing sociopolitical subcultures. *Small Group Behavior,* 1977, **8,** 313–331.

Gintner, G., & Lindskold, S. Rate of participation and expertise as factors influencing leader choice. *Journal of Personality and Social Psychology,* 1975, **32,** 1085–1089.

Glass, D. C., Reim, B., & Singer, J. E. Behavioral consequences of adaptation to controllable and uncontrollable noise. *Journal of Experimental Social Psychology,* 1971, **7,** 244–257.

Glass, D. C., Singer, J. E., & Friedman, L. N. Psychic cost of adaptation to an environmental stressor. *Journal of Personality and Social Psychology,* 1969, **12,** 200–210.

Goldberg, M. L., Passow, A. H., & Justman, J. *The effects of ability grouping.* New York: Teachers College Press, 1966.

Goldberg, S. C. Influence and leadership as a function of group structure. *Journal of Abnormal and Social Psychology,* 1955, **51,** 119–122.

Goldman, M. A comparison of individual and group performance for varying combinations of initial ability. *Journal of Personality and Social Psychology,* 1965, **1,** 210–216.

Goldman, M., & Fraas, L. A. The effects of leader selection on group performance. *Sociometry,* 1965, **28,** 82–88.

Goldman, M., Stockbauer, J. W., & McAuliffe, T. G. Intergroup and intragroup competition and cooperation. *Journal of Experimental Social Psychology,* 1977, **13,** 81–88.

Goldman, W., & Lewis, P. Beautiful is good: Evidence that the physically attractive are more socially skillful. *Journal of Experimental Social Psychology,* 1977, **13,** 125–130.

Good, K. J. Social facilitation: Effects of performance anticipation, evaluation, and response competition on free associations. *Journal of Personality and Social Psychology,* 1973, **28,** 270–275.

Good, L. R., & Good, K. C. Similarity of attitudes and attraction to a social organization. *Psychological Reports,* 1974, **34,** 1071–1073.

Good, L. R., & Nelson, D. A. Effects of person-group and intra-group attitude similarity on perceived group attractiveness and cohesiveness. *Psychonomic Science,* 1971, **25,** 215–217.

Goodacre, D. M., III. The use of a sociometric test as a predictor of combat unit effectiveness. *Sociometry,* 1951, **14,** 148–152.

Goodlad, J. I. Classroom organization. In C. W. Harris (Ed.), *Encyclopedia of educational research.* New York: Macmillan, 1960. Pp. 223–225.

Goodman, D. W., Randolph, D. L., & Brown, H. J. D. Attitudinal group-centered counseling: Effects on openmindedness. *Small Group Behavior,* 1978, **9,** 403–408.

Goodnow, J. J. Determinants of choice-distribution in two-choice situations. *American Journal of Psychology,* 1955, **68,** 106–116.

Goodstadt, B. E., & Hjelle, L. A. Power to the powerless: Locus of control and the use of power. *Journal of Personality and Social Psychology,* 1973, **27,** 190–196.

Gordon, K. A study of aesthetic judgments. *Journal of Experimental Psychology,* 1923, **6,** 36–43.

Gordon, K. Group judgments in the field of lifted weights. *Journal of Experimental Psychology,* 1924, **7,** 389–400.

Graen, E., & Cashman, J. F. A role-making model of leadership in formal organizatons: A developmental approach. In J. G. Hunt & L. L. Larsen (Eds.), *Leadership Frontiers.* Kent, Ohio: Kent State University Press, 1975. Pp. 143–165.

Green, E. H. Friendships and quarrels among pre-school children. *Child Development,* 1933a, **4,** 237–252.

Green, E. H. Group play and quarreling among pre-school children. *Child Development,* 1933b, **4,** 302–307.

Green, R. B., & Mack, J. Would groups do better without social psychologists: A response to Buys. *Personality and Social Psychology Bulletin,* 1978, **4,** 561–563.

Greenberg, C. I., & Firestone, I. J. Compensatory responses to crowding: Effects of personal space intrusion and privacy reduction. *Journal of Personality and Social Psychology,* 1977, **35,** 637–644.

Greenberg, M. S. Role playing: An alternative to deception. *Journal of Personality and Social Psychology,* 1967, **7,** 152–157.

Greer, F. L. Small Group effectiveness. Institute Report No. 6, Contract Nonr-1229(00), Institute for Research in Human Relations, Philadelphia, 1955.

Griffitt, W. Interpersonal attraction as a function of self-concept and personality similarity-dissimilarity. *Journal of Personality and Social Psychology,* 1966, **4,** 581–584.

Griffitt, W., & Veitch, R. Preacquaintance attitude similarity and attraction revisited: Ten days in a fall-out shelter. *Sociometry,* 1974, **37,** 163–173.

Gross, E. Primary functions of the small group. *American Journal of Sociology,* 1954, **60,** 24–30.

Gross, E. Symbiosis and consensus as integrative factors in small groups. *American Sociological Review,* 1956, **21,** 174–179.

Grush, J. E. Audiences can inhibit or facilitate competitive behavior. *Personality and Social Psychology Bulletin,* 1978, **4,** 119–122.

Guetzkow, H., Alger, C. F., Brody, R. A., Noel, R. C., & Snyder, R. C. *Simulation in international relations.* Englewood Cliffs, N.J.: Prentice-Hall, 1963.

Guetzkow, H., & Dill, W. R. Factors in the organizational development of task-oriented groups. *Sociometry,* 1957, **20,** 175–204.

Guetzkow, H., & Simon, H. A. The impact of certain communication nets upon organization and performance in task-oriented groups. *Management Science,* 1955, **1,** 233–250.

Guilford, J. P., & Zimmerman, W. S. *The Guilford-Zimmerman Temperament Survey.* Beverly Hills: Sheridan Supply, 1949.

Gundlach, R. H. Effects of on-the-job experiences with Negroes upon racial attitudes of white workers in union shops. *Psychological Reports,* 1956, **2,** 67–77.

Gurnee, H. A comparison of collective and individual judgments of facts. *Journal of Experimental Psychology,* 1937, **21,** 106–112.

Gurnee, H. The effect of collective learning upon the individual participants. *Journal of Abnormal and Social Psychology,* 1939, **34,** 529–532.

Hackman, J. R. Effects of task characteristics on group products. *Journal of Experimental Social Psychology,* 1968, **4,** 162–187.

Hackman, J. R. Toward understanding the role of tasks in behavioral research. *Acta Psychologica,* 1969, **39,** 97–128.

Hackman, J. R., & Morris, C. G. Group tasks, group interaction process, and group performance effectiveness: A review and proposed integration. In L. Berkowitz (Ed.), *Advances in experimental social psychology.* Vol. 8. New York: Academic Press, 1975. Pp. 45–99.

Hackman, J. R., & Morris, C. G. Group process and group effectiveness: A reappraisal. In L. Berkowitz (Ed.), *Group processes.* New York: Academic Press, 1978. Pp. 57–66.

Hackman, J. R., & Vidmar, N. Effects of size and task type on group performance and member reactions. *Sociometry,* 1970, **33,** 37–54.

Haiman, F. S. Effects of training in group processes on open-mindedness. *Journal of Communication,* 1963, **13,** 236–245.

Hall, J., & Williams, M. S. A comparison of decision-making performances in established and ad hoc groups. *Journal of Personality and Social Psychology,* 1966, **3,** 214–222.

Hall, J., & Williams, M. S. Group dynamics training and improved decision making. *Journal of Applied Behavioral Science,* 1970, **6,** 27–32.

Halpin, A. W. The leader behavior and effectiveness of airplane commanders. In R. M. Stogdill and A. E. Coons (Eds.), *Leader behavior: Its description and measurement.* Columbus: Ohio State University Press, 1957. Pp. 52–64.

Hamilton, V. L. Obediance and responsibility: A jury simulation. *Journal of Personality and Social Psychology,* 1978, **36,** 126–146.

Harding, J., & Hogrefe, R. Attitudes of white department store employees toward Negro coworkers. *Journal of Social Issues,* 1952, **8,** 18–28.

Hare, A. P. Interaction and consensus in different sized groups. *American Sociological Review,* 1952, **17,** 261–267.

Hare, A. P. *Handbook of small group research.* (2d ed). New York: Free Press, 1976.

Hare, A. P., & Bales, R. F. Seating position and small group interaction. *Sociometry,* 1963, **26,** 480–486.

Harms, L. S. Listener judgments of status cues in speech. *Quarterly Journal of Speech,* 1961, **47,** 164–168.

Harris, B., Luginbuhl, J. E. R., & Fishbein, J. E. Density and personal space in a field setting. *Social Psychology,* 1978, **41,** 350–353.

Harris, C. W. (Ed.) *Problems in measuring change.* Madison: The University of Wisconsin Press, 1967.

Harrison, R. Cognitive change and participation in a sensitivity training laboratory. *Journal of Consulting Psychology,* 1966, **30,** 517–520.

Harrison, R., & Lubin, B. Personal style, group composition, and learning. *Journal of Applied Behavioral Science,* 1965, **1,** 286–301.

Harvey, O. J., & Consalvi, C. Status and conformity to pressures in informal groups. *Journal of Abnormal and Social Psychology,* 1960, **60,** 182–187.

Harvey, O. J., Hunt, D. E., & Schroder, H. M. *Conceptual systems and personality organization.* New York: Wiley, 1961.

Haythorn, W. The influence of individual members on the characteristics of small groups. *Journal of Abnormal and Social Psychology,* 1953, **48,** 276–284.

Haythorn, W. W. The composition of groups: A review of the literature. *Acta Psychologica,* 1968, **28,** 97–128.

Haythorn, W. W., Couch, A., Haefner, D., Langham, P., & Carter, L. F. The behavior of authoritarian and equalitarian personalities in groups. *Human Relations,* 1956a, **9,** 57–74.

Haythorn, W. W., Couch, A., Haefner, D., Langham, P., & Carter, L. F. The effects of varying combinations of authoritarian and equalitarian leaders and followers. *Journal of Abnormal and Social Psychology,* 1956b, **53,** 210–219.

Hearn, G. Leadership and the spatial factor in small groups. *Journal of Abnormal and Social Psychology,* 1957, **54,** 269–272.

Heider, F. *The psychology of interpersonal relations.* New York: Wiley, 1958.

Heller, J. F., Groff, B. D., & Solomon, S. H. Toward an understanding of crowding: The role of physical interaction. *Journal of Personality and Social Psychology,* 1977, **35,** 183–190.

Helson, H. Adaptation-level as a basis for quantitative theory of frames of reference. *Psychological Review,* 1948, **55,** 297–313.

Hemphill, J. K. Relations between the size of the group and the behavior of "superior" leaders. *Journal of Social Psychology,* 1950, **32,** 11–22.

Hemphill, J. K., & Sechrest, L. A comparison of three criteria of air crew effectiveness in combat over Korea. *American Psychologist,* 1952, **7,** 391.

Henchy, T., & Glass, D. C. Evaluation apprehension and the social facilitation of dominant and subordinate responses. *Journal of Personality and Social Psychology,* 1968, **10,** 446–454.

Hendrick, C., Giesen, M., & Coy, S. The social ecology of free seating arrangements in a small group interaction context. *Sociometry,* 1974, **37,** 262–274.

Hendricks, M., & Brickman, P. Effects of status and knowledgeability of audiences on self presentation. *Sociometry,* 1974, **37,** 440–449.

Hill, T. A. An experimental study of the relationship between opinionated leadership and small group consensus. *Communication Monographs,* 1976, **43,** 246–257.

Himber, C. Evaluating sensitivity training for teen-agers. *Journal of Applied Behavioral Science,* 1970, **6,** 307–322.

Hirota, K. Group problem solving and communication. *Japanese Journal of Psychology,* 1953, **24,** 176–177.

Hockbaum, G. M. The relation between group members' self-confidence and their reactions to group pressures to uniformity. *American Sociological Review,* 1954, **79,** 678–687.

Hoffman, L. R. Homogeneity of member personality and its effect on group problem-solving. *Journal of Abnormal and Social Psychology,* 1959, **58,** 27–32.

Hoffman, L. R. Group problem-solving. In L. Berkowitz (Ed.), *Group Processes.* New York: Academic Press, 1978. Pp. 67–100.

Hoffman, L. R., & Maier, N. R. F. Quality and acceptance of problem solutions by members of homogeneous and heterogeneous groups. *Journal of Abnormal and Social Psychology,* 1961, **62,** 401–407.

Hoffman, L. R., & Maier, N. R. F. Valence in the adoption of solutions by problem-solving groups: Concept, method, and results. *Journal of Abnormal and Social Psychology,* 1964, **69,** 264–271.

Hollander, E. P. Authoritarianism and leadership choice in a military setting. *Journal of Abnormal and Social Psychology,* 1954, **49,** 365–376.

Hollander, E. P. Conformity, status, and idiosyncrasy credit. *Psychological Review,* 1958, **65,** 117–127.

Hollander, E. P. Competence and conformity in the acceptance of influence. *Journal of Abnormal and Social Psychology,* 1960, **61,** 365–369.

Hollander, E. P. *Leadership dynamics.* New York: The Free Press, 1978.

Hollander, E. P., & Julian, J. W. Contemporary trends in the analysis of leadership processes. *Psychological Bulletin,* 1969, **71,** 387–397.

Hollander, E. P., & Julian, J. W. Studies in leader legitimacy, influence, and innovation. In L. Berkowitz (Ed.), *Advances in Experimental Social Psychology.* Vol 5. New York: Academic Press, 1970. Pp. 33–69.

Hollander, E. P., Julian, J. W., & Perry, F. A. Leader style, competence, and source of authority as determinants of actual and perceived influence. Technical report No. 5. ONR Contract 4679, SUNY at Buffalo, 1966.

Hollander, E. P., & Webb, W. B. Leadership, followership, and friendship: An analysis of peer nominations. *Journal of Abnormal and Social Psychology,* 1955, **50,** 163–167.

Homans, G. C. *The human group.* New York: Harcourt, Brace & World, 1950.

Hong, L. K. Risky shift and cautious shift: Some direct evidence on the culture-value theory. *Social Psychology,* 1978, **41,** 342–346.

Hoogstraten, J., & Vorst, H. C. M. Group cohesion, task performance, and the experimenter expectancy effect. *Human Relations,* 1978, **31,** 939–956.

Hoppe, C. M. Impersonal aggression as a function of subject's sex, subject's sex role identification, opponent's sex, and degree of provocation. *Journal of Personality,* 1979, **47,** 317–329.

Horowitz, M. J., Duff, D. F., & Stratton, L. O. Body buffer zone. *Archives of General Psychiatry,* 1964, **11,** 651–656.

Horwitz, M. The recall of interrupted group tasks: An experimental study of individual motivation in relation to group goals. *Human Relations,* 1954, **7,** 3–38.

Howells, L. T., & Becker, S. W. Seating arrangement and leadership emergence. *Journal of Abnormal and Social Psychology,* 1962, **64,** 148–150.

Hrycenko, I., & Minton, H. L. Internal-external control, power position, and satisfaction in task-oriented groups. *Journal of Personality and Social Psychology,* 1974, **30,** 871–878.

Hurwitz, J. I., Zander, A. F., & Hymovitch, B. Some effects of power on the relations among group members. In D. Cartwright & A. Zander (Eds.), *Group dynamics: Research and theory.* Evanston, Ill.: Row, Peterson, 1953. Pp. 483–492.

Husband, R. W. Cooperative versus solitary problem solution. *Journal of Social Psychology,* 1940, **11,** 405–409.

Ickes, W., & Barnes, R. D. The role of sex and self-monitoring in unstructured dyadic interactions. *Journal of Personality and Social Psychology,* 1977, **35,** 315–330.

Indik, B. P. Organization size and member participation: Some empirical tests of alternatives. *Human Relations,* 1965, **18,** 339–350.

Ingham, A. G., Levinger, G., Graves, J., & Peckham, V. The Ringlemann effect:

Studies of group size and group performance. *Journal of Experimental Social Psychology,* 1974, **10,** 371–384.

Iscoe, I., Williams, M., & Harvey, J. Modification of children's judgments by a simulated group technique: A normative developmental study. *Child Development,* 1963, **34,** 963–978.

Izard, C. E. Personality similarity and friendship. *Journal of Abnormal and Social Psychology,* 1960a, **61,** 47–51.

Izard, C. E. Personality similarity, positive affect, and interpersonal attraction. *Journal of Abnormal and Social Psychology,* 1960b, **61,** 484–485.

Jackson, E. F. Status consistency and symptoms of stress. *American Sociological Review,* 1962, **27,** 469–480.

Jackson, J. M., & Saltzstein, H. D. The effect of person-group relationships on conformity processes. *Journal of Abnormal and Social Psychology,* 1958, **57,** 17–24.

Jacobs, R. C., & Campbell, D. T. The perpetuation of an arbitrary tradition through several generations of a laboratory microculture. *Journal of Abnormal and Social Psychology,* 1961, **62,** 649–658.

Jahoda, M. Race relations and mental health. In UNESCO, *Race and science.* New York: Columbia, 1961.

James, J. A preliminary study of the size determinant in small group interaction. *American Sociological Review,* 1951, **16,** 474–477.

Janis, I. L. *Victims of groupthink.* Boston: Houghton Mifflin, 1972.

Janssens, L., & Nuttin, J. R. Frequency perception of individual and group successes as a function of competition, coaction, and isolation. *Journal of Personality and Social Psychology,* 1976, **34,** 830–836.

Jellison, J. M., & Zeisset, P. J. Attraction as a function of the commonality and desirability of a trait shared with another. *Journal of Personality and Social Psychology,* 1969, **11,** 115–120.

Jenness, A. The role of discussion in changing opinion regarding a matter of fact. *Journal of Abnormal and Social Psychology,* 1932, **27,** 279–296.

Johnson, D. W., Johnson, R. T., & Skon, L. Student achievement on different types of tasks under cooperative, competitive, and individualistic conditions. *Contemporary Educational Psychology,* 1979, **4,** 99–106.

Johnson, M. P., & Ewens, W. Power relations and affective style as determinants of confidence in impression formation in a game situation. *Journal of Experimental Social Psychology,* 1971, **7,** 98–110.

Johnson, R. H., Jr., & Hunt, J. J. *Rx for team teaching.* Minneapolis: Burgess, 1968.

Jones, S. E., & Aiello, J. R. Proxemic behavior of black and white first-, third-, and fifth-grade children. *Journal of Personality and Social Psychology,* 1973, **25,** 21–27.

Julian, J. W., Hollander, E. P., & Regula, C. R. Endorsement of the group spokesman as a function of his authority, competence, and success. *Journal of Personality and Social Psychology,* 1969, **11,** 42–49.

Jurma, W. E. Leadership structuring style, task ambiguity, and group member satisfaction. *Small Group Behavior,* 1978, **9,** 124–134.

Kandel, D. B. Similarity in real-life adolescent friendship pairs. *Journal of Personality and Social Psychology*, 1978, **36**, 306–312.

Kanekar, S., & Rosenbaum, M. E. Group performance on a multiple-solution task as a function of available time. *Psychonomic Science*, 1972, **27**, 331–332.

Kano, S. Task characteristics and network. *Japanese Journal of Educational Social Psychology*, 1971, **10**, 55–66.

Kano, S. A change of effectiveness of communication networks under different amounts of information. *Japanese Journal of Experimental Social Psychology*, 1977, **17**, 50–59.

Kanter, R. M. Some effects of proportions on group life: Skewed sex ratios and responses to token women. *American Journal of Sociology*, 1977, **82**, 965–990.

Katz, D. Morale and motivation in industry. In W. Dennis (Ed.), *Current trends in industrial psychology*. Pittsburgh: The University of Pittsburgh Press, 1949. Pp. 145–171.

Katz, I., Roberts, S. O., & Robinson, J. M. Effects of difficulty, race of administrator, and instructions on Negro digit-symbol performance. *Journal of Personality and Social Psychology*, 1965, **2**, 53–59.

Katz, R. The influence of job longevity on employee reactions to task characteristics. *Human Relations*, 1978, **31**, 703–725.

Kaul, T. J., & Bednar, R. L. Conceptualizing group research: A preliminary analysis. *Small Group Behavior*, 1978, **9**, 173–191.

Kawamura-Reynolds, M. Motivational effects of an audience in the content of imaginative thought. *Journal of Personality and Social Psychology*, 1977, **35**, 912–919.

Kelley, E. L. Consistency of adult personality. *American Psychologist*, 1955, **10**, 659–681.

Kelley, H. H. Communication in experimentally created hierarchies. *Human Relations*, 1951, **4**, 39–56.

Kelley, H. H. Two functions of reference groups. In G. E. Swanson, T. M. Newcomb, & E. L. Hartley (Eds.), *Readings in social psychology* (2 ed). New York: Holt, 1952. Pp. 410–414.

Kelley, H. H., & Arrowood, A. J. Coalitions in the triad: Critique and experiment. *Sociometry*, 1960, **23**, 231–244.

Kelley, H. H., & Thibaut, J. W. Group problem solving. In G. Lindzey & E. Aronson (Eds.), *The handbook of social psychology* (2d ed.) Vol. 4. Reading, Mass.: Addison-Wesley, 1969. Pp. 1–101.

Kendon, A. Some functions of gaze direction in social interaction. *Acta Psychologica*, 1967, **26**, 22–63.

Kent, R. N., & McGrath, J. E. Task and group characteristics as factors influencing group performance. *Journal of Experimental Social Psychology*, 1969, **5**, 429–440.

Kerckhoff, A. C., & Davis, K. E. Value consensus and need complementarity in mate selection. *American Sociological Review*, 1962, **27**, 295–303.

Kernan, J. P. Laboratory human relations training: Its effect on the "personality" of supervisory engineers. *Dissertation Abstracts*, 1964, **25**, 665–666.

Kerr, N. L., Davis, J. H., Meek, D., & Rissman, A. K. Group position as a function of member attitudes: Choice shift from the perspective of social decision scheme theory. *Journal of Personality and Social Psychology*, 1975, **31**, 574–593.

Kidd, J. S., & Campbell, D. T. Conformity to groups as a function of group success. *Journal of Abnormal and Social Psychology*, 1955, **51**, 390–393.

Killian, L. M. The significance of multiple-group membership in disaster. *American Journal of Sociology*, 1952, **57**, 309–314.

Kipnis, D. The effects of leadership style and leadership power upon the inducement of an attitude change. *Journal of Abnormal and Social Psychology*, 1958, **57**, 173–180.

Kipnis, D. Does power corrupt? *Journal of Personality and Social Psychology*, 1972, **24**, 33–41.

Kipnis, D., & Vanderveer, R. Ingratiation and the use of power. *Journal of Personality and Social Psychology*, 1971, **17**, 280–286.

Kleck, R. Physical stigma and task-oriented interaction. *Human Relations*, 1969, **22**, 51–60.

Kleck, R. E., & Rubenstein, C. Physical attractiveness, perceived attitude similarity, and interpersonal attraction in an opposite-sex encounter. *Journal of Personality and Social Psychology*, 1975, **31**, 107–114.

Klein, A. L. Changes in leadership appraisal as a function of the stress of a simulated panic situation. *Journal of Personality and Social Psychology*, 1976, **34**, 1143–1154.

Kleiner, R. J. The effect of threat reduction upon interpersonal attractiveness. *Journal of Personality*, 1960, **28**, 145–155.

Klinger, E. Feedback effects and social facilitation of vigilance performance: Mere coaction vs. potential evaluation. *Psychonomic Science*, 1969, **14**, 161–162.

Knight, H. C. A comparison of the reliability of group and individual judgments. Unpublished master's thesis, Columbia University, 1921. (Cited in Lorge et al., 1958.)

Konecni, V. J., Libuser, L., Morton, H., & Ebbesen, E. B. Effects of a violation of personal space on escape and helping responses. *Journal of Experimental Social Psychology*, 1975, **11**, 288–299.

Knowles, E. S. Boundaries around group interaction: The effect of group size and member status on boundary permeability. *Journal of Personality and Social Psychology*, 1973, **26**, 327–331.

Knox, R. E., & Safford, R. K. Group caution at the race track. *Journal of Experimental Social Psychology*, 1976, **21**, 317–324.

Koch, J. L. Managerial succession in a factory and changes in supervisory patterns: A field study. *Human Relations*, 1978, **31**, 49–58.

Kogan, N., & Wallach, M. A. Group risk taking as a function of members' anxiety and defensiveness. *Journal of Personality*, 1967, **35**, 50–63.

Komorita, S. S., & Brinberg, D. The effects of equity norms in coalition formation. *Sociometry*, 1977, **40**, 351–361.

Komorita, S. S., & Chertkoff, J. M. A bargaining theory of coalition formation. *Psychological Review*, 1973, **80**, 149–162.

Komorita, S. S., & Kravitz, D. A. The effects of alternatives in bargaining. *Journal of Experimental Social Psychology*, 1979, **15**, 147–157.

Komorita, S. S., & Meek, D. D. Generality and validity of some theories of coalition formation. *Journal of Personality and Social Psychology,* 1978, **36,** 392–404.

Komorita, S. S., & Moore, D. Theories and processes of coalition formation. *Journal of Personality and Social Psychology,* 1976, **33,** 371–381.

Komorita, S. S., Sheposh, J. P., & Braver, S. L. Power, the use of power, and cooperative choice in a two-person game. *Journal of Personality and Social Psychology,* 1968, **8,** 134–142.

Krail, K. A., & Leventhal, G. The sex variable in the intrusion of personal space. *Sociometry,* 1976, **39,** 170–173.

Kravitz, D. A., Cohen, J. L., Martin, B., Sweeney, J., McCarty, J., Elliott, E., & Goldstein, P. Humans would do better without other humans. *Personality and Social Psychology Bulletin,* 1978, **4,** 559–560.

Krebs, D., & Adinolfi, A. A. Physical attractiveness, social relations, and personality style. *Journal of Personality and Social Psychology,* 1975, **31,** 245–253.

Krupat, E. A re-assessment of role playing as a technique in social psychology. *Personality and Social Psychology Bulletin,* 1977, **3,** 498–504.

Kukla, A. Preferences among impossibly difficult and trivially easy tasks: A revision of Atkinson's theory of choice. *Journal of Personality and Social Psychology,* 1975, **32,** 338–345.

Kutner, D. H., Jr. Overcrowding: Human responses to density and visual exposure. *Human Relations,* 1973, **26,** 31–50.

LaFrance, M., & Mayo, C. Racial differences in gaze behavior during conversations: Two systematic observational studies. *Journal of Personality and Social Psychology,* 1976, **33,** 547–552.

Lakin, M. Experiential groups: The uses of interpersonal encounter, psychotherapy groups, and sensitivity training. Morristown, N.J.: General Learning Press, 1972.

Lamm, H., & Myers, D. G. Group-induced polarization of attitudes and behavior. In L. Berkowitz (Ed.), *Advances in experimental social psychology.* Vol. 11. New York: Academic Press, 1978. Pp. 145–195.

Lanzetta, J. T., & Roby, T. B. Effects of work-group structure and certain task variables on group performance. *Journal of Abnormal and Social Psychology,* 1956, **53,** 307–314.

Lanzetta, J. T., & Roby, T. B. Group learning and communication as a function of task and structure "demands." *Journal of Abnormal and Social Psychology,* 1957, **55,** 121–131.

Lasswell, T. E. The perception of social status. *Sociology and Social Research,* 1961, **45,** 170–174.

Latane, B., & Darley, J. M. Group inhibition of bystander intervention in emergencies. *Journal of Personality and Social Psychology,* 1968, **10,** 215–221.

Latane, B., Eckman, J., & Joy, V. Shared stress and interpersonal attraction. *Journal of Experimental Social Psychology,* 1966, **1,** 80–94.

Latane, B., & Rodin, J. A lady in distress: Inhibiting effects of friends and strangers in bystander intervention. *Journal of Experimental Social Psychology,* 1969, **5,** 189–202.

Laughlin, P. R., & Bitz, D. S. Individual versus dyadic performance on a disjunctive task as a function of initial ability level. *Journal of Personality and Social Psychology,* 1975, **31,** 487–496.

Laughlin, P. R., Branch, L. G., & Johnson, H. H. Individual versus triadic performance on a unidimensional complementary task as a function of initial ability level, *Journal of Personality and Social Psychology,* 1969, **12,** 144-150.

Laughlin, P. R., Kerr, N. L., Davis, J. H., Halff, H. M., & Marciniak, K. A. Group size, member ability, and social decision schemes on an intellective task. *Journal of Personality and Social Psychology,* 1975, **31,** 522–535.

Lawler, E. J., & Youngs, G. A., Jr. Coalition formation: An integrative model. *Sociometry,* 1975, **38,** 1–17.

Lawson, E. D. Reinforced and non-reinforced four-man communication nets. *Psychological Reports,* 1964a, **14,** 287–296.

Lawson, E. D. Reinforcement in group problem-solving with arithmetic problems. *Psychological Reports,* 1964b, **14,** 703–710.

Lawson, E. D. Change in communication nets, performance, and morale. *Human Relations,* 1965, **18,** 139–147.

Leavitt, H. J. Some effects of certain communication patterns on group perform-ance. *Journal of Abnormal and Social Psychology,* 1951, **46,** 38–50.

Lecuyer, R. Space dimensions, the climate of discussion and group decisions. *European Journal of Social Psychology,* 1975, **5,** 509–514.

Lefcourt, H. M., & Ladwig, G. W. The effect of reference groups upon Negroes' task persistence in a biracial competitive game. *Journal of Personality and Social Psychology,* 1965, **1,** 668–671.

Lefkowitz, M., Blake, R. R., & Mouton, J. S. Status factors in pedestrian violation of traffic signals. *Journal of Abnormal and Social Psychology,* 1955, **51,** 704–706.

Leierson, M. Power and ideology in coalition behavior: An experimental study. In S. Groenings (Ed.), *The Study of Coalition Behavior.* New York: Holt, Rinehart and Winston, 1970.

Lenski, G. E. Status crystallization: A non-vertical dimension of social status. *American Sociological Review,* 1954, **19,** 405–413.

Lenski, G. E. Social participation and status crystallization. *American Sociological Review,* 1956, **21,** 458–464.

Leonard, R. L., Jr. Self-concept and attraction for similar and dissimilar others. *Journal of Personality and Social Psychology,* 1975, **31,** 926–929.

Leuba, C. J. An experimental study of rivalry in young children. *Journal of Comparative Psychology,* 1933, **16,** 367–378.

Levine, J. M., Saxe, L., & Harris, H. J. Reaction to attitudinal deviance: Impact of deviate's direction and distance of movement. *Sociometry,* 1976, **39,** 97–107.

Levinger, G., & Schneider, D. J. Test of the "risk is a value" hypothesis. *Journal of Personality and Social Psychology,* 1969, **11,** 165–169.

Levinger, G., Senn, D. J., & Jorgensen, B. W. Progress toward permanence in courtship: A test of the Kerckhoff-Davis hypothesis. *Sociometry,* 1970, **33,** 427–443.

Lewin, K. *Principles of topological psychology.* New York: McGraw-Hill, 1936.

Lewin, K. Forces behind food habits and methods of change. *Bulletin of the National Research Council*, 1943, **108**, 35–65.

Lewin, K. *Resolving social conflicts*. New York: Harper, 1948.

Lewin, K. *Field theory in social science*. New York: Harper, 1951.

Lewin, K. Studies in group decision. In D. Cartwright & A. Zander (Eds.), *Group dynamics: Research and theory*. Evanston, Ill.: Row, Peterson, 1953. Pp. 285–301.

Lewin, K., Dembo, T., Festinger, L., & Sears, P. S. Level of aspiration. In J. McV. Hunt (Ed.), *Personality and the behavior disorders*. New York: Ronald, 1944. Pp. 333–378.

Lewin, K., Lippitt, R., & White, R. K. Patterns of aggressive behavior in experimentally created "social climates." *Journal of Social Psychology*, 1939, **10**, 271–299.

Lewis, S. A., Langan, C. J., & Hollander, E. P. Expectation of future interaction and the choice of less desirable alternatives in conformity. *Sociometry*, 1972, **35**, 440–447.

Lieberman, M., Yalom, I., & Miles, M. The group experience project: A comparison of ten encounter technologies. In L. Blank, G. Gottsegen, & M. Gottsegen (Eds.), *Encounter: Confrontation in self and interpersonal awareness*. New York: Macmillan, 1971.

Lieberman, M. A., Yalom, I. D., & Miles, M. B. *Encounter groups: First facts*. New York: Basic Books, 1973.

Lindskold, S., Albert, K. P., Baer, R., & Moore, W. C. Territorial boundaries of interacting groups and passive audiences. *Sociometry*, 1976, **39**, 71–76.

Linton, R. *The study of man*. New York: Appleton-Century-Crofts, 1936.

Lipman, A. Building design and social interaction. *The Architects Journal*, 1968, **147**, 23–30.

Lippitt, R., Polansky, N., Redl, F., & Rosen, S. The dynamics of power. *Human Relations*, 1952, **5**, 37–64.

Lippitt, R., & White, R. K. The "social climate" of children's groups. In R. G. Barker, J. Kounin, & H. Wright (Eds.), *Child behavior and development*. New York: McGraw-Hill, 1943. Pp. 485–508.

Litman-Adizes, T., Fontaine, G., & Raven, B. H. Consequences of social power and causal attribution for compliance as seen by powerholder and target. *Personality and Social Psychology Bulletin*, 1978, **4**, 260–264.

Little, K. B. Personal space. *Journal of Experimental Social Psychology*, 1965, **1**, 237–247.

Loo, C. M. The effects of spatial density on the social behavior of children. *Dissertation Abstracts*, 1972, **7**, 41–89.

Lorge, I., Aikman, L., Moss, G., Spiegel, J., & Tuckman, J. Solutions by teams and by individuals to a field problem at different levels of reality. *Journal of Educational Psychology*, 1955, **46**, 17–24.

Lorge, I., Fox, D., Davitz, J., & Brenner, M. A survey of studies contrasting the quality of group performance and individual performance, 1920–1956. *Psychological Bulletin*, 1958, **55**, 337–372.

Lorge, I., & Solomon, H. Two models of group behavior in the solution of eureka-type problems. *Psychometrika*, 1955, **20**, 139–148.

Lott, A. J., & Lott, B. E. Group cohesiveness, communication level, and conformity. *Journal of Abnormal and Social Psychology,* 1961, **62,** 408–412.

Lott, A. J., & Lott, B. E. Group cohesiveness and individual learning. *Journal of Educational Psychology,* 1966, **57,** 61–73.

Lott, D. F., & Sommer, R. Seating arrangements and status. *Journal of Personality and Social Psychology,* 1967, **7,** 90–95.

Luchins, A. S., & Luchins, E. H. On conformity with true and false communications. *Journal of Social Psychology,* 1955, **42,** 283–304.

Luckiesh, M. *Seeing.* Cleveland: Lighting Research Laboratory, 1931.

Lundgren, D. C. Interpersonal needs and member attitudes toward trainer and group. *Small Group Behavior,* 1975, **6,** 371–388.

Lundgren, D. C., & Knight, D. J. Trainer style and member attitudes toward trainer and group in T-groups. *Small Group Behavior,* 1977, **8,** 47–64.

Lyman, S. M., & Scott, M. B. Territoriality: A neglected sociological dimension. *Social Forces,* 1967, **15,** 236–249.

McClelland, D. C., Atkinson, J. W., Clark, R. A., & Lowell, E. L. *The achievement motive.* New York: Appleton-Century-Crofts, 1953.

McCurdy, H. G., & Lambert, W. E. The efficiency of small human groups in the solution of problems requiring genuine co-operation. *Journal of Personality,* 1952, **20,** 478–494.

McDavid, J. W. Personality and situational determinants of conformity. *Journal of Abnormal and Social Psychology,* 1959, **58,** 241–246.

McDavid, J. W., & Harari, H. *Social psychology: Individuals, groups, societies.* New York: Harper & Row, 1968.

McDavid, J. W., & Sistrunk, F. Personality correlates of two kinds of conforming behavior. *Journal of Personality,* 1964, **32,** 420–435.

McGrath, J. E., & Altman, I. *Small group research.* New York: Holt, 1966.

McGrath, J. E., & Julian, J. W. Interaction process and task outcome in experimentally-created negotiation groups. *Journal of Psychological Studies,* 1963, **14,** 117–138.

McGuire, J. M. Aggression and sociometric status with preschool children. *Sociometry,* 1973, **36,** 542–549.

McLeish, J., & Park, J. Outcomes associated with direct and vicarious experience in training groups: I. Personality changes. *British Journal of Social and Clinical Psychology,* 1972, **11,** 333–341.

McNeel, S. P. Training cooperation in the prisoner's dilemma. *Journal of Experimental Social Psychology,* 1973, **9,** 335–348.

McNeel, S. P., Sweeney, J. D., & Bohlin, P. C. Cooperation and competitive goals: A social-comparison analysis. *Psychological Reports,* 1974, **34,** 887–894.

MacNeil, M. K., & Sherif, M. Norm change over subject generations as a function of arbitrariness of prescribed norms. *Journal of Personality and Social Psychology,* 1976, **34,** 762–773.

Mabry, E. A. Sequential structure of interaction in encounter groups. *Human Communication Research,* 1975, **1,** 302–307.

Mack, R. W. Ecological patterns in an industrial shop. *Social Forces,* 1954, **32,** 351–356.

Macy, J., Jr., Christie, L. S., & Luce, R. D. Coding noise in a task-oriented group. *Journal of Abnormal and Social Psychology,* 1953, **48,** 401–409.

Madsen, D. B. Issue importance and choice shifts: A persuasive arguments approach. *Journal of Personality and Social Psychology,* 1978, **36,** 1118–1127.

Maier, N. R. F. The quality of group decisions as influenced by the discussion leader. *Human Relations,* 1950, **3,** 155–174.

Maier, N. R. F. An experimental test of the effect of training on discussion leadership. *Human Relations,* 1953, **6,** 161–173.

Maier, N. R. F., & Hoffman, L. R. Organization and creative problem solving. *Journal of Applied Psychology,* 1961, **45,** 277–280.

Maier, N. R. F., & Solem, A. R. The contribution of a discussion leader to the quality of group thinking: The effective use of minority opinions. *Human Relations,* 1952, **5,** 277–288.

Maier, N. R. F., & Solem, A. R. Improving solutions by turning choice situations into problems. *Personnel Psychology,* 1962, **15,** 151–157.

Maissonneuve, J., Palmade, G., & Fourment, C. Selective choices and propinquity. *Sociometry,* 1952, **15,** 135–140.

Mandler, G., & Sarason, S. B. A study of anxiety and learning. *Journal of Abnormal and Social Psychology,* 1952, **47,** 166–173.

Mann, L. The effect of stimulus queues on queue-joining behavior. *Journal of Personality and Social Psychology,* 1977, **35,** 437–442.

Mann, R. D. A review of the relationships between personality and performance in small groups. *Psychological Bulletin,* 1959, **56,** 241–270.

Mann, R. D. Dimensions of individual performance in small groups under task and socio-emotional conditions. *Journal of Abnormal and Social Psychology,* 1961, **62,** 674–682.

Marine, G. I've got nothing against the colored, understand. *Ramparts,* 1966, **5,** 13–18.

Markel, N. N., Bein, M. F., Campbell, W. W., & Shaw, M. E. The relationship between self-rating of expressed inclusion and speaking time. *Language and Speech,* 1976, April/June, 117–120.

Markus, H. The effect of mere presence on social facilitation: An unobtrusive test. *Journal of Experimental Social Psychology,* 1978, **14,** 389–397.

Marple, C. H. The comparative susceptibility of three age levels to the suggestion of group versus expert opinion. *Journal of Social Psychology,* 1933, **10,** 3–40.

Marquart, D. I. Group problem solving. *Journal of Social Psychology,* 1955, **41,** 103–113.

Marquis, D. G., Guetzkow, H., & Heyns, R. W. A social psychological study of the decision-making conference. In H. Guetzkow (Ed.), *Groups, leadership and men.* Pittsburgh: Carnegie Press, 1951. Pp. 55–67.

Marshall, J. E., & Heslin, R. Boys and girls together: Sexual composition and the effect of density and group size on cohesiveness. *Journal of Personality and Social Psychology,* 1975, **31,** 952–961.

Marston, W. M. Studies in testimony. *Journal of Criminal Law and Criminology,* 1924, **15,** 5–31.

Martens, R., & Landers, D. M. Evaluation potential as a determinant of coaction effects. *Journal of Experimental Social Psychology,* 1972, **8,** 347–359.

Mathis, A. G. "Trainability" as a function of individual valency pattern. In D. Stock & H. A. Thelen (Eds.), *Emotional dynamics and group culture.* Washington, D.C.: National Training Laboratories, 1958.

Matlin, M. W., & Zajonc, R. B. Social facilitation of word associations. *Journal of Personality and Social Psychology,* 1968, **10,** 455–460.

Mausner, B. Studies in social interaction: III. Effect of variation in one partner's prestige on the interaction of observer pairs. *Journal of Applied Psychology,* 1953, **37,** 391–393.

Mead, M. *Male and female: A study of the sexes in a changing world.* New York: Morrow, 1949.

Mehrabian, A., & Diamond, S. G. Effects of furniture arrangement, props, and personality on social interaction. *Journal of Personality and Social Psychology,* 1971a, **20,** 18–30.

Mehrabian, A., & Diamond, S. G. Seating arrangement and conversation. *Sociometry,* 1971b, **34,** 281–289.

Meisels, M., & Guardo, C. J. Development of personal space schemata. *Child Development,* 1969, **40,** 1167–1178.

Mellinger, G. D. Interpersonal trust as a factor in communication. *Journal of Abnormal and Social Psychology,* 1956, **52,** 304–309.

Messé, L. A., Aronoff, J., & Wilson, J. P. Motivation as a mediator of the mechanisms underlying role assignments in small groups. *Journal of Personality and Social Psychology,* 1972, **24,** 84–90.

Meunier, C., & Rule, B. G. Anxiety, confidence, and conformity. *Journal of Personality,* 1967, **35,** 498–504.

Meyer, H. H. Factors related to success in the human relations aspect of workgroup leadership. *Psychological Monographs,* 1951, **65,** No. 3 (Whole No. 320).

Meyer, J. P., & Pepper, S. Need compatibility and marital adjustment in young married couples. *Journal of Personality and Social Psychology,* 1977, **35,** 331–342.

Michener, H. A., Fleishman, J. A., & Vaske, J. J. A test of the bargaining theory of coalition formation in four-person groups. *Journal of Personality and Social Psychology,* 1976, **34,** 1114–1126.

Michener, H. A., & Lawler, E. J. Endorsement of formal leaders: An integrative model. *Journal of Personality and Social Psychology,* 1975, **31,** 216–223.

Michener, H. A., & Tausig, M. Usurpation and perceived support as determinants of the endorsement accorded formal leaders. *Journal of Personality and Social Psychology,* 1971, **15,** 364–372.

Miles, M. B. Changes during and following laboratory training: A clinical-experimental study. *Journal of Applied Behavioral Science,* 1965, **1,** 215–242.

Milgram, S. Behavioral study of obedience. *Journal of Abnormal and Social Psychology,* 1963, **67,** 371–378.

Milgram, S. Group pressure and action against a person. *Journal of Abnormal and Social Psychology,* 1964, **69,** 137–143.

Milgram, S. Liberating effects of group pressure. *Journal of Personality and Social Psychology,* 1965, **1,** 127–134.

Milgram, S. *Obedience to authority.* New York: Harper & Row, 1974.

Mill, C. R. Personality patterns of sociometrically selected and sociometrically rejected male college students. *Sociometry,* 1953, **16,** 151–167.

Miller, A. G. Role playing: An alternative to deception? A review of the evidence. *American Psychologist,* 1972, **27,** 623–636.

Miller, E. L. Job attitudes of national union officials: Perceptions of the importance of certain personality traits as a function of job level and union organizational structure. *Personnel Psychology,* 1966, **19,** 395–410.

Miller, N., Butler, D. C., & McMartin, J. A. The ineffectiveness of punishment power in group interaction. *Sociometry,* 1969, **32,** 24–42.

Mills, T. M. Power relations in three-person groups. *American Sociological Review,* 1953, **18,** 351–357.

Mills, T. M. *The sociology of small groups.* Englewood Cliffs, N.J.: Prentice-Hall, 1967.

Mintz, N. Effects of esthetic surroundings: II. Prolonged and repeated experience in a "beautiful" and an "ugly" room. *Journal of Psychology,* 1956, **41,** 459–466.

Mitchell, R. R. Relationships between personal characteristics and change in sensitivity training groups. *Small Group Behavior,* 1975, **6,** 414–420.

Mixon, D. Instead of deception. *Journal for the Theory of Social Behavior,* 1972, **2,** 147–177.

Mixon, D. Temporary false belief. *Personality and Social Psychology Bulletin,* 1977, **3,** 479–488.

Montgomery, R. L., Hinkle, S. W., & Enzie, R. F. Arbitrary norms and social change in high- and low-authoritarian societies. *Journal of Personality and Social Psychology,* 1976, **33,** 698–708.

Moore, J. C., Jr., Johnson, E. B., & Arnold, M. S. C. Status congruence and equity in communication networks. *Sociometry,* 1972, **35,** 519–537.

Moore, O. K., & Anderson, S. B. Search behavior in individual and group problem solving. *American Sociological Review,* 1954, **19,** 702–714.

Moos, R. H. & Speisman, J. C. Group compatibility and productivity. *Journal of Abnormal and Social Psychology,* 1962, **65,** 190–196.

Moran, G. Dyadic attraction and orientational consensus. *Journal of Personality and Social Psychology,* 1966, **4,** 94–99.

Moreno, J. L. *Who shall survive.* Washington, D.C.: Nervous and Mental Disease Publishing Company, 1934.

Moreno, J. L. *Psychodrama.* New York: Beacon House, 1946.

Morgan, C. P., & Aram, J. D. The preponderance of arguments in the risky shift phenomenon. *Journal of Experimental Social Psychology,* 1975, **11,** 25-34.

Morris, C. G. Effects of task characteristics on group process. Technical Report No. 2, AFOSR Contract AF 49 (638)-1291, University of Illinois, 1965.

Morris, C. G., & Hackman, J. R. Behavioral correlates of perceived leadership. *Journal of Personality and Social Psychology,* 1969, **13,** 350–361.

Morris, W. N., & Miller, R. S. The effects of consensus-breaking and consensus-pre-empting partners on reduction of conformity. *Journal of Experimental Social Psychology,* 1975, **11,** 215–223.

Morse, N. C., & Reimer, E. The experimental change of a major organizational variable. *Journal of Abnormal and Social Psychology,* 1956, **52,** 120–129.

Mortensen, C. D. Should the group have an assigned leader? *Speech Teacher,* 1966, **15,** 34–41.

Moscovici, S., & Zavalloni, M. The group as a polarizer of attitudes. *Journal of Personality and Social Psychology,* 1969, **12,** 125–135.

Movahedi, S. Role playing: An alternative to what? *Personality and Social Psychology Bulletin,* 1977, **3,** 489–497.

Muehleman, J. T., Bruker, C., & Ingram, C. M. The generosity shift. *Journal of Personality and Social Psychology,* 1976, **34,** 344–351.

Mulder, M. Group-structure and group-performance. *Acta Psychologica,* 1959a, **16,** 356–402.

Mulder, M. Power and satisfaction in task-oriented groups. *Acta Psychologica,* 1959b, **16,** 178–225.

Mulder, M. Communication structure, decision structure and group performance. *Sociometry,* 1960, **23,** 1–14.

Mulder, M., Van Dijk, R., SoutenDijk, S., Stelwagen, T., & Verhagen, J. Non-instrumental liking tendencies toward powerful group members. *Acta Psychologica,* 1964, **22,** 367–386.

Murnighan, J. K., Komorita, S. S., & Szwajkowski, E. Theories of coalition formation and the effects of reference groups. *Journal of Experimental Social Psychology,* 1977, **13,** 166–181.

Murphy, A. J. A study of the leadership process. *American Sociological Review,* 1941, **6,** 674–687.

Murphy-Berman, V., & Berman, J. The importance of choice and sex in invasions of interpersonal space. *Personality and Social Psychology Bulletin,* 1978, **4,** 424–428.

Myers, D. G. Polarizing effects of social comparison. *Journal of Experimental Social Psychology,* 1978, **14,** 554–563.

Myers, D. G., & Lamm, H. The polarizing effect of group discussion. *American Scientist,* 1975, **63,** 297–303.

Myers, D. G., & Lamm, H. The group polarization phenomenon. *Psychological Bulletin,* 1976, **83,** 602–627.

Myers, R. K. Some effects of seating arrangements in counseling. Unpublished doctoral dissertation, University of Florida, Gainesville, 1969.

Nadler, E. B. Yielding, authoritarianism, and authoritarian ideology regarding groups. *Journal of Abnormal and Social Psychology,* 1959, **58,** 408–410.

Nadler, E. B., & Fink, S. L. Impact of laboratory training on socio-political ideology. *Journal of Applied Behavioral Science,* 1970, **6,** 79–92.

Nahemow, L., & Lawton, M. P. Similarity and propinquity in friendship formation. *Journal of Personality and Social Psychology,* 1975, **32,** 205–213.

Nakamura, C. Y. Conformity and problem solving. *Journal of Abnormal and Social Psychology,* 1958, **56,** 315–320.

Near, J. P. Comparison of developmental patterns in groups. *Small Group Behavior,* 1978, **9,** 493–506.

Nesbitt, P. D., & Steven, G. Personal space and stimulus intensity at a southern California amusement park. *Sociometry,* 1974, **37,** 105–115.

Neville, B. W. Interpersonal functioning and learning in the small group. *Small Group Behavior,* 1978, **9,** 349–361.

Newcomb, T. M. The prediction of interpersonal attraction. *American Psychologist,* 1956, **11,** 575–586.

Newcomb, T. M. *The acquaintance process.* New York: Holt, 1961.

Newman, B. M. The development of social interaction from infancy through adolescence. *Small Group Behavior,* 1976, **7,** 19–32.

Nickols, S. A. A study of the additivity of variables influencing conformity. Unpublished doctoral dissertation, University of Florida, Gainesville, 1964.

Novak, D. W., & Lerner, M. J. Rejection as a consequence of perceived similarity. *Journal of Personality and Social Psychology,* 1968, **9,** 147–152.

O'Dell, J. W. Group size and emotional interaction. *Journal of Personality and Social Psychology,* 1968, **8,** 75–78.

O'Dell, S., & Seiler, G. The effects of short-term personal growth groups on anxiety and self-perception. *Small Group Behavior,* 1975, **6,** 251–271.

Okun, M. A., & Di Vesta, F. J. Cooperation and competition in coacting groups. *Journal of Personality and Social Psychology,* 1975, **31,** 615–620.

O'Neill, M. S., & Alexander, J. F. Family interaction patterns as a function of task characteristics. *Journal of Applied Social Psychology,* 1971, **1,** 163–172.

Ort, R. S. A study of role-conflicts as related to happiness in marriage. *Journal of Abnormal and Social Psychology,* 1950, **45,** 691–699.

OSS Assessment Staff. *The Assessment of Men.* New York: Rinehart, 1948.

Page, R. C., & Kubiak, L. Marathon groups: Facilitating the personal growth of imprisoned, black female heroin abusers. *Small Group Behavior,* 1978, **9,** 409–416.

Palmer, F. H., & Myers, T. I. Sociometric choice and group productivity among radar crews. *Proceedings of the American Psychological Association,* 1955.

Palmer, G. J., Jr. Task ability and effective leadership. Technical Report No. 4, Contract Nonr 1575(05), Louisiana State University, 1962a.

Palmer, G. J., Jr. Task ability and successful and effective leadership. Technical Report No. 6, Contract Nonr 1575(05), Louisiana State University, 1962b.

Palmore, E. B. The introduction of Negroes into white departments. *Human Organization,* 1955, **14,** 27–28.

Parsons, T. An outline of the social system. In T. Parsons, E. Shils, K. D. Naegele, & J. R. Pitts (Eds.), *Theories of society.* New York: Free Press, 1961. Pp. 30–79.

Parsons, T., Bales, R. F., & Shils, E. A. *Working papers in the theory of action.* Glencoe, Ill.: Free Press, 1953.

Parten, M. B. Social participation among preschool children. *Journal of Abnormal and Social Psychology,* 1932, **27,** 243–269.

Patel, A. A., & Gordon, J. E. Some personal and situational determinants of yielding to influence. *Journal of Abnormal and Social Psychology,* 1960, **61,** 411–418.

Patterson, M. L., Kelly, C. E., Kondracki, B. A., & Wulf, L. J. Effects of seating arrangement on small-group behavior. *Social Psychology Quarterly,* 1979, **42,** 180–185.

Patterson, M. L., Roth, C. P., & Schenk, C. Seating arrangement, activity, and sex differences in small group crowding. *Personality and Social Psychology Bulletin,* 1979, **5,** 100–103.

Patterson, M. L., & Schaeffer, R. E. Effects of size and sex composition on interaction distance, participation, and satisfaction in small groups. *Small Group Behavior,* 1977, **8,** 433–442.

Paulus, P. B., Annis, A. B., Seta, J. J., Schkade, J. K., & Matthews, R. W. Density does affect task performance. *Journal of Personality and Social Psychology,* 1976, **34,** 248–253.

Paulus, P. B., Cox, V., McCain, G., & Chandler, J. Some effects of crowding in a prison environment. *Journal of Applied Social Psychology,* 1975, 5, 86–91.

Paulus, P. B., & Murdoch, P. Anticipated evaluation and audience presence in the enhancement of dominant responses. *Journal of Experimental Social Psychology,* 1971, **7,** 280–291.

Pepitone, A., & Kleiner, R. J. The effects of threat and frustration on group cohesiveness. *Journal of Abnormal and Social Psychology,* 1957, **54,** 192–199.

Perlmutter, H. V., & de Montmollin, G. Group learning of nonsense syllables. *Journal of Abnormal and Social Psychology,* 1952, **47,** 762–769.

Pessin, J., & Husband, R. W. Effects of social stimulation on human maze learning. *Journal of Abnormal and Social Psychology,* 1933, **28,** 148–154.

Piaget, J. *The moral judgment of the child.* New York: Basic Books, 1954.

Polansky, N., Lippitt, R., & Redl, F. An investigation of behavioral contagion in groups. *Human Relations,* 1950, **3,** 319–348.

Preston, M. Note on the reliability and validity of group judgment. *Journal of Experimental Psychology,* 1938, **22,** 462–471.

Preston, M. G., & Heintz, R. K. Effects of participatory vs. supervisory leadership on group judgment. *Journal of Abnormal and Social Psychology,* 1949, **44,** 345–355.

Pruitt, D. G., & Teger, A. I. The risky shift in group betting. *Journal of Experimental Social Psychology,* 1969, **5,** 115–126.

Rabbie, J. M., & Bekkers, F. Threatened leadership and intergroup competition. *European Journal of Social Psychology,* 1978, **8,** 9–20.

Rabbie, J. M., Benoist, F., Oosterbaan, H., & Visser, L. Differential power and effects of expected competitive and cooperative intergroup interaction on intragroup and outgroup attitudes. *Journal of Personality and Social Psychology,* 1974, **30,** 46–56.

Radke, M., & Klisurich, D. Experiments in changing food habits. *Journal of the American Dietetics Association,* 1947, **23,** 403–409.

Raper, A. *The tragedy of lynching.* Chapel Hill: University of North Carolina Press, 1933.

Rapoport, A., & Kahan, J. P. When three is not always two against one: Coalitions in experimental three-person games. *Journal of Experimental Social Psychology,* 1976, **12,** 253–273.

Raven, B. H., & Rietsema, J. The effects of varied clarity of group goal and group path upon the individual and his relation to the group. *Human Relations,* 1957, **10,** 29–44.

Read, P. B. Source of authority and the legitimization of leadership in small groups. *Sociometry,* 1974, **37,** 189–204.

Read, W. H. Upward communication in industrial hierarchies. *Human Relations,* 1962, **15,** 3–15.

Reckman, R. F., & Goethals, G. R. Deviancy and group orientation as determinants of group composition preferences. *Sociometry,* 1973, **36,** 419–423.

Reddy, W. B. On affection, group composition, and self-actualization in sensitivity training. *Journal of Consulting and Clinical Psychology,* 1972a, **38,** 211–214.

Reddy, W. B. Interpersonal compatibility and self-actualization in sensitivity training. *Journal of Applied Behavioral Science,* 1972b, **8,** 1–5.

Reddy, W. B., & Beers, T. Sensitivity training . . . and the healthy become self-actualized. *Small Group Behavior,* 1977, **8,** 525–532.

Reddy, W. B., & Byrnes, A. The effects of interpersonal group composition on the problem solving behavior of middle managers. *Journal of Applied Psychology,* 1972, **56,** 516–517.

Reilly, M. E. A case study of role conflict: Roman Catholic Priests. *Human Relations,* 1978, **31,** 77–90.

Reitan, H. T., & Shaw, M. E. Group membership, sex-composition of the group, and conformity behavior. *Journal of Social Psychology,* 1964, **64,** 45–51.

Rice, S. A. *Quantitative methods in politics.* New York: Knopf, 1928.

Riecken, H. W. The effect of talkativeness on ability to influence group solutions of problems. *Sociometry,* 1958, **21,** 309–321.

Rittle, R. H., & Bernard, N. Enhancement of response rate by the mere physical presence of the experimenter. *Personality and Social Psychology Bulletin,* 1977, **3,** 127–130.

Roby, T. B. The influence of subgroup relationships on the performance of group and subgroup tasks. *American Psychologist,* 1952, **7,** 313–314.

Roby, T. B. Computer simulation models for organization theory. In E. V. Vroom (Ed.), *Methods of organizational research.* Pittsburgh: Pittsburgh Press, 1967. Pp. 171–211.

Roby, T. B. *Small group performance.* Chicago: Rand McNally, 1968.

Roethlisberger, F. J., & Dickson, W. J. *Management and the worker.* Cambridge, Mass.: Harvard, 1939.

Rokeach, M. *The open and closed mind.* New York: Basic Books, 1960.

Romer, D., Bontemps, M., Flynn, M., McGuire, T., & Gruder, C. L. The effects of status similarity and expectation of reciprocation upon altruistic behavior. *Personality and Social Psychology Bulletin,* 1977, **3,** 103–106.

Rose, A. *Union solidarity.* Minneapolis: The University of Minnesota Press, 1952.

Rosenbaum, L. L., & Rosenbaum, W. B. Morale and productivity consequences of group leadership style, stress, and type of task. *Journal of Applied Psychology,* 1971, **55,** 343–348.

Rosenbaum, M. E., & Blake, R. R. Volunteering as a function of field structure. *Journal of Abnormal and Social Psychology,* 1955, **50,** 193–196.

Rosenberg, L. A. Group size, prior experience, and conformity. *Journal of Abnormal and Social Psychology,* 1961, **63,** 436–437.

Rosenberg, S., Erlick, D. E., & Berkowitz, L. Some effects of varying combinations of group members on group performance measures and leadership behaviors. *Journal of Abnormal and Social Psychology,* 1955, **51,** 195–203.

Ross, I., & Zander, A. Need satisfaction and employee turnover. *Personnel Psychology*, 1957, **10**, 327–338.

Ross, L. D., Amabile, T. M., & Steinmetz, J. L. Social roles, social control, and biases in social-perception processes. *Journal of Personality and Social Psychology*, 1977, **35**, 485–494.

Ross, M., Layton, B., Erickson, B., & Schopler, J. Affect, facial regard, and reactions to crowding. *Journal of Personality and Social Psychology*, 1973, **28**, 69–76.

Rousseau, J. J. *Contrat social ou principes du droit politique*. Paris: Librairie Garnier Frères, 1772.

Ruhe, J. A. The effects of varying racial compositions upon attitudes and behavior of supervisors and subordinates in simulated work groups. Unpublished doctoral dissertation, University of Florida, Gainesville, 1972.

Ruhe, J. A. Effect of leader sex and leader behavior on group problem-solving. *Proceedings of the American Institute for Decision Sciences, Northeast Division*, May, 1978, pp. 123–127.

Ruhe, J. A., & Allen, W. R. Differences and similarities between black and white leaders. *Proceedings of the American Institute of Decision Sciences, Northeast Division*, April, 1977, pp. 30–35.

Ruhe, J. A., & Eatman, J. Effects of racial composition on small work groups. *Small Group Behavior*, 1977, **8**, 479–486.

Runyan, D. L. The group risky-shift effect as a function of emotional bonds, actual consequences, and extent of responsibility. *Journal of Personality and Social Psychology*, 1974, **29**, 670–676.

Russo, N. F. Connotations of seating arrangements. *Cornell Journal of Social Relations*, 1967, **2**, 37–44.

Ruzicka, M. F., Palisi, A. T., & Berven, N. L. Use of Cattell's three panel model: Remedying problems in small group research. *Small Group Behavior*, 1979, **10**, 40–48.

Ryan, E. D., & Lakie, W. L. Competitive and noncompetitive performance in relation to achievement motive and manifest anxiety. *Journal of Personality and Social Psychology*, 1965, **1**, 342–345.

Rychlak, J. F. The similarity, compatibility, or incompatibility of needs in interpersonal selection. *Journal of Personality and Social Psychology*, 1965, **2**, 334–340.

Ryen, A. H., & Kahn, A. Effects of intergroup orientation on group attitudes and proxemic behavior. *Journal of Personality and Social Psychology*, 1975, **31**, 302–310.

Saha, S. K. Contingency theories of leadership: A study. *Human Relations*, 1979, **32**, 313–322.

Sakurai, M. M. Small group cohesiveness and detrimental conformity. *Sociometry*, 1975, **38**, 340–357.

Sampson, E. E. Studies of status congruence. In L. Berkowitz (Ed.), *Advances in experimental social psychology*. Vol. 4. New York: Academic Press, 1969. Pp. 225–270.

Sanders, G. S. An integration of shifts toward risk and caution in gambling situations. *Journal of Experimental Social Psychology*, 1978, **14**, 409–416.

Sanders, G. S., & Baron, R. S. The motivating effects of distraction on task performance. *Journal of Personality and Social Psychology,* 1975, **32,** 956–963.

Sanders, G. S., & Baron, R. S. Is social comparison irrelevant for producing choice shifts? *Journal of Experimental Social Psychology,* 1977, **13,** 303–314.

Sanders, G. S., Baron, R. S., & Moore, D. L. Distraction and social comparison as mediators of social facilitation effects. *Journal of Experimental Social Psychology,* 1978, **14,** 291–303.

Sapolsky, A. Effect of interpersonal relationships upon verbal conditioning. *Journal of Abnormal and Social Psychology,* 1960, **60,** 241–246.

Sarbin, T. R., & Allen, V. L. Role theory. In G. Lindzey & E. Aronson (Eds.), *The handbook of social psychology* (2d ed.) Vol. 1. Reading, Mass.: Addison-Wesley, 1968. Pp. 488–567.

Sasfy, J., & Okun, M. Form of evaluation and audience expertness as joint determinants of audience effects. *Journal of Experimental Social Psychology,* 1974, **10,** 461–467.

Schachter, S. Deviation, rejection, and communication. *Journal of Abnormal and Social Psychology,* 1951, **46,** 190–207.

Schachter, S. *The psychology of affiliation.* Stanford, Calif.: Stanford University Press, 1959.

Schachter, S., Ellertson, N., McBride, D., & Gregory, D. An experimental study of cohesiveness and productivity. *Human Relations,* 1951, **4,** 229–238.

Schaible, T. D., & Jacobs, A. Feedback III: Sequence effects. Enhancement of feedback acceptance and group attractiveness by manipulation of the sequence and valence of feedback. *Small Group Behavior,* 1975, **6,** 151–173.

Schanck, R. L. A study of a community and its groups and institutions conceived of as behaviors of individuals. *Psychological Monographs,* 1932, **43,** No. 2 (Whole No. 195).

Scheidel, T. M., & Crowell, L. Idea development in small discussion groups. *Quarterly Journal of Speech,* 1964, **50,** 140–145.

Scheidel, T. M., & Crowell, L. Feedback in small group communication. *Quarterly Journal of Speech,* 1966, **52,** 273–278.

Schein, E. H. The development of organization in small problem-solving groups. Final Report, Sloan Project No. 134, Massachusetts Institute of Technology, 1958.

Schein, E. H., & Bennis, W. G. *Personal and organizational change through group methods: A laboratory approach.* New York: Wiley, 1965.

Schelling, T. C. The strategy of conflict: Prospectus for a reorientation of game theory. *Journal of Conflict Resolution,* 1958, **2,** 203–264.

Schiffenbauer, A., & Schiavo, R. S. Physical distance and attraction: An intensification effect. *Journal of Experimental Social Psychology,* 1976, **12,** 274–282.

Schlenker, B. R. Social psychology and science. *Journal of Personality and Social Psychology,* 1974, **29,** 1–15.

Schlenker, B. R., Bonoma, T., Tedeschi, J. T., & Pivnick, W. P. Compliance to threats as a function of the wording of the threat and the exploitativeness of the threatener. *Sociometry,* 1970, **33,** 394–408.

Schlenker, B. R., Nacci, P., Helm, B., & Tedeschi, J. T. Reactions to coercive and reward power: The effects of switching influence modes on target compliance. *Sociometry,* 1976, **39,** 316–323.

Schlenker, B. R., & Tedeschi, J. T. Interpersonal attraction and the exercise of coercive and reward power. *Human Relations,* 1973, **25,** 427–439.

Schlosser, M. Liking as a function of physical attractiveness and task performance. Unpublished master's thesis, University of Florida, Gainesville, 1969.

Schneider, F. W. Differences between Negro and white school children in conforming behavior. Unpublished doctoral dissertation, University of Florida, Gainesville, 1968.

Schutz, W. C. What makes groups productive? *Human Relations,* 1955, **8,** 429–465.

Schutz, W. C. *FIRO: A three dimensional theory of interpersonal behavior.* New York: Rinehart, 1958.

Schutz, W. C. On group composition. *Journal of Abnormal and Social Psychology,* 1961, **62,** 275–281.

Schutz, W. C. *The Interpersonal Underworld.* Palo Alto: Science and Behavior Books, 1966.

Schutz, W. C. *JOY: Expanding human awareness.* New York: Grove Press, 1967.

Schutz, W. C., & Allen, V. L. The effects of a T-group laboratory on interpersonal behavior. *Journal of Applied Behavioral Science,* 1966, **2,** 265–286.

Scioli, F. P., Jr., Dyson, J. W., & Fleitas, D. W. The relationship of personality and decisional structure to leadership. *Small Group Behavior,* 1974, **5,** 3–22.

Scott, W. E., Jr., & Cherrington, D. J. Effects of competitive, cooperative, and individualistic reinforcement contingencies. *Journal of Personality and Social Psychology,* 1974, **30,** 748–758.

Seashore, S. E. *Group cohesiveness in the industrial work group.* Ann Arbor: The University of Michigan Press, 1954.

Seeman, W., & Marks, P. A. The behavior of the psychologist at a choice point. *American Scientist,* 1962, **50,** 538–547.

Segal, M. W. A reconfirmation of the logarithmic effect of group size. *Sociometry,* 1977, **40,** 187–190.

Seghers, C. E. Color in the office. *The Management Review,* 1948.

Senn, D. J. Attraction as a function of similarity-dissimilarity in task performance. *Journal of Personality and Social Psychology,* 1971, **18,** 120–123.

Shaffer, D. R., & Sadowski, C. This table is mine: Respect for marked barroom tables as a function of gender of spatial marker and desirability of locale. *Sociometry,* 1975, **38,** 408–419.

Shaffer, J. B. P., & Galinsky, M. D. *Models of group therapy and sensitivity training.* Englewood Cliffs, N.J.: Prentice-Hall, 1974.

Shaffer, L. S. On the current confusion of group-related behavior and collective behavior: A reaction to Buys. *Personality and Social Psychology Bulletin,* 1978, **4,** 564–567.

Shapiro, E. G. Effect of expectations of future interaction on reward allocations in dyads: Equity or equality. *Journal of Personality and Social Psychology,* 1975, **31,** 873–880.

Shaver, K. G. *Principles of social psychology.* Cambridge, Mass.: Winthrop Publishing Co., 1977.

Shaw, Marjorie E. A comparison of individuals and small groups in the rational solution of complex problems. *American Journal of Psychology,* 1932, **44,** 491–504.

Shaw, M. E. Some effects of problem complexity upon problem solution efficiency in different communication nets. *Journal of Experimental Psychology,* 1954a, **48,** 211–217.

Shaw, M. E. Some effects of unequal distribution of information upon group performance in various communication nets. *Journal of Abnormal and Social Psychology,* 1954b, **49,** 547–553.

Shaw, M. E. A comparison of two types of leadership in various communication nets. *Journal of Abnormal and Social Psychology,* 1955, **50,** 127–134.

Shaw, M. E. Some effects of irrelevant information upon problem-solving by small groups. *Journal of Social Psychology,* 1958a, **47,** 33–37.

Shaw, M. E. Some motivational factors in cooperation and competition. *Journal of Personality,* 1958b, **26,** 155–169.

Shaw, M. E. Acceptance of authority, group structure, and the effectiveness of small groups. *Journal of Personality,* 1959a, **27,** 196–210.

Shaw, M. E. Some effects of individually prominent behavior upon group effectiveness and member satisfaction. *Journal of Abnormal and Social Psychology,* 1959b, **59,** 382–386.

Shaw, M. E. A note concerning homogeneity of membership and group problem solving. *Journal of Abnormal and Social Psychology,* 1960, **60,** 448–450.

Shaw, M. E. Group dynamics. *Annual Review of Psychology,* 1961a, **12,** 129–156.

Shaw, M. E. Some factors influencing the use of information in groups. *Psychological Reports,* 1961b, **8,** 187–198.

Shaw, M. E. Implicit conversion of fate control in dyadic interaction. *Psychological Reports,* 1962, **10,** 758.

Shaw, M. E. Some effects of varying amounts of information exclusively possessed by a group member upon his behavior in the group. *Journal of General Psychology,* 1963, **68,** 71–79.

Shaw, M. E. Communication networks. In L. Berkowtiz (Ed.), *Advances in experimental social psychology.* Vol 1. New York: Academic Press, 1964. Pp. 111–147.

Shaw, M. E. Social psychology and group processes. In J. B. Sidowski (Ed.), *Experimental methods and instrumentation in psychology.* New York: McGraw-Hill, 1966. Pp. 607–643.

Shaw, M. E. Scaling group tasks: A method for dimensional analysis. *JSAS Catalog of Selected Documents in Psychology,* 1973a, **3,** 8. (MS No. 294).

Shaw, M. E. Changes in sociometric choices following forced integration of an elementary school. *Journal of Social Issues,* 1973b, **29,** 143–158.

Shaw, M. E., Ackerman, B., McCown, N. E., Worsham, A. P., Haugh, L. D., Gebhardt, B. M., & Small, P. A., Jr. Interaction patterns and facilitation of peer learning. *Small Group Behavior,* 1979, **10,** 214–223.

Shaw, M. E., & Ashton, N. Do assembly bonus effects occur on disjunctive tasks? A test of Steiner's theory. *Bulletin of the Psychonomic Society,* 1976, **8,** 469–471.

Shaw, M. E., Ashton, N. L., & Worsham, A. P. Personal space: A re-examination.

Paper presented at the meetings of the Southeastern Psychological Assoc., Atlanta, 1978.

Shaw, M. E., & Blum, J. M. Group performance as a function of task difficulty and the group's awareness of member satisfaction. *Journal of Applied Psychology,* 1965, **49**, 151–154.

Shaw, M. E., & Blum, J. M. Effects of leadership styles upon group performance as a function of task structure. *Journal of Personality and Social Psychology,* 1966, **3**, 238–242.

Shaw, M. E., & Breed, G. R. Effects of attribution of responsibility for negative events on behavior in small groups. *Sociometry,* 1970, **33**, 382–393.

Shaw, M. E., & Briscoe, M. E. Group size and effectiveness in solving tasks varying in degree of cooperation requirements. Technical Report No. 6, ONR Contract NR 170-266, Nonr-580(11), University of Florida, 1966.

Shaw, M. E., & Costanzo, P. R. *Theories of social psychology.* New York: McGraw-Hill, 1970.

Shaw, M. E., & Gilchrist, J. C. Repetitive task failure and sociometric choice. *Journal of Abnormal and Social Psychology,* 1955, **50**, 29–32.

Shaw, M. E., & Gilchrist, J. C. Intra-group communication and leader choice. *Journal of Social Psychology,* 1956, **43**, 133–138.

Shaw, M. E., & Harkey, B. Some effects of congruency of member characteristics and group structure upon group behavior. *Journal of Personality and Social Psychology,* 1976, **34**, 412–418.

Shaw, M. E., & Nickols, S. A. Group effectiveness as a function of group member compatibility and cooperation requirements of the task. Technical Report No. 4, ONR Contract NR 170-266, Nonr-580(11), University of Florida, 1964.

Shaw, M. E., & Penrod, W. T., Jr. Does more information available to a group always improve group performance? *Sociometry,* 1962a, **25**, 377–390.

Shaw, M. E., & Penrod, W. T., Jr. Validity of information, attempted influence, and quality of group decisions. *Psychological Reports,* 1962b, **10**, 19–23.

Shaw, M. E., & Penrod, W. T., Jr. Group effectiveness as a function of amount of "legitimate" information. *Journal of Social Psychology,* 1964, **62**, 241–246.

Shaw, M. E., & Reitan, H. T. Attribution of responsibility as a basis for sanctioning behavior. *British Journal of Social and Clinical Psychology,* 1969, **8**, 217–226.

Shaw, M. E., & Rothschild, G. H. Some effects of prolonged experience in communication nets. *Journal of Applied Psychology,* 1956, **40**, 281–286.

Shaw, M. E., Rothschild, G. H., & Strickland, J. F. Decision processes in communication nets. *Journal of Abnormal and Social Psychology,* 1957, **54**, 323–330.

Shaw, M. E., & Shaw, L. M. Some effects of sociometric grouping upon learning in a second grade classroom. *Journal of Social Psychology,* 1962, **57**, 453–458.

Shaw, M. E., & Tremble, T. R., Jr. Effects of attribution of responsibility for a negative event to a group member upon group process as a function of the structure of the event. *Sociometry,* 1971, **34**, 504–514.

Shaw, M. E., & Wagner, P. J. Role selection in the service of self-presentation. *Memory and Cognition,* 1975, **3**, 481–484.

Sheley, K., & Shaw, M. E. Social power: To use or not to use? *Bulletin of the Psychonomic Society,* 1979, **13**, 257–260.

Shelley, H. P. Level of aspiration phenomena in small groups. *Journal of Social Psychology*, 1954, **40**, 149–164.

Sherif, M. *The psychology of social norms*. New York: Harper, 1936.

Sherif, M., & Hovland, C. I. *Social judgment*. New Haven, Conn.: Yale University Press, 1961.

Sherif, M., & Sherif, C. W. *Groups in harmony and tension*. New York: Harper & Row, 1953.

Sherif, M., & Sherif, C. W. *An outline of social psychology* (rev. ed.). New York: Harper & Row, 1956.

Sherrod, D. R. Crowding, perceived control, and behavioral aftereffects. *Journal of Applied Social Psychology*, 1974, **4**, 171–186.

Shevitz, R. N. *Leadership acts: IV. An investigation of the relation between exclusive possession of information and attempts to lead*. Columbus: Ohio State University Research Foundation, 1955.

Shure, G. H., Rogers, M. S., Larsen, I. M., & Tassone, J. Group planning and task effectiveness. *Sociometry*, 1962, **25**, 263–282.

Shuter, R. Proxemics and territoriality in Latin America. *Journal of Communication*, 1976, **26**, 46–52.

Silverstein, C. H., & Stang, D. J. Seating position and interaction in triads: A field study. *Sociometry*, 1976, **39**, 166–170.

Singer, J. E., & Shockley, V. L. Ability and affiliation. *Journal of Personality and Social Psychology*, 1965, **1**, 95–100.

Sistrunk, F., & McDavid, J. W. Sex variable in conforming behavior. *Journal of Personality and Social Psychology*, 1971, **17**, 200–207.

Slater, P. E. Role differentiation in small groups. *American Sociological Review*, 1955, **20**, 300–310.

Slater, P. E. Contrasting correlates of group size. *Sociometry*, 1958, **21**, 129–139.

Sleight, R. B., & Tiffin, J. Industrial noise and hearing. *Journal of Applied Psychology*, 1948, **32**, 476–489.

Small, P. A., Jr. Science education: Simulation methods for teaching process and content. *Federations Proceedings*, 1974, **33**, 2008–2010.

Small, P. A., Jr. Small group learning situations: Two questions—and one answer. *Association of American Medical Colleges Education News*, 1975, **3**, 1 & 5.

Smelser, W. T. Dominance as a factor in achievement and perception in cooperative problem solving interactions. *Journal of Abnormal and Social Psychology*, 1961, **62**, 535–542.

Smith, C. R., Williams, L., & Willis, R. H. Race, sex, and belief as determinants of friendship acceptance. *Journal of Personality and Social Psychology*, 1967, **5**, 127–137.

Smith, H. W. Small group interaction at various ages: Simultaneous talking and interruptions of others. *Small Group Behavior*, 1977, **8**, 65–74.

Smith, K. H. Changes in group structure through individual and group feedback. *Journal of Personality and Social Psychology*, 1972, **24**, 425–428.

Smith, P. B. Attitude changes associated with training in human relations. *British Journal of Social and Clinical Psychology*, 1964, **3**, 104–112.

Smith, P. B. Social influence processes and the outcome of sensitivity training. *Journal of Personality and Social Psychology*, 1976, **34**, 1087–1094.

Smith, R. J., & Cook, P. E. Leadership in dyadic groups as a function of dominance and incentives. *Sociometry*, 1973, **36**, 561–568.

Smith, S., & Haythorn, W. W. Effects of compatibility, crowding, group size, and leadership seniority on stress, anxiety, hostility, and annoyance in isolated groups. *Journal of Personality and Social Psychology*, 1972, **22**, 67–79.

Smith, W. P. Power structure and authoritarianism in the use of power in the triad. *Journal of Personality*, 1967, **35**, 64–90.

Smith, W. P., & Bordonaro, F. Self-esteem and satisfaction as affected by unexpected social status placement. *Sociometry*, 1975, **38**, 223–246.

Smith, W. P., & Leginski, W. A. Magnitude and precision of punitive power in bargaining strategy. *Journal of Experimental Social Psychology*, 1970, **6**, 57–76.

Sommer, R. Studies in personal space. *Sociometry*, 1959, **22**, 247–260.

Sommer, R. *Personal space: The behavioral basis of design.* Englewood Cliffs, N.J.: Prentice-Hall, 1969.

Sorenson, J. R. Group member traits, group process, and group performance. *Human Relations*, 1973, **26**, 639–655.

Sorrentino, R. M., & Boutillier, R. G. The effect of quantity and quality of verbal interaction on ratings of leadership ability. *Journal of Experimental Social Psychology*, 1975, **11**, 403–411.

Sorrentino, R. M., & Sheppard, B. H. Effects of affiliation-related motives on swimmers in individual versus group competition: A field experiment. *Journal of Personality and Social Psychology*, 1978, **36**, 704–714.

Spector, P. E., Cohen, S. L., & Penner, L. A. The effects of real vs. hypothetical risk on group choice-shifts. *Personality and Social Psychology Bulletin*, 1976, **2**, 290–293.

Spence, R. B. Lecture and class discussion in teaching educational psychology. *Journal of Educational Psychology*, 1928, **19**, 454–462.

Spencer, H. *Principles of sociology.* New York: Appleton, 1876.

Speroff, B., & Kerr, W. Steel mill "hot strip" accidents and interpersonal desirability values. *Journal of Clinical Psychology*, 1952, **8**, 89–91.

Spielberger, C. D. Theory and research on anxiety. In C. D. Spielberger (Ed.), *Anxiety and behavior.* New York: Academic Press, 1966.

Spielberger, C. D., Gorsuch, R. L., & Lushene, R. E. *State-Trait Anxiety Inventory Manual.* Palo Alto: Consulting Psychologists Press, 1969.

St. Jean, R. Reformulation of the value hypothesis in group risk taking. *Proceedings of the 78th Annual Convention of the American Psychological Association*, 1970, **5**, 339–340.

Stager, P. Conceptual level as a composition variable in small-group decision making. *Journal of Personality and Social Psychology*, 1967, **5**, 152–161.

Steele, F. I. Personality and the "laboratory style." *Journal of Applied Behavioral Science*, 1968, **4**, 25–46.

Stein, R. T. Identifying emergent leaders from verbal and nonverbal communications. *Journal of Personality and Social Psychology*, 1975, **32**, 125–135.

Steiner, I. D. *Group process and productivity.* New York: Academic Press, 1972.

Steiner, I. D., & Rajaratnam, N. A model for the comparison of individual and group performance scores. *Behavioral Science*, 1961, **6**, 142–147.

Steinzor, B. The spatial factor in face-to-face discussion groups. *Journal of Abnormal and Social Psychology,* 1950, **45,** 552–555.

Stephenson, G. M., & Kniveton, B. K. Interpersonal and interparty exchange: An experimental study of the effect of seating position on the outcome of negotiations between teams representing parties in dispute. *Human Relations,* 1978, **31,** 555–566.

Stevenson, H. W., & Cruse, D. B. The effectiveness of social reinforcement with normal and feebleminded children. *Journal of Personality,* 1961, **29,** 124–135.

Stevenson, H. W., & Odom, R. D. The effectiveness of social reinforcement following two conditions of social deprivation. *Journal of Abnormal and Social Psychology,* 1962, **65,** 429–431.

Stewart, F. A. A study of influence in Southtown: II. *Sociometry,* 1947, **10,** 273–286.

Stires, L. K. Leadership designation and perceived ability as determinants of the tactical use of modesty and self-enhancement. *Dissertation Abstracts International,* 1970, **30A,** 35–51.

Stogdill, R. M. Personal factors associated with leadership: A survey of the literature. *Journal of Psychology,* 1948, **25,** 35–71.

Stogdill, R. M. Leadership, membership and organization. *Psychological Bulletin,* 1950, **47,** 1–14.

Stogdill, R. M. *Individual behavior and group achievement.* New York: Oxford University Press, 1959.

Stogdill, R. M. *Leadership: A survey of the literature. I. Selected topics.* Greensboro, N.C.: Smith Richardson Foundation, 1968.

Stogdill, R. M. *Handbook of leadership.* New York: The Free Press, 1974.

Stogdill, R. M., Shartle, C. L., Scott, E. L., Coons, E. A., & Jaynes, W. E. *A predictive study of administrative work patterns.* Columbus: Ohio State University, Bureau of Business Research, 1956.

Stokols, D. A social-psychological model of human crowding phenomena. *Journal of the American Institute of Planners,* 1972, **38,** 72–83.

Stolte, J. F. Power structure and personal competence. *Journal of Social Psychology,* 1978, **106,** 83–92.

Stoner, J. A. F. A comparison of individual and group decisions involving risk. Unpublished master's thesis, Massachusetts Institute of Technology, 1961. (Cited in Wallach, Kogan, & Bem, 1962.)

Stoner, J. A. F. Risky and cautious shifts in group decisions: The influence of widely held values. *Journal of Experimental Social Psychology,* 1968, **4,** 442–459.

Storms, M. D., & Thomas, G. C. Reactions to physical closeness. *Journal of Personality and Social Psychology,* 1977, **35,** 412–418.

Stotland, E., & Cottrell, N. B. Similarity of performance as influenced by interaction, self-esteem, and birth order. *Journal of Abnormal and Social Psychology,* 1962, **64,** 183–191.

Stotland, E., Cottrell, N. B., & Laing, G. Group interaction and perceived similarity of members. *Journal of Abnormal and Social Psychology,* 1960, **61,** 335–340.

Stouffer, S. A., Suchman, E. A., DeVinney, L. C., Star, S. A., & Williams, R. M.,

Jr. *The American soldier: Adjustment during army life.* Vol. 1. Princeton, N.J.: Princeton University Press, 1949.

Strodtbeck, F. L., & Hook, L. H. The social dimensions of a twelve man jury table. *Sociometry,* 1961, **24,** 397–415.

Stroop, J. R. Is the judgment of the group better than that of the average member of the group? *Journal of Experimental Psychology,* 1932, **15,** 550–562.

Strupp, H. H., & Hausman, H. J. Some correlates of group productivity. *American Psychologist,* 1953, **8,** 443–444.

Suedfeld, P., & Rank, A. D. Revolutionary leaders: Long-term success as a function of changes in conceptual complexity. *Journal of Personality and Social Psychology,* 1976, **34,** 169–178.

Suls, J. M., & Miller, R. L. Ability comparison and its effects on affiliation preferences. *Human Relations,* 1978, **31,** 267–282.

Sundstrom, E., & Altman, I. Field study of territorial behavior and dominance. *Journal of Personality and Social Psychology,* 1974, **30,** 115–124.

Swingle, P. G. Illusory power in a dangerous game. *Canadian Journal of Psychology/Review of Canadian Psychology,* 1968, **22,** 176–185.

Sykes, R. E., Larntz, K., & Fox, J. C. Proximity and similarity effects on frequency of interaction in a class of naval recruits. *Sociometry,* 1976, **39,** 263–269.

Tannenbaum, R., & Massarik, F. Leadership: A frame of reference. *Management Science,* 1957, **4,** 1–19.

Taylor, D. W., & Faust, W. L. Twenty questions: Efficiency of problem solving as a function of the size of the group. *Journal of Experimental Psychology,* 1952, **44,** 360–363.

Taylor, J. A. A personality scale of manifest anxiety. *Journal of Abnormal and Social Psychology,* 1953, **48,** 285–290.

Tedeschi, J. T., Lindskold, S., Horai, J., & Gahagan, J. P. Social power and the credibility of promises. *Journal of Personality and Social Psychology,* 1969, **13,** 253–261.

Tedesco, J. F., & Fromme, D. K. Cooperation, competition, and personal space. *Sociometry,* 1974, **37,** 116–121.

Teger, A. I., Pruitt, D. G., St. Jean, R., & Haaland, G. A. A reexamination of the familiarization hypothesis in group risk taking. *Journal of Experimental Social Psychology,* 1970, **6,** 346–350.

Teichman, Y. Predisposition for anxiety and affiliation. *Journal of Personality and Social Psychology,* 1974, **29,** 405–410.

Tennis, G. H., & Dabbs, J. M., Jr. Sex, setting and personal space: First grade through college. *Sociometry,* 1975, **38,** 385–394.

Terborg, J. R., Castore, C., & DeNinno, J. A. A longitudinal field investigation of the impact of group composition on group performance and cohesion. *Journal of Personality and Social Psychology,* 1976, **34,** 782–790.

Terman, L. M. *Manual for concept mastery test.* New York: Psychological Corporation, 1956.

Terman, L. M., & Miles, C. C. *Sex and personality: Studies in masculinity and feminity.* New York: McGraw-Hill, 1936.

*The White House transcripts.* New York: Bantam Books, 1974.

Thelen, H. A. Group dynamics in instruction: The principle of least group size. *School Review*, 1949, **57**, 139–148.

Thelen, H. A. Classroom grouping. In A. Yates (Ed.), *Grouping in education*. New York: Wiley, 1966. Pp. 143–150.

Thibaut, J. W. An experimental study of the cohesiveness of underprivileged groups. *Human Relations*, 1950, **3**, 251–278.

Thibaut, J. W., & Gruder, C. L. Formation of contractual agreements between parties of unequal power. *Journal of Personality and Social Psychology*, 1969, **11**, 59–65.

Thibaut, J. W., & Kelley, H. H. *The social psychology of groups*. New York: Wiley, 1959.

Thibaut, J. W., & Strickland, L. Psychological set and social conformity. *Journal of Personality*, 1956, **25**, 115–129.

Thibaut, J. W., Strickland, L. H., Mundy, D., & Goding, E. F. Communication, task demands, and group effectiveness. *Journal of Personality*, 1960, **28**, 156–166.

Thie, T. W. The efficiency of the group method. *English Journal*, 1925, **14**, 134–137.

Thomas, E. J., & Fink, C. F. Models of group problem solving. *Journal of Abnormal and Social Psychology*, 1961, **68**, 53–63.

Thorndike, R. L. On what type of task will a group do well? *Journal of Abnormal and Social Psychology*, 1938, **33**, 408–412.

Thurstone, L. L., & Chave, E. J. *The measurement of attitudes*. Chicago: The University of Chicago Press, 1929.

Tinker, M. A. Illumination standards for effective and comfortable vision. *Journal of Consulting Psychology*, 1939, **3**, 11–19.

Tjosvold, D., & Sagaria, D. D. Effects of relative power of cognitive perspective-taking. *Personality and Social Psychology Bulletin*, 1978, **4**, 256–259.

Toch, H. *The social psychology of social movements*. Indianapolis: The Bobbs-Merrill Co., 1965.

Torrance, E. P. Some consequences of power differences on decision making in permanent and temporary three-man groups. *Research Studies*, Washington State College, 1954, **22**, 130–140.

Torrance, E. P. "Structure" can improve the group behavior of five-year-old children. *The Elementary School Journal*, *1971b*, **72**, 102–106.

Travis, L. E. The effect of a small audience upon eye-hand coordination. *Journal of Abnormal and Social Psychology* 1925, **20**, 142–146.

Travis, L. E. The influence of the group upon the stutterer's speed in free association. *Journal of Abnormal and Social Psychology*, 1928, **23**, 45–51.

Tresselt, M. E. The influence of amount of practice upon the formation of a scale of judgment. *Journal of Experimental Psychology*, 1947, **37**, 251–260.

Triandis, H. E., Hall, E. R., & Ewen, R. B. Member heterogeneity and dyadic creativity. *Human Relations*, 1965, **18**, 33–55.

Triplett, N. The dynamogenic factors in pacemaking and competition. *American Journal of Psychology*, 1897, **9**, 507–533.

Trope, Y. Seeking information about one's own ability as a determinant of choice among tasks. *Journal of Personality and Social Psychology,* 1975, **32,** 1004–1013.

Trope, Y., & Brickman, P. Difficulty and diagnosticity as determinants of choice among tasks. *Journal of Personality and Social Psychology,* 1975, **31,** 918–925.

Trotter, W. *Instincts of the herd in peace and war* (rev. ed.). London: Allen, 1920.

Tuckman, B. W. Personality structure, group composition, and group functioning. *Sociometry,* 1964, **27,** 469–487.

Tuckman, B. W. Developmental sequences in small groups. *Psychological Bulletin,* 1965, **63,** 384–399.

Tuckman, B. W. Group composition and group performance of structured and unstructured tasks. *Journal of Experimental Social Psychology,* 1967, **3,** 25–40.

Tuckman, J., & Lorge, I. Individual ability as a determinant of group superiority. *Human Relations,* 1962, **15,** 45–51.

Tuddenham, R. D. The influence of a distorted norm upon individual judgment. *Journal of Psychology,* 1958, **46,** 227–241.

Tuddenham, R. D., MacBride, P., & Zahn, V. The influence of the sex composition of the group upon yielding to a distorted norm. *Journal of Psychology,* 1958, **46,** 243–251.

Turney, J. R. The cognitive complexity of group members, group structure, and group effectiveness. *Cornell Journal of Social Relations,* 1970, **5,** 152–165.

Tyler, T. R., & Sears, D. O. Coming to like obnoxious people when we must live with them. *Journal of Personality and Social Psychology,* 1977, **35,** 200–211.

Uesugi, T. T., & Vinacke, W. E. Strategy in a feminine game. *Sociometry,* 1963, **26,** 75–88.

Valenti, A. C., & Downing, L. L. Differential effects of jury size on verdicts following deliberation as a function of the apparent guilt of a defendant. *Journal of Personality and Social Psychology,* 1975, **32,** 653–655.

Valentine, K. B., & Fisher, B. A. An interaction analysis of verbal innovative deviance in small groups. *Speech Monographs,* 1974, **41,** 413–420.

Valiquet, M. I. Individual change in a management development program. *Journal of Applied Behavioral Science,* 1968, **4,** 313–325.

Vallacher, R. R., Callahan-Levy, C. M., & Messe, L. A. Sex effects on bilateral bargaining as a function of interpersonal context. *Personality and Social Psychology Bulletin,* 1979, **5,** 104–108.

VanTuinen, J. J., & McNeel, S. A test of the social facilitation theories of Cottrell and Zajonc in a coaction situation. *Personality and Social Psychology Bulletin,* 1975, **1,** 604–607.

Van Zelst, R. H. Sociometrically selected work teams increase production. *Personnel Psychology,* 1952a, **5,** 175–186.

Van Zelst, R. H. Validation of a sociometric regrouping procedure. *Journal of Abnormal and Social Psychology,* 1952b, **47,** 299–301.

Vinacke, W. E. Sex roles in a three-person game. *Sociometry,* 1959, **22,** 343–360.

Vinacke, W. E., & Arkoff, A. Experimental study of coalitions in the triad. *American Sociological Review,* 1957, **22,** 406–415.

Vinacke, W. E., Crowell, D. C., Dien, C., & Young, V. The effect of information about strategy on a three-person game. *Behavioral Science,* 1966, **11,** 180–189.

Vinokur, A., & Burnstein, E. Effects of partially shared persuasive arguments on group-induced shifts: A group problem-solving approach. *Journal of Personality and Social Psychology,* 1974, **29,** 305–315.

Vinokur, A., & Burnstein, E. Depolarization of attitudes in groups. *Journal of Personality and Social Psychology,* 1978, **36,** 872–885.

Wahrman, R. Status, deviance, sanctions, and group discussion. *Small Group Behavior,* 1977, **8,** 147–168.

Wahrman, R., & Pugh, M. D. Sex, nonconformity and influence. *Sociometry,* 1974, **37,** 137–147.

Walker, T. G. Leader selection and behavior in small political groups. *Small Group Behavior,* 1976, **7,** 363–368.

Wallach, M. A., & Kogan, N. The roles of information, discussion, and consensus in group risk taking. *Journal of Experimental Social Psychology,* 1965, **1,** 1–19.

Wallach, M. A., Kogan, N., & Bem, D. J. Group influence on individual risk taking. *Journal of Abnormal and Social Psychology,* 1962, **65,** 75–86.

Wallach, M. A., Kogan, N., & Bem, D. J. Diffusion of responsibility and level of risk taking in groups. *Journal of Abnormal and Social Psychology,* 1964, **68,** 263–274.

Wallach, M. A., & Wing, C. W., Jr. Is risk a value? *Journal of Personality and Social Psychology,* 1968, **9,** 101–106.

Walster, E., Aronson, V., Abrahams, D., & Rottman, I. Importance of physical attractiveness in dating behavior. *Journal of Personality and Social Psychology,* 1966, **4,** 508–516.

Walters, R. H., & Karal, P. Social deprivation and verbal behavior. *Journal of Personality,* 1960, **28,** 89–107.

Walters, R. H., & Ray, E. Anxiety, social isolation, and reinforcer effectiveness. *Journal of Personality,* 1960, **28,** 358–367.

Ware, J. R., & Barr, J. E. Effects of a nine-week structured and unstructured group experience on measures of self-concept and self-actualization. *Small Group Behavior,* 1977, **8,** 93–100.

Warriner, C. H. Groups are real: A reaffirmation. *American Sociological Review,* 1956, **21,** 549–554.

Watson, D. Reinforcement theory of personality and social system: Dominance and position in a group power structure. *Journal of Personality and Social Psychology,* 1971, **20,** 180–185.

Watson, D., & Bromberg, B. Power, communication, and position satisfaction in task-oriented groups. *Journal of Personality and Social Psychology,* 1965, **2,** 859–864.

Watson, D. L. Effects of certain social power structures on communication in task-oriented groups. *Sociometry,* 1965, **28,** 322–336.

Watson, G. B. Do groups think more effectively than individuals? *Journal of Abnormal and Social Psychology,* 1928, **23,** 328–336.

Wegner, D. M., & Schaefer, D. The concentration of responsibility: An objective self-awareness analysis of group size effects in helping situations. *Journal of Personality and Social Psychology,* 1978, **36,** 147–155.

Weigel, R. G., & Corazzini, J. G. Small group research: Suggestions for solving common methodological and design problems. *Small Group Behavior,* 1978, **9,** 193–220.

Weston, S. B., & English, H. B. The influence of the group on psychological test scores. *American Journal of Psychology,* 1926, **37,** 600–601.

Wheaton, B. Interpersonal conflict and cohesiveness in dyadic relationships. *Sociometry,* 1974, **37,** 328–348.

Wheeler, L., & Nezlek, J. Sex differences in social participation. *Journal of Personality and Social Psychology,* 1977, **35,** 742–754.

White, K. R. T-groups revisited: Self-concept change and the "fishbowling" technique. *Small Group Behavior,* 1974, **5,** 473–485.

Whyte, W. F. *Street corner society.* Chicago: The University of Chicago Press, 1943.

Whyte, W. F. The social structure of the restaurant. *American Journal of Sociology,* 1949, **54,** 302–308.

Whyte, W. H., Jr. *The organization man.* Garden City, N.Y.: Doubleday, 1957.

Wiley, M. G. Sex roles in games. *Sociometry,* 1973, **36,** 526–541.

Wilke, H., Kuyper, H., Rouwendal, J., & Visser, G. Preference for prospective interaction. *European Journal of Social Psychology,* 1978, **8,** 377–382.

Wilke, H., Pruyn, J., & De Vries, G. Coalition formation: Political attitudes and power. *European Journal of Social Psychology,* 1978, **8,** 245–261.

Willems, E. P., & Clark, R. D., III. Shift toward risk and heterogeneity of groups. *Journal of Experimental Social Psychology,* 1971, **7,** 304–312.

Willerman, B., & Swanson, L. Group prestige in voluntary organizations. *Human Relations,* 1953, **6,** 57–77.

Williams, R. M., & Mattson, M. L. The effect of social groupings upon the language of pre-school children. *Child Development,* 1942, **13,** 233–245.

Willis, F. N., Jr. Initial speaking distance as a function of the speaker's relationship. *Psychonomic Science,* 1966, **5,** 221–222.

Willis, R. H. Coalitions in the tetrad. *Sociometry,* 1962, **25,** 358–376.

Willis, R. H., & Joseph, M. L. Bargaining behavior. I. "Prominence" as a predictor of the outcome of games of agreement. *Conflict Resolution,* 1959, **3,** 102–113.

Winch, R. F. The theory of complementary needs in mate selection: A test of one kind of complementariness. *American Sociological Review,* 1955, **20,** 52-56.

Winter, S. K. Developmental stages in the roles and concerns of group co-leaders. *Small Group Behavior,* 1976, **7,** 349–362.

Wolosin, R. J., Sherman, S. J., & Till, A. Effects of cooperation and competition on responsibility attribution after success and failure. *Journal of Experimental Social Psychology,* 1973, **9,** 220–235.

Worchel, P. Catharsis and the relief of hostility. *Journal of Abnormal and Social Psychology,* 1957, **55,** 238–243.

Worchel, S., Andreoli, V. A., & Folger, R. Intergroup cooperation and intergroup attraction: The effect of previous interaction and outcome of combined effort. *Journal of Experimental Social Psychology,* 1977, **13,** 131–140.

Worchel, S., Lind, E. A., & Kaufman, K. H. Evaluations of group products as a function of expectations of group longevity, outcome of competition, and publicity of evaluations. *Journal of Personality and Social Psychology*, 1975, **31**, 1089–1097.

Worchel, S., & Teddlie, C. The experience of crowding: A two-factor theory. *Journal of Personality and Social Psychology*, 1976, **34**, 30–40.

Worchel, S., & Yohai, S. M. L. The role of attribution in the experience of crowding. *Journal of Experimental Social Psychology*, 1979, **15**, 91–104.

Wright, F. The effects of style and sex of consultants and sex of members in self-study groups. *Small Group Behavior*, 1976, **7**, 433–456.

Wyer, R. S., Jr. Effects of incentive to perform well, group attraction, and group acceptance on conformity in a judgmental task. *Journal of Personality and Social Psychology*, 1966, **4**, 21–26.

Wyer, R. S., Jr. Behavioral correlates of academic achievement: Conformity under achievement- and affiliation-incentive conditions. *Journal of Personality and Social Psychology*, 1967, **6**, 255–263.

Wyer, R. S., & Malinowski, C. Effects of sex and achievement level upon individualism and competitiveness in social interaction. *Journal of Experimental Social Psychology*, 1972, **8**, 303–314.

Yuker, H. E. Group atmosphere and memory. *Journal of Abnormal and Social Psychology*, 1955, **51**, 17–23.

Zajonc, R. B. The requirements and design of a standard group task. *Journal of Experimental Social Psychology*, 1965a, **1**, 71–88.

Zajonc, R. B. Social facilitation. *Science*, 1965b, **149**, 269–274.

Zajonc, R. B., & Sales, S. M. Social facilitation of dominant and subordinate responses. *Journal of Experimental Social Psychology*, 1966, **2**, 160–168.

Zajonc, R. B., & Taylor, J. J. The effects of two methods of varying group task difficulty on individual and group performance. *Human Relations*, 1963, **16**, 359–368.

Zaleska, M. Individual and group choices among solutions of a problem when solution verifiability is moderately low. *European Journal of Social Psychology*, 1978, **8**, 37–53.

Zander, A. Group aspirations. In D. Cartwright & A. Zander (Eds.), *Group dynamics: Research and theory (3d ed.)*. New York: Harper & Row, 1968. Pp. 418–429.

Zander, A. *Motives and goals in groups*. New York: Academic Press, 1971.

Zander, A., & Cohen, A. R. Attributed social power and group acceptance: A classroom experimental demonstration. *Journal of Abnormal and Social Psychology*, 1955, **51**, 490–492.

Zander, A., & Havelin, A. Social comparison and interpersonal attraction. *Human Relations*, 1960, **13**, 21–32.

Zander, A., & Medow, H. Individual and group levels of aspiration. *Human Relations*, 1963, **16**, 89–105.

Zander, A., & Newcomb, T., Jr. Group levels of aspiration in United Fund campaigns. *Journal of Personality and Social Psychology*, 1967, **6**, 157–162.

Zander, A., & Wulff, D. Members' test anxiety and competence: Determinants of a group's aspirations. *Journal of Personality*, 1966, **34**, 55–70.

Zeleny, L. D. Characteristics of group leaders. *Sociology and Social Research,* 1939a, **24,** 140–149.

Zeleny, L. D. Sociometry of morale. *American Sociological Review,* 1939b, **4,** 799–808.

Zeleny, L. D. Experimental appraisal of a group learning plan. *Journal of Educational Research,* 1940, **34,** 37–42.

Ziller, R. C. Four techniques of group decision making under certainty. *Journal of Applied Psychology,* 1957a, **41,** 384–388.

Ziller, R. C. Group size: A determinant of the quality and stability of group decisions. *Sociometry,* 1957b, **20,** 165–173.

Zimbardo, P. The human choice: Individuation, reason, and order versus deindividuation, impulse, and chaos. In W. Arnold, & M. Levine (Eds.), *Nebraska symposium on motivation, 1969.* Lincoln: University of Nebraska Press, 1970. Pp. 237–307.

Zimmer, J. L., & Sheposh, J. P. Effects of high status and low status actor's performance on observers' attributions of causality and behavioral intentions. *Sociometry,* 1975, **38,** 395–407.

# Name Index

# Subject Index